The Beginnings of Jewishness

HELLENISTIC CULTURE AND SOCIETY

General Editors: Anthony W. Bulloch, Erich S. Gruen, A. A. Long, and Andrew F. Stewart

The Beginnings of Jewishness

Boundaries, Varieties, Uncertainties

Shaye J. D. Cohen

UNIVERSITY OF CALIFORNIA PRESS

Berkeley / Los Angeles / London

University of California Press
Berkeley and Los Angeles, California

University of California Press, Ltd.
London, England

© 1999 by
The Regents of the University of California

First Paperback Printing 2000

Library of Congress Cataloging-in-Publication Data
Cohen, Shaye J. D.
    The beginnings of Jewishness : boundaries, varieties,
uncertainties / Shaye J. D. Cohen
        p.   cm.—(Hellenistic culture and society ; 31) S. Mark Taper
Foundation imprint in Jewish studies)
    Includes bibliographic references and index.
    ISBN 0-520-21141-3 (alk. paper)
    ISBN 0-520-22693-3 (pbk: alk. paper)
    1. Judaism—History—Post-exilic period, 586 B.C.–210 A.D.
2. Jews—Identity—History—To 1500 A.D.   3. Proselytes and
proselyting, Jewish—History—To 1500 A.D.   4. Interfaith
marriage—History—To 1500 A.D.   I. Title.   II. Series.
III. Series: S.
Mark Taper Foundation imprint in Jewish studies.
BM176.C614   1999
296'.09'014—dc21   99-39899
                                                            CIP

Printed in the United States of America

08   07   06   05   04   03   02   01   00
9   8   7   6   5   4   3   2   1

For

Zahava, Jonathan, Ezra, and Hannah.

May their Jewishness always be secure.

Contents

Acknowledgments

This book is the product of the labor of many years, and I would like to thank my numerous friends and colleagues who over a protracted period have assisted me by reading drafts of my work, providing references, correcting errors, and making helpful suggestions. In particular, I owe a specific debt to the following individuals:

The original publication of chapter 2 was much improved by the suggestions and criticisms of David Konstan, Joseph Mélèze-Modrzejewski, and Jerzy Linderski. Several rabbinic references were provided by Hebert Basser, Marc Bregman, and Ranon Katzoff. An early version of chapter 3 was given a close reading by Willy Clarysse and Roger Bagnall, thanks to whose comments I shortened the chapter substantially (by removing most of what they thought was wrong). A penultimate version was read and heavily annotated by Erich Gruen, although I have foolishly rejected most of his advice. I am also grateful to John Oates of Duke University for sharing an unpublished paper with me ("The Greeks in Egypt") and for answering a number of questions. The original publication of chapter 4 was improved by the comments of Troels Engberg-Pedersen, chapter 5 by George Nickelsburg. An early version of chapter 6 was read by Seth Schwartz. Chapter 7 was originally presented at the World Congress of Jewish Studies in August 1989 in Jerusalem, and its original publication benefited from the ensuing discussion, especially the comments of Moshe Herr, Reuven Kimelman, and Lawrence Schiffman. It has also benefited from the suggestions and criticisms of Morton Smith and Richard Kalmin. Chapter 8 was read by

Saul Olyan. The original publication of chapter 9 benefited from the suggestions and advice of David Cherry, Leonard Gordon, and Sarah Pomeroy. In revising the original I have benefited from the comments of David Kraemer and Israel Francus. The original publication of the first part of chapter 10 was much improved by the criticisms and suggestions of Israel Francus and Richard Kalmin. I am particularly grateful to Professor Francus for annotating the essay carefully, catching several errors, and forcing me to sharpen my arguments. The original publication of appendix D benefited from the suggestions and advice of J. Louis Martyn; my work was facilitated by the exemplary cooperation of the staff of the library of Union Theological Seminary in New York.

Many of these essays were originally written when I was a faculty member of the Jewish Theological Seminary in New York. I would like to thank the Seminary for supporting my work, most especially through the Nisson Touroff Fund and the Abbell Publication Fund, and for sustaining a community of people who respect and value the study of Judaism.

Chapters 1 and 6, as well as the prologue and the epilogue, have not been published previously. The remaining chapters, in one form or another, have already been published, and even if many of them have been thoroughly reconceived, revised, and rewritten, I am grateful to the holders of the original copyright for permitting their republication here. The original publications were:

Chapter 2: "'Those Who Say They Are Jews and Are Not': How Do You Know a Jew in Antiquity When You See One?" in *Diasporas in Antiquity,* ed. Shaye J. D. Cohen and Ernest Frerichs, Brown Judaic Studies, no. 288 (Atlanta: Scholars Press, 1993) 1–45.

Parts of chapters 3 and 4: "Religion, Ethnicity, and 'Hellenism' in the Emergence of Jewish Identity in Maccabean Palestine," in *Religion and Religious Practice in the Seleucid Kingdom,* ed. Per Bilde et al. (Aarhus: Aarhus University Press, 1990) 204–223.

Chapter 5: "Crossing the Boundary and Becoming a Jew," *Harvard Theological Review* 82 (1989) 13–33. Copyright 1989 by the President and Fellows of Harvard College. Reprinted by permission.

Chapter 7: "The Rabbinic Conversion Ceremony," *Journal of Jewish Studies* 41 (1990) 177–203.

Chapter 8: "The Prohibition of Intermarriage: From the Bible to the Talmud," *Hebrew Annual Review* 7 (1983) [= *Essays in Honor of Robert Gordis*] 23–39.

Chapter 9: "The Origins of the Matrilineal Principle in Rabbinic Law," *Association for Jewish Studies Review* 10 (1985) 19–53.

Chapter 10, first part: "Can a Convert to Judaism Have a Jewish Mother?" in *Torah and Wisdom: Studies in Jewish Philosophy, Kabbalah, and Halacha in Honor of Arthur Hyman,* ed. Ruth Link-Salinger (New York: Shengold, 1992) 19–31.

Chapter 10, second part: "Can a Convert to Judaism Say 'God of Our Fathers'?" *Judaism* 40 (1991) 419–428. Copyright 1991 American Jewish Congress.

Appendix D: "Was Timothy Jewish (Acts 16:1–3)? Patristic Exegesis, Rabbinic Law, and Matrilineal Descent," *Journal of Biblical Literature* 105 (1986) 251–268. Copyright Society of Biblical Literature.

I also would like to thank Erich Gruen for accepting this book in the series Hellenistic Culture and Society.

I originally wanted to dedicate this book to my wife, Miriam. My debt to her is incalculable, and not a day goes by without my being grateful to her for sharing her life with me. Miriam, however, suggested that I should dedicate the book to my children. I agreed, and proposed "For my children, without whom this book would have been completed years ago." This sentiment is entirely true, but the dedication that I have chosen instead reflects more clearly some of the love and the hopes that I have for them.

Shaye J. D. Cohen
Brown University
Providence, Rhode Island

A Note on *God* and Parentheses

In English we customarily capitalize the word *God* when referring to the God of monotheistic religions, and keep the word lowercase when referring to the gods of polytheists. In this book I have adopted a more ecumenical perspective. I try to reflect the perspective of the original authors of the texts I am treating. When a Jewish text refers to the *God* of Israel and the *gods* of the gentiles, I capitalize the former and write the latter lowercase, because for Jews the God of Israel is the only God whereas the gods of the nations are not gods at all. When, however, Tacitus states that converts to Judaism "despise the *Gods*," I capitalize the word because for Tacitus these Gods are Gods.

In translating ancient texts I have placed in parentheses words that are unstated in the original but implied; in those cases where a literal English translation would sound cryptic but where the meaning of the original is quite clear, I have placed the absent but implied words in parentheses. In contrast, I have placed in square brackets words that are neither present nor implied in the original but which I have added for purposes of clarity or explanation. I have similarly bracketed words that I have added in cases where the original is corrupt or defective.

Jews and Others

According to an old joke, there are two kinds of people in the world: those who divide the world into two kinds of people, and those who do not. Jews are in the former category; like numerous other groups, both ancient and modern, Jews see the world in bipolar terms: Jews versus gentiles, "us" versus "them." This dualistic view of the world is not only a product of European ghettos or a response to Christian anti-Judaism; it is well attested in Graeco-Roman antiquity. Rabbinic literature is filled with statements that contrast "Israel" with "the nations."[1] Even Greek-speaking Jews, who might be thought to have been more "hellenized" than their rabbinic brethren, hence more integrated into the culture and society of the larger world, shared this perspective. Philo of Alexandria, perhaps the best-educated and most literate representative of Egyptian Jewry, wrote that "both Alexandria and the whole of Egypt had two kinds of inhabitants, us and them"—that is, us Jews and those non-Jews (Egyptians and Greeks). Josephus often refers to "us Jews," in the first-person plural, and contrasts Jews with "gentiles."[2] A Greek inscription from Tlos (Lycia, Asia Minor), apparently from the end of the first century C.E., reads as follows:

Ptolemy son of Leukios of Tlos erected at his own expense this tomb from the foundations, himself and on behalf of his son, Ptolemy the second, son

---

1. S. Stern, *Jewish Identity* chap. 1; Gary G. Porton, *Goyim: Gentiles and Israelites in Mishnah-Tosefta,* Brown Judaic Studies, no. 155 (Atlanta: Scholars Press, 1988).

2. Philo, *Against Flaccus* 43; Josephus, *AJ* 20.157, 259 (us *Ioudaioi*), and 262 (*Ioudaioi* and *allophuloi*). These phrases appear throughout the Josephan corpus.

1

of Leukios, on the occasion of the completion of the archonship among
us Jews, so that it (the tomb) shall be for all the Jews, and no one else is
allowed to be buried in it. If anyone shall be discovered burying someone,
he shall owe to the people of Tlos [a fine of *x* amount of money].[3]

The Jews in the city of Tlos constituted an organized community. Ptolemy son of Leukios erected a tomb for the Jews of the city in honor of
his son on the occasion of his completion of the archonship, or presi-
dency, of the community.[4] The tomb is for Jews only; anyone caught
burying a non-Jew in the tomb will be fined, the fine to be paid to the
city of Tlos.[5] Ptolemy son of Leukios is a man of Tlos, a proud citizen
of his city. Although he does not call himself a Jew, his social horizons
are defined by his Jewishness. The phrase "among us Jews" reveals a
strong public identification with the Jewish community, which defined
itself as an "us." And wherever there is an "us," there also is a "them."

Now to the two questions that form the heart of this book: first,
what is it that makes us *us* and them *them*? That is, what is it that makes
a Jew a Jew, and a non-Jew a non-Jew? The answer to this question will
lead directly to the second question: can one of "them" become one of
"us"; that is, can a gentile become a Jew? These questions are, of
course, large and complex, immediately leading to other large and complex questions, and I do not pretend to have answered fully any of them,
let alone all of them. My goal is more modest: to understand the questions and to appreciate their complexity. I am not a total agnostic, however; in this book I shall advance conjectures, defend theses, and argue
for and against certain points. These conjectures, theses, and points do,
I think, help illuminate the Jewish experience in the past and the present, and explain some otherwise puzzling aspects of Jewish law and so-

---

3. *CIJ* no. 757; I follow the text of *Tituli Asiae Minoris* II.2 no. 612. See too Schürer,
History 3.32–33. I have translated *Ioudaioi* in this inscription as "Jews," although perhaps
"Judaeans" would be more accurate.

4. The inscription is somewhat obscure on a number of points: "himself" (*autos*) apparently means "for himself." The meaning of *huper tou huiou autou Ptolemaiou b tou
Leukiou,* translated here as "on behalf of his son, Ptolemy the second, son of Leukios," is
not clear; did Ptolemy son of Leukios have a son named "Ptolemy son of Leukios"? See
the discussion by Frey in *CIJ.* The text does not state that the archonship was exercised
by the son; was it exercised by the father? Schürer, *History* 3.33, translates "in thanksgiv-
ing for his son's attainment to *archonteia,*" but *teloumenas* surely implies fulfillment or
completion, not attainment.

5. Protection of graves from violation through the imposition of a fine is common in
sepulchral inscriptions from Roman Asia Minor in general, and Jewish sepulchral inscriptions from Roman Asia Minor in particular. See Trebilco, *Jewish Communities* 213 n. 13.

ciety. Still, I cannot claim to have penetrated to the inner mystery of Jewish identity or "Jewishness," the qualities that make a Jew a Jew.

In part I, entitled "Who Was a Jew?" my thesis is that Jewish identity in antiquity was elusive and uncertain for two simple reasons. First, there was no single or simple definition of *Jew* in antiquity. Indeed, the Greek word *Ioudaios,* usually translated as "Jew," often is better translated as "Judaean," and the concepts "Jew" and "Judaean," in turn, need clarification. Second, there were few mechanisms in antiquity that would have provided empirical or "objective" criteria by which to determine who was "really" a Jew and who was not. Jewishness was a subjective identity, constructed by the individual him/herself, other Jews, other gentiles, and the state. As I discuss in chapter 1, Herod the Great illustrates well both of these reasons. Herod's Jewishness is a function of the meanings we impute to the word *Ioudaios.* Herod was either a Jew or a non-Jew—or both. Chapters 2 and 3 are devoted to the explication of these two difficulties. Were there social mechanisms in antiquity by which you could tell who was a Jew and who wasn't? Were Jews distinctive because of their costume, hairstyle, language, or body type? The observance of ritual helps create and maintain a sense of community among those who participate in the ritual, but were all those who participated in Jewish rituals necessarily Jewish? In chapter 2 I argue that the answer to all these questions is no. In most places and most of the time, individual Jews were not distinctive; it was easy for a gentile to pass as a Jew, and for a Jew to pass as a gentile—if that is what you wanted to do and if you knew what to do. Chapter 3 is a philological study of the word *Ioudaios.* My thesis is that the original meaning of the word is "Judaean," a meaning that never completely disappears but that in the latter part of the second century B.C.E. is supplemented by a "religious" or "cultural" meaning: "Jew."

Behind the philological shift from "Judaean" to "Jew" is a significant development in the history of Judaism: the emergence of the possibility that a gentile could be enfranchised as a citizen in the household of Israel, either politically or religiously. This is the theme of part II, "The Boundary Crossed: Becoming a Jew." In chapter 4 I argue that under the influence of Hellenistic culture and politics the Hasmoneans refashioned the Judaean state into a league that would allow the incorporation of non-Judaeans. At more or less the same time, the progression from ethnicity to religion had advanced to the point where individual gentiles who came to believe in the God of the Jews were accepted as Jews themselves. These two models of "conversion," political enfranchisement and religious change, are the products of the Hasmonean period. But these two modes hardly exhaust the different ways by which a gentile can cross the boundary and become a Jew. In chapter 5 I discuss seven such ways, beginning with those that do not necessarily imply that the gentile is becoming a Jew, and ending with those that do. The boundary was fluid and not well marked; we must allow for a variety of competing definitions and for the influence of the perspective of the observer. These factors are particularly relevant when we try to define "judaizing," the subject of chapter 6. If I see a gentile doing things that I think are characteristic (or ought to be characteristic) of Jews, I may regard that gentile as a "judaizer," but this judgment reveals nothing about the self-definition of the alleged "judaizer" or, indeed, about the judgments that other observers, both Jewish and gentile, may make of this alleged "judaizer." Many scholars have discussed "judaizing" in early Christianity as if the concept were clearly defined, but it is not. Finally in chapter 7 I come to the rabbinic definition of conversion as exemplified by the rabbinic conversion ceremony. The point of the ceremony is to provide a means for society to verify that the formal requirements for conversion (as established by the rabbis) have been met. By accepting the people of Israel and the commandments of the Torah a gentile could become a Jew ("Israelite" in rabbinic terminology). The precision that the rabbis introduced, or attempted to introduce, into the definition of conversion contrasted with the social reality of the preceding centuries, and perhaps of their own period as well.

In part III, entitled "The Boundary Violated: The Union of Diverse Kinds," I discuss the effect of intermarriage on Jewishness. One of the well-known hallmarks of classical Judaism is its prohibition of sexual union, whether marital or nonmarital, between Jews and non-Jews. I briefly survey the history of this prohibition in chapter 8. But what if the prohibition is violated? What is the status of the resulting offspring? According to rabbinic law, the status of the offspring of intermarriage is determined by the mother: a Jewish mother bears a Jewish child, a non-Jewish mother bears a non-Jewish child. This puzzling law, which is first attested explicitly in the Mishnah, is the subject of chapter 9. I argue that the explanations that are usually advanced for this law are entirely inadequate, and I propose two other explanations—which, alas, are probably inadequate too. I suggest that the rabbis may have been influenced by the Roman law of persons, and may have regarded sex between a Jew and a gentile as a union of diverse kinds, which, at least in the plant and animal kingdoms, is prohibited by the Torah. In chapter 10 I treat the interpretation of a mishnaic text that stands at the intersection of several of the concerns of this book: matrilineal descent, conversion, the status of the convert, and the notion of Jewishness.

•   •   •

Parts II and III of this book, and various sections of part I as well, are studies of the imagination. Jewishness, like most—perhaps all—other identities, is imagined; it has no empirical, objective, verifiable reality to which we can point and over which we can exclaim, "This is it!" Jewishness is in the mind. In the felicitous phrase of Benedict Anderson, we are speaking of an "imagined community."[6]

Sociologists agree that ethnic or national identity is imagined; it exists because certain persons want it to exist and believe that it exists. It can be willed into and out of existence. So far all agree. However, exactly what needs to be imagined to create and maintain an ethnic or national identity is the subject of ongoing debate and discussion. In an influential article published in 1969, Frederik Barth argued that an ethnic group was made by its boundaries—the ways in which it demarcates itself and distinguishes itself ("us") from others ("them"):

The nature of continuity of ethnic units is clear: it depends on the maintenance of a boundary. The cultural features that signal the boundary may change, and the cultural characteristics of the members may likewise be transformed, indeed, even the organizational form of the group may change—yet the fact of continuing dichotomization between members and outsiders allows us to specify the nature of continuity, and investigate the changing cultural form and content.[7]

In other words, the boundary makes the group. The "cultural stuff" enclosed by the boundary is almost accidental to the identity of the group, since it is not the essence of ethnicity. The group can change its culture and its organization, but it maintains its continuity as long as its boundaries are intact.

Barth is certainly correct that boundaries are essential to ethnicity. Any ethnic group that gives itself a name is implicitly or explicitly naming itself in opposition to some other named group, claiming that its members are not the members of some other group, and asserting that its members constitute an "us" versus the members of other groups who constitute a "them." Without these boundaries it is hard to speak

6. B. Anderson, *Imagined Communities.* For Anderson (6), a nation is "an imagined political community."

7. Frederik Barth, ed., *Ethnic Groups and Boundaries: The Social Organization of Cultural Difference* (Bergen: Universitets Forlaget, 1969) 14.

of a group as a group at all. What is more problematic, however, is Barth's separation of the culture (customs, values, habits, language, etc.) of a group from its identity. Surely the boundary erected by a group to maintain and protect its identity is an expression of that group's culture. A social boundary cannot exist without the "stuff" that it encloses. It is not the boundary that makes the group; it is the group that makes the boundary. Hence a study of identity needs to focus not just on boundaries but also on the territory that it encircles.[8] Throughout this book I shall refer to the Jews (or Judaeans) as constituting a "people"—an *ethnos,* or "ethnic group"—and I shall speak of the boundary that separates Jews from non-Jews, but my assumption is that the boundary is an expression of Jewish identity, not synonymous with it.

What is an ethnic group? In a non-Barthian mode Anthony D. Smith writes as follows:

An ethnic group is distinguished by four features: the sense of unique group origins, the knowledge of a unique group history and belief in its destiny, one or more dimensions of collective cultural individuality, and finally a sense of unique cultural solidarity. For short, we may define the "*ethnie*" or ethnic community as a social group whose members share a sense of common origins, claim a common and distinctive history and destiny, possess one or more distinctive characteristics, and feel a sense of collective uniqueness and solidarity.[9]

Of these four features, three are entirely in the mind: a *sense* of common origins, a *knowledge* or *belief* in a distinctive history, and a *sense* of solidarity. The fourth feature, the possession of one or more distinctive characteristics, seems at first to be empirical and objective, but it too, in large part, is a creation of mind. Which dimension of the collective culture of the group shall be defined as defining and distinctive? Religion? Language? Skin color? Dress? Food? Livelihood? The decision to deem some of these factors as essential and others as insignificant—that is, the decision to regard as a "boundary" one cultural indicator but not another—is, in fact, a decision, a product of the same discriminatory fac-

8. For a critique of Barth, see S. Stern, *Identity* 135–138 and 197–198, and, more briefly, A. D. Smith, *Ethnic Origins* 49 and 97.

9. Anthony D. Smith, *The Ethnic Revival* (Cambridge: Cambridge University Press, 1981) 66. Smith returns to this in chapter 2 of *Ethnic Origins,* where this list of four is expanded somewhat and presented with less emphasis on the element of imagination; on page 32 he writes: "*ethnie* (ethnic communities) may now be defined as named human populations with shared ancestry myths, histories, and cultures, having an association with a specific territory and a sense of solidarity."

ulties that gave birth to the other three features of ethnic identity. Smith goes on to remark:

It is the myth of a common and unique origin in time and place that is essential for the sense of ethnic community.

Whether the group in fact shares a common and unique origin does not much matter; what matters only is that the members believe that the group shares a common and unique origin in a specific place at a specific moment.

A similar approach is taken by Ernest Gellner, who defends the following two propositions:

Two men are of the same nation if and only if they share the same culture, where culture in turn means a system of ideas and signs and associations and ways of behaving and communicating.

Two men are of the same nation if and only if they recognize each other as belonging to the same nation. In other words, *nations maketh man;* nations are artefacts of man's convictions and loyalties and solidarities.[10]

Gellner uses the term "nation" to mean what I have been calling ethnic group. Here the group is said to cohere on the basis of common culture and collective will. A nation is a nation if its members want it to be one; the members of a nation are those who share the common culture. For Gellner, then, one of the two essential characteristics of a nation is a product of mind, while the other is "objective" only in the sense that it focuses on some verifiable traits—but which traits need to be verified is, in turn, a question for the collective mind of the nation to determine.

The Jews (Judaeans) of antiquity constituted an *ethnos,* an ethnic group.[11] They were a named group, attached to a specific territory, whose members shared a sense of common origins, claimed a common and distinctive history and destiny, possessed one or more distinctive characteristics, and felt a sense of collective uniqueness and solidarity. The sum total of these distinctive characteristics was designated by the Greek word *Ioudaïsmos.* As we shall see, the most distinctive of the distinctive characteristics of the Jews was the manner in which they worshiped their God, what we today would call their religion. But *Ioudaïsmos,* the ancestor of our English word *Judaism,* means more

10. Ernest Gellner, *Nations and Nationalism* (Ithaca: Cornell University Press, 1983) 7; for further discussion see 53–62.

11. See chapter 3 below. On the meaning of *ethnos* in antiquity, see *Lexikon der alten Welt,* s.v. "Ethnos" (by F. Gschnitzer), and Anthony J. Saldarini, *Matthew's Christian-Jewish Community* (Chicago: University of Chicago Press, 1994) 59–61 and 78–81.

than just religion. For ancient Greeks and contemporary social scientists, "religion" is only one of many items that make a culture or a group distinctive. Perhaps, then, we should translate *Ioudaismos* not "Judaism" but "Jewishness." In this book I am attempting to understand how the Jews of antiquity drew the boundary between themselves and the gentiles, and thus to understand their conceptions of "Jewishness."

•   •   •

In modern times Jewishness has become problematic. Numerous books and articles have appeared under the heading "Who Is a Jew?" Every time the state of Israel considers a change in the Law of Return, or ponders the Jewishness of a group of immigrants, newspapers and magazines, both in Israel and abroad, are filled with articles, editorials, and advertisements on Jewish identity. The extraordinary growth of intermarriage in the United States, which in turn has occasioned the Reform movement's embrace of a patrilineal reckoning of Jewishness (while still retaining the traditional matrilineal reckoning), has further fueled the discussion. Behind the debates of the late twentieth century are the developments of the nineteenth. The Emancipation and the restructuring of European society meant the collapse of the intellectual, political, and social boundaries that traditionally had kept Jews "in" and gentiles "out." Reform Jews argued that Judaism was a religion, Zionists that it was a nationality, and Bundists that it was a peoplehood. Intellectuals and philosophers of all stripes created new systems that mediated between these extremist positions. Although this book ostensibly is about the Jews of antiquity, I am fully aware of its contemporary relevance. The uncertainty of Jewishness in antiquity curiously prefigures the uncertainty of Jewishness in modern times. The ancients lived in a pre-rabbinic world, while we live in a post-rabbinic world. I devote the epilogue to reflection on these matters.

Of course, in our postmodern, polyethnic, multinational, multilingual, politically correct, and socially fractured world, Jews are not the only group whose boundaries are threatened and whose identity is unsure. An interesting parallel to the Jewish dilemma is provided by, to pick only one example out of many possibilities, Blacks in America. In 1991 F. James Davis published a fascinating book titled *Who Is Black? One Nation's Definition*. Davis shows that the "one-drop rule," according to which anyone with a single drop of Black blood in his/her veins is to be regarded as Black, did not become widely accepted in the United States until the latter part of the nineteenth century. For a long time many states used other rules; some states even validated a class of "mulattoes" to serve as a buffer between whites and Blacks. In the end, however, the one-drop rule triumphed, not only among whites (who had created it) but also among Blacks, many of whom had initially opposed it. Thus, in the United States, there are no mulattoes; the color line permits only two possibilities: white and Black. (By curious coincidence, rabbinic law, which does not subscribe to a one-drop rule, also does not permit mulattoes: a person is either a Jew or a non-Jew; there are no "half-Jews.") Persons who by ancestry are more white than Black, who "look" more white than Black, whose social connections are more white than Black, whose manner of speech is more white than Black—can or must, nonetheless, see themselves as Black, and even be seen by others, both white and Black, as Black. Citizens of other countries, which do not have the one-drop rule, are thoroughly puzzled by a system that insists on the Blackness of people who do not "look" Black at all and who, if they lived outside the United States, would not be considered Black.

As the population of the United States continues to become more diverse, as more and more "Browns" enter the population alongside Blacks and whites, and as genetic mixing among all these groups continues to increase, more and more people will question whether a single drop of Black blood necessarily makes a person Black. In a *New York Times* story titled "Black Identity in the 1990's," members of the Black community wonder aloud whether Blackness is a function of skin color, ancestry, culture, class, politics, or some combination of these. Even the federal government, according to another *New York Times* story, is beginning to rethink its system of racial classification. Perhaps it will institute a "multiracial" category, and yet other categories for people who are dark skinned but not Black. Who, then, is Black? And, no less important, who has the power to decide? [12]

Taxonomic questions are everywhere. Mirroring our uncertainty about Jewishness and Blackness is a growing uncertainty about the classification of the members of the animal kingdom. In 1992 the *New*

12. Racial mixing: *New York Times,* July 4, 1996, p. A16 ("Number of Black-White Couples Is Rising Sharply"); *New York Times Magazine,* July 7, 1996, p. 50 ("An Ethnic Trump"); *New York Times,* July 20, 1996, p. A1 ("Multiracial Americans Ready to Claim Their Own Identity"). Black identity: *New York Times,* November 30, 1991, p. A1. Federal government: *New York Times,* July 8, 1994; July 6, 1996, p. A1; December 6, 1996, p. A25; May 16, 1997 ("Few Choose Multiracial Census Category"); July 9, 1997 ("Panel Balks at Multiracial Census Category"); October 30, 1997 ("New Categories on Race and Ethnic Makeup Adopted by Administration"). A genetic marker has been discovered that links Jews, Arabs, Turks and Armenians. What this means is still unknown. See *New York Times,* August 22, 1997 ("Gene from Mideast Ancestor May Link Four Disparate Peoples").

York Times Magazine ran a story entitled "Could the Red Wolf Be a Mutt?" The issue that came before the Environmental Protection Agency is the status of the red wolf, an endangered species found only in Texas and parts of the southeastern United States. Is it, in fact, a species, on a par with other wild canine species? Is it a subspecies? Or is it the product of crossbreeding between coyotes and gray wolves, hence a hybrid, a mulatto, a mutt, and not a species at all? The question pits geneticists, who have determined by DNA testing that the red wolf is, genetically at least, a coyote–gray wolf hybrid, against field biologists (naturalists), who are sure that the red wolf is neither a coyote nor a gray wolf but a species in itself. Similarly, genetic testing of guinea pigs suggests that these animals, long seen as members of the order of rodents, are not rodents at all. Members of an order are all supposed to have descended from a common ancestor; they are monophyletic. (In this respect a taxonomic order—for example, the order of rodents—is akin to an ethnic group, the crucial difference between them being that rodents descend from a single remote ancestor but don't know it, whereas members of an ethnic group suppose they descend from a single remote ancestor even though they don't.) Yet recent genetic testing shows that guinea pigs cannot have descended from this putative ancestor. Hence we must conclude either that a taxonomic order can allow for multiple lines of descent (that is, an order can be polyphyletic), a conclusion that flouts the standard definition of *order,* or guinea pigs are not rodents, a conclusion that flouts accepted wisdom. The verdict is not yet in.[13]

Once upon a time we knew who was a Jew, who was a Black, what was a red wolf, and what was a rodent. Now we are not so sure. Genetics testing has even called into question the fundamental taxonomic divide between male and female. "Who Is Female? Science Can't Say," runs a headline.[14] It is not just Jews, then, who wonder about their identity and their proper taxonomic classification. Until geneticists discover the long-elusive Jewish gene,[15] Jewishness will remain a social construction—a variable, not a constant. In this book I hope to illuminate the beginnings of Jewishness.

13. Red wolf: *New York Times Magazine,* June 14, 1992, p. 30. Guinea pigs: *New York Times,* June 13, 1996, p. A1.

14. *New York Times,* February 16, 1992, sec. 4, p. 6.

15. Which, of course, does not exist. See A. E. Mourant et al., *The Genetics of the Jews* (Oxford: Oxford University Press, 1978); Raphael and Jennifer Patai, *The Myth of the Jewish Race,* rev. ed. (Detroit: Wayne State University Press, 1989). Recent attempts to identify a genetic marker of priestly descent ("Finding Genetic Traces of Jewish Priesthood," *New York Times,* January 7, 1997) do not impress me.

PART I

Who Was a Jew?

CHAPTER I

Was Herod Jewish?

Who was a Jew in antiquity? How was "Jewishness" defined? In their minds and actions the Jews erected a boundary between themselves and the rest of humanity, the non-Jews ("gentiles"), but the boundary was always crossable and not always clearly marked. Gentiles do not always behave as they might be expected to behave: a gentile might associate with Jews, or observe Jewish practices, or "convert" to Judaism. Jews do not always behave as they might be expected to behave: a Jew might cease associating with Jews, or cease observing Jewish practices, or deny Judaism outright. Such gentiles and Jews have crossed the boundary, or, at least, raise serious questions about the boundary and its efficacy in keeping Jews "in" and gentiles "out." Or a Jew might threaten the boundary through marriage with a gentile: in such a situation, is the Jew still a Jew? Has the gentile partner somehow become a Jew? What is the status of the offspring of this union?

The "Jewishness" of all these boundary crossers had to be determined by various jurisdictions and groups. The organized Jewish community, the municipal or provincial governments, and the imperial government each had an interest in determining whether a given individual was a Jew. For example, if in the year 80 C.E. a gentile in Ephesus converted, or claimed to have converted, to Judaism, the local Jewish community would have had to determine whether it would accept him or her as a member; the municipal government would have had to determine whether this person could now enjoy the privileges that traditionally had been extended to Jews; and the imperial government would have had to determine whether this person was now subject to the Jewish tax levied upon all Jews in the Roman empire as punishment for the war of 66–70 C.E. Had the conversion taken place before 70 C.E., when the Jerusalem temple was still standing, the priests would have had to determine whether this person, once a gentile, was now to be treated as a Jew and allowed to join other Jews in the inner precincts. There is no reason to assume that all these jurisdictions would necessarily have reached identical conclusions in every case, or to assume that the boundary definition used by the Jewish community of Ephesus would necessarily have been identical with that which was operative in the other organized Jewish communities of Asia Minor, or, for that matter, of Italy, Syria, Egypt, North Africa, Judaea, and Babylonia.

The convert's social status too was subject to conflicting judgments. How did this person, born a gentile, see him/herself? How was this person seen by his/her spouse, relatives, friends, and other gentiles? How was this person seen by native-born Jews? Once again, there is no reason to assume that these questions will have received uniform answers. A gentile who engaged in "judaizing" behavior may have been regarded as a Jew by gentiles, but as a gentile by Jews. A gentile who was accepted as a convert by one community may not have been so regarded by another. Nor should we assume that the converts of one community were necessarily treated like those of another, because the Jews of antiquity held a wide range of opinions about the degree to which the convert became just like the native born.

Even if we leave aside for a moment all these problematic boundary crossers, we are still left with a serious puzzle: the meaning of the word *Jew* itself. The predecessors of the English word *Jew*, Greek *Ioudaios* and Latin *Iudaeus*, were originally ethnic-geographic terms, like "Egyptian," "Syrian," "Cappadocian," "Thracian," and so forth. Thus instead of "Jews" we should, in many cases, speak rather of "Judaeans," the residents of Judaea (geography), who constitute the *ethnos*, "nation" or "people," of the Judaeans (ethnicity). Similarly, Egyptians are those who reside in Egypt and constitute the nation or people of the Egyptians. At some point in their history Greek *Ioudaios* and Latin *Iudaeus* came to have another meaning: a *Ioudaios* is anyone who venerates the God of the temple of Jerusalem and observes his laws. In other words, a *Ioudaios* is a Jew, a term designating "culture" or "religion." Here *Ioudaios* parts company with "Egyptian," "Syrian," "Cappadocian," "Thracian," and so on because none of those terms ever became normative terms of "culture" or "religion." Thus, were the "Jews" of antiquity an ethnic group? A geographic group? A religious group? Or, perhaps, all three? This book is devoted to puzzling out the answers to these questions.

In this brief chapter I would like to illustrate the problematic nature of "Jewishness" by focusing on one specific case. I will keep the scholarly apparatus to a minimum as slight compensation for the fact that in all subsequent chapters I do not. My illustrative example is Herod the Great, king of Judaea for thirty-four years (37–4 B.C.E.), builder extraordinaire, and the murderer of his wives and children.[1]

Numerous different sources attest that Herod the Great was a *Ioudaios*—that is, a Judaean, a member (and king) of the ethnic-geographic polity constituted by the inhabitants of Judaea. Thus Plutarch, in his *Life of Antony,* gives a list of the kings who supported Antony against Octavian; these included Archelaus of Cappadocia, Philadelphus of Paphlagonia, Mithridates of Commagene, Malchus of Arabia, and "Herod of Judaea" (*Hērōdēs ho Ioudaios*). The labels on Italian wine amphorae discovered at Masada indicate that the wine was destined for Herod *Iudaicus,* Herod of Judaea.[2] In his narrative Josephus regularly refers to Herod as "king of the Judaeans," and even has Herod address a crowd in Jerusalem as "my kinsmen" (or, perhaps, "my fellow tribesmen"). Herod tells them that "our fathers" had built the temple. These Josephan passages also clearly imply that Herod the Judaean was also, as would be expected, a Jew—that is, someone who venerates the God whose temple is in Jerusalem. When the temple was being rebuilt, Josephus reports, Herod did not enter the sacred precincts because he was not a priest; in fact all the laborers on the project had to be priests.[3] Herod was not a priest, but, in Josephus' estimation at least, clearly was a Judaean and a Jew.

Herod's Judaeanness/Jewishness was conceded even by those who might have had reason to deny it. Not long before the outbreak of the war in 66 C.E., there were riots in the city of Caesarea, sparked by a feud between the two dominant groups in the city. Here is the report of the *Jewish Antiquities:*

There arose also a quarrel between the Jewish and Syrian inhabitants of Caesarea on the subject of equal civic rights. The Jews claimed that they had

---

1. For a parallel discussion of this question but with a different focus and a different purpose, see Albert Baumgarten, "On the Legitimacy of Herod and His Sons as Kings of Israel" (in Hebrew), in *Jews and Judaism in the Second Temple, Mishna, and Talmud Period: Studies in Honor of Shmuel Safrai,* ed. I. Gafni et al. (Jerusalem: Yad Izhak Ben-Zvi, 1993) 31–37. For a brief discussion, see Richardson, *Herod* 52–53.

2. Plutarch, *Life of Alexander* 61.3 = M. Stern, *Authors* no. 267; Cotton and Geiger, *Masada II* 147–148. On *Iudaicus,* see chapter 3 below, note 21.

3. King of the Judaeans: *AJ* 15.311; "my kinsmen" (*andres homophuloi*): *AJ* 15.382; "our fathers": *AJ* 15.385; Herod not a priest: *AJ* 15.420.

the precedence because the founder of Caesarea, their king Herod, had been of Jewish descent; the Syrians admitted what they said about Herod, but asserted that Caesarea had before that been called Strato's Tower, and that before Herod's time there had not been a single Jewish inhabitant in the city.[4]

The parallel report in the *Jewish War* is slightly different:

Another disturbance occurred at Caesarea, where the Jewish portion of the population rose against the Syrian inhabitants. They claimed that the city was theirs on the ground that its founder, king Herod, was a Jew. Their opponents admitted the Jewish origin of its second founder [more literally: Their opponents admitted that its founder was a Jew], but maintained that the city itself belonged to the Greeks, since Herod would never have erected the statues and temples which he placed there had he destined it for Jews.[5]

Both translators take *Ioudaios* here to mean "Jew," so that the quarrel is between "Jews" and Syrians (who, in the *Jewish War* passage, are synonymous with "Greeks"), and Herod is declared to be a "Jew" or "of Jewish descent." I would prefer to take the term throughout in the sense "Judaean," so that the quarrel is between "Judaeans" and Syrians, and Herod is declared to be a "Judaean" or "Judaean by birth" (or "Judaean by descent"). The struggle in Caesarea is between two ethnic groups vying for power. The last word of the *Jewish War* excerpt, however, is perhaps best kept as *Jews,* because here religious sensitivities are at issue: Judaeans ("Jews") would not tolerate statues and temples, but Greeks (that is, Greek-speaking polytheists) would welcome them.

Let us return to Herod. In the *Jewish War* passage, the Judaeans of Caesarea claim that Herod, the founder of the city, was a Judaean. In the *Jewish Antiquities* they claim that Herod was "Judaean by birth"— that is, a real Judaean, a genuine Judaean.[6] In both passages the Syrians concede the point, and try to establish their claims to political dominance on other criteria. Clearly, it would have been to the Syrians' advantage to deny Herod's Judaeanness and to claim that Herod was by birth something else, not Judaean, but they made no such denials or claims; by the 60s C.E. everyone seems to have known that Herod had been a *Ioudaios.*

But how did Herod come to be a Judaean/Jew? Josephus gives two contrasting explanations:

4. *AJ* 20.173, trans. Feldman.
5. *BJ* 2.266, trans. Thackeray.
6. S. J. D. Cohen, "*Ioudaios to genos*" 32 and 35.

There was a certain friend of Hyrcanus, an Idumaean called Antipater, who, having a large fortune and being by nature a man of action and a trouble-maker, was unfriendly to Aristobulus and quarreled with him because of his friendliness to Hyrcanus. Nicolas of Damascus, to be sure, says that his family belonged to the leading Jews who came to Judaea from Babylon. But he says this in order to please Antipater's son Herod, who became king of the Jews by a certain turn of fortune . . . This Antipater, it seems, was first called Antipas, which was also the name of his father, whom King Alexander (Jannaeus) and his wife appointed governor of the whole of Idumaea, and they say he made friends of the neighboring Arabs and Gazaeans and Ascalonites, and completely won them over by many large gifts.[7]

Herod was son of Antipater, but who was Antipater? Nicolas of Damascus, resident adviser, tutor, and intellectual at the court of Herod, contended that Herod's family descended from the blue bloods who came to Judaea from Babylon (in the Persian period).[8] In American terms, Nicolas is saying that Herod's ancestors arrived on the *Mayflower*. Josephus argues that Nicolas is lying in order to flatter his employer; Herod was not the first or the last autocrat who was unhappy with his pedigree and commissioned a court historian to discover a better one. Nicolas complied. What is important about the fabrication is that it reveals that Herod realized that his real pedigree was inadequate to assure him of an unassailable claim to the epithet *Ioudaios*.

Josephus contends that Herod was really an Idumaean.[9] He was the son of Antipater the Idumaean, scion to a family that had long been prominent in Idumaean politics and close to the Hasmonean dynasty. The family also had connections with "the neighboring Arabs and Gazaeans and Ascalonites." But Josephus has also said that Herod was a Judaean; how did the Idumaeans come to be Judaeans? Josephus explains:

Hyrcanus also captured the Idumaean cities of Adora and Marisa, and after subduing all the Idumaeans, permitted them to remain in their country so long as they had themselves circumcised and were willing to observe the laws of the Judaeans. And so, out of attachment to their ancestral land, they submitted to circumcision and to having their manner of life in all other

---

7. *AJ* 14.8–10, trans. Marcus.

8. The information in parentheses is not stated, but I assume that this is what is meant; the author of *Yosippon* also understood Nicolas to mean "in the time of Ezra and Nehemiah" (*Yosippon* 1.146, ed. Flusser).

9. See too *BJ* 1.123. Qumran Scroll 4Q491 may also allude to Herod as an Idumaean (Edomite); see M. Smith, *Studies* 2.74–75.

respects made the same as that of the Judaeans. And from that time on they have continued to be Judaeans.[10]

In chapter 4 below I shall treat this passage in some detail. In the 120s B.C.E. John Hyrcanus incorporated the Idumaeans into the Judaean state. The Idumaeans became Judaeans, except that they also still remained Idumaeans. Politically, they became Judaeans, citizens in the Judaean state (or Judaean League). Religiously, they became Jews, at least to the extent that they were expected to observe the laws and customs of the Judaeans. Ethnically, however, they remained as they had been, Idumaeans, just as the Galileans retained their own ethnic-geographic identity even after becoming Judaeans/Jews.

For some Judaeans, especially "genuine" Judaeans from the "real" Judaea (the district around Jerusalem), Idumaeans like Herod would always be outsiders, a combination of parvenus and country bumpkins. Antigonus the Hasmonean tried to convince the Romans that "it would be contrary to their own notion of right if they gave the kingship to Herod who was a commoner and an Idumaean, that is, a half-Jew." Herod suffers from two genealogical liabilities, according to Antigonus: he is a commoner (a nonpriest) and an Idumaean. "Half-Jew" is Marcus' translation of *hēmiioudaios,* but surely "half-Judaean" is the intent here.[11] Antigonus is commenting not on Herod's religiosity but on his pedigree: Idumaeans are Judaeans, but from the perspective of the Hasmoneans (who had themselves once been parvenus and country bumpkins) they are only half-Judaeans, because they remain Idumaeans. Needless to say, the Romans ignored Antigonus' argument. But to counter such attitudes Herod had his official biographer invent for him a full Judaean, non-Idumaean, ancestry.

In common parlance a "half-ethnic" is a half-breed, a mestizo or mulatto—that is, the offspring of parents of dissimilar ethnicity. Hence when we say that someone is "half-Italian," we mean that one of her parents is Italian and that the other is not. By the same logic we may speak of someone who is one-quarter or one-eighth Black (a quadroon, an octoroon). Therefore it is important to note that when Herod's detractors called him a "half-Judaean," they were not referring to the dissimilar ethnicity of his parents. Herod was a half-Judaean because his fa-

10. *AJ* 13.257–258.
11. *AJ* 14.403. Goodman, *Who Was a Jew?* 10, writes: "In another passage, which is theologically incomprehensible (at least to me), Josephus affirmed that the Idumaeans . . . were now 'half-Jews.'" The term "half-Jew" may be theologically incomprehensible, but the term "half-Judaean" is fully comprehensible.

ther Antipater was an Idumaean—that is, a half-Judaean. There is no reference here to Herod's mother; her ancestry seems to be irrelevant. According to rabbinic law, however, the status of the offspring of inter-marriage follows the status of the mother. And who was Herod's mother? A woman named Kypros (or Kypris), "of an illustrious Arab family."[12] According to rabbinic law Herod will have been a gentile be-cause he was the son of a non-Jewish woman who is not reported to have converted; neither Antipater nor Herod nor Antigonus nor Jose-phus knew this, of course, because the matrilineal principle did not yet exist in the first century B.C.E. or first century C.E., as I shall discuss in chapter 9 below. Herod was a "half-Judaean/Jew" through his father.

Later generations elaborated yet other genealogies for Herod the Great. In the middle of the second century C.E. Justin Martyr wrote his *Dialogue with Trypho,* a defense of Christianity and an attack on Ju-daism. The book revolves around the interpretation of the Hebrew Bible (the "Old Testament"), Justin insisting that the Jews have com-pletely misunderstood its intent and its message. As one of his many proofs of the truth of Christianity, Justin cites Genesis 49:10: *The scepter shall not depart from Judah . . . until that which is laid up in store for him shall come* (translation based on the Septuagint). Justin, and in-deed virtually all subsequent Christian exegetes, argued that these ob-scure words meant that the Messiah would be the last king of Judah: af-ter the arrival of the Messiah, Israel would no longer have any royal office. And since after the birth and passion of Jesus the Jews no longer have any king or prophet, here is proof that the biblical prophecy has been fulfilled and that Jesus is the Christ. Justin is aware of a possible Jewish objection: we lost our kingship even before the birth and passion of Jesus. Justin responds, "For though you affirm that Herod, after whom he [Jesus] suffered, was an Ascalonite, nevertheless you admit that there was a high priest in your nation . . . also you had prophets" (*Dialogue with Trypho* 52). Thus even if the Jews are right that Herod was an Ascalonite, and that they had lost their kingship even before the arrival of Jesus, nevertheless the prophecy is fulfilled by the fact that Jews had priests and prophets until the arrival of Jesus, after which they were lost in the destruction of the temple in 70 C.E.

The Jewish-Christian debate concerning the interpretation of Gene-sis 49:10 is not our concern here, even if I shall have to refer to it again in a moment; what is important for us is that Justin contends that the Jews say that Herod, presumably Herod the Great, was a native of the

12. *BJ* 1.181 and *AJ* 14.121.

Philistine city of Ascalon. No extant Jewish source makes this claim about Herod, but the attribution of the claim to Jews is not impossible, and perhaps not implausible. When and why the Jews will have invented the story, we do not know. How they came to associate Herod with Ascalon, we also do not know. Perhaps the fact that the Herodian family had connections with "the neighboring Arabs and Gazaeans and Ascalonites," as Josephus said, gave rise to the polemic that Herod was an Ascalonite himself. Perhaps.[13]

Sextus Julius Africanus, a Christian writer who lived two generations after Justin (ca. 160 – ca. 240 c.e.), has a fuller version of the Ascalon story:

When Idumaean brigands attacked the city of Ascalon in Palestine, among their other spoils they took away captive from the temple of Apollo, which was built on the walls, Antipater the child of a certain Herod, a temple slave, and since the priest was unable to pay ransom for his son, Antipater was brought up in the customs of the Idumaeans and later was befriended by Hyrcanus the high priest of Judaea.[14]

Here we are told that Antipater, father of Herod, was from the Philistine city of Ascalon, where his father (that is, Herod's grandfather) served as a priest or temple slave. As a young boy he was captured by the Idumaeans and was raised by them. The story does preserve some vestige of a connection between Herod and Idumaea, but the bottom line is that Herod is not Idumaean and not half-Judaean/Jewish—he is not Jewish at all! He is Ascalonite.

A different story appears in the Babylonian Talmud:

Herod was a slave of the Hasmonean house.
He set his eyes on a young girl (of the house).
One day he heard a heavenly voice which said, "Any slave who rebels today, will succeed."
He rose up and killed all his masters, and spared (only) that young girl.
When she saw that he wished to marry her, she ascended the roof and said aloud, "Anyone who comes and says that he is from the Hasmonean house, he is (really) a slave, because none of them is left except me." She threw herself down from the roof to the ground (and died) . . .

13. In "Die frühchristliche Überlieferung über die Herkunft der Familie des Herodes," *Annual of the Swedish Theological Institute* 1 (1962) 109–160, Abraham Schalit argues that this story derives from Jewish anti-Herodian propaganda of Herod's own time. This is possible, of course, but Schalit's conjectures leave me unconvinced. The story may be a Christian invention imputed to the Jews. See below for an analogous development.

14. Eusebius, *Ecclesiastical History* 1.7.11 (quoting Julius Africanus).

He said, "who expounds the verse *be sure to set as king over yourself one of your own people; (you must not set a foreigner over you, one who is not your kinsman*) (Deut. 17:15)? The sages."

He rose up and killed all the sages . . .[15]

In this story "Herod" is clearly Herod the Great, and the Hasmonean princess is clearly Mariamme. Herod is a slave of the Hasmonean house; we are meant, of course, to understand that he is a *gentile* slave. As a slave and a gentile, Herod realizes he is disqualified for kingship by Deuteronomy 17:15, which requires a king to be a "kinsman" (or "brother") to his Jewish subjects. How old this piece of anti-Herodian propaganda might be, I cannot say; the Talmud cites the story anonymously, and there is no telling how long the story circulated before being incorporated in the text. The talmudic story shares with Justin the idea that Herod was not a legitimate Judaean king, and with Africanus the idea that Herod was a gentile, but the Talmud knows nothing of Herod's origin in Ascalon (or, for that matter, in Idumaea).

Our last story combines motifs from Justin and the Talmud. The story is found in the Slavonic version of Josephus, a product of the thirteenth century. The origins and history of this version are much debated, but the following story, which has no parallel in the genuine writings of Josephus, is certainly of Christian origin:

At that time the priests mourned and grieved one to another in secret. They dared not [do so openly for fear of] Herod and his friends.

For [one Jonathan] spoke: "The law bids us have no foreigner for king. Yet we wait for the Anointed, the meek one, of David's line. But of Herod we know that he is an Arabian, uncircumcised. The Anointed will be called meek, but this [is] he who has filled our whole land with blood. Under the Anointed it was ordained for the lame to walk, and the blind to see, and the poor to become rich. But under this man the hale have become lame, the seeing are blinded, the rich have become beggars . . ."

But one of them, by name Levi, wishing to outwit them, spoke to them . . . Overcome with shame, he fled to Herod and informed him of the speeches of the priests which they had spoken against him. But Herod sent by night and slew them all . . .[16]

15. Bava Batra 3b, in Aramaic.

16. H. St. J. Thackeray, *Josephus: The Jewish War* (Loeb Classical Library) 3.636–638, replacing the Greek text at *BJ* 1.364–370. For an alternative translation, see *La prise de Jérusalem de Josèphe le Juif: Texte vieux-russe*, ed. V. Istrin, A. Vaillant, and P. Pascal, 2 vols. (Paris: Institut d'Etudes Slaves, 1934–1938) 1.54–57. On the Slavonic Josephus, see E. Bickerman, "Sur la version vieux-russe de Flavius Josèphe," in Bickerman, *Studies* 3.172–195.

Jonathan the priest wants to believe that Herod is the Anointed one, the Messiah, but is unable to square Herod's pedigree and accomplishments with those promised by the prophets: the Messiah is to be of David's line, but Herod is an Arabian; the Messiah is to be meek, but Herod is cruel; the Messiah is to perform miracles, but Herod has brought disaster. The idea that Jews believed, or wanted to believe, that Herod was the Messiah is the product of Christian exegesis of Genesis 49:10. As I discussed above in connection with Justin, Christians argued that the verse predicted the end of Judaean kingship in the person of Jesus Christ; since Jews deny the kingship of Christ, they must believe that the verse refers instead to Herod the Great, the last king of the Jews; and if for Christians the referent of the verse is the Messiah, then for Jews too the referent of the verse must be the Messiah. Hence, Christian exegetes concluded, Jews must believe that Herod was the Messiah. Needless to say, no Jew in ancient or medieval times is known to have thought of Herod as the Messiah, but this fact did not stop Christian authors, like the author of the Slavonic Josephus, from imputing this belief to them.[17]

In the Christian story the priests take the place of the sages in the rabbinic story. In both stories those who explicate the Deuteronomic verse *you must not set a foreigner over you [as king]* are slain by Herod. In the rabbinic story the victims are the sages, in the Christian story the priests. Both sages and priests agree that Herod is a foreigner who may not rule over Israel; the rabbis think Herod was a gentile slave, while the priests in the Slavonic Josephus think Herod was "an Arabian, uncircumcised." Perhaps the association of Herod with Arabia was invented in the same manner as Herod's association with Ascalon. Perhaps the fact that the Herodian family had connections with "the neighboring Arabs and Gazaeans and Ascalonites," as Josephus said, gave rise to the polemic that Herod was an Arab himself. And how did the Slavonic Josephus come to the idea that Herod was "uncircumcised"? The simplest explanation, surely, is that "uncircumcised" means simply "gentile."[18] The crucial point for the author was to emphasize Herod's non-Jewishness, and describing him as uncircumcised effectively made that point. The juxtaposition of "Arab" with "uncircumcised" is somewhat jarring, since it seems likely that (many) Arabs in antiquity practiced cir-

17. See Bickerman, "La version vieux-russe," 3.187–189, and esp. idem, "Les Hérodiens," in Bickerman, *Studies* 3.22–33.

18. This is Jewish usage, common in the Middle Ages; cf. M. Nedarim 3:11.

cumcision, but a medieval romance writer did not have to trouble himself with the facts. We may assume that the historical Herod, as both an Idumaean and a Judaean, was circumcised.[19]

In sum, was Herod the Great Jewish? The historical Herod certainly was Jewish—that is, a member of the community of those who revere the God whose temple is in Jerusalem. Herod even built a magnificent temple for this God. Herod may have been a Jew, but he was also a "bad" Jew. Most forms of ancient Judaism, I think, would have disapproved of Herod's murder of his wives and children. The largesse he bestowed on pagan temples, cities, and festivals, and his other violations of the ancestral laws, provoked hostile comment in antiquity.[20] If Herod was held accountable to the laws and customs of Judaism, it can only be because he regarded himself, and was regarded by other Jews, as a Jew. The fact that he often failed this standard implies that he was a "bad" Jew. Herod was also an Idumaean, born of an Idumaean father, but insofar as the Idumaeans had been incorporated into the Judaean polity approximately fifty years before his birth, Herod was also a Judaean. He was a member of the Idumaean subdivision of the Judaean polity; Judaeans from Jerusalem sneered at this "half-Judaean" parvenu, but he was Judaean nonetheless. In response his apologist Nicolas denied his Idumaean roots and argued that Herod was a blue-blooded Judaean whose ancestors had arrived on the Judaean equivalent of the *Mayflower*. If we apply the criteria of later rabbinic law, Herod was a gentile, because he was the son of a gentile woman. Indeed, later stories in both Christian and Jewish sources claim that Herod was a gentile, although they do not derive this status from his mother. Herod invented a blue-blooded Judaean extraction for himself, whereas his opponents (at least those who lived a safe distance after him) invented a non-Judaean extraction for him. In sum, depending on whom you ask, Herod was either a *Ioudaios* (that is, a Judaean and Jew), a blue-blooded Judaean, an Idumaean and therefore not a Judaean, an Idumaean and therefore also a Judaean, an Idumaean and therefore a half-Judaean, an Ascalonite, a gentile slave, an Arab, or—the Messiah!

Herod was not a typical Jew of antiquity, and this range of opinions about a single individual is, we may assume, highly unusual. We may also be sure that this range of opinions was occasioned by subsequent Jew-

19. On the circumcision of Arabs, see chapter 2 below, note 77.

20. For example, *AJ* 15.267–276 and 326–330; 16.1–5; 19.328–329. On Herod's Judaism, see Richardson, *Herod* 240–261, and chapter 4 below, note 76.

ish reflection on Herod's rule, rather than by contemporary views of his Jewishness. Still, this case exemplifies several important points. First, it shows the ambiguity inherent in the word *Ioudaios:* it is a political term, an ethnic-geographic term, and a religious term. I shall return to this in chapter 3. Second, it shows that Jewishness is a function of both ethnicity (birth) and religion (culture), a point to which I shall return in chapters 4 and 10 below. Third, it shows that the definition of conversion is a complicated matter (did the Idumaeans "really" become Judaeans/Jews?), a point to which I shall return in chapter 5. Fourth and last, it shows that manipulation of genealogy was relatively easy in antiquity, since there were no genealogical records or written documentation by which a Jew could prove that he really was Jewish; I shall return to this point in my next chapter.

CHAPTER 2

"Those Who Say They Are Jews and Are Not"

How Do You Know a Jew in Antiquity When You See One?

Yes, God has marked them in their very natures. Clearly, a Jew has something about him that makes him immediately recognizable and distinguishable from other people. They rouse disgust and horror.

Grosses Vollständiges Universal Lexikon

God has marked them [the Jews] with certain characteristic signs so that one can recognize them as Jews at the first glance, no matter how hard they try to disguise themselves.

J. J. Schudt, *Jüdische Merckwürdigkeiten*

In the New Testament book of Revelation the risen Jesus appears in a vision to John of Patmos and instructs him to write letters to the protecting angels of the seven churches of Asia Minor. The letter to the church in Philadelphia includes the following lines:

I know that you have but little power, and yet you have kept my word and have not denied my name. Behold, I will make those of the synagogue of Satan who say that they are Jews and are not, but lie—behold, I will make them come and bow down before your feet, and learn that I have loved you.

The epigraphs are from, respectively, *Grosses Vollständiges Universal Lexikon* (Lepizig/Halle, 1735), cited in Frank E. Manuel, *The Broken Staff: Judaism through Christian Eyes* (Cambridge: Harvard University Press, 1992) 251; and J. J. Schudt, *Jüdische Merckwürdigkeiten* (1714–1718), cited in J. Trachtenberg, *The Devil and the Jews* (New Haven: Yale University Press, 1943) 228 n. 26.

A similar phrase appears in the letter to the church in Smyrna ("I know your tribulation and your poverty . . . and the slander by those who say that they are Jews and are not, but are a synagogue of Satan"). Who are these people who say that they are Jews but are not? The simplest and likeliest explanation is that Jews are meant.[1] The author of Revelation believes that the title "Jew" (*Ioudaios*) is an honorable designation and properly belongs only to those who believe in Christ, just as Paul says that the real Jew is not the one outwardly with circumcision in the flesh but the one inwardly with circumcision in the heart and spirit.[2] The Jews are slandering and persecuting the nascent and relatively powerless churches of Smyrna and Philadelphia, and as a result the Jews are deemed to be "synagogues of Satan."

Christian appropriation of the name *Ioudaios* did not end in the first century, of course. Augustine knows Christians who still call themselves *Iudaei,* and the Bishop of Hippo explains to them that Christians can and should be called Israel, but not *Iudaei,* even though in theory this name belongs to them as well.[3] Between the late first century, the date of Revelation, and the late fourth or early fifth century, the period of Augustine, the separation of Jews from Christians, and Christians from Jews, proceeded apace, so that much that was true for Augustine of Hippo was not true for John of Patmos (and vice versa!).[4] For Revela-

1. Rev. 3:8–9 and 2:9. Adela Yarbro Collins, "Insiders and Outsiders in the Book of Revelation," in *"To See Ourselves As Others See Us": Christians, Jews, "Others" in Late Antiquity,* ed. Jacob Neusner and Ernest S. Frerichs (Atlanta: Scholars Press, 1985) 187–218, at 204–210 (an expanded version of an article that appeared in *HTR* 79 [1986] 308–320, at 310–314). See 205 n. 88 for a list of scholars who argue that non-Christian Jews are meant, and 205 n. 89 for a list of scholars who argue that certain kinds of Christians are meant. Collins herself persuasively defends the first position. For a parallel, note the long recension of the letters of Ignatius (probably late fourth century), which uses *pseudoioudaioi* to mean "Jews"; see J. B. Lightfoot, ed., *The Apostolic Fathers: Clement Ignatius and Polycarp,* pt. 2, vol. 3 (London: Macmillan, 1889–1890; reprint, Peabody, Mass.: Hendrickson, 1989) 160 and 212.

2. Rom. 2:28–29; cf. Phil. 3:3. Perhaps Revelation is following the Philonic view that the name *Judah,* the progenitor of the name *Ioudaios,* means "confession of praise to God." Only those who believe in Christ confess God, and therefore only those who believe in Christ deserve the name Jew. See the Philonic passages listed by J. W. Earp in volume 10 of the Loeb edition of Philo (Cambridge: Harvard University Press, 1962) 357 note *a.* Many church fathers followed this view; see de Lange, *Origen* 32 n. 29, and Scherer, *Origène* 168–169. Unless I am mistaken Philo nowhere associates *Ioudaios* with Judah, but we may assume that he and other first-century Jews knew the connection; see *AJ* 11.173 and Justin, *Historiae Philippicae* 36.2.5 = M. Stern, *Authors* no. 137.

3. Augustine, Epistle 196 (= CSEL 57 pp. 216–230).

4. Tertullian already remarks *neque de consortio nominis cum Iudaeis agimus* (*Apology* 21:2).

tion *Ioudaios* is a theological category:[5] real *Ioudaioi* are those who believe in Christ. For Augustine *Judaeus* ought to be a theological category, but instead it is a sociological category; Christians are the true *Judaei* but will create too much confusion if they use that title. Let the Jews have it.

The striking phrase "those who say they are Jews and are not" may well have been a current expression in the first century. It will have applied originally to gentiles who "act the part of Jews" but are not in fact Jews, and was deliberately and cleverly misapplied by Revelation to the Jews themselves.[6] The phrase illustrates the ambiguities inherent in Jewish identity and "Jewishness," especially in the diaspora. In the Judaean homeland (at least until the fourth century C.E.) Jewishness (Judaeanness?) for Jews was natural, perhaps inevitable, but in the diaspora Jewishness was a conscious choice, easily avoided or hidden, sometimes welcomed by society at large, sometimes tolerated, and sometimes harassed. In this chapter I am interested in the social dynamics of "Jewishness" in the Roman diaspora in the last century B.C.E. and the first centuries C.E. How was Jewishness expressed? What did a Jew do—or not do—in order to demonstrate that she/he was not a gentile? If someone claimed to be a Jew, how could you ascertain whether the claim was true? In sum, how did you know a Jew in antiquity when you saw one?[7]

Social Mechanisms That Did Not Make Jews Distinctive

I begin with a discussion of those factors that did *not* render Jews distinctive. Many Greek and Roman authors talk about Jews and Judaism, usually focusing on those characteristics that make Jews

5. The word *Ioudaios* appears in Revelation only in these two passages.
6. I owe this excellent suggestion to David Konstan. For those who "act the part of Jews" but are not in fact Jews, see the passage of Epictetus cited and discussed below.
7. In his *Who Was a Jew?* Schiffman ignores these social questions entirely and focuses exclusively on the history of rabbinic law, as if rabbinic law were the only legal system in antiquity that had an interest in defining Jewishness and as if legal history were social history. In my discussion I occasionally cite rabbinic texts, which, of course, derive from Palestine and/or Babylonia. These citations are entirely for the sake of confirmation, contrast, or illustration; I am not interested here in the manifestations of Jewishness in rabbinic Palestine and Babylonia.

and Judaism peculiar, different from what these authors take to be "normal."[8] It is striking to note, then, what these authors do *not* say. Not a single ancient author says that Jews are distinctive because of their looks, clothing, speech, names, or occupations. I shall now discuss each of these points.

LOOKS

The Romans, and the Greeks before them, noted that foreign peoples often looked different from themselves: they were peculiarly tall or short, hairy or smooth, dark or fair. The Romans also noted peculiar styles of hair and beard.[9] But not a single ancient author comments on the distinctive size, looks, or coiffure of the Jews. In Europe from the high Middle Ages until the early modern period, Jewish men were recognizable by their beards. The Cistercian abbot Richalm of Schönthal (early thirteenth century) said that he was sometimes called a Jew because of his beard; in 1748 Emperor Frederick II of Prussia forbade Jews from shaving their beards, so that they could not pass as gentiles. But no ancient author comments on the Jewish beard.[10] The rabbis prohibited a certain type of haircut because in their estimation it was quintessentially gentile, an "Amorite custom," and in one rabbinic legend a rabbi adopts this haircut precisely in order to be able to pass as a gentile, infiltrate the councils of state, and thwart some anti-Jewish decrees; perhaps we might conclude that at least some rabbis followed this prohibition, but we surely cannot conclude that non-rabbinic Jews did.[11] In any case even the rabbis do not enjoin a distinctive Jewish hairstyle. Apparently Jews looked "normal."[12]

8. The material is easily surveyed in M. Stern, *Authors.*

9. Balsdon, *Romans and Aliens* 214–219.

10. Richalm: Giles Constable, cited by *Apologiae Duae: . . . Bvrchardi . . . Apologia de Barbis,* ed. R. B. C. Huygens, *CChr* cont. med., no. 62 (Turnholt: Brepols, 1985) 54 n. 25 (my thanks to Robert Somerville for pointing me to this passage); Frederick: *Encyclopaedia Judaica* 13:1291, s.v. "Prussia." The Jewish beard is the subject of a forthcoming monograph by Elliot Horowitz.

11. Prohibition: T. Shabbat 6:1 22L (and parallels); see the commentary of Lieberman, *Tosefta Ki-Fshutah* ad loc. pp. 80–81. Legend: B. Me'ilah 17a.

12. Cf. M. Smith, *Studies* 1.100: "I do not recall any ancient reference to a man's being recognized, from his physical appearance, as a Jew, except when the recognition was an inference from circumcision." Marcus Aurelius (cited by Ammianus Marcellinus, in M. Stern, *Authors* no. 506) is said to have noted a peculiar Jewish odor or stench (*Iudaeorum fetentium*). The idea that Jews have a peculiar smell will recur frequently in the Middle Ages, but no one in antiquity suggests that Jews are recognizable by their odor! The notion that Jews look different—that is, different from other white Europeans—by reason

Papyri of the Ptolemaic period regularly contain descriptions of the physical appearance of parties or witnesses to contracts. A few such descriptions of *Ioudaioi* are extant:

1. Apollōnios, aged about thirty-five, tall, honey-colored skin, with rather bright eyes and protruding ears

2. Sōstratos, aged about thirty-five, of middle height, honey-colored skin . . . with a scar over his right eyebrow

3. Jōnathas, aged about . . . , of middle height, honey-colored skin

4. Apollōnios, aged about thirty-eight, of middle height, honey-colored skin

5. Philopatros, aged about fifty-three, . . . honey-colored skin, long-faced, with a scar . . . , a bald forehead

6. Diagoras, aged about . . . , of middle height, honey-colored skin, round-faced, snub-nosed, somewhat nearsighted

7. Nikopolē, aged about twenty-two, of middle height, honey-colored skin, broad-faced, . . . mouth

8. Dōsitheos, aged about thirty-five, of middle height, honey-colored skin, a bald forehead, long-faced

9. Dōsitheos, aged about thirty-eight, of middle height, honey-colored skin, a bald forehead, with light eyes, no hair on the face

10. Philoumenē, aged about fifty, of middle height, honey-colored skin, round-faced, a mole on the chin on the right side, a scar under . . .

11. Pythoklēs, aged about . . . , tall, dark-colored skin, with deeply set eyes, a mole on the neck on the left side

12. Menestratos, aged about thirty-six, of middle height, honey-colored skin, long-faced, a mole on the cheek near the nose on the right side

13. Philistiōn, aged about . . . , tall, honey-colored skin, long-faced, a scar on the right eyebrow

---

of their hair, skin, face, or nose became widespread only in the nineteenth century, although the notion has roots in earlier, medieval conceptions. See the numerous works of Sander L. Gilman on the body of the Jew in the nineteenth century—for example, Sander Gilman, "The Jewish Nose: Are Jews White? Or, The History of the Nose Job," in *The Other in Jewish Thought and History*, ed. Laurence Silberstein and Robert Cohn (New York: New York University Press, 1994) 364–401.

14. Theodōros, aged about twenty-*x*, of middle height, honey-colored skin, straight-nosed, with deeply set eyes[13]

There is nothing "Jewish" about any of these descriptions. A distinguished papyrologist writes: "Nothing we find here [in these descriptions] . . . can help us distinguish a Jew from a Greek."[14] Circumcision was, of course, the one obvious corporeal indication of Jewishness, but Ptolemaic descriptions of free persons list only features visible on the head and neck; apparently it was unseemly to inspect the body of a free person any more closely.[15] In a society in which public nudity was uncommon, and the inspection of the bodies of free persons was deemed inappropriate, circumcision, or its absence, was not a usable marker of identity. I shall return to this below.

CLOTHING

Clothing is an extension of identity. Roman clothing was distinctive, and the Roman magistrate who wore Greek clothing in public was subject to ridicule, at least in Republican times. Romans mocked the crude clothing of the northerners (Celts and Germans), while the Greeks mocked the outlandish costumes of the Persians.[16] Slaves would normally be clothed in a distinctive manner, to distinguish them from free persons. Within Jewish society of rabbinic times, at least some rabbis wore distinctive clothing that marked them out as rabbis.[17]

13. On physical descriptions in Ptolemaic papyri, see Clarysse, *Petrie Papyri* 49–55. For the descriptions of 1–2, see *CPJ* 23 (182 B.C.E.); for 3–5, see Kramer, CPR 18, no. 7; for 6–9, see Kramer, CPR 18, no. 8; for 10–13, see Kramer, CPR 18, no. 9, and cf. no. 11; for 14, see Kramer, CPR 18, no. 11. Clarysse and Kramer provide abundant bibliography.

14. Mélèze-Modrzejewski, *Jews of Egypt* 114.

15. Clarysse, *Petrie Papyri* 54. Slaves, in contrast, were inspected from head to toe, and identifying marks, including circumcision (and the lack of circumcision), were noted; see, for example, *CPJ* no. 4.

16. Balsdon, *Romans and Aliens* 219–222.

17. Slaves: pseudo-Xenophon, *Constitution of the Athenians* 1.10, is offended by the fact that in Athens slaves and commoners dressed alike and were indistinguishable. Rabbis: Genesis Rabbah 82:8 (984T-A) is a story about two disciples who in a time of persecution "changed their dress." This story is usually understood to mean that the disciples changed their clothing so that they would not be recognized as Jews (see, for example, Theodor's commentary ad loc. and *Shulhan Arukh, Yoreh Deah* 157:2), but it is more likely that the story simply means that the disciples were trying to hide their status as rabbis. Normally disciples of sages (like philosophers) were immediately recognizable by their clothing (see Sifrei Deuteronomy 343 [400F] and parallels), but these disciples tried to hide their standing as rabbis in order to escape a persecution that was directed primarily at the sages.

But Jews did not wear distinctive Jewish clothing. Second Maccabees reports that Jewish ephebes in Hellenistic Jerusalem wore the petasos, the broad-rimmed Greek hat worn by youths in the gymnasium, but no ancient author refers to a distinctively Jewish hat, or any other item of distinctively Jewish clothing. The archaeological finds of the Bar Kokhba period reveal that the Jews of Palestine in the first and second centuries C.E. wore clothing that was indistinguishable from that of non-Jews.[18] Tertullian, living in Carthage at the end of the second century C.E., writes that Jewish women could be recognized as Jews by the fact that they wore veils in public. I think it likely, or at least plausible, that Jewish women wore veils in public in the eastern Roman empire, but in the eastern Roman empire many women wore veils in public, and Jewish women would hardly have been distinctive for doing what many other women did. Perhaps in Carthage, a western town, the veils of Jewish women made them distinctive, but I know of no other evidence for the easy recognizability of Jews, either male or female, in antiquity.[19]

18. Petasos: 2 Macc. 4:12. The fullest discussion remains that of Samuel Krauss, *Talmudische Archäologie*, 3 vols. (Leipzig: G. Fock, 1910) 1:127–207, and *Qadmoniyot Ha-Talmud*, 4 vols. (Tel Aviv: Dvir, 1945) vol. 2,2; see too Juster, *Les juifs* 2:215–220; Goodenough, *Jewish Symbols* 9:168–174; Yadin, *Bar Kochba* 66–85 (note esp. 69: "The most important contribution of these textiles . . . was in giving us for the first time a complete set of clothes of the first and second centuries A.D., worn by the Jews of Palestine, which . . . reflect also the fashions throughout the Roman Empire of those days"); Gildas Hamel, *Poverty and Charity in Roman Palestine* (Berkeley: University of California Press, 1990) 57–93 ("Poverty in Clothing"); Sanders, *Judaism* 123–124; D. Edwards, "Dress and Ornamentation," *Anchor Bible Dictionary* (1992) 2.232–238. Cf. Israel Abrahams, *Jewish Life in the Middle Ages* (Philadelphia: Jewish Publication Society, 1911; frequently reprinted) 273–290 ("Costume in Law and Fashion"), esp. 280: ". . . it may be asserted in general that there was no distinctive Jewish dress until the law [of the Christian state] forced it upon the Jews." Cf. Mendel and Thérèse Metzger, *Jewish Life in the Middle Ages* (New York: Alpine Fine Arts Collection, 1982) 111–150 ("Costume"), esp. 138: "Contrary to what might be expected, there was no tradition of clothing peculiar to Jews" (see too p. 150). At *AJ* 18.61 the Loeb translation refers to "Jewish garments," but the translation is misleading; Pilate simply has his soldiers wear "their robes"—that is, civilian attire. The text does not imply that there is Jewish attire.

19. Tertullian, *De Corona* 4.2 (= *CChr* 1:1043–1044), writes: *apud Judaeos tam sollemne est feminis eorum velamen capitis ut inde noscantur*. (Tertullian makes the same point in *De Oratione* 22 = *CChr* 1:270). Claude Aziza correctly notes that the literary context in both the *De Corona* and the *De Oratione* suggests that Tertullian derived his "evidence" from the Hebrew Bible, not from his observation of contemporary Jewish women. Nevertheless, Aziza insists that Tertullian indeed provides reliable evidence about contemporary Jewish women. Aziza supports this contention by appeal to M. Shabbat 6:6, but that Mishnah partly confirms (Jewish women veil themselves) and partly contradicts (the head coverings worn by Jewish women are the same as those of their gentile neighbors) what Tertullian says. See Claude Aziza, *Tertullien et le judaïsme* (Paris: Les Belles Lettres, 1977) 20–21. On the veiling of women in public see Ramsay MacMullen, "Women in Public in the Roman Empire," in his *Changes in the Roman Empire: Essays in*

On the contrary, there is much evidence that Jews, whether male or female, were not easily distinguished from gentiles.

Some examples follow. In the romantic and novelistic retelling of Scripture attributed to the Jewish writer Artapanus, the Egyptian king Chenephres "ordered the Jews to be clothed with linen and not to wear woolen clothing. He did this so that once they were so marked, they could be harassed by him." Without such a publicly visible mark, there was no way to distinguish Jews from the rest of the population.[20] According to the novella known as 3 Maccabees, when Ptolemy Philopator ordered the Jews to be registered and marked as slaves, he wanted to have them branded with an ivy leaf, "the emblem of Dionysus"; here too without such a publicly visible mark there was no way to distinguish Jews from the rest of the population.[21] In the Alexandrian riots in the time of Caligula, the mob arrested Jewish women and brought them to the theater, but by mistake seized many non-Jewish women as well; obviously, Jewish women could not be easily distinguished from non-Jewish.[22] Similarly, the Babylonian Talmud reports that R. Ada b. Ahavah once spotted a woman in the market wearing a *krabalta,* an outlandish piece of clothing not precisely identifiable but obviously inappropriate for a daughter of Israel. The good rabbi, thinking the woman to be a Jew, tore off her *krabalta,* but was chagrined to discover that the woman was a gentile (and a member of the royal family). The

---

the Ordinary (Princeton: Princeton University Press, 1990) 162; on the veiling of Arab women, see R. de Vaux, "Sur le voile des femmes dans l'orient ancien," *Revue biblique* 44 (1935) 397–412. Jewish women in Palestine too seem to have been veiled in public, but I know of no ancient evidence that would confirm Tertullian's statement that they were distinctive because of their veils. A medieval passage of uncertain date and provenance contrasts the habits of Roman with Jewish women; see Daniel Sperber, *A Commentary on Derech Erez Zuta Chapters Five to Eight* (Tel Aviv: Bar Ilan University Press, 1990) 123. In the Roman West women seem as a rule not to have veiled themselves; hence the Jewish women of Carthage, who probably hailed from the East, appeared distinctive because they maintained the mores of their countries of origin. W. H. C. Frend, citing the passage from Tertullian, writes: "The Jew seems even at that time [the second century C.E.] to have been distinguished by his dress, his food, his dwelling in a separate quarter of the town," but this statement is much exaggerated; see Frend, *Martyrdom and Persecution in the Early Church* (New York: New York University Press, 1967) 146 with n. 53. On head covering for women, see Ilan, *Jewish Women* 129–132.

20. Artapanus, frag. 3 par. 20, in Holladay, *Fragments* 1:216–217. I am grateful to Albert Pietersma for reminding me of this passage. The passage seems to be an etiological explanation for the origin of the prohibition of wearing wool and linen together (Deut. 22:11).

21. Maccabees 2:29.

22. Philo, *Against Flaccus* 96. Contrast the passage of Tertullian cited above.

rabbi was fined four hundred zuz.[23] At the opening of Justin Martyr's *Dialogue with Trypho the Jew,* Trypho recognizes Justin immediately as a philosopher (because he is wearing the garb of a philosopher), but Justin has to ask Trypho, "Who are you?" and has to be told, "I am called Trypho and I am a Hebrew of the circumcision." Without such a statement, Justin would not have known Trypho to be either a Jew or circumcised.

In sum, the silence of the texts indicates that Jews were not distinctive because of their clothing.[24] This silence is striking because ancient Jewish sources describe two distinctively Jewish items of clothing: tzitzit and tefillin. Jesus, the Pharisees, and presumably other pietists in the land of Israel wore tzitzit in public, tasseled fringes affixed to the four corners of one's garment in accordance with the injunctions of Numbers 15:37–41 and Deuteronomy 22:12. Tzitzit of the period of Bar Kokhba have been discovered in the Judaean desert. The Pharisees and other pietists in the land of Israel also wore tefillin in public, usually called "phylacteries"—small leather containers strapped to the head and arm and containing several excerpts from the Torah, notably the Shema and (in some versions) the Ten Commandments. Tefillin have been discovered at Qumran.[25]

According to one rabbinic legend of Babylonian provenance a pious Jew working as a jailer kept his Jewishness secret by wearing black shoes (apparently Babylonian Jews did not wear black shoes) and by not wearing tzitzit.[26] According to another statement Jews ought not to sell to a gentile a garment fringed with tzitzit because, R. Judah explains, the gentile might don the garment, accost an unsuspecting Jew, and kill

23. B. Berakhot 20a (a reference I owe to Herb Basser). I follow the reading of the Munich manuscript.

24. According to Y. Demai 4:6 24a, the men of Jerusalem were accustomed to wear robes in the Roman style. See the discussion of the passage by Daniel Sperber, "Melilot V" (in Hebrew), *Sinai* 91 (1982) 270–275, a reference I owe to Marc Bregman. All in all it is striking to note the large number of Greek and Latin words used by the rabbis to denote items of clothing.

25. See the evidence, references, and bibliography assembled by Schürer, *History* 2:479–481. On the tzitzit see Yadin, *Bar Kochba* 81–84. Following Epiphanius, Goodenough argues that *phylacteria* in Matt. 23:5 means not "tefillin" but "stripes of purple cloth appliqué"; see Goodenough, *Jewish Symbols* 9:171–172. It is not clear whether the tassels that appear on the clothing of some of the painted figures of the Dura-Europus synagogue are tzitzit or merely tassels; see Carl H. Kraeling, *The Excavations at Dura-Europus: The Synagogue* (New Haven: Yale University Press, 1956; reprint, New York: Ktav, 1979) 81 n. 239.

26. B. Taanit 22a; on black shoes see B. Sanhedrin 74b, Tosafot, s.v. *"afilu."*

him.[27] Thus, in rabbinic piety, tzitzit could serve as a marker to distinguish Jew from gentile and, indeed, to hamper intimate relations between Jewish men and gentile women.[28] In the rabbinic imagination tefillin could serve the same function.[29] The Letter of Aristeas mentions both tzitzit and tefillin; Philo and Josephus also mention tefillin.[30] Greek-speaking Jews in the diaspora thus knew of tzitzit and tefillin, but, unlike the rabbis, they never referred to them as markers of Jewish identity.

Why do outsiders not mention either tzitzit or tefillin? We have three possibilities: (1) Jews who, like diaspora Jews, came into contact with outsiders did not wear tzitzit and tefillin in public, and perhaps not at all; (2) Jews did wear tzitzit and tefillin, but outsiders did not find them remarkable; or (3) Jews wore tzitzit and tefillin in an inconspicuous manner so as not to attract the attention of outsiders. I think that the first explanation is by far the most plausible. According to one rabbinic passage, togas and two other specific forms of Roman (Greek?) clothing were exempt from the commandment of tzitzit; romanized Jews—who probably would not have listened to the rabbis anyway—were under no obligation to wear tzitzit. The rabbis also reveal that the *ammê ha'aretz*—the "people of the land," who lived outside of rabbinic control and were frequently excoriated by the rabbis for their improper conduct—did not wear either tzitzit or tefillin.[31]

To summarize these first two points: Jews were not distinctive either by their looks or by their clothing. Jews of Antioch looked Antiochene, Jews of Alexandria looked Alexandrian, Jews of Ephesus looked Ephesian, and the Jews of Rome looked like just another exotic group from the East.

SPEECH

The Jews of the diaspora in the Middle Ages created a number of distinctive Jewish "languages": Judaeo-Arabic, Judaeo-

27. B. Menahot 43a (a reference I owe to Ranon Katzoff). The Talmud also supplies another explanation for the rule, but its meaning is not clear.

28. B. Menahot 44a (and parallels).

29. R. Joshua removes his tefillin so as not to be recognized as a Jew (*AdRN* B 19 21a-b). On tzitzit and tefillin as identity markers in rabbinic texts, see S. Stern, *Jewish Identity* 67–71.

30. Aristeas 157–158; Josephus, *AJ* 4.213. Unless I am mistaken neither Philo nor Josephus mentions tzitzit. On Philo's tefillin see Naomi G. Cohen, *Philo Judaeus: His Universe of Discourse* (Frankfurt: Peter Lang, 1995) 144–155; on his omission of tzitzit, 167–177.

31. Togas: Sifrei Deuteronomy 234 (266–267F). *Ammê ha'aretz*: B. Berakhot 47b.

German (Yiddish), Judaeo-Greek, Judaeo-Spanish (Ladino), Judaeo-Persian. The Jews of antiquity, however, did not. The common language of the Jews of the Roman empire (perhaps including Palestine) was Greek. Literate Jews (like Philo) spoke a literate Greek, while illiterate Jews spoke a Greek that was the target of sneers from the educated.[32] There is no evidence at all for a "Jewish Greek," or even for Jewish slang.[33] In 215 C.E. the emperor Caracalla orders the expulsion from Alexandria of all Egyptians who have fled to the city and "who can easily be detected . . . For genuine Egyptians can easily be recognized among the linen-weavers by their speech, which proves them to have assumed the appearance and dress of another class; moreover in their mode of life their far from civilized manners reveal them to be Egyptian countryfolk."[34] No Greek or Roman ever made such comments about Jews; Jews spoke Greek like everyone else.[35]

NAMES

The Tosefta remarks: "Writs of divorce that come (i.e., that are brought to the land of Israel) from overseas are valid, even if the names (of the witnesses) are like the names of the gentiles, because Israel(ites) overseas (have) names like the names of the gentiles."[36] Some diaspora Jews had Jewish or Hebrew names, but many, perhaps most, had names that were indistinguishable from those of the gentiles, a fact that is confirmed by the epigraphical and archaeological record. Many Jews in antiquity, in both the land of Israel and the diaspora, had two names, one gentile and the other Jewish; when they used their gentile names their Jewishness was well hidden.[37]

---

32. Cleomedes: M. Stern, *Authors* no. 333.

33. In contrast, German Jews of the lower and rural classes created a distinctive Jewish German slang that even non-Jewish Germans adopted; see Werner Weinberg, *Die Reste des Jüdischdeutschen* (Stuttgart: Kohlhammer, 1969).

34. *Select Papyri* no. 215.

35. Kurt Treu, "Die Bedeutung des griechischen für die Juden im römischen Reich," *Kairos* 15 (1973) 123–144; G. H. R. Horsley, "The Fiction of Jewish Greek," *New Documents Illustrating Early Christianity* 5 (1989) 5–40; S. Schwartz, "Language."

36. T. Gittin 6:4 270L (and parallels). The Yerushalmi ad loc. asks how we can be sure that the witnesses are, in fact, Jews; see below.

37. Diaspora Jews showed a fondness for certain names, or certain kinds of names, and some diaspora Jews used Hebrew names. Still, outsiders did not comment on the peculiar names of the Jews, probably because Jews who came into contact with outsiders did not have peculiar names. On names of Jews in antiquity see Juster, *Les juifs* 2:221–234; Naomi G. Cohen, "Jewish Names as Cultural Indicators in Antiquity," *Journal for the Study of Judaism* 7 (1976) 97–128; Solin, "Juden und Syrer" 636–647 and 711–713;

On the importance of distinctive Jewish names and language for the maintenance of Jewish identity in the diaspora, the rabbis comment as follows:

> R. Huna said in the name of Bar Qappara,
> Because of four things were the Israelites redeemed from Egypt:
> because they did not change their names;
> and they did not change their language;
> and because they did not speak ill (of each other);
> and because none of them was sexually promiscuous.
> "Because they did not change their names":
> They went down (to Egypt) Reuben and Simeon, and they came up Reuben and Simeon.
> They did not call Reuben "Rufus," Judah "Lollianus," Joseph "Justus,"[38] and Benjamin "Alexander."[39]

This midrash sees the sojourn of the Israelites in Egypt as prefiguring the exile/diaspora. Presumably the midrash is commenting negatively on the status quo; the Israelites of old were redeemed but we are not, because the Israelites of old merited redemption but we—that is, all Jews, not just the Jews of the diaspora—do not. We have changed our names, we have changed our language, we do speak ill of each other, and we are sexually promiscuous (i.e., certain members of our community have sexual relations with gentiles).[40] The Jews of both the

---

Reynolds and Tannenbaum, *Jews and Godfearers* 93–105; Leonard Rutgers, *The Jews in Late Ancient Rome* (Leiden: Brill, 1995) 139–175.

38. All the manuscripts of Leviticus Rabbah read LYSTS—that is, *lēstēs* (the Greek word for "brigand")—but I presume that the initial "L" is an erroneous duplication from the previous word (LYWSP), and that the name that is intended is YSTS, that is, Justus.

39. Leviticus Rabbah 32:5 747–748M and numerous parallels. See S. Stern, *Jewish Identity* 161–162. In a note to the parallel in Pesiqta de Rav Kahana, Beshallah p. 83b ed. Buber (= p. 182 ed. Mandelbaum), Buber refutes a popular paraphrase of this midrash that adds the clause "because they did not change their clothing." Buber comments (n. 66): "This our sages of blessed memory never said." In all likelihood Buber is correct, although some later versions do, in fact, read "because they did not change their clothing"; see the variants assembled and discussed in Menahem M. Kasher, *Torah Shelemah* 8 (5714 = 1954) 239, and 9 (5715 = 1955) 116 (I owe this reference to Herb Basser and Marc Bregman). Buber's note was directed against his ultra-Orthodox contemporaries of the sort described in Michael K. Silber, "The Emergence of Ultra-Orthodoxy: The Invention of Tradition," in *The Uses of Tradition,* ed. Jack Wertheimer (Cambridge: Harvard University Press, 1992) 23–84, esp. 68–72.

40. That this is the meaning of *parutz ba'ervah* is demonstrated by the subsequent discussion in the midrash.

diaspora and the land of Israel changed their names and changed their language.

OCCUPATIONS

As is well known in modern western societies, certain professions and trades have attracted inordinately large numbers of Jews. As is also well known, in medieval Christian Europe Jews were allowed to pursue only a limited number of occupations. In antiquity, however, Jews did not segregate themselves, and were not segregated by general society, in their occupations. The economic profile of the Jews of antiquity seems to have been identical to that of their gentile neighbors, whether in the diaspora or in the land of Israel. Jews in Rome were widely reputed to be beggars, but no ancient source suggests that all beggars were Jews or that all Jews were beggars.[41] Jews perhaps abstained from certain occupations that would have brought them into contact with the gods and religious ceremonies of the gentiles, but, as far as is known, they did not concentrate in particular professions or devote themselves to particular trades. There were no "Jewish" occupations in antiquity.[42]

ROMANS CAN PASS AS JEWS
WITHOUT DIFFICULTY

Jews and gentiles in antiquity were corporeally, visually, linguistically, and socially indistinguishable. Even the sages of the rabbinic academy could not discern Romans in their midst. This story is from the Sifrei on Deuteronomy:

Once the (Roman) government sent two soldiers and said to them,
Go and make yourselves Jews, and see what is the nature of their Torah.
They went to R. Gamaliel in Usha,
and they read Scripture, and they studied the Mishnah, midrash, laws
    and narratives.
When the time came for them to leave, they (the soldiers) said to them
    (the school of R. Gamaliel),
All of the Torah is fine and praiseworthy,
except for this one matter which you say,

41. Johanan Hans Lewy, "Jewish Poor in Ancient Rome" (in Hebrew), in his *Studies in Jewish Hellenism* (Jerusalem: Bialik Institute, 1969) 197–203.
42. Reynolds and Tannenbaum, *Jews and Godfearers* 116–123.

An object stolen from a gentile is permitted (to be used), but (an
   object stolen) from a Jew is prohibited,
but this matter we shall not report to the government.[43]

In the two parallel versions of this story, the command to "make
yourselves Jews" is absent: the Roman officials come as Romans and
leave as Romans.[44] They are not spies but inspectors. These versions of
the story, however, present a problem: how could the sages teach Torah
to gentiles? The Talmud explicitly says: "Transmitting words of Torah
to a gentile is prohibited," and R. Yohanan says; ". . . a gentile who
studies Torah is liable to the death penalty."[45] This problem, which
bothered the medieval commentators, also bothered the editor of the
Sifrei, who solved it by having the Roman officers "make themselves
Jews."[46] Thus R. Gamaliel taught the Romans Torah because R. Gamaliel and his colleagues believed the Romans to be Jews.

"Make yourselves Jews" probably means not "convert to Judaism"
but "pretend to be Jews" or "disguise yourselves as Jews." It is hard to
imagine Romans pretending to be Jews, entering a rabbinic academy,
there to study the entire rabbinic curriculum, without once blowing
their cover or revealing their true identity. Their accents, their looks,
their initial ignorance of things Jewish and rabbinic (an ignorance that
we may freely assume must have been quite impressive)—did none of
this give them away? Apparently not. Some medieval copyists had such
difficulty with this that they understood "make yourselves Jews" to
mean "pretend to be converts" (or, less likely, "make yourselves con-

---

43. Sifrei Deuteronomy 344 401F and parallels. On this story see Catherine Hezser,
Form, Function, and Historical Significance of the Rabbinic Story in Yerushalmi Neziqin
(Tübingen: Mohr [Siebeck], 1993) 15–24.

44. Y. Bava Qamma 4:3 4b; B. Bava Qamma 38a.

45. B. Hagigah 13a and B. Sanhedrin 59a.

46. See Tosafot on Bava Qamma 38a s.v. "*qaru.*" A slightly different version of R. Yohanan's statement (not, of course, ascribed to R. Yohanan) appears in Sifrei Deuteronomy
345 402F, just one page after our story. Thus the editor of the Sifrei certainly knew, and
approved of, the prohibition of teaching Torah to gentiles, and it is likely that the phrase
"make yourselves Jews" is a redactional addition by the editor of the Sifrei to a preexist-
ing story. See Steven Fraade, *From Tradition to Commentary* (Albany: State University of
New York Press, 1991) 51–53, esp. 51 n. 129. Saul Lieberman argues that the phrase is an interpolation in the Sifrei, but I (following Fraade) am not convinced. The strongest argument that the phrase is an interpolation is overlooked by Lieberman: the ending of the
story should have contained a reference to the revelation of the officers' "true" identity:
"when the time came for them to leave, they revealed themselves and said to R. Gamaliel
etc." The absence of an unmasking may imply that no deception was involved. But I am
still not convinced. On the prohibition of Torah study by a gentile, see chapter 7 below,
note 84.

verts") and substituted *gerim* for *yehudim*.[47] According to this "correction," the Romans presented themselves to R. Gamaliel as converts, and R. Gamaliel would have had no difficulty in accepting them as such.

If my analysis is correct, this story, as redacted by the editor of the Sifrei, told of Roman soldiers pretending to be Jews and successfully surviving the scrutiny of R. Gamaliel and his colleagues. If you knew what to say and do, apparently it was easy to pass as a Jew.

Did Circumcision Make Jews Distinctive?

Would not circumcision have made Jews distinct and recognizable? The question is complicated and requires extended discussion. I begin with the obvious: even if circumcision is an indication of Jewishness, it is a marker for only half of the Jewish population (in the eyes of the ancients the more important half, of course, but still, only half). How you would know a Jewish woman when you saw one remains open.[48]

In certain times and places circumcision would have functioned as a marker—or the marker—of Jewishness (or, in the language of the Theodosian Code, *nota iudaica*),[49] but not in all times and not in all places. On the Jewish side, circumcision became *the* marker of Jewish identity—at least in Judaea—in the Maccabean period. Jews are those who are circumcised, Greeks are those who are not; "apostate" Jews try to hide their circumcision through epispasm, the "stretching" or

47. I am arguing that *yehudim* is the more difficult, hence the more original, reading. *Gerim*, however, has more and better support than *yehudim* (see Fraade, *From Tradition to Commentary* 214 n. 129). On the rabbinic avoidance of the locution "being made a Jew," see chapter 5 below, note 70.

48. Unless her veil would give her away; see Tertullian above. Strabo, *Geography* 16.2.37, repeated at 16.4.9 and 17.2.5 (= M. Stern, *Authors* nos. 115, 118, and 124), writes that the Jews practice circumcision on men and excision (*ektomē*) on women. I assume that Strabo is mistaken, the victim of an incorrect ethnography. Philo says that excision is practiced by Egyptians, not Jews (*Questions on Genesis* 3.47). See my "Why Aren't Jewish Women Circumcised?" *Gender and History* 9 (1997) 560–578.

49. Codex Theodosianus 16.8.22 (Theodosius II, 20 October 415 C.E.) = Linder, *Roman Imperial Legislation* no. 41. The term *nota* reflects *'ot* (sign) of Gen. 17:11 and *sēmeion* (sign) and *sphragis* (seal) of Rom. 4:11. The notion of circumcision as a "sign" of Jewish distinctiveness was much developed in the Christian Middle Ages; see Ruth Mellinkoff, *The Mark of Cain* (Berkeley: University of California Press, 1981) 91–96. On page 96 she quotes Peter Riga, *Aurora* 448, *pro signo cunctis est resecata cutis,* "His skin [better: foreskin] has been cut [better: cut back] as a sign to everyone."

"drawing down" of the remains of the foreskin so that the penis would have the look of an uncircumcised organ. Those who joined the Maccabean state were circumcised as well. I shall return to all this in chapter 4 below. Greek historians recounting the Maccabean conquests knew the importance of circumcision to the Maccabees, but over a century had to elapse before outsiders began to associate circumcision with Judaism in the diaspora. That association is first documented by one Latin writer in Rome in the second half of the first century B.C.E. (Horace) and by a string of Latin writers from the middle of the first century C.E. to the first quarter of the second century C.E. (Persius, Petronius, Martial, Suetonius, Tacitus, Juvenal).[50]

Horace (65–8 B.C.E.) once humorously refers to "the clipped Jews."[51] Persius (34–62 C.E.) mocks the man who fears the Sabbath, "turning pale at the Sabbath of the skinned" (lit., "you turn pale at the skinned Sabbath").[52] In the *Satyricon* of Petronius (mid–first century C.E.) a group of characters is trying to figure out how to disembark from a ship without being recognized. The suggestion is made that they dye themselves with ink to appear to be Ethiopian slaves. The suggestion is rejected as inadequate; a good disguise requires more than mere skin coloring. "Circumcise us too so that we look like Jews, and bore our ears to imitate Arabians, and chalk our faces till Gaul takes us for her own sons."[53] A remarkable epigram, probably but not certainly by Petronius, states that if a Jew (*Iudaeus*) does not "cut back with a knife the region of his groin" and "unloose by art the knotted head" (i.e., skillfully remove the knot [= foreskin] from the head of the penis), "he shall wander from his ancestral city, cast forth from his people."[54] These

50. On epispasm see Hall, "Epispasm," and Rubin, "Stretching of the Foreskin." Greek historians: Timagenes (M. Stern, *Authors* no. 81), Strabo (M. Stern, *Authors* nos. 100 and 115), and Ptolemy (M. Stern, *Authors* no. 146). Latin authors: good survey in Schäfer, *Judeophobia* 93–105.

51. *Curtis Iudaeis,* Horace, *Satires* 1.9.69–70 = M. Stern, *Authors* no. 129. Latin *curtus* = Greek *kolobos;* see *Corpus Glossariorum Latinorum,* ed. Loewe-Goetz, 7:299 s.v. For *kolobos* used to describe a type of circumcision, see Strabo, *Geographica* 16.4.9 = M. Stern, *Authors* no. 118, and note 78 below.

52. *Recutitaque sabbata palles,* Persius, *Satires* 5.184 = M. Stern, *Authors* no. 190. *Cutis* means simply "skin" or "leather," but can mean "foreskin"; see Adams, *Sexual Vocabulary* 73. Therefore *recutitus* means "with the (fore)skin removed."

53. *Etiam circumcide nos ut Iudaei videamur,* Petronius, *Satyricon* 102:14 = M. Stern, *Authors* no. 194.

54. *Ni . . . ferro succiderit inguinis oram et nisi nodatum solverit arte caput, exemptus populo patria migrabit ab urbe,* Petronius, frag. no. 37 = M. Stern, *Authors* no. 195. *Patria* is the excellent emendation of E. Courtney, *The Poems of Petronius,* American Classical Studies, no. 25 (Atlanta: Scholars Press, 1991) 70. Stern accidentally omits the translation for *et nisi nodatum solverit arte caput. Caput* = *glans penis;* see Adams, *Sexual*

two texts refer in the first instance to the Jews in their ethnic homeland (Judaeans, rather than Jews), but we may presume that Petronius intended the passages to have relevance to the Jews of Rome too. In a third passage Petronius refers to a "skinned" slave; we cannot be sure that the slave was Jewish.[55] Martial (end of the first century C.E.) complains that Caelia, a Roman girl, bestows her favors on the men of many nations, including "skinned Jews," but not on Romans.[56] In a vicious attack on a rival in both poetry and love, Martial describes him (four times in only eight lines!) with the offensive word *verpus*. *Verpus* means "with the glans of the penis exposed," the glans being exposed either because of erection or because of circumcision.[57] This poetic rival, this *verpus*, "born in the very midst of Jerusalem," he says, buggers his slave and has the nerve to deny it! Martial knows that his readers know that anyone born in Jerusalem will be circumcised, hence the pun of the poem: the rival is *verpus* because he is circumcised and because he lusts for a boy.[58] Two other epigrams may refer to Jews and circumcision, but the texts are difficult to interpret, and require extended discussion.[59]

For these four poets Jews are those who are circumcised, and those who are circumcised are, or look like, Jews. None of them associates circumcision with any other people. We should not exaggerate, of course; the perspective of these four poets was not universal even in Rome. Many other Latin writers of the same period in Rome mention—or even discuss at some length—Jews or Judaea but say nothing about circumcision.[60] Other natives of the "Orient," in addition to Jews, may well have persisted in observing their ancestral custom in Rome. Celsus,

---

Vocabulary 72, and cf. Rutilius Namatianus, *De Reditu Suo* 1.388 (= M. Stern, *Authors* no. 542), *(gens) quae genitale caput propudiosa metit.*

55. *Recutitus est,* Petronius, *Satyricon* 68.8 = M. Stern, *Authors* no. 193.

56. *Nec recutitorum fugis inguina Iudaeorum,* Martial, *Epigrams* 7.30.5 = M. Stern, *Authors* no. 240. Book 7 was published in 92 C.E.; see Sullivan, *Martial* 39.

57. Exposed because of erection: Catullus 47.4 (*verpus Priapus*), and cf. Martial 11.46.2 where *verpa* means erect penis. Exposed because of circumcision: Juvenal 14.104 (see below). The same ambiguity obtains in the parallel Greek words *psōlos/psōlē;* see K. J. Dover, *Greek Homosexuality* (Cambridge: Harvard University Press, 1978; reprint, 1989) 129. For an excellent discussion of these words see Adams, *Sexual Vocabulary* 12–14. See next note.

58. Martial 11.94 = M. Stern, *Authors* no. 245. *Verpus* often is used in connection with aggressive homosexual love; see Adams, *Sexual Vocabulary,* and Kay, *Martial Book XI* 258 (commentary on 11.94). On *pedicare* see Adams, *Sexual Vocabulary* 123–125. Book 11 was published at the end of 96 C.E.; see Sullivan, *Martial* 46.

59. See appendices A and B.

60. Circumcision is not mentioned by Cicero, Varro, Ovid, Valerius Maximus, Seneca, Pliny the Elder, Valerius Flaccus, Silius Italicus, Quintilian, or Statius, although all of these Latin authors living in Rome have something to say about Jews or Judaea.

a medical writer living in Rome in the middle of the first century C.E., describes a medical procedure by which a man whose glans is bare "can cover it for the sake of a pleasing appearance." The glans might be bare for natural reasons (i.e., from birth), or "in someone who after the custom of certain nations has been circumcised."[61] Jews are not mentioned. Thus the Jews are not the only nation to practice circumcision (see further below), but in Rome in the first century the Jews became particularly and peculiarly associated with it.

The barbs of the satirists seem innocuous, but they, and the attitude they represent, paved the way for a radical decision by the Roman state: any circumcised person in the city of Rome would be assumed by the state to be a Jew, and whoever was assumed by the state to be a Jew was liable to the *fiscus Iudaicus,* the "Jewish tax" levied on Jews throughout the empire as war reparations for the revolt of 66–70 C.E. Suetonius (first half of the second century C.E.) reports the following about the emperor Domitian:

Besides other (taxes), the Jewish tax was levied with the utmost vigor; (both) those who lived a Jewish life without registering (themselves as Jews), as well as those who concealed their origin and did not pay the tribute levied on their nation, were prosecuted as subject to the tax. I recall being present in my youth when a ninety-year-old man was examined by the procurator before a very crowded court to see whether he was circumcised.[62]

This story concerns those who say that they are not Jews but are; that is, they say they are not liable to the Jewish tax but are. Suetonius refers to two categories of people: those who "live a Jewish life" but have not declared themselves to be, or registered themselves as, Jews; and those who were born Jews but who mask their Jewish birth so that they would not have to pay the tax imposed on their nation. Members of the first category were not native Jews but converts to Judaism or "judaizers," whereas members of the second category were native Jews who did not lead a Jewish life. Unfortunately Suetonius does not tell us what this ninety-year-old man did (or refrained from doing) so as to arouse the suspicions of the authorities, or whether the man was in fact

61. *Qui quarundam gentium more circumcisus est,* Celsus, *De Medicina* 7.25.1. Celsus refers to an author named Iudaeus (M. Stern, *Authors* nos. 150–151) but otherwise does not mention Jews anywhere in his book. *Decoris causa* echoes Herodotus 2.37.2 (having a foreskin is *euprepēs*).

62. Suetonius, *Domitian* 12.2 = M. Stern, *Authors* no. 320. I have modified the Loeb translation of Rolfe (reprinted by Stern) in order to make it more literal.

circumcised, or what decision was rendered. Nor does Suetonius tell us whether the old man was suspected of belonging to the first category (i.e., of being a convert or a judaizer) or the second (i.e., of being an unobservant Jew or an apostate).[63] In either case, apparently, circumcision would have been seen as unmistakable proof of Jewishness, since it would have indicated either Jewish birth (circumcision being performed on the eighth day after birth) or Jewish life or both. In the eyes of the state, at least under Domitian (81–96 C.E.) and at least in Rome, if you were circumcised you were Jewish.[64] Presumably no one but Jews would continue to circumcise their sons.

Why did the Jews persist in practicing circumcision when no one, or hardly anyone, else in Rome did? The historian Tacitus, writing in the first decade of the second century C.E., explains:

These rites (i.e., frequent fasts, the Sabbath, unleavened bread), whatever their origin, can be defended by their antiquity; their other customs are sinister and abominable, and owe their persistence to their depravity: for the worst rascals among other peoples, renouncing their ancestral religions, always kept sending tribute and contributing to Jerusalem, thereby increasing the wealth of the Jews. Further, the Jews are extremely loyal toward one another, and always ready to show compassion, but toward every other people they feel only hate and enmity. They sit apart at meals and they sleep apart, and although as a nation they are prone to lust, they abstain from intercourse with foreign women; yet among themselves nothing is unlawful. They instituted circumcision of the genitalia so that they could be recognized by their difference. Those who are converted to their ways follow the same practice, and the earliest lesson they receive is to despise the Gods, to disown their country, and to regard their parents, children, and brothers as of little account.[65]

I have quoted this passage in full because its tone and general outlook are as significant as its specifics. Tacitus conceives of the Jews as a secret

---

63. First category: Smallwood, *Jews under Roman Rule* 377. Second category: Goodman, "Nerva" 40–41. For discussion of this passage see Williams, "Domitian," and Schäfer, *Judeophobia* 113–116.

64. We cannot be sure that this episode took place in Rome, but it is likely that it did. Nerva's coinage *fisci iudaici calumnia sublata* was issued under senatorial auspices in Rome, suggesting that Domitian's abusive exactions were practiced there. The date of the incident is c. 88–92 C.E. See Stern's commentary. How did non-Jews who practiced circumcision fare under Domitian? Perhaps there were not many left.

65. Tacitus *Histories* 5.5.1–2 = M. Stern, *Authors* no. 281. See Stern's commentary ad loc. for a rich collection of parallels from both Jewish and non-Jewish texts (add Philostratus, Life of Apollonius 5.33 = M. Stern, *Authors* no. 403).

and sinister society, hostile to the civilized order and opposed to everything that the Romans hold sacred and dear.[66] Although, or perhaps because, they are hostile to outsiders, they attract a constant flow of converts, who increase their numbers, augment their wealth, and render
them all the more dangerous. I shall return to this motif below. And
how do the members of this secret society, whether natives or converts,
recognize each other? Through circumcision. "They instituted circumcision of the genitalia so that they could be recognized by their difference."[67] Tacitus' contemporary Juvenal (first quarter of the second century C.E.) has a similar conception of Judaism and circumcision.[68] Early
Christianity too was widely regarded by its critics as a sinister and secret
society whose members would recognize each other by a secret sign unknown to outsiders.[69] According to Tacitus, circumcision began as a
sign by which Jews would recognize each other; by Tacitus' own time
it had become a sign by which outsiders would recognize Jews.

Thus in the city of Rome in the first century C.E., certainly in the latter part of the century, circumcision served as a marker of Jewishness.
But in the eastern parts of the empire, at least until the first century C.E.,
circumcision cannot have served as such a marker because it was practiced by non-Jews as well as Jews. Balancing the literary tradition that
associates circumcision exclusively with the Judaeans, a tradition exemplified by the Latin writers surveyed above,[70] is the literary tradition that
associates circumcision with Egypt and with nations influenced by
Egypt, among them the Jews. Herodotus (mid fifth century B.C.E.) says
that the Colchians, Egyptians, and Ethiopians "are the only nations that
have from the first practiced circumcision," and that the Phoenicians
and the Syrians of Palestine learned the custom from the Egyptians,
whereas the Syrians of the river valleys of Asia Minor learned it from the

66. For a brilliant analysis of this motif see Yohanan Hans Lewy, "Tacitus on the Antiquities of the Jews and Their Manners" (in Hebrew), in his *Studies in Jewish Hellenism*
115–189, esp. 164–179.

67. *Circumcidere genitalia instituerunt ut diversitate noscantur.*

68. Juvenal, *Satires* 14.96–106 = M. Stern, *Authors* no. 301. Converts allow their foreskins to be cut (*mox et praeputia ponunt;* for this sense of *ponere* see *Oxford Latin Dictionary* s.v., definition 6b) and lead only the circumcised to the desired fountain (*quaesitum
ad fontem solos deducere verpos*). *Verpus* here must mean "circumcised"; I see no alternative (see above).

69. Lewy, "Tacitus" 173 n. 249, cites Caecilius in Minucius Felix, *Octavius* 2:9: Christians recognize each other by a secret sign in the body.

70. The tradition first appears in Strabo, for whom circumcision is a sign not of hostility to other nations but of superstition (*deisidaimonia*). See Strabo, *Geographica* 16.2.37
= M. Stern, *Authors* no. 115. The other Strabonian references to Jewish circumcision are
in the Herodotean tradition; see M. Stern, *Authors* nos. 118 and 124.

Colchians.[71] That the Herodotean phrase "the Syrians of Palestine" means "the Jews (Judaeans) of Palestine" is assumed by Diodorus of Sicily, argued by Josephus, and repeated by the philosopher Celsus in the middle of the second century C.E.[72] In this literary tradition, the practice of circumcision is characteristic of the Egyptians, the Jews (Judaeans), and other nations as well.

How many of these nations preserved this ancestral ritual through the Hellenistic and Roman periods is not clear. Herodotus already remarks that Phoenicians who mingle with the Greeks no longer circumcise their sons.[73] But the practice did not die out. A Phoenician author of the Roman period writes that Kronos, the God of the Phoenicians, circumcised himself to atone for his castration of his father Ouranos. The intent of this statement surely is to explain the origins of the Phoenician practice of circumcision, a question that was still alive at the time of the author.[74] According to Philo "not only the Jews but also the Egyptians, Arabs, and Ethiopians and nearly all those who inhabit the southern regions near the torrid zone are circumcised," whereas "the nations which are in the northern regions . . . are not circumcised."[75] Josephus is probably more accurate: not the Egyptians but the Egyptian priests continued the practice of circumcision, a fact that is confirmed by papyrological documents of the second century C.E.[76] Jerome (ca. 400 C.E.) confirms that still in his day the Arabs practice

---

71. Herodotus 2.104.2–3 = M. Stern, *Authors* no. 1. For a good discussion of this passage, see Lloyd, *Herodotus, Book II* 2:157–159 (commentary on Herodotus 2.36.3) and 3:22–25 (commentary on 2.104.2–3). On the practice of circumcision by nations other than the Jews see Stern's commentary on M. Stern, *Authors* nos. 1 and 511; Schürer, *History* 1:537–540; and Jack M. Sasson, "Circumcision in the Ancient Near East," *JBL* 85 (1966) 473–476 (a reference I owe to Saul Olyan).

72. Diodorus of Sicily 1.28.2–3 = M. Stern, *Authors* no. 55; and 1.55.5 = M. Stern, *Authors* no. 57; Josephus, *AJ* 8.262 and *CAp* 1.169–17; Celsus cited by Origen, *Against Celsus* 1.22 = M. Stern, *Authors* no. 375 (pp. 233 and 265).

73. Herodotus 2.104.4.

74. Philo of Byblos cited by Eusebius, *Praeparatio evangelica* 1.10.33 (= Jacoby, *FGrH* 790 F 2); see Albert Baumgarten, *The Phoenician History of Philo of Byblos* (Leiden: Brill, 1981) 222. I am grateful to Saul Olyan for reminding me of this passage.

75. Philo, *Questions on Genesis* 3.48 (Loeb edition, supp. 1, p. 243).

76. *CAp* 2.141. On the circumcision of Egyptian priests see Stern's commentary on M. Stern, *Authors* no. 1; Colson's supplementary note to Philo, *On the Special Laws* 1.2; L. Mitteis and U. Wilcken, *Grundzüge und Chrestomathie der Papyruskunde*, vol. 1, pt. 2 (Leipzig: Teubner, 1912) nos. 74–77; *Select Papyri*, nos. 244 and 338; and the edition by Maarit Kaimio of a *Beschneidungsantrag* (ca. 156 C.E.) in P. Rainer Cent. = *Festschrift zum 100-jährigen Bestehen der Papyrussammlung der österreichischen Nationalsbibliothek Papyrus Erzherzog Rainer* (Vienna: Brüder Hollinek, 1983) no. 58, pp. 339–342; P. J. Sijpesteijn and K. A. Worp, "Urkunde bezüglich Beschneidung," *Aegyptus* 67 (1987) 46–52 (I owe these last two references to K. Worp).

circumcision.[77] We may assume that in the first century C.E. in portions of Asia Minor, Syria, Arabia, and perhaps Egypt, circumcision will not have been unusual and certainly will not have been a Jewish peculiarity. There is no certainty that Jewish circumcision looked exactly like Egyptian or Arab circumcision, but we may presume that in these regions circumcision alone was not an unmistakable marker of Jewishness.[78]

The situation will have changed markedly during the reign of Hadrian (117–137 C.E.). Precisely when and why the emperor Hadrian issued a general prohibition of circumcision is debated, but that he did so is beyond dispute. In the Roman-Jewish war that erupted in the wake of this prohibition (commonly known as the war of Bar Kokhba or Bar Kosba), circumcision was understood by both sides to be a marker of Jewishness; some Jews tried to remove it through epispasm.[79] Hadrian's successor, the emperor Antoninus Pius, issued a rescript permitting the Jews to circumcise their sons; that is, the general prohibition remained in place but the Jews were granted an exemption.[80] Thenceforth throughout the Roman empire, even in the east, at least for the next century or so, circumcision would be a fairly secure sign of Jewishness. Justin Martyr, in his *Dialogue with Trypho the Jew,* written not long after the Hadrianic persecution, tells his Jewish interlocutor, "You (Jews) are recognized among other people by nothing other than your circumcision in the flesh."[81]

77. Cited by Stern in his commentary on M. Stern, *Authors* no. 1. See too Sozomen 6.38.11, p. 299, ed. J. Bidez, rev. G. C. Hansen (GCS 50). The Slavonic version of the *Jewish War* has one of the priests call Herod "an Arabian, uncircumcised" (H. St. J. Thackeray, *Josephus: The Jewish War* [Loeb Classical Library] 3.636). See chapter 1 above. On the circumcision of Arabs see also chapter 7 below, note 73.

78. It is not clear exactly how much was cut or cut off in Egyptian circumcision; see Lloyd, *Herodotus, Book II* 2:158. Not all circumcisions are the same; see Rubin, "Stretching of the Foreskin," passim, and Dulière, "La seconde circoncision." Note Jubilees 15:33, which polemicizes against some Jews who circumcise their sons but leave on them some of the flesh of their circumcision; clearly they were not circumcising correctly. Similarly Strabo 16.4.17 (776) and Diodorus 3.32.4 distinguish between *peritemnomenoi* and *koloboi tas balanous;* they do not agree on the distinction, but the fact that there is a distinction shows that there are different ways of doing circumcision.

79. On the Hadrianic decree see the pages of Stern and Schürer cited above in note 71 (with bibliography); see too Peter Schäfer, *Der Bar Kokhba Aufstand* (Tübingen: Mohr [Siebeck], 1981) 8–50 and 233–235, and Alfredo M. Rabello, "Il problema della 'circumcisio' in diritto romano fino ad Antonino Pio," in *Studi in onore di Arnaldo Biscardi* (Milan: Cisalpino-Goliardica, 1982) 2:187–214. On the rabbinic evidence for epispasm see the full discussion in Rubin, "Stretching of the Foreskin."

80. Linder, *Roman Imperial Legislation* no. 1. Egyptian priests too were granted an exemption; see above.

81. Justin, Dialogue 16.3.

The situation will have changed markedly again when the Syrian Elagabalus became emperor in 218 C.E. He circumcised himself as well as several of his companions in honor of his Syrian God.[82] Perhaps this action indicates that circumcision had never died out completely among some portions of the Syrian population, but it certainly indicates that the Hadrianic prohibition was no longer in force.

Thus in certain times and places in antiquity, if you saw a circumcised person you could be fairly sure that he was a Jew, but in other times and places, you could not.[83] In contemporary western culture the organ on which circumcision is practiced is generally kept hidden from the sight of other men. If this was true in antiquity as well, how often would you have had the opportunity to see the circumcision of another person? In the classical period (fifth and fourth centuries B.C.E.) the Greeks noted that the readiness to appear naked in public was a distinctively Greek characteristic not shared by those whom the Greeks called barbarians.[84] In the words of some these barbarians, "There is no man more despicable than he who goes naked in public."[85] The Romans at first shared the barbarian aversion to public nudity,[86] but by the period of the empire they had combined the Greek gymnasium with the Roman bath and had come to terms with nudity as a regular feature of public life. In the gymnasia and the baths the wellborn would regularly be seen nude by their peers and their social inferiors; the lowborn, of course, routinely would have had their bodies exposed to the eyes of others, even outside the gymnasium and the bath, and this very fact was confirmation of their inferior status.[87]

The degree to which Jews participated in the culture of the gymnasium is a question that I cannot address here. Clearly some Jews did

---

82. Dio Cassius 80.11.1 (Loeb ed., vol. 9, pp. 456–457).

83. The daughter of Pharaoh, when she saw Moses' circumcision, realized that the boy must be an Israelite; see B. Sotah 12b and the discussion in Ginzberg, *Legends* 5:399 n. 51. I ignore here the statistically insignificant cases of gentiles being circumcised, and Jews not being circumcised, for medical reasons. For the former see Josephus, *CAp* 2:143 and cf. M. Stern, *Authors* no. 539. For the latter see T. Shabbat 15.8 70–71L (and parallels) and cf. M. Nedarim 3:11 (reference to "the uncircumcised ones of Israel").

84. Herodotus 1.10.3; Thucydides 1.6.5; Plato, *Republic* 5.452c.

85. Sifrei Deuteronomy 320 367F (and parallels). See now Michael Satlow, "Jewish Constructions of Nakedness in Late Antiquity, *JBL* 116 (1997) 429–454.

86. Romans would cover their loins in public: Dionysius of Halicarnassus 7.72.2–3.

87. Peter Brown, "Late Antiquity," in *A History of Private Life*, vol. 1, *From Pagan Rome to Byzantium*, ed. Paul Veyne (Cambridge, Mass.: Belknap, 1987) 245–246. T. Berakhot 2:14 9L imagines that a field laborer might be naked or wearing only a thong; see Hamel, *Poverty and Charity*.

participate.[88] If they experienced jibes from their uncircumcised colleagues[89] they had three choices: grin and bear (bare) it; stay home; or undergo epispasm. Other Jews, offended by the public nudity of the gymnasium, had no interest in participating and kept themselves—and their circumcisions—home. How the Jews of the diaspora fared in the baths is not known. Certainly the rabbinic Jews of Palestine went to the baths,[90] and we may presume that diaspora Jews did so too. Here then you would have your chance to see if someone was circumcised.[91] Outside the bath, however, you would never know (unless you were dealing with a slave or another lowborn person, whose naked body you would be able to see often).

A final point. Whether or not circumcision is an infallible or a usable indicator of Jewishness, there is no evidence that the Jews in antiquity ever actually used it as a means of detecting fellow Jews.[92] The midrash imagines that Joseph, when revealing himself to his brothers, really did reveal himself: he proves his identity by showing his circumcision.[93] But surely Jewish men were not in the habit of showing each other their circumcisions. Here is an excerpt from a cycle of stories about Antoninus, the legendary Roman emperor who was a good friend of the Jews and a disciple of Rabbi Judah the Patriarch, known simply as Rabbi:

> Antoninus said to Rabbi, will you let me eat of leviathan in the world to come?
> He (Rabbi) said to him, yes.
> He (Antoninus) said to him, from the Paschal lamb you will not let me eat, but you will let me eat of leviathan?

88. H. A. Harris, *Greek Athletics and the Jews* (Cardiff: University of Wales, 1976); Trebilco, *Jewish Communities* 176–177.

89. The Roman poets surveyed above have a mocking tone toward circumcision. Apion too mocked circumcision (Josephus, *CAp* 2.137 = M. Stern, *Authors* no. 176); Philo, *Special Laws* 1.2, reports that circumcision is widely "laughed at."

90. For example, M. Avodah Zarah 3:4. See Yaron Eliav, "Did the Jews at First Abstain from Using the Roman Bathhouse?" (in Hebrew), *Cathedra* 75 (1995) 3–35 (I am grateful to Shaya Gafni for this reference). Even in Jewish bathhouses men would be naked in the presence of other men; see T. Berakhot 2:20 10L.

91. In the bath one normally would be able to tell if a neighbor was circumcised; see Martial 7:82 = M. Stern, *Authors* no. 243 (if indeed *verpus* here means circumcised; see appendix B below). In rabbinic baths too people are nude: B. Shabbat 10a. Josephus reports that the Hellenizers concealed their circumcision in order to be Greeks even when unclothed (*AJ* 12.41, cf. 1 Macc. 1:11). *BJ* 2.161 reports that Essene women wore a garment while bathing, men a loincloth; this implies that non-Essenes were naked while bathing.

92. The Maccabees roamed the countryside checking to see whether babies were circumcised; later, we imagine, they roamed the countryside checking the Idumaeans and Ituraeans. Clearly these are special cases.

93. Genesis Rabbah 93.8 (93.10) 1160T-A.

He (Rabbi) said to him, what can I do for you, when concerning the
Paschal lamb it is written (in Exod. 12:48) *but no uncircumcised per-
son may eat of it.*
When he heard this, he (Antoninus) went and was circumcised.
He (Antoninus) came (back) to him (and) said to him, my master, look
at my circumcision.
He (Rabbi) said to him (Antoninus), never in my life have I looked at
my own—(shall I look) at yours?[94]

True, Rabbi Judah the Patriarch was unusually abstemious in this matter,[95] but it is striking that there is not a single attested case in antiquity
of Jewish communal leaders checking the circumcision of a supposed
Jew.[96] Even R. Gamaliel and company did not check the circumcision
of the Roman spies (inspectors?) that came to the academy (see above).
The shock that emerges from Suetonius' story quoted above might imply that even the Romans did not regularly check circumcisions publicly; the Romans, at least, had the authority to do so if they needed to,
but the Jews did not. From the Jewish side circumcision was not a useful marker of Jewishness.

Were There Official Lists or Registers of Jews?

If, then, circumcision was neither infallible nor usable as
a marker of Jewishness, was there some other "empirical" or "objective" way by which Jewishness could be confirmed? Or, to phrase the
question more specifically, if someone claimed to be Jewish by birth,
could his or her pedigree be checked? If someone claimed to be a convert, could this claim somehow be verified? In sum, were genealogical
registers and records of conversions kept at the temple or at local community archives and synagogues?

94. Y. Megillah 1:12 72b = Y. Megillah 3:2 74a. For discussion see my "The Conversion of Antoninus," in *The Yerushalmi in Its Greco-Roman Environment,* ed. Peter Schäfer
(forthcoming).

95. Burton Visotzky, "Three Syriac Cruxes," *JJS* 42 (1991) 167–175, at 175 = Burton
Vistozky, *Fathers of the World* (Tübingen: Mohr [Siebeck], 1995) 158–159.

96. The Talmud has many stories of rabbis checking the pedigrees of Jews and supposed Jews, but, as far as I know, no story about rabbis checking circumcisions. In the
rabbinic imagination Abraham stands at the gate to Gehenna, refusing entry to the circumcised and allowing only the uncircumcised (and Jews who have had sex with gentiles)
to enter (B. Eruvin 19a and Genesis Rabbah 48:8 483T-A). A gatekeeper checking circumcision is a product of fantasy with no analogue in the real life of rabbinic society.

I cannot treat these questions here in any detail. There is abundant and probative evidence that priests (*kohanim*) kept careful genealogical records both before and after the destruction of the second temple, and that they carefully checked (or were expected to check) the pedigree of their marriage partners. When the temple was still standing, these records apparently were public and were maintained in the temple.[97] Whether lay Jews too were similarly obsessed with their genealogies is not as clear. In any case, virtually all the evidence on the question either derives from, or refers to, the land of Israel.[98] In the Roman diaspora, certainly after 70 C.E., there is no evidence for obsession with genealogical purity and hardly any evidence for public archives and archival records. A lone papyrus from Egypt refers to "the archive of the Jews" (13 B.C.E.), in which apparently wills were filed; a lone inscription from Hierapolis in Phrygia refers to "the archive of the Jews" (second or third century C.E.), where apparently copies of tomb-violation inscriptions were recorded.[99] Public archives may have existed in various communities, then, but there is no sign that they were repositories of demographic data or were used to verify status claims. Various individuals may have kept private family genealogies, but there were no public archives that would have been of use.

A register for converts is even less likely to have existed. Julius Africanus would have us believe that in the time of Herod, "the Hebrew families, and those traceable to proselytes such as Achior the Ammonite and Ruth the Moabite, and the mixed families which had come out of Egypt"—all these were "enrolled in the archives."[100] The plausibility of this claim is not enhanced by its reference to Achior the Ammonite, a fictional character of the book of Judith; Ruth the Moabite, a fictional (or, at least, legendary) character of the book of Ruth, and scarcely a convert or proselyte in the later sense of the word; and the mixed mul-

97. Lieberman, *Hellenism* 172. On the concern of the priests to maintain family purity, see Adolph Büchler, *Studies in Jewish History* (London: Oxford University Press, 1956) 64–98.

98. Schürer, *History* 2:240–242, and Joachim Jeremias, *Jerusalem in the Time of Jesus* (Philadelphia: Fortress, 1969) 214–216 and 275–283. Babylonian Jews prided themselves on the purity of their pedigree (boasting that it was superior even to that of the Jews of the land of Israel—B. Qiddushin 69b and 71b), but as far as I know they never refer to a *megillat yohasin* like that mentioned in M. Yevamot 4:13.

99. *CPJ* no. 143.7–8; *CIJ* no. 775. *CIJ* no. 776 and nos. 778–779 (also Hierapolis) and *CIJ* no. 741 (Smyrna) refer to "the archive," but it is not clear if the reference is to "the archive of the Jews" or to the local municipal archives.

100. *Anagraptōn en tois archeiois*, Julius Africanus cited by Eusebius, *Historia Ecclesiastica* 1.7.13 (trans. K. Lake) = Routh, *Reliquiae Sacrae* 2:236 and notes ad loc.

titudes who left Egypt with the Israelites, people who lived (insofar as we can say anything positive about them) approximately one thousand or twelve hundred years before the time of these archives. Furthermore, before the rabbinic innovations of the second century of our era, conversion to Judaism was entirely a private and personal affair. The conversion was not supervised or sponsored by anyone, and there were no established standards that had to be met (except for the act itself—circumcision).[101] A register for converts before the second or third century C.E. is impossible to conceive; a register for converts after the second or third century C.E. is conceivable but undocumented.

In sum, genealogical investigation would have been based not on documents but on the memory of oral informants.[102] This investigation will have been slow and uncertain. Without documentary records on which to rely, it is easy to see how genealogies could be forgotten, falsified, or improved. Herod the Great could try to pass himself off as a Judaean blue blood, a descendant of the Jews who returned from Babylonia in the time of the Persians, while his opponents would call him a "half-Jew" or a "slave."[103] Paul would declare himself to be a well-bred Jew of the tribe of Benjamin, but his opponents (probably after his death) would declare him to be a gentile by birth and a convert.[104]

But even if the Jews of antiquity possessed written genealogical records, we should not exaggerate their significance or utility. The legitimate offspring of Roman citizens were enrolled in public registers, as were all those who received grants of Roman citizenship,[105] but

101. See chapter 7 below.

102. Cf. B. Ketuvot 28b and Y. Ketuvot 2:10 26d (and parallels) regarding the *qetzitzah* ceremony. Memory, not documents, as a rule forms the basis of proof for the Attic orators as well; see Adele Scafuro, "Witnessing and False Witnessing: Proving Citizenship and Kin Identity in Fourth Century Athens," in *Athenian Identity and Civic Ideology*, ed. Alan Boegehold and Adele Scafuro (Baltimore: Johns Hopkins University Press, 1994) 156–198.

103. Nicolaus of Damascus cited by Josephus, *AJ* 14.9 = M. Stern, *Authors* no. 90; see Stern's commentary ad loc. See chapter 1 above.

104. Epiphanius, *Panarion* 30.16.8–9 (citing the Ebionite *Ascents of James*). This motif is absent from Gerd Luedemann, *Opposition to Paul in Jewish Christianity* (Minneapolis: Fortress, 1989), which treats material up to about 200 C.E.; in all likelihood the motif is a polemical invention from the third or fourth century.

105. Registration of offspring: A. N. Sherwin-White, *Roman Society and Roman Law in the New Testament* (Oxford: Clarendon, 1963) 146–149; *Fontes Iuris Romani Antejustiniani* III no. 1–5; Marcus Aurelius, *Historia Augusta* 9.7–8. Registration of citizenship grants: *Fontes Iuris Romani Antejustiniani* III no. 6–8. In general see Carroll A. Nelson, *Status Declarations in Roman Egypt* (Amsterdam: A. M. Hakkert, 1979); Jane Gardner,

doubts and uncertainties were not unusual. According to Suetonius the emperor Claudius prohibited noncitizens from adopting Roman nomenclature and passing themselves off as citizens.[106] Three Alpine tribes thought that they had been granted Roman citizenship and were dismayed to discover that they had not; Claudius retroactively gave them citizenship.[107] One hundred years later, the rule book of the chief finance officer of the province of Egypt threatens punishment for those who style themselves incorrectly—that is, who adopt Roman names although they are not citizens. It also threatens punishment for those Egyptians who after the death of their father declare (falsely) that their father had been a Roman citizen.[108] The jurists deal with the status problems that arise from cases of marriage in which one partner is misinformed about the status of the other.[109]

If you knew what to do and say, it must have been easy to pass as a Roman citizen, public registers or no public registers. If a person in antiquity claimed to be a Roman citizen, apparently he was believed without investigation. In Acts' story of Paul's arrest and trial, Paul merely has to declare that he is a Roman citizen and he is immediately believed; he produces no documentation and is never asked to prove his status. There must have been many people who said they were Romans but were not.[110] And there may well have been many people who said they were Jews but were not.

"Proofs of Status in the Roman World," *Bulletin of the Institute of Classical Studies* (London) 33 (1986) 1 ff.; *NewDocs* 6 (1992) sec. 17.

106. S. Claudius 25, *peregrinae condicionis homines vetuit usurpare Romana nomina dumtaxat gentilicia. Civitatem romanam usurpantes in campo esquilino securi percussit.*

107. *Fontes Iuris Romani Antejustiniani* I no. 71 = E. M. Smallwood, *Documents Illustrating the Principates of Gaius Claudius and Nero* (Cambridge: Cambridge University Press, 1967) no. 368.

108. Gnomon of the Idios Logos 42–43. Cf. the Ptolemaic prohibition of changing one's name or ethnic origin: Mélèze-Modrzejewski, "Le statut des Hellènes" 244.

109. Gaius, *Institutes* 1.67–75, 87; 2.142–143; Ulpian 7.4; Gnomon of the Idios Logos 39, 46, 47.

110. Perhaps Paul was one of them; see the cautious doubts of Wolfgang Stegemann, "War der Apostel Paulus ein römischer Bürger?" *Zeitschrift für das neutestamentliche Wissenschaft* 78 (1987) 200–229, and the discussion in *NewDocs* 6 (1992) sec. 20. Martin Hengel comes to Paul's defense in "Der vorchristliche Paulus," in *Paulus und das antike Judentum,* ed. Martin Hengel and Ulrich Heckel (Tübingen: Mohr [Siebeck], 1991) 177–291, at 193–208.

Social Mechanisms That Made (or Might Have Made) Jews Distinctive

If, then, circumcision was neither an infallible nor a usable marker of Jewishness; if there were no genealogical records that would have proven who was a Jew and who was not; and if the Jews of antiquity looked like everyone else, spoke like everyone else, were named liked everyone else, and supported themselves like everyone else, how did you know a Jew in antiquity when you saw one? There were two methods by which you might have established plausibility or probability. You might reasonably conclude that people you see associating with Jews are themselves Jews, and you might reasonably conclude that people you see observing Jewish laws are Jews. These conclusions would be plausible or probable, to be sure, but not probative, as I shall now explain.

JEWISH BY ASSOCIATION

You might reasonably conclude that people you see associating with Jews are themselves Jews. This argument has some merit especially if the Jews of antiquity as a rule kept themselves separate from gentiles. Many anti-Jewish writers refer to Jewish misanthropy (hatred of the rest of humanity) and separateness, analogues to the charge of "clannishness" that would be advanced against Jews in modern times. In the passage cited above Tacitus says of the Jews that "toward every other people they feel only hate and enmity. They sit apart at meals and they sleep apart, and although as a nation they are prone to lust, they abstain from intercourse with foreign women." "Those who are converted to their ways," Tacitus continues, are taught "to despise the Gods, to disown their country, and to regard their parents, children, and brothers as of little account." Many other sources too speak of the separation of Jews from gentiles, especially at table. In the book of Acts, Peter tells the Roman centurion: "You yourselves know how unlawful it is for a Jew to associate with or to visit anyone of another nation."[111] If in fact diaspora Jews separated themselves rigorously from their gentile

---

111. Acts 10:28. On separation at meals, see Barclay, *Diaspora* 434–437.

neighbors, you could reasonably assume that people you see associating with Jews are themselves Jews.

We may be sure that many, if not most, diaspora Jews observed the Jewish food laws at least to some degree, abstaining from pork, blood, and meat "sacrificed to idols," and that these observances were a barrier to free social intercourse between Jews and gentiles, but we may not conclude that many or most diaspora Jews sought complete separation from their gentile environment. On the contrary. The bulk of the evidence suggests that the musings of the anti-Jewish writers are highly exaggerated and that diaspora Jews maintained their Jewish identity even as they integrated themselves into gentile society.[112] Even Tacitus—Juvenal too—admits that the Jews attracted converts, a fact that clearly implies that the Jews did not separate themselves from their neighbors and that the boundary between Jews and gentiles was crossable. Clearly this is not the place for a full discussion of this question, which has already generated a substantial bibliography; the evidence is abundant and unequivocal.[113]

From the rabbinic perspective diaspora Jews did not follow an ethic of separation from gentiles. The Tosefta comments:

R. Simeon b. Eleazar says,
Israel(ites) in the diaspora are worshipers of idolatry.[114]
How?
A gentile makes a (wedding) feast for his son and goes and invites all
     the Jews who dwell in his city—
even though they (the Jews) eat and drink from their own, and their
     own steward stands and serves them,
(nevertheless) they are worshipers of idolatry,
as it is written *(You must not make a covenant with the inhabitants of the*
     land, for they will lust after their gods and sacrifice to their gods) and
     invite you and you will eat of their sacrifices (Exod. 34:15).[115]

---

112. Food laws: Sanders, *Jewish Law* 272–283. Maintenance of Jewish identity and integration into gentile society: see the essays of A. T. Kraabel, now conveniently collected in *Diaspora Jews and Judaism: Essays in Honor of, and in Dialogue with, A. Thomas Kraabel,* ed. J. Andrew Overman and Robert S. MacLennan (Atlanta: Scholars Press, 1992); Trebilco, *Jewish Communities* passim, esp. 173–183; Rajak, "Jews and Christians"; Barclay, *Diaspora,* is a fine and finely nuanced study of this theme.

113. See Feldman, *Jew and Gentile,* for full bibliography. The frequency of intermarriage between Jews and non-Jews in antiquity is unknown; see chapter 8 below, note 12.

114. Some manuscripts and testimonia read "worshipers of idolatry in purity."

115. T. Avodah Zarah 4(5):6 466Z. For discussion of the manuscript variants and parallels, see Zvi Aryeh Steinfeld, "On the Prohibition of Eating with a Gentile" (in Hebrew), *Sidra: A Journal for the Study of Rabbinic Literature* 5 pp. 131–148.

According to R. Simeon b. Eleazar, even if diaspora Jews observe the laws of kashruth, avoiding prohibited foods and foods cooked by gentiles, nevertheless their diaspora setting will inevitably bring them into intimate social contact with gentiles and thereby to social settings (like wedding feasts) that feature idolatry.[116] R. Simeon b. Eleazar, of course, is right. Diaspora Jews, even when maintaining their identity, did (and do!) routinely find themselves in intimate contact with gentiles.

Contact with gentiles took place even in the institutional life of the Jewish community. Gentiles participated in the annual festival, celebrated by the Alexandrian Jewish community, commemorating the completion of the Septuagint.[117] The pilgrimage festivals at the temple in Jerusalem attracted not only large numbers of Jews from the diaspora but also large numbers of gentiles who came to watch.[118] The synagogues of the Roman diaspora were open to gentiles, and some—perhaps many—gentiles actually attended services. This was true for Asia Minor in the first century (if we may trust the book of Acts), and for Antioch and Syria in the fourth.[119] The Jewish community of Aphrodisias established a charitable organization that was administered (?) by a small group of Jews and proselytes, and supported (?) in part by a large number of gentiles titled "venerators of God" (usually translated as "God-fearers," *theosebeis*). As I shall discuss in chapter 5, these "venerators of God" probably had no formal standing in the community (any more than "righteous gentiles," gentiles who are honored by the state of Israel for saving Jews during the Holocaust, have any formal standing either in the Jewish community or the state of Israel today), but they were recognized by the community for their assistance and clearly were on good terms with the Jews of the city.

---

116. Cf. Canon 7 of the Council of Ancyra (314 C.E.) (ed. Mansi, vol. 2, p. 516): Christians who have attended pagan feasts require penance, even if they brought and ate their own food. This text was first brought to my attention by my student Susan Holman, although I now see that it was cited too in Rajak, "Jews and Christians" 255 n. 19 (following Baer).

117. Philo, *Life of Moses* 2.41.

118. Josephus, *BJ* 6.427; cf. John 12:20. Cf. too Menander Rhetor in M. Stern, *Authors* no. 446. See below.

119. Asia Minor: Acts 13 and 17:17. Antioch and Syria: Wilken, *John Chrysostom* 66–94 ("The Attraction of Judaism"); *Apostolic Constitutions* 8.47.65 and 8.47.71. Cf. Martyrdom of Pionius 13: "I understand also that the Jews have been inviting some of you to their synagogues" (H. A. Musurillo, *The Acts of the Christian Martyrs* [Oxford: Clarendon, 1972] 152–153). An inscription from Panticapaeum also seems to suggest that "God-fearers" had a place in the synagogue of the community; see Reynolds and Tannenbaum, *Jews and Godfearers* 54.

There is one further aspect of Jewish separatism that needs to be considered. In antiquity diaspora Jews tended to live in Jewish neighborhoods. These were not "ghettos," of course, but "ethnic neighborhoods"; members of ethnic minorities tended (and still tend) to live in proximity to each other because they were comfortable in each other's presence and felt that their interests were better protected if they were massed as a group.[120] In Rome the trans-Tiber region now called Trastevere was an ethnic neighborhood with many Jews.[121] In Alexandria, Josephus says, the successors to Alexander the Great set aside for the Jews "their own district, so that they could live a life of greater purity by mixing less with strangers"; Strabo reports that "a great part of the city [of Alexandria] has been set aside for this *ethnos*," and Philo reports that "the city [of Alexandria] has five sections named after the first letters of the alphabet; two of these are called 'Jewish' (*Ioudaïkai*) because most of the Jews inhabit them (or: because most of the inhabitants are Jews), though in the rest also there are not a few Jews scattered about."[122] Smaller settlements too had Jewish neighborhoods; Oxyrhynchos had a street or district called "Jewish" (*Ioudaïkē*), as did Hermoupolis.[123] In the Ptolemaic period the Egyptian towns of Trikomia and Samareia had large numbers of Jews who probably lived in Jewish neighborhoods.[124] In Hellenistic times the Jews on the island of Delos lived in a quarter that was unsullied by the presence of any pagan temple.[125] The Jews (some Jews?) of Acmonia (in Phrygia) may have lived (if an inscription has been rightly interpreted) in "the neighborhood of those of the First-Gate."[126]

---

120. The Jews of course are hardly unique in this respect. See *CPJ* vol. 1, p. 5 n. 14. Not a single non-Jewish author, not even Tacitus, comments on the fact that Jews tended to live together in Jewish neighborhoods; the phenomenon apparently was not distinctive. On Jewish neighborhoods, see Barclay, *Diaspora* 117–118 and 331–332.

121. Philo, *Embassy to Gaius* 23.155; see commentary by Smallwood, *Philonis Alexandri* 234, and Leon, *Jews of Ancient Rome* 135–139. On the Trastevere region see Ramsay MacMullen, "The Unromanized in Rome," in *Diasporas in Antiquity*, ed. Shaye J. D. Cohen and Ernest Frerichs, Brown Judaic Studies, no. 288 (Atlanta: Scholars Press, 1993) 47–64.

122. Josephus, *BJ* 2.488; Strabo cited by Josephus, *AJ* 14.117 = M. Stern, *Authors* no. 105; Philo, *Against Flaccus* 8.55; further references and discussion in Schürer, *History* 3:43–44.

123. *CPJ* no. 454 and no. 468; cf. no. 423. Modern scholars have deduced that Apollinopolis Magna (Edfu) too had a Jewish quarter, but there is no explicit ancient reference; see *CPJ* vol. 2, pp. 108–109.

124. Trikomia: Clarysse, "Trikomia," and Harrauer, CPR 13, p. 44. Samareia: Kramer, CPR 18, p. 100.

125. Bruneau, "Israelites" 504.

126. Trebilco, *Jewish Communities* 78–80 with n. 101.

How Jewish were these "Jewish neighborhoods"? Neighborhoods that merited the name *Ioudaïke* may have been exclusively Jewish,[127] but there is no evidence that Jews had the legal or social power to exclude gentiles from their streets. In fact, the two papyrological references to the Jewish district in Oxyrhynchos describe land purchases in the district by non-Jews! At least here the name *Ioudaïke* seems to have been given after the Jews no longer lived there; it was the street or neighborhood where Jews formerly had lived. (Similarly, numerous European towns still have a Jews' Lane, or a Judengasse or a Rue des Juifs, although no Jew has lived there for centuries.) In any case, only few *Ioudaïkai* are known; in most cities Jewish neighborhoods will not have been exclusively Jewish. The Trastevere region of ancient Rome was home to many ethnic groups, not just Jews. And in some locations there may well have been no "Jewish neighborhood" at all; perhaps most of the Jews of these places lived in close proximity to each other, but their street or district did not attain a Jewish character.[128] It is striking that not one of the archaeologically attested synagogues from the Roman diaspora was situated in an archaeologically identifiable "Jewish neighborhood."[129]

One passage of the Yerushalmi (the Palestinian Talmud) may imply that presence in a Jewish neighborhood is sufficient to establish a presumption of Jewishness. The Yerushalmi asks: since the Jews of the diaspora use gentile names (see above), how can we ascertain the Jewishness of gentile-named witnesses on writs of divorce that are sent from the diaspora to the land of Israel?

R. Bibi says in the name of R. Asi,
(We know that the witnesses are Jewish) only if he (the scribe)[130] writes as the place (of origin of the divorce) "in the *Ioudaïke*."[131]
If there is no *Ioudaïke*, (he should write) "in the synagogue."
If there is no synagogue, he should gather together ten (Jewish) people (and write the divorce in their presence).[132]

---

127. But note the ambiguity in the Philonic passage just quoted.

128. "Antioch had no special Jewish quarter as had Alexandria," writes David Flusser, *Encyclopedia Judaica* 3:71, s.v. "Antioch." The same conclusion emerges from Carl H. Kraeling, "The Jewish Community of Antioch," *JBL* 51 (1932) 130–160, at 140–145.

129. For the archaeological evidence see L. Michael White, *Building God's House in the Roman World* (Baltimore: Johns Hopkins University Press, 1990) 60–101 ("Synagogues in the Graeco-Roman Diaspora").

130. Or, if not the scribe, the messenger who is bringing the divorce from abroad.

131. Alternative translation: writes (as the place of origin of the divorce) "in the place of the *Ioudaïke*."

132. Y. Gittin 1:1 43b.

If a divorce was written in a *Ioudaïkē,* or a synagogue, or before ten (male) Jews, the Yerushalmi says that we may presume that the witnesses are Jews, even if they have gentile names. The meaning of *Ioudaïkē* is not certain; it may mean "Jewish district," the same meaning it has in Philo's description of Alexandria and the papyrological documents emanating from Oxyrhynchos and Hermoupolis.[133] If so, the Yerushalmi is saying that even gentile-named people in a Jewish district can be presumed to be Jews. This presumption is not compelling, as I have just tried to explain. It is possible, however, that *Ioudaïkē* in the Yerushalmi means not "Jewish district" but "Jewish court," or some other communal Jewish institution.[134] If this is correct, the Yerushalmi is saying that even gentile-named people who appear in a document issued by a communal Jewish institution can be presumed to be Jews. This presumption makes a great deal of sense. Only Jews will have submitted themselves to the authority of communal Jewish courts.[135]

In sum: people associating with Jews were not necessarily Jews themselves. Even people assembled in a synagogue or present in a Jewish neighborhood were not necessarily Jews themselves. In the Roman diaspora social mingling between Jews and gentiles was such that, without inquiring or checking, you could not be sure who was a Jew and who was not.

JEWISH BY OBSERVANCE

You might reasonably conclude that people you see observing Jewish laws are Jews. The Romans understood that the observance of Jewish laws was an essential aspect of Jewishness. Thus in 49–48 B.C.E. the proconsul L. Lentulus granted special privileges to Roman citizens in Ephesus who were Jews (*Ioudaioi*), and defined the category "Jews" to mean "those who have and observe Jewish sacred things," or "whoever seem to me to have and observe Jewish sacred things." I am not sure exactly what these phrases mean, but it is clear that if someone wanted to be treated as a Jew by the state he had to behave as a Jew— that is, observe Jewish laws.[136] According to Dio Cassius, a historian of

133. See Saul Lieberman, *Studies in Palestinian Talmudic Literature* (in Hebrew), ed. David Rosenthal (Jerusalem: Magnes, 1991) 475–476, and *Tosefta K'Fshuta* 8.790–791 (on Gittin).

134. See Lieberman, *Studies.*

135. The nature and authority of these courts—indeed, their very existence—are not my concern here.

136. Josephus, *AJ* 14.228 and 234; cf. too 14.237 (the clause *an autōi phanē* is parallel to *moi . . . edokoun* in 234; correct accordingly Marcus' translation in the Loeb) and 240.

the early third century C.E., "from that time forth [i.e., after 70 C.E.] it was ordered that the Jews who continued to observe their ancestral customs should pay an annual tribute of two denarii to Jupiter Capitolinus."[137] Only Jews who observed the ancestral customs were, at least at first, subject to the tax; it was the wicked Domitian who tried to extend the tax even to those who did not observe the laws (see above).

Thus the Jewishness of Jews expressed itself primarily, at least in the eyes of outsiders, via the observance of Jewish practices. This fact is confirmed by the word *ioudaïzein,* "to judaize," whose history and meaning are the subject of chapter 6 below. "To judaize" in antiquity does not mean to dance in a peculiar manner, or to dress in a peculiar manner, or to speak quickly, or to gesticulate with the hands while speaking; nor does it mean to lend money at interest, a meaning it will have in the Middle Ages; rather it means to abstain from pork, to refrain from work on the Sabbath, or to attend synagogue. What makes Jews distinctive, and consequently what makes "judaizers" distinctive, is the observance of the ancestral laws of the Jews.

Therefore if you see someone observing Jewish rituals, you might reasonably conclude that the person is Jewish.[138] The Tanhuma, a medieval midrash of uncertain date, tells the following story. Astrologers predicted that two people seen leaving the city of Tiberias would not return home because they would be bitten by a snake and die. When they returned home safely the astrologers asked them, "What did you do today"? They replied, "We did nothing today except for what we are accustomed to do: we recited the Shema and we prayed (the Eighteen Benedictions)." The astrologers replied to them, "You are Jews? The words of astrologers have no effect on you, because you are Jews."[139] In this story the astrologers had no idea that the people were Jewish; they did not recognize them by their clothing, gait, speech, or even by the fact that they were seen leaving the city of Tiberias, a city that was al-

---

On these laws see Christiane Saulnier, "Lois romaines sur les juifs," *Revue biblique* 88 (1981) 161–198, at 168–169.

137. Dio Cassius 66.7.2 = M. Stern, *Authors* no. 430.

138. And if you see someone not observing Jewish rituals, you might reasonably conclude that the person is not Jewish. Cf. Tanhuma Balaq 24 ed. Buber (and numerous parallels): a restaurateur sees that a customer neither washes his hands nor recites a benediction before eating, and deduces (incorrectly, it turns out) that the customer is a gentile. The aphorism on which the story depends is in B. Hullin 106a and Yoma 83b. I am grateful to Herb Basser for reminding me of this story.

139. Tanhuma (nidpas) Shoftim 10 p. 114a. I thank Ranon Katzoff for bringing this text to my attention and pointing out how it differs from its parallels (see next note).

most exclusively Jewish. The astrologers realized that the men were Jews only when they heard that they recited the Shema. Recitation of the Shema is presumptive proof of Jewishness.[140]

But is practice of Jewish laws inevitably proof of Jewishness? Dio Cassius writes that "[the citizens of the country] have been named Jews (*Ioudaioi*). I do not know how this title came to be given them, but it applies also to all the rest of mankind, although of alien race, who are devoted to their customs."[141] Dio is not necessarily talking about "converts"; he does not even mention circumcision. For Dio anyone devoted to Jewish ways is called a Jew.

Anyone who has read Plato knows the critical difference between "being" and "being called," between "name" and "nature." According to Dio if you are devoted to Jewish ways you are called a Jew, but are you a Jew? Some ancient texts clearly make the distinction between "being" a Jew and being "called" a Jew.[142] Ptolemy, an otherwise unknown biographer of Herod the Great, writes that Jews and Idumaeans differ in that Jews "are so originally and naturally" whereas Idumaeans were called Jews only when they were conquered by the Jews and compelled to follow Jewish laws.[143] Revelation, in the passages treated at the beginning of this chapter, speaks of people who call themselves Jews but really are not. A contemporary of John of Patmos, the philosopher Epictetus, writes:

Why, then, do you call yourself a Stoic [if you are a student of Epicurus], why do you deceive the multitude, why do you act the part of a Jew when you are Greek? Do you not see in what sense men are severally called Jew, Syrian, or Egyptian? For example, whenever we see a man facing two ways

140. It is striking that the Tanhuma shifts the burden of the story from the protective power of good deeds (like reciting the Shema, giving charity, respecting one's neighbor), the point of the parallels in Y. Shabbat 6:10 8d and B. Shabbat 156b, to the protective power of Jewishness.

141. Dio Cassius 37.17.1 = M. Stern, *Authors* no. 406.

142. Cf. Ignatius, *Letter to the Magnesians* 4: "It is proper not only to be called Christians but (also) to be (Christians)" (*prepon estin mē monon kaleisthai khristianous alla kai einai*). Cf. too Ignatius, *Letter to the Romans* 3 and *Letter to the Ephesians* 15 with the commentary of W. R. Schoedel ad locc. This distinction might also be attested in a Miletus theater inscription whose exact interpretation has been disputed. If it means "For those Jews who are also known as Venerators of God," the inscription is referring to gentiles who are known as Jews because of their veneration of the God of the Jews. But this interpretation of the inscription is only one of several possibilities; see Reynolds and Tannenbaum, *Jews and Godfearers* 54, and my brief discussion in chapter 5 below.

143. Ammonius, *De adfinium vocabulorum differentia* no. 243 = M. Stern, *Authors* no. 146. See my discussion in chapter 4 below.

at once,[144] we are in the habit of saying, "He is not a Jew, he is only acting the part." But when he adopts the attitude of mind of the man who has been baptized and has made his choice, then he both is a Jew in fact and is also called one. So we also are counterfeit "Baptists," ostensibly Jews, but in reality something else.[145]

Whether Epictetus has Christian Jews or regular Jews in mind here does not much matter for my purposes. Epictetus is interested in the correct application of names, and knows of people who act the part of Jews (or Judaeans, *Ioudaioi*), are called Jews, but are not Jews.[146] They become Jews only when they have made their choice and have been baptized; before that, they are prevaricators. Unfortunately Epictetus does not describe how one "acts the part of a Jew." Presumably one does so by observing one or another of the Jewish laws. In his life of Cicero, Plutarch, another contemporary of John of Patmos, reports an anecdote according to which the orator asked a suspected "judaizer" why he, "a Jew," involved himself in a case featuring a pig. For Plutarch a "judaizer" who abstains (or could be thought to abstain) from pork can be called a Jew.[147] Even rabbinic literature is aware that non-Jews can be called Jews under certain circumstances. "Anyone who denies idolatry acknowledges the entire Torah" is a widely repeated rabbinic statement. One version of it reads: "Anyone who denies idolatry is called a Jew."[148]

Thus all those who observe Jewish laws (or who "deny idolatry") could be called Jews and could be known as Jews, even if they were not Jews and even if they did not necessarily see themselves as Jews. Seneca the Elder reports that in his youth certain foreign rites were expelled

144. Oldfather in the Loeb, followed by Stern, translates "halting between two faiths," but this translation is too theological. My translation is based on Epictetus' use of the same word (*epamphoterizein*) in 4.2.4–5 (a passage similar to this one).

145. Arrian, *Dissertations of Epictetus* 2.19–21 = M. Stern, *Authors* no. 254.

146. In its first occurrences in this paragraph, *Ioudaios* seems to be used in the sense "Judaean." *Ioudaios* is contrasted with Greek, Syrian, and Egyptian. A non-Judaean, by adopting some of the manners of the Judaeans, is acting the part of a Judaean. The ethnic-geographic meaning is still paramount. But the final occurrences of *Ioudaios* seem to be used in the sense "Jew." By adopting the "attitude of mind of the man who has been baptized and has made his choice," a non-*Ioudaios* becomes a *Ioudaios*—that is, a Jew. For a discussion of the difference between "Judaean" and "Jew," and, indeed, for further discussion of this passage, see chapter 3 below.

147. M. Stern, *Authors* no. 263. See my discussion of this story in chapters 5 and 6 below.

148. *Kol hakofer ba'avodah zarah niqra yehudi*, B. Megillah 13a. Cf. Y. Nedarim 3:4 38a and B. Nedarim 25a (and parallels); Sifrei Numbers 111 p. 116 ed. Horovitz; Sifrei Deuteronomy 54 p. 122 ed. Finkelstein; cf. Mekhilta Shirah 8 on Exod. 15:11, p. 142 ed. Horovitz-Rabin. For a discussion of this passage, see chapter 5 below.

from the city of Rome; Seneca is probably referring to Tiberius' expulsion in 19 C.E. of both the Jews and the adherents of the Egyptian God Isis. Abstention from certain animal foods, Seneca continues, was sufficient to establish a presumption of guilt—that is, a presumption of being an adherent of one of the proscribed rites. As a result Seneca, on the advice of his father, abandoned his vegetarianism.[149] A vegetarian could easily be regarded as a Jew and be punished accordingly.

There is abundant evidence that in the first centuries of our era some—perhaps many—gentiles, whether polytheist or Christian, attended Jewish synagogues, abstained from work on the Sabbath, and perhaps observed other Jewish rituals as well. These gentiles are often called "God-fearers" by modern scholars, but the debate about the precise meaning and application of this term ought not to obscure the fact that such gentiles existed. If so, not everyone you saw observing a Jewish ritual would necessarily have been a Jew. Even people who, on account of their observance of Jewish laws, were widely regarded as Jews and called Jews were not necessarily Jews and did not necessarily see themselves as Jews. The observance of Jewish laws was perhaps a somewhat more reliable indicator of Jewishness than presence in a Jewish neighborhood or association with known Jews, but it was hardly infallible.[150]

A STORY FROM THE BABYLONIAN TALMUD

The fallibility of observance as an indicator of Jewishness is well illustrated by a story from the Babylonian Talmud:

There was a gentile[151]
who went up to Jerusalem and ate the Paschal sacrifices.

149. Seneca, *Epistulae Morales* 108.22 = M. Stern, *Authors* no. 189.

150. Although some gentiles donated money to Jewish institutions, perhaps those rituals that would have demanded an expenditure of money will have been the clearest indicators of Jewishness. Perhaps the best statement of Jewishness for a diaspora Jew in the pre–70 C.E. period was the (annual?) payment of two drachmas to the Jerusalem temple. Outsiders noticed the large amounts of money that were raised by this self-imposed Jewish "tax." Converts to Judaism would pay as well as natives (see Tacitus, cited above), but we may presume that nonconverts did not. If you contributed your two drachmas to the temple, you were declaring yourself to be a Jew, and you were declaring your desire to be seen as a Jew. Contrast the social dynamic of the *fiscus Iudaicus,* briefly discussed above: if you were obligated to pay the *fiscus Iudaicus,* you were seen by the Roman state as a Jew, whether or not you saw yourself as one. Mandell misses the point entirely in her "Who Paid the Temple Tax?"

151. The vulgate printed text reads "Aramaean," but all the manuscripts read "gentile."

(When he returned home) he said, it is written (in the Torah) *No for-eigner shall eat of it* (Exod. 12:43), *no uncircumcised person may eat of it* (Exod. 12:48), but I, I have eaten of the very best (of it)!

R. Judah b. Beteira said to him,[152] did they give you a piece of the fat-tail?

He said to him, no.

(R. Judah replied, in that case you did not really get the best of it.) When you go up there (next time), say to them, give me a piece of the fat-tail.

When he went up (to Jerusalem), he said to them, give me a piece of the fat-tail.

They said to him, (That is impossible!) The fat-tail ascends to heaven (i.e., the fat-tail is consumed completely on the altar).

They said to him, who said to you (to speak) thus?

He said to them, R. Judah b. Beteira.

They said (to themselves), what is this before us? (Why would R. Judah have suggested to this man that he make such a request?)

They investigated him and they found that he was a gentile and they killed him.

They sent (a message) to R. Judah b. Beteira, peace to you, R. Judah b. Beteira, for you are in Nisibis but your net is cast in Jerusalem.[153]

The likelihood that this story is historical—that is, that it describes actual events in a manner more or less resembling the way they took place—is remote.[154] The story seems to assume that the Paschal sacrifice was slaughtered and roasted by the priests, who would dispense portions of meat to the populace, as if the Paschal sacrifice were like a regular peace offering. But the Paschal sacrifice was unique; it was permitted to be, and apparently often was, slaughtered by the laity, and the meat would be roasted not on the temple altar by the priests but at various locations on the temple mount by the lay participants themselves.[155] Further difficulties: wouldn't this gentile have wondered that

152. The manuscripts provide various interpolations to explain how the gentile's comment became known to R. Judah.

153. B. Pesahim 3b. For manuscript variants, see *Gemara Shelemah: Pesahim*, ed. Barukh Naeh and Menahem M. Kasher (Jerusalem: Torah Shelemah Institute, 1960).

154. The only point in the story that is confirmed elsewhere is the association of R. Judah ben Beteira with Nisibis. See Jacob Neusner, *History of the Jews in Babylonia*, vol. 1, *The Parthian Period*, 2d ed. (Leiden: Brill, 1969) 46–52.

155. The Paschal lamb was slaughtered in the temple court (the *azarah*, M. Pesahim 5:5–7), to which a gentile was prohibited access, but the actual roasting took place either on the temple mount (*har habayit*, M. Pesahim 5:10) or in all Jerusalem (not stated explicitly in the Mishnah, but cf. M. Pesahim 7:9 and 7:12 with Albeck's note), and the eating took place anywhere in Jerusalem, to which gentiles were permitted access (M. Kelim 1:8). Cf. Schürer, *History* 2:252 n. 55, and Sanders, *Judaism* 136–137.

R. Judah b. Beteira was assisting him to trick the priests?[156] Why did not R. Judah b. Beteira go himself to Jerusalem to bring a Paschal sacrifice and there tell the priests of this miscreant?[157] At least, why did he not send a message via someone else?[158] The anecdote is story and folktale, not history, and we are not to ask such questions of stories and folktales. Fictional or not, sensible or not, the story has an important point. The story demonstrates the superiority of the disciples of Moses to the sons of Aaron. Without the assistance of R. Judah b. Beteira—a rabbi in the diaspora!—the priests are incapable of protecting the sacred.[159]

Let us ignore the fictional and polemical nature of the story and put ourselves in the priests' position. According to the book of Acts, Paul was accused of bringing a gentile into the temple; whether the accusation is true we do not know.[160] According to this rabbinic story a gentile was able to deceive the priests (and apparently all the Jews around him) and to partake of the Passover. The priests were the custodians of the temple, but they could hardly be expected to check all those who entered the sacred precincts, certainly not at the pilgrimage festivals, when the crowds were immense. The Pauline episode apparently took place at or around the time of Pentecost.[161] Passover in particular attracted large numbers of people. According to Josephus, Cestius Gallus once took a census and counted 255,600 Paschal sacrifices; according to the parallel rabbinic story, 600,000 Paschal sacrifices were counted. Both the rabbis and Josephus agree that on average each sacrifice was to serve a group (*havurah* in rabbinic parlance) of ten people. Thus, according to Josephus, there were at least 2,556,000 people in Jerusalem for the Passover, and according to the rabbis there were 6 million![162] These numbers do not include gentile visitors who came to watch but

156. To avoid this difficulty see the ingenious interpretation of R. Solomon Luria (the Maharshal), followed by the Maharsha, ad loc.

157. See Tosafot s.v. "*me'alyah.*"

158. Probably because the storyteller wants to employ the dramatic but common motif of the deceived messenger who brings a message that will lead to his own death. See Stith Thompson, *Motif Index of Folk Literature*, 6 vols. (Bloomington: Indiana University Press, 1932–1936) motif K978, the "Uriah letter motif."

159. The deferential attitude of temple priests to rabbinic sages is a motif that appears elsewhere in rabbinic historiography, but neither the motif nor its historicity needs to be investigated here.

160. See appendix C.   161. Acts 20:16.

162. Josephus, *BJ* 6.423–425; T. Pisha 4:15 166L; see commentary of Lieberman, *Tosefta K'Fshutah* ad loc. Josephus and the rabbis agree that the Passover sacrifice was normally eaten by a group of ten or more; even R. Yosi, who permits Paschal sacrifices for individuals (M. Pesahim 8:7), would, I think, agree that individual sacrifices were not the norm.

could not participate.[163] So impressive were the proceedings that according to one rabbinic story Roman soldiers would convert on the fourteenth day of Nisan in order to be able to partake of the Paschal sacrifice in the evening.[164] Here, then, is a city teeming with native Judaeans, Jews from abroad, longtime converts and recent converts, gentile sightseers and gentile venerators of God. How were the priests to distinguish Jew from gentile, especially on the Passover, when all the slaughtering and sacrificing had to be completed in the space of only several hours? Josephus even tells a story of one Passover when Samaritans took advantage of the confusion, slipped into the temple, and scattered the dust of pulverized bones everywhere, seeking to render the temple impure.[165]

Gentiles were permitted to enter the temple mount, but were prohibited from entering the actual temple precincts, which were marked off by a low balustrade (*soreg* in rabbinic parlance). A Greek inscription warned gentiles that they faced death if they violated the sacred precincts with their presence:

No gentile may enter within the screen and the enclosure around the temple. Whoever shall be caught (doing so) shall be responsible for his own death which follows.[166]

The priests will have been entrusted with the duty of protecting the temple from foreign contagion, but in the final analysis the priests did not keep gentiles out of the temple as much as well-intentioned and respectful gentiles kept themselves out of the temple (just as well-intentioned and respectful impure Jews kept themselves out of the temple until purified).[167] No doubt their good intentions and respectful attitude were strengthened by their fear: if caught they would die, as the inscription warned, whether by lynching or by judicial execution or by divine visitation.[168] No doubt gentiles who were determined to en-

---

163. Josephus, *BJ* 6.427; cf. John 12:20.

164. T. Pisha 7:14 182L (and parallels; see Lieberman's commentary ad loc.). See my discussion in "Proselyte Baptism."

165. *AJ* 18.30; the text is corrupt and is variously construed.

166. Schürer, *History* 2:285 n. 57. D. R. Schwartz suggests that the inscription was meant to exclude converts as well as gentiles, and he may well be correct; see Schwartz, "Priestly View of Descent" 165–166.

167. On the exclusion of the impure from the temple by the priests see A. I. Baumgarten, "Josephus on Essene Sacrifice," *JJS* 45 (1994) 169–183, esp. 171–172. For a good illustration of the self-exclusion of reverent gentiles, see Josephus, *AJ* 3.319.

168. Peretz Segal, "The Penalty of the Warning Inscription from the Temple of Jerusalem," *Israel Exploration Journal* 39 (1989) 79–84. The story about Paul in Acts (see

ter the temple could do so, just as Richard Francis Burton and other westerners have disguised themselves as Muslims and gone on pilgrimage to Mecca, blending in with the crowds.[169] If a gentile knew how to pass as a Jew, and certainly if that gentile was in the company of a Jewish accomplice (like Paul), he (or she) would have had no difficulty in entering the temple precincts and/or joining a *havurah* to partake of the Paschal sacrifice.

The rabbinic story concludes: "They investigated him (lit., they investigated after him, *badqu batreh*) and they found that he was a gentile and they killed him." It is most unfortunate that the story does not explain how they investigated him or what exactly they investigated. Perhaps they checked to see whether or not he was circumcised—the gentile apparently was not circumcised, to judge from the glee with which he recited the prohibition *no uncircumcised person may eat of it*— but it is more likely that they investigated his pedigree.[170] As I discussed above, there is no evidence that Jews checked circumcision as proof of Jewishness.[171]

Conclusions

"Thus are Israel: whithersoever one of them goes, he is unable to say that he is not a Jew. Why? Because he is recognizable (or: because he is recognized)."[172] In the words of R. Abin, "A woman is able to hide herself (among gentiles) and say 'I am a gentile,' but a man is unable to hide himself (among gentiles) and say 'I am a gentile.'"[173]

---

appendix C) suggests execution by lynching, whereas our rabbinic story suggests judicial execution. See now Torrey Seland, *Establishment Violence in Philo and Luke: A Study of Non-conformity to the Torah and Jewish Vigilante Reactions* (Leiden: Brill, 1995).

169. Edward Rice, *Captain Sir Richard Francis Burton* (New York: Scribner's, 1990).

170. Cf. M. Qiddushin 4:4–5. In its other occurrences on B. Pesahim 3b, the phrase *badqu batreh* clearly refers to genealogical investigation. Similarly, *badqu aharav* in Y. Megillah 4:12 75c.

171. Of course here there are two issues: "Jewishness" and circumcision. The two are not identical, because even an uncircumcised Jew who ate of the Paschal sacrifice would violate Exod. 12:48. See Mekhilta Pisha 15 57H-R with the note ad loc.

172. *Shehu nikkar*, Song of Songs Rabbah on Song of Songs 6:11 (p. 35b ed. Vilna); cited by Salo Baron, "Problems of Jewish Identity," *Proceedings of the American Academy for Jewish Research* 46–47 (1979–1980) 33–67, at 52 n. 23.

173. Y. Avodah Zarah 2:1 40c. The commentaries differ on the explanation for a man's inability to disguise himself; some say (see *Pilpula Harifta* on R. Asher, Avodah Zarah,

But according to another rabbinic statement, even Jewish women were recognizable.

R. Phinehas said,

It happened that two harlots of Ashkelon were quarreling. In the course of the quarrel one said to the other, "You should not go out because you look like a Jew."

They subsequently became reconciled, and the [other] one said, "I forgive you everything you said except the remark that I look like a Jew."[174]

Unfortunately none of these texts explains exactly what makes a Jew (either male or female) recognizable and unassimilable. In this chapter I have argued that, rabbinic evidence to the contrary notwithstanding, the diaspora Jews of antiquity were not easily recognizable—if, indeed, they were recognizable at all. Jews looked like everyone else, dressed like everyone else, spoke like everyone else, had names and occupations like those of everyone else, and, in general, closely resembled their gentile neighbors. Even circumcision did not always make male Jews distinctive, and as long as they kept their pants on, it certainly did not make them recognizable. Like many other diaspora peoples ancient and modern, the Jews of antiquity succeeded in maintaining their identity without becoming conspicuous.

How, then, did you know a Jew in antiquity when you saw one? The answer is that you did not.[175] But you could make reasonably plausible inferences from what you saw. First, if you saw someone associating with Jews, living in a (or the) Jewish part of town, married to a Jew, and, in general, integrated socially with other Jews, you might reasonably conclude that that someone was a Jew. Second, if you saw someone performing Jewish rituals and practices, you might reasonably conclude

---

chap. 2, par. 4) it is because of his circumcision, while others (see the *Pnei Moshe* in the Yerushalmi ad loc.) think it is because of his hair and beard.

174. Lamentations Rabbah 1:39 on Lam. 1:11, p. 38a ed. Buber (who offers an alternative rendering to the one presented here, which is the translation in the Soncino Press edition).

175. Barclay, *Diaspora* 429 n. 40, objects that I have underplayed the role of social networks in creating and maintaining identity. I do not, of course, deny that Jewish communities will have been distinctive, clearly marked off as a group from non-Jewish groups, but in this chapter I have focused on the individual. On an individual-by-individual basis, the establishment of Jewishness is not clear at all. I am arguing that our modern scholarly difficulty in distinguishing Jews from non-Jews in antiquity faithfully mirrors the thinness of the boundary between Jews and gentiles in antiquity. Cf. Alice Bij de Vaate and Jan Willem van Henten, "Jewish or Non-Jewish? Some Remarks on the Identification of Jewish Inscriptions from Asia Minor," *Bibliotheca Orientalis* 53 (1996) 16–27.

that that someone was a Jew. Each of these conclusions would have been reasonable, but neither would have been certain, because gentiles often mingled with Jews and some gentiles even observed Jewish rituals and practices. As a result, these reasonable conclusions would lead you to label some gentiles as Jews. Some ancient authors distinguish between "truly being a Jew" and "acting the part of a Jew," or between "truly being a Jew" and "being called a Jew." By observing Jewish practices and by associating with Jews, gentiles will have been called Jews and will have been mistaken as Jews.

Some gentiles will have been called Jews, others will have called themselves Jews. In situations where status as a Jew conferred privilege and/or esteem, that status will have been coveted by outsiders, and we may be sure that as a result some non-Jews converted to Judaism and others simply declared themselves to be Jews. The Jews of Rome and of the cities of Asia Minor and Syria enjoyed a wide range of legal privileges, and at times were socially and economically prominent; in the Roman legal system the Jews of Egypt occupied a place above that of Egyptians. In these environments gentiles would have had strong incentive to declare themselves to be Jews, and it would have been relatively easy for them to do so, especially in places where the Jewish community was large.

CHAPTER 3

Ioudaios, Iudaeus,
Judaean, Jew

Our nation of the children of Israel is a nation only by virtue of its laws.

Saadia Gaon, *The Book of Beliefs and Opinions*

Greek *Ioudaios* and Latin *Iudaeus* (or *Iudeus*) are usually translated as "Jew." Indeed, the English word *Jew* (like the German *Jude,* French *juif,* etc.) ultimately derives from the Greek via the Latin. Behind the Greek word lies the Hebrew *Yehudi,* also usually translated as "Jew." These translations, however, are sometimes misleading, because in contemporary speech the English word *Jew* has a range of meanings different from that of its ancient forerunners. English *Jew* is primarily a "religious" term: a Jew is someone who believes in (or is supposed to believe in) and practices (or is supposed to practice) Judaism, as opposed to a Catholic, Lutheran, Episcopalian, Hindu, Muslim, and so forth. In some contexts the designation "Jew" may also have "ethnic" overtones, although it never has a geographic meaning and, outside of the state of Israel, seldom has a political one.

In contrast Greek *Ioudaios* (pl., *Ioudaioi*), Latin *Iudaeus* (pl., *Iudaei*), and Hebrew *Yehudi* (pl., *Yehudim*) are originally, and in antiquity primarily, ethnic-geographic terms, designating the eponymous inhabitants of the land of *Ioudaia/Yehudah.* Like Egyptians, Edomites, Syr-

---

The epigraph is from Saadia Gaon, *The Book of Beliefs and Opinions,* book 3, chap. 7, trans. Samuel Rosenblatt (New Haven: Yale University Press, 1948) 158.

ians, Lydians, Thracians, Cappadocians, and so forth, *Ioudaioi* constitute a people or nation (*ethnos* in Greek) living on its ancestral land. In this chapter my thesis is that all occurrences of the term *Ioudaios* before the middle or end of the second century B.C.E. should be translated not as "Jew," a religious term, but as "Judaean," an ethnic-geographic term.[1] In the second half of the second century B.C.E. the term *Ioudaios* for the first time is applied even to people who are not ethnic or geographic Judaeans but who either have come to believe in the God of the Judaeans (i.e., they have become "Jews") or have joined the Judaean state as allies or citizens (i.e., they have become "Judaeans" in a political sense). Behind this semantic shift lies a significant development in the history of Judaism. In the next chapter I shall argue that it was only in the Maccabean period that the ethnic-geographic self-definition was supplemented by religious (or "cultural") and political definitions, because it was only in this period that the Judaean *ethnos* opened itself to the incorporation of outsiders. In this chapter I discuss the development of the word *Ioudaios*.

The Meanings of *Ioudaios*

The original meaning of the Hebrew term *Yehudi*, hence of the Greek term *Ioudaios*, is "a member of the tribe of Judah," but this meaning seems to have disappeared from common usage by the Hellenistic period. As Josephus explains, "From the time they went up from Babylon they were called by this name (*Ioudaioi*) after the tribe of Judah."[2] In the period of interest to us, the word *Ioudaios* (fem., *Ioudaia*; pl., *Ioudaioi*) has three basic meanings:[3]

1. a Judaean (a function of birth and/or geography)
2. a Jew (a function of religion or culture)
3. a citizen or ally of the Judaean state (a function of politics)

1. M. Smith, *Studies* 1.264: ". . . in the Babylonian and Persian periods, the term 'Judean' added to its former tribal and territorial meanings, the new religious one of 'Jew.'" I think Smith has dated this shift too early. Smith returns to the meaning of *Ioudaios* in *Studies* 1.101 and 1.280–281.

2. *AJ* 11.173.

3. I omit the use of *Ioudaios* or *Iuda* as a personal name ("Judah"), for which see Louis Robert, *Hellenica* 1 (1940) 28–29, and Kraemer, "The Term 'Jew,'" 48–52.

There may well be other meanings too, but we lack a detailed and so-phisticated study of the term *Ioudaios*. In particular, the use of the plural *hoi Ioudaioi* must be distinguished from the use of the singular *Ioudaios;*[4] self-designation must be distinguished from designations imposed by others; official public designations must be distinguished from unofficial private ones; the relationship between the term *Ioudaios/oi* and the terms *Hebraios* and *Israel* must be determined; and the oc-currences of the terms must be catalogued by chronology, geography, and language. None of this has yet been done.[5] Here I shall briefly discuss and document each of the meanings I have outlined, primar-ily by appeal to the works of Josephus, and then I shall survey all the occurrences of the term *Ioudaios* before the end of the first century B.C.E. The purpose of this exercise is to demonstrate that before about 100 B.C.E. *Ioudaios* always and only meant "Judaean" in sense 1.

I. A *IOUDAIOS* IS A JUDAEAN (A FUNCTION OF BIRTH AND/OR GEOGRAPHY)

First and foremost, a *Ioudaios* is a Judaean—that is, a member of the Judaean people or nation (*ethnos* in Greek, or a similar term) living in the ethnic homeland of Judaea (*Ioudaia* in Greek).[6] The

4. For the distinction between the plural and the singular, cf. the term *Hellēnes* ("Greeks"), which frequently appears in the papyri of the Ptolemaic period, although in-dividuals are seldom designated as *Hellēn* (Harrauer, CPR 13, p. 42).

5. On the term *Ioudaios* see Tomson, "Names," and Runia, "Philonic Nomenclature" 14–20, esp. 14 n. 45. Solin, "Juden und Syrer" 647 n. 150, correctly notes that Lowe, "Who Were the *Ioudaioi*," overemphasizes the geographic aspect, virtually ignores the ethnic aspect, and too cleanly separates the geographic from the religious aspect. But Lowe's discussion is good nonetheless; on Josephus see Lowe, "Who Were the *Ioudaioi*" 104–105. The recent study by Graham A. P. Harvey, *The True Israel: Uses of the Names Jew, Hebrew and Israel in Ancient Jewish and Early Christian Literature* (Leiden: Brill, 1996), is disappointing. Harvey reaches a correct conclusion on Josephus (see p. 61; "His *Ioudaioi* are those who either live in or originate from *Ioudaia*"), but he omits the texts in CPJ, CIJ, and M. Stern, *Authors*, and is insufficiently rigorous in his analyses. It is of-ten stated in the scholarly literature that *Ioudaios* bears a negative valence, but this asser-tion reflects the valence of *Jew, juif,* and *Jude* in modern times, which in turn was influenced by Christianity's assessment of Judaism. A negative valence is nowhere in evi-dence in any of the texts surveyed here. Some ethnic terms in antiquity did, indeed, carry negative overtones (for a good example see G. F. Franko's convincing distinction between the Latin terms *Poenus*, with negative valence, and *Carthaginiensis*, with neutral or posi-tive valence; *Classical Philology* 89 [1994] 153–158), but in non-Christian sources *Ioudaios* was not one of them.

6. Bickerman, *Greek Age*, 124. On ethnic terminology and conception, see Barclay, *Diaspora* 405–408.

historian Polybius defines the *ethnos* of the Judaeans as "those who dwell around the temple that is called 'Hierosolyma.'" Numerous Seleucid documents preserved by 1 Maccabees are addressed to the *ethnos* of the *Ioudaioi*—that is, "the nation of the Judaeans." The Romans too saw the Judaeans as an *ethnos*. Josephus regularly uses *Ioudaios/oi* to mean "Judaean(s)," so much so that the Josephan phrase *Ioudaios to genos* always means "Judaean by birth," not "Jewish by birth."[7]

As an ethnic-geographic term, *Ioudaios* is parallel to terms like Egyptian, Cappadocian, Thracian, Phrygian, and so forth, which are both ethnic and geographic. In certain contexts, of course, the ethnic meaning may have primacy over the geographic, while in other contexts the geographic meaning may have primacy over the ethnic, but both meanings are present. (Below I shall discuss cases where the "ethnic" meaning completely overshadows the geographic, and cases where the geographic meaning supplants, or allegedly supplants, the ethnic.) As an ethnic-geographic term, *Ioudaios* is best translated as "Judaean." The onomastic link between people and land is explained by Josephus (in the continuation of the passage cited just above): "As this tribe [the tribe of Judah] was the first to come to those parts, both the people themselves and the country have taken their name from it." Almost four hundred years before Josephus, Clearchus of Soli, a disciple of Aristotle (ca. 300 B.C.E.), makes a similar point: "The Judaeans take their name from their place, for the place that they inhabit is named Judaea."[8]

As an ethnic-geographic term "Judaean" is more ambiguous than Phrygian, Egyptian, Lydian, and other such terms because Judaea is the name of both a country and a district. The writings of Josephus show that Judaea is the name both of the entire land of Israel, including its districts Idumaea, Judaea, Samaria, Galilee, and Peraea, and also of a specific district, Judaea, in contrast with the other districts Idumaea, Samaria, Galilee, and Peraea.[9] Thus, a Judaean sometimes can be contrasted with an Idumaean, Galilean, Peraean, or Samarian. This usage is attested most clearly in the following passage from the *Jewish War:*

7. Polybius: M. Stern, *Authors* no. 32 = *AJ* 12.135–136. Seleucid documents: 1 Macc. 8:23, 10:25, 11:30, 11:33, 13:36, 15:2. Romans: R. R. R. Smith, "*Simulacra Gentium:* The *Ethne* from the Sebasteion at Aphrodisias," *JRS* 78 (1988) 50–77, at 55. Josephus: S. J. D. Cohen, "*Ioudaios to genos.*"

8. Josephus, *AJ* 11.173; Clearchus in M. Stern, *Authors* no. 15 = Josephus, *CAp* 1.179. Greek scholars in antiquity debated the identity of the Iouda, from whom *Ioudaia* received its name. See M. Stern, *Authors* nos. 53, 137 (par. 5), 249, 259.

9. For the contrast see, for example, *BJ* 2.95–96, 247; 3.35–58; *AJ* 13.50; 17.318–319. On narrow and broad Judaea, see Stern's discussion on *Authors* no. 142.

A countless multitude ran together [to Jerusalem] from Galilee and from Idumaea, from Jericho and from Peraea beyond the Jordan, but the genuine nation from Judaea itself exceeded them in both number and eagerness.[10]

The nation from Judaea itself is genuine in that the name Judaeans is entirely appropriate to them, while it is only partly appropriate for Galileans, Idumaeans, and Peraeans. The latter groups are Judaeans insofar as they inhabit the land of Judaea broadly defined and are members of the nation of the Judaeans broadly defined, but insofar as they do not live in Judaea narrowly defined and are not members of the nation of the Judaeans narrowly defined—Galileans like Idumaeans can be said to constitute an *ethnos* of their own[11]—they are not Judaeans. Only the Judaeans of Judaea narrowly defined are Judaeans in all respects. In several other passages too Josephus explicitly or implicitly distinguishes Judaeans from Galileans and Idumaeans, but in other passages Josephus includes both of these groups among the Judaeans.[12]

Many Judaeans, of course, lived in the diaspora. For them the geographic component of the name *Ioudaios* was much attenuated, to be sure, but sometimes was still present. When the citizens of Antioch petition Titus for permission to expel the Judaeans from the city, the future emperor refuses their request on the grounds that the fatherland of the Judaeans has just been destroyed and there is no place to receive them. Philo refers to Jerusalem as "the mother city" of Judaeans throughout the world, and thinks of the diaspora as a series of "colonies" sent out from the mother country. During the reign of Alexander Jannaeus, Cleopatra, queen of Egypt, was contemplating an attack on

---

10. *BJ* 2.43 (my translation). "Genuine nation" is *gnēsios laos.* The parallel in *AJ* 17.254 is worded somewhat differently but probably means the same thing.

11. *BJ* 2.510; 4.105, 243, 272; *AJ* 15.257.

12. Idumaeans: The Idumaean contingent is explicitly grouped among the *Ioudaioi* in *BJ* 6.148. It is Antigonus, not Josephus, who calls Herod "an Idumaean, that is, a half-Judaean" (*AJ* 14.403); see my discussion in chapter 1 above. Of course before the Hasmonean conquests the Idumaeans are not *Ioudaioi* (*AJ* 11.61; 12.327–328, 353). Galileans: *Galilaioi* are *Ioudaioi*: *BJ* 2.232 (but note that the parallel in *AJ* 20.118 makes no such implication); 3.229 (frequently in this section, beginning with 3.110, Josephus alternates between *Ioudaioi* and *Galilaioi*); *AJ* 13.154 (Demetrius supposes that Jonathan will not let the Galileans be attacked because they are "his"; text somewhat shaky); 18.38 (the foundation of Tiberias violates the ancestral usages of the *Ioudaioi*); 20.43 (a *Ioudaios* from Galilee); Josephus, *Vita* 74 (*Ioudaioi* live in Caesarea Philippi—or are these *Ioudaioi* "Judaeans"?); 113 (Josephus refers to the Galileans as *Ioudaioi*). *Galilaioi* are not *Ioudaioi*: *AJ* 20.120 (contrast between *Galilaioi* and *to plēthos tōn Ioudaiōn*); *Vita* 346 (Sepphoris forbade any of its citizens from serving with the *Ioudaioi*); 349 (no city of *Ioudaioi* near Tiberias); cf. *Vita* 221 (*Ioudaios* probably means Judaean).

Judaea, but was warned by her general Ananias, who was a Judaean himself, that "any injustice done to this man [Jannaeus] will make all us Judaeans your enemies." The Letter of Aristeas views Judaeans everywhere as the "citizens" of the polity governed by Eleazar, the high priest of Jerusalem. Two centuries after Eleazar, Hyrcanus II, high priest of Jerusalem, refers to the Judaeans of Ephesus as "his citizens." Wherever they may be, Judaeans are "citizens" of their nation.[13]

If the geographic meaning of *Ioudaios* became attenuated in diaspora settings, the ethnic meaning came to the fore. Throughout antiquity Jews of the diaspora were members of local associations or corporations. At first these associations were defined ethnically; that is, membership will have been open primarily or exclusively to people who themselves were, or whose ancestors had been, members of the ethnic-geographic polity of Judaea. Until the time of Augustus, and perhaps even after, the Alexandrian Jewish community was headed by a "head of the nation" (*ethnarch* or *genarch*). The emperor Claudius addresses "the Judaeans in Alexandria," even referring to them explicitly as a "nation." Many scholars have argued that some or all of the Jews of Alexandria constituted an ethnic corporation. Several inscriptions mention "the ethnic corporation of the Judaeans in Berenike." In several places in the Greek diaspora the Jews called their local community *laos,* "the people," which seems to be an ethnic self-designation.[14]

The clearest evidence for the ethnic character of these organizations

13. Titus: *BJ* 7.109 (fatherland is *patris*). Philo: the classic text is *Legatio ad Gaium* 281–282, although the concept of *mētropolis* appears elsewhere too; see Willem Cornelis van Unnik, *Das Selbstverständnis der jüdischen Diaspora* (Leiden: Brill, 1993) 127–137. Cleopatra: *AJ* 13.354. Letter of Aristeas 3, 36 (= *AJ* 12.46, Ptolemy to Eleazar), 44 (= *AJ* 12.54, Eleazar to Ptolemy). Hyrcanus II: *AJ* 14.226. On the Jewish conceptions of diaspora, see now Isaiah M. Gafni, *Land, Center, and Diaspora: Jewish Constructs in Late Antiquity* (Sheffield: Sheffield Academic Press, 1997).

14. On these ethnic associations, usually called *ethnos, laos,* or *politeuma,* see Schürer, *History* 3:87–91. On the term *laos,* see L. Robert, *Hellenica* 11–12 (1960) 260–261. *Ethnarch* or *genarch:* Strabo in M. Stern, *Authors* no. 105 = *AJ* 14.117, and Philo, *Against Flaccus* 74. For discussion see the commentary on M. Stern, *Authors* no. 105, and Schürer, *History* 3:92–93. Claudius: *AJ* 19.281 and 284. Claudius' reference to the "nationhood" of the Judaeans is obscured by Feldman's translation in the Loeb edition. In his historical essays Philo frequently refers to the *Ioudaioi* of Alexandria. Whether the Judaeans in Alexandria constituted an ethnic corporation (a *politeuma*) is strongly debated; for a classic statement of the old view (in the affirmative), see Tcherikover, *CPJ* 1:6 n. 16. For newer views (in the negative), see G. Lüderitz, "What Is the Politeuma," in *Studies in Early Jewish Epigraphy,* ed. Jan Willem van Henten and Pieter Willem van der Horst (Leiden: Brill, 1994) 183–225, and C. Zuckerman, "Hellenistic *Politeumata* and the Jews—a Reconsideration," *Scripta Classica Israelica* 8–9 (1985–1988) 171–185. Berenike: Gert Lüderitz, *Corpus jüdischer Zeugnisse aus der Cyrenaika* (Wiesbaden: L. Reichert, 1983) no. 70–72 (the community also calls itself *synagōgē*).

is their name. *Hoi Ioudaioi* is the most common way by which "the Judaeans" of specific places identify themselves. Papyri and inscriptions document the existence of "the Judaeans" in various towns in Hellenistic Egypt.[15] Here is an example from the second half of the second century B.C.E.:

On behalf of king Ptolemy and queen Cleopatra the sister and queen Cleopatra the wife, the Judaeans of Xenephyris (dedicated) the gateway of the synagogue building when Theodore and Achillion were presiding.[16]

Theodore and Achillion presided over the community of Judaeans of Xenephyris when the construction took place. Who were these Judaeans? In all likelihood they were born in Egypt, but were Judaeans, the descendants of ethnic Judaeans who had immigrated to Egypt. Literary evidence confirms the archaeological. Roman documents preserved by Josephus refer to "the Judaeans in Delos" and "the citizen-Judaeans resident in the city (of Sardis)."[17] If "the Judaeans" constituted the community of a given place, then any individual member will have been a "Judaean." In a petition to the Roman prefect in 5–4 B.C.E., Helenos son of Tryphon first described himself as "an Alexandrian," but then erased that self-designation and substituted "a Judaean, of the (Judaeans) from Alexandria."[18] Helenos was a Judaean, a member of the association of Judaeans in Alexandria.

Even in the absence of a formal corporation or association of "Judaeans," individuals will have identified themselves, or have been identified by others, as Judaeans. These will have included émigrés from Judaea as well as their descendants who may never have stepped foot in Judaea. For the latter, as for the ethnic corporations of Judaeans, the geographic component of the term "Judaean" is a historical memory at best, and the ethnic component is paramount.

The ethnic reference of "Judaean" was so strong that both the Judaeans themselves and the Greeks and Romans had a sense that all Judaeans everywhere somehow belonged to a single group. (This sense is an integral part of a definition of "ethnic group"; see my prologue above.) Strabo remarks that the Judaeans "have made their way already into every city, and it is not easy to find any place in the habitable world

15. Tcherikover, *CPJ* 1:8; Schürer, *History* 3:87–88; *JIGRE,* index.

16. *JIGRE* no. 24. The word for "synagogue building" is *proseukhē.*

17. Delos: *AJ* 14.213; Sardis: *AJ* 14.259. *AJ* 13.213 refers to *hoi Ioudaioi en Dēlōi kai tines tōn paroikōn Ioudaiōn;* the meaning of the latter phrase is not clear.

18. *Para Helenou . . . Ioudaiou tōn apo Alexandreias, CPJ* 151. The translation in *CPJ,* "a Jew of Alexandria," misses the *tōn.*

that has not received this nation and in which it has not made its power felt." In a letter attributed by Aristeas to Ptolemy Philadelphus, the king expresses his wish to bestow benefactions on "all the Judaeans in the civilized world and their descendants." A letter attributed by Josephus to the emperor Claudius includes a reference to "the Judaeans throughout the empire under the Romans." In these passages "the Judaeans" constitute an "ethnic" category, not a political or administrative one, since no empire-wide political structure embracing all Judaeans ever existed in either the Hellenistic or early Roman empires.[19]

Thus the ethnic meaning of "Judaean" remained even when the geographic meaning waned. Whether the inverse of this proposition is also true is not clear. Might "Judaean" be used as a geographic term without any ethnic reference at all? When Greek or Latin authors wished to indicate the geographic position of a natural landmark (a river, a mountain, a plain, etc.) or of an army, they would regularly use adjectives ending in -ikos (Greek) or -icus (Latin). For example, in his *Histories* Tacitus refers to the *Iudaicus exercitus,* "the Judaic army," which means "the (Roman) army in Judaea" (not "the army of Judaeans"). Similarly, Tacitus refers to the *Syriacae legiones,* "the Syriac legions," which means "the (Roman) legions in Syria" (not "the legions of Syrians"). Roman generals celebrating triumphs took these geographic adjectives as cognomens (*Germanicus, Numidicus, Macedonicus, Parthicus,* etc.). These cognomens are entirely geographic: the triumphator was declaring himself to be not Parthian but Parthic, the celebrant of a triumph in Parthia.[20] As far as I have been able to determine, -ikos (-icus) adjectives were not generally used to indicate the geographic origins of named, individual people.[21] Might, then, the ethnic-geographic adjective be used in its stead? Might *Ioudaios* designate someone who is in or from Judaea but is not necessarily an ethnic Judaean?

19. Strabo on the Judaean nation (*phulon*): M. Stern, *Authors* no. 105 = *AJ* 14.115. Philadelphus: Letter of Aristeas 38. Claudius: *AJ* 19.288.

20. Kajanto, *Latin Cognomina* 52.

21. Adjectives ending in -ikos (-icus) were sometimes used as names, especially names of slaves, alongside the more common ethnic-geographic adjectives, apparently with no difference in meaning; thus, the epitaphs of the city of Rome document as names both *Ion (Ionis)* and *Ionicus, Macedo* and *Macedonicus, Syrus* and *Syriacus,* and so forth. Solin, *Die griechischen Personennamen* 1.566–648. Wine amphorae have been discovered at Masada that were marked *regi Herodi Iudaico;* see Cotton and Geiger, *Masada II* 147–148. This probably should be translated as "for king Herod of Judaea" and seems to reflect Greek usage. Cf. Appian, *Mithr.* 83, *tois persikois basileusin;* Plutarch, *Comp. Cimon et Lucull.* 3 *dia tōn Arabikōn basileōn;* and the numerous other examples assembled by W. Dittenberger, *Hermes* 42 (1907) 20–21.

Apparently not. In formal or legal usage the term "Judaeans," when used with reference to the district of Judaea, would apply only to the members of the nation of Judaeans of Judaea. Other inhabitants of the district would be called "those from Judaea" or "those residing in Judaea." When describing the ethnic conflicts in Judaea in the first century C.E., Josephus refers to the one side as "Judaeans" and the other as either "Syrians" or "Greeks."[22] These Greeks lived in Judaea (broadly defined) but were not "Judaeans." In formal, literary usage, ethnic-geographic adjectives and nouns, in both singular and plural, seem always to have retained their ethnic component.[23] However, in nonformal usage, ethnic-geographic adjectives and nouns seem to have been used occasionally, at least in the Roman period and at least in the singular, with sole reference to the geographic meaning and with no reference to the ethnic meaning. A character in Josephus is first introduced as "a Judaean from Babylonia" but is immediately thereafter referred to as "the Babylonian," not because he was Babylonian but because he was from Babylonia.[24] Many of the epitaphs of the catacombs of Beth Shearim (third and fourth centuries C.E.) refer to the origin of the deceased: Antiochene, Beritian (of Beirut), Caesarean, Iamouritan (of the town Yahmur, near Sidon), Palmyrene, Sidonian, and Tyrian.[25] We may well ask whether any of these deceased Judaeans were citizens of the municipal polities indicated; it is likely that the adjectives simply commemorate the geographic origin of the deceased. An epitaph from the Jewish

22. For example, *BJ* 2.266–267 (Syrians and Greeks are synonymous); cf. *AJ* 18.374 and *AJ* 20.173.

23. Saul Levin, "Ethnic Classes in Greek and English," *TAPA* 81 (1950) 130–152, at 151: "Greek usage parallels English enough to support the conclusion that *ethnica* are not employed to indicate mere residence in a certain place, or provenance therefrom. If no more than that is intended, both languages have prepositional expressions, or the equivalent. *Ethnica* imply membership in a class thought to have recognizable traits." In contrast, W. Peremans, "Sur la *Domestica Seditio* de Justin," *L'antiquité classique* 50 (1981) 628–636, at 633, writes: "le terme *Aiguptioi* peut désigner soit des Egyptiens de race . . . soit des personnnes qui habitent l'Egypte, sans être Egyptien d'origine." Peremans cites as support Polybius 27.9.12, the story of the boxer Cleitomachus of Thebes, who was almost bested at the Olympic games by his opponent Aristonicus, an athlete supported by Ptolemy of Egypt. Cleitomachus sways the crowd against his opponent: "Would they prefer to see an Egyptian (*Aiguption*) conquer the Greeks and win the Olympian crown, or to hear a Theban and Boeotian proclaimed by the herald as victor?" This passage does not support Peremans' point for two reasons. First, it is possible, as many scholars have assumed, that Aristonicus was indeed an Egyptian. Second, even if Aristonicus was a Greek from Egypt, the passage makes the most sense if Cleitomachus is deliberately pretending that his opponent is an Egyptian, for Egyptians were widely despised by the Greeks.

24. *AJ* 17.24, 26 and 29.

25. *Beth Shearim II,* index, p. 228.

cemetery at Joppa declares the deceased (if the inscription has been correctly deciphered) to have been an "Egyptian"—that is, someone from Egypt.[26] Similarly, even in formal usage, the term "Alexandrian" seems to have indicated only place of origin or domicile, not political status.[27]

Might then "Judaean," at least in nonformal, nonliterary usage, describe someone "from Judaea," even if that person was neither an ethnic "Judaean" nor a "Jew"? Perhaps so, perhaps not. Inscriptions provide several possible examples, but not a single case in which "from Judaea" is the only or best interpretation of *Ioudaios/a*. A. T. Kraabel has suggested that an inscription from Smyrna (first half of the second century C.E.) that refers to *hoi pote Ioudaioi,* usually rendered as "the former Jews," be rendered instead as "people formerly of Judaea" (i.e., "immigrants from Palestine, now doing their civic duty as residents of Smyrna").[28] This interpretation is not likely, however, because people from Judaea living in Smyrna would be called simply "Judaeans," or "those from Judaea" (*hoi ek Ioudaias*). By definition *Ioudaioi* in Smyrna are "former Judaeans"—they are in Smyrna! It is unlikely that the plural *hoi . . . Ioudaioi,* which is an official designation, would reflect nonformal usage. It is more likely (this is a conjecture) that *hoi pote Ioudaioi* means "the former members of the association of *Ioudaioi.*" The inscription is a list of citizens who have made donations to the municipal treasury; between the making of the gift (ten thousand drachmas) and the erection of the inscription, we may suppose that the association of *Ioudaioi* in Smyrna was dissolved (for unknown reasons), and the inscription acknowledges this fact. Even if my explanation is incorrect, surely this enigmatic inscription does not constitute evidence that *Ioudaios* could function as a geographic designation without any ethnic connotation.[29]

2. A *IOUDAIOS* IS A JEW (A FUNCTION OF RELIGION OR CULTURE)

A *Ioudaios* is someone who believes (or is supposed to believe) certain distinctive tenets, and/or follows (or is supposed to fol-

26. *JIGRE* no. 149.

27. On the meaning of *Alexandreus,* see Delia, *Alexandrian Citizenship* 9 and 45. This point is debated, of course.

28. *CIJ* no. 742 and Kraabel, "Roman Diaspora" 455.

29. Kraabel's interpretation is hesitantly endorsed by Solin, "Juden und Syrer" 649, followed by van der Horst, *Epitaphs* 69 n. 24, who also suggests one or two other inscriptions that may attest the geographic meaning. My objection is endorsed by Barclay, *Diaspora* 333.

low) certain distinctive practices; in other words, a *Ioudaios* is a Jew, someone who worships the God whose temple is in Jerusalem and who follows the way of life of the Jews.[30] In Josephus' description of the conversion of the royal house of Adiabene, Izates realizes that "to be truly a *Ioudaios*" is impossible without circumcision, but his mother warns him that his subjects will not tolerate rule by a king who is a *Ioudaios*. In this passage, which speaks about conversion to Judaism, the ethnic-geographic meaning of *Ioudaios* is entirely absent, and only a religious meaning is intended. A gentile can become a Jew. Similarly, several converts to Judaism in antiquity were commemorated on their epitaphs as "Jews."[31]

The religious meaning is evident too in another Josephan passage: "He [Felix] sent to her [Drusilla] one of his friends, a *Ioudaios* named Atomos, a Cyprian by birth."[32] This is the only Josephan passage in which a person is said to be both a *Ioudaios* and a member by birth of another ethnic-geographic group (in this case, Cyprians). It is possible, if unlikely, that *Ioudaios* here has a geographic meaning (Atomos is ethnically a Cyprian but is residing in Judaea), but surely it is much simpler to take *Ioudaios* as a religious term (Atomos is a Cyprian but a Jew). The passage, then, is analogous to Mark 7:26: "the woman was Greek, a Syro-Phoenician by birth." The term "Greek" (*Hellēn/Hellēnis*) is no less ambiguous than *Ioudaios*, as I shall discuss in chapter 4, but the presence of an unambiguous ethnic-geographic term ("Syro-Phoenician") implies that "Greek" should be construed here as a cultural term, which in Jewish settings means "pagan."

The Judaean communities in the cities of the Graeco-Roman diaspora were usually organized as associations. As I remarked above, these associations at first were defined ethnically: they will have incorporated as members ethnic Judaeans and their descendants. It is likely that in the

---

30. Exactly which beliefs and which practices were essential to Jewish identity was never clearly spelled out by the Jews of antiquity. As a result of this vagueness, the term *Ioudaios* could be used to designate a variety of individuals and a variety of behaviors. I shall discuss this ambiguity in chapter 5 below.

31. Adiabene: *AJ* 20.38–39. Converts: see chapter 5 below, note 74. The epitaph of *Sara Ioudea hosia* is the only one in *Beth Shearim* to contain the word *Ioudea (Ioudaia)*, and the editors therefore suggest that Sara perhaps was a proselyte; see *Beth Shearim* II no. 158 and III p. 31. Cf. Kraemer, "The Term 'Jew,'" 38–48; van der Horst, *Epitaphs* 68–72. Of course, many proselytes memorialized in epitaphs are not labeled *Ioudaioi.*

32. *AJ* 20.142. The text is somewhat uncertain: some testimonia read "one of his Jewish friends" (*tōn heautou philōn Ioudaiōn*) rather than "one of his friends, a Jew" (*tōn heautou philōn Ioudaion*); some manuscripts read "Simon" instead of "Atomos." On the phrase *to genos* in Josephus, see S. J. D. Cohen, "*Ioudaios to genos.*"

course of time (chronology is vague) associations that once had been defined ethnically came to be defined religiously: they will have incorporated as members all those of whatever ethnic extraction (although we may be sure that members of Judaean extraction will have been preponderant) who wished to worship the God of the Judaeans. In the mid first century B.C.E. a Roman official implicitly equated the (ethnic) association of Judaeans on Delos with the religious association of the Jews of Rome.[33] In the high Roman empire the usual designation of the Jewish communities of the diaspora was *synagōgē* ("community," "congregation"), rather than the ethnic designations that had been common earlier. This shift reflects "a change of emphasis, from the characterization of Jewish communities as ethnic groups to one which reflected their character as private religious associations."[34]

The corporations of the Egyptians and Syrians on Delos and elsewhere in the Hellenistic age underwent a similar development. Originally ethnic in character, they gradually were redefined in religious terms. Thus the worshipers of Isis in Greece about 300 B.C.E. called themselves "Egyptians," presumably because they were ethnic Egyptians, but by the second century B.C.E. on Delos they had redefined themselves as the nonethnic association of "Isiasts" (worshipers of Isis). Other Egyptian Gods on Delos (Sarapis, Osiris, Anoubis) also had clubs of devotees (Sarapiasts, Osiriasts, Anoubiasts).[35] Similarly, the Syrians in Delos originally called themselves "the association of the Syrian club members . . . whom the Goddess has assembled"; as the worship of the Goddess attracted Alexandrians, Athenians, Italians, and other non-Syrians—that is, as the association lost its ethnic character—they dropped the name "Syrians." They called themselves "the worshipers."[36] As we shall see in the next chapter, the Judaeans of Judaea in the second cen-

33. *AJ* 14.215; religious association is *thiasos*.

34. Schürer, *History* 3:91. The earlier ethnic designations had been *politeuma, laos,* and *ethnos.*

35. *Aiguptioi,* worshipers of Isis, in Athens, 333–332 B.C.E.: Vidman, *Sylloge* no. 1; in Eretria, ca. 300 B.C.E.: Vidman, *Sylloge* no. 73. Isiastai, etc.: Vidman, *Sylloge* index pp. 346–350.

36. For the inscription with the phrase *to koinon tōn thiasitōn tōn Surōn . . . hous sunēgage hē theos,* see G. Siebert, "Sur l'histoire du sanctuaire des dieux syriens à Délos," *Bulletin de correspondance hellénique* 92 (1968) 359–374; on the expansion of the Syrian cult, see Philippe Bruneau, *Recherches sur les cultes de Délos à l'époque hellénistique* (Paris: de Boccard, 1970) 472. It is not clear if the Phoenicians too broadened their base as did the Syrians; the associations of the Herakleistai and Poseidoniastai seem to have remained ethnic. See J. Teixidor, *The Pagan God* (Princeton: Princeton University Press, 1977) 42–46.

tury B.C.E. also began to redefine their community in terms of "religion" (the worship of the God whose temple is in Jerusalem), but neither in the homeland nor in the diaspora did the Judaeans give themselves a new name to reflect this development. Even in the diaspora they remained "Judaeans."

3. A *IOUDAIOS* IS A CITIZEN OR ALLY OF THE JUDAEAN STATE (A FUNCTION OF POLITICS)

Any citizen or ally of the Judaean state was, or could be regarded as, a Judaean. Josephus reports Hyrcanus' conquest of Idumaea as follows:

Hyrcanus also captured the Idumaean cities of Adora and Marisa, and after subduing all the Idumaeans, permitted them to remain in their country so long as they had themselves circumcised and were willing to observe the laws of the Judaeans. And so, out of attachment to their ancestral land, they submitted to circumcision and to having their manner of life in all other respects made the same as that of the Judaeans. And from that time on they have continued to be Judaeans.[37]

Ethnically, of course, the Idumaeans are not Judaeans, but by joining the Judaeans they have become known as Judaeans and become Judaeans. I shall treat this Josephan report at some length in chapter 4. My conclusion there is that the Idumaeans and the Judaeans merged in an alliance, and, since the Judaeans were the dominant partner in this alliance, the allies too became known as Judaeans, just as all members of the Achaean League were known (in some contexts) as Achaeans, all the nations of Italy were known (in some contexts) as Romans, and so forth. Ancient armies frequently consisted of troops of diverse backgrounds, but historians would ignore this ethnic diversity and simply speak of Romans, Syrians, Parthians, and so forth.

A similar phenomenon can be seen perhaps also in another context There is a slight but real possibility that "Judaeans" in Ptolemaic Egypt (third to second centuries B.C.E.) and in the late Roman empire (mid fourth century C.E.) constituted a troop within the imperial army. The evidence for either of these possibilities is fragmentary, ambiguous, and subject to conflicting interpretations. I shall discuss the evidence for the

37. *AJ* 13.257–258.

Ptolemaic case below; the evidence for the Roman case has been discussed in a recent article by David Woods.[38] If either of these possibilities is correct, we must allow for the possibility that individuals might be known as Judaeans not because they are ethnic or geographic "Judaeans" or "Jews," but simply because they are members of a certain troop of soldiers that had once consisted of Judaeans and therefore kept the name "Judaean" even after its ethnic composition had changed. The Judaean group bestowed the Judaean name on all its members.

The Development of the Term *Ioudaios*

In this section I survey the earliest occurrences of the word *Ioudaios* (and, for the sake of completeness, the word *Yehudi*) in order to demonstrate that before the end of the second century B.C.E. *Ioudaios* never means "Jew." It is always used as an ethnic-geographic term, parallel to Egyptian, Phrygian, Phoenician, and other such terms.

LITERARY EVIDENCE:
HEBREW AND ARAMAIC TEXTS

In the Tanakh the plural *Yehudim* occurs several dozen times, mostly in the books of Esther and Jeremiah. The Aramaic equivalent (*Yehuda'in* or *Yehudayê*) occurs in the book of Daniel. The word means "Judaeans," whether "members of the tribe of Judah" or "people of the kingdom of Judah." They may be living either in Judaea (as in the book of Ezra) or in exile (as in the books of Esther and Daniel).[39] An individual member of these Judaean communities would himself be called a *Yehudi,* as Mordecai is throughout the book of Esther ("Mordecai the Judaean"), and Daniel is in the Prayer of Nabonidus discovered at Qumran. (Aside from this passage, the authors of the Qumran scrolls do not use the term *Yehudi* or its Aramaic equivalent.) The Greek translators usually render *Yehudi* with *Ioudaios;* in Jeremiah 34:9 they correctly translate it as "a man from Judah."[40] The meaning

---

38. David Woods, "A Note concerning the *Regii Emeseni Iudaei,*" *Latomus* 51 (1992) 404–407. The argument is based on an inscription whose restoration and interpretation are uncertain; see *JIWE* no. 6.

39. The *Yehudaye* of Dan. 3:8 and 3:12 correspond to the *bene yehudah* of 1:6.

40. Jer. 34:9 = LXX 41:9, *andra ex iouda.* The Codex Alexandrinus has "Israel."

"Judaean" persists even to Roman times. A marriage contract of 122–125 C.E. declares itself to have been executed "according to the law of Moses and the Judaeans (*Yehuda'in*)."[41] A *Yehudi* is a Judaean.

The same conclusion results from a survey of the Aramaic documents discovered at Elephantine. An island in the Nile River located in southernmost Egypt (just north of the Aswan High Dam), Elephantine was the site of a military colony in Persian times (sixth to fourth centuries B.C.E.). Virtually all of our information about this colony, and its companion colony on the mainland (Syene, the ancient name of Aswan), derives from a series of Aramaic documents discovered there.[42] The garrison was polyethnic; the soldiers were Babylonian, Caspian, Khorazmian, Medean, Persian, Aramean, and, last but not least, Judaean. Several documents refer to "the Judaean troop" (*hayla yehudaya*), or simply "the Judaeans," and a fair number of individuals (both men and women) are also designated as "Judaean." Although the origins and history of the community are obscure, we may presume that the ancestors of the Judaeans who appear before us in the Aramaic documents of the fifth century B.C.E. migrated to Egypt from Judaea, and there maintained their distinctiveness as a military ethnic community. Most of those designated as "Judaeans" bear names compounded with YHW, the name of the God of Israel. A slight puzzle is presented by the fact that various individuals labeled themselves in some documents as "a Judaean of Elephantine," in others as "an Aramean" (or "a Syenian," or "an Aramean of Syene"), as if these designations were synonymous, or at least fully compatible.[43] Surely the simplest explanation of this phenomenon is *not* that "Judaean" is a religious term and "Aramean" an ethnic term, but that the Judaean troop was a subset of the larger and ethnically variegated Aramean garrison.

These Aramaic documents of Elephantine form an interesting contrast with the Greek papyri of Ptolemaic Egypt, which I shall survey below. Both sets of documents identify "Judaean" soldiers in the employ

41. H. Cotton, "A Cancelled Marriage Contract from Judaea," *JRS* 84 (1994), at 82 n. 179, citing Jonas Greenfield.

42. See Porten, *Archives* and "Jews in Egypt." The standard edition of the texts, which supersedes all others, is now Porten and Yardeni, *Textbook.*

43. Thus, a petition calls five of the leaders of the Judaean community "Syenians": Porten and Yardeni, *Textbook* A4.10 (= Cowley 33). If a contract is supplemented correctly, Mibtahiah explicitly calls herself both a Judaean and an Aramean: Porten and Yardeni, *Textbook* B5.5 (= Cowley 43). Mahseiah son of Yedaniah in some documents is called "an Aramean of Syene," in others "a Judean who is in the fortress of Elephantine": Porten and Yardeni, *Textbook* B2.1–11.

of the non-Egyptian (in the one case, Persian; in the other, Macedonian) king of Egypt. In both sets of documents the majority of people designated as "Judaean" seem to have been Judaean in reality, the descendants of immigrants from Judaea to Egypt, although both sets of documents raise difficult, usually unanswerable, questions about the "Judaeanness" of certain specific individuals: is a Judaean name necessarily an indication of Judaeanness? Is a non-Judaean name necessarily an indication of non-Judaeanness?[44] The important point for us about this military colony is that the community was constituted ethnically and designated as "Judaean."

LITERARY EVIDENCE:
JUDAEAN/JEWISH AUTHORS IN GREEK

Graeco-Jewish authors of the Hellenistic period frequently refer to *Ioudaioi*.[45] Almost without exception the term means "Judaeans," living either in the land of Judaea or outside it. Thus, for example, as I just noted, the Septuagint regularly uses *Ioudaioi* to translate *Yehudim* or other biblical expressions for "men of Judah." The Letter of Aristeas refers to *Ioudaia* as the land of the *Ioudaioi* and has the Egyptian king show favor to all the *Ioudaioi* throughout the world—that is, to all the Judaeans who have emigrated from Judaea for other parts.[46] The same usage appears in pseudo-Hecataeus. Eupolemus and Artapanus regularly refer to Moses as the leader of the Judaeans in Egypt—that is, the people who after the Exodus would become the Judaeans.[47]

The development of the term *Ioudaios* from "Judaean" to "Jew" is evident in a comparison of four works that, according to the guesses and conjectures of modern scholarship, were written within a generation or two of each other: Susanna, Bel and the Dragon, 1 Maccabees, and 2 Maccabees. All four use the term *Ioudaios,* but only in 2 Maccabees does the word come to mean "Jew."

44. For a full discussion see Porten, *Archives,* although Porten tries hard to make the community as normatively Jewish as possible. Porten always translates *Yehudi* as "a Jew."

45. Albert-Marie Denis, *Concordance grecque des pseudépigraphes d'ancient testament* (Louvain: Université Catholique, 1987) 432.

46. Aristeas 6 (*genos*), 11 (comparison of *Ioudaioi* with *Aiguptioi*), 12 (*Ioudaia* is the land of the *Ioudaioi*), 22–24, 35–36 (the *Ioudaioi* who have settled in Egypt are Eleazar's *politai*), 38 (show favor to all the *Ioudaioi* throughout the *oikoumene*), 308, 310 (*politeuma*).

47. Artapanus also has a brief if incomprehensible note regarding the name *Ioudaioi* (Eusebius PE 9.18.1 = Holladay, *Fragments* 1.204–205).

The original language and date of composition of the books of Susanna and Bel and the Dragon, two of the additions to the book of Daniel in the Greek version, are most obscure. Both books are extant in two versions, the "Septuagint" (LXX) and "Theodotion"; in both cases the former is shorter, less polished, and less dramatic than the latter, but the deviations between the versions are far more numerous and pronounced in Susanna than in Bel and the Dragon. I accept the common view that the Septuagint version of both stories is a product of the second half of the second century B.C.E. and that the version of Theodotion is a revision of the Septuagint.[48]

I begin with Susanna. Two wicked elders are inflamed with lust for Susanna, the beautiful and virtuous heroine. The elders try to have their way with her, but Susanna resists. Verses 22–23 run as follows in the LXX version (translated by Carey A. Moore):

The Jewess [*Ioudaia*] said to them, "I know if I do this thing, it'll be my death, and if I don't do it, I'll not escape your hands. But it's better for me not to do it and so fall into your hands than sin in the Lord's sight."[49]

What is the meaning of *Ioudaia* here? Moore translates "Jewess," but why should Susanna be identified as a Jewess? Her attackers are no less "Jewish" than she is. We may presume that Theodotion was puzzled by this question and therefore omitted the word "Jewess" (*Ioudaia*), substituting "Susanna." The key to the passage is provided by verses 56–57 (also translated by Moore).

And he [Daniel] said to him [one of the wicked elders], "Why was your progeny corrupted like Sidon and not like Judah? Beauty has beguiled you—petty lust! And this is how you have been treating the daughters of Israel; and being afraid of you, they had relations with you two. But this daughter of Judah would not tolerate your villainous sickness."[50]

The elder's behavior indicates that he is of the seed of Sidon more than he is of the seed of Judah. In contrast Susanna has behaved as a true

---

48. It is possible, if not likely, that both stories circulated for a long time before being redacted in Greek, but of this pre-Septuagint (Hebrew? Aramaic?) version not a trace is extant. No fragment of Susanna or Bel and the Dragon has yet been discovered among the Qumran scrolls, in spite of the exertions of Milik to the contrary; see J.-T. Milik, "Daniel et Susanne à Qumran?" in *De la Tōrah au Messie: Études . . . offertes à Henri Cazelles*, ed. M. Carrez et al. (Paris: Desclée, 1981) 337–359. For a discussion of the origins of the book of Susanna, see C. A. Moore, *Daniel, Esther, and Jeremiah* 28–29 and 77–92; Engel, *Susanna-Erzählung*. For a discussion of the origins of Bel and the Dragon, see C. A. Moore, *Daniel, Esther, and Jeremiah.*

49. C. A. Moore, *Daniel, Esther, and Jeremiah* 99.

50. C. A. Moore, *Daniel, Esther, and Jeremiah* 114.

daughter of Judah; daughters of Israel have succumbed to the elders' threats, but not Susanna. The contrast between "Israel" and "Judah" is stark and somewhat puzzling, but what is clear is that a son or daughter of Judah behaves virtuously, even in the face of temptation (unlike the elders) or compulsion (like Susanna).[51] Surely this explains why Susanna is called a *Ioudaia* in verse 22. In her resistance to the elders, she shows that she is a *Ioudaia*. The word should be translated not as "Jewess" but as "daughter of Judah," or, perhaps, "Judaean."[52]

Bel and the Dragon actually consists of two stories, in each of which Daniel demonstrates to the Persian king the silliness of idol worship. In the first story Daniel proves that the great statue of Bel does not actually eat the offerings that are placed before him, and in the second Daniel destroys the dragon (or serpent) of Babylon by feeding it a vile concoction. When the Babylonians heard that Daniel, with the king's approval, had destroyed the great dragon whom they revered, they concluded that "the king has become a *Ioudaios*," for "he has destroyed Bel, and killed the dragon, and slaughtered the priests."[53] The king's denial of the Babylonian gods makes him a *Ioudaios*. Certainly the meaning "Jew" fits the verse well, and the verse would seem to exemplify the rabbinic adage "Anyone who denies idolatry is called a Jew."[54] But within the context of the book of Daniel (and this is the context of Bel and the Dragon), surely the phrase should be translated as "the king has become a Judaean"—that is, the king is behaving like a Judaean, like Daniel who is "of the sons of Judah" (Dan. 1:6) or "from

51. Theodotion here substitutes "Canaan" for "Sidon," but otherwise is rather close to the LXX. On the contrast of "Israel" with "Judah," see Engel, *Susanna-Erzählung* 126–127, and C. A. Moore, *Daniel, Esther, and Jeremiah* 111–112.

52. Engel, *Susanna-Erzählung* 98–99 and 178–179, suggests that "Susanna the *Ioudaia*" is meant to represent the people of Judaea, the "Jews"; for a sustained reading of the book from this perspective see Amy-Jill Levine, "'Hemmed In on Every Side': Jews and Women in the Book of Susanna," In *Reading from this Place,* vol. 1, *Social Location and Biblical Interpretation in the United States,* ed. F. F. Segovia and M. A. Tolbert (Minneapolis: Fortress, 1995) 175–190. This allegorical (or typological) reading does not convince me. In any case, at least Engel too saw the connection between *Ioudaia* and Judaea. If Susanna had a Hebrew original it would have read *ha-yehudiyah* (thus D. Heller cited in Kahana, *Hasefarim hahitzonim* 1.566), a word that is not attested in the Tanakh (1 Chron. 4:18 is corrupt).

53. Bel and the Dragon 28. For the Greek text see Joseph Ziegler, *Susanna, Daniel, Bel et Draco,* Septuaginta Vetus Testamentum Graecum, vol. 15, no. 2 (Göttingen: Vandenhoeck & Ruprecht, 1954) 220, and Angelo Geissen, *Der Septuaginta Text des Buches Daniel Kap. 5–12 zusammen mit Susanna, Bel et Draco* (Bonn: Habelt, 1968) 274.

54. B. Megillah 13a; see chapter 5 below, note 37. I discuss this Bel and the Dragon passage again in chapter 5.

Judaea" (Dan. 1:6 LXX). The Babylonians complain that the king is behaving not like a Babylonian who reveres the ancestral Gods but like a Judaean who reviles them. Thus in this passage the fundamental meaning remains "Judaean," but, insofar as the passage recognizes that the fundamental distinctiveness of the Judaeans lies in their denial of other gods, the meaning "Jew" is beginning to emerge.

I turn now to the books of Maccabees. First Maccabees, a history of the Maccabean dynasty, was written either during the high priesthood of John Hyrcanus (134–104 B.C.E.) or shortly after it. The book was originally written in Hebrew, but our knowledge of the work derives exclusively from the Greek translation, probably prepared by a member of the Maccabean party not long after the book itself was composed. Second Maccabees, a history of the attacks on the Jerusalem temple and the wars fought in its defense between 175 and 161 B.C.E., claims to be an epitome of a five-volume history by Jason of Cyrene. That history, however, has otherwise disappeared without a trace and is no longer recoverable, since there is no secure way to distinguish between the work of the epitomator and his source. The epitome (hereafter cited simply as 2 Maccabees) was written before the Roman conquest of Jerusalem in 63 B.C.E., but how much before is not known. For the sake of argument I shall assume that 2 Maccabees, like 1 Maccabees, was written in Judaea about 100 B.C.E. Both books cite Seleucid and other official documents, most of which are authentic and thus certainly predate 100 B.C.E.

First Maccabees uses the plural *Ioudaioi* many times, and in all of these occurrences the meaning is "Judaeans." Many official Seleucid and Roman documents in 1 Maccabees are addressed to the "people" or "nation" or "crowd" of the Judaeans. The documents concern Judaeans, either in Judaea or outside it.[55] The narrator usually designates the heroes of the book as "Israel" or "those of Israel," but occasionally calls them *Ioudaioi*. In these passages too the meaning seems to be "Judaeans" consistently.[56] Where the Greek has *Ioudaioi*, the Hebrew original will have been *(ha)Yehudim*, which, as I discussed above, everywhere and always in the Tanakh means "Judaeans," either the men of Judaea living in Judaea or the men of Judaea living in exile.

In one passage, however, *Ioudaios* appears in the singular. First Mac-

55. Documents in 1 Maccabees referring to *Ioudaioi*: 8:20 (*plēthos*), 23, 27 (*ethnos*), 29 (*dēmos*), 31; 10:23, 25 (*ethnos*), 29, 33, 34, 36; 11:30, 33 (*ethnos*); 12:3 (*ethnos*), 6 (*dēmos*), 21; 13:36 (*ethnos*), 42; 14:20 (*dēmos*), 22; 15:1, 2 (*ethnos*), 17 (*dēmos*).

56. Narrative passages in 1 Maccabees with *Ioudaioi*: 4:2; 11:47–51; 14:33, 34, 37, 40, 41, 47.

cabees 2:15–25 (with some omissions) runs as follows in the New Revised Standard Version:

(15) The king's officers who were enforcing the apostasy came to the town of Modein to make them offer sacrifice. (16) Many from Israel came to them; and Mattathias and his sons were assembled. (17) Then the king's officers spoke to Mattathias as follows: "You are a leader, honored and great in this town, and supported by sons and brothers. (18) Now be the first to come and do what the king commands, as all the gentiles and the people of Judah and those that are left in Jerusalem have done. Then you and your sons will be numbered among the friends of the king . . ." (19) But Mattathias answered and said in a loud voice: ". . . (22) We will not obey the king's words by turning aside from our religion to the right hand or to the left." (23) When he had finished speaking these words, a Jew came forward in the sight of all to offer sacrifice on the altar in Modein, according to the king's command. (24) When Mattathias saw it, he burned with zeal and his heart was stirred. He gave vent to righteous anger; he ran and killed him on the altar. (25) At the same time he killed the king's officer who was forcing them to sacrifice, and he tore down the altar.[57]

Like numerous other versions, the NRSV translates *anēr Ioudaios* in verse 23 as "a Jew." So does Emil Schürer in his standard history of the period; Jonathan Goldstein in the Anchor Bible edition ("a Jewish man"); Joseph Sievers in his recent study of the Maccabean party; and many others.[58] At first glance, the translation seems unobjectionable: the verse describes the dramatic moment when "a Jew" was prepared to sacrifice to a pagan god but was cut down by Mattathias, filled with zeal for the Torah. But since *Ioudaioi* in 1 Maccabees never means "Jews," it is unlikely that *Ioudaios* should mean "Jew." In 1 Maccabees 2:23 *anēr Ioudaios* should be translated not as "a Jew" but as "a man of Judah" or "a Judaean."[59] The Hebrew original will have been *ish Yehudi*, a phrase that in Zechariah 8:23 means "a man of Judaea" and that in Esther 2:5 means "a man from Judaea."[60] In the Greek version Zechariah

---

57. *The New Oxford Annotated Bible*, ed. B. Metzger and R. Murphy (New York: Oxford University Press, 1991), p. 190 in the Apocrypha.

58. Schürer, *History* 1.157; Goldstein, *I Maccabees* 230; Joseph Sievers, *The Hasmoneans and Their Supporters* (Atlanta: Scholars Press, 1990) 30; Hengel, *Zeloten* 156, writes: "Als nun in Modein ein Israelit dem Aufruf des Königs Folge leisten"—this is German usage. Hugo Bevenot, *Die beiden Makkabäerbücher* (Bonn, 1931) 59, translates "einer von den Juden."

59. In the footnote to 1 Macc. 2:23 *The New Oxford Annotated Bible* suggests that *Ioudaios* "here perhaps means 'Judean.'"

60. See the rendering of 1 Macc. 2:23 in Kahana, *Hasefarim hahitzonim* 2.106. The Judaean reference of these verses is confirmed by the references to Jerusalem in Zech. 8:22 and Esther 2:6.

8:23 is translated *anēr Ioudaios,* precisely the same as in our passage of Maccabees, and Esther 2:5 is translated similarly: *anthrōpos Ioudaios.*

Modein, the site of the dramatic confrontation, was just outside Judaea (narrowly defined).[61] In verse 18 the king's officer tells Mattathias and the assembled crowd that "the people of Judah"[62] had acceded to the king's orders, and in verse 23 one of these Judaean men, who had accompanied the officer in his foray outside of Judaea, approached the altar in order to set an example for the assembled throng of non-Judaeans. No doubt this man was one of those Judaean "renegades" who had made a covenant with the gentiles and followed the edict of the king, thereby gaining the opprobrium of 1 Maccabees.[63] In Modein this man was an outsider twice over: he was a Judaean, probably from Jerusalem, intruding into the affairs of a village remote from Jerusalem,[64] and he was an advocate of gentile ways in a bastion of country piety. No wonder he was unwelcome in Modein.

Ioudaioi occurs even more frequently in 2 Maccabees than in 1 Maccabees, and here too the meaning is "Judaeans." The first verse of the book, the salutation of a letter written in 124–123 B.C.E., contains greetings "to (our) brethren the *Ioudaioi* in Egypt" from "the brethren the *Ioudaioi* in Jerusalem and in the land of Judaea"; a second letter has a similar salutation. The meaning "Judaeans" is clear. These documents are of Judaean provenance, and Seleucid documents continue this usage.[65] The narrator, too, regularly uses *Ioudaioi* to mean the citizens of Judaea and occasionally uses the term to designate Judaeans living outside Judaea.[66]

---

61. This is the simple implication of 1 Macc. 2:6 (I am not convinced by Goldstein's note ad loc.). If it was in Judaea, it was near its outermost limits.

62. *Hoi andres Iouda;* the Hebrew will have been *anshei Yehudah.*

63. 1 Macc. 1:11, 1:43.

64. For a brilliant analysis of the social background to the emergence of the Maccabees, see Seth Schwartz, "A Note on the Social Type and Political Ideology of the Hasmonean Family," *JBL* 112 (1993) 305–309.

65. 1 Macc. 1:1; 1:10; cf. 2 Macc. 1:7, a reference to "we Judaeans." Seleucid documents: 2 Macc. 9:19; 11:16, 24, 27, 31, 34. The first of these references derives from a document (2 Macc. 9:19–27) that in all likelihood is a forgery; see Habicht, "Royal Documents" 5–7; idem, 2. *Makkabäerbuch* 246–247; M. Stern, *Documents* 22; Goldstein, *II Maccabees* 357–359. In contrast 11:22–26 and 27–33 are authentic.

66. Judaeans in Judaea: 2 Macc. 3:32; 4:11, 35 (contrast between *Ioudaioi* and "many other *ethnē*"); 5:23, 25; 6:1; 8:10–11 (synonymous with *tēs Ioudaias genos* in 8:9), 32, 34, 36; 9:4, 7, 15, 17, 18; 10:12, 14, 15, 24, 29; 11:2, 15, 16; 12:1, 3, 4, 8, 34, 40; 13:9, 18, 19, 23; 14:5, 6, 14, 37, 39; 15:2, 12. Cf. 2 Macc. 13:21 *ioudaikē taxis,* troop of Judaeans. Judaeans outside Judaea: 2 Macc. 4:36 (in Antioch); 6:8 (Ptolemais and Greek cities); 10:8 (*ethnos* of *Ioudaioi* presumably includes those outside Judaea too); 12:17 (in Charax); 12:30 (Scythopolis). 2 Maccabees also uses *Hebraioi* (7:31; 11:13; 15:37) and *Israel* (1:25–26; 9:5;

In at least one verse, however, 2 Maccabees uses *Ioudaioi* in a manner that clearly anticipates the meaning "Jews." Second Maccabees 6:1–11 (with some omissions) runs as follows in the New Revised Standard Version (I italicize all occurrences of the word *Ioudaioi,* translated here as "Jews"):

(1) Not long after this, the king sent an Athenian senator to compel the *Jews* to forsake the laws of their ancestors and no longer to live by the laws of God; (2) also to pollute the temple in Jerusalem and to call it the temple of Olympian Zeus, and to call the one in Gerizim the temple of Zeus-the-Friend-of-Strangers . . .

(3) Harsh and utterly grievous was the onslaught of evil. (4) For the temple was filled with debauchery and reveling by the Gentiles . . . (5) The altar was covered with abominable offerings . . . (6) People could neither keep the Sabbath, nor observe the festivals of their ancestors, nor so much as confess themselves to be *Jews.*

(7) On the monthly celebration of the king's birthday, they were taken, under bitter constraint, to partake of the sacrifices . . . (8) At the suggestion of the people of Ptolemais a decree was issued to the neighboring Greek cities that they should adopt the same policy toward the *Jews* and make them partake of the sacrifices, (9) and should kill those who did not choose to change over to Greek customs . . . (10) . . . two women were brought in for having circumcised their children. They publicly paraded them around the city, with their babies hanging at their breasts, and then hurled them down headlong from the wall. (11) Others who had assembled in the caves nearby, in order to observe the seventh day secretly, were betrayed to Philip and were all burned together . . .[67]

The numerous textual and historical problems raised by these verses are not our concern here. I am interested instead in the meaning of the word *Ioudaioi,* which occurs three times in this passage. In the last of these (verse 8) the word simply means "Judaeans" and refers to Judaeans living in Greek cities outside Judaea. In the first of these (verse 1) too the word simply means "Judaeans," but here apparently it refers to the inhabitants of Judaea broadly defined, even the people of Samaria who venerate the temple on Mount Gerizim. Similarly, in 5:22–23 the term "the people" (the *genos*) includes not only those of Jerusalem but also those of Gerizim.

The second of our three occurrences (verse 6) is far more intriguing

---

10:38; 11:6); these terms, in 2 Maccabees at least, have theological overtones absent from *Ioudaioi.*

67. *New Oxford Annotated Bible,* p. 239 in the Apocrypha.

than the other two: "People could . . . no[t] so much as confess themselves to be *Jews*." *Ioudaioi* cannot mean "Judaeans" here, because
why should Antiochus care if people identify themselves as Judaeans?
Ethnic-geographic identity seems to be irrelevant. Here, in contrast
with verses 1 and 8, the translation "Jews" seems right: people could not
identify themselves as "Jews."[68] Why not? Are we to understand that
the mere name "Jew" aroused the ire of the Seleucid state just as centuries later the mere name "Christian" aroused the ire of the Roman? I
assume not.[69] I presume that what is at stake here is the observance of
the Jewish laws. "People could not confess themselves to be Jews"
means that they could not declare themselves to be practitioners of the
ancestral laws, the laws of God (6:1).[70]

What ancestral laws are intended? Perhaps the phrase simply summarizes what has come previously: "to confess oneself to be a Jew" means
to observe the laws of temple, Sabbath, and festivals. However, verse 6
can also be understood as foreshadowing what follows. "People could
neither keep the Sabbath" adumbrates 6:11, which describes how
people who gathered in a cave in order to observe the Sabbath were
burned to death. People could not "observe the festivals of their ancestors" adumbrates 6:7–9, which describes how people were compelled
to observe the king's birthday, a festival of Dionysus, and the festivals
of Greek cities. If this is right, then the final phrase, people could not
"so much as confess themselves to be Jews," adumbrates 6:10, which
describes how two women were executed for having circumcised their
sons. Antiochus proscribed circumcision, thus preventing people from
"confessing themselves to be Jews."[71]

68. Cf. Zeitlin's comment ad loc.: "The term 'Jew' here connotes the meaning of ad-
hering to a particular religion." See Solomon Zeitlin, *The Second Book of Maccabees* (New
York: Harper and Bros. for Dropsie College, 1954) 152.

69. In his commentary Grimm assumes the opposite: "Niemand dürfte sagen: ich bin
zwar Jude, habe aber die griechische Religion angenommen; selbst der Name Juden sollte
getilgt werden"; see Carl L. W. Grimm, *Das zweite, dritte, und vierte Buch der Maccabäer*
(Leipzig: Hirzel, 1857) 110. Goldstein, *II Maccabees* 276, suggests that the phrase may be
hyperbole.

70. In addition to suggesting that the phrase may be hyperbole (see previous note),
Goldstein, *II Maccabees* 276, also suggests that the phrase might refer to the recitation of
the Shema.

71. To strengthen this interpretation Jan Willem van Henten brings to my attention
Assumption of Moses 8:1, which describes how a king will "hang on the cross those who
confess circumcision" (*qui confitentes circumcisionem in cruce suspendit*). If "to confess
circumcision" means "to confess Judaism," it is a close parallel to 2 Macc. 6:6; see Johannes Tromp, *The Assumption of Moses: A Critical Edition with Commentary* (Leiden:

All ancient peoples, including Egyptians, Syrians, Lydians, Athenians, and Corinthians, had ancestral laws and customs, practices and beliefs. The phrase "to live (or: conduct public life, *politeuesthai*) in accordance with ancestral laws (*patrioi nomoi*)" recurs frequently in Hellenistic diplomacy and politics.[72] The Judaeans were hardly unique, or even unusual, in this regard. What made the Judaeans ("Jews") unique, however, is the essential role that these ancestral laws and beliefs would come to assume in the construction of Judaean identity. This point is evident in the subtle but significant shift in emphasis in the meaning of the word *Ioudaios* between 2 Maccabees 6:1 and 6:6. In the former passage, the word is to be translated as "Judaean"; the Judaeans have ancestral laws by which they live and conduct their public life. In the latter the word is to be translated as "Jew"; the essence of "being" a Jew is the observance of the ancestral laws.

"Confessing oneself to be a Jew" involves more than just circumcision and the observance of the other ancestral laws. As 6:1 says, the laws of the *Ioudaioi* are from God. Being a Jew also means believing in the God of the Jews, the one true God, creator of heaven and earth. Near the end of his life, afflicted by God with severe torments and hoping for divine mercy, Antiochus pledges to grant various boons to the Judaeans: the city of Jerusalem shall be free, the Judaeans shall be the equals of the citizens of Athens, the holy sanctuary shall be adorned with the finest ornaments, and the sacrificial cult shall be maintained at royal expense. "In addition to all this he also would become a Jew (*Ioudaion esesthai*) and would visit every inhabited place to proclaim the power of God."[73] We may presume that Antiochus is offering God a theological conversion, not a change in domicile or political affiliation. That is, he promises that he will become a Jew, a worshiper of the true God, but he does not intend to become a Judaean, a member of the

---

Brill, 1993) 217. A slight obstacle to this interpretation is the fact that v. 10 is linked by *gar* to v. 9 (thus NRSV reads "(9) . . . and should kill those who did not choose to change over to Greek customs. One could see, therefore, the misery that had come upon them. (10) For example, two women were brought in for having circumcised their children . . ."), but this does not mean that the content of the verse cannot have been adumbrated in v. 6.

72. Bickerman, *Studies* 2.44–85; Bernd Schröder, *Die "vaterlichen Gesetze"* (Tübingen: Mohr [Siebeck], 1996).

73. 2 Macc. 9:13–17. Note that this sentiment is absent from the subsequent document, which is a forgery (see note 65). Goldstein, *II Maccabees* 356, suggests that the vow to become a Jew was probably inferred from the king's gratitude to "God" (in the singular, 9:20).

house of Israel living on God's holy land. After all, Antiochus is a Macedonian king and intends to remain one. Thus, in both 6:6 and 9:17 *Ioudaios* means "Jew,"[74] the first attested examples of this usage.

LITERARY EVIDENCE:
GREEK AND LATIN AUTHORS

Usage of the term *Ioudaios* by Greek and Latin authors is easily surveyed in the three-volume collection edited by Menahem Stern, *Greek and Latin Authors on Jews and Judaism*. Volume 1, which contains texts from the fifth century B.C.E. to about 100 C.E. ("from Herodotus to Plutarch"), is of particular relevance here. Before the middle of the first century B.C.E., all authors who speak of *Ioudaioi* (Hecataeus of Abdera [ca. 300 B.C.E.] is the first)[75] are speaking of Judaeans, the ethnic inhabitants of Judaea.[76] The *Ioudaioi* are often contrasted or paired with other ethnic-geographic groups, and are explicitly called an *ethnos*.[77] The singular *Ioudaios* occurs once: Clearchus of

74. In addition to the common usage of an ambiguous word, dramatic irony and a satisfying sense of closure link these two verses. At the beginning of the persecution one could not even declare oneself to be a Jew, but at the end even the archenemy pledged to become one. A crucial bridge between these verses (pointed out to me by Jan Willem van Henten) is provided by 7:37, the final declaration of the last and youngest of the seven martyrs: "I . . . give up body and life for the laws of our ancestors, appealing to God to show mercy soon to our nation and by trials and plagues to make you confess that he alone is God." This prayer, which speaks of "confessing" (*exhomologein*) God, clearly looks back to 6:6, the prohibition of confessing (*homologein*) oneself to be a Jew, and looks forward to 9:17, Antiochus' promise "to become a Jew."

75. Hecataeus in Diodorus of Sicily 40.3 = M. Stern, *Authors* no. 11. In the text printed by M. Stern, *Authors* no. 4, Theophrastus explicitly refers to *Ioudaioi,* but there are good reasons to doubt the text. Gifford and Nauck seclude the word; it is syntactically difficult, and is rendered suspect by the fact that Theophrastus nowhere uses *Ioudaia* (Stern p. 9) and nowhere else mentions *Ioudaioi*. Even if the word *Ioudaios* is not original, Theophrastus probably is speaking of Judaeans, but the matter is not nearly as certain as Stern allows it to be. See the discussion in Jean Bouffartigue and Michel Patillon, *Porphyre de l'abstinence*, vol. 2 (Paris: Les Belles Lettres, 1979) 58–67. In any case, the word here clearly means "Judaeans."

76. For references to Judaea (*Ioudaia*), see Hecataeus no. 11 par. 2; Manetho no. 19 par. 90 and no. 21 par. 228 (Manetho mentions *Ioudaia* but not *Ioudaioi*). For references to Judaeans (*Ioudaioi*), see Hecataeus no. 11; pseudo-Hecataeus no. 12 (even if the passage is not genuine Hecataeus, the meaning of *Ioudaioi* is the same: Judaeans); Megasthenes no. 14; Berossus no. 17; Hermippus nos. 25, 26; Mnaseas no. 28; Agatharchides no. 30; Polybius no. 32; Laetus no. 39; Posidonius no. 44; Alexander Polyhistor no. 51a; Diodorus of Sicily nos. 55, 57, 58, 63, 64, 66.

77. Paired with other ethnic-geographic groups: Berossus no. 17 par. 137 (Phoenicians, Syrians, and "the nations of Egypt"); Hermippus no. 25 par. 165 (Thracians) and no. 26

Soli, a disciple of Aristotle (ca. 300 B.C.E.), describes "a Judaean by birth from Coele Syria" who was traveling in Asia Minor.[78] In other words, before the middle of the first century B.C.E., *Ioudaios/oi* in the writings of Greek authors always means "Judaean(s)," the ethnic inhabitants of Judaea. The growth of the Judaean diaspora is evident in the fact that after the middle of the first century B.C.E. various authors, notably Cicero and Strabo, use the term to designate Judaeans living outside Judaea. The former speaks of the *Iudaei* of Rome, Italy, the provinces, and Jerusalem: they constitute one nation, whose habit of sending gold every year to Jerusalem was a "barbaric superstition."[79] Strabo refers to the *Ioudaioi* not just of Judaea (whom he pairs or contrasts with Ituraeans, Idumaeans, Syrians, Cilicians, Phoenicians) but of other places too: Egypt, Cos, Cyrene—indeed, "the entire inhabited world." Even in the diaspora they constitute a tribe or an *ethnos*.[80] In the first century C.E. *Ioudaios* is used routinely in these two senses (Judaean of Judaea and Judaean outside Judaea). The word remains an ethnic-geographic term.[81]

Many of these texts recognize, of course, that the Judaeans have peculiar ancestral usages and a peculiar manner of worshiping God, but this recognition does not detract from the fact that Judaeans were per-

---

(Greeks); Mnaseas no. 28 par. 112 (Idumaeans); Diodorus no. 58 (Egyptians, Greeks, Arians, Getae), no. 66 (Medes, Iberians, Nabatean Arabs). *Ethnos:* Hecataeus no. 11 par. 4; Agatharchides no. 30b; Polybius no. 32; Diodorus of Sicily nos. 55, 58, 63.

78. *Genos Ioudaios*—that is, a member of the *ethnos* of the *Ioudaioi;* M. Stern, *Authors* no. 15 = Josephus, *CAp* 1.179.

79. Cicero no. 68 par. 69 (*gens*) and no. 70 par. 10 (*natio*).

80. *Ioudaioi* of Judaea: Strabo nos. 100, 101, 103, 106, 107, 108, 110 (*Ioudaioi,* Syrians, Cilicians, Phoenicians), 111 (*Ioudaioi,* Idumaeans, Gazaeans, Azotians), 114 (Jerusalem metropolis of *Ioudaioi*), 115 (Idumaeans were Nabataeans but joined the Judaeans), 120. *Ioudaioi* of Egypt: Strabo nos. 99, 105 (*phylon* and *ethnos*). *Ioudaioi* of Cos: Strabo no. 102 (at Cos Mithridates seized the money of the *Ioudaioi;* Josephus argues, perhaps correctly, that these must be the *Ioudaioi* of Asia). *Ioudaioi* of Cyrene, Egypt and the entire *oikoumenē:* Strabo no. 105. H. L. Jones, the editor of Strabo's *Geography* in the Loeb edition, usually translates *Ioudaioi* as "Judaeans."

81. Varro no. 72a (*gens*); Asinius Pollio no. 76; Timagenes no. 81; Nicolas of Damascus nos. 84, 85, 88, 90, 92, 97 (*ethnos*), 86; Horace nos. 127, 128 (*Iudaeus Apella*), 129; Livy nos. 131, 133, 135; Pompeius Trogus nos. 136, 137, 138, 139; Ovid no. 141 (*Iudaeus Syrus,* to be translated as "Judaean of Syria," cf. no. 142 *Palaestinus Syrus*); Ptolemy no. 146 (*Ioudaioi,* Idumaeans, Phoenicians, Syrians); Valerius Maximus no. 147; On the Sublime no. 148; Seneca no. 149; Ptolemy of Mendes no. 157; Lysimachus no. 158 (*laos*); Apion nos. 163c, 165, 166, 167, 168, 169, 170, 171, 172; Chaeremon no. 178; Columella no. 185; Seneca no. 186 (*gens*); Petronius nos. 194, 195; Erotianus no. 196 (*Ioudaioi,* Egyptians); Pliny nos. 208, 214 (*gens*), 221, 223; Frontinus no. 229; Martial no. 246; Damocritus no. 247; Nicarchus no. 248; Epictetus nos. 252, 253 (*Ioudaioi,* Syrians, Egyptians, Romans), 254; Plutarch nos. 256, 257, 258, 260, 262, 264, 266, 267 (Herod the *Ioudaios*), 268, 272.

ceived primarily as an ethnic-geographic group. A good illustration of this perception is provided by a series of Roman documents preserved by Josephus in book 14 of the *Jewish Antiquities*. Scholars have long debated the authenticity and accuracy of these documents, but I think it is safe to assume that the documents are substantially authentic even if we cannot securely identify Josephus' source and even if we can be sure that the transcriptions that lie before us in the text of Josephus are often corrupt.[82] I have cited many of these documents above in my discussion of the use of *Ioudaioi* as a designation for diaspora communities. One group of documents concerns the exemption of the Judaeans of Ephesus from military service. One of the these documents runs as follows:

Lucius Lentulus, consul, declares. In consideration of their religious scruples I have released [from military service] those Judaeans in Ephesus who are Roman citizens and have appeared to me to have and to practice Judaic (rites). Dated the twelfth day before the calends of July (19 June 49 B.C.E.).[83]

The Judaeans in Ephesus constitute, as usual, an ethnic community of migrants from Judaea and their descendants. Judaeans who are Roman citizens would normally be obligated to serve in the Roman army, but because of their religious scruples (or "superstition") the Judaeans of Ephesus are exempted from this obligation. To whom does this exemption apply? Only to those Judaeans who seem to the consul "to have and to observe Judaic (rites)."[84] I am not sure exactly what this means, but it is clear that if a Judaean wanted to enjoy an exemption granted to Judaeans, he had to behave as a Judaean—that is, observe the Judaean laws. Those Judaeans in Ephesus who no longer, at least in the eyes of the consul, "had and practiced Judaic rites" could not claim to be barred from military service by their religious scruples. Here then is recognition that Judaeans have peculiar religious scruples, which, at least in the diaspora, some Judaeans observe and others apparently do not. The Judaeans remain in Roman eyes an ethnic-geographic community.

82. Christiane Saulnier, "Lois romaines sur les juifs," *Revue biblique* 88 (1981) 161–198; Miriam Pucci Ben Zeev, "Greek and Roman Documents from Republican Times in the *Antiquities:* What Was Josephus' Source?" *Scripta Classica Israelica* 13 (1994) 46–59, and eadem, "Did the Jews Enjoy a Privileged Position in the Roman World?" *Revue des études juives* 154 (1995) 23–42.

83. *AJ* 14.234, part of *AJ* 14.225–240.

84. Cf. *AJ* 14.228, 237 (the clause *an autōi phanē* is parallel to *moi . . . edokoun* in 234; correct accordingly Marcus' translation in the Loeb), 240.

The end of the first century C.E. witnesses for the first time the emergence of *Ioudaios* as a religious term, a designation for anyone who venerates the God of the Judaeans. Epictetus refers to someone "who has been baptized," thereby becoming a Jew both in fact and in name—a passage I discussed in chapter 2.[85] This passage deals with converts, those who have crossed the boundary separating Jews from gentiles. It was not until the end of the first century C.E. that Greek and Roman writers recognized that one could become a Jew by changing one's beliefs and practices.[86]

DOCUMENTARY EVIDENCE: INSCRIPTIONS AND PAPYRI

Ioudaioi, both individuals and communal associations, appear regularly in the private and public records preserved on stone and papyrus. Inscriptional evidence for *Ioudaioi* derives from the entire Mediterranean basin, whereas papyrological evidence derives mainly from Egypt. I begin with the inscriptions.

Inscriptions. Many Greek inscriptions, especially from Hellenistic Egypt and Roman Asia Minor, refer to "the *Ioudaioi*" of a given place. I have briefly treated these references above. Here I shall discuss the first occurrences of the singular *Ioudaios*. The earliest comes from Oropos, a small city on the border between Attica and Boeotia, from the Amphiareion, the temple dedicated to Amphiaraos, a local God-hero. The text is undated, but the letterforms point to a date in the first half of the third century B.C.E.

. . . Phrynidas (will release) Moschos to be free, dependent on no man. But if anything happens to Phrynidas before the time elapses, let Moschos go free wherever he wishes. To Good Fortune.

WITNESSES:

Athenodoros son of Mnaskikon, an Oropian

Biottos son of Eudikos, an Athenian

Charinos son of Anticharmos, an Athenian

Athenades son of Epigonos, an Oropian

Hippon son of Aeschylos, an Oropian

---

85. M. Stern, *Authors* no. 254.
86. Goodman, "Nerva."

Moschos son of Moschion, a *Ioudaios,* having seen a dream, at the command of the God Amphiaraos and Hygieia, (set up this inscription); just as Amphiaraos and Hygieia have commanded (him) to write it on a stele and to set it up at the altar.[87]

In the first paragraph (the first part of which is lost) Phrynidas manumits Moschos, with the provision that Moschos continue to remain obligated for a set number of years to perform some services for his former master. Should the master die before those years have elapsed, his heirs do not inherit his claim on Moschos' services, and the former slave becomes completely free. The second paragraph lists the five witnesses who attest to the transaction. Three are men of Oropos, two are men of Athens. The most interesting paragraph is the third, somewhat prolix and not entirely grammatical. Moschos explains what led him to write this inscription: the Gods of the temple (Amphiaraos himself and Hygieia, "Health") appeared to him in a dream and commanded him to do so. Perhaps the dream was vouchsafed to Moschos while he spent a night in the temple, sleeping there in the hope of obtaining a cure or a message from the Gods.[88] In any case, following the divine command, Moschos had the inscription engraved and set up near the altar.

The third paragraph also reveals two important facts about Moschos the former slave: his father's name, and his own origin. His father's name, Moschion, is a derivative of his own; both Moschos and Moschion mean "calf" and are common Greek names.[89] Moschos is, or at least claims to be, a *Ioudaios.* The context indicates that this must be translated as "Judaean." The witnesses were Athenian and Oropian, and Moschos himself was Judaean. In what sense was Moschos Judaean? Perhaps he was Judaean only geographically: he (or his father) hails from Judaea. If this is correct, we cannot be sure that Moschos was "Jewish"—that is, an adherent of the God whose temple is in Jerusalem; he could have been a gentile (a "Syrian" or an "Arab," for example) as easily as he could have been a "Jew."[90] However, as I remarked above,

87. Text and translation: Lewis, "Greek Jew"; Lifshitz, *CIJ,* no. 711b. See too *SEG* 15 (1958) no. 293, and Millar in Schürer, *History* 3:65. My translation is based on those of Lewis and Lifshitz.

88. This suggestion is Lewis'.

89. Of course, as a freed slave, Moschos did not have a legal father, since slaves lack paternity. Thus, the legal part of the document (first paragraph) simply refers to Moschos. But in the nonlegal part of the document, Moschos' own self-description, there is no reason why he should not style himself "son of Moschion."

90. Not all the inhabitants of Judaea, certainly not in the first half of the third century B.C.E., were Jews. Similarly, not all "Jerusalemites" in the second century B.C.E. are necessarily "Jewish"; see Millar in Schürer, *History* 3:25 (regarding *CIJ* no. 749).

Ioudaios in the sense "inhabitant of Judaea" is nowhere attested and seems very unlikely in the Hellenistic period. Surely, then, he was Judaean both geographically and ethnically. We may wonder how an ethnic Judaean permitted himself to erect an inscription in a Greek temple and boast of receiving a dream from two Greek Gods, but we must allow Judaeans to behave in a manner of which we disapprove. As David M. Lewis remarks, Moschos, "the first Greek Jew of whom we know," is "thoroughly assimilated to his Greek environment."[91] No matter what we think of Moschos, *Ioudaios* here certainly means "Judaean."

Ioudaios next appears in two manumission inscriptions from Delphi, some one hundred years after the Moschos inscription. The first, erected between 170 and 156 B.C.E., records the manumission (in the form of a sale to the God Apollo) of "three female slaves, whose names are Antigonē, by birth a *Ioudaia,* and her daughters Theodora and Dorothea, for the price of seven minas of silver." The second, dated to 162 B.C.E., records the manumission (in the form of a sale to the God Apollo) of "a male slave, whose name is Ioudaios, by birth a *Ioudaios,* for the price of four minas of silver."[92] The descriptive phrase "by birth a *Ioudaios*" clearly has nothing to do with "religion." It is a legal description of the origin of the slaves: they were born in Judaea, land of the *Ioudaioi.* Delphic manumissions regularly record the place of birth of slaves being manumitted: they are listed as Cappadocian, Thracian, Aetolian, Phrygian, and so forth. Second-generation slaves are recorded as "home-born" or "born-within"—that is, born within the house.[93] If a manumitted slave is described as *Ioudaios* (or *Ioudaia*), it is because the slave is Judaean, not because the slave is Jewish.

When we move forward a few hundred years and look at the inscriptions of late antiquity (third to fifth centuries C.E.), a clear shift is evi-

91. Lewis, "Greek Jew." Cf. J. Robert and L. Robert, "Bulletin epigraphique," *Revue des études grecques* 69 (1956) no. 121, where the authors call Moschos "exemple frappant de dénationalisation." See too Barclay, *Diaspora* 321–322.

92. *CIJ* nos. 709 and 710; Millar in Schürer, *History* 3.65.

93. For manumissions at Delphi, see *Fouilles de Delphes III: Epigraphie Fascicule II: Inscriptions du trésor des Athéniens,* ed. M. G. Colin (Paris: Fontemoing, 1909–1913) nos. 119–133, and *Fascicule III: Inscriptions depuis le Trésor des Athéniens jusqu'aux bases de Gélon,* ed. G. Daux and A. Salac (Paris: de Boccard, 1932) passim. For the phrase *to genos oikogenēs,* see, from fascicule II, nos. 14, 17, 18, 40, 41, 48, 53, 139, 141, 268, 269, 290, 313, 366, [397], 427; for the phrase *to genos endogenēs,* see 133, 137, 337, 368; for the phrase *to genos engenēs,* see no. 39. These phrases show that *to genos* must mean "by birth," not "by race" or "by nation." (The adjectives *oikogenēs, endogenēs,* and *engenēs* also occur without *to genos.*) These inscriptions are of the second century B.C.E.

dent. In some inscriptions the precise meaning of *Ioudaios* is unclear, and in others the ethnic-geographic meaning seems to remain predominant, but in many, both Greek and Latin, east and west, the word *Ioudaios* has come to mean "Jew," an adherent of the Jewish religion.[94] In fact, phrases like "who conducted his entire manner of life in accordance with Judaism" and "a fearer of the Jewish religion" now receive epigraphical attestation.[95] One Latin inscription (fourth century) invokes the wrath of the Gods against anyone who would deface the inscription (and, presumably, the monument). Which Gods? "Whatever the Romans or the Jews or the Christians or the barbarians worship." "Romans" are the pagans within the Roman empire (a Greek inscription would have used the term "Hellenes"), "barbarians" are those without. The Jews (*Iudei*) and the Christians (*Crissiani*) are the monotheists.[96] A fifth-century inscription from northern Italy reads, in part: "Here lies Petrus, also called Papario, son of Olympius the Jew, and the only one of his people who deserved to reach the grace of Christ." Here, then, is a Jew by birth who accepted Christian baptism. *Iudaeus* clearly means "Jew."[97]

Papyri. I turn now to the evidence of the papyri of Ptolemaic Egypt. The material is easily surveyed in volume 1 of the *Corpus Papyrorum Judaicarum,* edited by Victor Tcherikover (with the addition of some papyri that have appeared after the publication of the Corpus).[98]

Ioudaios is but one of several dozen ethnic-geographic (or, in the case of Greek cities, political-geographic) designations that occur in the

94. Kraemer, "The Term 'Jew.'"

95. *Poleiteusamenos pasan poleiteian kata ton Ioudaismon, CIJ* no. 694 (Stobi, Macedonia); *religioni Iudeicae metuenti, JIWE* no. 9 (Pola, northern Italy).

96. I follow the reconstructed text of Rudolf Egger, *Von Römern, Juden, Christen, und Barbaren,* Sitzungsberichte der Österreichische Akademie der Wissenschaften, vol. 247, no. 3 (Vienna: H. Böhlaus, 1965). This fourfold distinction must have been a commonplace; it recurs in *Paralipomena* 41 in F. Halkin, *Sancti Pachomii Vitae Graecae,* Subsidia Hagiographica, no. 19 (Brussels: Peeters, 1932) = *Pachomian Koinonia II: Pachomian Chronicles and Rules,* trans. A. Veilleux (Kalamazoo, Mich.: Cistercian Publications, 1981) 66. A different reading of the inscription is presented by Lifshitz, *CIJ* 62–63, no. 680a. "Gods" is *numina.*

97. Lifshitz, *CIJ* 49–50, no. 643a = *JIWE* no. 8. Instead of "the only one of his people" perhaps we should translate *ex gente sua* as "the only one of his family."

98. I. Fikhman is now preparing a volume of addenda to *CPJ.* I have no doubt that I have not located all the published *Ioudaioi,* but I hope that I have not missed anything significant.

papyri: Achaean, Athenian, Amphipolitan, Antiochian, Boeotian, Carian, Lycian, Macedonian, Persian, Paphlagonian, and so forth.[99] In both public and private documents, *Ioudaios* is functionally indistinguishable from the other ethnic terms, and consequently should always be understood in an ethnic-geographic sense: "Judaean," not "Jew."

Even if *Ioudaios* is properly translated as "Judaean," however, some ambiguities and uncertainties remain, because the meaning of all these ethnic-geographic designations is the subject of ongoing scholarly debate: are they real or fictive; that is, do their bearers really descend from the indicated ethnic or political group, or not? Do the terms denote legal status, social status, military status, or are they simply marks of identification, denoting no status at all? There is general agreement among scholars that some ethnic-geographic terms changed their meaning over time. A good example is provided by the cavalry units of the Ptolemaic army, which were ethnically named ("Thessalians and other Greeks," "Thracians," "Mysians," "Persians," and "Macedonians" are attested). Originally, we may presume, the horsemen of each of these units actually were of the ethnic origin indicated by the name of their troop, but by the end of third century B.C.E. this was no longer true. In the case of the cavalry, at least, the ethnic-geographic terms have become "pseudo-ethnics." (Similarly, as several scholars have noted, originally all the soldiers in the Irish, Welsh, and Scottish regiments of the British army really were Irish, Welsh, or Scottish, but after a certain point this was no longer true, even if the names of the regiments did not change. Not all Welsh Fusiliers are Welsh.)[100] Thus the

---

99. The program of the *Corpus Papyrorum Judaicarum*, which ignores everyone except *Ioudaioi* and those with "Jewish" names, obscures this fact. For a good example of a document that cannot be properly interpreted without being considered as a whole, but which is presented only in part in the *Corpus*, see *CPJ* no. 31 with the comments in Kasher, *Hellenistic and Roman Egypt* 53–54. There is an enormous literature on the ethnic-geographic designations of the documents of Ptolemaic Egypt and on the social conditions that they reflect. I do not pretend to have mastered the relevant literature, but I have learned much from the following works (even if they are contradictory on various points): Bickermann, "Heimatsvermerk"; Tcherikover, *CPJ* 1.11–15 and 51 n. 10; Oates, "Status Designation"; Boswinkel and Pestman, *Archives privées de Dionysios,* 34–63; Mélèze-Modrzejewski, "Le statut des Hellènes"; Goudriaan, *Ethnicity;* Vandersleyen, "Suggestion"; Kramer, CPR 18, pp. 69–73 and 79–80; Bilde et al., *Ethnicity;* Hanson, "Egyptians, Greeks." My discussion here simply confirms Bickerman's observation (*Greek Age* 82) that "when we find [in the papyri] the qualification 'Jew' or 'Jewess,' the term refers to nationality, not religion, which was irrelevant to the Ptolemaic administration. A Jew was a man from Judaea."

100. Goudriaan, *Ethnicity* 106. An American analogy would be sports teams with "ethnic" names. Most of the football players on the "Fighting Irish" of Notre Dame are

second half of the third century B.C.E. witnesses such anomalies as "Diphilos, a Thracian" of the troop of "Thessalians and other Greeks," and "Ptolemy, a Macedonian" of the troop of "Persians and *xxxx*" (the full name of the troop is lost).[101] By the middle of the second century B.C.E., "Persian," "Macedonian," "Thracian," and perhaps other terms as well no longer were true ethnics (i.e., they no longer indicated the actual ethnic origins of their bearers),[102] even in the absence of any reference to the cavalry, and perhaps even in the absence of any connection with military service.

Closely associated with some of these ambiguities is the phrase *tēs epigonēs,* which frequently modifies these ethnic terms (e.g., "Athenian *tēs epigonēs,*" "Thracian *tēs epigonēs,*" etc.). Meaning literally "of the succession" or "of the following generation," the phrase has been understood in two radically different ways: according to some scholars it is evidence of association with the military, while according to others it is evidence of nonassociation with the military. Tcherikover gives a brief statement of the first view:

Soldiers, settled in *cleruchies* . . . , took wives from among the natives, and so a younger generation, having a military tradition from its very birth, grew up in the settlements. This younger generation was called the Epigone (*epigonē*). Since the Epigone served as permanent source of new enlistments, the term acquired the significance of an "army of reserves." Every soldier, when giving his name for any official purpose, was obliged to record his origin (Macedonian, Thracian, etc.) and state whether he was a regular soldier (with details of detachment, hipparchy and the like) or belonged to the Epigone.[103]

---

not Irish; most of the basketball players on the Boston Celtics are not Celtic; most of the baseball players on the Cleveland Indians are not Indian; and so forth.

101. On the ethnic hipparchies, see Kramer, CPR 18, pp. 79–80; Diphilos: CPR 18 no. 10.197; Ptolemy: CPR 18 no. 15.298–299. See Kramer's useful display of the evidence on pp. 64–65. For other anomalies cf. "Ptolemarchos, a Macedonian" of the troop of "Thessalians and other Greeks" (Peremans, *Prosopographia Ptolemaica* 2.2743) and "Chaereas, a Pergamene [or: Pergean]" of the "hipparchy of Thracians" (Peremans, *Prosopographia Ptolemaica* 2.2745).

102. This clarification is needed because Bickermann, "Heimatsvermerk" 223, means something different when he calls the ethnics "false." Unless I am mistaken, Bickermann nowhere doubts that the ethnic terms denote the real ethnic origins of their bearers; for Bickermann the terms are false only in a juridical or legal sense; that is, the terms do not always correspond to political reality, even if they correspond to ethnic reality. Some scholars (notably Goudriaan) have misinterpreted Bickermann.

103. Tcherikover, *CPJ* 1 p. 13.

As a result, in the *Corpus* Tcherikover includes among "Jewish Soldiers and Military Settlers" anyone labeled *Ioudaios tēs epigonēs*, even if there is no other evidence for a connection with the army.[104] Tcherikover, however, did not fully grasp the implications of this view, for if men of "the Epigone" were soldiers in reserve by virtue of their birth, then the ethnic group to which they belong must also be a function of their military status. Two distinguished papyrologists write:

During the first period [before the second half of the second century B.C.E.], the "Persians of the *epigone*" were destined to serve as "Persians" in the army, the "Jews of the *epigone*" as "Jews," etc.[105]

In other words, if *Ioudaioi tēs epigonēs* are soldiers, then *Ioudaios* is not primarily an ethnic designation but a military title, just as (in this view) "Persian" is not primarily an ethnic designation but a military title. And, just as not all soldiers and settlers designated "Persians" were necessarily real Persians, perhaps not all those designated *Ioudaioi* were necessarily real "Judaeans."[106] If this is correct, we have just recovered a new meaning of the term *Ioudaios*: a designation of military status in Ptolemaic Egypt.

This conclusion, however, has no basis at all if we accept the alternate interpretation of the phrase *tēs epigonēs*. In 1963 John Oates argued that *tēs epigonēs* "signifies a person who has no governmental or military position and means 'civilian' or 'private individual.'"[107] Thus, whereas in the first view the phrase "of the Epigone" modifies the ethnic designation that it follows (indicating that the military-ethnic status of the father has been inherited by the son), in the alternate interpretation it does not.[108] The status indicated by the ethnic designation, whether real or fictive, has nothing to do with the status indicated by the phrase "of the Epigone." Thus in this interpretation a *Ioudaios tēs epigonēs* is someone who is (or claims to be) a *Ioudaios* and who is not serving in

104. Similarly, Launey, *Recherches* 2.1232–1235, includes *Ioudaioi tēs epigonēs* in his prosopography of soldiers.

105. Boswinkel and Pestman, *Archives privées de Dionysios* 59: "Durant la première période, les 'Perses de l'*epigonè*' étaient destinés à servir comme 'Perses' dans l'armée, les 'Juifs de l'*epigonè*' comme 'Juifs', etc."

106. Vandersleyen doubts whether "Persian" was ever a true ethnic, a view that is contested by W. Clarysse in a forthcoming publication.

107. Oates, "Status Designation" 116; Oates' position is endorsed by Vandersleyen, "Suggestion."

108. Hence Oates, "Status Designation," places a comma between *Persēs* and *tēs epigonēs*.

a military or government function. As a result, in the *Corpus,* Tcherikover should *not* have included among "Jewish Soldiers and Military
Settlers" those labeled *Ioudaios tēs epigonēs,* because none of them has
any connection with the military. Whether *Ioudaios* (and the other ethnic designations followed by *tēs epigonēs*) is a true or a fictive ethnic designation must be determined either on a case-by-case basis or on the basis of general considerations; the phrase "of the Epigone" provides not
a clue.

In sum, even if we may be certain that *Ioudaios* in Ptolemaic documents should always be translated as "Judaean," we cannot be sure that
all these "Judaeans" were really ethnic Judaeans from Judaea or their
descendants. It is as impossible to prove that they were as it is to prove
that they were not. I am struck by the fact that so few scholars have even
considered the possibility that *Ioudaios* might be, occasionally at least,
a pseudo-ethnic, and that not all *Ioudaioi* were in fact "Judaeans."[109]
The hesitation to raise this possibility is, I presume, the result of the notion that Jews are, and have always been, "different," "distinctive," and
unassimilable. The degree to which the Jews (Judaeans) of the diaspora
in antiquity were, in fact, different, distinctive, and unassimilable is a
difficult question, which I have already treated in chapter 2. I argued
that, in fact, individual Judaeans abroad were not so different from their
neighbors and not so easily recognized. Clearly, however, it is unwarranted to *assume* that all *Ioudaioi* must have been real *Ioudaioi,* and that
only other ethnic-geographic designations may have been fictive.

Of course there is some evidence that the ethnic designation *Ioudaios*
was not used capriciously. Many *Ioudaioi* bear Hebrew names (e.g.,
Jonathan, Judah, Joseph, Samuel, John) or names compounded with
theos (God) that seem entirely appropriate to real Judaeans (e.g.,
Theodotos, Dōsitheos, Theogenēs, Theophile, Theodore, Timothy).
There is no conclusive evidence that *Ioudaios* ever served as a pseudo-
ethnic. No one in Ptolemaic Egypt is ever identified as both a *Ioudaios*
and a member of some other ethnic community, either simultaneously
or sequentially.[110] There is no clear evidence for a regiment or troop of
Ioudaioi whose name could atrophy and be applied to soldiers of non-

109. The possibility is raised and dismissed by Launey, *Recherches* 550 n. 3; Kasher,
"Civic Status" 108; and Honigman, "Birth" 96.

110. I do not consider *CPJ* 417 (a text of 59 C.E., concerning three *Ioudaioi Persai tēs
epigonēs*) to be an exception, because by the Roman period the phrase "Persian of the
Epigone" was no longer an ethnic designation; it designated the legal status of a borrower
whose property could be attached by a creditor without restriction.

Judaean origin.[111] The papyri document not a single case in which a *Ioudaios* marries a non-*Ioudaios*. No doubt intermarriages took place, but in the written record *Ioudaioi* marry other *Ioudaioi* or individuals of no ethnic designation. Members of other ethnic groups, in contrast, are commonly seen marrying someone outside their ethnic group.[112] Last, virtually all of the dozens of ethnic designations that regularly appear in the documents of the third and second centuries B.C.E. disappear by the Roman period—with the notable exception of *Ioudaios*.[113] All the others had folded into "Greeks" or "Egyptians." This fact implies that, at least by the late Ptolemaic and early Roman periods, *Ioudaioi* constituted a clearly definable group.

Conclusion

Greek *Ioudaios*, Latin *Iudaeus*, and Hebrew *Yehudi* are almost always translated as "Jew," but in all occurrences of the term before the end of the second century B.C.E. this translation is wrong, because before that point these words always and everywhere mean "Judaean," not "Jew." "Judaean" is an ethnic-geographic term: a Judaean is a member of the Judaean people (*ethnos*) and hails from Judaea, the ethnic homeland. In the diaspora a "Judaean" is a member of an association of those who hailed originally from the ethnic homeland; a person might be a Judaean even if he or she had not been born in Judaea

111. Kasher argues that *Ioudaioi* in Ptolemaic Egypt formed their own military units, as they had at Elephantine under the Persians, but I am not convinced by his arguments; conclusive evidence is lacking. See Kasher, *Hellenistic and Roman Egypt* 38–48.

112. I owe this observation to John Oates. On the frequency of intermarriage, see chapter 8 below, note 12, and Tcherikover, commentary on *CPJ* 128 and 144. Kramer, CPR 18 p. 70 n. 225, writes: "Der bisher einzige Papyrus, der eine Mischehe dokumentiert, ist *CPJ* I 46," but I fail to see how that papyrus documents mixed marriage. "Marriages between 'Hellenes', under which heading the Jews fell, and native Egyptians were a very rare occurrence in Hellenistic Egypt, " writes Joseph Mélèze-Modrzejewski in "Jewish Law and Hellenistic Legal Practice," in *An Introduction to the History and Sources of Jewish Law,* ed. N. S. Hecht et al. (Oxford: Clarendon, 1996) 86, but the incidence of intermarriage between *Ioudaioi* and other *Hellenes* is not known. Marriages among Hellenes in Egypt were common; so too marriages between citizens of different Greek cities were common in the late Hellenistic and Roman periods (Oliver, *Marcus Aurelius* 50–53).

113. On the disappearance of the ethnic designations, see Bickermann, "Heimatsvermerk" 239. On the persistence of *Ioudaios* (and "Arab"), see Hanson, "Egyptians, Greeks" 137–139 (although her reference to "Semites" is misleading, since there were no Semites and no antisemitism in antiquity).

or ever set foot there. Like all other ethnic-geographic groups, Judaeans have their own language, customs, institutions, dress, cuisine, religion, and so on, but no one of these characteristics is necessarily more important than any other in defining a "Judaean." Texts describing Judaeans may deal with their religion or way of life, but this fact does not change the primary meaning of the concept "Judaean." In contrast, "Jew" (at least in English) is a religious term: a Jew is someone who venerates the God of the Judaeans, the God whose temple is in Jerusalem (the capital of Judaea). "Jew," then, denotes culture, way of life, or "religion," not ethnic or geographic origin.

In the Hellenistic period, virtually all "Judaeans" will have been Jews; that is, virtually all the members of the Judaean *ethnos* will have worshiped the God whose temple is in Jerusalem. During the persecution by Antiochus Epiphanes some Judaeans become "apostates" and no longer worshiped the ancestral God properly—at least from the joint perspective of our extant sources and the Maccabees. Out of the clash between Judaism (the ways of the Judaeans) and Hellenism (the ways of the Greeks) emerged two new definitions of *Ioudaios* that for the first time allowed gentiles the opportunity to join the Judaean people. The first definition was political: the Judaeans form a political community and could extend citizenship even to nonnatives. Such newly enfranchised citizens themselves became *Ioudaioi* or Judaeans. They still retained their prior ethnicity and much of their prior religion and culture, but they joined the Judaean people and declared loyalty to the God of the Judaeans. This political definition of Judaean identity gave the Hasmoneans an institutional mechanism by which to deal with (some of) their allies and to turn (some of) their conquests into allies. With the demise of the Hasmonean empire, this political definition faded as well, but left behind clear traces in later Jewish reflections on the meaning and process of conversion to Judaism.

The second definition was cultural (or "religious"): the Judaeans form a religious community and could extend membership to nonnatives who believe in the God of the Judaeans and observe his precepts. A non-Judaean could become a *Ioudaios* by joining the Judaeans in venerating the one true God, the God whose temple is in Jerusalem. Second Maccabees 6:6 and 9:17, the first witness to this new conception and new terminology, mark an important turning point in the history of the word *Ioudaios* and, indeed, in the history of Judaism. As is well known, 2 Maccabees is the first work to use the word *Ioudaïsmos*. We are tempted, of course, to translate this as "Judaism," but this translation is too narrow, because in this first occurrence of the term, *Ioudaïsmos* has not yet been reduced to a designation of a religion. It means rather "the aggregate of all those characteristics that make Judaeans Judaean (or Jews Jewish)." Among these characteristics, to be sure, are practices and beliefs that we would today call "religious," but these practices and beliefs are not the sole content of the term. Thus *Ioudaïsmos* should be translated not as "Judaism" but as Judaeanness.[114] Its antonym is the adoption of foreign ways or "paganness," and, more particularly, *Hellēnismos*, the adoption of "Greek" ways.[115] It is a conflict between "Judaism," the ways of the Judaeans, and "Hellenism," the ways of the Greeks (even if 2 Maccabees never juxtaposes the two terms). The creation of the word *Ioudaïsmos* is an important moment in the development of Jewish self-identity and in the birth of Jewishness, but even more striking is the use of the old word *Ioudaios* in a new way. Second Maccabees is the first work to use *Ioudaïsmos* and the first work to use *Ioudaios* in the sense of "Jew."

In the next chapter I shall treat both of these new definitions of Judaeanness. What is their origin, and what is their connection to the events of the second century B.C.E.?

114. 2 Macc. 2:21; 8:1; 14:38. See Amir, "*Ioudaismos*." Habicht translates "die jüdische Sache."

115. *Allophulismos*, 4:13; 6:25; *Hellēnismos* 4:13.

PART II

The Boundary Crossed

Becoming a Jew

CHAPTER 4

From *Ethnos* to Ethno-religion

*It is clear that a person of a certain descent may become attached
to people of another descent . . . Such a person comes to be known
as having the same descent as those to whom he is attached and is
counted one of them . . . In the course of time the original descent
is almost forgotten.*
     Ibn Khaldûn, *The Muqaddimah: An Introduction to History*

In the previous chapter I argued that the history of the
word *Ioudaios* demonstrates that before the second or first century
B.C.E. we can speak not of "Jewishness" but of "Judaeanness." "Judaeanness" was a function of birth and geography; *Ioudaioi* belonged to
the *ethnos* of Judaeans in Judaea. Even when Judaeans left their homeland to live in the diaspora, they maintained themselves as ethnic associations. Ethnic (or ethnic-geographic) identity is immutable; non-
Judaeans cannot become Judaeans any more than non-Egyptians can
become Egyptians, or non-Syrians can become Syrians. However, in the
century following the Hasmonean rebellion two new meanings of "Judaeans" emerge: Judaeans are all those, of whatever ethnic or geographic
origins, who worship the God whose temple is in Jerusalem (a religious
definition), or who have become citizens of the state established by the
Judaeans (a political definition). In contrast with ethnic identity, reli-

The epigraph is from Ibn Khaldûn, *The Muqaddimah: An Introduction to History*,
translated by F. Rosenthal, abridged and edited by N. J. Dawood (Bollingen Series/Prince-
ton University Press, 1967) 100.

gious and political identities are mutable: gentiles can abandon their false gods and accept the true God, and non-Judaeans can become citizens of the Judaean state. Thus, with the emergence of these new definitions in the second century B.C.E., the metaphoric boundary separating Judaeans from non-Judaeans became more and more permeable. Outsiders could become insiders. In the previous chapter I studied this phenomenon philologically; in this chapter, the first of four on gentiles becoming Jews, I study the phenomenon historically. In the first part of the chapter I analyze the incorporation of the Idumaeans within the Hasmonean state, the earliest evidence for the idea that "citizenship" in the Judaean state can be conferred on outsiders. In the second part of the chapter I analyze the statements in Judith, 2 Maccabees, and related works, which suggest that gentiles can believe in the God of the Jews and thus become Jews themselves. I shall argue that neither of these innovations can be explained as developments of biblical institutions and ideas, and that both of them become explicable only within the context of Hellenistic culture.

Change of Citizenship

The earliest evidence for the incorporation of outsiders within the Judaean state and the identification of Judaeanness with citizenship is the Hasmonean conquest of the Idumaeans about 128 B.C.E. This episode requires extended discussion, because our evidence is fragmentary and contradictory, and has received remarkably varied interpretations by modern scholars.

THE INCORPORATION OF THE IDUMAEANS WITHIN THE HASMONEAN STATE

In the *Jewish War* Josephus mentions briefly Hyrcanus' conquests in Idumaea but says nothing about the treatment of the inhabitants. His silence on this subject is due presumably to the brevity of his account. The *Jewish Antiquities,* however, reports the following:

Hyrcanus also captured the Idumaean cities of Adora and Marisa, and after subduing all the Idumaeans, permitted them to remain in their country so long as they had themselves circumcised and were willing to observe the laws of the Judaeans. And so, out of attachment to their ancestral land, they submitted to circumcision and to having their manner of life in all other respects made the same as that of the Judaeans. And from that time on they have continued to be Judaeans.[1]

This passage should be studied in conjunction with Josephus' description of Aristobulus' conquest of part of the Ituraeans in 104–103 B.C.E.:

In his reign of one year with the title of Philhellene he conferred many benefits on his country, for he made war on the Ituraeans and acquired a good part of their territory for Judaea and compelled the inhabitants, if they wished to remain in their country, to be circumcised and to live in accordance with the laws of the Judaeans.[2]

Josephus makes clear that the incorporation of "all" the Idumaeans and "a good part of" the Ituraeans into the Judaean state was not entirely voluntary. The inhabitants were given a choice: if they did not wish to be incorporated they could leave, but if they wished to continue living on their land, they would have to accept circumcision and the obligation to live according to the Judaean laws. The choice was real; both alternatives were harsh but bearable. The Idumaeans and the Ituraeans accepted incorporation, but, Josephus reports (at least in the manuscript reading adopted by all modern editors), in the days of Alexander Jannaeus (ca. 83 B.C.E.) the noncitizen inhabitants of Pella did not. As a result they were expelled and the city was destroyed.[3] Confirmation of the nonvoluntary nature of their incorporation is provided by the fact that almost one hundred years later some Idumaeans were not content with living according to the customs of the Judaeans:

Costobar was an Idumaean by birth and was one of those first in rank among them, and his ancestors had been priests of Koze whom the Idumaeans believe to be a god. Hyrcanus had altered their way of life to the customs and laws of the Judaeans. When Herod took over royal power he appointed Costobar governor of Idumaea and Gaza, and gave him in marriage his sister Salome . . . Costobar gladly received these favors . . . [but] did not think that it was proper for him to carry out the orders of Herod, who was his

1. *AJ* 13.257–258; cf. *BJ* 1.63.
2. *AJ* 13.318.
3. *AJ* 13.397: "They [the forces of Alexander Jannaeus] destroyed this city [Pella] because the inhabitants did not promise to change over to the ancestral customs of the *Ioudaioi*." Kasher, *Jews and Hellenistic Cities* 158, astutely observes that Jannaeus had no hope of converting the Greek citizens (*politai*) of the town; his offer, rather, was extended to the noncitizen inhabitants (*hoi enoikountes*) who, he thought, might be willing to join the *Ioudaioi*, just as the Idumaeans and Ituraeans had done. Some manuscripts and testimonia read "although the inhabitants promised" instead of "because the inhabitants did not promise." This reading is not necessarily wrong and deserves further consideration than it has received.

ruler, or for the Idumaeans to adopt the customs of the Judaeans and be subject to them.[4]

Costobar, an Idumaean noble with an Idumaean name (as Josephus explains, Cos or Koz is the Idumaean god), was plotting to find a way to escape Jewish customs and thereby Jewish domination (ca. 34 B.C.E.). "Idumaism" was not yet dead. It still flourished in Egypt, and Costobar was hoping that it would flourish yet again in Idumaea itself.[5] Sixty years after the death of Herod, the name Costobar was still in use in the Herodian family.[6]

The non-Josephan sources, however, present a somewhat different picture. Here is Strabo on the Idumaeans:

The Idumaeans are Nabataeans, but owing to a sedition they were banished from there, joined the *Ioudaioi*, and shared in the same customs with them.[7]

And here is Strabo (drawing on Timagenes) on the Ituraeans:

He [Aristobulus] had a kindly nature and was wholly given to modesty, as Strabo also testifies on the authority of Timagenes, writing as follows. "This man was a kindly person and very serviceable to the Judaeans, for he acquired additional territory for them, and brought over a portion of the Ituraean nation, whom he joined to them by the bond of circumcision."[8]

According to Strabo, the incorporation of both the Idumaeans and the Ituraeans into the Judaean state was voluntary. The Idumaeans left the Nabataeans and joined the Judaeans on their own initiative. The account of the incorporation of the Ituraeans does not mention compulsion, but refers instead to Aristobulus' mild character. None of the possible translations of the ambiguous word *ōikeiōsato*, translated here as "brought over," suggests that Aristobulus resorted to violence; rather he "brought them over," or "won them over," or "established friendship with them," or "established an alliance with them," or "established kinship with them." Thus Strabo understands the union of the Judaeans with the Idumaeans and the Ituraeans as one of friendship, the Idumaeans vol-

---

4. *AJ* 15.253–255.

5. On "Idumaism" in Egypt, see Fraser, *Ptolemaic Alexandria* 1.280–281; Rapaport, "Iduméens en Égypte."

6. *AJ* 20.214.

7. Strabo, *Geography* 16.2.34 = M. Stern, *Authors* no. 115.

8. *AJ* 13.319 = M. Stern, *Authors* no. 100; the reference to Timagenes is in M. Stern, *Authors* no. 81.

untarily assuming the same customs as the Judaeans, and the Ituraeans being attached to the Judaeans by the "bond" of circumcision.[9]

A friendly alliance between the Judaeans and the Idumaeans is perhaps implied as well by the following cryptic remark of Alexander Polyhistor.

> Judaea. Alexander Polyhistor (says that the name derives) from the children of Semiramis, Juda and Idumaea.[10]

Like many other ethnographers, Polyhistor did not hesitate to employ fanciful etymologies to explain exotic geographic names. Thus the name "Judaea" is said to derive from two eponymous heroes, Juda and Idumaea, the sons of the glorious Semiramis. Since this fragment has no hint of any rivalry or hostility between the brothers, it seems to suggest that Judaea is the peaceful agglomeration of Judaeans and Idumaeans. (I freely admit that this passage provides only ambiguous evidence—or perhaps no evidence!—for our problem.)

In contrast, an author named Ptolemy, date and identity uncertain, whose works are lost except for the following quotation, depicts the incorporation of the Idumaeans as entirely compulsory:

> Judaeans and Idumaeans differ, as Ptolemy states in the first book of his "On Herod the King." Judaeans are those who are so originally and by nature. The Idumaeans, on the other hand, were not Judaeans originally but Phoenicians and Syrians; having been subjugated by them [the Judaeans] and compelled to be circumcised, to contribute (taxes) to the nation, and to follow the same laws, they were called Judaeans.[11]

Ptolemy and Strabo agree that the Idumaeans originally were not Judaeans but Nabataeans (Strabo) or Phoenicians and Syrians (Ptolemy). But on two important points Ptolemy and Strabo differ. First, Ptolemy says that Judaeans were such "originally" (or "from the beginning") and "by nature" (*hoi ex archēs phusikoi*), whereas Strabo believes that Jews originally were Egyptians.[12] Second, Ptolemy says that the Idumaeans have been subjugated by the Judaeans, whereas Strabo says that the Idumaeans joined the Judaeans voluntarily.

---

9. The poet Philo also refers to circumcision as a *desmos* (but in the plural); see Eusebius, *Praeparatio Evangelica* 9.20.1 = frag. 1 line 5 ed. Holladay.

10. M. Stern, *Authors* no. 53.

11. M. Stern, *Authors* no. 146.

12. M. Stern, *Authors* no. 105 par. 118; no. 115 sec. 34; no. 124. Ammonios, our source for this fragment of Ptolemy, similarly distinguishes Thebans, the original settlers of Boeotia, from *Thebageneis*, later settlers who were added to the Boeotians by the Thebans (Ammonius no. 231), and distinguishes Italians, the original (*hoi arkhēthen*) settlers of the land, from *Italiotai*, Greek settlers who came later (Ammonios no. 252).

In chapter 2 I emphasized the Platonic distinction between "being" and "being called." Is there a contradiction between Ptolemy's statement that the Idumaeans "were called" Judaeans, and Josephus' statement that the Idumaeans "have continued to be Judaeans"? Probably not. Josephus makes abundantly clear that the Idumaeans always retained their own ethnic identity. Costobar was "an Idumaean by birth." Even when the Idumaeans came to the aid of the Zealots in Jerusalem in 67–68 C.E., they constituted their own *ethnos*. Similarly, the Ituraeans probably maintained their ethnic identity as well, at least at first. Soaemus "the Ituraean" served in the Herodian court. However, the converted Ituraeans quickly disappear from the record; perhaps they were swallowed up by the more numerous Galileans (*Galilaioi*), who also, Josephus carefully notes, formed their own *ethnos* distinct from that of the Judaeans.[13] Thus when Josephus says that the Idumaeans "have continued to be Judaeans," he probably means that they worshiped at the temple in Jerusalem and adopted the ways of the Judaeans (a religious sense), and that they became part of the Judaean state (a political sense). When Ptolemy says that the Idumaeans "were called Judaeans," he probably is speaking in a political sense. They were called Judaeans because they were thoroughly subjugated by the Judaeans. If *suntelein eis to ethnos* be translated as "to be counted among the nation"—that is, "to belong to the nation as members"—rather than "to contribute (taxes) to the nation," Ptolemy might be thought to be suggesting that Idumaeans attained full equality with Judaeans, but it is more likely that he is using the word *ethnos* loosely. The Idumaeans belong as members to the *ethnos*—that is, the state controlled by the Judaeans. On this point, Josephus and Ptolemy are in agreement; the Idumaeans came to be called Judaeans and have continued to be Judaeans.

In sum: three sources, three opinions. (1) According to Strabo, the union between the Judaeans and the Idumaeans was completely voluntary, with the initiative coming from the Idumaeans. Similarly, according to Strabo, the union between the Judaeans and the Ituraeans was entirely cordial, with the initiative coming from the Judaeans. (2) According to Josephus neither union was voluntary or cordial; the Idumaeans and Ituraeans, forced to choose between expulsion from their homeland and incorporation into the Judaean state, decided to accept circumcision and Judaean ways. A century later some Idumaean nobles

13. Idumaeans constitute their own *ethnos: BJ* 4.272; cf. 4.243. Soaemus the Ituraean: *AJ* 15.185. Galileans: *BJ* 2.510 and 4.105.

like Costobar were not happy with the results. (3) According to Ptolemy the union between the Judaeans and the Idumaeans was entirely compulsory: the Judaeans subjugated the Idumaeans and compelled them to be circumcised and adopt Jewish ways. Ptolemy does not say that Maccabean troops roamed the Idumaean countryside forcibly circumcising all uncircumcised males whom they would encounter, but he says nothing that would exclude this possibility.[14] Whether Ptolemy would have interpreted the union between the Judaeans and the Ituraeans in the same manner is not known.

Aside from the direct literary testimony of Josephus, Strabo, and Ptolemy, two additional pieces of evidence need to be considered. First, several Idumaean colonies are mentioned in Egyptian papyri. The Idumaeans seem to have arrived in Egypt in the last quarter of the second century B.C.E., probably as a result of the Hasmonean conquests. They probably came from Marisa and maintained their ancestral loyalty to Koz (= Apollo). This suggests that some Idumaeans preferred to leave their country rather than live under Judaean domination and adopt the Judaean laws.[15]

Second, Josephus says that circumcision was a new practice introduced to the Idumaeans and Ituraeans by the Judaeans. Ptolemy confirms this statement for the Idumaeans.[16] But both sources are probably wrong on this point, because in all likelihood the Idumaeans and Ituraeans practiced circumcision long before they came into contact with the Judaeans. Herodotus writes that "the Syrians in Palestine" practice circumcision; Josephus argues that Herodotus can only have meant the Jews, but there is no reason to accept this narrow interpretation. The Judaeans will have been only one among various Syrian peoples that practiced circumcision.[17] A verse in Jeremiah seems to imply that the Edomites as well as various other neighboring peoples were circumcised like the Judaeans.[18] Many ancient texts state that the Arabs practiced circumcision; the Ituraeans were Arabs, and we may presume that they followed the practice of their kinsmen.[19] In 257 B.C.E. in Palestine, Toubias

---

14. Cf. Judah in 1 Macc. 2:46.

15. Rapaport, "Iduméens en Égypte" 75–77.

16. Strabo does not mention circumcision in connection with the Idumaeans, and the phrase he uses in connection with the Ituraeans, *desmōi synapsas tēi . . . peritomēi*, does not reveal whether circumcision is novel.

17. Herodotus 2.104.3 = M. Stern, *Authors* no. 1; *AJ* 8.262 and *CAp* 1.168–171.

18. Jer. 9:24–25; the verse can be construed in various ways. See below, note 38.

19. On the circumcision of the Idumaeans and Ituraeans, see Kasher, *Jews, Idumeans* 56–57; M. Smith, "Gentiles," 1.272. On the passage of Herodotus, and on circumcision in

sent Apollonius a gift of a eunuch and four slave boys; two of the boys were circumcised, two were not. The letter that announced the gift provides no clue on the ethnic origins of the slaves, but there is no reason to assume that the circumcised boys were Jews and the uncircumcised ones were not.[20] Perhaps the more Hellenized Idumaeans (like the citizens of Adora and Marisa) and Ituraeans were not circumcised, but many Idumaeans and Ituraeans, perhaps most, will have been circumcised even before the Hasmonean conquest.

Most modern historians, recounting the conquests of the Maccabees, ignore Strabo and Ptolemy and follow Josephus. Some interpret Josephus as if he said what Ptolemy said. Thus for example the revised version of Schürer reads: "[John Hyrcanus] took the Idumaean towns of Adora and Marisa and forced the Idumaeans to submit to circumcision and to accept the Jewish law." Some seem not to notice that Josephus' account is not consistent with those of Strabo and Ptolemy. Recently, however, some historians have argued that Strabo's account provides an important corrective to Josephus, even if the manner in which the two accounts are to be combined remains the subject of debate. I tentatively offer the following conjectural reconstruction, which at least has the merit of accounting for all the available evidence.[21]

Seeing the growing power of the Hasmonean state, the rural Idumaeans sought an alliance with the Judaeans. Perhaps they were seeking to make the best of the inevitable; perhaps they wanted allies to protect

---

the Near East in Hellenistic and Roman times, see chapter 2 above, text at notes 71–78; on the circumcision of the Arabs, see chapter 2 above, note 77, and chapter 7 below, note 73.

20. *CPJ* no. 4.

21. Historians ignore Strabo and Ptolemy and follow Josephus: see, for example, Will and Orrieux, *Ioudaïsmos-Hellènismos* 194–196, and Doron Mendels, *The Land of Israel as a Political Concept in Hasmonean Literature* (Tübingen: Mohr [Siebeck], 1987) 57–81 (note Jubilees' repeated assertions, discussed by Mendels [75–76], of the kinship of Edom and Israel). The citation from Schürer, *History,* is 1:207. Some historians seem not to notice inconsistency between Josephus, Strabo, and Ptolemy: see, for example, Hengel, *Zeloten* 202; Israel Shatzman, "The Hasmoneans in Greco-Roman Historiography," *Zion* 57 (1992) 5–64, at 32–34 (Timagenes) and 34–40 (Strabo); M. Stern, "Timagenes of Alexandria as a Source for the History of the Hasmonean Monarchy," in *Jews and Judaism in the Second Temple, Mishna and Talmud Period: Studies in Honor of Shmuel Safrai,* ed. I. Gafni et al. (Jerusalem: Yad Izhak ben Zvi, 1993) 3–15, at 8–10. Strabo as corrective to Josephus: Rappaport, "Hellenistic Cities"; Kasher, *Jews, Idumeans* 46–77; M. Smith, "Gentiles"; Richardson, *Herod* 54–62. All the available evidence: I ignore here the testimony of *AJ* 13.275, which seems to say that the men of Marisa were "colonists and allies of the *Ioudaioi.*" The text is probably corrupt; for various suggestions see Marcus' note ad loc. and the extended discussion by A. Schalit, *A Complete Concordance to Flavius Josephus,* supp. 1, *Namenwörterbuch zu Flavius Josephus* (Leiden: Brill, 1968) 130–133.

them from exploitation by the Hellenized cities; perhaps they felt a real sympathy with the anti-Seleucid and anti-Hellenistic posture of the Maccabees; perhaps they realized the political, economic, and military advantages that would accrue to them as a result of joining a larger and more prosperous state. Like the Judaeans they had practiced circumcision for centuries, and it was a relatively simple matter to declare their loyalty to the God of the Jews and to his laws (Strabo).[22] After the Maccabees attacked and captured Adora and Marisa,[23] the two cities of Idumaea, they offered the citizens a choice between expulsion and incorporation into the Judaean state. Since these cities were strongly Hellenized, many of their citizens, as in pre-Maccabean Jerusalem, no longer practiced circumcision although they were still loyal to their ancestral god Koz. Some of the citizens accepted circumcision (Josephus), but many chose instead to flee to Egypt (papyrological evidence). Ptolemy's claim that the Idumaeans were compelled to be circumcised and to adopt Jewish laws is a simplified account of what these urban Idumaeans experienced. As a result of all this, the Idumaeans joined the Judaeans (Strabo), have continued to be Judaeans (Josephus), and were called Judaeans (Ptolemy).

For the incorporation of the Ituraeans we have much less evidence. The simplest way to resolve the conflict between Strabo and Josephus is to assume that Strabo's account is primary. Aristobulus, king of the Judaeans, established friendship or an alliance with part of the nation of the Ituraeans. The two peoples were joined together on the basis of circumcision, a practice current among the Ituraeans for centuries but now endowed with new meaning. The willingness of the Ituraeans can be explained by the same explanations offered above in connection with the Idumaeans. Josephus, however, who was somewhat uncomfortable with

22. I follow Kasher, *Jews, Idumeans* 56–57, in distinguishing the rural Idumaeans from the citizens of Adora and Marisa, but my reconstruction differs from his. Kasher cannot decide whether Josephus basically agrees with Ptolemy (48, 69) or not (65–66). On those pages where he regards Josephus as agreeing with Ptolemy, Kasher argues that the Josephan account is anti-Maccabean propaganda, but the account seems to give an accurate depiction of the Maccabean treatment of Adora and Marisa. Kasher's frequent appeal to rabbinic evidence (50–53, 60–62, 65 n. 66, 67 n. 70) is useless because the Maccabees were not beholden to rabbinic law. On the cultural similarities of the Idumaeans and the Judaeans, cf. E. Eshel and A. Kloner, "An Aramaic Ostracon of an Edomite Marriage Document from Maresha, Dated 176 B.C.E." (in Hebrew), *Tarbiz* 63 (1994) 485–502, which shows the great similarity of the Edomite marriage contract with the later Judaean one.

23. The capture of Marisa (Maresha) by the Hasmoneans is confirmed by archaeology: Amos Kloner, "Underground Metropolis: The Subterranean World of Maresha," *Biblical Archaeology Review* 23, no. 2 (1997) 24–35 and 67.

the idea that the Maccabean state had expanded through voluntary association,[24] wanted to portray the incorporation of the Ituraeans, like the incorporation of the Idumaeans, as involuntary.

Thus the rural Idumaeans joined the Judaeans on their own initiative, the citizens of Adora and Marisa joined the Judaeans at the threat of expulsion, and the Ituraeans joined the Judaeans at the initiative of the ruler of the Judaeans. None of these groups became ethnic Judaeans. Insofar as they became citizens in a state dominated by the Judaeans, they became Judaeans themselves in a political sense, and obligated themselves to observe the ways of the Judaeans. The glue that held this union together was common hatred of "the Greeks" and the readiness of these nations to adopt the way of life and name of the Judaeans.

Hyrcanus' incorporation of the Idumaeans into the Judaean state, and Aristobulus' incorporation of the Ituraeans, are unprecedented actions not explicable on the basis of any previous Hasmonean policy. The Hasmoneans of the first generation (Judah, Jonathan, Simon) cleansed the temple and Jerusalem of "idolatry," but outside Jerusalem their ardor to purify the land was neither consistent nor sustained: Judah burned the sacred precincts of Atargatis at Carnaim in the Gaulan, Judah tore down the altars and destroyed the graven images in Azotus, Jonathan and Simon burned the temple of Dagon at Azotus, and Simon expelled the citizens of Gazara from their city, cleansed the houses of their idolatry, and settled the city with law-observant Jews. Sometimes they expelled populations from positions of military importance: Jonathan and Simon expelled the inhabitants of Beth Zur, Simon expelled the inhabitants of Joppa. Our sources give no indication that the Hasmoneans in any of their other numerous conquests and depredations were determined to wipe out either idolaters or idolatry.[25] Nowhere in either 1 or 2 Maccabees is there a hint that pagan inhabitants of the Holy Land were "Judaized," either by compulsion or otherwise. Clearly this is not the place for a full discussion of the Hasmonean conquests, but the novelty of Hyrcanus' and Aristobulus' actions is apparent.[26]

24. S. J. D. Cohen, "Respect for Judaism" 423.

25. Atargatis at Carnaim: 1 Macc. 5:43–44//2 Macc. 12:26. Azotus: 1 Macc. 5:68. Dagon at Azotus: 1 Macc. 10:84, 11:4. Gazara: 1 Macc. 13:43–48 and 14:34. Beth Zur: 1 Macc. 11:66. Joppa: 1 Macc. 13:11. If the passage in *CAp* 1.193 is pseudo-Hecataeus rather than Hecataeus (= M. Stern, *Authors* no. 12), as is argued by Bezalel Bar-Kochva, *Pseudo-Hecataeus, "On the Jews"* (Berkeley: University of California Press, 1997) 97–101, it may obliquely refer to a sustained Hasmonean policy of temple destruction ("when temples and altars were erected in the country by its invaders, the Jews razed them all to the ground").

26. Will and Orrieux, *Ioudaïsmos-Hellènismos* 189–190, speak of a Hasmonean policy of "homogénéité culturelle." This is plain fantasy, as is documented by the Hasmonean

Whence comes this novel policy? Perhaps it was born simply of expediency; the Hasmonean rulers appreciated the political, economic, and military advantages that would accrue to the Judaean state as a result of the incorporation of outsiders. Perhaps these advantages were no less obvious to the rural Idumaeans and Ituraeans (see above), thus explaining their readiness to adopt the ways of the Judaeans. These advantages and realities perhaps explain why the Hasmoneans did what they did, but not how they did it. How did the Hasmoneans come to the idea of making the Idumaeans and Ituraeans into Judaeans?

BIBLICAL MODELS

The Hasmonean policy was not derived from the pages of the Tanakh. In the Tanakh the peoples conquered by the Israelites were not "converted" or turned into Israelites. God enjoined upon the Israelites the destruction of the Canaanites, not their incorporation or conversion. When they conquered Canaan the Israelites sinned by allowing the Canaanites to persist, but no one attempted to impose Israelite ways on them or convert them. Even in the heyday of the empire of David and Solomon, subjugated nations were compelled to pay tribute; they were not compelled or cajoled to worship Israel's God or to follow Israelite ways. Conquered nations were to remain separate and subordinate.[27]

In the conquest narratives, the story of the Gibeonites is perhaps the most relevant for our purposes (Joshua 9). A Canaanite group (Josh. 9:7), the Gibeonites feared for their lives when the Israelites approached. They therefore sent a delegation to the Israelites; the delegates, pretending to be from a distant country and claiming to have heard of the power of the God of the Israelites, sued for a treaty with the Israelites. Joshua and the elders agreed. When they discovered the deception, the Israelites were furious but were bound by their oath not to harm the Gibeonites. They cursed the Gibeonites and pressed them into service as slaves to the temple and the community. Thus in some measure the

---

treatment of the Greek cities. Many scholars have argued that the Hasmonean conquests spawned anti-Judaic sentiment among their victims, giving rise to "anti-semitism" (Schäfer, *Judeophobia* 178–179), but if my reading of the evidence is correct, this argument needs to be rethought.

27. I am aware, of course, of the numerous historical problems associated with the biblical account of the conquest of Canaan, but these do not concern me here. My question is: are there any narratives or laws in the Tanakh that might have inspired the Hasmoneans in their foreign policy?

Gibeonites were incorporated into the community as underlings, but they remained distinct; because "the Gibeonites were not of Israelite stock, but a remnant of the Amorites," they were massacred by King Saul. Perhaps, by the Persian period, under the name of *netinim,* they found a more secure place for themselves in Israelite society, but they still remained distinct and inferior.[28] Neither the enslavement of the Gibeonites nor the conquest narratives of the Tanakh would have inspired the Hasmoneans to incorporate the Idumaeans and Ituraeans in the Judaean state and regard them as "Judaeans."

The pages of the Tanakh provide abundant documentation for the presence of resident aliens within Israelite society. A "mixed multitude" is said to have accompanied the Israelites on the exodus from Egypt. In the narratives about David and Saul we encounter numerous foreigners either in the army or at court: Doeg the Edomite, Ittai of Gath, Zeleq the Ammonite, Uriah the Hittite, and numerous others.[29] Needless to say, there is no hint that any of these people ever "converted"[30] or were ever regarded as Israelites. They were foreigners, and like *metics* (resident aliens) in classical Athens, foreigners they always remained. Perhaps in the course of time they or their children might have succeeded in assimilating into the dominant society, but there was no formal procedure or process by which this result could be attained.

Similarly, numerous laws in the Torah refer to the "resident alien" (*gēr*). In the earliest literary strata the *gēr*'s social inequality is treated by the legislator; alongside the widow and orphan the *gēr* is a potential victim of abuse and consequently in need of protection and help. In contrast, the priestly sources ("P" and "H") are primarily concerned to establish legal equality between the *gēr* and the native; phrases like "there shall be one law for you, the native and the *gēr* alike" appear frequently in the priestly texts. But even the priestly legislators prescribe no ritual or vehicle by which a *gēr* can ever become not-a-*gēr*. If the resident alien wishes to eat of the Paschal sacrifice, he must first circumcise all the males of his household. The circumcision does not make the resident alien into a native, however; rather, it gives him the right to participate in a ritual that would otherwise be closed to him. He remains a resident

28. Gibeonites: Joshua 9 and 2 Sam. 21:2. *Netinim:* Joseph P. Healey, "Nethinim," *Anchor Bible Dictionary* (1992) 4.1085–1086.

29. "Mixed multitude": Exod. 12:38, cf. Num. 11:4. Doeg: 1 Sam. 21:8. Ittai (and the foreign mercenaries): 2 Sam. 8:18 and 15:18–22. Zeleq the Ammonite: 2 Sam. 23:37. Uriah the Hittite: 2 Sam. 11:3 and 23:39.

30. Even if Ittai swears by YHWH (2 Sam. 15:21).

alien.[31] As Bickerman remarks, "Oriental civilizations had no concept of naturalization." [32]

Some scholars argue that the legal equality between the *gēr* and the native envisioned by the priestly legislators demonstrates that the notion of "religious conversion" existed already in the sixth century B.C.E., as if *gēr* in these texts had already come to mean "convert," as it would in rabbinic texts. I disagree, because P is emphasizing only legal equality for the resident alien. Whether and how the *gēr* is to become part of the people of Israel is nowhere indicated. The *gēr* remains a legally unassimilable foreign element. Indeed, the social setting of P's references to the *gēr* is unknown, and to import the notion of "conversion" into the text is simply unwarranted by the available evidence. These scholars are influenced by the translation of the Septuagint, but their interpretation of the Septuagint is not necessarily correct. In those passages of the Torah that emphasize the social inequality of the resident alien, the Septuagint usually translates *gēr* with *paroikos*, Greek for "resident alien"; in those passages of the Torah that emphasize the legal equality of the resident alien, the Septuagint usually translates *gēr* with *prosēlutos*, a new word in Greek. What force the word "proselyte" had in the third and second centuries B.C.E. we cannot be sure; it did not necessarily mean "convert." By rabbinic times, to be sure, exegetes could securely distinguish those passages that spoke about the "resident alien" (*gēr toshav*) from those that spoke about the convert (*gēr tzedeq*), but the Septuagint in the third century B.C.E. is not necessarily aware of the developments that the rabbis will later be able to take for granted.[33] Whether the Hasmoneans read the Septuagint, and, if they did, what they would have made of the strange word *prosēlutos*, I do not know. The important point is that although the Torah is aware of the existence of "resident aliens" amid the people of Israel, neither the Hebrew text nor the Septuagint advocates the absorption of such aliens or prescribes any means by which such absorption could be effected. The Hasmoneans did not derive their policy from the narratives and laws about the resident alien.

Various texts of the Persian period refer to gentiles who have "at-

---

31. Exod. 12:43–49.

32. Bickerman, *Greek Age* 81. For a full and careful discussion of *gēr*, see van Houten, *Alien*. On the distinction between ethnic assimilation and religious conversion see Y. Kaufmann, *Golah ve Nekhar* (Tel Aviv: Dvir, 1934) 1.227–256.

33. On the word *gēr* in the priestly texts, see van Houten, *Alien* chap. 5. On *proselytos* in the LXX, see van Houten, *Alien* 179–183, and Overman, "God-Fearers" 18–19.

tached themselves" either to the Lord or to Israel.[34] Isaiah 56 refers to the foreigners who have "attached themselves to the Lord to minister to him." Zechariah predicts that "in that day many nations will attach themselves to the Lord and become his people." Isaiah 14:1, a text dated by virtually all scholars to the post-exilic period, prophesies that "strangers (*hagēr*) shall join (*venilvah*) them and shall cleave to the House of Jacob." The meaning of these visions is not entirely clear; are the gentiles to be slaves, proselytes, or "righteous gentiles"?[35] All of these passages address the eschatological age, when the earth is filled with knowledge of the Lord, and a new cosmic order is being created. Whether gentiles in the historical present were recognizing God and attaching themselves to his people is not known. Isaiah 56, in particular, seems to suggest that the foreigners who have attached themselves to Israel in the preeschatological present have been excluded from the temple and the temple cult. The first and only passage in the Tanakh that would seem to refer clearly to the social integration of the gentile in the historical present is Esther 9:27: "the Judaeans undertook and irrevocably obligated themselves and their descendants, and all who might join them, to observe these two days in the manner prescribed and at the proper time each year." Here we have Judaeans (*yehudim*), and gentiles who attach themselves (*nilvim aleihem*) to them; all alike constitute the community of those bound by the law of the Purim festival. This is an interesting and important passage, but it does not predate the Hasmonean period by very much, if at all; it is part of a section that is usually regarded as a secondary or tertiary expansion of the book. In sum: these passages show that in the Persian period, with the destruction of the temple, the disappearance of the tribal system, the emergence of a diaspora, the weakening of the connection between the people and the land, and the gradual elaboration of non-temple-oriented forms of religiosity comes the beginning of the idea that gentiles could somehow attach themselves to the people of Israel by attaching themselves to Israel's God. Here then are harbingers of the idea of conversion, in both its religious and its social sense, but the idea itself is not yet in evidence.[36]

34. Ezra 6:21 and Neh. 10:29 are sometimes taken as references to gentile adherents, but I think that the phrase "all who separate themselves from the impurity of the nations of the lands" does not refer to gentiles. Cf. Ezra 10:11 and Neh. 9:2 and 13:3.

35. In addition to Isa. 14:1–2 and 56:1–8 and Zech. 2:15, see Isaiah 49, 60–61, and 66, and Zechariah 14 (date uncertain: Hellenistic?). For a good and thorough discussion see Donaldson, "Proselytes or 'Righteous Gentiles'?" On Isaiah 56, see Kaufmann, *Religion of Israel* 136–139.

36. On Esther 8:17 see my discussion in chapter 6 below. Ruth is not a "religious convert"; she is a foreigner whose foreignness remains even after she has attempted to adopt

The only chapter in the Tanakh that might have some direct bearing on the Judaization of the Idumaeans and Ituraeans is Genesis 34. After raping Dinah, the daughter of Jacob, Shechem son of Hamor wishes to set matters right by marrying her. Dinah's brothers pretend to be interested in his proposal. They respond "with guile," agreeing to the marriage on condition that the Shechemites be circumcised. "Then we will give our daughters to you and take your daughters to ourselves; and we will dwell among you and become as one kindred (or: one nation, *'am*)." The Shechemites were fooled; they circumcised themselves and during their recuperation were massacred by Simeon and Levi. This dramatic story, with its emphasis on circumcision, its (apparent) prohibition of intermarriage, its militant hostility toward foreigners who oppress the children of Israel, and its assurance that Israelites will triumph if their cause is just (even if their methods are not)—this story struck a responsive chord among many Jews of the second century B.C.E. Witness its extensive treatment in Jubilees, Testament of Levi, the poet Theodotus, and other writers.[37] The story also has partial analogies with the incorporation of the Idumaeans and Ituraeans: a neighboring tribe/group is prepared to join the Judaeans, and the Judaeans are prepared to accept the union on condition that the outsiders accept circumcision. But this story surely cannot have inspired Hyrcanus and Aristobulus to do what they did, because the story and the history have such different conclusions. In the story the offer of the sons of Jacob "to become one nation" with the Shechemites on the basis of circumcision is insincere and guileful, as the subsequent events make clear. In Hasmonean history the offer is sincere and the union is lasting. Genesis 34 played a background role at best in the formulation of the policy of Hyrcanus and Aristobulus.

In particular, what the Hasmoneans may have derived from Genesis 34 is that circumcision is an essential ethnic marker. If other peoples are to forge a single nation or kinship group with the Israelites, they must be circumcised. Circumcision is necessary but is not sufficient; the circumcision of non-Israelites does not ipso facto make them Israelites. Several biblical texts recognize the fact that other nations too practice

---

the ways of her surroundings; see Y. Kaufmann, *Toledot ha-emunah ha-yisraelit* (Jerusalem: Bialik and Dvir, 1955; frequently reprinted) 2.211–214. The phrase *nilvim* appears in the Code of Damascus 4.3 (eschatological reference).

37. Collins, "Epic of Theodotus"; Pummer, "Genesis 34"; Standhartinger, "Perspektive Dinas"; D. Mendels, *The Land of Israel as a Political Concept in Hasmonean Literature* (Tübingen: Mohr [Siebeck], 1987) 109–116; Pieter van der Horst, "Samaritans and Hellenism," in van der Horst, *Hellenism* 53–54. See chapter 8 below, note 70.

circumcision. Jeremiah 9:24–25 seems to say that the circumcision of the men of Judah is no better than, or different from, the circumcision of the men of Egypt, Edom, Amon, Moab, and the desert.[38] Genesis 17, a text that most modern scholars attribute to "P," slightly after Jeremiah, attributes covenantal value to Israelite circumcision and ascribes its origin to a command from God to Abraham. But Genesis 17 also has Abraham circumcise his son Ishmael and his male household slaves; we may presume that the author of Genesis 17 did not intend to argue that Ishmaelites were Israelites! Israelite circumcision was covenantal, but the circumcision of other nations was not. The author of Genesis 17 does not address this problem; hundreds of years later the rabbis would explain that intentionality affects the value of circumcision. Jewish circumcision is covenantal because it is intended to be covenantal, whereas the circumcision of gentiles is not. Most modern scholars emphasize that Genesis 17, part of "P," was written in the exilic community in Babylonia, and that circumcision was invested with covenantal meaning in that milieu in order to heighten Judaean identity in exile and separate the Judaeans from the Babylonians (who did not practice circumcision). But while circumcision could serve as a marker of differentness vis-à-vis some nations, like the Babylonians and, later, the Greeks, it could also serve as a marker of commonality vis-à-vis other nations, like the Ishmaelites, the Idumaeans, and the Ituraeans.[39]

The Hasmoneans would also have learned from the prophetic literature of the exile that circumcision was essential for anyone who would enter the temple. Ezekiel complained that the Israelites permitted "aliens, uncircumcised of spirit and uncircumcised of flesh," to enter the temple; only the Levites and priests have permission to do so. Isaiah promised that "the uncircumcised and the impure" shall never again enter Zion.[40] If a gentile would enter the temple, he had to be circumcised. This is a question not of covenant but of blemish and impurity. From all this the Hasmoneans would readily have concluded that if the Idumaeans and Ituraeans wanted to join the Judaeans and share their

38. I say "seems to say" because the verses are ambiguous and can be interpreted in various ways. In particular, the Septuagint understands 9:25b to mean "all the nations are uncircumcised in the flesh."

39. The tension within Genesis 17 between competing conceptions of circumcision, specifically between a covenantal conception of circumcision and a noncovenantal one, has led various scholars to argue that the chapter is composite; see, for example, Klaus Grünwaldt, *Exil und Identität: Beschneidung, Passa, und Sabbat in der Priesterschrift* (Frankfurt: A. Hain, 1992). On intentionality and circumcision, see chapter 7 below at notes 72–75.

40. Ezek. 44:6–10; Isa. 52:1.

name, they would have to be circumcised. Those of them who were already circumcised had the necessary mark. Circumcision would permit them to enter the temple and participate in all the public cultic ceremonies demanded by the God of the Judaeans. Perhaps too the Hasmoneans, like the rabbis after them, would have deduced from Exodus 12:43–49 that circumcision is the critical marker that distinguishes the alien from the naturalized citizen. The text requires circumcision of a resident alien who would eat of the Paschal sacrifice, but the text can easily be read to mean that once the resident alien has been circumcised, he is to be treated before the law just like the native born. Circumcision effaces the distinction between alien and native.

Thus, the biblical record and Israelite history provide warrant for the absorption of "aliens" and the association of circumcision with that absorption. They may also explain how the Hasmoneans came to see circumcision both as a crucial marker of Judaean identity and as a ritual that might unify the Judaeans with some of their neighbors. But neither the biblical record nor Israelite history would have inspired the Hasmoneans with the novel idea of incorporating alien peoples within the community of Israel and bestowing the name "Judaeans" upon them. The origins of this idea derive from elsewhere.

JUDAISM AS *POLITEIA*

The Greek word *politeia* means in the first instance "citizenship," the quality of being a citizen (a *politēs*). By extension the word also refers to the institutions and conventions within which a citizen exercises his citizenship. In the latter sense the word is often translated as "constitution," but in many texts the translation "law of the land" or "way of life" would be better.[41] The *politeia* of an individual is his citizenship; the *politeia* of a state is its way of doing things.

The Judaeans too had their own way of life, given to them by their lawgiver Moses. Hecataeus is the first (ca. 300 B.C.E.) Greek writer to describe Moses and his "constitution," and his description is the first of many.[42] Upon his conquest of Judaea in 200 B.C.E. Antiochus III decreed: "Let all those from this nation conduct their way of life (*politeia*) in accordance with their ancestral laws." The decree is the first official

41. De Romilly, *Rise and Fall* 69–76; J. Bordes, *"Politeia" dans la pensée grecque jusqu'à Aristote* (Paris: Les Belles Lettres, 1982).

42. Diodorus of Sicily 40.3.3 = M. Stern, *Authors* no. 11.

document extant that demonstrates that the ancestral laws of the Judae-ans—that is, the laws of the Torah—constituted the law of the land. Both Philo and Josephus explicitly label Judaism a *politeia* and speak of outsiders who become insiders by adopting the *politeia* of the Judaeans. In a passage cited above, Josephus remarks that Hyrcanus had altered the way of life (*politeia*) of the Idumaeans to make it conform to the customs and laws of the Judaeans.[43]

If the ancestral laws of the Judaeans constituted their *politeia*, then the Judaeans themselves, not only in Judaea but even in the diaspora, will have been *politai* or "citizens." The Letter of Aristeas views Judae-ans everywhere as the "citizens" of the polity governed by Eleazar, the high priest of Jerusalem. Eleazar has benefited not only his own circle but also "the citizens in various places." When writing to Eleazar, Ptol-emy Philadelphus refers to the Judaeans of Egypt as "your citizens," and in his response Eleazar refers to them as "our citizens." Similarly, two centuries after Philadelphus and perhaps a century after the Letter of Aristeas, Hyrcanus II, high priest of Jerusalem, refers to the Judaeans of Ephesus as "his citizens."[44] Judaeans are "citizens," and Jewishness is their citizenship.

Unlike birth, *politeia,* in both the sense "way of life" and "citizen-ship," is mutable. The best constitution is the one that endures un-changed through the centuries, but the Greeks knew that such *politeiai* were rare because most constitutions undergo change, evolving from one form to another. In the *Against Apion* Josephus argues that one of the proofs for the superiority of the Jewish *politeia* is its constancy; none of the Greek constitutions has resisted the forces of change as suc-cessfully as the Jewish one.[45] Antiochus IV Epiphanes and his support-ers tried without success to destroy, change—or cause the Judaeans to abandon—the ancestral *politeia* and the ancestral laws. After their suc-cessful revolt the Judaeans were granted the right to "follow their laws as before" and to "conduct their *politeia* in accordance with their an-

---

43. Antiochus III: *AJ* 12.142. "Proselytes" are so called, Philo says (*On the Special Laws* 1.9.51), because "they have come to a new and God-loving *politeia*," and Josephus has a similar conception (S. J. D. Cohen, "Respect for Judaism" 425–427). I shall return to the Philonic passage below. On Philo's fondness for *politeia*, see Barclay, *Diaspora* 173. Hyrcanus altered the *politeia* of the Idumaeans: *AJ* 15.253.

44. Letter of Aristeas 3, 36 (= *AJ* 12.46, Ptolemy to Eleazar), 44 (= *AJ* 12.54, Eleazar to Ptolemy); *AJ* 14.226 (Hyrcanus II). In *AJ* 13.287 Strabo says that Jews of the district of Onias remained faithful to the queen because their *politai* Chelkias and Ananias were in favor with the queen.

45. S. J. D. Cohen, "History and Historiography."

cestral customs."[46] If a "constitution" or "way of life" was mutable, so was "citizenship." Individuals and groups could obtain a "citizenship" that was not theirs by birth. "The *polis* . . . invented the concept of naturalization, that is, the change of nationality by will and fiat."[47]

Here, then, is the key to the novel policy of the Hasmoneans. By accepting the Greek definition of their way of life as a *politeia*, and by separating "citizenship" from ethnicity, the Hasmoneans discovered a way to incorporate gentiles into the Judaean polity. The idea that the Idumaeans and Ituraeans could somehow adopt membership in the Judaean state, and somehow become Judaean themselves through the observance of the Judaean way of life, presumes the definition of Judaeanness as a way of life and as a citizenship. Idumaeans and Ituraeans could be granted citizenship in the Judaean polity. Greek political thinking provides not only the mechanism for the incorporation of outsiders but also a background in which the Hasmonean development fits perfectly. As I shall discuss below, the last centuries B.C.E. witness the removal of ethnicity from the concept of "Hellene"; city-states were more open to the incorporation of outsiders as citizens than they had ever been before;[48] many city-states joined together to form leagues. Indeed, the formation of the Greek leagues provide a striking parallel— and perhaps a source—for the policy of the Hasmoneans toward the Idumaeans and Ituraeans.[49]

Polybius describes the Achaean League in these terms:

. . . not only have they [the Peloponnesians] formed an allied and friendly community, but they have the same laws, weights, measures, and coinage, as well as the same magistrates, senate, and courts of justice, and the whole Peloponnesus only falls short of being a single city in the fact of its inhabitants not being enclosed by one wall, all other things being, both as regards the whole and as regards each separate city, very nearly identical.[50]

46. The ancestral *politeia:* 2 Macc. 4:11, 6:1. The ancestral laws: 1 Macc. 2:19, 3:29; 2 Macc. 6:1, 8:17. To "follow their laws as before": 1 Macc. 6:59. To "conduct their *politeia* in accordance with their ancestral customs": 2 Macc. 11:25.

47. Bickerman, *Greek Age* 87.

48. In the Hellenistic period many Greek cities for the first time extended their citizenship to outsiders; see J. K. Davies, "The *Polis* Transformed" 309.

49. I owe this insight to Morton Smith, who develops it brilliantly in his "Gentiles." Earlier, in his "Rome and Maccabean Conversions," Smith had argued that the Hasmoneans adopted the Roman practice of granting citizenship to their allies and conquests (a view followed too by Goodman, *Mission and Conversion* 61), but Smith himself came to recognize that the Roman policy is probably an analogy to, rather than a source for, the Hasmonean practice.

50. 2.37.10–11, trans. Paton.

Aside from the same laws, weights, measures, and so forth, the league also had a "common temple and holy place"—the enclosure of Zeus Homarios near Aegium.[51] The league grew through a combination of voluntary affiliation, persuasion, and force:

... while some of the Peloponnesians chose to join it [the Achaean League] of their own free will, it won many others by persuasion and argument, and those whom it forced to adhere to it when the occasion presented itself suddenly underwent a change and became quite reconciled to their position.[52]

In sum, Polybius says, "both these two peoples [the Arcadians and Laconians] and the rest of the Peloponnesians have consented to change not only their political institutions [politeia, perhaps "mode of life"] for those of the Achaeans, but even their name." In his life of Aratus of Sicyon, Plutarch makes the same point: "though the people of Sicyon were Dorians, they voluntarily assumed the name and constitution [politeia, perhaps "citizenship" or "mode of life"] of the Achaeans."[53]

The parallels between the Achaean League and the Judaean League formed by Hasmoneans are numerous and striking.[54] By joining the Judaeans, the Idumaeans and Ituraeans changed not only their way of life and citizenship (politeia) but also their name, just as the Sicyonians and other Peloponnesians did when joining the Achaean League. The Judaean League grew through a combination of voluntary affiliation, persuasion, and force, just as the Achaean League did. In both cases, even those incorporated by force generally came to accept their status (witness the fact that in the great war against the Romans, the Idumaeans went to Jerusalem to aid their Judaean brethren). Like the Achaean League, the Judaean League was united by common laws, practices, magistrates, and, last but not least, a common temple and holy place. The Judaean League was not Greek, of course, and I am not suggesting that it was governed in a Greek manner; clearly it was not. Even if it issued coins in the name of the "League of the Judaeans" (in Hebrew, hever hayehudim), it was not "democratic" in the way that the Achaean League was. Nevertheless, the Judaean League—a union of Judaeans, Idumaeans, and Ituraeans—had a Greek character: it was based on a Greek political theory and was paralleled, if not inspired, by a Greek po-

51. Polybius 2.39.6.   52. 2.38.7, trans. Paton.
53. Polybius 2.38.4; Plutarch, *Aratus* 9.4.
54. I am aware, of course, that Polybius' account of the Achaean League has its share of exaggerations and cannot be trusted in all its details. Modern discussion of these problems—none of which, I am happy to note, affects my discussion—begins with Walbank's commentary ad loc.

litical form. By conceiving of Judaism as a *politeia*—a way of life and a citizenship—that could be extended to the Idumaeans and Ituraeans, Hyrcanus and Aristobulus were working within a decidedly Hellenistic framework.

Change of Belief

THE EARLIEST CONVERSIONS

Two texts of the Hasmonean period are the earliest references to conversion to Judaism—that is, the process by which gentiles change their theology and adopt exclusive allegiance to the one true God, the God of the Jews. Both of these literary references are unambiguous, but both are also fictional. Perhaps their very fictionality attests to the reality of conversion in the authors' social setting—after all, the authors want their stories to be believed—but that reality is conjectural. Firm evidence for actual converts emerges only in the first century C.E.

Second Maccabees, probably written around 100 B.C.E., recounts how Antiochus Epiphanes proscribed Jewish observances, made war on the Judaeans, and profaned the temple in Jerusalem. Near the end of his life, afflicted by God with severe torments and hoping for divine mercy, Antiochus promises to grant various boons to the Judaeans: the city of Jerusalem shall be free, the Judaeans shall be the equals of the citizens of Athens, the holy sanctuary shall be adorned with the finest ornaments, and the sacrificial cult shall be maintained at royal expense. "In addition to all this he also would become a Jew and would visit every inhabited place to proclaim the power of God."[55] This legendary story is an account of a religious conversion, or at least of a proffered religious conversion. If God takes pity on Antiochus, the human king promises to become a Jew and to proclaim the power of the divine king throughout the world. This is not an account of a change of ethnicity or geography. Antiochus does not intend to become a Judaean, a member of the house of Israel living on God's holy land; he is a Macedonian king and intends to remain one. Nor is this an account of a change of citizenship; unlike the Idumaeans and Ituraeans, Antiochus is not proposing to take out citizenship in the Judaean state. He does not intend to become circumcised or to observe the Judaean laws. He simply intends

55. 2 Macc. 9:13–16; quoted verse is 2 Macc. 9:17.

to become a Jew, a worshiper of the one true God. As I remarked in chapter 3 above, this passage is one of the earliest attestations of the word *Ioudaios* in the sense of "Jew."

The book of Judith, which is probably contemporary (more or less) with 2 Maccabees, reports that "when Achior [an Ammonite general] saw all that the God of Israel had done, he believed firmly in God, and was circumcised, and joined the house of Israel, remaining so to this day." This passage is no less fictional than the passage about Antiochus, but differs from it substantially. Antiochus' Jewishness was to be expressed by his becoming a wandering Jew, proclaiming the power of God, whereas Achior's is expressed through his incorporation into the house of Israel. Like the Idumaeans and Ituraeans, Achior is circumcised and joins the house of Israel ("becomes a Jew"), but unlike them, he is also said to believe firmly in God. His belief derives from the miraculous deliverance of Israel he has just witnessed.[56]

In the first century of our era Philo clearly describes conversion in theological terms:

Having laid down laws for members of the same nation, he (Moses) holds that the incomers too should be accorded every favor and consideration as their due, because abandoning their kinsfolk by blood, their country, their customs and the temples and the images of their gods, and the tributes and honors paid to them, they have taken the journey to a better home, from idle fables to the clear vision of truth and the worship of the one and truly existing God.[57]

Behind Philo's account are the two fictional stories of the Hasmonean period. In all three, the essential part of becoming a Jew is to believe in the God of the Jews.

BIBLICAL MODELS

Does the Hebrew Bible contain the idea that a non-Israelite can somehow become an Israelite by believing in the one true God? The answer is no. The Tanakh has adumbrations, intimations, harbingers of the idea, but not the idea itself.

According to numerous passages in the Torah and the Prophets, God chose the Israelites to be his people and the Israelites chose God to be their Lord. Such a conception provides an ideological basis for conver-

56. Jth. 14:10.
57. Philo, *On the Virtues* 20.102–103, trans. Colson.

sion, because the link between God and his people is not "natural" but "covenantal" and would seem to allow others too to choose God to be their Lord. The Israelites became a nation by standing at the foot of Mount Sinai and binding themselves to God and the Torah through an oath. Could not gentiles too bind themselves by oath to God and the Torah and thereby make themselves into Israelites? Just as God once chose the Israelites to be his treasured people, could not God continue to choose individuals from among the nations to join his treasured people? Thus the Torah has the raw material for a theology of conversion, and indeed in the second century C.E. the rabbis exploit the analogy between converts and the Israelites at Mount Sinai.[58] But in the biblical period this theology of conversion remained inchoate. The tribal structure, the myth of common descent from a single set of ancestors, and the link between God, people, and land all conspired to prevent the growth of an ideology of conversion. Just as there was no established mechanism by which to allow outsiders to become insiders, as I discussed above, there was no established mechanism by which to recognize gentiles who had come to respect Israel's God.[59]

The narrators of the Hebrew Bible knew, or knew of, such gentiles. Non-Israelites can bless Israel's God, can sacrifice to him, can be impressed by his power and miracles, and can acknowledge him as God, perhaps the greatest of Gods, but they do not thereby become Israelites or join the holy people or abandon their ancestral Gods. In a famous vision a prophet foresaw a time when the nations would stream to Jerusalem to learn the ways of the Lord.[60] As I discussed briefly above, some seers of the exilic and postexilic periods (sixth to fourth centuries B.C.E.) forecast a utopian future in which the gentiles would recognize God, worship in his temple, and either serve the Israelites or "attach themselves" to them. But in none of these texts, even in the eschatological visions, is there a sense that non-Israelites somehow become Israelites through acknowledging the God of the Israelites. None of these texts precisely parallels 2 Maccabees' story about Antiochus Epiphanes and

---

58. Israelites and God choose each other: Deut. 26:17–19. Covenantal oath at Mount Sinai: Exodus 19 and 24. Rabbinic analogy: the three requirements for conversion (circumcision, immersion, and sacrifice) are said to derive from the experience of the Israelites at Mount Sinai; see B. Keritot 9a and parallels.

59. Once again, I follow Kaufmann (see above note 32).

60. Non-Israelites can bless Israel's God: Exod. 18:10, 1 Kings 5:21 and 10:9; can sacrifice to him: Exod. 18:12, cf. Mal. 1:11; can be impressed by his power and miracles: Josh. 2:9–10, 1 Kings 8:42–43, 2 Kings 17:32–33, Dan. 3:31–33; can acknowledge him as God, perhaps the greatest of Gods: Exod. 18:11, Josh. 2:11, 2 Kings 5:15, Ezra 1:2, Dan. 4:34 and 6:27–28. Famous vision: Isa. 2:1–4, cf. Mic. 4:1–5.

Judith's story about Achior. For the idea that gentiles can become Jews or can join the house of Israel through a change in theology, the Hasmonean period provides the earliest attestation. What is the source of this idea?

JUDAISM AS RELIGION AND CULTURE

The Greeks divided the world in two: Hellenes and barbarians. According to Herodotus, Hellenes were linked together by four elements: common blood, common language, common modes of worshiping the Gods, and a common way of life.[61] Of these four elements, the first, common blood, is immutable (ascribed), while the latter three are mutable (achieved). In the fourth century B.C.E., with the rise of the Macedonians and the creation of the Hellenistic empires, the Greeks deemphasized the immutable and emphasized the mutable elements. Thus redefined, Hellenism ("Greekness") became a world culture. Barbarians could not change their birth or their blood, but they could learn to speak Greek; indeed, the fundamental root meaning of the verb "to hellenize" is "to speak Greek" (see chapter 6 below). They could also learn to worship the Greek Gods, or, at least, to assign Greek names to their traditional divinities, and to adopt the Greek way of life (Greek clothing, art, architecture, etc.). By speaking Greek, worshiping the Greek Gods, and following a Greek way of life, barbarians became Hellenes. Thus "Hellene" changed from an ethnic or ethnic-geographic term to a cultural term. At the beginning of this process, even before the conquests of Alexander, Isocrates explained:

Our city (Athens) has so much surpassed other men in thought and speech that her students have become the teachers of others, and she has made the name of Greeks to seem to be no more of race/birth (*genos*) but of thought, so that those who share our education, more than those who share a common nature (*physis*), are to be called Hellenes.[62]

Thus Greekness (or "Hellene-ness") became a function of culture rather than genealogy.[63] In Ptolemaic Egypt this theory had political con-

---

61. Herodotus 8.144.2.   62. Panegyricus 50.

63. Wolfgang Will and Richard Klein, *Reallexikon für Antike und Christentum*, vol. 14 (1988), s.v. "Hellenen," 375–445, esp. 388. Polybius 1.67.7 refers to the offspring of Greek fathers and barbarian mothers as *mixhellenes,* not because of their non-Greek descent but because of their inability to speak Greek. According to Dionysius Halicarnassus 1.89.4, the Achaeans near the Pontus have unlearned their Greekness (*to hellēnikon*): they no longer speak Greek, observe Greek customs, or worship the Greek Gods; they have become the fiercest of the barbarians although they are of pure Greek stock.

sequences; in Ptolemaic documents the category "Hellene" included many non-Greek peoples—for example, Judaeans. If you spoke Greek and were not Egyptian, you were a Hellene.[64]

Like Hellenes, Judaeans too were linked together originally by common blood, common language, a common mode of worshiping God, and a common way of life. Much more than "Hellene," "Judaean" always retained its ethnic component; even in rabbinic times Jews imagined themselves as an *ethnos,* a descent group linked together by common blood, and, as I shall discuss in chapter 10 below, this fact was to be an obstacle to the complete enfranchisement of converts. In contrast with "Hellene," "Judaean" did not retain a linguistic meaning at all. The verb "to judaize" (*ioudaïzein*) never· means "to speak Hebrew" (see chapter 6 below). Modern nationalisms are frequently linguistic nationalisms; modern ethnic groups or nationalities frequently define themselves by the language they speak. But neither the Israelites nor the Judaeans of antiquity laid much emphasis on their distinctive language as an essential component of their corporate identity. Nehemiah became upset when sons born of intermarriage within the Jerusalem community could not speak "Judaean," but in the Hellenistic and Roman periods few Judaeans shared his outrage. A Hellene had to speak Greek, but a Judaean did not have to speak Hebrew.[65]

Even if "Judaean" always retained its ethnic meaning, in the Hasmonean period common mode of worship and common way of life became much more important in the new definition of Judaean/Jew. Just as a barbarian could become a Hellene through speaking Greek and adopting a Greek way of life, a gentile could become a Jew through worshiping the God of Jerusalem (i.e., believing firmly in God) and/or adopting a Judaean way of life (i.e., observing the ancestral laws of the Judaeans). Antiochus Epiphanes promised to do the former; Achior the Ammonite did both the former and the latter. It was this Hasmonean redefinition of Judaism that permitted Josephus at the end of the first century c.e. to state that the constitution established by Moses was not

---

64. Mélèze-Modrzejewski, "Le statut des Hellènes." For the philosophers, if you were virtuous, you were Greek. Cf. Plutarch, *On the Fortune of Alexander* 329C: Alexander bade his followers to consider "as akin to them all good men, and as foreigners only the wicked; they should not distinguish between Grecian and foreigner by Grecian cloak and targe, or scimitar and jacket; but the distinguishing mark of the Grecian should be seen in virtue, and that of the foreigner in iniquity; clothing and food, marriage and manner of life they should regard as common to all, being blended into one by ties of blood and children." A slightly different formulation of the same sentiment is attributed by Strabo 1.4.9 to Eratosthenes.

65. Neh. 13:24. S. Schwartz, "Language."

only a *genos*—a nation, a "birth"—but also "a choice in the manner of life."[66] It was this Hasmonean redefinition that led a Jewish author in the first century C.E. to the logical, if radical, conclusion that Jewishness is not ethnic at all but is completely a function of belief: "for he is not a real *Ioudaios* who is one outwardly . . . [but] he is a *Ioudaios* who is one inwardly."[67] In his commentary on this Pauline passage, Origen, a Christian exegete and philosopher of the mid third century C.E., writes as follows:

The noun *Ioudaios* is the name not of an *ethnos* but of a choice (in the manner of life). For if there be someone not from the nation of the Jews, a gentile, who accepts the ways of the Jews and becomes a proselyte, this person would properly be called a *Ioudaios*.[68]

Paul was prepared to shear Jewishness of all its ethnic connotations,[69] but most Jews, in antiquity at least, were not prepared to go as far as Paul on this trajectory; for them *Ioudaios* never entirely lost its ethnic meaning.

Second Maccabees presents the conflict between the Judaeans and their opponents as, inter alia, the attempt by the latter to have the former "go over" to "Greek ways."[70] If Judaeans could go over to Greek ways, why could not Greeks go over to Judaean ways? If Judaeans could become Greeks, why could not Greeks become Judaeans? Influenced by Greek culture, and at the same time in opposition to it, the Judaeans redefined Judaism (Jewishness) so that it too could become a portable culture. The notion of Hellene was completely sundered from any connection with the land or people of Greece; the notion of *Ioudaios* was

66. *CAp* 2.210. The same language appears in Philo, *On Abraham* 251, concerning Hagar: an Egyptian by *genos* but a Hebrew by *proairesis*. Josephus has the Samaritans declare that they "differ from the *Ioudaioi* in birth (*genos*) and in customs (*ethē*)" (*AJ* 12.261).

67. Rom. 2:28–29. For an extended discussion of this motif in Paul, see Daniel Boyarin, *A Radical Jew: Paul and the Politics of Identity* (Berkeley: University of California Press, 1994).

68. Scherer, *Origène* 134 (I am grateful to Robert Wilken for bringing this text to my attention). Origen's contrast (*genos* vs. *proairesis*) is exactly that of Philo.

69. When it suits him, of course, Paul can play up his "ethnic" connections. In Gal. 2:15 Paul includes himself among those who are "*Ioudaioi* by birth (or: nature, *phusei*)," and in Phil. 3:5 he describes himself as "of the people (*genos*) of Israel . . . a Hebrew born of Hebrews." I cannot discuss these passages here.

70. 2 Macc. 4:10, 15; 6:9. This perspective also appears in an official Seleucid document quoted by the author (11:24). This document is authentic and is to be attributed to Antiochus V; see Habicht, "Royal Documents" 12. The same perspective appears in a document of Antiochus IV quoted by Josephus, *AJ* 12.263, and in Tacitus, *Histories* 5.8.2.

not completely sundered from all connection with the land or people of Judaea, but was opened up sufficiently to become, like "Hellene," a cultural term, designating a way of life. One could be a Macedonian and a Hellene, a Syrian and a Hellene, a Cappadocian and a Hellene. Similarly, one could be a Macedonian and a Jew, a Syrian and a Jew, a Cappadocian and a Jew. If one worshiped the God of the Judaeans and/or followed the ancestral laws of the Judaeans, one became a Jew. The struggle between "Jewishness" and "Greekness" was a struggle between two cultures, one completely shorn of its ethnic and geographic roots, the other partly so. Conversion to Judaism thus emerges as an analogue to conversion to Hellenism.

Conclusion: The Redefinition of Jewish Identity in the Hasmonean Period

The persecution of Judaism by Antiochus Epiphanes and its aftermath bestowed new prominence on laws and rituals that would separate Jews from non-Jews. The forging of a new Jewish identity in the Hasmonean period was partly the product of an ethic of separation from, and hostility toward, gentiles.[71] In an account that otherwise has only positive things to say about Moses and the constitution he established, Hecataeus (ca. 300 B.C.E.) writes that Moses introduced a way of life that was "somewhat unsociable and hostile to foreigners."[72] Hecataeus' major point is not that the Jews hate foreigners but that the laws of the Jews are different from those of all other nations.[73] In any case, however Hecataeus is understood, the fact remains that only from the end of the second century B.C.E. do Greek writers emphasize the Jews' refusal to mix with others or dine with them.[74] Diaspora Jews had always had to work out strategies by which to maintain their identity, but in the middle and second half of the second century B.C.E. the Jews of Judaea too—or, perhaps more accurately, some Jews of Judaea—be-

---

71. Schwarz, *Identität*.

72. *Apanthropon tina kai misoxenon* (Diodorus of Sicily 40.3.4. = M. Stern, *Authors* no. 11).

73. Gager, *Moses* 35.

74. Apollonius Molon cited in Josephus, *CAp* 2.258 = M. Stern, *Authors* no. 50; Diodorus of Sicily 34/35.1–4 = M. Stern, *Authors* no. 63 (from Posidonius?). Manetho cited in Josephus, *CAp* 1.239 = M. Stern, *Authors* no. 21 refers to separation from the Egyptians, and says nothing about separation from all humanity.

gan to emphasize their distinctiveness vis-à-vis the gentiles and to highlight those rituals and practices that would separate them from the nations of the world.[75]

But we should not allow the ethic of separation to obscure the other side of the coin. The Hasmonean period witnesses for the first time in the history of Judaism the establishment of processes by which outsiders can become insiders, non-Judaeans can become Judaeans, and non-Jews can become Jews. Our sources describe two such processes; these ultimately blend and become one, but in the second century B.C.E. they are still easily distinguished. The first is change of citizenship, or political enfranchisement; the second is change of belief, or religious conversion. The key to each of these processes is the limitation of the role of ethnicity in Judaean identity. Ethnicity is closed, immutable, an ascribed characteristic based on birth. But by investing Judaean identity with political or cultural (religious) content, the Hasmoneans were able to give outsiders an opportunity to attain membership in Judaean society.

The key to the new idea of change of citizenship or political enfranchisement is the Greek concept of *politeia,* which means, among other things, both "citizenship" and "public way of life." The Hasmonean state extended Judaean citizenship to the Idumaeans and Ituraeans, two neighboring peoples, thus incorporating them in a Judaean League. Many of the Idumaeans and Ituraeans voluntarily associated themselves with the Hasmoneans, although not a few had to be "convinced" to join. Some Idumaeans fled to Egypt rather than become part of a state dominated by the Judaeans. As price for membership the Hasmoneans demanded that the Idumaeans and Ituraeans be circumcised and follow the laws of the Judaeans. Since most of the Idumaeans and Ituraeans were already circumcised, this was not particularly onerous, and the Idumaeans and Ituraeans clearly thought that the advantages to be gained by the alliance outweighed the cost. Modern scholars regularly refer to this event as the forced conversion of the Idumaeans and Ituraeans, but this is wrong on two counts. First, most of the Idumaeans and Ituraeans seem to have joined voluntarily. The historiographical tradition surrounding the event is complex and contradictory, but the simplest way to make sense of it is to assume that the bulk of the enfranchisement was voluntary and that later writers, for various reasons, took the compulsory experience of the few and turned it into the experience of the

---

75. Thus the uniqueness of the Torah is known to Ben Sira, but separation from the gentiles is not, in spite of 33:11–12 and 36:1–12.

many. If, as is likely, most of the Idumaeans and Ituraeans were circumcised even before their alliance with the Hasmoneans, they could not have been forcibly circumcised by them. Second, this was not a conversion in a religious sense. No one demanded of the Idumaeans and Ituraeans belief in the God of the Jews. No doubt the Idumaeans, as part of the price for joining the Judaean League, accepted the God of the Judaeans and agreed to abide by his laws (at least some of them), but they also were able to retain a measure of their old Idumaean culture and religion. Witness Herod the Great himself, whose loyalty to the God of Jerusalem did not prevent him from building temples to several other Gods as well.[76] Political enfranchisement had religious repercussions, to be sure, but a change in *politeia* was primarily a change in citizenship, public behavior, and politics.

Aside from change of citizenship, the Hasmonean period attests for the first time the idea of religious conversion: by believing in the God of the Jews and following his laws, a gentile can become a Jew. Whereas theological change was a secondary effect of the incorporation of the Idumaeans and Ituraeans, here it is central. This idea first appears in literary texts written in the Hasmonean period, and does not seem to have been an institution of state policy; rather, individual gentiles could now convert to Judaism by changing their beliefs. If the first process betrays the influence of the Greek notion of *politeia,* this process is a close analogue to the growth of Hellenism itself. Greekness once had been a function of birth and geography, but in the Hellenistic period it became a function of language and culture. Similarly, Jewishness (Judaeanness) once had been a function of birth and geography but now in the Hasmonean period it became a function of religion and culture. Anyone could become a Hellene or a *Ioudaios* through a change in values and culture. However, whereas Greekness was completely shorn of its ethnic and geographic connections, Jewishness was not. For most *Ioudaioi* in antiquity, the ethnic definition was supplemented, not replaced, by the religious definition. Jewishness became an ethno-religious identity.[77]

The outward manifestations of political enfranchisement and reli-

76. On Herod the Great's Judaism, as representative of the Judaism of the newly enfranchised *Ioudaioi,* see Smith, "Gentiles" 1.302–309.

77. I borrow the term "ethno-religious identity" from John A. Armstrong, *Nations before Nationalism* (Chapel Hill: University of North Carolina Press, 1982) 201–203. The word *ethno-religion* is a mixed Greek-Latin hybrid, hence scorned by purists, but I cannot think of anything better. Even purists use words like *dysfunctional, hyperactive, Tyrannosaurus rex.*

gious conversion are the same: circumcision and the observance of the ancestral laws of the Judaeans. Hence we understand the ease with which the two processes were identified and confused. Philo, for example, can say that proselytes "have come to a new and God-loving *politeia*."[78] And, of course, we should not be too insistent on separating "religion" from "ethnicity" in antiquity, when the ancients had a much more organic conception of these matter than do we. Nevertheless, it is clear that the emphases of the two processes differ. In the first, circumcision is a sign of membership in the people. Observance of the ancestral laws is a demonstration of the acceptance of communal norms. In the second, circumcision, like the observance of all the other ancestral laws, is a sign of subservience to God's will. In chapter 7 I shall return again to the different symbolic values attached to circumcision, and in chapter 5 I shall return to the different ways of "crossing the boundary" that separates Jews from gentiles. The contrasting implications of these two processes are occasionally evident even in material that significantly postdates the Hasmonean period.

The incorporation of the Idumaeans and Ituraeans into the Jewish polity, and the emergence of religious conversion, show that separation from gentiles was only one aspect of the new Jewish self-definition. Circumcision was a mark of difference vis-à-vis the Greeks, but a link with neighboring peoples. In order to resist the forces of assimilation, Judaism became like Hellenism, a citizenship and a way of life open to people of diverse origins. The Idumaeans and Ituraeans apparently were more willing to accept *Ioudaismos* than *Hellenismos*. Thus even as they were becoming more "nationalistic" and "particularistic," the Judaeans/Jews were becoming more "universalistic" by extending citizenship to other peoples and allowing individuals to convert to Judaism. The Hasmonean hostility to Hellenistic culture should not be exaggerated. The history of colonialism in the nineteenth and twentieth centuries shows that it usually was the most "westernized" and best-educated elements of the subjugated populations that led the rebellions against colonialist rule. In order to be successful nationalists, rebels have to know the culture of the imperialists.[79] The Hasmoneans, secure in their knowledge that the Jewish *politeia* was true and the Hellenic *politeia* was false, were not afraid to use the ideas, techniques, and weap-

78. See note 43 above.

79. A. D. Smith, *Ethnic Origins* 56–57, sees Jewish resistance movements to Seleucid and Roman rule as classic instances of "ethnicism." On the role of colonial mulattoes in resistance movements, see B. Anderson, *Imagined Communities.*

ons of their enemies. They established festivals and had themselves installed as high priests by vote of the populace, a decidedly Hellenic way of doing things. Members of their entourage wrote works in Greek and in Greek literary form. To find a place for themselves in the Hellenistic world, the Hasmoneans even invented a fake genealogy for the Judaeans, which claimed that they were the long-lost cousins of the Spartans. By understanding the Jewish way of life in Greek terms, they redefined Jewish identity and were able, for the first time, to naturalize outsiders in the Jewish commonwealth. As Elias Bickerman remarked, "The real Hellenization of the Seleucid empire, outside Asia Minor, began only after the end of Seleucid domination, when the hellenizing process was taken over by the native rulers."[80]

80. Bickerman, *Greek Age* 302.

CHAPTER 5

Crossing the Boundary
and Becoming a Jew

*In a village in Hesse the peasants enjoyed a stewlike bean soup
(probably a form of Schalet). When questioned about what they
were eating, they would laugh and say, "Today I'm a Jew."*
Marion A. Kaplan, *The Making of the Jewish Middle Class*

In chapter 4 I argued that in the second century B.C.E. the
Judaeans/Jews opened their boundary and allowed outsiders to enter
either by accepting the God of the Jews or by becoming citizens in the
Judaean state. In this chapter I would like to explore further the various
ways by which a gentile in antiquity (mid second century B.C.E. to the
fifth century C.E.) became less a gentile and more a Jew. How did a gentile cross the boundary that separates "the nations of the world" from
Jews (Judaeans)? How did a gentile "become a Jew" in the eyes of the
gentile him/herself, in the eyes of contemporary gentiles, and in the
eyes of contemporary Jews? I propose to describe and classify seven
forms of behavior by which a gentile demonstrates respect or affection
for Judaism. I begin with forms that do not imply that the gentile is "becoming a Jew," and I end with those that do. These forms are not necessarily sequential; they are not "stages" in a process. Nor are these
forms mutually exclusive; a gentile might easily behave in such a way so
as to be able to be classified in more than one category simultaneously.

The epigraph is from Marion A. Kaplan, *The Making of the Jewish Middle Class* (New
York: Oxford University Press, 1991; reprint, 1994) 73.

I freely admit that the paucity of evidence, and the frequent obscurity of the meager evidence that does exist, give a tentative character to my analysis; my seven categories are chiefly of heuristic value. The chapter concludes with a sample of three conversion stories and a discussion of "God-fearers." For the sake of convenience I translate the word *Ioudaios* throughout as "Jew."

A gentile can show respect or affection for Judaism in seven ways: by (1) admiring some aspect of Judaism; (2) acknowledging the power of the God of the Jews or incorporating him into the pantheon; (3) benefiting the Jews or being conspicuously friendly to Jews; (4) practicing some or many of the rituals of the Jews; (5) venerating the God of the Jews and denying or ignoring all other gods; (6) joining the Jewish state or community; (7) converting to Judaism and "becoming a Jew."

1. Admiring Some Aspect of Judaism

Some gentile polytheists admired various aspects of Judaism. Josephus writes that throughout the world gentiles "attempt to imitate our unanimity, our liberal charities, our devoted labor in the crafts, our endurance under persecution on behalf of our laws"—and this is aside from the adoption of Jewish customs (see below). Many Greek and Roman writers describe Judaism or Jewish heroes in positive terms. In a passage preserved by Augustine, Varro states that the aniconic worship of the Jews accurately reflects the original and admirable piety of humanity, before the vulgar began to worship visible and tactile images. An intellectual of the first century C.E. cited the opening verse of the Septuagint as an example of high or noble style. Moses was widely believed to have been a distinguished legislator.[1] Such admiration, easily paralleled in the Greek and Roman reactions to other oriental or exotic religions, is unexceptional and does not necessarily indicate any peculiar closeness to Judaism.

---

1. Josephus: *CAp* 2.283—probably an exaggeration. M. Stern, *Authors* no. 72 (Varro) and no. 148 (On the Sublime). Cf. too M. Stern, *Authors* no. 115 (Strabo). On the figure of Moses, see John Gager, *Moses in Greco-Roman Paganism* (Nashville: Abingdon, 1972). For a brief survey of the image of Judaism in classical authors, see Menahem Stern, "The Jews in Greek and Latin Literature," in *Compendia Rerum Judaicarum ad Novum Testamentum: Section I: The Jewish People in the First Century,* ed. Samuel Safrai et al., 2 vols. (Philadelphia: Fortress, 1976), 2.1101–1159.

2. Acknowledging the Power
of the God of the Jews

Many gentiles in antiquity recognized that the God of the Jews was a powerful God. The authors of the magical papyri routinely invoke the "God of Abraham, Isaac, and Jacob," "Iao Sabaoth," and so forth. In the second century C.E. one intellectual, a disciple of the orator Herodes Atticus, quoted two verses from Deuteronomy 28 in the warning curse he included in the epitaph for his son. This gentile knew that a curse backed by the authority of the God of the Jews would likely be effective.[2] Graeco-Jewish literature is filled with stories about gentiles, usually kings or other dignitaries, who witness some manifestation of the power of the God of the Jews and as a result venerate the God and acknowledge his power.[3] The most spectacular example is Heliodorus, an emissary of Seleucus IV, who tried to seize the treasury of the Jerusalem temple but was thwarted by a miraculous display of divine might. Heliodorus learned an important lesson; "he bore testimony to all men of the deeds of the supreme God, which he had seen with his own eyes."[4]

The reverent gentile appears in the Hebrew Bible too. Jethro hears the story of the miraculous exodus from Egypt and declares: "Blessed be the Lord . . . Now I know that the Lord is greater than all Gods." Hiram king of Tyre is so impressed by Solomon that he declares: "Blessed be the lord God of Israel who made heaven and earth."[5] In the book of Daniel, King Nebuchadnezzar addresses the seer and proclaims: "Truly your God is God of Gods and lord of kings, and a revealer of mysteries." Even bolder proclamations are put in the mouths of Cyrus, Darius, and Artaxerxes.[6]

---

2. Louis Robert, "Malédictions funéraires grecques," in *Comptes rendus de l'Académie des inscriptions et belles-lettres* (1978) 241–289, at 244–252. I am not convinced by Robert's argument that the orator, one Flavius Amphicles, was a monotheist. It is possible that the curse inscriptions from Rheneia were written by a polytheist who, like Amphicles, used the language of the Septuagint to make his curse effective; this possibility is not sufficiently appreciated by Adolf Deissmann, *Light from the Ancient East* (New York: George Doran, 1927) 413–424. The curses of Deuteronomy were well known and widely feared; see Trebilco, *Jewish Communities* 60–69.

3. See S. J. D. Cohen, "Alexander the Great" 56–60 and "Respect for Judaism" 412–415.

4. 2 Macc. 3:35–39.

5. Exod. 12:10–11; 2 Chron. 2:11, an expansion of 1 Kings 5:21 (Hebrew verse numeration).

6. Nebuchadnezzar: Dan. 2:47; cf. 3:28 and 4:34–37. Cyrus: Bel and the Dragon 41. Darius: Dan. 6:25–27. Artaxerxes: Greek Esther 16:16.

In a somewhat different vein, many gentiles incorporated the God of the Jews into their pantheon. In the Hellenistic and early Roman periods numerous dignitaries offered sacrifices or gifts to the God of the Jews at his temple in Jerusalem. Even Alexander the Great was said to have done so. If the dignitary was the ruler of the Jews, the political meaning of his gesture was clear; by sacrificing to the God of the Jews, he confirmed his sovereignty over the Jews because he represented the people before their God.[7] The theological meaning of the gesture was clear as well. The Jews are a respectable nation, and their God is a respectable deity. An empire has many nations and many gods. More striking, perhaps, is the conduct of private gentiles, people who were not generals or monarchs or officials, who worshiped in the Jerusalem temple or sent money to support it. Josephus mentions gentiles from across the Euphrates who came to the temple to bring a sacrifice, and God-venerating gentiles from Asia and Europe who enriched the temple with their donations. The Gospel of John mentions Greeks who went up to worship at the temple at the Passover.[8] Conduct that was normal or expected of an enlightened and benevolent monarch was exceptional for a private citizen,[9] and these gentiles perhaps should be assigned to category 5 below rather than here.

The destruction of the temple in 70 C.E. meant that gentiles (like Jews!) could no longer sacrifice in Jerusalem to the God of the Jews, but they still could recognize the God as one of the supreme deities of the world. The oracle at Claros declared that Iao (here identified with Dionysus) is "the highest of all the Gods."[10] The early third century C.E. provides two spectacular (and perhaps fictional) examples of this trend: the emperor Elagabalus included Judaism and Christianity among the religions to be incorporated in the cult of the God Heliogabalus on the Palatine Hill, and the emperor Alexander Severus maintained a private chapel for Apollonius, Christ, Abraham, and Orpheus, each of whom pointed the way to the supreme God.[11] Private individuals could adopt the same theology. Many Neoplatonists identified the God of the Jews

7. See S. J. D. Cohen, "Alexander the Great" 46 n. 13 and 58 n. 48, "Respect for Judaism" 413 n. 14.

8. *AJ* 3.318–319; *AJ* 14.110; John 12:20.

9. See S. J. D. Cohen, "Respect for Judaism" 427.

10. Macrobius, *Saturnalia* 1.18.20; the translation is that of H. W. Parke, *Greek Oracles* (London: Hutchinson, 1967) 147. On the identification of the God of the Jews with Dionysus, see M. Smith, "Wine God in Palestine."

11. M. Stern, *Authors* nos. 518 and 522. Similarly, the Theosophy of Tübingen no. 44, a fifth-century collection of oracular sayings, classes Hermes, Moses, and Apollonius as having status equal to that of the Gods (Mitchell, *Anatolia* 2.36 n. 211).

with the father of all the Gods; Numenius even argued that the teachings of Plato were basically the same as those of Moses, and frequently supported his arguments by quotations from the works of Moses and the prophets.[12] Of course, the identification of the Jewish God with the supreme God long antedates the syncretism of the high Roman empire. Herodotus had already sought Greek equivalents for the oriental deities he encountered, and after the Jews became part of the Hellenistic world, their God too had to be fitted to the Greek pantheon. For who was this God if not Zeus or Dionysus with another name (or with no name at all)?[13]

A related but more elusive phenomenon is the use by gentiles of Jewish religious language (or, more accurately, religious language that "sounds" Jewish). In Pergamon, perhaps in the second century C.E., one Zopyros erected an altar to "God the lord, the eternal existent one." Zopyros' respect for God is couched in terms that seem to derive from the Hebrew Bible. Similarly, in Pamphylia in the first or second century C.E., an altar was dedicated "To the God (who is) not false and not made with hands." This description of God seems to be the product of Jewish conceptions; Jewish polemic dismissed idols as false, man-made gods, but this altar is dedicated to the true God who cannot be crafted by human artisans. The religiosity that inspired these dedications is a puzzle. Were Zopyros and the dedicant of Pamphylia simple polytheists who used Jewish religious language while unaware of its connections and implications, or were they polytheists who incorporated the God of the Jews into their pantheon, or were they monotheists devoted exclusively to the one true God, the God of the Jews (see category 5)? These questions cannot be answered with any certainty.[14]

Numerous inscriptions and altars are dedicated to God "the most high" (*Hypsistos*), the God who harkens to prayer (*epēkoos*), the one God, the one and only God, the one God in heaven, and so forth. Whether any of these phrases is evidence of Jewish influence or connection with

---

12. M. Stern, *Authors* nos. 363–369.

13. Identification with Zeus: Letter of Aristeas 15–16; cf. Celsus in Origen, *Against Celsus* 5.41 = M. Stern, *Authors* no. 375 (p. 256 in the Greek, p. 286 in the English). Identification with Dionysus: Plutarch in M. Stern, *Authors* no. 258, and Tacitus *Histories* 5.5.5 = M. Stern, *Authors* no. 281; Smith, "Wine God in Palestine." Anonymous God: see Lucan and Numenius in M. Stern, *Authors* nos. 191 and 367.

14. Zopyros: E. Bickerman, "Altars of Gentiles," in Bickerman, *Studies* 2.324–346, esp. 2.337–342; Gerhard Delling, "Die Altarinschrift eines Gottesfürchtigen in Pergamon," *Novum Testamentum* 7 (1964) 73–80; Siegert, "Gottesfürchtige" 143–144. Altar in Pamphylia: Pieter van der Horst, "A New Altar of a Godfearer?" *JJS* 43 (1992) 32–37 = van der Horst, *Hellenism* 65–72; see also Levinskaya, *Book of Acts* 81–82.

Judaism is much debated. A series of inscriptions in western Asia Minor attests to the worship of "the good angel" or "the divine angel." Polytheists, especially in the high Roman empire, especially in Asia Minor, believed, no less than Jews and Christians, that there was one supreme God who communicated with the world through the intermediation of an "angel" (the Greek word for "messenger") or "angels." It seems unlikely that this belief is the result of either Jewish or Christian influence, but the religious vocabulary in which the belief is expressed as well as the cultic manifestation of the belief may be evidence for the absorption of Jewish (Christian?) language and practices. The possibility is real but the point cannot be proven.[15]

The conceptual distinction between gentiles who acknowledge the power of the God of the Jews and/or incorporate him into the pantheon (category 2) and gentiles who venerate the God of the Jews and deny or ignore other gods (category 5) is clear, at least in theory. The gentiles of category 2 do not stand in any special relationship either with the Jews or with the God of the Jews. They behave as "normal" polytheists behave when confronted by a foreign God and a foreign religion; their attitude toward the God of the Jews is easily paralleled by their attitude toward other Gods. They remain polytheists. Jethro in spite of his declaration, Alexander the Great in spite of his sacrifice, Heliodorus in spite of his "conversion" experience, and Numenius in spite of his theology remain gentiles and polytheists. Augustine comments that Alex-

---

15. Cult of *Hypsistos:* T. Drew-Bear and C. Naour, "Divinités de Phrygie," *ANRW* 2.18.3.1907–2044, at 2032–2043; Trebilco, *Jewish Communities* 127–140; J. Ustinova, "The *Thiasoi* of Theos Hypsistos in Tanais," *History of Religions* 31 (1991) 150–180; Mitchell, *Anatolia* 36–39; Levinskaya, *Book of Acts* 83–103. Cult of angels: Sheppard, "Pagan Cults of Angels"; *NewDocs* 5 (1989) 72–73 and 136; *NewDocs* 6 (1992) 206–209; M. Ricl, *Epigraphica Anatolica* 19 (1992) 71–102 (non vidi); see further M. Smith, "A Note on Some Jewish Assimilationists: The Angels," in M. Smith, *Studies,* vol. 2. In general see Bickerman, *Studies* 2.337–342, and Mitchell, *Anatolia* 43–51, esp. 45–46 (angels) and 49–50 (*Hypsistos*). The difficulties involved in distinguishing Jewish from "judaizing" from polytheist are evident in a paragraph in Mitchell, *Anatolia* 49: "A vow to Theos Hypsistos found at Yenice köy on the territory of Phrygian Acmonia has been identified as a Jewish or Judaizing text on the grounds that the same site has produced an unquestionable Jewish epitaph . . . A virtually identical dedication to Theos Hypsistos found in another village on Acmonia's territory, where no other Jewish evidence is to hand, is regarded as pagan . . . it is prudent to be cautious about assuming that otherwise undistinctive dedications to Theos Hypsistos are necessarily pagan. The chance discovery of a Jewish text from the same site would alter the picture." According to Mitchell, Theos Hypsistos inscriptions are to be regarded as Jewish if there is evidence for a Jewish presence in their surrounding, and as pagan if there is no evidence for a Jewish presence (with the proviso that such evidence may always turn up). In other words, there is no way to tell whether a dedication to Theos Hypsistos is Jewish or pagan.

ander the Great "did indeed offer sacrifices in the temple of God, not because he was converted to his worship through true piety, but because he thought through impious vanity that God ought to be worshiped together with false gods."[16] In contrast, the gentiles of category 5 have adopted some degree of exclusive loyalty to the one God, the God of the Jews. They have become "monotheists."

3. Benefiting the Jews or Being Conspicuously Friendly to Jews

From the sixth century B.C.E. to the twentieth century C.E. the Jews have lived, with a few relatively brief exceptions, under the dominion of gentile powers. Many of these powers in antiquity were benevolently disposed toward the Jews. Monarchs, generals, and public officials bestowed favors on the Jews, protected their rights, and granted their requests. In many cases the benefaction was preceded by the offering of a sacrifice at the temple in Jerusalem (see above). Jewish storytellers told elaborate tales about dramatic meetings between Jewish sages and gentile kings in which the king honors the sage and grants the Jews a variety of favors: a high priest with Alexander, Yohanan ben Zakkai with Vespasian, Rabbi Judah the Patriarch with Antoninus, and Samuel with Shapur.[17] The Jews of Berenike (Cyrenaica) honored a local Roman official named M. Tittius for executing his responsibilities in a manner "well disposed toward the Jews of our commu-

---

16. *On the City of God* 18.45.2. In contrast, the midrash argues that Jethro was a proselyte; see Bamberger, *Proselytism* 182–191; Judith R. Baskin, *Pharaoh's Counsellors*, Brown Judaic Studies, no. 47 (Atlanta: Scholars Press 1983) 45–74; Porton, *Stranger* 64–65. The same opinion was occasionally advanced regarding Nebuchadnezzar, Cyrus, and, especially in the Middle Ages, Alexander the Great (see note 25 below).

17. High priest with Alexander: see S. J. D. Cohen, "Alexander the Great." The bibliography on Yohanan ben Zakkai and Vespasian is immense; see, for example, Jacob Neusner, *Development of a Legend* (Leiden: Brill, 1970). Antoninus: David Z. Hoffman, "Die Antoninus-Agadot im Talmud und Midrasch," *Magazin für die Wissenschaft des Judenthums* 19 (1892) 33–55 and 245–255; Bamberger, *Proselytism* 248–250; Lieberman, *Greek in Jewish Palestine* 78–80; Martin Jacobs, *Die Institution des jüdischen Patriarchen* (Tübingen: Mohr [Siebeck], 1995) 125–154. On Shapur see G. Wewers, "Israel zwischen den Mächten: Die rabbinischen Traditionen über König Schabhor," *Kairos* 22 (1980) 77–100. On the motif in general see Moshe D. Herr, "The Historical Significance of the Dialogue between Jewish Sages and Roman Dignitaries," in *Scripta Hierosolymitana 22: Studies in Aggadah and Folk Literature*, ed. J. Heinemann (Jerusalem: Magnes, 1971) 123–150 (Herr seems not to realize that he is studying not history but a literary motif).

nity."[18] Local dignitaries might benefit the Jews through gifts to the community. For example, Tation daughter of Straton son of Empedon from her own resources constructed the assembly hall and the enclosure of the synagogue in Phocaea, and thus she "bestowed a gift on the Jews." Julia Severa, the high priestess of the cult of the emperor in Acmonia in the first century C.E., built a synagogue for the Jews of her town.[19] Clearly these gentiles respected Judaism, but there is no reason to assume that they had any special affection for it. Tolerant monarchs routinely benefited many of the native populations that together constituted the polyethnic empires of antiquity. Dignitaries might have had any of a number of reasons to associate with Jews, support them, or bestow a gift on the local Jewish community.[20]

From a theological perspective gentiles who acknowledge the power of the God of the Jews (category 2) are closer to Judaism than those who simply treat the Jews kindly (category 3), but from a social perspective the gentiles of category 3 are closer because they have a friendly relationship with the Jewish community. As a result, both gentiles and Jews could regard these gentiles as "pro-Jewish" even if they had no real evidence that such was the case. The Alexandrian nationalists who regarded imperial rule as (among other evils) too pro-Jewish, on the grounds that the Romans consistently supported Jewish rights, called one Roman emperor "the cast-off son of the Jewess Salome," and suggested that another was overly influenced by his senate that was packed with "impious Jews."[21] We may doubt whether either of these claims was true.

18. Lüderitz, *Corpus jüdischer Zeugnisse* no. 71; for discussion see Martha W. B. Bowsky, "M. Tittius Sex. F. Aem. and the Jews of Berenice," *American Journal of Philology* 108 (1987) 495–510.

19. Tation: *CIJ* 2.738 = *NewDocs* 1 (1976) 111 = Lifshitz, *Donateurs* no. 13; Mitchell, *Anatolia* 31 n. 176. Julia Severa: *CIJ* 2.766 = Lifshitz no. 33; Trebilco, *Jewish Communities* 58–60; Mitchell, *Anatolia* 9. Cf. Luke 7:5, and T. Megillah 2:16 352L = B. Erkhin 6a ("if a gentile donates a beam to a synagogue . . .").

20. A. Thomas Kraabel correctly notes that the donation of a synagogue does not necessarily make Julia Severa a "God-fearer"; see "Roman Diaspora" 456. Here is a parallel from a much later time. At some point prior to 1611 (perhaps in the fifteenth century) a Christian woman donated a vegetable garden to the Jewish community of Worms. Obviously this woman did not have any animosity toward the Jews, but her gift was the result more of her own charitable inclinations (she also donated a pond to the Christian poor of the town) than of any "judaizing." See *Wormser Minhagbuch des R. Jousep (Juspa) Schammes,* ed. Benjamin Hamburger and Erich Zimmer (Jerusalem: Mifal Torat Chachme Aschkenas, 1988) par. 192 (p. 228 with n. 6).

21. *CPJ* no. 156d line 12 and no. 157 lines 42–50. Numerous modern analogies suggest themselves. Alexander Severus was vilified by his opponents as "a Syrian archisynagogue," perhaps because of his pro-Jewish leanings (M. Stern, *Authors* no. 521).

The Jews too tended to regard gentile benefactors as motivated by some special affection for, or devotion to, Judaism, but, again, we may doubt whether this perspective is true. The point is demonstrated already by the biblical account of Cyrus. The founder of the Persian empire had his own good reasons for benefiting the Judaeans, just as he had his own good reasons for benefiting the temple of Marduk in Babylon. But in the eyes of the Judaeans the only way that Cyrus' actions could be understood was to imagine that the king recognized that he was enjoying the largess of "the God of heaven" and was commanded by the God to build him a temple in Jerusalem.[22] Centuries later, Philo suggested that Petronius, the governor of Syria who refused to follow Caligula's instructions to erect a statue in the temple, was motivated not only by his innate kindness and gentleness but also by his affection for Judaism:

He had himself, apparently, some glimmerings of Jewish philosophy and religion. He may have studied it in the past because of his interest in culture, or after his appointment as governor of those countries which have large numbers of Jews in all their cities, namely Asia and Syria; or his mind may have been so disposed through some voluntary, instinctive, and spontaneous inclination of its own towards things worthy of serious attention.[23]

It is most unlikely that Cyrus permitted the rebuilding of the Jerusalem temple because he feared the God of heaven, the God of the Jews. It is also unlikely, or at least completely unnecessary to believe, that Petronius protected the Jews because he felt some special attraction to the Jewish religion.[24] The culmination of this understandable but unhistorical Jewish perspective is the statement of some storytellers that the gentile kings who benefited the Jews (e.g., Alexander the Great) converted to Judaism![25]

22. Ezra 1:2. Of course, it is possible that the Hebrew version of the Cyrus decree in Ezra 1:2–4 is inspired by propaganda issued directly by Cyrus' court. In either case, the author of Ezra 1 chose to believe not only that Cyrus was working under divine direction but also that Cyrus himself recognized this fact.

23. Philo, *Legation to Gaius* 33.245, trans. Smallwood.

24. Although some scholars seem to accept Philo's suggestion; see Smallwood's commentary ad loc.; M. Stern's commentary on *Authors* no. 435; Feldman, *Jew and Gentile* 310 and 349. Contrast the cautious doubts of Siegert, "Gottesfürchtige" 149.

25. On the conversion of Alexander to Judaism (or is it Christianity?), see my "Alexander the Great" 59–60, and esp. Gerhard Delling, "Alexander der Grosse als Bekenner des jüdischen Gottesglaubens," *JSJ* 12 (1981) 1–51. See note 16 above.

4. Practicing Some or
Many of the Rituals of the Jews

In a series of passages, Philo and Josephus boast that gentiles throughout the world, from ancient times to the present, have adopted Jewish practices and display "a devotion to our religion." Josephus adds: "There is not one city, Greek or barbarian, nor a single nation, to which our custom of abstaining from work on the seventh day has not spread, and where the fasts and the lighting of lamps and many of our prohibitions in the matter of food are not observed."[26] Seneca laments that "the customs of this accursed race have gained such influence that they are now received throughout all the world. The vanquished have given laws to their victors."[27] For all the obvious exaggeration of the boast and the lament, they reflect some measure of reality. In the city of Rome, at least, in the latter part of the first century B.C.E. and throughout the first century C.E., some gentiles of both the upper and lower classes observed the Sabbath by lighting lamps and fasting. In the following centuries Sabbath observance extended to gentiles in Egypt and Asia Minor as well.[28] Some gentiles in Asia Minor frequented synagogues on the Sabbath and perhaps observed other Jewish laws as well. Josephus has a cryptic reference to "Greeks who honor our practices because they are unable to refute them." And, of course, later centuries provide abundant evidence for the observance of Jewish rituals in the churches of Syria and Asia Minor.[29] The existence of such gentiles meant that observance of Jewish rituals did not always establish a presumption of Jewishness; a gentile might be mistaken for a Jew, as I discussed in chapter 2.

A gentile who observes Jewish rituals might be mistaken for a Jew, or might be deliberately and polemically regarded as a Jew. According to an anecdote in Plutarch's life of Cicero, anyone who abstains from pork, or who can humorously be thought of as abstaining from pork, can be called a "Jew."[30] Dio Cassius, a historian of the early third century C.E.,

26. Philo, *Life of Moses* 2.17–24 and *Hypothetica;* Josephus, *CAp* 1.162–167 and 2.281–284.

27. M. Stern, *Authors* no. 186.

28. Tcherikover, *CPJ* 3:43–87.

29. *AJ* 3.217. It is possible that some Christians in Antioch had themselves circumcised: John Chrysostom, *Adversus Judaeos* 2.2 (859), and Wilken, *John Chrysostom* 75.

30. M. Stern, *Authors* no. 263. See my discussion of this anecdote in chapter 6 below.

makes a related point explicitly. He writes: "[The citizens of the country] have been named Jews (*Ioudaioi*). I do not know how this title came to be given them, but it applies also to all the rest of mankind, although of alien race, who emulate their customs."[31] Dio distinguishes the *Ioudaioi* of the ethnic homeland ("Judaeans") from the non-ethnic *Ioudaioi* ("Jews"), who are so called because they follow the customs of the ethnic Judaeans. Dio is not necessarily talking about "converts"; he does not even mention circumcision. For Dio anyone devoted to Jewish (Judaean) ways is called a Jew. The members of the Jewish community and the gentiles themselves who observed the Jewish rituals probably would have disputed this liberal use of the name "Jew." They would have said that a gentile who follows Jewish ways is nothing more than a gentile who follows Jewish ways, just as other gentiles affected the ways of Isis, Mithras, or one of the philosophical schools without actually "converting" (see my conclusion below). But in the eyes of some outsiders—and, perhaps in Dio's time, in the eyes of gentile society in general—the practice of Jewish rituals puts the practitioner over the boundary that separates Judaism from the rest of the world. In the Ciceronian anecdote the application of the name "Jew" to gentile observers of Jewish practices is clearly meant to be ironic and polemical; in the passage of Dio the tone seems dry and matter-of-fact. In both cases the gentile is deliberately being called a Jew. I shall return to this polemical usage at the end of my discussion of the next category.

5. Venerating the God of the Jews and Denying or Ignoring All Other Gods

Some Jewish texts describe a category of gentiles who were so devoted to the God of the Jews that they venerated him (almost) exclusively even if they did not observe his laws. Philo's obscure and much debated discussion of uncircumcised "proselytes" (or "epelytes") probably refers to gentiles of this type. The proselyte "is one who circumcises not his uncircumcision but his desires and sensual pleasures and the other passions of the soul . . . But what is the mind of the proselyte if not alienation from belief in many gods and familiarity with honoring the one God and father of all?"[32] These proselytes apparently do

---

31. M. Stern, *Authors* no. 406. "Emulate" translates *zēlousi*.
32. *Questions and Answers on Exodus* 2.2, trans. Marcus, slightly modified.

not observe the Jewish laws (they remain uncircumcised); instead they renounce polytheism, worship the one God, and follow a philosophic way of life.

The romance *Joseph and Asenath*, probably written in Egypt by a contemporary of Philo, describes Asenath as a proselyte of this type. She destroys her idols, renounces polytheism, and becomes a servant of the one God. The text says nothing about her observance of Jewish laws (except for her abstention from sacrifices offered to idols).[33] Numerous legends recount how Abraham, the archetype of all proselytes, destroyed his father's idols and was the first to recognize the one God. Practically all these legends discuss Abraham's monotheism, not his observance of Jewish rituals.[34] The author of 2 Maccabees gleefully imagines Antiochus Epiphanes on his deathbed beseeching God for assistance in return for a promise that "he would become a Jew and would visit every inhabited place to proclaim the power of God." For Antiochus "being a Jew" means proclaiming the power of the God of the Jews.[35] The princes of the royal house of Adiabene are said by Josephus "to have venerated God" before becoming circumcised and practicing the Jewish laws. Before their circumcision the princes studied the Torah but did not practice it; after their circumcision (their "conversion") the princes ran the risk of being regarded by their subjects as devotees of foreign customs.[36] Here, then, are gentiles who were devoted to the God of the Jews but who were not devoted to his laws.

Various strands of rabbinic tradition seem to be familiar with this "monotheistic proselyte." "Anyone who denies idolatry acknowledges

33. Asenath destroys her idols: 9:2, 10:13–14. Becomes a servant of God: 12–13.

34. *Joseph and Asenath:* see Chesnutt, *Death to Life,* and note 40 below. Abraham as model proselyte: Philo, *On the Virtues* 39.219; Y. Bikkurim 1:4 64a. Abraham destroys his father's idols and believes in the one God: Jubilees 12; Apocalypse of Abraham 1–8; cf. Testament of Job 2–5; and numerous other versions. Abraham's "philosophic" recognition of God: Philo, *On the Virtues* 39.212–218; Josephus, *AJ* 1.154–157. For a discussion of these passages see W. L. Knox, "Abraham and the Quest for God," *HTR* 28 (1935) 55–60; Louis H. Feldman, "Abraham the Greek Philosopher in Josephus," *TAPA* 99 (1968) 143–156; and Dieter Georgi, *The Opponents of Paul in Second Corinthians* (Philadelphia: Fortress, 1986) 49–60.

35. 2 Macc. 9:17. For a discussion of this passage and its significance, see chapter 3 above.

36. "Venerate God" (*to theon sebein*): *AJ* 20.34 and 41; circumcision and observance of the Jewish laws: *AJ* 20.17, 35, and 38. *AJ* 20.44 clearly implies that before their circumcision the princes studied the Torah but did not practice it; see S. J. D. Cohen, "Respect for Judaism" 420 n. 34; Reynolds and Tannenbaum, *Jews and Godfearers* 50; Daniel Schwartz, "God, Gentiles, and Jewish Law: On Acts 15 and Josephus' Adiabene Narrative," in *Geschichte — Tradition — Reflexion: Festschrift für Martin Hengel I: Judentum,* ed. Hubert Cancik et al. (Tübingen: Mohr [Siebeck], 1996) 263–282, at 265–272. Devotees of foreign customs: *AJ* 20.47, 75–77.

the entire Torah" is a widely repeated rabbinic statement. One version of it reads: "Anyone who denies idolatry is called a Jew." [37] According to one opinion, at least, a gentile attains the status of a "resident alien" and may live in the land of Israel only after renouncing idolatry.[38] Similarly, all versions of the "Noahide laws," the practices that a gentile must avoid in order to be reckoned a "righteous gentile," include the prohibition of idolatry. By avoiding idolatry and by observing some ethical norms a gentile fulfills all that one strand of rabbinic Judaism requires of him or her.[39] Perhaps the polemic against idolatry, which recurs with some regularity in Graeco-Jewish literature, and the appeal to the gentiles to lay aside their images, which appears only seldom, are connected with this ideology.[40]

None of these texts, not even Philo's account of these "proselytes," implies that gentiles of this sort were members of a Jewish community.[41] No doubt Jews rejoiced when gentiles cast aside their idols and came to believe in the one true God, the God of the Jews, but such rejoicing did not necessarily mean that such gentiles became Jews in a social sense. Theological conversion was not social conversion. We may presume that

37. B. Megillah 13a ("is called a Jew"); Y. Nedarim 3:4 38a and B. Nedarim 25a (and parallels); Sifrei Numbers 111 (116H); Sifrei Deuteronomy 54 (122F); cf. Mekhilta Shirah 8 on Exod. 15:11 (142H–R). See Segal, *Babylonian Esther Midrash* 2.20–21.

38. Y. Yevamot 8:1 8d and B. Avodah Zarah 64b (*gēr toshav*).

39. T. Avodah Zarah 8:4; B. Sanhedrin 56b; David Novak, *The Image of the Non-Jew in Judaism* (Lewiston, Me.: Edwin Mellen, 1983), esp. 3–51 and 107–165.

40. Polemic against idolatry: see especially Sibylline Oracles 3.8–45 and 545–572; 5.484–500; 12:291–292; and Wisd. of Sol. 12:23–15:19, with the commentary of David Winston, *The Wisdom of Solomon,* Anchor Bible (Garden City, N.Y.: Doubleday, 1979) ad loc.; and the Abraham traditions listed in note 34 above. The problems raised by the "apostolic decree" in Acts 15, by Paul's concept of "law" and "justification," and by the ethical maxims of pseudo-Phocylides and the Sibylline Oracles cannot be discussed here.

41. Peder Borgen suggests that the Philonic passage quoted above is answering the question "When does a person receive status as a proselyte in the Jewish community and cease to be a heathen?" He goes on to state that "Philo uses an ethical criterion for deciding who has the status of proselyte within the Jewish community. This ethical conversion of the heathen also meant a sociological change from a pagan context to a Jewish one." I see none of this in the text of the *Questions on Exodus.* Elsewhere Philo does discuss some of the sociological aspects of conversion (see below), but not here. See Borgen, "The Early Church and the Hellenistic Synagogue," *Studia Theologica* 37 (1983) 55–78, esp. 66–67 (with bibliography on the passage) = Borgen, *Philo, John, and Paul* (Atlanta: Scholars Press, 1987) 207–232, esp. 219–220. Other scholars too have suggested that some proselytes might have remained uncircumcised. I am not convinced. For a partial rebuttal of Neil McEleney, "Conversion, Circumcision, and the Law," *New Testament Studies* 20 (1974) 328–333, see John Nolland, "Uncircumcised Proselytes?" *JSJ* 12 (1981) 173–194, and Heikki Räisänen, *Paul and the Law* (Philadelphia: Fortress, 1986) 40–41. See too Birnbaum, *Judaism* 200. On the alleged rabbinic evidence for this position, see chapter 7 below, at note 49.

these gentiles did not see themselves as Jews in a social sense—that is, as members of a Jewish community. They acknowledged the truth of the God of the Jews but remained, in their own eyes, gentiles, just as gentiles who practiced Jewish rituals (category 4) remained, in their own eyes, gentiles. Other gentiles, however, who observed the peculiar behavior of these gentiles might have concluded that they were Jews. As I discussed above, according to an anecdote in Plutarch's life of Cicero, anyone who abstains from pork, or who can humorously be thought of as abstaining from pork, can be called a "Jew." The historian Dio Cassius thinks that anyone devoted to Jewish (Judaean) ways is called a Jew. Similarly, if a gentile destroyed his ancestral gods and declared exclusive loyalty to the God of the Jews, his neighbors might have regarded him as a Jew. When the Babylonians heard that Daniel, with the king's approval, had destroyed the great dragon whom they revered, they concluded that "The king has become a Jew" (or, more accurately, "The king has become a Judaean"), for "he has destroyed Bel, and killed the dragon, and slaughtered the priests."[42] Neither the narrator of the story nor Daniel regarded the Persian king as a Judaean/Jew; he was Persian. Even the Babylonians, perhaps, if pressed, would have admitted that the king was not really a Judaean/Jew. He simply has behaved like one.

Anyone who believes as the Jews believe or who acts as the Jews act can, for purposes of humor or polemic, be labeled a Jew. This usage is abundantly attested in the internecine conflicts of early Christianity: "Jew" and "Judaizer" became epithets by which one side could denigrate the theology or rituals of the other. I shall discuss this in my next chapter. Such a polemical usage of ethnic labels is readily paralleled in antiquity. Various writers of Old Comedy mocked the Athenian politician Lycurgus as an "Egyptian": he was presented onstage wearing an Egyptian cloak, and Egyptians were called "his countrymen." Lycurgus, of course, was not an Egyptian, but he could be mocked as one because he was devoted to Isis and apparently was instrumental in the foundation of the first temple to Isis in Athens.[43] Just before the battle of Actium, in a speech put into his mouth by the historian Dio Cassius, Octavian says of Mark Antony that he "has abandoned all his ancestors' habits of life, has emulated all alien and barbaric customs," and "Therefore let no one count him a Roman, but rather a rank Egyptian, nor call him An-

---

42. Bel and the Dragon 28: *ioudaios gegonen ho basileus*. See my discussion of this passage in chapter 3 above.

43. R. Kassel and C. Austin, *Poetae Comici Graeci* 4 (1983) 137 (Cratinus frag. no. 32); Vidman, *Sylloge* 4, commentary on no. 1.

tony, but rather a Serapion."[44] Antony, of course, was not an Egyptian, but his Egyptophilia was so extreme that Octavian (Dio?) could suggest that he be regarded as an Egyptian. Similarly, the Babylonians could claim that Darius has become a Judaean, and Dio could claim that anyone who follows the observances of the Jews is called a Jew.

6. Joining the Jewish Community

Some gentiles became members of, or at least achieved an intimate status within, the Jewish community, without undergoing a religious "conversion." Perhaps they underwent a nominal conversion, but their conversion was not the result of a religious experience or of a newly gained devotion to the God of the Jews. They are of several types.

a. Early Christianity grew in part through the conversions of entire households to the new faith. The conversion of a master or mistress would bring along the conversion of children, slaves, retainers, and perhaps spouse.[45] The Tosefta imagines a case where a master converts to Judaism and converts his slaves too.[46] We may be sure that the involuntary members of the household had substantially less enthusiasm, at least at first, for the new religion than did the chieftain who initiated the conversion, but all alike became members of the new community. In the Byzantine period several Arabian tribes converted to Judaism (see below for one such case), but ancient Judaism provides no parallel.[47] As far as I know the only attested conversion of an entire household to Judaism is the case of Valeria described in several rabbinic accounts. She converted to Judaism with her female slaves; because of a legal technicality some of her slaves became free upon their conversion, but they continued to serve her nevertheless.[48] According to a ninth-century midrash, not only did

44. Dio Cassius 50.25.3 and 50.27.1: *mēt' oun Rōmaion einai tis auton nomizetō alla tina Aiguption*. "Emulated" translates *ezēlōkota*.

45. Wayne Meeks, *The First Urban Christians* (New Haven: Yale University Press, 1983) 75–77; cf. Kraemer, "The Term 'Jew,'" 45.

46. T. Qiddushin 5:11 297L.

47. Salo W. Baron, *A Social and Religious History of the Jews* (New York: Columbia University Press, 1957), 3:63–72, 196–206, and 323–330; Gordon Newby, *A History of the Jews of Arabia* (Columbia: University of South Carolina Press, 1988) 33–77. Aryeh Kasher suggests a parallel in the conversion of the Ituraeans, but I see no need for this conjecture; see Kasher, "Jews and Itureans in the Hasmonean Period" (in Hebrew), *Cathedra* 33 (1984) 18–41, esp. 30–31.

48. Mekhilta Pisha 15 on Exod. 12:48 (57H–R) and parallels. See Bamberger, *Proselytism* 104 n. 193 and 234; Porton, *Stranger* 128–129.

the sailors of the book of Jonah become converts (after all, Scripture declares: "the men feared the Lord greatly; they offered a sacrifice to the Lord and they made vows"), but they even brought their wives and children along to convert with them.[49]

b. More common is the simple case of the acquisition of a gentile slave by a Jew. A male slave would be circumcised and, upon manumission, attain the status of a proselyte. That the Jews of late antiquity actually followed this practice is strongly suggested by the imperial legislation that, beginning with Antoninus Pius, repeatedly forbade it.[50] A female slave too would attain the status of a proselyte upon manumission. These slaves, even if they assented to their conversion (as the Talmud requires them to do), cannot have been motivated by a deep or sincere love for the God of Abraham. They were converted to Judaism for the religious convenience of their owners. And yet they were accepted as proselytes after their manumission, and even before that they were regarded, by rabbinic law at least, as proselytes in the making.[51]

c. As I discussed at some length in chapter 4, the Idumaeans and Ituraeans became Judaeans, citizens in the Judaean state (or Judaean League). Their enfranchisement entailed the observance of circumcision (which they already observed) and the other Judaean laws, as well as the worship of the God of the Judaeans, but the union between the Judaeans and the Idumaeans and Ituraeans was primarily political, not theological. Scholars routinely speak of the incorporation of the Idumaeans and Ituraeans in terms of religious conversion, but this is wrong. It was not a religious conversion but a social and political integration into the Jewish state. In the year 66 C.E. an incident took place in Jerusalem that illustrates the same point. Upon being captured by the rebels, the commander of the Roman garrison, one Metilius, saved his life by promising "to judaize as far as circumcision."[52] The meaning of this striking phrase is not entirely clear, as I shall discuss in chapter 6, but Metilius seems to mean that he will defect from the Romans, join the Jews, and have himself circumcised as proof of his new loyalty. The God of the Judaeans has no part in Metilius' calculations.

d. Some gentiles joined the Jewish community either for the sake of, or through, marriage. Josephus records that Azizus king of Emesa was circumcised for the sake of marriage with Drusilla, and Polemo

---

49. Jon. 1:16; Pirqe de Rabbi Eliezer 10, pp. 72–73, trans. Friedlander. Cf. the medieval story of a gentile priest who converts to Judaism and is followed by thousands of his followers: Moses Gaster, *The Exempla of the Rabbis* (1924; reprint, New York: Ktav, 1968) no. 131 = Midrash haGadol on Exod. 2:16 (this story awaits analysis).

50. See M. Stern's commentary on *Authors* no. 511, and Linder, *Roman Imperial Legislation* 80–82.

51. Flesher, *Oxen*.   52. *BJ* 2.454.

king of Cilicia for the sake of marriage with Berenike.[53] The sincerity of these conversions can be gauged by subsequent events: Berenike abandoned Polemo and he therefore abandoned his Judaism. As I shall discuss in chapter 7 below, rabbinic law prohibits conversion for the sake of marriage or any other nonreligious consideration, but this law is irrelevant in pre-rabbinic times and may have been easily ignored even after it was decreed. (See the story cited below.)

In some cases a gentile may have joined the Jewish community through marriage even without conversion. If a gentile man married a Jewish woman, in all likelihood he would not thereby enter the Jewish community, since a wife would normally join her husband's house and family. In contrast, if a gentile woman was married to a Jewish man, she too was supposed to join her husband's house and family, thereby becoming part of the community to which her husband belonged. There was no ritual of conversion; the act of marriage to a Jewish husband was de facto an act of conversion—that is, an act of integration into the Jewish community (I shall return to this point in my conclusion). She probably would have been regarded by her contemporaries, and probably would have regarded herself as well, not as a Jew but as a gentile; in the case of divorce, she would have returned to her father's house and her gentile origins. Her children of course were Jewish, because they were the offspring of a Jewish father. This system is presumed by various sources of the first century C.E. (Josephus, Philo, New Testament), but the rabbis of the second century C.E. presume a different system entirely. According to rabbinic law, the status of the offspring of intermarriage follows that of the mother. The rabbis do have a ritual for the conversion of women: if a gentile wife converts to Judaism, then she and the children she bears after her conversion would be Jewish. If she does not convert, neither she nor her children are Jewish. This rabbinic innovation is the subject of chapter 9 below.

7. Converting to Judaism and "Becoming a Jew"

Conversion to Judaism entails three elements: practice of the Jewish laws (category 4); exclusive devotion to the God of the Jews (category 5); and integration into the Jewish community (category 6).

53. *AJ* 20.139 and 145–146. In contrast Syllaeus the Nabatean (*AJ* 16.225) and Epiphanes son of the king of Commagene (*AJ* 19.355 and 20.139) refused circumcision and there

The three elements are stated forthrightly by the book of Judith. When Achior the Ammonite "saw all that the God of Israel had done, he believed firmly in God, and was circumcised, and joined the house of Israel, remaining so to this day."[54] The same three elements appear implicitly in Tacitus and Juvenal. Tacitus writes that the Jews "instituted the circumcision of the genitalia in order to be recognizable by their difference. Those who cross over into their manner of life adopt the same practice, and, before anything else, are instructed to despise the Gods, disown their native land, and regard their parents, children, and brothers as of little account." Juvenal too sees in conversion the denial of all other Gods (the worship of nothing but the clouds), the practice of the Jewish laws (notably circumcision), and hostility toward all non-Jews.[55]

Most descriptions of conversion, however, mention only one or two of the three elements. In several passages, Philo praises the proselytes (or epelytes) for having the courage to abandon "their kinsfolk by blood, their country, their customs, and the temples and the images of their gods, and the tributes and honors paid to them," and to undertake the "journey to a better home, from idle fables to the clear vision of truth and the worship of the one and truly existing God." Moses "commands all members of the nation to love the incomers, not only as friends and kinsfolk but as themselves in body and soul." For Philo, then, the crucial elements of conversion are the denial of all other gods, the belief in the God of Israel, and integration into the Israelite polity (*politeia*).[56] It is striking that Philo does not explicitly associate the process of conversion with the observance of the special laws, notably circumcision; we may presume that Philo would have required the proselyte, upon acquiring membership in the Israelite polity, to observe all the laws observed by the Israelites, including circumcision, but the initial process of conversion does not seem to include circumcision.[57] In a much briefer

---

fore were denied permission to marry princesses of the Herodian house. I shall return to Syllaeus in chapter 7 below. On the conversion of women for the sake of marriage, see Ilan, *Jewish Women* 211–214.

54. Jth. 14:10.

55. Tacitus, *Histories* 5.5.2 = M. Stern, *Authors* no. 281; Juvenal, *Satires* 14.96–106 = M. Stern, *Authors* no. 301.

56. *On the Virtues* 20.102–21.108, 34.182, 39.212–219; *On the Special Laws* 1.9.51–55 and 4.34.178. See the discussion by Birnbaum, *Judaism* 193–219.

57. In the passage cited above from the *Questions on Exodus,* Philo explicitly says that the proselyte is not circumcised and omits any reference to the abandonment of his previous family and integration into the community. As always in Philo, it is difficult to determine when Philo is giving scriptural exegesis and when he is reflecting the practices of Alexandrian Jewry. See above note 36.

description the author of the Apocalypse of Baruch sees proselytes as "people who have left their vanities to take refuge under your wings" and "those who began by not knowing and who then knew life, and mixed themselves in the race apart among the peoples."[58]

Josephus nowhere says explicitly that conversion to Judaism entails the rejection of the gods. Instead he defines conversion to mean the adoption of the practices and customs of the Jews. And of all the practices and customs of the Jews, Josephus singles out circumcision. For him "to adopt the customs of the Jews" and "to be circumcised" are synonymous expressions.[59] As I discussed in the previous chapter, in the second century B.C.E. circumcision achieved prominence, for Jews and gentiles alike, as *the* Jewish ritual, and in subsequent centuries many gentile writers (e.g., Tacitus and Juvenal) confirmed Josephus' (and Paul's!) view that the acceptance of circumcision is the acceptance of Judaism. Although they knew that circumcision was practiced by other nations too (as I discussed in chapter 2 above), these writers persisted in regarding the ritual as quintessentially Jewish, probably because the Jews themselves so regarded it. The Greek-speaking Jews of the second-temple period and the Hebrew- (and Aramaic-) speaking Jews after 70 C.E. debated the meaning of circumcision and the ritual's exact place in the conversion process, but as far as is known no Jewish community in antiquity (including Philo's) accepted as members male proselytes who were not circumcised. Perhaps the God of the Jews would be pleased with gentiles who venerated him and practiced some of his laws, and perhaps in the day of the eschaton gentiles would not need to be circumcised to be part of God's holy people, but if those gentiles wanted to join the Jewish community in the here and now, they had to accept circumcision.[60]

The third element of the conversion process is the integration of the

---

58. Apocalypse of Baruch 41:1–5 and 42:4–5.

59. Cf. Josephus, *Vita* 113 with 149; see S. J. D. Cohen, "Respect for Judaism" 420–421.

60. On the status of gentiles in the days of the eschaton, see the fine discussion of Donaldson, "Proselytes or 'Righteous Gentiles'?" For discussions of the meaning of circumcision see Philo, *On the Special Laws* 1.1–11, and B. Nedarim 31b–32a (and parallels). On the Philonic passage see Richard Hecht, "The Exegetical Contexts of Philo's Interpretation of Circumcision," in *Nourished with Peace: Studies in Hellenistic Judaism in Memory of Samuel Sandmel*, ed. Frederick Greenspahn et al. (Chico, Calif.: Scholars Press, 1984) 51–79. On the place of circumcision in the conversion process see chapter 7 below. In general see John J. Collins, "A Symbol of Otherness: Circumcision and Salvation in the First Century," in *"To See Ourselves as Others See Us": Christians, Jews, "Others," in Late Antiquity*, ed. Jacob Neusner and E. Frerichs (Atlanta: Scholars Press, 1985) 163–186.

proselyte into the Jewish community.[61] Josephus comments that the Jews of Antioch "always drew to their religious ceremonies a great multitude of Greeks whom they made in some way a part of themselves."[62] This integration would be manifest in various ways. Whatever separation the Jews observed in their dealings with gentiles would no longer affect the proselyte. The proselyte would be counted as a member of the synagogue, would be allowed to participate in the sacred meals,[63] would be expected to bring his or her legal cases before the communal authorities and to pay his or her share of the communal taxes (local impositions as well as the offerings to the central institutions in the land of Israel, the temple, and the patriarch),[64] would be allowed to sit with the Jews in the theater, and after death would be buried in proximity to other Jews. In sum, the proselyte was just like the native born.

In the eyes of outsiders a proselyte not only could be called a Jew but actually became one. Epictetus says of a convert to Judaism that he is "a Jew in fact and is also called one."[65] The Life of Septimius Severus reports that the emperor prohibited his subjects from "becoming Jews." Ambrosiaster writes that "proselytes" are those "who have been made Jews."[66] The Gospel according to Philip opens with the statement "A Hebrew makes another Hebrew, and such a person is called *proselyte*."[67] In the *Acts of Pilate,* upon being asked by Pilate to define "proselyte," the high priests reply: "They were born children of Greeks, and now

61. Two imperial laws of the fourth century see conversion primarily in terms of social integration. See Theodosian Code 16.8.1 (18 Oct. 315), *si quis vero ex populo ad eorum* [i.e., *Iudaeorum*] *nefariam sectam accesserit et conciliabulis eorum se adplicaverit,* and Theodosian Code 16.8.7 (3 July 357 [?]), *si quis . . . ex Christiano Iudaeus effectus sacrilegis coetibus adgregetur.* See Linder, *Roman Imperial Legislation* nos. 8 and 12.

62. *BJ* 7.45. In "Respect for Judaism" 417, I argued that the passage refers to converts; Goodman, *Mission and Conversion* 87 n. 58, argues that the passage refers to adherents, "God-fearers." Perhaps.

63. On these sacred meals see Josephus, *AJ* 14.215–216, and Schürer, *History* 3:145.

64. S. Mandell asks an excellent question in her article "Who Paid the Temple Tax When the Jews Were under Roman Rule?" *HTR* 77 (1984) 223–232. Unfortunately, she makes many unwarranted assumptions (e.g., she assumes that only Pharisees and rabbis observed the ancestral laws) and does not appreciate the social dynamics of the question.

65. M. Stern, *Authors* no. 254. See chapter 2 above at note 145.

66. Life of Severus = M. Stern, *Authors* no. 515 (*Iudaeos fieri sub gravi poena vetuit*); pseudo-Augustine (Ambrosiaster), *Questions on the Old and New Testament* 81 (CSEL 50.137, ed. A. Souter) (*fieri Iudaeos*). Cf. too Ambrosiaster, *Liber Quaestionum* 115.14 (CSEL 50.323): *Et quid illud est, ut, cum tanta multitudo Iudaeorum sit per totum mundum, nemo inmutetur ex his ut fiat gentilis, cum videamus ex paganis, licet raro, fieri Iudaeos?*

67. Translated by Wesley Isenberg in *Nag Hammadi Codex II, 2–7,* ed. Bentley Layton (Leiden: Brill, 1989) 1.191; *The Nag Hammadi Library,* ed. James Robinson, 3d ed. (San Francisco: Harper, 1990) 141.

have become Jews." [68] In the eyes of outsiders even those who have not
"converted" to Judaism can be said to have "become Jews." Gentiles
with an unusual attachment to the God of the Jews or who practiced
Jewish rituals could be called "Jews" by other gentiles, as we have seen,
but proselytes had an even stronger claim to the name. Tacitus and Juvenal clearly regard proselytes as gentiles who have rejected gentile
society and joined the sinister and tight-knit group of the Jews. In the
eyes of outsiders, then, a proselyte not only "was called" but also "became" a Jew. [69]

Proselytes became citizens or "members" of the Jewish polity, but in
the eyes of the Jews did the proselytes "become" Jews? Apparently not.
Ancient Jewish sources put this locution exclusively in the mouths of
gentiles; otherwise, Jewish texts, in both Hebrew and Greek, use other
terms to describe the process of conversion. [70] Numerous passages in

68. *Acts of Pilate* 2.4: *Hellēnōn tekna egennēthēsan kai nun gegonasin Ioudaioi.* For
the Greek text see Constantinus Tischendorf, *Evangelia Apocrypha* (Leipzig: Avenarius et
Mendelssohn, 1853) 214–216. For a translation see Schneemelcher, *New Testament Apocrypha*, 1.512; cf. too Montague Rhodes James, *The Apocryphal New Testament* (Oxford:
Clarendon, 1924; reprint, 1972) 98–99.

69. The language of "becoming a Jew" or "being made" a Jew is paralleled by the language of "becoming a Christian" or "being made" a Christian. Cf. Tertullian, *Apology* 3.1,
3.3, and esp. 18, *fiunt non nascuntur Christiani,* "Christians are made, not born," and the
numerous parallels cited ad loc. by J. E. B. Mayor in his edition of the *Apology* (Cambridge, 1917) 265. Cf. *genesthai Khristianous:* Martyrdom of Pionius 7.3, and council of
Laodicea, canon 31; *Ioustinos humas epoiēse Khristianous:* Acts of Justin 4.5 (ed. Musurillo p. 44); cf. Evagrius, *Altercatio Legis inter Simonem Judaeum et Theophilum Christia-
num,* ed. E. Bratke (CSEL 35, pt. 1 [1904]), p. 2: *aut, si tu me hodie reviceris, facito Chris-
tianum; aut, ego te cum superavero, faciam Nazoraeum Iudaeum.* Jewish and Christian
usage echoes the classical. Aristotle refers to *hoi poiētoi politai,* those who have been made
citizens (*Politics* 3.1275a6; cf. 3.1275b30). Apollodorus [Demosthenes], *Against Neaera*
59.88, speaks of making someone an Athenian (*poiēsasthai Athēnaion*). According to
Plutarch, "the Lacedaemonians made him a Spartan" (*Life of Dion* 17.4; cf. 49.4). Ennius,
Annales frag. 5.4 (= Otto Skutsch, *The Annals of Q. Ennius* [Oxford: Clarendon, 1985],
p. 84, line 157) writes *cives Romani tunc facti sunt Campani;* cf. Livy 8.17.12 (*Romani
facti*).

70. A convert says *mit'abad yehuda'i,* "I wish to be made a Jew," in Tanhuma Huqat
(nidpas) 6 (p. 79b), *na'aseiti Yisrael,* "I was made an Israelite," in Tanhuma Shoftim (nidpas) 10 (p. 114a); a gentile requesting conversion says *ya'asuni giyoret,* "let them make me
a convert" (many testimonia have *ya'asuni ivriyah,* "let them make me a Hebrew"), in
B. Menahot 44a (see below note 77); the Roman governor Turnus Rufus asks his father
through necromancy, *abba, min demayytat, itabadt yehudi,* "Father, did you become a Jew
[lit., were you made a Jew] after your death?" in Genesis Rabbah 11.5 (94T–A). Only
gentiles and converts use this locution (in spite of the fact that Gen. 12:5, *and the souls
that they had made in Haran,* was commonly taken to refer to the making of converts;
Genesis Rabbah 39:14 378–379T–A and parallels); rabbinic Jews spoke of conversion in
other ways (see chapter 7 below). It was only in the Middle Ages that the verb *lehityahed,*

Philo and in rabbinic literature praise the proselyte and enjoin upon Jews the equitable treatment of those who have entered their midst.[71] Josephus writes that "kinship is created not only through birth but also through the choice of the manner of life." The rabbis state that when the conversion ceremony is complete the proselyte is "like an Israelite in all respects."[72] But none of these passages demonstrates that the proselyte achieved real equality with the native born. Even Philo clearly implies in one passage that proselytes are decidedly inferior to natives.[73] The proselyte probably had an ambiguous status in the Jewish community. Many epitaphs and synagogue inscriptions attach the label "the proselyte" after the name of the person being commemorated.[74] This practice highlights the ambiguity. On the one hand, the Jewish community accorded "membership" status to the proselyte; he or she could obtain honor and power in his or her adopted community. On the other hand, the membership status of the proselyte was anomalous, and the proselyte felt obligated (was obligated?) to call attention to this fact. According to the *Acts of Pilate* the high priests, who have just explained that proselytes "have become Jews," take it as obvious that the testimony of native-born Jews is more reliable than that of the incomers. In the communities that produced and preserved the Qumran scrolls and rabbinic literature, both of which were heavily influenced by priestly conceptions of pedigree and descent, proselytes did not attain equality with the native born. Two Qumran texts prohibit the proselyte (*gēr*)

---

taken from Esther 8:17, was used to mean "to convert to Judaism" (just as in Christian Greek *ioudaïzein* was used to mean "to become a Jew"). See, for example, Tanhuma Yitro (nidpas) 7 (93a),and Midrash Yelamdenu on Kedoshim, ed. Wertheimer, *Batei Midrashot*, 1.171.

71. See above, note 56. Love for incomers is also endorsed by pseudo-Phocylides 39; see the discussion of Pieter van der Horst, *The Sentences of Pseudo-Phocylides* (Leiden: Brill, 1978) 139–140. For a survey of rabbinic attitudes toward proselytes see Bamberger, *Prosylityism* 149–173; Porton, *Stranger*.

72. Josephus: *CAp* 2.210. Conversion ceremony: B. Yevamot 47b. See chapter 7 below.

73. *Life of Moses* 1.147; see McKnight, "Lion Proselytes," and idem, *Light* 92–96. Chesnutt, *Death to Life* 111–115, argues that one of the purposes of *Joseph and Asenath* is to teach that the proselyte is to be considered a full-fledged member of the Israelite community.

74. The Aphrodisias inscription (see below, note 99) lists three proselytes. Rome: Leon, *Jews of Ancient Rome* nos. 21, 68, 202, 222, 256, 462, and 523. Venosa: *CIJ* 576. Cyrene: Lüderitz, *Corpus jüdischer Zeugnisse* no. 12. Jerusalem: Pau Figueras, *Decorated Jewish Ossuaries* (Leiden: Brill, 1983) 16 nn. 135–136. Dura: Joseph Naveh, *On Stone and Mosaic: The Aramaic and Hebrew Inscriptions from Ancient Synagogues* (Jerusalem: Carta, 1978) no. 88; T. Ilan, "New Ossuary Inscriptions from Jerusalem," *Scripta Classica Israelica* 11 (1991–1992) 149–159, at 150, 154–155; Figueras, "Epigraphic Evidence"; Levinskaya, *Book of Acts* 25–26. See too chapter 3 above, note 31.

from entering the temple; another records that the people of Israel are divided into four groups: priests, Levites, Israelites, and proselytes.[75] According to the Mishnah, a proselyte should not say "Our God and God of our fathers" in his prayers, nor should he recite the Deuteronomic formula "from the land you have sworn unto our fathers to give us." This important text is the subject of chapter 10 below.

In the eyes of outsiders a proselyte or convert was a gentile who became a Jew. But in the eyes of (some?) Jews, a gentile who converted to Judaism became not a Jew but a proselyte—that is, a Jew of a peculiar sort. How the proselytes saw themselves is unknown. If they voluntarily added "the proselyte" on their inscriptions, they knew that they were different from the native Jews. Some proselytes assumed Jewish names upon their conversion, indicating a real desire to adopt a new identity and to "become Jews."[76]

Three Conversion Stories

In order to illustrate some of the problems in defining "conversion," I present here three conversion stories from late antiquity. Even after the rabbis had defined the process of conversion and instituted a formal conversion ceremony (see chapter 7 below), the nature and meaning of the conversion experience could vary widely.

My first story comes from the Sifrei on Numbers, a rabbinic work of uncertain date but generally ascribed to the third century C.E. The story is attributed to R. Nathan, a figure of the mid second century C.E.:

75. Exclusion from temple: 4Q Florilegium (John M. Allegro, *Discoveries in the Judaean Desert of Jordan V: Qumran Cave 4* [Oxford: Clarendon, 1968] pp. 53–57 no. 174) and Yadin, *Temple Scroll* 39:5 and 40:6; see my discussion in chapter 8 below, note 36. Four groups: Damascus Covenant 14:3–6; cf. M. Qiddushin 4:1 and Sifrei Deuteronomy 247 (276F). It is possible that *gēr* in the Qumran texts means not "proselyte" but "resident alien." On the inequality of the proselyte, see Schwartz, *Agrippa* 124–130. In Covenant of Damascus 11.2 a gentile proselyte even after conversion is still called *ben hanekhar;* see P. R. Davies, "Who Can Join" 138–140.

76. Explicit evidence for change of name: Leon, *Jews of Ancient Rome* no. 462 (Felicitas becomes Peregrina) and no. 523 (Veturia Paulla becomes Sarra). Implicit evidence is provided by the inscriptions that commemorate a proselyte with a Jewish name; in all likelihood the proselyte received the Jewish name after conversion. See the inscriptions from Aphrodisias, Cyrene, and Jerusalem listed in note 74 above. T. Gittin 6:4 (270L) seems to say that gentiles would change their names upon conversion to Judaism, but might continue to use their gentile names at least in some situations.

It once happened that a man, who was careful to observe the commandment of *tzitzit* (fringes), heard that there was a prostitute in (one of) the cities of the sea who would receive four hundred pieces of gold as her hire. He sent her four hundred pieces of gold and she set a time with him.

When the time came, he went and sat at the doorway to her house. Her maid came and said to her, "That man for whom you set a time—he is sitting at the doorway to the house." She replied, "Let him come in." When he entered, she spread out for him seven mattresses of silver and one of gold. She herself was on the topmost. Between each and every mattress was a step stool of silver; the topmost one was of gold. When they arrived at the moment for the act, his four fringes seemed to him like four witnesses and struck him on the face. Immediately he withdrew and sat down on the ground. She too withdrew and sat down on the ground.

She said to him, "By the Love goddess of Rome, I will not release you unless you tell me what imperfection you have seen in me."

He said to her, "By the temple service, I have not seen any imperfection in you; there is no beauty like yours in the entire world. But the Lord our God has commanded us to observe an easy commandment, and Scripture states concerning it *I am the Lord your God, I am the Lord your God,* twice. *I am the Lord your God:* I am the one who in the future will pay your reward; *I am the Lord your God:* I am the one who in the future will exact punishment."

She said to him, "By the temple service, I will not release you until you write for me your name, the name of your city, and the name of the school in which you study Torah."

He wrote for her his name, the name of his city, the name of his teacher, and the name of the school in which he studied Torah.

She arose and liquidated all her property; (she gave) a third to the government, a third to the poor, and a third she took with her. She came and stood in the school of R. Hiyya [in some readings: R. Meir]. She said to him, "Master, convert me."[77]

He said to her, "Perhaps you have set your eyes on one of the students?"
She took out for him the writing that she had.

He (R. Hiyya) said to him (the student),[78] "Arise and take possession of your purchase. Those mattresses that she had spread out for you illicitly, she shall spread out for you licitly. This is her reward in this world—in the next world, I do not know how much."[79]

---

77. This is the reading of the Sifrei (*rabbi gayyereni*). The vulgate printed edition as well as the Munich manuscript of the Bavli read: "Master, issue a command and let them make me a convert" (*rabbi tzaveh alai veya'asuni giyoret*); three manuscripts and several medieval testimonia read: "Master, issue a command and let them make me a Hebrew woman" (*veya'asuni ivriayh/ivrit*).

78. Some testimonia have "He said to her" and change the gender of the following pronouns.

79. Sifrei Numbers 115 (128–129H), on Num. 15:41. There are numerous minor differences in the parallel version in B. Menahot 44a that do not concern us here.

This is rich and wonderful story, which I cannot analyze in full here.[80] The story clearly was inspired by Numbers 15:39: *That shall be your fringe; look at it and recall all the commandments of the Lord and observe them, so that you do not follow your heart and eyes after which you go whoring.* Scripture states that fringes save from metaphorical whoring; the midrash states that fringes save from real whoring. Not only do fringes save a pious man from sin, they even win over a gentile to Judaism. The gentile who is won over is not just any gentile; she is a gentile of the sort who would be reckoned least likely to convert. Like the conversion of prostitutes in Christian hagiography,[81] the conversion of this prostitute demonstrates the power of repentance and the ability of the spirit to conquer the body.

An especially remarkable feature of the story is the ease with which R. Hiyya (R. Meir?) accepts the former prostitute as a convert. He is aware that she is interested in marrying one of his students, but apparently he allows her to convert anyway. (As I have already noted, the Babylonian Talmud prohibits conversion for the sake of matrimony.) Nor does the story have the master instruct the woman in the ways of Judaism (contrast the level of instruction expected by the Babylonian Talmud; see chapter 7 below). What is the woman's motivation? This woman, who was the object of desire by men around the world, wants the one man who was able to resist her charms. Perhaps we are meant to understand that she realized the truth of Judaism from the fact that it was the Torah that gave the student the power to resist. Since this story concerns a woman, it is no surprise that it includes marriage. A happy conversion of a gentile woman is a conversion that ends in marriage.

Our second story comes from Sozomen, a Christian historian of the first half of the fifth century C.E. In his account of the reign of Valens (364–378 C.E.) he includes a digression on the history of the Arabs, which includes the following:

This . . . tribe . . . took its origin and had its name from Ishmael, the son of Abraham; and the ancients called them Ishmaelites after their progenitor.

---

80. For two good discussions see Warren Harvey, "The Pupil, the Harlot, and the Fringe Benefits," *Prooftexts* 6 (1986) 259–271, and A. Goshen-Gottstein, "The Commandment of *Tzitzit*, the Prostitute, and the Exegetical Story," in *Mahshevet Hazal* (Rabbinic thought), ed. T. Groner and M. Hirschman (Haifa: University of Haifa, 1990) 45–58. See too Porton, *Stranger* 61 and 205, and Ilan, *Jewish Women* 81 n. 82.

81. Benedicta Ward, *Harlots of the Desert* (Kalamazoo, Mich.: Cistercian Publications, 1987); Ruth Mazo Karras, "Holy Harlots: Prostitute Saints in Medieval Legend," *Journal of the History of Sexuality* 1 (1990) 3–32.

As their mother Hagar was a slave, they afterwards, to conceal the opprobrium of their origin, assumed the name of Saracens, as they were descended from Sara, the wife of Abraham. Such being their origin, they practice circumcision like the Jews, refrain from the use of pork, and observe many other Jewish rites and customs . . . As is usual, in the lapse of time, their ancient customs fell into oblivion, and other practices gradually got the precedence among them. Some of their tribe afterwards happening to come into contact with the Jews, gathered from them the facts of their true origin, returned to their kinsmen, and inclined to the Hebrew customs and laws. From that time on, until now, many of them regulate their lives according to the Jewish precepts.[82]

Sozomen is convinced that the Saracens (whose name is given a wonderful folk etymology) are Ishmaelites, and therefore originally had a manner of life exactly like that of their cousins, the Jews.[83] Proof of this is the fact that they practice circumcision and abstain from pork. As for the rest of the Jewish laws and customs, the Saracens forgot them in the course of time and were corrupted by the worship of other gods. However, a group of Saracens, through contact with some Jews, became conscious of their Abrahamic origins and adopted all the Hebrew/Jewish customs and laws. A literal translation of the last sentence of the excerpt is: "From that time until now many among them live Jewishly."

The "conversion" of the Saracens, as narrated by Sozomen, has three features of interest. First, the motivation for the conversion is not readily paralleled in any other ancient conversion story. This is not an ecstatic conversion brought about by a dream, a vision, or a miracle; this is not a philosophical conversion brought about by a contemplation of eternal verities; this is not a marital conversion brought about by the prospect of marital union; it is an ethnographic conversion, if I may use that term, in which a tribe is convinced that it must change its ways if it is to be true to its own origins (which it believes had somehow been forgotten in the course of time). Second, this is a group "conversion." No doubt members of the group will have differed widely in enthusiasm and

82. Sozomen 6.38.10–13, p. 299, ed. J. Bidez, rev. G. C. Hansen (GCS 50). The translation is that of Chester Hartranft in *A Select Library of Nicene and Post-Nicene Fathers*, ed. P. Schaff and H. Wace (New York: Christian Literature Co., 1890; frequently reprinted) 2.375. On Sozomen's digression on the Arabs, see Irfan Shahid, *Byzantium and the Arabs in the Fourth Century* (Washington, D.C.: Dumbarton Oaks, 1984) 274–277 and *Byzantium and the Arabs in the Fifth Century* (Washington, D.C.: Dumbarton Oaks, 1989) 167–180.

83. On "Ishmaelism," see Shahid, *Byzantium and the Arabs in the Fifth Century* 179–180; F. Millar, "Hagar, Ishmael, Josephus, and the Origins of Islam," *JJS* 44 (1993) 23–45.

commitment to the new way (which claims to be old). Many will have simply followed the sheik; whatever the sheik does, they do. Several different occurrences of such group conversions to Judaism are attested in Arabia in late antiquity.[84]

Third, it is not at all clear that the Saracens have joined the Jewish community and become "Jews." They now live in the Jewish manner; they observe the customs and laws of the Hebrews; but have they become Jews? They remain Saracens. Their tribal structure remains intact; they are no more part of the Jewish community now than they had been previously. From the Jewish perspective the Saracens have not converted to Judaism so much as they have begun to "judaize." Perhaps travelers coming upon the Saracens would now characterize them as "Jews" on the basis of their Jewish observances, and perhaps the Saracens, if asked to identify themselves, would reply that they were Jews (or would they say Ishmaelites? Hebrews? sons of Abraham?), but have they really become Jews? If gentiles begin to observe Jewish laws and customs, do they ipso facto become Jews? We have already seen, both in this chapter and in chapter 2, that in some contexts the answer is yes, but in others the answer is no.[85]

My third story is an excerpt from a homily *On Dreams,* written about 614 C.E. by Antiochus the Monk; the point of the homily is that dreams can often mislead those who believe them. He proves the point by telling the following story:

There was a certain monk on Mount Sinai who demonstrated great continence by being locked away in his cell for many years. Later, tricked by the revelations and dreams of the devil, he fell away into Judaism and the circumcision of the flesh. At first the devil often showed him dreams that were true, and having thus snared his benighted mind, the devil finally showed him the multitude of the martyrs, apostles, and all the Christians, shrouded in darkness and filled with every shame. On the other side were Moses, the prophets, and the God-hated [or: God-hating] multitude of the Jews, illuminated with a great light and bearing themselves in joy and gaiety. Having seen these things this unfortunate monk immediately rose up and left the holy mountain. He arrived in Palestine and went to Noaras and Libuas,[86] the headquarters of the Jews, and having told them his devilish apparitions,

---

84. See note 47 above.

85. Millar, "Hagar" 42–43, calls the incident a "reconversion" to Judaism.

86. Noaras seems to be No'aran, not far from Jericho; see Michael Avi-Yonah, *Gazetteer of Roman Palestine* (Jerusalem: Institute of Archaeology, 1976) 84; *Sefer Ha-Yishuv,* ed. S. Klein (1939; reprint, Jerusalem: Yad Ben Zvi, 1978) 109 (which transcribes the story). Libuas is Livias (Bet haramtha).

he was circumcised and became a Jew. He took a wife and publicly taught doctrines for the Jews against the Christians. I myself and many of the monks saw him. Not three years have passed since his wretched death, when he gave up the ghost [lit., when he snapped his soul]. After vomiting for years he became worm-eaten and expired. Seeing him, I and several pious monks, we lamented much. For he was a pitiful sight, a man who had become gray through asceticism and old through (ascetic) toils, but who was sporting with women, eating the defiled meats of the Jews, speaking unholy words, blaspheming Christ, insulting the holy baptism—(someone) whom the lawless Jews called "a second Abraham" [or: whom the lawless Jews renamed "Abraham"].[87]

In this story we seem to be in the Middle Ages: there is a strong and clear division between Judaism and Christianity, and between Jews and Christians. This is a good example of what has been called "ecstatic" conversion: impelled by a dream and by a new burning sense that what had previously been thought true was really false, and that what had previously been thought false was really true, the monk converts to Judaism and immediately sets out to harass and persecute his former coreligionists. The conversion takes place under the aegis of the Jewish community; the monk is circumcised and becomes a Jew.[88] In all these respects the story prefigures, for example, the conversion of Bodo-Eleazar in the ninth century or Andreas of Bari in the eleventh.

In sum, three conversion stories, three modes of conversion. Whatever the historical value of these stories, they show that the category of "conversion" covers a wide variety of phenomena. The ecstatic conversion of the monk, the tribal conversion of the Saracens, the marital conversion of the prostitute—all of these are "conversions," but they differ markedly from each other. The monk clearly became a Jew, as did the prostitute, but the former was motivated by a revelation and the latter by the desire for matrimony. In contrast with both, the Saracens clearly remained Saracen; they did not undergo any social conversion into Jewish society. Perhaps they should be called "judaizers" (see next chapter).

87. PG 89:1689D–1692A. For older scholarship on the story see Louis I. Newman, *Jewish Influence on Christian Reform Movements* (New York: Columbia University Press, 1925) 429 with n. 14. My attention was first drawn to this story by Derwas Chitty, *The Desert a City* (1966; reprint, Crestwood, N.Y.: St. Vladimir's Seminary Press, 1977) 154, who writes from a partisan monastic perspective. For a partisan Jewish perspective on Judaea in the early seventh century, see Michael Avi-Yonah, *The Jews of Palestine* (Oxford: Blackwell, 1976) 259–261 (who does not cite our story).

88. The Greek is *perietmēthē kai ioudaise,* precisely as in the LXX of Esther 8:17, but although there the verb *ioudaïzein* means "to side with the Jews," here it must mean "to become a Jew," a postclassical Christian usage. See chapter 6 below.

All three have crossed the boundary, but not all three have become Jews, and the two that have, have not become Jews in the same way.

Conclusions: Gentiles, "God-Fearers," Converts, and Jews

A convert (or proselyte) is a gentile who has become a Jew. How does a gentile become a Jew? Too often conversion is understood in terms of theology alone, or of theology and practice alone, but in this chapter I have emphasized the social aspects of conversion.[89] A gentile becomes a Jew by being integrated into Jewish society. In discussing conversion to Islam, Richard Bulliet writes:

. . . formal conversion, in the sense of utterance of the confession of faith, is not as significant as what might be termed social conversion, that is, conversion involving movement from one religiously defined social community to another . . . What is implied by the term social conversion is individual rather than communal action. Having performed the act of conversion, the convert henceforth saw his identity in terms of the new religious community of which he had become a member. This possibility, in turn, implies or presupposes a society in which social security was normally defined in religious terms as opposed, say, to tribal or national terms.[90]

As we have seen in chapter 4, the redefinition of Jewish society in religious (and political) terms, as opposed to tribal or ethnic (what Bulliet calls "national") terms, was a product of the second half of the second century B.C.E. Social conversion became possible then, not before. Of the seven categories treated above, the final two exemplify social conversion: joining the Jewish community, even in the absence of any theological or religious commitment (category 6), and joining the community through theological conversion and ritual commitment (category 7). From the Jewish perspective, without social conversion—that is, without the integration of a gentile into Jewish society—there is no conversion at all; the gentile remains a gentile.

89. For a similar approach, see E. V. Gallagher, "Conversion and Community in Late Antiquity," *Journal of Religion* 73 (1993) 1–15, who argues that conversion is not a single dramatic moment but a continuing transformation through ritual practice within a community. In contrast, see, for example, McKnight, *Light*, 90–101, a chapter entitled "Levels of Adherence," which, in spite of the sociological jargon cited on p. 90, sees conversion simply in terms of accepting God (see too 34 ff.).

90. Bulliet, *Conversion* 33–34.

Social conversion does not necessarily mean equality between the convert and the native born, of course. Non-Arab converts to Islam in the first century or so of Islam's growth could not attain equality with Arab Muslims because they lacked the blood lineage that was the focus of tribal honor and loyalty.[91] Similarly, gentile converts to Judaism could not attain full equality with the native born because they lacked the blood lineage that was an essential part of the ethnic part of the Jewish self-definition (see chapter 10 below). More significant than the residual discrimination against converts was the readiness of the Jewish community (and of Jewish communities) to accept as members people who were not born as Jews.

What must a gentile do in order to achieve social integration into the Jewish community? The only empirical or "objective" requirement that our sources reveal is circumcision for men. Circumcision can signal either theological conversion (cf. Achior in Judith)—that is, acceptance of belief in the God of the Jews—or commitment to observe the Jewish laws (as in Josephus, for whom "to be circumcised" and "to adopt the customs of the Jews" are synonymous), or the assumption of membership or citizenship within the community (as in the case of the Idumaeans and Ituraeans). No matter what its import, circumcision was essential; without it social conversion for men was impossible.

And what of women? What was their sign of social conversion? I am not sure. In rabbinic times immersion in water (baptism) served this purpose, but no source of the second-temple period knows anything about immersion as a ritual of conversion for either men or women (see chapter 7 below). There was no ritual, then, that could serve as a sign for women the way that circumcision could serve as a sign for men. Perhaps originally a woman's social setting was a sign of her status. The Covenant of Damascus ordains that a member of the sect may not "sell his male slave or female slave to gentiles, because they (the slaves) have come with him into the covenant of Abraham."[92] In the case of male slaves, the ordinance is clearly referring to circumcision, the Abrahamic covenant that, according to Genesis 17, is to be performed on slaves as well as on free-born Israelites. But how has a female slave entered into the covenant of Abraham? Perhaps female slaves are automatically brought into the covenant by being the property of an Israelite master. Similarly,

---

91. Bulliet, *Conversion* 41.

92. Covenant of Damascus 12.10–11: *ve et avdo ve et amato al yimkor lahem asher ba'u imo bivrit avraham*. P. R. Davies, "Who Can Join" 139–140, argues correctly that this means not that slaves are members of the sect, but that they are members of the "first covenant" (*brit rishonim*, Covenant of Damascus 3.10 and 6.2), the covenant with all Israel.

if a gentile woman was married to a Jewish man, the fact of marriage established the fact of social conversion. (As so often in ancient society, a woman's personhood is established only through a relationship with a man, whereas a man's is established on his own.) No conversion ritual was required. As a dutiful wife she would abandon her ancestral gods and automatically accept the religion of her husband.[93]

A wife's loyalty to her husband's religion would last as long as her loyalty to her husband. After executing his son Alexander, Herod sent Alexander's wife Glaphyra back to her father, Archelaus of Cappadocia; her next husband was Juba king of Libya. When the wife of Herod Antipas discovered that her husband was planning to take a second wife, she fled to her father, Aretas king of Petra. The idea of "conversion to Judaism" seems entirely irrelevant to the biography of these aristocratic women. As long as they were the wives of Judaean princes, they were part of Judaean society. However, at some point in the late first or second century C.E., the idea arose that gentile women (wives) too must convert; if they do not convert, they remain gentiles, even if married to a Jewish husband. (A woman's personhood is beginning to emerge.) Immersion in water would signal a gentile woman's change of status. Immersion became *a* conversion ritual for men and *the* conversion ritual for women. These developments are attested for the first time only in rabbinic texts.[94]

A particularly obscure point is the status of women who are said to have followed Judaism while being married to gentile husbands. Josephus mentions two such women: Fulvia the Roman matron and Helena the queen of Adiabene. Fulvia is said to have "entered [or: drawn near to] the Jewish practices," and Helena is said to have "been brought over to their (the Jews') laws." In another passage Josephus remarks that "all of their wives [in Damascus], except for a few, had gone over to the Jewish religion." Here, then, are gentile women married to gentile husbands but who are said to have adopted Jewish laws or the Jewish religion.[95] If Josephus means "conversion" (what I have called category 7), how should this be understood? There certainly is no social conversion here, and it is hard to imagine how a wife could observe the rituals of

93. Cf. Plutarch, *Moralia* 140D = *Advice to Bride and Groom* 19: "It is becoming for a wife to worship and to know only the Gods that her husband believes in." For an egregious exception see *AJ* 18.340–352.

94. Glaphyra: *AJ* 17.11 and 349–350. Herod Antipas: *AJ* 18.109. On the history of conversion of women, see Daube, *Ancient Jewish Law* chap. 1, and the conclusion of chapter 9 below.

95. Fulvia: *AJ* 18.82. Helena: *AJ* 20.35. Damascus: *BJ* 2.560.

Judaism without the consent and cooperation of her husband.[96] Perhaps Josephus simply means that the women practice some Jewish rituals (category 4) or venerate the God of the Jews (category 5) but have not actually "converted." Could a free woman convert to Judaism in a non-marital setting before the second century C.E.?[97] If the answer is yes, how should a female convert be distinguished from a female "God-fearer" or "sympathizer"? The answer is not clear.

Gentiles who expressed admiration for some aspect of Judaism (category 1) or who acknowledged the power of the God of the Jews (category 2) were acting as "normal" polytheists and would hardly have attracted any attention to themselves. Gentiles who were conspicuously friendly to Jews (category 3), who practiced the rituals of the Jews (category 4), or who venerated the God of the Jews, denying or ignoring all other gods (category 5)—these gentiles had an unusual attachment to Judaism, were sometimes called "Jews" by other gentiles, and may even have thought of themselves as "Jews" to one degree or another. Would (the) Jews too have called them "Jews"? We cannot be sure, but I would argue that the answer is no.

The Jews of antiquity in both Greek and Hebrew termed these gentiles, or at least some of them, "fearers of God" or "venerators of God" (my preferred translation of *theosebeis*), a usage attested in Josephus, Acts, rabbinic literature, and several inscriptions.[98] (The fact that *Jewish* venerators of the Jewish God could also be designated "God-venerators" merely introduces some uncertainty in the interpretation of certain inscriptions, but the basic point remains.) Three Jewish communities are known to have accorded some measure of recognition to gentile "venerators of God." The recently published inscription from Aphrodisias lists (on side A) a group that consists of eighteen people, of whom three are proselytes, two are God-venerators, and the rest (we presume)

96. Cf. 1 Cor. 7:12–16.

97. Of course, *Joseph and Asenath* is the obvious proof text: Asenath "converts" even before she marries Joseph. But Asenath's conversion is at first "theological," what I have called category 5 (hence I treated Asenath in my discussion of that category); she does not achieve social conversion until she marries Joseph. This point is not appreciated by Chesnutt, *Death to Life* 165 n. 42.

98. The terms are *theosebeis, sebomenoi ton theon, phoboumenoi ton theon,* and *yirē shamayim.* For a full collection of material see Siegert, "Gottesfürchtige"; the commentary of Reynolds and Tannenbaum, *Jews and Godfearers,* on the Aphrodisias inscription, esp. 48–66; Feldman, *Jew and Gentile* chap. 10; Levinskaya, *Book of Acts* passim, esp. 52–80 and 117–135. A comparable use of the Latin term *metuens* is poorly attested. Christians too could use the term *theosebēs;* see J. M. Lieu, "The Race of the God-Fearers," *JTS* 46 (1995) 483–501, and Ernest Diehl, *Inscriptiones Latinae Christianae Veteres* (reprint, Berlin: Weidmann, 1961) no. 2953.

are native-born Jews. The nature of the group is not clear, because the meaning of the heading of the inscription is obscure. It seems to be a charitable organization sponsored by the Jewish community, but it also declares itself to be a society of those who (if the Greek has been interpreted properly) "continually praise"; the object of their praise is not stated but is probably the God of the community. This is not a synagogue, however, but some other Jewish communal institution, and in this institution two (gentile) God-venerators have a place.[99] At Miletus a section of the municipal theater was reserved (if the inscription has been correctly interpreted) for "Jews and God-venerators."[100] An inscription from Panticapaeum (in the Bosporus) refers (if the inscription has been correctly emended) to "the synagogue of the Jews and the God-venerators."[101]

The Jewish communities of these Greek cities allowed outsiders either to join as members (to become proselytes) or to affiliate loosely (to become "God-venerators"). Such an arrangement is hardly unusual. In Rome in the first century B.C.E. the Goddess Isis exerted a powerful attraction on many poets and intellectuals who remained under her spell but did not undergo conversion.[102] Similarly, philosophical schools in antiquity won souls through "conversion" but more often attracted "hangers-on" who adopted some but not all of the tenets of the school.[103] In a public inscription a professional corporation of Ravenna at the time of Diocletian listed the members and officers of the group as well as the "affiliates" or "sympathizers."[104] But the example of Aph-

99. Reynolds and Tannenbaum, *Jews and Godfearers; SEG* 41 (1991) no. 918. On the nature of the institution, see Margaret Williams, "The Jews and Godfearers Inscription from Aphrodisias," *Historia* 41 (1992) 297–310.

100. Hildebrecht Hommel, "Juden und Christen im kaiserzeitlichen Milet," *Mitteilungen des deutschen archäologischen Instituts zu Istanbul* 25 (1975) 167–195, esp. 184–187. The exact rendering of the inscription is debated; see Reynolds and Tannenbaum, *Jews and Godfearers* 54.

101. Heinz Bellen, "*Synagoge ton Ioudaion kai theosebon:* Die Aussage einer bosporanischen Freilassungsinschrift," *Jahrbuch für Antike und Christentum* 8–9 (1965–1966) 171–176. For a different reading see Irina Levinskaya, "The Inscription from Aphrodisias and the Problem of God-Fearers," *Tyndale Bulletin* 41 (1990) 312–318 = Levinskaya, *Book of Acts* 70–80.

102. F. Solmsen, *Isis among the Greeks and Romans* (Cambridge: Harvard University Press, 1979) 83: "There is an acceptance of the cult of Isis which falls short of conversion. For want of a better name we may think of it as an emotional conquest."

103. Paul Veyne, *A History of Private Life,* vol. 1, *From Pagan Rome to Byzantium,* trans. A. Goldhammer (Cambridge, Mass.: Belknap, 1987) 225–226. For the phrase "to become a Pythagorean" (*Pythagoreios genesthai*), see Didodorus of Sicily 10.11.1.

104. Members: *ordo;* officers: *patroni, matres;* "affiliates" or "sympathizers": *amatores.* See A. Donati, *Epigraphica* 39 (1977) 27–40 = *L'année épigraphique* 1977, no. 265.

rodisias, Miletus, and Panticapaeum—if the inscriptions have been correctly emended and interpreted—hardly proves that everywhere gentile "venerators of God" were accorded recognition by local Jewish communities, much less that they could "join" the communities and become members. (Similarly, in our time "righteous gentiles," gentiles who rescued Jews during the Holocaust, have been honored by the state of Israel, but that honor does confer on them any formal standing either in the Jewish community or the Jewish state or in any Jewish synagogue.) In Aphrodisias, in Miletus, and in other cities of western Asia Minor, the Jewish communities saw themselves—and, by the second century C.E. at least, were seen by their gentile neighbors—as part of general society. These communities attracted sympathizers of all sorts and accorded them some recognition under the title "venerators of God." In the Jewish communities of other cities "God-venerators" may not have been a public title at all; it remained a private designation for righteous people, both Jewish and gentile. In yet other cities (e.g., Alexandria in the first century C.E.) the relations between the Jewish community and the general society were not nearly so open and friendly, and in these communities we may doubt whether there were any sympathizers, and whether those few who did exist attained recognition of any kind.[105]

The term "God-venerator" is primarily theological. In the eyes of the Jewish community these gentiles "venerate God," but whether they really were venerators of the God of the Jews, and whether they saw themselves as venerators of the God of the Jews, are questions that cannot be answered. The Jews of antiquity are entitled to view their friends and benefactors in any way they choose, and from their perspective any gentile well disposed toward Jews or Judaism might be called a "venerator of God" (see Philo's account of the governor Petronius, cited above under category 3), but their perspective should not determine ours. That "veneration of God" can have a nontheological reference is confirmed by analogy with the word *judaize* (*ioudaizein*), which I shall discuss at length in the next chapter. The word is best known from Paul's letter to the Galatians, where it means "to adopt the customs and/or manners of the Jews," but it also means "to give political support to the Jews, to side with the Jews." Gentiles who benefact the Jews and support them (category 3) might have been derided as "judaizers" (or Jews!) by un-

---

105. Neither Philo nor any of the Jewish works commonly ascribed to Alexandrian provenance names a specific individual who was a "God-venerator" or a proselyte. I do not discuss here the relative numbers of "God-venerators" or the role of "God-venerators" in the book of Acts.

sympathetic observers, but would have been called "venerators of God" by the Jews. Side B of the Aphrodisias inscription contains two long lists of names, the first of fifty-five people, all apparently native Jews, and the second of fifty-two persons, under the heading "and these are the God-venerators." Clearly the two God-venerating gentiles listed on side A of the inscription, in the company of three proselytes and thirteen native-born Jews, stand in much more intimate relationship with the Jewish community than do the fifty-two God-venerating gentiles of side B, who seem to be donors, and nothing more. Yet both the gentiles of side A who praise (God?) and help direct the charitable organization and the gentiles of side B who simply support it are equally called "God-venerators." There is absolutely no reason to assume that all "venerators of God" throughout the Roman empire over the course of several centuries followed a single fixed pattern of practice and belief, when there are many ways in which gentiles can express their veneration.[106]

106. Contrast the discussion of Reynolds and Tannenbaum, *Jews and Godfearers* 48–66, and the conclusion of Siegert, "Gottesfürchtige" 163. The distinction between the *theosebeis* of side A and those of side B was well observed by J. Murphy-O'Connor, "Lots of God-Fearers?" *Revue biblique* 99 (1992) 418–424, esp. 423–424.

CHAPTER 6

Ioudaïzein, "to Judaize"

*Wie man heutigen Tages im Deutschen für beschneiden
"jüdschen" oder "jüdischen" sagen hört.*
Bar Amithai, *Ueber die Beschneidung in historischer und
dogmatischer Hinsicht*

The verb *ioudaïzein,* "to judaize," consists of two elements: the noun stem *iouda-* and the verb stem *-izein.* The verb then is of the same class as *mēdizein,* "to medize," *attikizein,* "to atticize," and numerous other such verbs that are securely attested in classical, non-Jewish, non-Christian Greek. I shall first study this verb family as a whole and then turn to the specific meanings of *ioudaïzein.*[1]

The *-izein* Verb Family

Verbs in the *-izein* family have three basic meanings: (a) to give political support (a political meaning); (b) to adopt customs or

The epigraph is from Bar Amithai, *Ueber die Beschneidung in historischer und dogmatischer Hinsicht* (Frankfurt: Hermann, 1843) 12

1. There have been many studies of Christian "judaizing," but I know of no previous study of the word *ioudaïzein* in antiquity. On the word in European languages in the Middle Ages and Renaissance, see Newman, *Jewish Influence* 1–4, and esp. Dán, "'Judaizare.'" I was aided immeasurably in identifying *-izein* verbs by Paul Kretschmer and

manners (a cultural meaning); (c) to speak a language (a linguistic meaning).[2]

    a. *To give political support.* Thus "to medize" (*mēdizein*), perhaps the oldest of these verbs,[3] means to give political support to the Medes or Persians—that is, to side with the Medes (and "Medism," *mēdismos,* denotes political support for the Medes). Similarly, "to arcadize" (*arkadizein*) means to side with the Arcadians, "to cappadocize" (*kappadokizein*) means to side with the Cappadocians, "to orchomenize" (*orkhomenizein*) means to side with the Orchomenians, and "to arabize" (*arabizein*) means to side with the Arabs.[4]

    b. *To adopt customs or manners.* Thus "to phoenicize" (*phoinikizein*) denotes the adoption of the customs and manners of the Phoenicians—in this case, "unnatural vice."[5] Similarly, "to cilicize" (*kilikizein* and *enkilikizein*) means to adopt the manners of the Cilicians—that is, to be cruel and treacherous[6] or to cheat someone; "to sicelize" (*sikelizein, katasikelizein*) means to adopt the manners of the Sicilians—that is, to dance or play the rogue; "to chalcidize" (*khalkidizein*) means to adopt the manners of the Chalcidians—that is, to engage in pederasty or parsimony; "to lesbize" (*lesbizein* or *lesbiazein*) means to adopt the manners of Lesbos—that is, to perform fellatio;[7] "to bergaïze" (*bergaizein*) means to adopt the manners of the people of Berga in Thrace—that is, to tell tall tales; "to sybarize" (*subarizein* or *subriazein*) means to adopt the manners of the people of Sybaris—that is, to live a luxuriant life.[8]

Ernst Locker, *Rückläufiges Wörterbuch der griechischen Sprache* (Göttingen: Vandenhoeck & Ruprecht, 1944; reprint, 1963) 607–623. I am certain that I have missed several verbs and I intentionally ignore most compound forms, but I hope that I have cited enough for illustrative purposes.

    2. In this section I rely heavily on LSJ. In the notes I cite either the earliest or the most important source for the indicated meaning. References that consist solely of the name of an author or authors are cited on the authority of LSJ; references that are given in full have been checked and verified by me. Thus "Xenophon" means that LSJ lists Xenophon as the earliest or most important source for the indicated meaning; "Xenophon, *Hellenica* 4.1.1" means that Xenophon is the earliest or most important source for the indicated meaning and that I have verified the reference.

    3. *Mēdizein* and *mēdismos* are the models for *attikizein* and *attikismos* in Thucydides 3.62 and 64.

    4. *Mēdizein:* Herodotus; *arkadizein:* Polyaenus; *kappadokizein:* Appian; *orkhomenizein:* Hellanicus; *arabizein:* Suda.

    5. "Unnatural vice" is the translation of LSJ. The verb means "to mouth the vaginal or anal orifice"; see Jocelyn, "*Laikazein*" 18.

    6. *Kilikismos* means "drunken butchery" (Theopompus).

    7. "Lesbianism" in antiquity means the mouthing of the penis, not the erotic interplay of two women. See Jocelyn, "*Laikazein*" 18 n. 66 and 31–34.

    8. *Phoinikizein:* Lucian; *kilikizein:* Eustathius, Old Comedy; *kilikizein:* Theophrastus,

c. *To speak a language.* Thus "to syrize" (*surizein*) means to speak Syrian, "to thracize" (*thrakizein*) means to speak Thracian, and "to illyrize" (*illurizein*) means to speak Illyrian. The linguistic meaning is also paramount in the verb "to hellenize" (*hellēnizein*), whose original meaning is "to speak Greek" or "to speak Greek correctly," in contrast with "to barbarize" (*barbarizein*), to speak a non-Greek language or to speak Greek incorrectly.[9] (Similarly "Hellenism," *hellēnismos,* means pure Greek style, a term used by Greek grammarians, in contrast with "barbarism," *barbarismos.*)

b. and c. Some verbs have both a cultural and a linguistic meaning: "to scythize" (*skuthizein*), to talk Scythian or to drink immoderately or to shave the head; "to thessalize" (*thessalizein*), to speak Thessalian or adopt the customs of the Thessalians; "to egyptize" (*aiguptiazein*), to speak Egyptian or to adopt the manners of the Egyptians— that is, to be sly and crafty;[10] "to cretize" (*krētizein*), to speak like a Cretan or adopt the manner of the Cretans—that is, to lie;[11] "to lydize" (*ludizein*), speak Lydian or to adopt the manners of the Lydians; "to dorize" (*dōrizein* or *dōriazein*), to speak Doric Greek or to dress like a Dorian; "to chaldaize" (*khaldaïzein*), to speak Chaldean or to adopt the manner of the Chaldees—that is, to believe in astrology.[12]

a. and b.; a. and c. Some verbs combine a political meaning with a cultural or linguistic one. Thus "to laconize" (*lakōnizein*) denotes either to side with the Spartans or to adopt the customs of the Spartans, notably paederasty; "to boeotize" (*boiōtizein* or *boiōtiazein*) denotes either to side with the Boeotians or to speak Boeotian; "to atticize" (*attikizein*) (like the noun *attikismos,* "Atticism") de-

---

Old Comedy; *khalkidizein:* Hesychius, comedy; *lesbizein:* Aristophanes; *bergaïzein:* Strabo; *subarizein:* Aristophanes.

9. *Surizein:* Sextus Empiricus, Lucian; *thrakizein:* a grammarian of the second century C.E.; *illurizein:* Stephanus of Byzantium; *hellēnizein:* Plato, Aristotle; *barbarizein:* Herodotus, Plato. Goudriaan, *Ethnicity* 92 n. 6, argues that in P. Col. Zen. 66 (256–255 B.C.E.) *hellēnizein* probably means "to speak Greek" rather than "to act like a Greek." Cf. *graikizein,* "to speak Greek" (a grammarian of the second century C.E.). Hesychius glosses *akhaïzein* with *hellēnizein,* but I do not know what this means. In addition to its linguistic meaning, *barbarizein* can also mean "to side with the barbarians, that is, the Persians" (Xenophon).

10. Cf. too *aiguptiasmos,* imitation of the Egyptians (Eustathius).

11. And *ktrētismos* means "Cretan behavior"—that is, lying (Plutarch).

12. *Skuthizein:* Himerius, Hieronymus Rhodius, Euripides. *Thessalizein:* Parthenius, Dio Chrysostom, Aelian. *Aiguptiazein:* Lucian, Old Comedy. *Krētizein:* Dio Chrysostom, Polybius, Plutarch. *Ludizein:* Hipponax, Aristophanes. *Dōrizein* or *dōriazein:* Theocritus, Anacreontea. *Khaldaïzein:* Philo, *De Somniis* 1.161 (speak Chaldean), *De Mutatione Nominum* 16; *De Migratione* 184; *Quis rerum heres* 99; *De Abrahamo* 70 and 77 (believe in astrology); as far as I know, the verb occurs only in Philo (see Wong, "Philo's Use of *Chaldaioi*").

notes either to side with the Athenians or to speak Attic Greek;[13]
"to macedonize" (*makedonizein*) denotes either to side with
the Macedonians or to speak Macedonian; and "to romize" (*hrōmaïzein*) denotes either to side with the Romans or to speak
Latin.[14]

In all these verbs the noun stem is the name of a region or an *ethnos*.
By the fourth century B.C.E. the noun stem of the verb could even be
the name of an individual: "to pythagorize" (*pythagorizein*), to be a disciple of Pythagoras; "to aristotelize" (*aristotelizein*), to follow or imitate
Aristotle; "to demosthenize" (*dēmosthenizein*), to imitate Demosthenes; "to sisyphize" (*sisuphizein*), to act like Sisyphus—that is, be sly and
unscrupulous; "to homerize" (*homērizein*), to imitate Homer; "to athe-
nize" (*athēnaïzein*), to be as wise as Athena; "to sinopize" (*sinopizein*),
to behave like the courtesan Sinope. These verbs have, of course, a cultural meaning, but verbs of this formation could also be used with a
political meaning: "to philippize" (*philippizein*), to side with Philip of
Macedon (cf. "Philippism," *philippismos*); "to seleucize" (*seleukizein*),
to side with Seleucus; and "to hannibize" (*annibizein*), to side with
Hannibal.[15]

When describing political or cultural behavior, the verbs generally
have as their subjects people from whom such behavior would not be
expected: Medes do not medize, Greeks do. Spartans do not lakonize,
non-Spartans do.[16] The verbs refer not to a change of essence but to
a change of behavior, not "to be" but "to be like." *Mēdizein* means
neither "to be a Mede" nor "to become a Mede," but "to act like a
Mede."[17] However, when describing linguistic behavior, the verbs can
have as their subjects either outsiders or members of the *ethnos* to which
the verb refers. *Hellēnizein,* "to speak Greek," is regularly used to describe the speech of either Hellenes or non-Hellenes. Similarly, *make-*

13. For the linguistic meaning cf. too *enattikizein, exattikizein, hupattikizein,* and
huperattikizein.

14. *Lakōnizein:* Xenophon, Plato, Demosthenes, Aristophanes; *boiōtizein* or *boiōtiazein:* Xenophon, Aeschines; *attikizein:* Thucydides, three comedians of fifth and fourth
centuries B.C.E.; *makedonizein:* Polybius, Plutarch; *hrōmaïzein:* Appian; *megarizein* in
Aristophanes can be construed with either a political ("to side with the Megarians") or
linguistic ("to speak the dialect of Megara") meaning.

15. *Pythagorizein:* Antiphon; *aristotelizein:* Strabo; *dēmosthenizein:* Plutarch; *sisuphizein:* Phrynichus; *homērizein:* Libanius; *athēnaïzein:* Eustathius; *sinopizein:* Hesychius;
philippizein: Demosthenes, Aeschines; *seleukizein:* Polyaenus; *annibizein:* Plutarch.

16. Plato, *Protagoras* 342b–c; Xenophon, *Hellenica* 4.8.18; Demosthenes 54.34.

17. Similarly, the verb *gunaikizein* means "to act like a woman," not "to be a woman."

donizein, "to speak Macedonian," can be used to describe the speech of either Macedonians or non-Macedonians. Anyone who speaks Latin can be the subject of *hrōmaïzein.*[18]

On the whole, when these verbs bear a cultural meaning, they have a negative valence. Since they describe behavior that is unexpected or paradoxical, they have a nasty or a comic edge; they frequently appear in comedy.[19] The grammarian Suetonius (better known as the biographer of the first Caesars), in his book *On Insults,* writes that "insults in the form of verbs have been made from the names of nations (*ethnē*), cities, and demes. From the names of nations: for example, *kilikizein* . . . *aiguptiazein* . . . *krētizein.* From the names of cities: for example, *lesbiazein* . . ."[20] Verbs of this sort are insulting, or at least funny. When bearing a political meaning, these verbs, occasionally at least, can also have negative valence: *mēdizein* is clearly an abusive term. In contrast, when bearing a linguistic meaning, these verbs seem to be entirely neutral. An exception to this pattern is the verb *hellēnizein.* From the Greek perspective, it was a good thing for barbarians not only to speak Greek but also to adopt the customs and manners of the Greeks. Philo expresses the Greek viewpoint when he fulsomely praises the emperor Caligula for "hellenizing" (here a transitive verb, *aphellēnizein*) the most important parts of the barbarian world. For other Jews, however, "Hellenism" and "to hellenize" were not positive attributes but negative.[21]

The Meanings of *Ioudaïzein*

Now I turn to *ioudaïzein.* By analogy with the other *-izein* verbs, *ioudaïzein* ought to have three basic meanings: (1) a political meaning, "to give political support to the Judaeans"—that is, to side with them (and "Judaism," *Ioudaïsmos,* ought then to denote this po-

18. *Hellēnizein,* of Hellenes: Plato, *Charmides* 159a, *Protagoras* 328a; Aristotle; of non-Hellenes: Plato, *Meno* 82b referring to a house-born slave, *hellēn men esti kai hellēnizei;* Aeschines 3.172. *makedonizein,* of Macedonians: Plutarch, *Antonius* 27; of non-Macedonians: Athenaeus 3.122a (of Attic writers who use Macedonian words). *Hrōmaïzein:* Appian, *Hannibalic War* 41; Philostratus, *Life of Apollonius* 5.36.

19. Similarly, in Latin *graecissare, graecari,* and *pergraecari* all appear in Plautus.

20. Jean Taillardat, *Suétone Peri Blasphēmiōn, Peri Paidiōn: Extraits byzantins* (Paris: Les Belles Lettres, 1967) 62–63.

21. Philo, *Legatio* 147; on the Jewish reaction to Hellenism, see chapter 4 above.

litical support); (2) a cultural meaning, "to adopt any of the distinctive customs and manners of the Judaeans"; and (3) a linguistic meaning, "to speak the language of the Judaeans." These are the meanings that the word *ought* to have, but the attested meanings are somewhat different, perhaps because the word is so seldom used by non-Christian authors. In Christian texts *ioudaïzein* almost always has a cultural meaning, and the customs and manners to which the verb refers derive from the "religious" sphere. The word appears only five times in non-Christian texts; four of these five passages can be satisfactorily construed with either the political or the cultural meaning. The political meaning combined with the cultural is attested in at least one Christian text, but is nowhere attested unambiguously by itself.[22] The linguistic meaning is never attested, whether ambiguously or not; when Josephus wished to say "to speak Hebrew," he used the verb *hebraïzein*.[23] I shall now survey the meanings of *ioudaïzein* in classical, Jewish, and Christian Greek.

IOUDAÏZEIN IN CLASSICAL GREEK

The word *ioudaïzein* appears only once in classical (i.e., non-Jewish non-Christian) Greek.[24] In his *Life of Cicero* Plutarch tells the following anecdote:

Verres is the Roman word for a castrated porker; when, accordingly, a freedman named Caecilius, who was subject to judaizing, wanted to thrust aside the Sicilian accusers and denounce Verres himself, Cicero said, "What has a Jew to do with a *Verres?*"[25]

Because Caecilius was "subject to judaizing," a mode of behavior of which Plutarch clearly disapproves,[26] Cicero could call him a *Ioudaios*, a

22. Similarly, the noun *ioudaïsmos* is never used with a political meaning.

23. *BJ* 6.96; Thackeray ad loc. in the Loeb edition astutely compares Acts 21:40 and 22:2. *Yehudit* in 2 Kings 18:26 is translated by the LXX as *ioudaïsti;* but *ioudaizein* does not mean "to speak Hebrew."

24. It may appear twice if Eusebius is accurately citing Alexander Polyhistor; see below.

25. *Life of Cicero* 7.6 = M. Stern, *Authors,* no. 263.

26. Perrin in the Loeb edition, followed by M. Stern, translates *enokhos tōi ioudaïzein* "suspected of Jewish practices," but this translation is wrong because *enokhos* does not mean "suspected." Plutarch commonly uses *enokhos* with the dative to describe people who are subject to a certain influence, usually an influence of which Plutarch disapproves (subject to love/lust: *Cimon* 4.9, *Galba* 12.1, *Agesilaus* 20.6; subject to vice: 542D, 965E; "subject to Orphic rites," *Alexander* 2.7; subject to epilepsy, *Caesar* 17.2; subject to pollution, *Pericles* 33.1). Presumably here too *enokhos* suggests that Plutarch does not approve of judaizing. The other standard meaning is "guilty" or "guilty of" something (70E,

Jew. The joke assumes that everyone knows that a *Ioudaios* has nothing to do with a pig, but what precisely is meant by *ioudaïzein*? Not clear. It might mean, and has usually been taken to mean, "to observe Jewish practices," including, we may presume, the abstention from pork: Caecilius judaized by abstaining from pork and Cicero mocks him as a Jew associating with a pig. To an outsider, especially an abusive outsider, anyone who observes, or can be thought to observe, Jewish practices can be called a judaizer or a Jew.[27] There is nothing wrong with this interpretation, but the verb could just as easily mean "to side with the Jews in their political struggles in Rome." Cicero himself (i.e., the real Cicero) attacks the Jews of Rome because of their (alleged) political power,[28] and *ioudaïzein* would make sense here as a political term. The joke also becomes sharper if Caecilius is someone who does not actually abstain from pork or observe Jewish practices: because of his association with Jews and support for them ("judaizing"), Caecilius can be called a Jew by his opponent and be mocked as possessing all the Jewish peculiarities. Thus I prefer the political meaning here, but the cultural meaning is certainly possible. The passage remains ambiguous.

IOUDAÏZEIN IN JEWISH GREEK

In Jewish Greek the word *ioudaïzein* appears only four times. The first instance is the Greek version of Esther 8:17. Here is the Hebrew text as translated in the New Jewish Version:

And in every province and in every city, when the king's command and decree arrived, there was gladness and joy among the Jews, a feast and a holiday. And many of the people of the land professed to be Jews, for the fear of the Jews had fallen upon them.

"Professed to be Jews" translates the Hebrew *mityahadim*. The simple meaning of the Hebrew (and, I think, of this English translation) is not that many non-Jews converted to Judaism but that they pretended to be Jews: they professed themselves to be something they were not. They did so because they feared for their lives; the Jews had just been given carte blanche by the king to kill their enemies, and therefore many gentiles pretended to be Jews in order to protect themselves. The Greek

---

632A, and 1117F). I identified these (and other) passages with the assistance of the *Thesaurus Linguae Graecae* database.

27. See chapter 5 above.

28. M. Stern, *Authors* no. 68.

translation of the crucial verb is *perietemonto kai ioudaïzon,* "they were circumcised and judaized." Many scholars have understood this to mean "they were circumcised and became Jews"—that is, converted to Judaism[29]—but this cannot be right, because, as I discussed above, *-izein* verbs indicate a change in behavior ("to be like"), not a change in essence ("to be"). *Ioudaïzein* with the meaning "convert to Judaism" is securely attested only in Christian authors (see below) and would seem to be impossible in a text of the second or first century B.C.E. Surely the Greek means that the gentiles either sided with the Jews (a political meaning) or adopted Jewish customs and manners (a cultural meaning). The presence of "they were circumcised" suggests that the cultural meaning is intended (the gentiles had themselves circumcised and observed various other Jewish customs and manners, all in order to show their affinity with the Jews),[30] but the political meaning can hardly be excluded (the gentiles had themselves circumcised, to show their affinity with the Jews, and judaized, supporting the Jews against their enemies).

Paul uses the verb in Galatians 2:14 in his attack on Peter: "If you, although a Jew (*Ioudaios*), live in the gentile manner and not Jewishly (*ethnikōs kai oukh ioudaïkōs*), how can you compel gentiles to judaize?" The structure of the sentence makes clear that "to judaize" here means "to live Jewishly," to follow the customs and manners of the Jews. (Similarly, *ioudaïsmos* in Galatians 1:13–14 means the observance of Jewish traditions.) The context suggests that no specific customs and manners are intended; Paul's attack is provoked by Peter's refusal to dine with gentiles, not by any overt attempt to force gentiles to observe Jewish laws. The verb seems to be used in a general sense: when gentiles adopt any distinctively Jewish customs and manners, they judaize. As I shall discuss below, this usage recurs frequently in later Christian writers.

Josephus uses *ioudaïzein* in two passages in close proximity in the

29. "They were circumcised and became Jews" is W. Lee Humphreys' translation in *The Harper Collins Study Bible* (New York: Harper Collins, 1993) 1494. For similar interpretations see E. A. Sophocles, *Greek Lexicon of the Roman and Byzantine Periods* (Boston: Little, Brown, 1870; frequently reprinted) 601; W. Gutbrod, *Theological Dictionary of the New Testament,* 10 vols. (Grand Rapids, Mich.: Eerdmans, 1964–1976) 3.383 ("Outside the NT *ioudaizein* implies conversion to Judaism, especially by circumcision"); Martin Hengel, *Jews, Greeks, and Barbarians* (Philadelphia: Fortress, 1980) 78; Feldman, *Jew and Gentile* 289 and 337 (contrast 343); and many others. This interpretation of the Greek has influenced the interpretation of the Hebrew; the Revised English Bible translates both the Hebrew and the Greek as "professed Judaism." The Lucianic version of the Greek, followed by Josephus, *AJ* 11.285, omits *kai ioudaizon:* the gentiles simply were circumcised.

30. Indeed, perhaps the Greek translators added "they were circumcised" precisely because of the ambiguity of the verb *ioudaïzein.*

Jewish War. In the fall of 66 C.E. the Roman garrison in Jerusalem was massacred by the revolutionaries, but the commander Metilius tried to save his life by promising "to judaize as far as circumcision" (*mekhri peritomēs ioudaïsein huposkhomenon*).[31] This passage is similar to the passage from Greek Esther: in both cases gentiles (or a gentile) circumcise and judaize in order to save themselves from death at the hands of Jews. The same ambiguity that obtains in the Greek Esther passage obtains here as well, except that here the linkage between the circumcision and the judaizing is expressed not by "and" but by "as far as." Metilius realized that "judaizing" was a broad concept, and was willing to go "as far as" circumcision in order to save himself. The meaning "to become a Jew" would fit nicely here: there are many ways of becoming a Jew, and many degrees to which one can become a Jew (see chapter 5), and Metilius promises to observe circumcision, an act that for Josephus (as for Paul and for many others in antiquity) is equivalent to observing the Jewish way of life in general.[32] This rendering certainly fits Josephus' words and conceptions, but can *ioudaïzein* mean "to become a Jew"? As I indicated above, I think the answer is no; such a meaning for the verb is unexpected and not yet attested in the time of Josephus.

We are left then with the same ambiguity that obtains in the Greek Esther: like the gentiles of the Persian empire, Metilius is promising either to side with the Jews (a political meaning) or to adopt Jewish customs and manners (a cultural meaning). The presence of "as far as circumcision" seems to suggest that the cultural meaning is intended (Metilius promises to adopt Jewish customs and manners, even circumcision, in order to be spared), and, if this is correct, Metilius is offering the functional equivalent of conversion: he promises to behave like a Jew in all respects, even circumcision. The political meaning, however, can hardly be excluded; I would argue that it is preferable. Metilius promises to defect from the Romans and to join the Jews, and as a sign of his change of politics he declares that he is prepared to go as far as circumcision. The political reading is perhaps supported by Josephus' use of the verb *hrōmaïzein* a few pages subsequently: the rebels "partly by force, partly by persuasion, brought over to their side those who were still romanizing" (*hoi eti hrōmaïzontes*).[33] Here the political meaning is unmistakable. Dio Cassius reports that during the siege of Jerusalem in

---

31. *BJ* 2.454.

32. For Josephus "to adopt the customs of the Jews" and "to be circumcised" are synonymous expressions. See chapter 5 above, note 51.

33. *BJ* 2.562.

70 C.E., some Roman soldiers went over to the Jewish side and were received kindly by the Jews.[34] Dio did not use the verb "judaize" to describe this activity, but no doubt he could have done so. Defection from the Romans to the Jews is "judaizing," and this is what Metilius did to save his life.[35]

The next instance of *ioudaïzein* occurs in Josephus' description of the troubles in Syria just before the outbreak of the war:

Frightful disorder took hold of the whole of Syria; every city was divided into two camps, and the safety of one party lay in their anticipating the other. They (the inhabitants of the cities of Syria) passed their days in blood, their nights, yet more dreadful, in terror. For, though believing that they had rid themselves of the Jews, they kept the judaizers under suspicion. And no one dared to kill offhand the ambiguous element in their midst, and it was feared as if it were truly foreign, although it was mixed.[36]

The cities of Syria were divided into two camps, Syrians versus Jews (*Ioudaioi*). The Syrians killed whatever Jews they could.[37] But on the boundary between the Syrians and the Jews were some liminal groups that the Syrians did not know how to treat. Josephus seems to say that there were two such liminal groups: the "judaizers," and the "ambiguous element" (*to par' ekastois amphibolon*).[38] The latter group was feared because it was "mixed" (*memigmenon*)—that is, of mixed ancestry,

34. Dio Cassius 66.5.4 = M. Stern, *Authors* no. 430. Similarly, Dio reports (69.13.2 = M. Stern, *Authors* no. 440) that in the war of 132–135 many foreigners joined the Jews "through eagerness for gain"; again, conversion to Judaism is not relevant here.

35. The conversion of Metilius to Judaism resembles the conversion of Russian soldiers to Islam upon capture by the Islamic rebels in Afghanistan; see "A Displaced Russian Has New Faith but No Home," *New York Times,* February 18, 1997, p. A4.

36. *BJ* 2.462–3. The translation is mine, based on that of Henry St. John Thackeray in the Loeb Classical Library.

37. *BJ* 2.461.

38. In "Respect for Judaism," I followed Thackeray's rendering of the passage and argued that the three terms *hoi ioudaizontes, to amphibolon,* and *(to)memigmenon* synonymously designated one group. In "The Gentiles" 1.316–317 n. 161, Morton Smith (correctly) rejects my rendering and instead (incorrectly) suggests that the passage refers to three separate groups. I think that this rendering is unlikely because the absence of the definite article before *memigmenon* implies that it modifies *amphibolon* and is not a new subject. Cf. the translation of Otto Michel and Otto Bauernfeind, *Flavius Josephus De Bello Judaico,* 4 vols. (Munich: Kösel, 1959; reprint 1982), 1.275: "man mochte zwar die nach beiden Seiten hinzweifelhafte Gruppe nicht ohne Weiteres umbringen, fürchtete sie aber doch auf Grund ihrer Verbindung mit den Juden, als seien sie wirklich Feinde." I now think that the passage refers not to one group or three groups but to two groups: the judaizers, and the ambiguous/mixed element. Morton Smith, *Palestinian Parties and Politics That Shaped the Old Testament* (New York: Columbia University Press, 1971) 239 n. 33, correctly objects to Thackeray's translation of *memigmenon* as "neutral."

people who would have been called *migades* by Polybius, *mixti* by Livy,[39] and *Mischlinge* by the Nazis. The "judaizers" may have been those who sided with the Jews in their political struggles or those who adopted Jewish customs and manners; on either account they were suspected, presumably of collaboration with the Jews, but were not killed. In support of the political interpretation is the thrust of the passage and, again, the use of "romanizers" a few pages subsequently. In support of the cultural interpretation is the story of the Jews of Damascus: the people of Damascus planned to massacre the Jews of the city but had to keep their plans secret because "all of their wives, except for a few, had gone over [or: were subject] to the Jewish religion" (*upēgmenas tēi Ioudaikēi thrēskeiai*). This would seem to be a good illustration of "judaizing."[40]

In sum: Paul's letter to the Galatians is the only text in Jewish Greek to use the verb *ioudaïzein* unambiguously in its cultural sense: to adopt the customs and manners of the Jews. Greek Esther uses the word once, and Josephus use it twice, and in all three instances the meaning of the word is ambiguous; most scholars have construed these passages with the cultural meaning, but in the two Josephan passages the political meaning seems preferable.

IOUDAÏZEIN IN CHRISTIAN GREEK

The word *ioudaïzein* appears more than eighty times in Christian Greek (and as a loan word in Christian Latin).[41] Christian Greek is rich in *-izein* verbs, with a whole series of neologisms: to pharisaize, to mosaize, to manichaize, to sabellize, to areianize, to sabellianize, to paulianize, to nestorianize, to christianize, to maronize, to pla-

---

39. Polybius 34.14.5 (Alexandrians are *migades*); Livy 38.17.9, referring to Gauls: *hi iam degeneres sunt, mixti.*

40. *BJ* 2.560. At Antioch too, Josephus says (*BJ* 7.45), the Jews "always drew to their religious ceremonies a great multitude of Greeks whom they made in some way a part of themselves" (*aei te prosagomenoi tais thrēskeiais polu plēthon Hellēnōn, kakeinous tropōi tini moiran autōn pepoiēnto*).

41. A computer search of the database of the Thesaurus Linguae Graecae CD-ROM #D (using TLG Workplace by Silver Mountain Software) yields eighty-five occurrences of the root *ioudaiz-* in Greek Christian literature from the first century to the fifth. This number does not include the various conjugated forms that contain *ioudais-*, passages not included in the TLG corpus (e.g., Canons of Laodicea 29), and Latin translations of lost Greek originals (e.g., Origen, *Commentariorum Serie*s on Matthew). In Latin *iudaizare* is used by Jerome, Augustine, Ambrosiaster, and Commodian. In this chapter I do not discuss all eighty-five-plus occurrences of the term; I discuss the entire range of meanings of the term, but I cite only representative passages.

tonize, to apolinarize, to epicurize, to samaretize, to philonize.[42] In all these Christian coinages the noun stem is the name of a teacher, usually pagan or heretical, or of a sect.[43] For Christian writers apparently the political meaning of the *-izein* verbs was in decline; the cultural meaning was dominant.

In Christian Greek *ioudaïzein* almost always has its cultural meaning: (a) to adopt the customs and manners of the Jews.[44] But within this definitional framework Christians invested the word with new meanings, new overtones, and a new specificity not previously attested. The specifically Christian meanings, in the order of their first attestation, are: (b) to be Jewish or to become Jewish; (c) to interpret the Old Testament "literally"; (d) to deny the divinity of Christ. In addition, in one passage *ioudaïzein* combines the "cultural" meaning with the political: (e) to give support to the Jews by adopting their customs and manners. Of course, there are also several passages in which the exact meaning of the word is not clear, and in any number of passages *ioudaïzein* is used with several meanings simultaneously, but all in all I think this fivefold distinction is useful.

a. *To adopt the customs and manners of the Jews.* Many Christian writers (e.g., Origen and Eusebius) use *ioudaïzein* as Paul did, in the general sense "to adopt the customs and manners of the Jews."[45] *Ioudaïzein* and its forms appear in the works of John Chrysostom at least thirty-six times. Thirty-three of these references occur in Chrysostom's commen-

42. *Pharisaïzein, mosaïzein, manichaïzein, sabellizein, areianizein, sabellianizein, paulianizein, nestorianizein, khristianizein, maronizein, platonizein, apolinarizein, epikourizein, samareitizein, philonizein.* I was aided immeasurably in identifying these verbs by Johannes B. Bauer and Anneliese Felber, *A Reverse Index of Patristic Greek* (Graz: Institut für Ökumenische Theologie und Patrologie an der Universität Graz, 1983) 176–180 (a list of words starred in *PGL*—that is, words not found in LSJ). *Philonizein* is attested for the first time in Suda (and therefore is listed in LSJ, not *PGL*), but it too, we may presume, is a Christian coinage.

43. These verbs are modeled on *pythagorizein. Mosaïzein* in *PGL* means "to speak like Moses," in contrast with *platonizein*, "to speak like Plato." On *khristianizein*, see below note 60.

44. *PGL*, s.v. "*ioudaïzein*," offers the following: "1. embrace, practice Judaism; 2. imitate the Jews; a. of Christians who observe Sabbath; b. of heretics who deny divinity of Christ; c. of those who will not go beyond letter of scripture." None of these definitions is incorrect, but the distinction between no. 1 and no. 2 is not clearly drawn, and many of the passages cited under no. 1 do not belong there.

45. Origen: E. Preuschen, ed., *Origenes: Der Johanneskommentar* (GCS IV; 1903) pp. 490 and 565 (commentary on John 1:13); Max Rauer, ed., *Die Homilien zu Lukas* (GCS IX; 1959) p. 298 (homily on Luke 10:38); Erich Klostermann, ed., *Matthäuserklärung* (GCS X, no. 1; 1935) p. 76 (on this passage see below). In his commentary on John liber 32:5 Origen quotes Gal. 2:4. Eusebius: Euseb., *Demonstratio Evangelica* 1.7 and 2.3.

taries and homilies on Galatians, Romans, Acts, and 1 Timothy,[46] and, unless I am mistaken, in all of these references the word has its general Pauline meaning.[47] In a passage in the *Acts of Pilate,* the Roman governor tells the Jews: "You know that my wife venerates God [or: is a God-venerator, *theosebēs estin*] and even judaizes [or: and judaizes rather much] with you." This ambiguous utterance apparently means that Mrs. Pilate as a consequence of her piety joins the Jews in the observance of Jewish customs and manners.[48]

In some texts *ioudaïzein* refers to specific Jewish customs and manners, and these almost always are well-known rituals of the "Old Testament." Ignatius is the first Christian author after Paul to use *ioudaïzein.* Just as in Paul "to judaize" parallels "to live Jewishly," in Ignatius it parallels "to live according to Judaism." The Ignatian use of the verb has been taken to refer to Jewish life in general, but the context suggests that the slighting of the Lord's Day (Sunday) in favor of the Sabbath is the specific issue at hand.[49] (Similarly, canon 29 of the Council of Laodicea prohibits Christians from "judaizing and resting on the Sabbath.")[50] In a work ascribed to Basil the verb refers to the observance of Jewish food taboos.[51] The verb appears three times in the *Against the Jews* (or *Against the Judaizing Christians*) of John Chrysostom. In one passage it refers to Christians who observe the (biblical) Jewish feasts and fasts.[52] Sabbath, food laws, feasts and fasts: the conspicuous Jewish observance of these rituals (and, of course, circumcision) gave Christians the impression that Judaism is synonymous with the Old Testament, and that Jews follow the injunctions of the Old Testament "liter-

46. One occurs in *De Sacerdotio* in a discussion of Galatians 2.

47. Similarly the verb appears in many patristic commentaries on, and discussions of, Galatians 2 and Acts (e.g., Ambrosiaster, Jerome, Augustine). See appendix D below.

48. *Kai mallon ioudaïzei sun humin;* the exact force of *sun humin* eludes me. Schneemelcher, *New Testament Apocrypha* 1.507, translates: "You know that my wife fears God and favours rather the customs of the Jews, with you."

49. Ignatius, Letter to the Magnesians 10:3 and 8:1. Magnesians 9 implies that Sabbath observance is the issue. In his commentary on Magnesians 9, William R. Schoedel considers and rejects this inference; see Schoedel, *Ignatius of Antioch: A Commentary* (Philadelphia: Fortress, 1985) 123. Our earliest commentator on Ignatius, however, the author of the so-called long recension, understood Magnesians 9 as a reference to the specifics of Sabbath observance; see Joseph B. Lightfoot, ed., *The Apostolic Fathers: Clement, Ignatius, Polycarp,* pt. 2, vol. 3 (London: Macmillan, 1889–1890; reprint, Peabody, Mass.: Hendrickson, 1989) 173.

50. Mansi, *Sacrorum Conciliorum etc.* (1759; reprint, 1901) 2:570. Cf. *sabbatizein,* which can be positive ("to observe the Christian Sabbath") or negative ("to observe the Jewish Sabbath"); see *PGL* s.v.

51. [Basil], *Constitutiones Asceticae, PG* 31:1416,3.

52. *PG* 48:934,56.

ally" (see below). A follower of Marcion would use the term "Judaist" (*ioudaïstēs,* a synonym for "judaizer") to smear anyone who believed that Jesus came to fulfill the law (the "Old Testament") and not to destroy it.[53]

In one of its occurrences in the *Against the Jews* of John Chrysostom, *ioudaïzein* refers to Christians who attend or venerate the synagogue of the Jews.[54] Here is something remarkable, the association of *ioudaïzein* with a nonscriptural practice (synagogal attendance and prayer are nowhere mentioned in the "Old Testament"). Thus John has expanded the meaning of the word from "to practice the rituals of the Old Testament" to "to practice the rituals of the Jews," a natural progression that would continue into the Middle Ages.

b. *To be Jewish or to become Jewish.* Clement of Alexandria, in order to rebut the argument that Christian sectarianism is evidence of Christian mendacity and falsehood, argues that Jews and philosophers too have many schools ("heresies"), "and you do not say that, as a result of the discord of your schools with each other, one should hesitate to be a philosopher or to be a Jew."[55] In his commentary on Matthew 23:15 Origen writes (the commentary is extant only in Latin translation) that the Pharisees and scribes "go about many places in the world in order to persuade aliens to judaize." According to Origen, Matthew's "to make a proselyte" means "to make aliens (*advenae;* lit., "foreigners, strangers," a translation of *prosēlytoi*) judaize"—that is, become Jews.[56] In his paraphrase of the poem of Theodotus, Eusebius (or is it Alexander Polyhistor?) writes that Jacob told Shechem and Hamor that he would not give Dinah in marriage to Shechem unless all the inhabitants of Shechem would "be circumcised and judaize" (*peritemnomenous iou-*

53. Adamantius, Dialogue 2.15 (ed. W. H. van de Sande Bakhuyzen, GCS 1901, p. 88 bottom). This is a fourth-century text. The Marcionite spokesman holds that our text of Matt. 5:17 is the work of a "Judaist" and that the correct text should read: "I have come not to fulfill the law but to destroy it." See Hans Dieter Betz, *The Sermon on the Mount: A Commentary* (Minneapolis: Fortress, 1995) 175–176. (*PGL,* s.v. "*Ioudaïstēs,*" incorrectly says "of Marcionites"; the term is used by a Marcionite to describe non-Marcionite Christians.)

54. *PG* 48:916,10.

55. *Oknein ētoi philosophein ē ioudaïzein* (Clement, *Stromateis* 7.15.89). Hort and Mayor translate "you do not say that one should hesitate to be a philosopher or a follower of the Jews," but I see no reason to distinguish between the force of the two verbs. *Philosophein* here means "to adhere to philosophy, to be a philosopher," and *ioudaïzein* means "to adhere to Judaism, to be a Jew." See Fenton J. A. Hort and Joseph B. Mayor, eds., *Clement of Alexandria Miscellanies Book VII* (London: Macmillan, 1902) 157.

56. *Circumeunt plurima loca mundi ut advenas iudaizare suadeant* (Origen, *Commentariorum Series* 16 on Matt. 23:15 [*Origenes Matthäuserklärung,* GCS XI, p. 29]).

daïsai). The reference to circumcision is biblical, of course, but the reference to judaizing is not, unless it be a paraphrase of the biblical "if you shall be like us" and "we shall become one people."[57] In any case, the meaning of *ioudaïzein* here is clear, since the poetic fragment that is being paraphrased has Jacob declare that "it is unlawful for Hebrews to bring home either sons-in-law or daughters-in-law from outside, but only one who proclaims to be of the same nation." Thus *ioudaïzein* here must mean "to become of the same nation (*genos*) as the Jews."[58] *Ioudaïzein* with the meaning "to become a Jew" recurs in Byzantine Greek.[59]

This is a new usage of the word. In classical Greek, *-izein* verbs mean not "to be" or "to become" but "to be like" (see above), so that in classical Greek *ioudaïzein* could not mean either "to be Jewish" or "to become Jewish." This Christian usage reflects the Pauline equation of "the Law" with "Judaism." Adopting Jewish customs and manners was not merely to imitate Jews, it was to become one of them. Observance of the Jewish laws was Judaism. The usage may also have been inspired by the Christian coinage of *khristianizein,* which means "to be a Christian" or "to be a good Christian." Thus Origen writes of those who "seek to combine being Christian [in the spirit] with being Jewish in the body."[60]

---

57. Gen. 34:15–16.

58. Eusebius, *Praeparatio Evangelica* 9.22.5–6 p. 514 ed. Mras; cf. Holladay, *Fragments* 2.116–117. In his note on the text (2.176 n. 82) Holladay writes: "Whether the term [*ioudaïsai*] is Theodotus' or Polyhistor's is uncertain." Following other scholars, Holladay suggests that Polyhistor is a more likely candidate than Theodotus, because the poet uses *Ebraioi* throughout, not *Ioudaioi* (even though the name of the poem is *Peri Ioudaiōn*). Holladay does not even consider the possibility that the term is Eusebius' (in other words, that Eusebius has modified Polyhistor's language), but if *ioudaïzein* here means "to become a Jew" it must be Eusebius' term, not Polyhistor's. Taken by itself *ioudaïzein* in the prose passage is ambiguous. It might mean "to side with the Jews" (political meaning), or it might mean "to observe the manners of the Jews" (cultural meaning) (cf. the Greek Esther passage cited above). Polyhistor certainly could have used *ioudaïzein* in either sense. However, when the prose passage is read in light of the poetic fragment, it becomes clear that *ioudaïzein* ought to mean "to become a Jew." If the person who wrote *ioudaïzein* realized what the word must mean in context, that person must be Eusebius; if the person who wrote it did not realize what it must mean in context, that person could be Polyhistor. Certainty is unattainable here, but I prefer Eusebius.

59. See Antiochus Monachus, *On Dreams* (ca. 614 C.E.), about a monk who has himself circumcised and "becomes a Jew" (*PG* 89:1689D-1692A). See chapter 5 above at note 87.

60. *Meta tou khristianizein hairoumenoi to sōmatikōs ioudaïzein* (Erich Klostermann, ed., *Matthäuserklärung* [GCS X, no. 1; 1935] 76 [on Matt. 16:6]). *Khristianizein* probably is a back formation from *khristianismos* (hence *khristianizein* rather than *khristizein;* cf. *sabellizein* and *sabellianizein*). The word originally meant "to be a good Christian" (Origen) and only later did it come to mean "to become a Christian" (Sozomen). In the-

c. *To interpret the Old Testament "literally."* In the passage just quoted, Origen continues:

They [i.e., those who seek to mix "being Christian" with "being Jewish"] neither take heed nor are wary of the leaven of the Pharisees and Sadducees (Matt. 16:6), but, against the wish of Jesus, who forbade it, they eat the bread of the Pharisees. And all, I think, who do not wish to think that "the law is spiritual" (Rom. 7:14) and has "a shadow of the good things to come" (Heb. 10:1) and is "a shadow of things to come" (Col. 2:17), and who do not seek "the good thing to come" of which each of the laws is a shadow— they neither take heed nor are wary of the leaven of the Pharisees.

"To be Jewish corporeally" means not to realize the truth of a Christological reading of the "Old Testament"—that is, to read the Law literally, "according to the bare letter" and without the benefit of Christian truth.[61] In another passage Origen explains that the Pharisees and Scribes who sit on the seat of Moses do not understand how to expound the law according to its spiritual meaning but rather are bound to the letter of the law.[62] For Origen a Christian who observes the rituals of the "Old Testament" and thereby becomes a Jew has been influenced (misled, Origen would say) by a literal reading of the text. In a passage indebted to Origen, Gregory of Nyssa argues that if a Christian "judaizes" by relying on the bare text of Scripture—that is, on the letter instead of the spirit—incorrect theology will be the result.[63] This usage seems to be first attested in Clement of Alexandria, who wrote a book entitled *Canon Ecclesiasticus, or Against the Judaizers.* This rather obscure title to a book otherwise almost completely lost has been plausibly interpreted to mean "[On the] typological correspondence between the Old Testament and the New Testament, against those Christians who say that the Old Testament has independent meaning and authority in the life of the church."[64] Jerome refers to *nostri iudaizantes,* Christians who apparently followed a literal reading of the biblical prophecies concerning the second coming and the end time.[65]

---

ory it should also be used of pagans who adopt the customs and manners of Christians and/or give political support to the Christians, but *PGL* lists no such usage.

61. Origen, ed. Klostermann, p. 75. See de Lange, *Origen* 32.

62. Origen, *Commentariorum Series* on Matt. 23:2 p. 16.

63. Gregory of Nyssa, *Against Eunomius* 12.

64. W. C. van Unnik, "The Nature of the *Canon Ecclesiasticus,*" in van Unnik, *Sparsa Collecta* 40–51; the main source is Eusebius, *Historia Ecclesiastica* 6.13.3. Rufinus renders "judaizers" with *qui Iudaicum sensum in scripturis sequuntur,* Jerome with *qui Iudaeorum sequuntur errorem.* See van Unnik 3.42.

65. Jerome, *In Isaiam* 35, *PL* 24:378 = *CChr* 73a p. 427; *In Isaiam* 49.14, *PL* 24:488 = *CChr* 73a p. 543. They are *iudaizantes* not only because of their literalism but also (and

d. *To deny the divinity of Christ.* Any Christology that was too "low"—
that is, that made the second person of the trinity too inferior to the
first—was attacked by its opponents as a "judaizing" theology, and its
proponents were dubbed "judaizers." The reason for this is not so much
that the Jews reject Jesus—after all, the Jews reject Jesus altogether, not
merely Jesus' divinity—but that Judaism as a theological abstraction
represents belief in a single undifferentiated God. Thus the Arian creed
"there was a time when Christ was not" was deemed "Jewish." Not
only Arius but Eunomius, Marcellus, and Sabellius "judaized" through
their denial of the preexistence and/or divinity of Christ.⁶⁶ Not only
were they called "judaizers," they were even called "Jews."⁶⁷ In contrast, any Christology that was too "high"—that is, that made the second person of the trinity too similar to the first—was attacked by its opponents as a "hellenizing" theology, and its proponents were dubbed
"hellenizers." "Hellenism"—that is, "paganism"—as a theological abstraction represents belief in many gods.⁶⁸

e. *To give support to the Jews.* In three passages of his *Against the Jews*
(or *Against the Judaizing Christians*) John Chrysostom uses *ioudaïzein*.
As I noted above, one passage refers to Christians who observe the Jewish feasts and fasts, and another refers to Christians who attend or venerate the synagogue of the Jews.⁶⁹ For John "judaizing" was a larger
problem than merely the observance of Jewish rituals; the problem was
consorting with the enemy:

When you observe someone judaizing, take hold of him, show him what he
is doing, so that you yourself may not share the risk he runs. If a soldier on
campaign abroad is caught siding with the barbarian and favoring the Per-

---

perhaps primarily) because their millenarian hopes closely resemble those of the Jews.
Apollinaris was called a "judaizer" on similar grounds; see Robert L. Wilken, *The Land
Called Holy* (New Haven: Yale University Press, 1992) 310.

66. Arians: Athanasius, *PG* 26:92,45, 124,3, 384,2; cf. 1085,42. Eunomius: Gregory of
Nyssa, *Against Eunomius;* Marcellus: Eusebius, *De Ecclesiastica Theologia* 2.14; Sabellians:
[Athanasius], *PG* 28:97,28. Cf. too Gregory of Nyssa, *Oratio Catechetica* proem (*PG*
45.10a) and other passages. On Judaism and Arianism see David T. Runia, "A Note on
Philo and Christian Heresy," *Studia Philonica Annual* 4 (1992) (= Brown Judaic Stud-
ies, no. 264) 65–74.

67. See *PGL* s.v. "Ioudaios." For additional passages see Joan E. Taylor, "The Phenomenon of Early Jewish Christianity: Reality or Scholarly Invention," *Vigiliae Christianae* 44 (1990) 313–334.

68. Cf. [Athanasius], *PG* 28:597,44: "if we believe in monarchy, we judaize; if in three
gods, we hellenize." For exactly the same sentiment see Gregory of Nazianzus, *PG*
36:320,24 and 628,41, and Gregory of Nyssa, *Ad Simplicium* 3.1 and *Refutatio confessio-
nis Eunomii* 109.

69. Jewish feasts and fasts: *PG* 48:934,56. Venerate the synagogue: *PG* 48:916,10.

sians in the midst of his troop, not only is he in danger but so also is everyone who was aware of how this man felt and failed to reveal him to the general. Since you are the army of Christ carefully seek and determine if any foreigner has mingled with you and[, if so,] make him known—not so that we might kill him, as they would do,[70] or punish him or take vengeance on him, but so that we might release him from his error and impiety and make him entirely ours.[71]

In this excerpt John is berating Christians who fast with the Jews on the Day of Atonement. But the fasting per se is not the problem; the problem is that these Christians are consorting with the killers of Christ.[72] John conceives of the issue in political terms, as is demonstrated by the parallel between *ioudaïzein* "to side with the Jews" and *barbarizein* "to side with the barbarians." A Christian who fasts on the Day of Atonement has judaized, that is, has sided with the Jews and, in effect, committed treason like a soldier on campaign who sides with the enemy; this Christian is now a foreigner in our midst (*allophulos*), and no longer ours.[73] This political conception of judaizing is evident elsewhere in the *Against the Jews* even in the absence of the word *ioudaïzein*.[74] Here then is one Christian author for whom *ioudaïzein* still has political overtones.[75]

---

70. "They" seems to refer to the generals (but why the plural?).

71. PG 48:849,55–850,6. I have followed Harkins' translation with some modifications; see Paul W. Harkins, *Saint John Chrysostom Discourses against Judaizing Christians*, The Fathers of the Church, no. 68 (Washington, D.C.: Catholic University of America, 1979) 16–17.

72. *PG* 48:849,24.

73. Cf. *PG* 48:875,59–60.

74. Here is *PG* 48:875,14–25 (I follow Harkins p. 78 with modifications). John again is attacking Christians who fast with the Jews: "Are you a Christian? Why, then, do you favor the Jews (*ta ioudaiōn zēlois*)? Are you a Jew, then? Why, then, do you trouble the church? Does not a Persian side with Persians (*ta persōn phronei*)? Does not a barbarian favor barbarians (*ta barbarōn zēloi*)? Does not an inhabitant of the Roman empire follow our way of life (*politeia*)? Tell me this. If anyone of those living among us is caught siding with them (*ta ekeinōn phronōn*) is he not immediately punished? . . . If someone among them is discovered to be following the laws of the Romans, again, will he not suffer the same punishment? How, then, do you expect to be saved by defecting to that unlawful way of life (*politeia*)?"

75. Similarly, Commodian (*Liber Instructionum* 1:37, CChr 128 p. 31) polemicizes against "pagans who judaize" (*Qui iudaeidiant fanatici*); their "judaizing" seems to consist of going to the Jews for instruction. For discussion see Simon, *Verus Israel* 331, and H. Schreckenberg, "Juden and Judentum in der altkirchlichen lateinischen Poesie," *Theokratia* 3 (1973–75) 82–94, esp. 84.

Conclusions

The verb *ioudaïzein* appears rather infrequently in non-Christian sources: once in classical Greek (Plutarch), once in Greek Esther, once in Paul, twice in Josephus. Approximately half of the eighty-plus attestations in ancient Christian literature are in passages directly inspired by the usage in Paul. It appears only three times in Chrysostom's *Against the Jews* (or *Against the Judaizing Christians*), a text that one might have thought would use the verb by the dozen. The term is used more widely by modern scholars than by our ancient sources.

The classical and Jewish uses of the term are all ambiguous (leaving aside Paul for a moment). The four passages yield good sense with either the cultural meaning ("to adopt the customs and/or manners of the Jews") or the political one ("to give political support to, or side with, the Jews"), and although modern scholars almost always construe the passages with the cultural meaning, the political meaning cannot be excluded. Indeed, in the Plutarchean passage and the two Josephan passages the political meaning seems preferable. In Plutarch the word has negative valence, as indeed most of the ethnic -*izein* verbs do in classical Greek, but in Jewish Greek the word is used neutrally. Two of the Jewish passages associate circumcision with "judaizing," but neither passage is speaking of conversion, and both passages see circumcision not as a "religious ritual" but as an "ethnic" practice of the Jews.

Christian usage is largely shaped by Paul. In Galatians Paul uses the word unambiguously in a cultural sense: to adopt the customs and/or manners of the Jews. For Paul and his Christian followers these manners and customs belong to the "religious" sphere: observance of the Sabbath and other holidays, abstention from various foods, and the like. By the third century C.E. Christian writers regularly associated "judaizing" with the observance of the laws of the "Old Testament" and the denial of the Christian "spiritual" reading of Scripture. By the fourth century they associated "judaizing" with the adherence to any Christology that did not accord a sufficient degree of divinity to the second person of the trinity. Paul, of course, was unfamiliar with these developments, as he was also unfamiliar with the notion of "Christianity" and its differentiation from "Judaism," but these Christian writers are treading a path that was begun by Paul. A striking Christian neologism is the usage of *ioudaïzein* in the sense of "to become a Jew" or "to be a Jew." The adoption of Jewish customs and manners was not merely to imitate Jews, it was to become one of them or to be one of them.

If *x* claims that *y* is judaizing, that claim is a primary source for *x*'s conception of Judaism (and, if *x* is a Christian, the statement is a primary source for *x*'s conception of what is inappropriate for Christianity), a secondary source for what *y* is doing, and no source at all for *y*'s conception of what he or she is doing. If *x* is a Christian, the tone of the word *ioudaïzein* is invariably polemical and abusive. For example, Athanasius and others claim that the Arians have judaized. This claim is a primary source for Athanasius' conception of Judaism and Christianity (Judaism is an undifferentiated monotheism and Christianity is not), a secondary source for Arianism, and no source at all for the Arian self-conception. It is likely that as a secondary source Athanasius is not totally reliable, since he was not interested in presenting a full and sympathetic portrait of Arianism. We may be sure that neither Arius nor the Arians thought of themselves as "judaizers" and of their theology as Jewish.[76] Not everyone accused of being a communist or of being a communist "sympathizer" in the United States in the late 1940s and early 1950s was actually a communist, or thought of him/herself as one.

If Christian *x* claims that Christian *y* is judaizing, that claim does not necessarily imply that *y* was influenced by contemporary Jews or Judaism. And even if the claim is meant to imply that *y* was consorting with Jews too much or adopting too many Jewish practices or beliefs, the implication might be false. *Υ* might be acting entirely on his/her own, without any contact with, or influence from, living Jews. Arius and the Arians were not influenced by contemporary Jews or Judaism.[77] Wherever *ioudaïzein* means to practice the rituals of the Old Testament, or to interpret the Old Testament literally, or to deny the divinity of Christ, the Judaism to which the verb is referring is an abstraction of Christian theology. From the Christian perspective (or, to be more accurate, from the specific Christian perspective of the writer who uses

---

76. In his massive study (931 pp.) of Arianism, *The Search for the Christian Doctrine of God* (Edinburgh: T. & T. Clark, 1988), R. P. C. Hanson nowhere even considers the possibility that Arius was a "judaizer." The index does not even have entries for *Judaism* or *judaizer*.

77. Thus the chapter titled "Arianismus und Judaismus" in Rudolf Lorenz, *Arius Judaizans?* Forschungen zur Kirchen- und Dogmengeschichte, no. 31(Göttingen: Vandenhoeck & Ruprecht, 1980) has the following footnote (141 n. 1): "Der Begriff 'Judaismus' wird hier im Sinne des altkirchlichen Vorwurfs an Arius gebraucht, er nähere sich in seiner Christologie jüdischen Vorstellungen." In other words, no modern scholar suggests that Arius was influenced by his contemporary Jews.

ioudaïzein in one of these senses) Judaism is the belief in a single unitary god and the literal observance of the laws of the "Old Testament."[78] Certainly no one familiar with rabbinic exegesis of Scripture
would claim that "the Jews" understand Scripture literally and observe
its laws literally.[79] No one familiar with Philonic theology would claim
that "the Jews" believe in a single unitary undifferentiated god. But the
church fathers are not referring to Judaism as a living social system; they
are using the concept simply as an antonym to Christianity.[80]

In recent years many scholars have pointed to Christian "judaizing"
as evidence for the continued vitality and attractiveness of Judaism in
late antique society, but the argument is overstated.[81] The Christian
impulse to observe the "Jewish" laws of "the Old Testament" is generated by ideas and tensions that are internal to Christianity, and does
not necessarily spring from Jewish influence or a desire to imitate Jews.
Thus, for example, if I may leave the narrow confines of the word
ioudaïzein for a moment, Christian observance of the Sabbath, of the
Levitical purity rules, of Easter on Pesach, of abstention from blood—
none of these was *necessarily* the product of Jewish influence or contact
with living Jews. Only in the minds of ancient critics of these practices—and in the minds of some modern scholars—would these observances be called "Jewish" and cited as evidence for the power of

78. When Christian writers complain of Jewish observances in the church, they usually focus on the customs listed in Col. 2:16, Rom. 14:17, and Gal. 4:10, all of these, of
course, being of biblical origin (food, drink, days, months, festivals, new moon, Sabbath).
Contrast, for example, the long text of Ignatius, Magnesians 9 (p. 173 ed. Lightfoot),
which lists the following Sabbath observances to be avoided by Christians: eating day-old
meats, drinking lukewarm drinks, walking no more than a measured distance, rejoicing
with dancing and clapping. All of these are nonbiblical, or at least are substantive exten-
sions of biblical requirements. Observances of this sort are not normally associated with
the verb *ioudaïzein*. Even the long text of Ignatius changes *ioudaïzein* to *ton pausthenta
ioudaismon epi dianoias ekhein* (p. 175 ed. Lightfoot).

79. Thus, for Erasmus at least, the term "Jewish" was associated not with literalism
but with scholasticism and legalism—in sum, Pharisaism. See Heiko Oberman, *The Roots
of Anti-Semitism* (Philadelphia: Fortress, 1984) 58 n. 76 and 59 n. 90 = "Three Sixteenth-
Century Attitudes to Judaism: Reuchlin, Erasmus, and Luther," in *Jewish Thought in the
Sixteenth Century,* ed. B. D. Cooperman (Cambridge: Harvard University Press, 1983) 358
n. 76 and 359 n. 90.

80. The same phenomenon can often be observed in medieval texts; see, for example,
Robert A. Markus, "The Jew as a Hermeneutic Device: The Inner Life of a Gregorian
Topos," in *Gregory the Great,* ed. John Cavadini (Notre Dame, Ind.: University of Notre
Dame Press, 1995) 1–15.

81. The source of the argument is Simon, *Verus Israel,* esp. chap. 11. The argument has
been developed and expanded by many scholars. For a recent assessment, see Miriam Taylor, *Anti-Judaism and Early Christian Identity* (Leiden: Brill, 1995).

Judaism.[82] The ancient polemical use of *judaize* and *judaizer* render these terms hopelessly vague and laden with enormous theological baggage, and therefore are best avoided except in discussion of ancient texts that actually use these words. To call a Christian practice "judaizing" is to label it, not to explain it.[83]

In the Middle Ages the verb "to judaize" was used to describe the conduct of those who rebelled against the state or who lent money at usurious rates of interest.[84] In the nineteenth century the transitive verb "to jew" entered English with the meaning "to bargain sharply with" or "to beat down in price" (cf. the English verbs "to welsh," "to gyp").[85] This verbal usage shows that Jews were thought of as rebels, moneylenders, and cheats. In contrast, in antiquity the customs and manners that made the Jews (Judaeans) distinctive were not their political or moral proclivities, their professions, their social habits, their manner of dancing and singing, speaking and dressing. Neither the verb *ioudaïzein* nor the noun *Ioudaios* ever refers to any of these.[86] What made Jews distinc-

---

82. See, for an egregious example, Feldman, *Jew and Gentile* 369–382, where various Christian reports of "judaizing" are cited as evidence for the Jewish success in winning sympathizers.

83. Thus, for example, Mitchell, *Anatolia* 35, writes: "Judaizing practices, notably the worship of angels, were to be found in the earliest evidence for Christianity in southern Phrygia . . . The later fruits of this close relationship between Anatolian Jews and the Christian communities . . . are clear in the Judaizing strain of Novatian Christianity." What makes the worship of angels "judaizing"? It is no less Christian than Jewish. Some Jews and some Christians (and some polytheists too) worshiped angels; some Jews and some Christians protested against the worship of angels. What makes this worship "Jewish"? If Mitchell means to imply that Christians learned from Jews to worship angels, he should present evidence that some Jews in Phrygia worshiped angels—evidence that, as far as I know, does not exist. To call angel worship "Judaizing" is simply a way of dismissing it as a form of Christianity that does not cohere with what we think Christianity is or ought to be. Similarly, why Mitchell calls Novatian Christianity "judaizing" is not clear (in spite of his treatment on pp. 46–47 and 96–108); would Mitchell call Arianism "judaizing"? Such confusion can also be found throughout Feldman, *Jew and Gentile*.

84. Dán, "'Judaizare'" 27.

85. If, indeed, "to welsh" derives from *Welsh,* and "to gyp" derives from *Gypsy.*

86. Ethnic-geographic designations can sometimes be applied to any individual, of whatever origin, who exhibits traits thought to be distinctive of the ethnic-geographic group. Thus, in antiquity, *Chaldean* regularly means "astrologer" (see LSJ s.v. and Wong, "Philo's Use of *Chaldaioi*"), and *Arab* sometimes means (in Egypt, at least) "policeman" (Hanson, "Egyptians, Greeks, Romans"). In the Hebrew Bible *Canaanite* sometimes means "merchant" (Isa. 23:8; Job 40:30; Prov. 31:24). Someone who is "a Scythian in speech" is a rude or rough person (Plutarch). In classical Athens a cheat might be called an "Egyptian" (David Whitehead, *The Ideology of the Athenian Metic* [Cambridge: Cambridge Philological Society, 1977] 112). In contrast, in pre-Christian antiquity *Ioudaios* never had a vocational or moral meaning.

tive in the eyes of outsiders (at least Christian outsiders, who provide the bulk of the evidence) was their "religion": circumcision, Sabbath, food laws, and so forth. But, as we have already seen in the previous chapter, crossing the boundary and becoming a Jew did not necessarily entail only religious practices and beliefs; one could also "judaize" by siding with the Jews, or being conspicuously helpful to them.

CHAPTER 7

The Rabbinic
Conversion Ceremony

The ceremony that marks the conversion of a gentile to
Judaism is depicted twice in ancient rabbinic literature, first in the Babylonian Talmud, tractate Yevamot 47a–b, and later, with substantial variations, in the post-talmudic tractate Gerim 1:1. This chapter is a study
of the origin and meaning of this ceremony.[1] I begin with a synoptic
translation of the two versions, and throughout the chapter I cite the
texts by the section divisions incorporated in my translation.[2] In order
to avoid confusion and to facilitate reference, the section divisions in the

---

1. The fullest previous study in English is Daube, *New Testament and Rabbinic Judaism* 113–140, but Daube's method and interests differ from mine. In particular, Daube
too readily assumes the antiquity of almost everything rabbinic, sees parallels where the
texts provide analogies (at best), and too quickly asserts that one parallel derives from, or
is somehow dependent on, the other. The text is also discussed by Porton, *Stranger* 98–
99 and 149–150.

2. I have translated both texts literally, sometimes at the expense of idiomatic English.
My translations are based on the following critical editions: *Tractate Yevamot*, ed. Abraham Liss (Jerusalem: Institute for the Complete Israeli Talmud, 1986) 2:193–199 (which
prints the text of the Vilna edition and provides a complete repertoire of variants from
manuscripts and testimonia), and *Seven Minor Tractates*, ed. Michael Higger (New York:
Bloch, 1930) 68–69. The version of Gerim printed in the Vilna edition of the Babylonian
Talmud is often corrupt, but in the description of the conversion ceremony it differs only
in various minor details from that of Higger. (Note too that Higger's paragraph numeration differs from that of the Vilna edition.) For translations of the Yevamot text, see (this
list is far from exhaustive): Strack and Billerbeck, *Kommentar* 1.110–111; G. F. Moore, *Judaism* 1.333–334; Bamberger, *Proselytism* 38–39; the translation of tractate Yevamot by
I. W. Slotki published by the Soncino Press of London (1936; frequently reprinted); Légasse, "Baptême juif" 10–11; Schiffman, "Crossroads" 122–123 = *Who Was a Jew?* 20. For
translations of (the Vilna edition of) Gerim, see Polster, "Talmudtraktat," and Maurice
Simon in *The Minor Tractates of the Talmud* (London: Soncino, 1965) 2.603–613. Both

Yevamot text are indicated by capital letters, in the Gerim text by lower-case letters.

THE TEXTS

B. Yevamot	Gerim

Our rabbis taught:

(A1)	A (potential) convert who approaches to be converted,	(a1)	Whoever desires to be converted,
		(a2)	they do not accept him immediately,
(A2)	they say to him:	(a3)	but they say to him:
(A3)	"Why have you decided to approach (us) to be converted?	(a4)	"Why do you wish to be converted?
(A4)	Do you not know that Israel(ites) at this time are pained, oppressed, harassed, and torn,	(a5)	Behold, you see that this nation is downtrodden and tortured more than all (other) nations,
(A5)	and that afflictions come upon them?"	(a6)	and that many diseases and afflictions come upon them,
		(a7)	and that they bury their children and grandchildren,
		(a8)	and they are killed because of (their observance of) circumcision and immersion and the remainder of the commandments,
		(a9)	and they do not practice their customs publicly like all the other nations?"
(A6)	If he says,	(a10)	If he says,
(A7)	"I know and am unworthy,"	(a11)	"I am unworthy to put my neck in the yoke of Him who spoke and the world came to be, blessed is he,"
(A8)	they accept him immediately.	(a12)	they accept him immediately.
		(a13)	But if he does not (answer thus), he is dismissed and wanders off.
cf. C1		(b1)	If he accepts upon himself
cf. D2		(b2)	they bring him down to the immersion house and they cover him with water until the place of his nakedness.

---

versions of the ceremony are translated and presented synoptically by Gavin, *Jewish Antecedents* 33–35; Samet, "Conversion" 326–327, presents the texts synoptically in Hebrew.

B. Yevamot

(B1)   And they make known to him a few of the light commandments and a few of the severe commandments.

(B2)   And they make known to him the sin of (the violation of the laws of) gleanings, the forgotten sheaf, the corner of the field, and the poor tithe.

cf. E1

(B3)   And they make known to him the punishment for (violation of) the commandments.

(B3a)   They say to him,

(B3b)   "Make sure you realize that, before you arrived at this measure,

(B3c)   if you had eaten forbidden fat you would not have been liable to punishment by *karet*;

(B3d)   if you had profaned the Sabbath you would not have been liable to punishment by stoning.

(B3e)   But now, were you to eat forbidden fat you would be liable to punishment by *karet*;

(B3f)   were you to profane the Sabbath you would be liable to punishment by stoning."

(B4)   And just as they make known to him the punishment for (violation of) the commandments, they make known to him their reward (for their fulfillment).

(B4a)   They say to him:

(B4b)   "Make sure you realize that the world to come was made only for the righteous,

Gerim

(c1)   They say to him a few of the details of the commandments,

(c2)   on condition that he contribute gleanings, the forgotten sheaf, the corner of the field, and the tithe.

(c3)   Just as they say to a man (a few of the details of the commandments), thus do they say (them) to a woman, on condition that she be careful (in her observance of) menstruation, bread-dough offering and the lighting of the (Sabbath) lamp.

cf. d2–7

B. Yevamot	Gerim
(B4c) and that Israelites at this time are not able to receive either the larger part of the good (that is due them) or the larger part of the chastisement (that is due them)."	
(B5) But they do not (speak) too much to him, nor are they too detailed with him.	
(C1) If he accepts,	cf. b1
(C2) they circumcise him immediately.	
(C2a) If shreds remain on him that impede the circumcision, they circumcise him a second time.	
(D1) When he has healed,	
(D2) they immerse him immediately,	cf. b2
(D3) and two disciples of the sages stand over him	
(D4) and make known to him a few of the light commandments and a few of the severe commandments.	
(D5) When he has immersed and risen (from the water),	(d1) When he has immersed and risen (from the water),
(D6) behold, he is like (an) Israel(ite) in all respects.	(d2) they speak to him kind words, words of comfort,
	(d3) "To whom have you attached yourself? Happy are you (for you have attached yourself) to Him who spoke and the world came to be, blessed is he.
	(d4) The world was created only for the sake of Israel,
	(d5) and only Israel were called children of God,
cf. B4b	(d6) and only Israel are dear before God.
	(d7) And all those (other) words that we said to you, we said them only to increase your reward."
	cf. c3
(E1) (In the case of) a woman,	Gerim (1:4) A man immerses a man [but does not immerse a woman]; a woman immerses a woman but (does) not (immerse) a man.
(E2) women make her sit in water up to her neck,	

B. Yevamot   Gerim

(E3)   and two disciples of the sages
        stand near her outside (the
        place of the immersion),

(E4)   and make known to her a few
        of the light commandments
        and a few of the severe
        commandments.

(F1)   A convert and an emanci-
        pated slave (follow the same
        procedure).

(F2)   And wherever a menstruant
        immerses, there a convert and
        an emancipated slave immerse.

(F3)   And every object that inter-
        poses (between the body and
        the water) during immersion
        (thereby invalidating the im-
        mersion), interposes (and in-
        validates the immersion) in the
        case of a convert, an emanci-
        pated slave, and a menstruant.

B. Yevamot 47a–b

As depicted in B. Yevamot, the conversion ceremony has
four parts:[3]

A. Presentation and examination;

B. Instruction;

C. Circumcision;

D. Immersion and further instruction.

The text concludes with two appendices:

E. Special rules for the immersion of a female convert;

F. Rules for the immersion of converts and emancipated slaves.

I shall analyze each of these sections briefly and then discuss the date of
the text.

3. Gavin, *Jewish Antecedents* 32.

A. PRESENTATION AND EXAMINATION

The text presumes that the potential convert will take the initiative by "approaching" or "coming"[4] to be converted. Exactly whom he is approaching is not entirely clear, since until section D the convert is addressed and instructed by the anonymous subjects of third-person-plural verbs.[5] He is greeted with a double question: "Why have you decided to approach (us) to be converted?" (A3) and "Do you not know that Israel(ites) at this time[6] are pained, oppressed, harassed, and torn, and that afflictions come upon them?" (A4–5). To this double question he replies with a double response: "I know and am unworthy" (A7, the only time in the ceremony that words are placed in the convert's mouth). The structure of this stylized conversation is *a-b-b-a*. To the second question, "Do you not know that Israel(ites) are pained?" he replies, "I know." To the first question, "Why have you decided to approach (us) to be converted?" he replies, "I am not worthy."[7] The exact force of this response is somewhat obscure; presumably it means something like "I am unworthy of being accepted as a convert" (see Gerim a11) or, as the commentator Rashi explains, "I am unworthy of joining such a persecuted lot." In any case, the potential convert is not grilled at any length about his motives and apparently need reveal only an attitude of modesty and contrition for the ceremony to proceed. "They accept him immediately" (A8); that is, they accept him as a candidate for conversion (a catechumen).

4. "To approach" (A1: *gēr habba lehitgayyer;* A3: *ma ra'ita shebata lehitgayyer*) is technical language for presenting oneself for membership or for approval. See Lieberman, *Greek in Jewish Palestine* 80; the Qumran Manual of Discipline 1.16 and 5.7–8, with the note of Saul Lieberman, "The Discipline in the So-Called Dead Sea Manual of Discipline," *JBL* 71 (1952) 199–206, at 202. See too M. Bekhorot 8:1; Mekhilta Amaleq 2 and 3 (1), 187H-R and 193H-R; Y. Yevamot 2:6 3d as emended by Lieberman, *Tosefta Ki-Fshutah* 10.407; and B. Bekhorot 30a cited below. Cf. the Greek verb *proserchesthai,* whence "proselyte."

5. Anonymous third-person-plural verbs (especially participles, as here) are common in the Mishnah and rabbinic literature generally.

6. That is, in this world, before the advent of the Messiah. The Vilna edition of the Talmud, following some manuscripts, adds the same phrase in section A: "A convert who approaches (us) to be converted *at this time,*" but the phrase is omitted there by numerous manuscripts and testimonia and is probably an addition inspired by the phrase's appearance in A4 and B4c and in such passages as B. Yevamot 24b and Keritot 9a.

7. Therefore I translate A7 as "I know *and* am unworthy," not "I know *but* am unworthy." The *a-b-b-a* structure was pointed out to me by Reuven Kimelman.

B. INSTRUCTION

The convert is to receive a fourfold instruction. "They make known to him" four bodies of information:

1. A few of the light commandments and a few of the severe commandments (B1);

2. The sin (or punishment) of violating the regulations concerning the agricultural tithes that support the poor (B2);[8]

3. The punishment for violation of the commandments (B3), notably eating forbidden food and desecrating the Sabbath (B3a–f);[9]

4. The reward for fulfillment of the commandments (B4), with special reference to the world to come (B4a–c).

This fourfold instruction does not mean, however, that the convert is to be told every detail about Judaism and Jewish life. On the contrary. The convert is to be instructed in only "a few" of the commandments (B1). "But they do not (speak) too much to him, nor are they too detailed with him" (B5).[10]

---

8. For these offerings to the poor see Lev. 19:9–10 and Deut. 14:28–29 and 24:19. Some manuscripts and testimonia read "second tithe" (*ma'aser sheni*) instead of "poor tithe" (*ma'aser 'ani*), but the context indicates that "poor tithe" is more likely to be the correct reading.

9. "Forbidden fat" (*helev*) in ancient rabbinic literature frequently represents the example par excellence of forbidden food. Sometimes, as here, the consumption of *helev* is coupled with the desecration of the Sabbath as twin paradigms of heinous behavior (Y. Yevamot 15:3 14d and parallels). The penalty of *karet* involved a court-inflicted whipping and an ill-defined divinely inflicted punishment.

10. The precise force of the Hebrew (*ve'eyn marbin alav ve'eyn medaqdeqin alav*) is obscure. The literal translation is "And they do not increase upon him nor are they exact upon him," implying a contrast between *rav*, "large, numerous, much," and *daq*, "small, narrow, thin." G. F. Moore, *Judaism*, translates: "This discourse should not, however, be too much prolonged nor go too much into particulars." Légasse, "Baptême juif," is similar: "Toutefois, on ne lui imposera pas un discours trop long ni trop détaillé"; as is Lazarus Goldschmidt, *Der babylonische Talmud* (Berlin: Verlag Biblion, 1929–1936): "Jedoch [rede man] auf ihn nicht zu viel ein und nehme es mit ihm nicht allzu genau." Perhaps the text is even more pointed. Bamberger, *Proselytism*, translates: "But we do not burden him with too long or too detailed an account." Another alternative: "But they do not make excessive (demands) upon him, nor do they (trouble) him with too many details." Slotki's translation—"He is not, however, to be persuaded or dissuaded too much"—is clearly wrong. M. Abegg suggests that *miqtzat* should be translated not as "a few" but as "some important" or "some of the best"; see his "Paul, 'Works of the Law,' and MMT," *Biblical Archaeology Review* 20, no. 6 (1994) 52 n.3. This is an interesting suggestion that requires further work. On the contrary, perhaps *miqtzat* should be translated as "some unimportant" or "some of the least"; see Genesis Rabbah 95.4 1190T-A with Theodor's note ad loc.

The convert is to be instructed in a few of the light commandments and a few of the severe commandments (B1). The distinction between "light" (or easy) commandments and "severe" (or difficult) commandments is well attested in rabbinic literature, but the exact force of the distinction in this context is not clear. The only commandments mentioned here explicitly are the agricultural tithes for the poor (B2) and the laws of forbidden food and the Sabbath (B3a–f). It is possible that the former are meant to illustrate the "light" commandments and the latter the "severe" commandments, but this interpretation (which was followed by Gerim c2) is unlikely because it ignores the literary structure of the text.[11] B2 is not subordinate to B1 but is parallel to it, and B3a–f is subordinate not to B1 but to B3, which in turn parallels B1. The "light" and "severe" commandments of B1 do not refer to the tithes of B2 and the food and Sabbath laws of B3a–f.

The prominence assigned to the agricultural tithes for the poor is peculiar. The Talmud understands B2 to refer to the sin of *neglecting* to separate the tithes, but does not explain why these rules should be preferred above the numerous other rules in the realms of charity and ethics, and why the instruction should emphasize the sin of neglect rather than simply the commandment to observe. It is more likely that B2 refers to the sin of *collecting* and *receiving* tithes when not eligible to do so. In a separate discussion the Talmud recognizes that a gentile might convert to Judaism in order to obtain gleanings, the forgotten sheaf, the corner of the field, and the poor tithe.[12] It is possible that B2 was added to our

---

11. Contrast Sifrei Numbers 115 (128H): "God began to decree upon them (the Israelites) a few of the light commandments and a few of the severe commandments, for example (*kegon*), the Sabbath, forbidden sexual relations, fringes, and phylacteries." Here it is clear that the enumerated commandments exemplify the categories "light" and "severe." For the distinction between "light" and "severe" commandments, see Urbach, *Sages* 345–346.

12. B. Yevamot 47a. In *CAp* 2.283 Josephus remarks that gentiles admire "our liberal charities." A midrash on Lev. 23:22 quoted by the Yalqut Shimeoni 645 (and cited by Polster, "Talmudtraktat" 23 n. 3) considers that a gentile might wish to become a proselyte (a *gēr;* or does the text mean a resident alien, a *gēr toshav?*) in order to collect the tithes for the poor. Many modern scholars have suggested that the liberality of Jewish charities was a major inducement for gentiles to convert to Judaism; see, for example, Baron, *Social and Religious History* 1.175, and Reynolds and Tannenbaum, *Jews and Godfearers* 55 and 86–87. The major difficulty with my explanation is that elsewhere the phrase clearly means "the sin of (neglecting to give) gleanings etc." (see especially T. Menahot 10:12 528Z). Another, if remote, possibility is that the text does refer to the sin of neglecting the tithes, and is based on a notion like that of R. Ebardimos b. R. Yosi in the Sifra: "Everyone who distributes gleanings, the forgotten sheaf, the corner of the field, and the poor tithe is considered as if the temple were standing and he had brought his

text on the basis of that talmudic discussion, but the reverse relationship (the talmudic discussion was inspired by B2) is just as possible. In
any case, the convert is warned of the sin of the unjustifiable collection
of the poor tithes not as an illustration of "light" commandments but
as an exhortation not to abuse his new status as a Jew.[13]

B3 concerns punishment for violation of the commandments, and B4
concerns rewards for their fulfillment. The two speeches together briefly
survey three of the most distinctive Jewish practices and beliefs: the Sabbath, forbidden foods, and belief in the world to come. However, the
little speech at B4c, which is supposed to be about rewards, refers to
both punishments and rewards and therefore is somewhat awkward in
its context. This suggests that B3a–f is secondary and that originally
B4a–c, with its reference to the world to come and to the inability of
Israel "at this time"[14] to sustain either its full reward or its full punishment, was the single speech for B3 and B4 together. When B3a–f
was added in order to balance B4a–c (so that punishment and reward
would each have separate speeches), B4 was given its resumptive opening ("And just as they make known to him the punishment for (violation of) the commandments")—an opening B4 did not need when it
followed directly on B3. The fact that both Gerim and the talmudic discussant on Yevamot 47b ignore B3a–f lends some support to this suggestion, but the strength of this support should not be overstated since
both Gerim and the talmudic discussant ignore many phrases and sections of the text.

Here in summary form is a possible literary history of this section.
The original text envisioned only three levels of instruction for the convert (B1—some of the commandments; B3—punishment; and B4—

---

sacrifices there." See Sifra on Lev. 23:22, p. 101c ed. Weiss, p. 450 in Vatican Codex Assemani 66 ed. Finkelstein. Since rabbinic law required a proselyte to bring a sacrifice at the
temple in order to become part of the temple community (see B. Keritot 9a and parallels), perhaps the poor tithes were seen as a surrogate offering. But many commandments
were homiletically declared to be equal or superior to the temple sacrifices, and the connection seems far-fetched.

13. Daube, *New Testament and Rabbinic Judaism* 127, correctly notes that rabbinic
law ordained "for the sake of peace" that even gentiles were not to be prevented from collecting the poor tithes (M. Gittin 5:8); nevertheless, the tithes were intended in the first
instance to benefit Jews. I do not understand Porton's explanation of the highlighting of
these agricultural tithes; see Porton, *Stranger* 99 and 149–150. These tithes "served as a
means of strengthening group cohesion and solidarity," but isn't this true also of virtually
all the commandments?

14. See note 6 above.

reward), and this short text was expanded by the addition of instruction in the agricultural tithes for the poor (B2), and by the insertion of two speeches: first a brief speech on the nature of divine reward and punishment (B4a–c), and later a longer speech on divine and human punishment (B3a–f with stylistic adjustment to B4). It is also possible that this literary history is completely wrong and that the text is a unity with no additions or interpolations at all.

C. CIRCUMCISION

If, after all this, the prospective convert indicates anew his willingness to accept (the commandments),[15] he is circumcised immediately (C2), and, if need be, repeatedly (C2a). It is possible that C2a is an addition inspired by other rabbinic passages that evince a concern for "shreds . . . that impede the circumcision,"[16] but there is no real evidence for this conjecture. In fact, C2a supports one of the larger purposes of the ceremony (see below).

D. IMMERSION AND FURTHER INSTRUCTION

"Immediately" after he has healed, "they" immerse him (D1–2). The immersion is supervised by two sages (D3, the first time the text provides a subject for the third-person-plural verbs) who instruct him (again) in "a few of the light commandments and a few of the severe commandments" (D4). The meaning of this phrase is no clearer here than it was the first time it appeared (B1). The reason for the duplication of B1 by D4 shall be discussed below. After he has completed the immersion (D5), he is "like (an) Israel(ite) in all respects" (D6), that is, the convert's obligation to observe the Torah is the same as that of the native.[17] The ceremony opens and closes with references to "Israel," although in A4 (as in B4c) the word refers to the collective, while in D6 it refers to the individual.

15. The formula of his acceptance is not given. An oath *might* be implied in the term *qibbel*.

16. M. Shabbat 19:6, cited on B. Yevamot 47b; T. Shabbat 15:4 69L; and parallels.

17. "Scripture has equated the convert with the native in all the commandments of the Torah" (Sifrei Numbers 71 67H and 109 113H, and Mekhilta Pisha 15 57H-R). Some testimonia here read *lekhal davar* instead of *lekhal devarav,* but the readings are synonymous; cf. B. Avodah Zarah 64b.

E. SPECIAL RULES FOR
THE IMMERSION OF A FEMALE CONVERT

In the case of a female convert (E1), the text provides a slight modification to the procedure outlined for men.

MEN		WOMEN	
(D2)	They immerse him immediately,	(E2)	Women make her sit in water up to her neck,
(D3)	and two disciples of the sages stand over him	(E3)	and two disciples of the sages stand near her outside (the place of the immersion),
(D4)	and make known to him a few of the light commandments and a few of the severe commandments.	(E4)	and make known to her a few of the light commandments and a few of the severe commandments.
(D5)	When he has immersed and risen (from the water),		
(D6)	behold, he is like (an) Israel(ite) in all respects.		

For both men and women immersion is performed in the nude (see F3) and, after initial entry into the water (D2//E2), is accompanied by instruction from two sages (D3–4//E3–4). Presumably D5 and D6 apply to men and women alike: after completing the immersion (D5)—that is, after submerging totally in the water and emerging—the convert, whether male or female, is deemed to be like an Israelite in all respects (D6). The only differences in the procedure for males and females is that the initial entry into the water is supervised by men for men and by women for women (see Gerim 1:4, cited above), and that the (male) instructors are kept at a safe distance when instructing women but stand in immediate proximity when instructing men. When receiving the instruction, the woman sits in the water up to her neck, thereby both maintaining her modesty and preventing words of Torah from being heard in the presence of nudity. Presumably men too would maintain their modesty while receiving the instruction; this point is not explicit in the text but is correctly deduced by Gerim b2.[18]

---

18. Cf. M. Berakhot 3:5. Some scholars have suggested that *tevilah* was not always total immersion and have cited E2 and b2 as evidence, but this argument ignores the parallelism between D2 and E2 and the distinction between the initial immersion of D2 (paralleled by E2) and the complete immersion of D5 (paralleled by Gerim d1). Whether early Christian baptism was "immersion" rather than "affusion" (pouring water on the initiate) or "aspersion" (sprinkling water on the initiate) need not be discussed here. For a brief discussion of the alternate possibilities, see E. Stommel, "Taufriten und Antike Badesit-

F. COMMON RULES FOR THE IMMERSION OF CONVERTS AND EMANCIPATED SLAVES

F1 states that "A convert and an emancipated slave (follow the same procedure)"; that is, both require immersion.[19] According to F2 and F3 the immersion of a menstruant is the paradigm for the immersion of converts and emancipated slaves. The immersion requires a *miqveh* or some other such body of water that a menstruant might use for her purification (F2), and no clothing, jewelry, or other object may interpose between the naked body and the water (F3).[20] Section F might be an addition.

THE DATE OF THE TEXT

The date of the text is difficult to determine. Not only is the text anonymous, but the discussion of the text in B. Yevamot 47b–48a is also anonymous. The names of various Palestinian and Babylonian authorities appear in that discussion, but all of them (with only one possible exception) are quoted from other contexts by the anonymous editor (the *setam*) and juxtaposed to our text. They do not address our text directly and therefore cannot help us date it or locate its origins.[21]

---

ten," *Jahrbuch für Antike und Christentum* 2 (1959) 5–14 (Stommel is one of those who misinterpret our passage). Gavin, *Jewish Antecedents,* avoids the duplicate immersion of D2 and D5 by translating the former "(he is) brought to baptism immediately," but this suggestion, while a philological possibility, ignores the parallel between D2 and E2.

19. In many respects in rabbinic law a slave is a convert-in-the-making, and an emancipated slave is a convert. The Mishnah often treats the two together, and sometimes uses language close to F1, except that F1 is in the singular and the Mishnah uses the plural; cf. M. Bikkurim 1:5 and Qiddushin 4:7. I do not discuss here the conversion of slaves. On slaves in the Mishnah and Tosefta, see Flesher, *Oxen.*

20. Cf. T. Miqva'ot 6:11 658Z: "Whatever interposes in (the immersion of) vessels, interposes (and thereby invalidates the immersion) in the case of a menstruant and a gentile at the time of immersion." Christian baptism too was to be performed in the nude, and was rendered invalid by interposition of objects between the body and the water; see van Unnik, *Sparsa Collecta* 299–317 ("Les cheveux défaits des femmes baptisées"). In contrast, according to Josephus, Essene women wore a garment while bathing, men a loincloth (*BJ* 2.161).

21. The anonymous editor cites R. Helbo, R. Hiyya b. Abba in the name of R. Yohanan (twice), R. Eleazar (the name is omitted in the Munich manuscript; some testimonia read *de'amar rabbi elazar,* thus confirming the fact that R. Eleazar is being quoted from elsewhere), and R. Jeremiah b. Abba in the name of Rav. None of these statements addresses our text. The *setam* also says (in reference to D3), "R. Yohanan told the reciter, '(From now on when you recite this *beraita*) recite "three" (instead of "two" in D3).'" If this quotation is genuine, R. Yohanan clearly knew the *beraita,* but the statement may have been invented and put in R. Yohanan's mouth by the *setam* in order to resolve the

The only firm *terminus ante quem* for the text (with all its additions and interpolations, if indeed there be any) is provided by its inclusion in the Babylonian Talmud (edited in the sixth to eighth centuries C.E.) and by its service as a source for Gerim (sixth to eighth century C.E.?; see below).

It is likely, however, that the text is what its introductory formula (*teno rabbanan*) claims it to be: it is a *beraita,* a text of Palestinian origin from the second or early third century C.E.[22] This conclusion is supported by several considerations: there are no indications that the text is not a *beraita;* the text has numerous linguistic parallels with the Mishnah and the Tosefta;[23] the text fits perfectly within the development of rabbinic law in the tannaitic period, as I shall discuss below; any number of Palestinian texts, both tannaitic and amoraic, presume either inquiry into a convert's motives or initial dissuasion of the convert or preconversion instruction, precisely as our text mandates.[24] The only reason not to regard the text as a genuine *beraita* is the fact that the text is not quoted in any source of Palestinian origin.[25] This objection has merit,

---

contradiction between D3 and R. Yohanan. A string of Babylonian *amora'im* (R. Sheshet, Raba, and R. Papa) is cited in the discussion of F1, but it is not clear that the authorities are really discussing F1 (their discussion revolves around a *beraita* cited on the bottom of B. Yevamot 47b), and even if they are, F1 might have circulated separately.

22. G. F. Moore, *Judaism* 1.333, suggests that section A4–5 refers to the Hadrianic persecution and therefore dates the *beraita* to that period ("after the war under Hadrian"). Moore is followed by Urbach, *Sages* 547; Baron, *Social and Religious History* 2.149–150; Schiffman, "Crossroads" 123 (who suggests that the passage might even refer to the war of 66–74 C.E.); and various other scholars (see Porton, *Stranger* 99 n. 73). But the argument is weak because at any point after the destruction of the temple in 70 C.E. ("at this time") the Jews could refer to their national afflictions. Further, the argument really has a basis only in the version of Gerim, which refers to execution because of the observance of circumcision (a8), but Gerim is secondary to the version in Yevamot and a8 can be explained in another way (see below).

23. See above notes 4, 16, 19, and 20. The proleptic use of "convert" in A1 (the meaning is "a gentile who is about to convert," or "a (potential) convert") is also mishnaic; cf. M. Hallah 3:6, Pesahim 8:8, Ketuvot 9:9, Hullin 10:4. A4–5 closely resembles the language used by R. Hannanya b. R. Gamaliel in a *beraita* in B. Yevamot 48b. "Two disciples of the sages" appear as representatives of a rabbinic court in M. Sotah 1:3 and M. Makkot 2:5. The admonition to the convert resembles in language and tone the admonition administered by the court to one about to take an oath (M. Sanhedrin 4:5; T. Sotah 7:2–4 190–192L and parallels). The phrase "behold, he (it) is like an *x* in all respects" appears numerous times in tannaitic texts: T. Terumot 1:3 107L and 3:1 116L; T. Ma'aser Sheni 1:14 246L; T. Yevamot 10:6 33L and 12:11 43L; etc.

24. Motive: T. Demai 2:5 69L. Dissuasion: Rav in Y. Qiddushin 4:1 65b. Motive and dissuasion: Mekhilta Amalek 3 2.172–173L = Amalek 1 193H-R. Preconversion instruction: Ruth Rabbah on 1:16–17. I shall discuss all these texts below.

25. Porton, *Stranger* 99 n. 77 and 150; I fully agree with Porton that these arguments are not "determinative."

but the Bavli (the Babylonian Talmud) is filled with allegedly Palestinian traditions that are not attested in sources of Palestinian provenance; some of these, no doubt, are Babylonian pseudepigraphs, but surely some are genuine. For what it is worth, I note that the rabbis of the second century were interested in determining boundaries between Jews and gentiles, and that the second century witnessed the creation and expansion of numerous conversion, initiation, and other such rituals in the Roman empire.[26] The second century provides both a rabbinic and a general cultural context for the ceremony described by this text. A definitive statement on the origin of this text is not possible, but I think it likely that the text is of Palestinian origin from the second century C.E., and this shall be my working hypothesis in the discussion below.

Tractate Gerim 1:1

Tractate Gerim is a work of unknown date; it almost certainly is post-talmudic (i.e., post–500 C.E.) and is first attested explicitly about 1300.[27] As depicted in Gerim, the conversion ceremony has four parts:

a. Presentation and Examination
b. Immersion
c. Instruction during the Immersion
d. Exhortation after the Immersion

I shall attempt to show that Gerim's version of the conversion ceremony is most easily explained on the assumption that it is dependent on B. Yevamot (or on some other version closely resembling that of Yevamot).[28]

26. Boundaries: Goodman, "Proselytising" 184; see chapter 9 below. Rituals: A. D. Nock, *Essays on Religion and the Ancient World*, ed. Z. Stewart (Cambridge: Harvard University Press, 1972) 1.53–54.

27. On the date of Gerim, see the brief discussions by Polster and Simon in the introductions to their translations. A much earlier date is advocated by M. B. Lerner, but I am not convinced. See Lerner, "The External Tractates," in *The Literature of the Sages First Part: Oral Tora*, ed. S. Safrai, CRINT II,3/1 (Philadelphia: Fortress, 1987) 400–401.

28. Against Urbach, *Sages* 547 n. 87, and Samet, "Conversion" 327. Bamberger, *Proselytism* 39, substantially underplays the distinctions between the two texts. That the author of Gerim used the Babylonian Talmud has yet to be demonstrated.

A. PRESENTATION AND EXAMINATION

This section follows the structure of Yevamot rather closely but contains many modifications and expansions. The Hebrew of a1 (*rotzeh*) and a4 is simpler than that of Yevamot A1 (*habba*) and A3.[29] Sections a2 and a13 are secondary expansions that make explicit what is implicit in the original: a convert should not be hindered if after the examination he decides to withdraw.[30]

In Yevamot the potential convert is told briefly about the sufferings of Israel (A4–5) and then at some length about the commandments (B1–4). In Gerim the gravamen of the instruction shifts from the commandments to the people of Israel. The opening speech about the sufferings of Israel (a5–9) and the closing speech about the threefold uniqueness of Israel (d4–6; contrast B4c) are much expanded, while the section on the commandments is much reduced (c). Many modern scholars have suggested that a7–9, which refer to persecution and have no parallel in Yevamot, must have been written during, or shortly after, the Hadrianic period,[31] but the argument is not convincing. Section a8 reads: "they are killed because of (their observance of) circumcision and immersion and the remainder of the commandments." This is not the place for a discussion of the ferocity and extent of the Hadrianic persecution, but even if we accept the reality of the persecution, nowhere does rabbinic literature claim that Hadrian interdicted the observance of immersion or that he issued an outright ban against "the remainder of the commandments."[32]

A more likely interpretation of a7–9 is suggested by Gerim 2:5, a different version of a *beraita* that appears in B. Yevamot 48b. The Gerim text runs as follows:

R. Hanina b. Gamaliel says,
Why are converts in a sorry state?

29. See note 4 above.
30. Similarly Maimonides, *Laws of Prohibited Intercourse* 14:5. Perhaps Gerim is based on the comment of the anonymous discussant on B. Yevamot 47b referring to A3–5: "If (as a result of hearing the speech) he wishes to leave, let him leave."
31. See note 22 above.
32. Lieberman argues that there was a persecution but no blanket prohibition against Jewish observances: see Saul Lieberman, "The Persecution of the Religion of Israel" (in Hebrew), in *Salo Baron Jubilee Volume*, 3 vols. (New York: American Academy for Jewish Research, 1974) 3.213–245. In contrast, Peter Schäfer, *Der Bar Kokhba Aufstand* (Tübingen: Mohr [Siebeck], 1981) chap. 7, argues that, beyond the decree against circumcision, there was no "persecution" at all. Both Lieberman and Schäfer agree that there is no evidence for a prohibition of immersion: Lieberman 3.215 n. 22 and Schäfer 206 and 212–213.

Because they calculate a year or two before (their conversion) that "I
    will collect my debts (with interest) and I will do my needs" (i.e., I
    will borrow whatever I need, because I know that after my conver-
    sion I will not have to repay the interest).
R. Yosi said to him,
If (they were afflicted) by a lack of money, your words would be cor-
    rect; but they bury their children and grandchildren, and many dis-
    eases and afflictions come upon them (and the offense you are de-
    scribing cannot account for such suffering).
But why are they in a sorry state?
Because of (their failure to observe) the seven Noahide commandments
    (before their conversion).

In this version R. Yosi's reply to R. Hanina contains a phrase ("they bury
their children and grandchildren, and many diseases and afflictions come
upon them") that is identical with a6–7 (except that the order of the
clauses is reversed).[33] The identity of language suggests that Gerim
thought that both texts were speaking about the same group of people.
Section a6–7 is speaking primarily not of the entire nation of Israel but
of converts to Judaism.

It is converts who are afflicted (a6) and bury their children (a7). It is
they who undergo circumcision and immersion and then undertake to
observe "the remainder of the commandments" (a8). In the second
century C.E. the emperor Hadrian prohibited circumcision altogether,
Antoninus Pius prohibited the circumcision of non-Jews (with few exceptions), and Septimius Severus prohibited (or at least is said to have
prohibited) conversion to Judaism. It was also illegal for a Jew to circumcise a non-Jew. The punishment for these crimes will have varied,
and for extensive periods the prohibitions seem not to have been enforced, but the death penalty was a real possibility in the pagan Roman
empire and especially in the Christian successor states of both East and
West. Thus Jews who accepted converts and the converts themselves
could indeed be said to be "killed because of (their observance of) circumcision and immersion and the remainder of the commandments"
(a8) and to be unable to "practice their customs publicly" (a9).[34] Section
a7–9 might have been written at a specific time when the death penalty

33. The phrase is reminiscent of T. Bava Metzia 3:25 79L. In B. Yevamot, R. Yosi's
reply is different, and R. Hannanya's question contains the clause "afflictions come upon
them."

34. On the prohibitions and punishments, see the classic discussion of Juster, Les juifs
1.254–271, and the comments (with bibliography) of Alfredo M. Rabello, "The Legal
Condition of the Jews in the Roman Empire," ANRW 2.13 (1980) 699–703. The laws are
collected by Linder, Roman Imperial Legislation. The Historia Augusta reports that Sep-

was actually being inflicted on converts, but it also could have been written at any point after the second century through the Middle Ages.

The convert's reply (a10–11) is fuller in Gerim than Yevamot (A6–7). The *a-b-b-a* structure is lost completely, but a new motif appears: God. The Yevamot text referred to God implicitly at several points but nowhere did so explicitly. Gerim remedied this startling omission (a11, d3, d5, d6). Maimonides would go even further in this direction.[35]

B. IMMERSION

If the potential convert accepts upon himself (the yoke of the commandments), he is brought to the "immersion house" and placed in water in order to cover his nakedness (b1–2). I have argued above that this requirement was deduced (correctly) from Yevamot E2.[36]

The renewed acceptance of the commandments in b1, which follows immediately upon an earlier statement of contrition and acceptance (a11), is unnecessary and indicates that Gerim derives from Yevamot, or a text much like that of Yevamot. In Yevamot the renewed acceptance is well motivated and appropriate, because the first acceptance (A7) precedes the instruction and the second (C1) follows it. By condensing and rearranging the material, Gerim has juxtaposed the two acceptances (a11 and b1), thus creating an unmotivated repetition absent from the original. Here is good evidence for the secondary character of Gerim's version.

In Gerim immersion is the central ritual act of the conversion ceremony. Circumcision is completely absent. Gerim knows that male converts must be circumcised (1:2; 2:1–2; 2:4)—circumcision is even mentioned by a8—but the conversion ceremony omits the requirement. This omission is in striking contrast with the version of Yevamot where circumcision is the central ritual (C2–2a). The precircumcision instruction of Yevamot (B) becomes instruction and exhortation during and after immersion in Gerim (c–d). This change can be explained in various ways:

timius Severus prohibited conversion to Judaism, but some scholars have doubted the reliability of this report; see M. Stern, *Authors* no. 515, and Anthony R. Birley, *Septimius Severus the African Emperor*, rev. ed. (New Haven: Yale University Press, 1988) 135.

35. Maimonides, *Laws of Prohibited Intercourse* 14:2: "and they make known to him the essentials of the religion—namely, the unity of God and the prohibition of idolatry. And they speak at some length about this matter."

36. I do not know why Gerim in turn forgot to include or otherwise paraphrase E2–3.

1. Circumcision was once a part of the Gerim text but fell out through manuscript corruption.

2. The omission of circumcision by Gerim was a literary device by which to eliminate the awkward and somewhat repetitious pre-circumcision and preimmersion instruction of Yevamot. (Gerim eliminates the duplicated instruction in "a few of the light commandments and a few of the severe commandments," B1, D4, and E4.) The omission of circumcision also allowed a greater evenness in the treatment of men and women, a tendency evident in c3. Gerim's intent was not to deemphasize circumcision but to produce a condensed and coherent version of the ceremony found in Yevamot. Circumcision was such an obvious part of the ritual that it could be presumed.[37]

3. Gerim developed the Yevamot ritual (or something like it) into two separate rituals, one for circumcision (now lost) and the other (preserved) for immersion.[38]

4. For Gerim circumcision was a precondition for conversion, a precondition that could be met by the mere removal, under whatever circumstances, of the requisite portion of skin. Circumcision was not accompanied by any ritual or ceremony; it did not require a specific intention or a religious setting. Its validity was a function of its efficacy; if it removed the foreskin, the circumcision was valid. Perhaps this was Gerim's conception of circumcision, a conception that was regnant in the pre-rabbinic and early tannaitic period (see below), and consequently Gerim did not provide for any circumcision ceremony or ritual.

Of these four possibilities, the former two are preferable because their implications are less radical than those of the latter. The suggestion of textual corruption is neither desperate nor far-fetched; the text of Gerim is in a poor state and contains more than its share of corrupted passages.[39] The second suggestion may seem inadequate, but cannot be rejected (or confirmed!) until the method and purpose of the entire tractate have been analyzed, an investigation that has not yet been undertaken. The latter two possibilities lead in totally new and unexpected

37. That circumcision is presumed is argued by Polster, "Talmudtraktat" 20.
38. I owe this suggestion to Prof. Morton Smith.
39. See note 2 above.

directions for which no evidence can be adduced. In particular, the notion that a pre-rabbinic or early tannaitic view of circumcision has somehow survived in a post-talmudic text, one that otherwise is so beholden to the text in Yevamot, is unlikely.

C. INSTRUCTION DURING THE IMMERSION

While the prospective convert is standing in the water, he is to be instructed "in a few of the details of the commandments" (c1), a slightly simpler formulation than B1 and D4. The agricultural tithes retain their peculiar prominence, except that here they are introduced by the phrase "on condition that" (*al menat she-*). Unless we are to believe that for Gerim the agricultural tithes for the poor are the absolute essentials of Judaism, the phrase would seem to have the force of "for example" or "specifically." That the agricultural tithes are an example of a detail that the convert is to be taught is an idea that Gerim will have derived from Yevamot, even if the literary structure of the original militates against this conclusion (see above). Women too need to be instructed (a logical deduction from Yevamot E1), and they should be instructed in commandments that obtain to them—namely, menstruation, bread-dough offering, and the lighting of the (Sabbath) lamp (c3).[40]

Gerim omits Yevamot's specification that the instruction during the immersion is to be performed by "two disciples of the sages" (D3 and E3). The number is perhaps omitted because the author of Gerim did not wish to arbitrate a dispute between a *beraita* and R. Yohanan (who, according to the Talmud, argued that the *beraita* should be emended from "two disciples" to "three"). The presence of sages is omitted because Gerim, like many later rabbinic authorities,[41] believed that even plain Jews could preside over a conversion; sages were not essential.

D. EXHORTATION AFTER THE IMMERSION

Gerim omits Yevamot's ringing declaration, "Behold, he is like (an) Israel(ite) in all respects" (D6), perhaps because Gerim knows of many laws that demonstrate the contrary (see Gerim 1–2 passim).

---

40. For "bread-dough offering" see Num. 15:17–21. This triad of women's commandments derives from M. Shabbat 2:6.

41. For example, Maimonides, *Laws of Prohibited Intercourse* 13:17 and 14:6. On R. Yohanan, see above, note 21.

Gerim instead has the convert hear words of congratulations and comfort after the completion of the conversion process, words that contrast (d7) with the sterner speech of a4–9. The content of d3–6 seems to have been inspired by Yevamot's speech (B4b) about the rewards of the commandments (although Gerim is more explicit than Yevamot about God, as I noted above, and less explicit about the world to come), but the setting is original. By ending with words of praise and hope for the new Jew, Gerim is using the ceremony to help integrate the convert into his or her new community—a point completely neglected by Yevamot.

Summary: B. Yevamot and Gerim

The date and literary history of the text in B. Yevamot 47a–b are obscure. In all likelihood the text is a Palestinian *beraita* of the second century, but it is possible that the text has experienced some expansions and interpolations. Because of the text's stylistic uniformity, however, the precise identification of these expansions and interpolations—if indeed there be any at all—is elusive. The most promising candidate for status as an interpolation is the speech B3a–f, which may be later than tractate Gerim. The date of that tractate is unknown (sixth to eighth centuries?), but its version of the conversion ceremony is best understood as a revision of a text much like that of Yevamot, if not that of Yevamot itself. Therefore Gerim is an important witness to the post-Yevamot, probably the post-talmudic, history of the ceremony, but is of no assistance in the reconstruction of its earliest stages. The following discussion of the purpose and history of the ceremony is based almost exclusively on the text of Yevamot.

The Purpose of the Rabbinic Conversion Ceremony

The rabbinic conversion ceremony had three major purposes: to regulate conversion; to ensure that the rituals were administered properly; and to ensure that a convert knew what awaited him/her. I shall elaborate on each of these separately.

TO REGULATE CONVERSION

As I discussed in chapter 4, in the second half of the second century B.C.E. citizenship in the Judaean state was opened to outsiders by the Hasmoneans. Idumaeans and Ituraeans became Judaeans, even if they still remained Idumaeans and Ituraeans. At the same time Judaean society began to accept as members gentiles who cast aside their false gods and believed in the one true God whose temple was in Jerusalem. Both the political and the religious incorporation were sealed by circumcision, in the first case representing political assimilation, in the second religious conversion. Aside from circumcision, there seems to have been no ritual or ceremony or symbol by which the newly enfranchised Judaean effected a transition to his new status. (*His* new status—not her new status, for there are no female converts yet.) Even without circumcision gentiles were sometimes regarded as Jews, and may even have regarded themselves as Jews, if they associated closely with, or benefacted, the Jews, or if they venerated the Jewish God "too much," or if they followed the Jewish laws. As I discussed in chapter 5, there were many ways to cross the boundary to become a Jew. There are no texts from the second-temple period that spell out a single set of practices that a gentile must perform or a single set of beliefs that a gentile must accept if he is to be regarded as a Jew by other Jews.[42] Circumcision aside, the boundary between Jew and gentile was fluid and not clearly marked.

In the second century C.E., animated by their passion for classifying and cataloguing persons, objects, and actions, the rabbis created the conversion ceremony that is preserved as a *beraita* in B. Yevamot 47a–b. The primary purpose of the ceremony was to introduce a measure of order and verifiability in a situation where previously chaos had reigned.[43] According to this text, conversion is effected through acceptance of the commandments, circumcision, and immersion, all three being done publicly. Thus the ceremony creates a single verifiable standard of conversion by which to distinguish between a gentile who has become a convert and a gentile who has not.

The first element is *acceptance of the commandments* (C1). This, we may assume, was the essence of "conversion" according to the authors of this text. Conversion means the acceptance of the Torah. Other rab-

---

42. See, for example, Chesnutt, *Death to Life* 155–165, and McKnight, *Light* 78–89.

43. The same tendency is conspicuous in the rabbinic laws regarding marriage and divorce.

binic texts state explicitly that conversions motivated by the prospect of matrimony, material gain, or other worldly consideration are suspect; according to some, invalid. Similarly, if the acceptance of the Torah was incomplete or insincere, the conversion was suspect; according to some, invalid. Whether our text would agree with these rulings, we cannot be sure, but its concern that the convert accept the obligatory nature of the commandments, with all their rewards and punishments, suggests that our text too would look askance at improper motivation and incomplete commitment.[44] By this definition, gentiles who simply practiced some or many rituals of the Jews (see category 4 in chapter 5 above) were not converts.

The second element is *circumcision*. This was the only ritual that, as far as is known, was demanded of all male converts by all non-Christian Jewish communities. As I have already discussed in chapter 5 above, gentiles might demonstrate their affection for Jews and Judaism in a number of different ways, but if they wished to attain full membership in a Jewish community, they had to be circumcised. Passages from Philo and Josephus that are cited by modern scholars as proof to the contrary prove no such thing. Righteous gentiles can certainly find favor in God's eyes even if they are not circumcised, and if they have come over to his exclusive worship they can be said, at least by Philo in one highly debated passage, to have become part of "Israel," but none of this implies "social conversion"—that is, the integration of the convert into the Jewish community.[45] In any event, all tannaitic texts that even incidentally refer to the requirements of conversion take circumcision for granted as a (or *the*) vehicle for conversion. This is true for Mishnah, Tosefta, and the Sifrei on Numbers.[46] The Yerushalmi (the Talmud of the land of Israel) cites a debate between R. Joshua and R. Eliezer about the relative importance of circumcision and immersion; both agree that circumcision is essential for conversion, but disagree concerning immersion. According to R. Eliezer a convert who has been circumcised but not immersed is nonetheless to be regarded as a convert, whereas R. Joshua says that immersion is no less essential than circumcision.[47]

---

44. Porton, *Stranger* 150, omits acceptance of the commandments from his paraphrase of the text. It is properly highlighted by Schiffman, *Who Was a Jew?* 21–23. On incomplete acceptance of the commandments, see below, note 79; on improper motivation, see below, note 85.

45. See chapter 5 above, note 41.

46. Mishnah Pesahim 8:8; T. Shabbat 15:9 71L; T. Pesahim 7:14 181–182L; T. Avodah Zarah 3:12 464Z; Sifrei on Numbers 108 112H (statement of Rabbi).

47. Y. Qiddushin 3.13 64d.

It is only the Bavli that gives us pause, for here—and only here—within the span of a single page we are told three times that some rabbis believe that immersion is essential for conversion but circumcision is not. First, in the Bavli's version of the debate between R. Eliezer and R. Joshua, the latter is attributed the view that a convert who has been immersed but not circumcised is nonetheless to be regarded as a convert; in other words, circumcision can be dispensed with, but immersion cannot. The view that the Yerushalmi had attributed to R. Joshua (that both immersion and circumcision are essential) is here attributed to "the sages." Second, in its analysis of the debate between R. Eliezer and R. Joshua, the anonymous discussant in the Bavli (the *setam*) argues that even R. Eliezer would agree that immersion alone is sufficient to make a convert a convert; the debate between the rabbis, we are told, centers on the question of whether circumcision alone *also* might be sufficient. To this question R. Eliezer says yes, and R. Joshua says no. Third, in its interpretation of a debate between R. Yosi and R. Judah on a separate but related matter, the (same?) anonymous discussant (the *setam*) argues that R. Judah believes that either circumcision or immersion is essential for conversion, whereas R. Yosi believes that both are essential. Here, then, are three authorities in the Bavli who believe that circumcision is not essential for conversion if immersion has been performed: R. Joshua, R. Eliezer as reinterpreted by the anonymous talmudic discussion, and R. Judah as reinterpreted by the anonymous talmudic discussion.[48]

There is abundant scholarly discussion of the view that the Bavli attributes to R. Joshua; many scholars see it as rabbinic confirmation of the fact that not all Jewish communities in the ancient world insisted on the circumcision of converts.[49] This argument is unconvincing. It assumes that the view that the Bavli has attributed to R. Joshua represents, or was supposed to represent, normative law—that is, a legal practice to be followed by living Jews in a real community. However, there is absolutely no evidence for this assumption. Both the Yerushalmi and Bavli cite several "case histories" to illustrate the legal issues under discussion; these stories feature converts who are said to have been circumcised but not to have been immersed. The general conclusion is that the conversions are valid nonetheless. Neither the Yerushalmi nor the

48. B. Yevamot 46a–b.

49. For a summary of some of the modern scholarly views, see Porton, *Stranger* 73 n. 15 and 94–96.

Bavli cites a single case of a convert who has been immersed but not circumcised; neither Talmud did so, because such a case did not require any discussion. Further, I would suggest that the view attributed to R. Joshua in the Bavli may have been invented for the sake of literary symmetry. In the Yerushalmi, R. Eliezer states that circumcision is essential and R. Joshua states that both immersion and circumcision are essential. One logical possibility is missing. The missing possibility was invented by the Bavli, attributed to R. Joshua, and R. Joshua's original view was attributed to the sages, indicating that it was meant to be the "correct" one. The *setam* in the Bavli followed suit in its reinterpretation of R. Eliezer and R. Judah, promoting a position that is an intellectual tour de force but which has no relevance to normative law.[50]

Even if my suggested interpretation is wrong, let us not exaggerate the significance of the Bavli's information. No rabbinic source of the land of Israel supports the view that a conversion can be effected by immersion without circumcision. R. Eliezer and R. Judah, as originally presented in the Bavli, do not need—and, I think, would disagree with— the reinterpretation of their views advocated by the anonymous voice of the Talmud. As for the Bavli's version of R. Joshua, it is contradicted by the Yerushalmi. Aside from this single page of the Bavli, nowhere else does the Bavli intimate that circumcision might not be essential for conversion. Everywhere else in the Bavli, it is assumed that circumcision is a hallmark of the people of Israel and that converts are circumcised like the native born.[51] I conclude that all the rabbinic communities of the land of Israel and, in all likelihood, all the rabbinic communities of Babylonia, just like all non-Christian Jewish communities known to us in the ancient world, would have insisted that converts be circumcised if they were to become members of the Jewish community.[52]

50. This is a prominent feature of discourse in the Bavli; see David Kraemer, *The Mind of the Talmud* (New York: Oxford University Press, 1990).

51. For rabbinic views of circumcision, see S. Stern, *Identity* 63–67; on the requirement of circumcision for conversion, see especially R. Judah the Patriarch in B. Keritot 9a (paralleled by Sifrei Numbers 108 112H).

52. Porton, *Stranger* 139–148 and 152–154, greatly exaggerates the degree of confusion and uncertainty in rabbinic texts regarding the place of circumcision in the conversion process. Porton confuses immersion with circumcision; debates regarding the former are not debates about the latter. Mishnah, Tosefta, Sifrei on Numbers, and Yerushalmi agree that circumcision is essential; it is only B. Yevamot 46a–b that suggests otherwise. According to Porton's own stated methodology, he should have concluded that it was the Bavli (and Babylonian Judaism?) that was unsure about the place of circumcision within the conversion process; how does the Bavli's uncertainty become the uncertainty of rabbinic Judaism as a whole? Porton's statement (148) that "it is impossible to determine

The third required element is *immersion*. In first-century Judaism immersion was the standard ritual of purification; all those entering the temple precincts immersed themselves first so as not to profane the sacred with any impurity.[53] Converts too, like the native born, would have needed to purify themselves before bringing or eating a sacrifice. Pietistic Jews (like John the Baptist and the Essenes) practiced immersion in other contexts and for other reasons as well, but immersion as a conversion ritual for gentiles is attested for the first time only in the letters of Paul and the book of Acts.[54] Whether Christian baptism derives from, or is basically identical to, Jewish immersion, or whether it derives from non-Jewish sources, or whether it is a unique feature of Christianity, is a much-debated question that I would like to avoid here.[55] The first evidence that gentile converts to non-Christian Judaism must immerse in water is a statement of Epictetus (first quarter of the second century C.E.), but the statement is not without some difficulties.[56] Immersion for converts is nowhere mentioned in the Mishnah, but is taken for

---

what the general or majority opinion was on this matter in any given period" is wrong, at least with regard to circumcision. Porton (148) also rejects my statement that all non-Christian Jewish communities would have demanded circumcision of their converts, but his objection fails. He assumes that R. Joshua in the Bavli represents the normative law of a community, but for this assumption—and it is just an assumption—he has no evidence. Porton himself elsewhere realizes the literary nature of many rabbinic disputes (*Stranger* 193–194 and 212).

53. M. Yoma 3:3, cf. M. Hagigah 2:5–6; T. Negaim 8:9 628Z. All Jews purify themselves in order to partake of the festival sacrifices: M. Sheqalim 8:1, M. Betzah 2:2 and M. Hagigah 3:6. Philo too assumes that all those entering the temple would be purified first (*On the Special Laws* 1.261); see Bickerman, *Studies* 2.89–90, and Sanders, *Judaism* 134–135. Cf. Acts 21 (Paul). Archaeologists have discovered numerous *miqvaot* (ritual baths) in and around the stairs leading to the temple.

54. Reasonably unambiguous references to the baptism of gentiles: 1 Cor. 1:13–17, 12:13; Gal. 3:27; Acts 8:12–13, 37–38; 10:47–48; 16:14–15 (or is Lydia a pious Jew?); 16:33.

55. For a review of older scholarship and an intelligent presentation of the issues, see H. H. Rowley, "Jewish Proselyte Baptism and the Baptism of John," in *From Moses to Qumran: Studies in the Old Testament* (New York: Association Press, 1963; originally published in 1940) 211–235. For more recent surveys see Légasse, "Baptême juif"; Gerhard Lohfink, "Der Ursprung der christlichen Taufe," *Theologische Quartalschrift* 156 (1976) 35–54; Gerhard Barth, *Die Taufe in frühchristlicher Zeit* (Neukirchen-Vluyn: Neukirchener, 1981); Robert Webb, *John the Baptizer and Prophet*, JSNT Supplement no. 62 (Sheffield: Sheffield Academic Press, 1991).

56. M. Stern, *Authors* no. 254. The text is rather cryptic, perhaps corrupt; see my discussion in chapter 2 above. Epictetus' failure to mention circumcision is puzzling, as Stern remarks. The exhortation of the fourth Sibylline Oracle to gentiles to "Wash your whole bodies in perennial rivers" (4.165) does not refer to a conversion ritual. The passage exhorts gentiles to lay aside their murders and ask forgiveness for their crimes, in the hope that God will decide as a result not to destroy the world. They are not being exhorted to convert to Judaism. In any case, the date of the passage is not much earlier than Epictetus.

granted by the Tosefta.[57] As we have just seen, in both the Bavli and
Yerushalmi, various sages, both *tannaim* and *amoraim*, debate whether
immersion is dispensable or not.

The emergence of immersion as a conversion ritual is no doubt to be
connected with the emergence of the possibility that women too could
convert to Judaism, not merely through marriage to a Jewish spouse but
in their own right. Josephus has several reports of women converting to
Judaism (or "drawing near to Jewish practices") in the mid first century
C.E., but does not mention the ritual or rituals that served to distinguish them from women who merely enjoyed following some Jewish
practices or associating with Jews. Perhaps they were not "converts" at
all; they did not undergo social conversion and they were not marked
by any conversion ritual. I have discussed this problem at the end of
chapter 5, even if I am not entirely sure how it should be solved. In any
event, rabbinic texts and traditions of the second century C.E. unambiguously attest for the first time the immersion of converts (both men
and women) and the conversion of women. The first is a precondition
for the second; the second, in turn, is a precondition for the matrilineal
principle, which also is attested for the first time in the second century
C.E. (see chapter 9 below).

Our *beraita* on B. Yevamot 47a–b, which requires both circumcision and immersion, fits perfectly within these developments. In common with all other tannaitic and Palestinian texts (and with the over-
whelming bulk of the Bavli too), it requires circumcision. It agrees with
R. Joshua (as presented in the Yerushalmi) and the sages (as presented
in the Bavli) that immersion is no less a requirement than circumcision.

Fourth, and last, our text not only requires acceptance of the commandments, circumcision, and immersion; it also requires that they be
performed publicly. In pre-rabbinic times (i.e., before the second century C.E.) conversion to Judaism was entirely a private affair. Conversions were not supervised or overseen by anyone, and there was no conversion ceremony. Circumcisions could be performed by anyone in any
manner (see below). Any gentile who followed (or pretended to follow)
Jewish practices could claim to be a convert. The creation of the rabbinic conversion ceremony meant that conversion was now a public affair. A gentile could no longer simply claim to be a convert and could
no longer convert to Judaism on his own. He (in the core of the text
the subject is a "he") must be able to provide proof of his conversion.
As the Sifra says, if a gentile comes before us and claims to be a convert,

57. S. J. D. Cohen, "'Proselyte Baptism.'"

"he must bring proof"—that is, proof that in fact he is a convert. In the parallel version in the Bavli, "proof" is explained to mean "he comes with his witnesses."[58] The conversion process involves formal interaction with native Jews (the anonymous "they" of the text). In the core of the text the identity of these Jews is deliberately left vague, perhaps because the rabbis were not yet willing or able to assert their exclusive control over the process. Anyone could speak to the convert, perhaps even a traveling salesman as in the Adiabene story in Josephus. The introduction of "two disciples of the sages" to do the instruction preceding the immersion (D3 and E3) is a further step (a later stage?) in the assertion of rabbinic control over the conversion process.

Our text is content with only *two* sages, to act as instructors and witnesses. According to a *beraita* cited just before our text, R. Judah (a *tanna,* mid second century C.E.) stated that "a convert who converts in a court, behold he is a (valid) convert. (If he converts) by himself, he is not a (valid) convert." If this be a genuine *beraita* and if the attribution to R. Judah be reliable, we may conclude that in the middle of the second century some sages were advocating that conversions take place before *three* people, not to act as witnesses but to serve as a court. In this conception conversion to Judaism was to be not only a public act but also a judicial act. This view did not gain ascendance immediately; Mishnah Sanhedrin 1:1–3, devoted to judicial matters that require a court of three, ignores conversion. In the middle of the third century, R. Yohanan declared (according to the testimony of R. Hiyya) that conversion required a tribunal of *three.* This view was confirmed in some case histories cited by both the Bavli and the Yerushalmi.[59] Confronted by a contradiction between our *beraita* and the ruling of R. Yohanan, the anonymous talmudic discussant adduces a (genuine?) claim of R. Yohanan that our text should be emended to read *three,* thus conceding that there is an irremediable conflict between the two positions. If the emendation attributed to R. Yohanan is, in fact, a genuine tradition emanating from that sage, we have a firm *terminus ante quem* for our text: it must precede R. Yohanan. In any case, all the parts of the conversion ceremony (acceptance of commandments, circumcision, immersion) take place before an audience of two or three.[60]

58. Sifra Qedoshim pereq 8:1 91aW; B. Yevamot 46b (bottom).

59. R. Hiyya in the name of R. Yohanan: B. Yevamot 46b, quoted at B. Yevamot 47b and B. Qiddushin 62b. Case histories: B. Yevamot 46b and Y. Yevamot 8:1 8d. For tribunals of three in the Bavli, cf. Bekhorot 30b and Avodah Zarah 64b.

60. Emendation: B. Yevamot 47b (see above, note 21). Samet, "Conversion" 325, misconstrues the texts concerning the requirement of three persons.

Verifiability was necessary. Rabbinic literature provides evidence that just outside the rabbinic orbit chaos still prevailed. R. Hiyya b. Abba (mid third century) visited Gabala (according to one version) or Tyre (according to another) and was confronted there by a case of a man who converted to Judaism through circumcision alone without immersion.[61] A similar case came before another rabbi of the same period.[62] R. Judah (mid second century) was confronted by the case of a self-made convert.[63] The Tosefta even considers the (theoretical) possibility that a gentile might convert himself, continue to live among gentiles, and not even know that work is prohibited on the Sabbath![64] From the rabbis' perspective chaos reigned "out there," and the creation of a formal conversion ceremony was one of their responses.[65]

TO ADMINISTER THE RITUALS PROPERLY

A second purpose of the ceremony was to ensure that the rituals of circumcision and immersion be performed properly, and this in two senses: first, that the technical requirements be met; second, that the rituals be performed with the proper intent. I shall discuss the first of these briefly, and comment on the second more extensively.

The conversion ceremony seeks to ensure that the technical requirements of circumcision and immersion are properly followed. This concern is evident in C2a (regarding circumcision) and F (regarding immersion). C2a reads: "If shreds remain on him that impede the circumcision, they circumcise him a second time." This is an allusion to the requirement that a circumcision include the tearing of the membrane under the foreskin so that the glans of the penis be entirely exposed, thus rendering epispasm (drawing down of penile skin over the glans to simulate a foreskin) impossible. This requirement, known as *periah*, is of uncertain origin but seems to have been instituted after the Hadrianic persecutions. C2a ordains that if, after the circumcision, any of the membrane covering the glans still remains, the convert must be circumcised again; that is, the offending membrane must be removed.[66] Regarding immer-

---

61. Gabala (in Nabataea): B. Yevamot 46a; Tyre: Y. Qiddushin 3:12 64d.

62. B. Yevamot 46b.   63. B. Yevamot 47a.

64. T. Shabbat 8:5 30L and parallels.

65. They also attempted to identify those areas whose Jewish population was "impure." See Y. and B. Qiddushin c. 4 passim.

66. On *periah* see Rubin, "Stretching of the Foreskin," and Dulière, "La seconde circoncision." On its origin, see Schürer, *History* 1.149 n. 28. Is *periah* known already to Jubilees 15:33? On *periah* in the Mishnah, see the texts cited in note 16 above. On the Hadrianic persecutions, see above, note 32.

sion, F2–3 ordains that immersion must take place in a *miqveh* or some other such body of water that a menstruant might use for her purification, and that no clothing, jewelry, or other object interpose between the body and the water.[67]

The conversion ceremony also seeks to ensure that the circumcision and the immersion be performed with the proper intent. This concern is evident in the insistence that circumcision follow immediately upon the instruction (C2) and that immersion be accompanied by renewed instruction even at the expense of some repetition (D3–4 and E3–4). This is a novel and important idea.

During the second-temple period circumcision was deemed efficacious no matter how, under what circumstances, or by whom it was performed. It was a surgical procedure, a physical operation on a piece of skin. The circumciser did not even have to be a Jew, let alone a priest or a sage.[68] Intention was irrelevant; involuntary circumcision was fine, too.[69] As long as his foreskin was removed, a man could present himself as a convert—or as a Jew. This view persists in the Mishnah and in rabbinic Judaism generally. Thus rabbinic law permits the conversion of children and the circumcision of slaves even against their will.[70] This position is well articulated by R. Yosi in a statement that is transmitted in three different versions: "where have we seen circumcision that is not for the sake of the covenant?" or "where have we seen that the Torah requires circumcision to be for the sake (of the covenant)?" or "Where have we found in the Torah that circumcision requires (proper) intent?"[71]

By R. Yosi's time (mid second century), however, a contrary position was emerging. Some rabbis distinguished circumcision, the removal of a piece of skin, from *berit* or "covenant," the removal of that same piece of skin but under religious auspices and for religious purposes. For a circumcision to be a *berit*, it must be performed by a Jew and with the intent of denoting subservience to the God of the Jews and his com-

---

67. See note 20 above.

68. In the Adiabene story Izates has himself circumcised by the court physician (Josephus, *AJ* 20.46).

69. Josephus claims that the Idumaeans and Ituraeans were compelled by the Hasmoneans to be circumcised (*AJ* 13.257–258 and 13.318–319). Even if this claim is false (see chapter 4 above), it shows that in Josephus' time the physical fact of circumcision, no matter what the circumstances under which it was perpetrated, sufficed for conversion.

70. Conversion of children: M. Ketuvot 1:2, 3:1, 4:3; B. Ketuvot 11a; B. Yevamot 60b; Y. Qiddushin 4:1 65b. Circumcision of slaves even against their will: B. Yevamot 48a and Y. Yevamot 8:1 8d.

71. T. Avodah Zarah 3:13 464Z; B. Avodah Zarah 27a; Y. Yevamot 8:1 9a.

mandments. If a circumcised gentile wishes to be converted to Judaism, a drop of blood must be drawn from his circumcised member, so that his circumcision can be deemed a *berit*. R. Judah, a contemporary of R. Yosi, seems to be the primary authority behind this view. He argues against R. Yosi that neither a gentile nor a Samaritan may circumcise a Jew, the former because he is not part of the covenant, the latter because he will not perform the ritual with the proper intent.[72]

As far as I can determine, this conception of circumcision is nowhere explicitly attested before the Tosefta's citation of the opinion of R. Judah. But there is one story in Josephus that suggests that this conception may already have been developing in the late first century B.C.E. In the Herodian period, various foreign princes married, or attempted to marry, into the royal house; in each case Josephus reports whether or not they were circumcised. The most interesting such case concerns Syllaeus the Arab who sought to marry Salome, sister of Herod the Great. Syllaeus was asked "to be enrolled in the Jewish customs"; this he refused to do, and the wedding was called off. It is possible that this phrase is a synonym for "to be circumcised," but since Syllaeus was an Arab it is likely that he was circumcised already; indeed, if he was being asked to be circumcised, Josephus should simply have said so. It is possible, therefore, that the text means that Syllaeus was asked to affirm, by one means or another, that his circumcision was now to be understood as a sign of allegiance to the Jewish laws—that is, a sign of Judaean citizenship. Whereas a century earlier the Hasmoneans could simply declare the circumcised Idumaeans and Ituraeans to be Judaeans, now Syllaeus had to make that declaration himself. Perhaps we see here for the first time the view that the intent of a circumcision affects its value. The circumcision of an Arab does not have the same effect as the circumci-

---

72. In T. Avodah Zarah 3:12 464Z, R. Meir and the sages debate whether a gentile may circumcise a Jew. The issue in question is whether a gentile can be trusted to perform the operation without intentionally killing or maiming the Jew in the process. B. Avodah Zarah 26b–27a quotes the opinion of R. Judah: "How do we know from scripture that circumcision performed by a gentile is invalid? Because it says, 'And you shall observe my covenant.'" In other words, circumcision performed by a gentile is invalid because the practitioner is not himself bound by the covenant; his harmful intentions are irrelevant. Similarly R. Judah (arguing against R. Yosi) invalidates a circumcision performed by a Samaritan because his intent is directed to Mount Gerizim. This debate concerns the circumcision of Jewish children, but presumably it applies to the circumcision of converts as well. Aware of R. Judah's view, R. Simeon b. Eleazar (second half of the second century) claimed that the House of Shammai required the drawing of blood from a prospective convert who had been circumcised before his conversion, while the House of Hillel did not require it (T. Shabbat 15:9 71–72L and parallels). The opinion ascribed to the House of Shammai agrees with that of R. Judah.

sion of a Jew. As the Talmud states, "A circumcised Arab and a circumcised Gibeonite may not eat of the Paschal sacrifice."[73] If this interpretation of Josephus is correct, we have an adumbration of the view that would later be attributed to R. Judah in the Tosefta.

Under the influence of R. Judah's view (which accords remarkably with that of Origen),[74] the conversion ceremony requires that circumcision be juxtaposed to instruction, so that both the convert and the circumciser be motivated properly. Also under the influence of this view, circumcision of converts came to be accompanied by a benediction, a development not yet known to our text.[75]

Immersion too, according to some sages, can be efficacious even without proper intent. Thus according to one opinion found in both Talmudim, a convert does not require (at least after the fact) a separate immersion for the sake of conversion, because we may presume that as a Jew the convert, whether male or female, would routinely immerse for purification after sexual discharge, and such immersion is sufficient for conversion as well.[76] Our *beraita*, however, insists that immersion be accompanied by instruction in the commandments so that the convert would be motivated properly.[77] The duplication of B1 by D4 and E4 is the result of this insistence.

TO ENSURE THAT THE CONVERT KNOWS WHAT AWAITS HIM/HER

In the ceremony the potential convert receives two kinds of instruction on his path to Judaism. In the first (A) he is told about

73. Syllaeus: *AJ* 15.225. "Enrolled" translates *engraphēnai*. Circumcised Arab: Mekhilta, Pisha 15, on Exod. 12:45 (54H-R, 1.122L) (R. Isaac); B. Yevamot 71a (R. Shemayah). On the circumcision of Arabs see chapter 2 above, note 77.

74. Origen, *Against Celsus* 5.47, trans. Chadwick: ". . . anyone who is circumcised (for one purpose) is entirely different from one who is circumcised for another purpose. For the purpose and law and intention of the man who performs the circumcision put the thing into a different category . . . Thus circumcision is different according to the different doctrines of the people who practice the rite."

75. B. Shabbat 137b (almost certainly an early medieval addition to the text of the Talmud; see Neil Danzig, *Introduction to Halakhot Pesuqot* (in Hebrew) (New York: Jewish Theological Seminary, 1993) 583 n. 265. There may be a reference to a benediction accompanying the immersion of converts in B. Pesahim 7b; see Tosafot s.v. "*al hatevilah.*"

76. See Bar Qappara in Y. Qiddushin 3:13 64d, and R. Asi and R. Joshua ben Levi in B. Yevamot 45b. These statements are misconstrued by Porton, *Stranger* 145 and 152 (who thinks they refer to immersion by the convert while still a gentile), but are explained correctly on p. 73.

77. Whether Christian baptism requires proper intent is the subject of Acts 19:2–6.

the trials and tribulations of being a Jew. If he is accepted for further instruction, he is told about the commandments and about rewards and punishments (B and D). If I may use an analogy from school life, the potential convert must first pass his admissions interview (A) before being instructed in the requirements for graduation (B and D). At first glance there seems to be a disparity between the toughness of the admissions interview, which seems intended to drive the convert away, or at least to discourage him, and the easiness of the graduation requirements, which seem intended not to discourage the convert. Let us look at this matter more closely.

The purpose of the formal instruction (B) was to inform the convert of what was expected of him. But exactly how much did a potential convert need to be told and how much did he have to accept? Rabbinic texts suggest several different answers. The maximalist position is taken by the following law (from the Babylonian Talmud, following the Tosefta and the Sifra), which makes clear that a convert must accept the entire Torah:

A gentile who approaches[78] (with the intent) to accept (all) the words of the Torah except for one, they do not accept him (as a convert). R. Yosi b. R. Judah says: (he is not to be accepted as a convert) even (if he rejects) one detail of the words of the sages.[79]

We may presume that the framers of this rule would insist that a convert explicitly accept all the words of the Torah; perhaps they would also insist that a convert receive extensive instruction in order to make sure that he would not reject any of the commandments, although any instruction in all the words of the Torah, including each and every rabbinic ordinance, would outlast the lifetime of any potential convert.

A more moderate position is taken by the midrashic expansions of Ruth 1:16–17. For the midrash, Ruth was the archetypal convert, and her declaration of fidelity to Naomi was understood to be a response to Naomi's instruction in Judaism. But in all these midrashic expansions Naomi's instruction remains brief and lacunose. In the fullest version of the midrash, adduced by the anonymous discussant on B. Yevamot 47b, Ruth acknowledges to Naomi her acceptance of the prohibition of exceeding the Sabbath limits, the prohibition of nonmarital intimacy between men and women, the 613 commandments, the prohibition of

78. *Sheba;* see note 4 above.
79. B. Bekhorot 30a; cf. Sifra, Qedoshim 8:3 91aW, and T. Demai 2:4–5 69L. Cf. too Sifrei Numbers 112 121H.

idolatry, the four modes of execution inflicted by the high court, and the two kinds of court-supervised burial—quite a mixed bag! Note that the 613 commandments are covered in only one sentence. Other versions of the midrash provide a different and shorter selection.[80] These midrashim are based on the exegesis of Scripture, not actual practice. They demonstrate, however, that the instruction of converts did not have to treat all the commandments in detail and could consist of a rather cursory summary of large issues.

The conversion ceremony in Yevamot is following (or establishing) the tradition found in the midrashim on Ruth. Only the prohibitions of agricultural tithes, Sabbath, and food are mentioned explicitly; as for the rest, "they do not (speak) too much to him, nor are they too detailed with him" (B5), because he is to be instructed in only "a few" of the commandments (B1 and D4). Perhaps the authors of the *beraita* would have agreed with R. Yosi that a convert is not to be accepted if he rejects "even one detail of the words of the sages,"[81] but they were not interested in assuring themselves that the convert has accepted "all" or "each and every" commandment, biblical and rabbinic. The primary concern here is to verify that the convert knows what awaits him, and for this purpose instruction in a "few" (representative) commandments would suffice. The rest he would learn later.[82]

There is perhaps yet another explanation for the rather scanty instruction that the convert receives.[83] As I remarked in chapter 2 above,

---

80. Ruth Rabbah on 1:16–17, ed. M. B. Lerner, in "Midrash Ruth Rabbah According to Ms. Oxford 164" (Ph.D. diss., Hebrew University, 1971) 76–78 (with references to parallels). See too the Targum on Ruth, ed. Etan Levine, in *The Aramaic Version of Ruth* (Rome: Biblical Institute Press, 1973) 22–24 and 56–62. Ruth Rabbah also refers to *hilkhot gērim*, "the laws (to be taught) to converts," but the meaning of the reference is obscure. On Ruth as the archetype for converts, see Bamberger, *Proselytism* 195–199, and D. R. G. Beattie, *The Book of Ruth in Jewish Exegesis* (Sheffield: JSOT Press, 1977).

81. Perhaps they would have disagreed. R. Yosi would reject a convert who refuses to accept even one detail (*diqduq*) of the words of the sages, but the authors of the *beraita* say explicitly "nor are they too detailed (*medaqdeqin*) with him."

82. In his paraphrase of B3, R. Moses of Coucy (ca. 1240) adds: "so that he will not say later, 'Had I known this, I would not have converted'" (*Sefer Mitzvot Gadol*, negative precepts, no. 116 [ed. Venice, 1547, 40d]). That a convert will learn much that is essential only after his conversion is recognized clearly in the stories about Hillel in B. Shabbat 31a; see Porton, *Stranger* 150 and 196–200.

83. I assume that the ceremony as described in the *beraita* is complete and does not presume any anterior instruction. One could argue, I suppose, that the ceremony is merely a public formal recognition of discussions, instruction, and experimentation that had been taking place privately. This is certainly true of modern conversions, but I do not see any reason to think that this is the setting in life of our text. As far as I have been able to determine, non-rabbinic sources do not reveal what, if anything, was taught to prospective converts. (I leave aside the numerous works that according to the fantasy of mod-

there is a rabbinic tradition that strongly disapproves of Torah study by gentiles. "Transmitting words of Torah to a gentile is prohibited" reads one adage; "a gentile who studies Torah is liable to the death penalty" reads another. If Jews may not teach gentiles Torah, and if gentiles may not study Torah, how should Jews deal with prospective converts? In the medieval period some Jews reached the extreme, if logical, conclusion: a convert may study Torah only after he has been circumcised and converted. A Jew may not instruct a gentile in Torah, even if that gentile is seeking to convert to Judaism! Our text is not as extreme; the potential convert is to receive instruction in some of the commandments, but not at great length or in great detail. He can continue his studies after he converts.[84]

The ethos presumed by the formal instruction (B) is one of openness and encouragement. The stern speech about the violation of the Sabbath and food laws (B3a–f)—if indeed it is not an interpolation altogether—is offset by the positive and reassuring tone of B4a–c. The convert is not to be overwhelmed by demands or information. The same attitude is evident in the ceremony's hesitation to investigate the convert's motives. He is asked, "Why have you decided to approach (us) to be converted?" (A3), but the question is not pursued. The anonymous "they" do not inquire whether the gentile is converting for some ulterior purpose like matrimony or financial gain. Such motives would disqualify the conversion according to R. Nehemiah (second half of the second century),[85] but our *beraita* is not interested in discovering reasons to reject the applicant or disqualify the conversion. He is to be accepted "immediately" (A8; cf. C2 and D2).

As I noted above, the opening speech (A3–5, the "admissions interview") might seem to be motivated by a different ethos, one of relative coolness toward the potential convert. As the anonymous discussant on B. Yevamot 47b says, "If (as a result of hearing the speech) he wishes to leave, let him leave, as R. Helbo said, 'Converts are as difficult for Israel

---

ern scholars served as "missionary tracts.") Note Testament of Joseph 4:4–8 (Potiphar's wife came to Joseph under pretense of receiving instruction, *katēchēsis*); the text may be Jewish or Christian (or both!).

84. On the prohibition of teaching Torah to a gentile, see chapter 2 above, at note 46. S. Stern, *Identity* 214 n.116, astutely connects that tradition with our *beraita*. The prohibition of teaching an applicant any of the sect's *mishpatim* in Covenant of Damascus 15:10–11 is probably to be explained differently: the applicant should not have an unfair advantage at his examination. Medieval prohibition: see Zohar, *Ahare Mot* on Leviticus 18:4 (3.73a ed. Vilna).

85. B. Yevamot 24b (R. Nehemiah); Y. Qiddushin 4:1 65b (anonymous *beraita*, cited below).

as scabs.'" Even as we are in the process of converting the gentile, we hope that he will go away. This negative attitude toward converts is attested in various places throughout rabbinic literature, but in all likelihood the conversion ceremony is not one of them. A "tough interview" does not necessarily mean that the interviewer wants the candidate to fail. As Gerim correctly explains, "And all those (other) words that we said to you (at the opening of the ceremony), we said them only to increase your reward" (d7). Monitory words serve only to heighten the resolve—and reward—of those committed to Judaism. The Talmud's interpretation is similarly ignored by the *Seder Elijah Rabbah,* a work of the tenth century. Referring to our text as a Mishnah, it states: "Thus have the sages taught in the Mishnah, 'A (potential) convert who approaches to be converted, they extend him a hand in order to have him enter under the wings of the (divine) presence.'"[86]

The monitory words of section A also serve to heighten the drama of the ceremony.[87] When Joshua attempted to dissuade the people from accepting the covenant with God, he surely would have been disappointed had the people answered anything other than "No, for we shall worship the Lord." His dissuasion was not real dissuasion.[88] Similarly, after the prospective convert has been told of the difficulties of being a Jew, surely the framers of this document would be disappointed were he to answer anything other than "I know and am unworthy" (A7). This ritualized discouragement and self-effacement are effective drama, and provide no evidence for rabbinic reluctance to accept converts.

Further evidence that this interpretation is correct comes from a passage in the Yerushalmi:

Someone who converts for the sake of love—whether it be a man for a woman or whether it be a woman for a man—and likewise converts (who convert for the sake) of the table of kings, and likewise converts (who convert out of the fear) of lions, and likewise (the) converts (of the days) of Mordecai and Esther—they do not accept them.

86. *Seder Elijah Rabbah* 6, p. 35 Ish Shalom (this passage is part of a long section of *Seder Elijah Rabbah* that is interpolated in Leviticus Rabbah; cf. Leviticus Rabbah 2:9 p. 49 Margalioth). Maimonides follows this interpretation as well; see *Laws of Prohibited Intercourse* 14:2.

87. This point became clear to me through a discussion with my student Robert Bohm.

88. Joshua 24:19–21. Origen realized that Josh. 24:15–18 is a good analogue to (Christian) catechism and conversion; see Origen, *Exhortation to Martyrdom* 17 = *Alexandrian Christianity,* ed. J. E. L. Oulton and H. Chadwick (Philadelphia: Westminster, 1954) 404–405.

Rav said,

The law is that they are converts. And they (the sages) do not push them
(away) as they push away (potential) converts at first, but they accept
them, for they (the converts) need a welcome reception, (for) perhaps
they converted for the Name.[89]

Rav's statement is significant because it attests the practice of dissuad-
ing potential converts, a practice exemplified in our *beraita*. Rav's statement may also help us understand the intent of that dissuasion. According to the first opinion, improperly motivated converts are not to be
accepted, whereas Rav (a first-generation *amora* active in both Babylonia and Palestine) says that they are to be accepted and welcomed.
There are numerous ambiguities and exegetical difficulties in this text,
but I cannot treat the text in detail here. The simplest way to construe
the passage is as follows.[90] According to the first opinion, improperly
motivated converts are not to be accepted as candidates for conversion
before the fact, and are not to be regarded as valid converts after the
fact. Rav basically agrees, except that Rav states that they may be accepted as candidates for a second or a renewed conversion. Regular first-
time converts are pushed away at first, but these second-time converts
are not to be pushed away. They are to be accepted (i.e., converted) and
accorded a welcome reception, because there is a chance that even in
their first conversion they had been motivated by a love of God (or: because there is a chance that in their second conversion they are motivated by a love of God).[91] This interpretation of Rav's view is supported
by a statement of the Yerushalmi elsewhere in connection with a debate
about the Samaritans. According to a common rabbinic view the Samaritans were improperly motivated converts (they converted out of fear of
lions). The Yerushalmi asks:

If someone converted not for the sake of heaven and afterward (would)
convert again for the sake of heaven—is it possible that they would not accept him (as a convert)? (No! Of course they accept him.)[92]

Someone who converted the first time for improper motives can convert a second time for proper motives; perhaps the very act of renewed
conversion is testimony to proper motivation.

89. Y. Qiddushin 4:1 65b.
90. Porton construes the text differently; see *Stranger* 74.
91. *yitgayyeru* would be smoother than *giyyeru*.
92. Y. Gittin 1:5 43c.

If my interpretation is correct, according to Rav the purpose of the dissuasion is not to chase away converts but to verify their motives. First-time converts need to be dissuaded at first, so that we can see if they are motivated by a love of God. Second-time converts need no dissuasion, because their renewed application shows that they had already converted, or will yet convert, for the sake of heaven. Their motives are not to be examined; they are to be welcomed warmly. Rav thus agrees with the Mekhilta:

If a person comes to you to be converted, and he comes only for the sake of heaven, you should draw him near and not keep him at a distance.[93]

Initial dissuasion is for the purpose of discovering the candidate's motivation, not for the purpose of chasing him away. I conclude that the Bavli's interpretation of part A of the conversion ceremony is incorrect. R. Helbo's position is not that of our *beraita*.

All in all, then, the authors of the ceremony are consistent in their attitude toward the potential convert. They are eager to accept him even if they wish to verify his sincerity and ensure that he knows what awaits him. Rabbinic Judaism in antiquity had a wide variety of attitudes toward converts and conversion, some even more friendly and open than that evident in our *beraita*, some decidedly less so.[94] The conversion ceremony in B. Yevamot 47a–b appears to occupy a median position.

Conclusion

The rabbinic conversion ceremony of B. Yevamot 47a–b is not—or, at least, is not primarily—an initiation ritual. It is not concerned with the spiritual state of the convert, his inner being, or the state of his soul. In this ceremony, by which a gentile converts to Judaism, there is no mention of God or of the eternality of the Torah.[95]

---

93. Mekhilta Amalek 3 2.172–173L = Amalek 1 193H-R.

94. More friendly and open: see, for example, the stories on B. Shabbat 31a and B. Menahot 44a (presented in chapter 5 above). For the variety of rabbinic attitudes toward converts and conversion see Bamberger, *Proselytism* chap. 9; Urbach, *Sages* 541–554; Goodman, "Proselytising"; Porton, *Stranger* 211–220.

95. The ceremony is not modeled on, or inspired by, any of the biblical ceremonies in which the Israelites confirm their covenant with God and pledge loyalty to his commandments (e.g., Exodus 24; Deuteronomy 27; 31:10–13; Joshua 24; Nehemiah 8–10).

96. But a resident alien in the land of Israel (a *gēr toshav*) must, in the rabbinic imagination at least, deny his idolatry (Y. Yevamot 8:1 8d; B. Avodah Zarah 64b). The

There is no denial of paganism or the pagan gods,[96] no repentance for the sins of a life lived under the sway of foreign deities, no abjuration of evil, no language of rebirth and renewal.[97] There is no review of the sacred history of the holy people, nor is there any prayer.[98] Even the theological underpinnings of the commandments are ignored; the midrash claims that conversion to Judaism is a reenactment of the revelation of the Torah on Mount Sinai, but our text contains no allusion to Sinai or revelation or covenant.[99] The ceremony is devoid of anything mystical, demonological, or "spiritual." The convert says a total of four words (A7). The ceremony centers around circumcision and immersion, but what meaning these rituals might have, and how they affect the body and soul of the convert, our text ignores completely.[100] In this ritual, by which a gentile becomes a member of the Jewish people, the Jewish community is conspicuously absent. Even if the number of sage in-

significance of the denial of idolatry (and, consequently, the anomaly of its omission here) is highlighted by this widely repeated comment: "Anyone who denies idolatry acknowledges the entire Torah" (see chapter 5 above, note 37).

97. Although there is an oft-repeated principle that "a convert is like a newborn infant" (B. Yevamot 48b and parallels; the principle is implicit in M. Negaim 7:1).

98. For example, some of the prayers recounted at Y. Berakhot 4:2 7d, which posit a contrast between the right path (the life of Torah) and the wrong, would have been appropriate (with only minor changes) for a new convert to recite. "I give thanks to you, O God, that you have placed my lot among those who sit in the house of study and the synagogues, and you have not placed my lot among (those who sit in) theaters and circuses. For I labor and they labor; I labor to inherit (a share in) the Garden of Eden, they labor for the pit of perdition." R. Hiyya b. Abba's prayer ("unify our hearts to fear your name, and keep us distant from all that you hate, and draw us near to all that love") is similar to the Manual of Discipline's statement (1:4) of the goals of the sect ("to love everything that he chose, and to hate everything that he detested"). Such prayers would demonstrate the change the convert has just undergone. The *Apostolic Constitutions* prescribes "Instruction for Catechumens" (7.39.2–4) and "A Prayer on behalf of the Catechumens" (8.6.5–8). If these texts are of Jewish origin, as some scholars have suggested, they presume a Jewish conversion ceremony very different from that of the rabbis, but the matter is uncertain and requires separate discussion. For a translation of the texts, see Charlesworth, *Old Testament Pseudepigrapha* 2.687 and 688–689 = David A. Fiensy, *Prayers Alleged to Be Jewish* (Chico, Calif.: Scholars Press, 1985) 88–89 and 92–95.

99. B. Keritot 9a and parallels. Anderson, "Status of the Torah" 12, remarks: "the author of the Community Rule has clearly seen an analogy between the entrance into the covenant of the sect and the entrance of the biblical Israelites into the Mosaic covenant." The correspondence is evident in the language of the Community Rule; not so the rabbinic conversion ceremony.

100. Medieval Jews, basing their work on passages from the Talmud and the midrashim, elaborated a mystical theology of circumcision; see Elliot R. Wolfson, *Circle in the Square* (Albany: SUNY Press, 1995) 29–48 ("Circumcision, Vision of God, and Textual Interpretation"). Morton Smith argues that the interpretation of circumcision as a mystery is to be dated to the first or second century C.E.; see *Clement of Alexandria and a Secret Gospel according to Mark* (Cambridge: Harvard University Press, 1973) 181–183.

structors is augmented from two to three, the ritual lacks an audience and a communal setting. There are no gifts, no meal, no benedictions, no rejoicing, no ritual by which the Jewish community blesses the convert and incorporates him/her into its midst.[101] The ceremony also lacks the symbolic actions and theatrical trappings that often accompany initiation rituals—for example, a procession, special garments, or some action that symbolizes the break with the past and the assumption of a new identity.[102] The rabbinic conversion ceremony lacks rites of separation, transition, and incorporation; in other words, it lacks virtually all the distinctive features of an initiation ritual.[103] It therefore bears little resemblance to Christian baptism rituals.[104]

If it is not an initiation ritual, what is it? I have argued that the ceremony, apparently the product of the second century C.E., was a vehicle by which the rabbis attempted to regulate and formalize what until then had been an entirely personal and chaotic process. The rabbis attempted to ensure that the ceremony was witnessed, that the convert received at

101. The benedictions to be recited at the circumcision of an infant involve a response by "those standing" at the ceremony (T. Berakhot 6:12–13 36–37L, Y. Berakhot 9:3 13a, and B. Shabbat 137b). For public parties at the *berit* of an infant, cf. Ecclesiastes Rabbah 3.2 (9b ed. Vilna). B. Shabbat 137b (in an early medieval interpolation; see note 75 above) also prescribes a benediction to be recited by the circumciser at the circumcision of a convert, but omits any response by "those standing" at the ceremony. Presumably, there were no guests.

102. For example, the ceremony might have made much of the convert's removal of clothing before immersion and might have required him to don special white garments afterward. Or the convert might have been required to break an object or to tear a piece of cloth to indicate his separation from his former family and way of life. Or he might have been required to change his name, as would become the practice in the Middle Ages. (Even in antiquity, converts to Judaism sometimes changed their names; see T. Gittin 6:4 270L; see chapter 5 above, note 76.) Symbolic actions figure occasionally in rabbinic rituals; cf. the *qetzatzah* (or *qetzitzah*) ceremony (B. Ketuvot 28b and Y. Ketuvot 2:10 26d and parallels).

103. The tripartite structure of rites of initiation was first described by Arnold van Gennep, *The Rites of Passage* (Chicago: University of Chicago Press, 1960; first published in 1909).

104. See R. J. Z. Werblowsky, "On the Baptismal Rite according to St. Hippolytus," *Studia Patristica* 2 (1957) 93–105, and idem, "A Note on Purification and Proselyte Baptism," in *Judaism, Christianity, and Other Greco-Roman Cults: Studies for Morton Smith,* ed. J. Neusner, 4 vols. (Leiden: Brill, 1975) 3.200–205. A connection between Jewish proselyte immersion and Christian baptism, and between the rabbinic conversion ceremony and the Christian baptismal liturgy, has been argued many times; see, for example, Daube, *New Testament and Rabbinic Judaism;* Gavin, *Jewish Antecedents* 33–35; and E. R. Hardy, "Jewish and Christian Baptism," in *A Tribute to Arthur Vööbus,* ed. Robert H. Fischer (Chicago: Lutheran School of Theology, 1977) 309–318. There are indeed some insignificant similarities, but the fundamental ethos of the two ceremonies differs markedly, as observed by Légasse, "Baptême juif."

least some modicum of instruction in the Jewish way, and that the rituals of circumcision and immersion were performed with the proper intent of both the convert and the persons supervising the conversion. The implementation of this regulation and "institutionalization" (if I may use the term loosely) would probably have had a negative impact on the ease with which conversions could have been performed, but the framers of this ceremony were certainly *not* inimically disposed toward either converts or conversion. On the contrary. The ceremony did not erect substantial barriers before the would-be convert. Its dissuasion was more ostensible than real, and its demands were relatively modest. There were others in rabbinic society who were much less friendly to converts than were the framers of this ceremony.

The ceremony, then, is a close analogue to the rabbinic ceremony by which a Jew becomes a member of the *havurah,* a fellowship or association of Jews who carefully observe the laws of purity. There too the candidate must be "accepted" by the group, and he must accept upon himself (according to the Bavli, before three members of the group) the obligation to observe all the rules of the group. If he rejects even one of the group's rules, he may not become a member. An initiate (if I may use that term) does not always know all the rules in advance; sometimes only after he is accepted as a member does he receive complete instruction. The effect of this ceremony is to change the legal status of the initiate. Before the ceremony he was presumed to ignore or flout the rules of purity; after the ceremony and becoming a member, he is presumed to observe them punctiliously. Thus both the conversion ceremony and the *havurah* ceremony are vehicles by which society affirms that the initiate has undergone a change of legal status based on the performance of, and the stated obligation to continue performing, certain legal norms. In neither ceremony is anyone cleansed, unburdened, reborn, re-created, reimagined, or refreshed.[105]

The exclusive focus on matters legal and the avoidance of matters theological reminds us of the Hasmonean incorporation of the Idumaeans and Ituraeans. "Conversion" is understood primarily in terms of enfranchisement. The potential convert is asked, "Why have you decided to approach (us) to be converted? Do you not know that Israel at this time are pained, oppressed, harassed, and torn, and that afflictions come upon them?" If the candidate says, "I know and am unworthy,"

---

105. Samet, "Conversion" 328, based on T. Demai 2:3–5 69L and B. Bekhorot 30b, correctly emphasizes the connection between the conversion ceremony and the *havurah* ceremony. For the rules of the *havurah* see T. Demai 2:2–14 68–71L.

he is accepted and is given instruction in "a few of the light command-ments and a few of the severe commandments." At the end of the cate-chism he is circumcised and becomes "like an Israelite in all respects." Here, then, are the same ingredients that we saw in Josephus: joining the people of Israel, observance of the laws, and circumcision. What is missing, from both Josephus and the rabbinic ceremony, is any associa-tion of enfranchisement with a change in belief or a change of spirituali-ty. Perhaps this is implicit in the rabbinic ceremony, but it certainly is not explicit.

In all likelihood the version of tractate Gerim (sixth to eighth cen-turies?) derives from one very much like that of B. Yevamot. In Gerim the ceremony is becoming less of a vehicle to ensure the compliance of legal norms and more of an initiation ritual. It contains several explicit references to God, shifts the focus of the opening instruction from the commandments to the people of Israel, and concludes with words of praise and hope for the new Jew. Here theological and "spiritual" con-cerns are evident, as they will be in the version of Maimonides.

PART III

The Boundary Violated

The Union of Diverse Kinds

CHAPTER 8

The Prohibition
of Intermarriage

Alienarum concubitu abstinent.
(They abstain from intercourse with foreign women.)

Tacitus, *Histories*

In this chapter I trace the history of the Jewish prohibition of intermarriage from the Bible to the Talmud,[1] with special attention to the history of the exegesis of the relevant verses of the Torah: Deuteronomy 7:3–4 (and Exodus 34:15), the prohibition of marriage with Canaanites; Deuteronomy 23:2–9, the prohibition of four nations from *entering the congregation of the Lord;* and Leviticus 18:21, the prohibition of sacrificing one's seed to Molekh, a prohibition that was occasionally interpreted as a reference to intermarriage. Last, I shall discuss Deuteronomy 21:10–14, the law of the beautiful war captive.

---

1. For the development of the prohibition of intermarriage, see Epstein, *Marriage Laws,* 145–219. L. Löw, "Eherechtliche Studien," in *Gesammelte Schriften,* ed. I. Löw (Szegedin, 1893; reprint, Hildesheim and New York, 1979; originally published in 1862) 3:108–200, and G. Kittel, "Das Konnubium mit den Nicht-Juden im antiken Judentum," *Forschungen zur Judenfrage* 2 (1937) 30–62, are still worth reading, but the former was written by a rabbi concerned about the rise of intermarriage among European Jewry, and the latter was written by a Nazi sympathizer eager to justify the Nuremberg legislation. J. D. Bleich, "The Prohibition against Intermarriage," in *Contemporary Halakhic Problems,* vol. 2 (New York: Ktav, 1983) 268–282, is a careful collection of talmudic and post-talmudic texts, but its naive fundamentalism and antihistorical pietism render its conclusions useless for the historian.

This law, which permits an Israelite warrior to marry a foreign woman, puzzled many later exegetes, for how could Moses have permitted intermarriage?

Deuteronomy 7:3–4

The classic prohibition of intermarriage is Deuteronomy 7:1–4:

When the Lord your God brings you to the land that you are about to invade and occupy, and He dislodges many nations before you—the Hittites, Girgashites, Amorites, Canaanites, Perizites, Hivites, and Jebusites, seven nations much larger than you—and the Lord your God delivers them to you and you defeat them, you must doom them to destruction: grant them no terms and give them no quarter. You shall not intermarry with them: do not give your daughters to their sons or take their daughters for your sons. For they will turn your children away from me to worship other gods, and the Lord's anger will blaze forth against you and He will promptly wipe you out.

Closely parallel is Exodus 34:11–17 (whose precise relationship to Deuteronomy is not our concern):[2]

I will drive out before you the Amorites, the Canaanites, the Hittites, the Perizites, the Hivites, and the Jebusites . . . You must not make a covenant with the inhabitants of the land, for they will lust after their gods and sacrifice to their gods and invite you, and you will eat of their sacrifices. And when you take wives from among their daughters for your sons, their daughters will lust after their gods and will cause your sons to lust after their gods.

The injunction upon the Israelites to slay the Canaanites and abominate Canaanite cultic practices appears elsewhere,[3] but the interdiction of marriage with the Canaanites appears only in these two sets of verses.

Does this prohibition apply to all gentiles or only to the seven Canaanite nations? The answer is clearly the latter.[4] Moses commands the

---

2. Exodus 34 is generally regarded as "J" reworked by "D."

3. Exod. 23:23–24; Deut. 12:1–3 and 20:16–18.

4. In his comment on this passage, Moshe Weinfeld, *Deuteronomy 1–11*, Anchor Bible (New York: Doubleday, 1991) 365, speaks of the prohibition "of mixed marriages," but he means the prohibition "of marriages with Canaanites"; see his further discussion, 377–380.

Israelites to destroy the seven Canaanite nations because they threaten Israelite religious identity and live on the land that the Israelites will conquer. Intermarriage with them is prohibited. The Ammonites and Moabites, somewhat more distant and therefore somewhat less dangerous, were not consigned to destruction and isolation; they were merely prohibited from *entering the congregation* (Deut. 23:4). The Egyptians and Edomites were even permitted *to enter the congregation* after three generations (Deut. 23:8–9). The meaning of the prohibition of "entering the congregation" is not at all clear, as I shall discuss below, but I presume that originally, at least, it was not a prohibition of intermarriage. Other nations, even further removed from the Israelite horizon, were presumably not subject to any prohibition.[5]

Internal biblical evidence confirms this narrow interpretation of Deuteronomy 7:3–4. The patriarchal narratives in Genesis condemn marriages between members of Abraham's clan and the indigenous Canaanite population.[6] Joshua warned the Israelites not to intermarry with the nations who remained in Canaan (Josh. 23:12), but his warning went unheeded (Judg. 3:1–7). Many nations tested the Israelites' loyalty to their God, but only the Canaanites caused the Israelites to sin through intermarriage. The rebuke delivered to Samson by his parents (Judg. 14:3: "Is there no one among the daughters of your own kinsmen . . . that you must go and take a wife from the uncircumcised Philistines?") indicates that some Israelites could frown upon an intermarriage even if it was not specifically prohibited, but a long time passed before this attitude was given legal expression. The transition from a narrow to an expansive interpretation of Deuteronomy 7:3 is implicit in Ezra 9:1–2:

When this was over, the officers approached me (Ezra), saying, "The people of Israel and the priests and Levites have not separated themselves from the peoples of the land, whose abhorrent practices are like those of the Canaanites, the Hittites, the Perizzites, the Jebusites, the Ammonites, the Moabites, the Egyptians, and the Amorites. They have taken their daughters as wives for themselves and for their sons, so that the holy seed has become intermingled with the peoples of the land . . ."

This passage combines the rhetoric of Leviticus 18 (the inhabitants of the land of Canaan commit "abominations") with the prohibitions of Deuteronomy 23 and Deuteronomy 7:3–4. The women whom the men

5. Does Deut. 25:17–19 assume that marriage with the Amaleqites was forbidden?
6. Gen. 24:3; 26:34–35; 27:46; 28:6–9; 34.

of Jerusalem had married were similar in their abominations to the Canaanites, Hittites, Perizites, and Jebusites, four of the seven nations enumerated in Deuteronomy 7:3–4. Whoever these women may have been, they certainly were not real Canaanites, Hittites, Perizites, and Jebusites, none of whom had been seen in Israel for centuries. Marriage with these women was prohibited not because they were Canaanites but because they were *like* Canaanites. Gentiles who are like Canaanites are the targets of the prohibition no less than the Canaanites themselves.[7]

This exegetical tack at first had few followers. As I shall discuss below, the Hasmonean period witnesses the emergence of proscriptions of, and polemics against, all forms of intermarriage, but it is striking that none of these proscriptions and polemics is based on Deuteronomy 7:3–4. If in this period there is a favorite proof text from the Torah, it is Leviticus 18:21.[8] Only in the first century C.E. in the works of Philo and Josephus does the expansive exegesis of Deuteronomy 7:3–4 reemerge. When discussing the laws of forbidden marriages, Philo writes the following:

But also, he [Moses] says, do not enter into the partnership of marriage with a member of a foreign nation, lest some day conquered by the forces of opposing customs you surrender and stray unawares from the path that leads to piety and turn aside into a pathless wild. And though perhaps you yourself will hold your ground . . . there is much to be feared for your sons and daughters. It may well be that they, enticed by spurious customs which they prefer to the genuine, are likely to unlearn the honor due to the one God.[9]

The reference to Deuteronomy 7:3–4 is implicit but unmistakable (note the reference to sons and daughters, the idea that intermarriage will led Israelites and their children away from God). Since the scriptural reason for the prohibition applies equally to all gentiles, Philo con-

---

7. Kaufmann, *Religion of Israel,* 4.337–339; Fishbane, *Biblical Interpretation* 115–118.

8. Proscriptions and polemics that ignore Deut. 7:1–4: Testament of Levi 9:10 and 14:5–8 (and elsewhere in the Testaments); Testament of Job 45:4; cf. Tobit 4:12–13. Deut. 7:1–4 and Exod. 34:11–17 are paraphrased without any remarkable additions in The Temple Scroll col. 2 (ed. Y. Yadin, 2:1–3), although the Temple Scroll 57:15–16 provides that a king may not marry a gentile wife. Similarly, the pseudo-Philonic *Liber Antiquitatum Biblicarum* has several passages condemning intermarriage, but none of them is connected with Deut. 7:3–4; see the passages assembled by M. R. James, *The Biblical Antiquities of Philo* 38, and by Louis H. Feldman in his prolegomenon to the reprint of James' work (New York: Ktav, 1971) xlvi. On Lev. 18:21 and its influence on Jubilees, see below.

9. *On the Special Laws* 3.29 (ed. Colson, vol. 7, pp. 492–493).

cludes that the prohibition itself applies equally to all gentiles. Josephus reaches the same conclusion.[10] The exegesis of Philo and Josephus, no less than that of Ezra, was determined by the antitraditional behavior of some of the Jews around them. Philo knew many Alexandrian Jews who intermarried or committed other forms of rebellion against the Jewish community.[11] The two speeches inserted by Josephus into his paraphrase of Numbers 25 (in the first speech the Midianite women persuade the Israelite men to have sex with them and worship their Gods; in the second speech Zimri explains why he is willing to accept their kind offer) suggest that he was familiar with the arguments of those Jews (in Rome?) who sought to legitimate intermarriage.[12] These two Graeco-Jewish authors indicate their disapproval of intermarriage by deeming it a violation of a Mosaic ordinance. In the first century C.E. Deuteronomy 7:3–4 was emerging as the central proof text for this argument.

Let us now turn to the rabbinic material. Rabbinic society was not much affected by intermarriage. The Yerushalmi has a rabbi castigate the Jews of Sepphoris (who, like the ancient Alexandrians, had a well-deserved reputation for contumacy and insolence) because many of them were committing "acts of Zimri"—that is, having sexual liaisons with gentiles.[13] The Bavli shows that some Jews on the other side of the Euphrates were guilty of the same crime. But sexual liaisons were

---

10. *AJ* 8.190–196; cf. 11.139–153.

11. Wolfson, *Philo* 1.73–85. Even if this description was shaped by Wolfson's familiarity with the Jewish scene in New York in the 1930s (see Leo Schwarz, *Wolfson of Harvard: Portrait of a Scholar* [Philadelphia: Jewish Publication Society, 1978] 155), it appears to be an accurate portrait of Alexandrian Jewry as well. On Jewish intermarriage in Ptolemaic Egypt, see chapter 3 above, note 112, and the studies of Mélèze-Modrzejewski cited in chapter 9 below, note 113.

12. *AJ* 4.134–138 and 145–149; see W. C. van Unnik, "Josephus' Account of the Story of Israel's Sin with Alien Women," in *Studies Presented to M. A. Beek* (Assen, Netherlands: van Gorcum, 1974) 241–261. Compare the argument advanced by the Roman official who was offended by R. Aqiba's refusal to accept the women who had been provided him for the evening (*AdRN* A 16, p. 32a ed. Schechter). To what extent the *Jewish Antiquities* reflects the concerns of the Jews of Rome is a difficult question. Tacitus, a Roman contemporary, could say of the Jews *alienarum concubitu abstinent* (*Histories* 5.5.2). The incidence of Jewish intermarriage in the Roman empire is not known. The church council of Elvira (Spain, 306 C.E.) and the Theodosian Code 16.8.6 (339 C.E.) and 3.7.2 = 9.7.5 (388 C.E.) prohibited intermarriages and other sexual liaisons between Jews and Christians, but these laws are not necessarily evidence for intermarriage. Feldman argues that the rate of intermarriage was low; see Feldman, *Jew and Gentile* 79. Barclay, *Diaspora* 107–108, 324–325, and 410–412, discusses intermarriage but does not attempt to estimate its incidence. A full collection of all evidence, both rabbinic and non-rabbinic, bearing on intermarriage in antiquity is a desideratum.

13. Y. Taanit 3:4 66c. See too chapter 2 above, note 40.

not intermarriage, and intermarriage was not, for the rabbis, a serious problem.[14] The prohibition of intermarriage does not appear in the Mishnah; even the prohibition of foreign liaisons seldom appears. The Yerushalmi too hardly discusses the prohibition, and when it does, it seems to say that Deuteronomy 7:3–4 refers only to the seven Canaanite nations.[15] Similarly, the named authorities of the Babylonian Talmud hardly discuss the prohibition, and when they do, as we shall see, they assume that Deuteronomy 7:3–4 applies only to the seven Canaanite nations.

The Talmudim are aware that the prohibition of intermarriage is a product of second-temple times. The emergence of the prohibition in the Hasmonean period, to be discussed below, is the historical "kernel" in the Palestinian tradition preserved in the Babylonian Talmud that "the Hasmonean Court" decreed that a Jewish man who has a private assignation with a gentile woman, let alone if he cohabits with her or marries her, deserves to be flogged for four reasons: intercourse with a menstruant, intercourse with a slave, intercourse with a gentile, and intercourse with a married woman (according to one opinion in the Talmud, the fourth reason is intercourse with a prostitute).[16] A similar antipathy toward gentiles motivated the revolutionaries of 66–70 C.E., and they too might have tried through "the Eighteen Decrees," ascribed by both Talmudim to the Houses of Hillel and Shammai, to prevent any social or sexual intercourse between Jews and gentiles.[17]

The rabbis of the Talmud thus recognized that the Torah is not the source for the general prohibition of intermarriage. This view is extended in a remarkable way by the Babylonian amora Rava. According

14. B. Berakhot 58a and Taanit 24b. See Lamentations Rabbah pp. 47a–b ed. Buber (the Jews could intermarry with the gentiles and thereby end their sufferings, but they remain loyal to God). The problem with the lineage of the Jews of Messene etc. is not intermarriage but *mamzērut* and improper divorces; see B. Qiddushin 71b–72b (and parallels). In areas outside the reach of rabbinic Judaism, intermarriage may have been much more common. See the rabbinic discussion on the family purity of the Jews of Palmyra and Mesopotamia: Y. Yevamot 1:6 3a–b; B. Yevamot 16a–17a; B. Qiddushin 71b–72b.

15. M. Sanhedrin 9:6; Y. Shabbat 1:7 3d and Sotah 1:8 17b. The interpretation of these Yerushalmi passages is disputed; see the commentators ad loc.

16. B. Avodah Zarah 36b and Sanhedrin 82a. The legal details of this decree are not entirely clear; see the Tosafot ad loc. On the menstrual impurity of gentile women, see M. Niddah 4:3 and Song of Songs Rabbah 1:1 [par. 10] (Solomon sins by having intercourse with his gentile wives while they are menstruant). The disagreement over the last point concerns the validity of marriage among gentiles; see next paragraph. Gentile women have the status of prostitutes: M. Yevamot 6:5.

17. Y. Shabbat 1:7 3c–d; B. Shabbat 17b; Hengel, *Zeloten* 190–229.

to rabbinic theory, only Jews possess the legal capacity to create marriages (*qiddushin*). Gentiles create a de facto status of marriage through sexual intercourse, but are incapable of creating a de jure status of marriage.[18] Consequently, Rava asked, how could Deuteronomy warn the Israelites not to *marry* the Canaanites when the Canaanites were legally incapable of marriage? He concluded that Deuteronomy 7:3–4 prohibits intermarriage only with Canaanites who have converted to Judaism. According to Rava, then, not only did Scripture fail to prohibit intermarriage with all gentiles, it even failed to prohibit intermarriage with Canaanites who remained Canaanites![19]

The opposite point of view is presented by the anonymous (*setam*) stratum of the Babylonian Talmud. This stratum, which postdates the period of the amoraim, is ultimately responsible for the shape and texture of the talmudic discussions. Among many other contributions, it elaborates the arguments of the named authorities, frequently by establishing casuistic distinctions between them, and it creates new debates by contrasting legal opinions that originally had been independent of each other. (We have already seen this stratum at work in my discussion of the debate between R. Joshua and R. Eliezer concerning the indispensability of circumcision for conversion.)[20] It is this stratum, then, that claims that R. Simeon b. Yohai (middle of the second century C.E.) interpreted Deuteronomy 7:3–4 as a general prohibition of intermarriage. The claim was based on the alleged readiness of R. Simeon to draw inferences from the reasons for the commandments.[21] Since the reason for the prohibition was *for they shall turn your son astray*—a reason that, as Philo and Josephus noted, applies equally to all gentiles—the Babylonian Talmud concluded in R. Simeon's name that the prohibition too applies equally to all gentiles. The conclusion was also suggested, I presume, by the tradition that R. Simeon deduced the

18. See chapter 9 below.

19. B. Yevamot 76a. Canaanites may convert to Judaism: B. Sotah 35b bottom (*hozrin biteshuvah*). Medieval Talmudists inquired whether Deut. 7:3–4 applied only to the Canaanites in the land of Israel or to all Canaanites everywhere, but as far as I know this refinement of the question is post-talmudic (if inspired by Sifre Deuteronomy 211 245F). See *Halakhot Gedolot,* vol. 2, pp. 520–521, ed. E. Hildesheimer (Jerusalem, 1971).

20. See chapter 7 above, note 50.

21. B. Qiddushin 68b and Yevamot 23a. Neither R. Simeon's extension of Deut. 7:3 to all gentiles nor his readiness to draw inferences from the reasons for the commandments appears in the Yerushalmi. We have no way of knowing whether the historical R. Simeon would have agreed with the opinions placed in his mouth by the Bavli (contrast the blithe certainty of Urbach, *Sages* 1.373–377). Our discussion was probably inspired by B. Bava Metzi'a 115a and Sanhedrin 21a (contrast Y. Sanhedrin 2:6 20c).

matrilineal principle from Deuteronomy 7:4.[22] Since the matrilineal principle applies to the offspring of all gentile women, not just Canaanites, it would seem that R. Simeon must believe that the prohibition of intermarriage applies to all gentiles, not just the seven nations of Canaan.[23]

Because the Babylonian Talmud nowhere states whether the alleged view of R. Simeon is correct, medieval scholars debated whether the prohibition of intermarriage with all gentiles was of biblical or rabbinic origin and whether Deuteronomy 7:3–4 prohibited only marriages (as Rava said) or nonmarital liaisons as well.[24] If any tendency can be detected in these later discussions, it is that the sins of Israel sometimes determined retrospectively the content of biblical revelation. In the Islamic East many Jews were engaged in the slave trade or owned slaves, and numerous questions arose concerning the sexual abuse of female slaves by their Jewish owners.[25] In response to these conditions, several sources of the period insist that a man who has intercourse with his female slave violates fourteen negative commandments of the Torah.[26]

Deuteronomy 23:2–9

Deuteronomy 23:2–9 prohibits the following groups from *entering the congregation of the Lord:* a man with mutilated genitalia, a *mamzer,* an Ammonite, a Moabite, an Edomite, and an Egypt-

22. See chapter 9 below.

23. Perhaps R. Simeon also believed that Deut. 7:2 (the command to exterminate the Canaanites) applies to all gentiles. Cf. Mekhilta on Exod. 14:7, 1.201L.

24. See, for example, Maimonides, *Laws of Prohibited Intercourse* 12:1, and the commentary of R. David Qimhi on 1 Kings 11:1. Aaron ben Elijah the Karaite (ca. 1300–1369), *Sefer mitzvot gadol gan eden* (Eupatoria, 1866) 147c, and other Karaites argue that Deut. 7:3–4 applies to all gentiles and that Moses listed the seven Canaanite nations only because they were the closest and the most likely to mingle with the Israelites. Robert Bellarmine (1542–1621), in his *De Sacramento Matrimonii* chap. 23 (in *Opera Omnia,* ed. J. Fèvre [Paris, 1873; reprint, Frankfurt, 1965] 5:117), argues, like Philo, Josephus, and R. Simeon, that the reason (*causa*) provided by Scripture shows that Deut. 7:3–4 applies to all gentiles: a Christian may not marry a non-Christian. The Karaites argued in this manner because they did not have a binding tradition upon which to rely for a general prohibition of intermarriage; Bellarmine argued in this manner because he wished to defend the right of the pope to grant dispensations (see Bellarmine p. 120).

25. Wacholder, "Proselyting of Slaves."

26. See chapter 9 below, note 131. This tendency is already evident in Targum Onqelos on Deut. 23:18.

ian (the latter two are permitted to enter the congregation after the third generation). What is the meaning of this prohibition?

The Mishnah and Talmud assume that these verses prohibit marriage; they understand *to enter the congregation of the Lord* to mean "to marry an Israelite."[27] If Deuteronomy 23:2–9 is a logical continuation of Deuteronomy 22:13–23:1 (a section dealing with marriage laws), the context would support this interpretation, but in the laws of Deuteronomy textual juxtaposition is not necessarily an indication of thematic connection.[28] The strongest support for this interpretation comes from elsewhere in the Bible. Solomon sinned by loving *many foreign women in addition to Pharaoh's daughter—Moabite, Ammonite, Edomite, Sidonian, and Hittite women, from the nations which the Lord had said to the Israelites None of you shall join them and none of them shall join you, lest they turn your heart away to follow their gods* (1 Kings 11:1–2). Here Deuteronomy 7:3–4 is combined with Deuteronomy 23:4 and 9.[29] Ezra 9:1 similarly combines Deuteronomy 7:3 with Deuteronomy 23:4 and 9.[30] In Nehemiah 13:23–28, Nehemiah attacks the sinful marriages of the Jews with Ashdodite, Ammonite, and Moabite women. His rhetorical outburst is dependent not only upon Deuteronomy 7:3–4 and 1 Kings 11:1–2, but also upon Deuteronomy 23:3–4.[31]

This was certainly not the interpretation accepted by the author of Ruth. Confronted by a biblical prohibition of intermarriage with Moabites and a biblical book that portrays such a marriage without the least sign of condemnation, the rabbis were forced to conclude that Deuteronomy 23:4 applies only to male Ammonites and Moabites, not female.[32] The harmony of sacred Scripture was maintained and the lineage of King David was freed from stigma, but this desperate exegesis had a cost. The exclusion of female Ammonites and Moabites from the Deuteronomic prohibition violates the simple meaning of the text and contradicts 1 Kings 11:1 and Nehemiah 13:23. If the author of

27. See, for example, M. Qiddushin 4:3.

28. Carmichael, *Laws of Deuteronomy* 67.

29. Sidonian women were really Canaanite (Gen. 10:15). On Solomon's sin, see S. J. D. Cohen, "Solomon," and Gary N. Knoppers, "Sex, Religion, and Politics: The Deuteronomist on Intermarriage," *Hebrew Annual Review* 14 (1994) 121–141.

30. In Ezra 9:1 *Emorite* is a mistake for *Edomite*, as many commentators have noted and as the Greek version confirms. Ezra 9:12 quotes Deut. 23:7. See Fishbane, *Biblical Interpretation* 116.

31. As Zech. 9:6 shows, Ashdodite = *mamzer;* see Ibn Ezra on Deut. 23:3 (followed by some modern commentators; see chapter 9 below, note 46). For the reuse of Deuteronomy 23 in 1 Kings 11 and in Nehemiah 13, see Fishbane, *Biblical Interpretation* 125–129.

32. M. Yevamot 8:3.

Ruth knew Deuteronomy 23:4 and regarded it as a sacred text that could not be contradicted—two debatable assumptions—he (she?) could not have understood the verse to refer to intermarriage. In fact, the Bible itself justifies a non-rabbinic interpretation of the phrase *to enter the congregation of the Lord*. "To enter the temple of the Lord" is the only meaning that will make sense in Lamentations 1:10: *She (Jerusalem) has seen her sanctuary invaded by nations which You have commanded that they may not enter your congregation*. The phraseology is the same as that of Deuteronomy 23:2–4 and 9, and a reference to marriage is clearly irrelevant. The same interpretation is perhaps assumed by Nehemiah 13:1–9.[33] An anonymous prophet assures the eunuch that in the end of days he will have a secure place in God's house (Isa. 56:3–5); the assurance was needed, because (as many commentators have noted) Deuteronomy 23:2 seemed to exclude eunuchs from the temple. Like many other gods, the God of Israel did not wish the maimed and the deformed, both animal (Lev. 22:17–25) and human (Lev. 21:16–24), to be brought into his presence.[34] Resident aliens and visiting foreigners could participate to some extent in the temple cult, but the *mamzer* and the four nations listed in Deuteronomy 23 were not welcome.[35]

(Some of) the Jews of Qumran followed this interpretation. In a text known as 4Q Florilegium, and in a parallel but mutilated passage of the Temple Scroll, the sectarian legislator prohibits the "Ammonite, Moabite, *mamzer*, foreigner, and proselyte" from entering the temple

33. Neh. 13:1–2 is a paraphrase of Deut. 23:4–6. It is followed by an ambiguous verse (13:3: *When they heard the teaching, they separated all the alien admixture from Israel*) and by the story (13:4–9) of the expulsion of Tobiah the Ammonite from the temple. If Neh. 13:4–9 is the logical continuation of 13:1–2, Nehemiah understood Deut. 23:3–4 to prohibit entry into the temple. He also understood it to refer to intermarriage; see above.

34. See further Tosefta Sukkah 4:23 277L. On the exclusion of maimed persons from the Jerusalem temple, see Saul Olyan, "'Anyone Blind or Lame Shall Not Enter the House': On the Interpretation of 2 Samuel 5:8b" *Catholic Biblical Quarterly* (1998).

35. On the participation of resident aliens and foreigners in the temple cult, see Exod. 12:43–50; Lev. 17:8–16 and 22:17–25; Num. 9:14 and 15:13–16; 1 Kings 8:41–43; contrast Ezek. 44:6–9. See Fishbane, *Biblical Interpretation* 141–143. This subject was intensely debated during late second-temple times. See I. Knohl, "The Acceptance of Sacrifices from Gentiles," *Tarbiz* 48 (1979) 341–345. In a law ascribed to Solon, *nothoi* (bastards) are excluded from the religious observances of the clan (Demosthenes 43:51 [*Against Macartatus*]); they are also excluded from the religious observances of a private foundation on Cos, ca. 300 B.C.E. (F. Sokolowski, *Lois sacrées des cités grecques* [Paris: de Boccard, 1969] no. 177, lines 144–149). For exclusions from Greco-Roman temples, see Bickerman, *Studies* 2.210–224.

to be built in the messianic future.[36] One rabbinic text similarly prohibits the *mamzer* from ever entering the city of Jerusalem; another text
prohibits a Jew from "making room" for a resident alien in Jerusalem.[37]
These texts clearly assume that the prohibitions of Deuteronomy 23:
2–9 refer to admission into the temple and/or holy city.

A different tack is taken by Philo and his followers. In numerous passages Philo interprets *to enter the congregation of the Lord* literally: to
join the Israelites in their assemblies and convocations, to participate
in their festivals and religious life.[38] One of these passages, a discussion
of Deuteronomy 23:8–9, clarifies Philo's intent: the Israelite may not
spurn an Egyptian after three generations, but should invite him into
the assembly, make him a member of the Jewish polity, and allow him
to share in the divine *logoi*.[39] In other words, the Egyptian may convert
to Judaism. Clement of Alexandria, Tertullian, and Origen also believe
that the literal meaning of *to enter the congregation* is "to be accepted as
a member of God's people" (which, for these church fathers, is the
Christian church).[40] The author of Judith, however, did not understand

36. Q Florilegium 1:4; Temple Scroll 39:5 and 40:6. For discussion see George J.
Brooke, *Exegesis at Qumran: 4Q Florilegium in Its Jewish Context*, JSOT Supplement
no. 29 (Sheffield, England: JSOT, 1985) 86 and 100–103; J. Baumgarten, "The Exclusion
of 'Netinim' and Proselytes in 4Q Florilegium," *Revue de Qumran* 8 (1972) 87–96 (reprinted in idem, *Studies in Qumran Law* [Leiden: Brill, 1977] 75–87), and "Exclusions
from the Temple: Proselytes and Agrippa I," *JJS* 33 (1982) 215–225; D. R. Schwartz,
"Priestly View of Descent." *Gēr* in 4Q Florilegium is usually translated as "proselyte," but
it may mean "resident alien" (note the reference to *zarim*, "strangers, outsiders," in line
5). See P. R. Davies, "Who Can Join" 136, and the brief note by Annette Steudel, *Der
Midrasch zur Eschatologie aus der Qumrangemeinde* (Leiden: Brill, 1994) 42–43 n. 5.
Deut. 23:2 appears also in *Miqtzat Ma'asei HaTorah* B 39–40 (p. 50 in DJD X), but it is
not clear to me whether the passage speaks of marriage or entry into the temple or both.
37. See G. Blidstein, "4Q Florilegium and Rabbinic Sources on Bastard and Proselyte," *Revue de Qumran* 8 (1975) 431–435. Blidstein discusses *AdRN* A 12 p. 27a; see also
AdRN A 35 p. 52b = T. Negaim 6:2 625Z, whose textual variants are assembled by
L. Finkelstein, "The Laws That Apply to Jerusalem" (in Hebrew), in *Alexander Marx Jubilee Volume* (New York: Jewish Theological Seminary, 1950) 351–369, at 352. *Gēr vetoshav*
in this text is probably hendiadys for "resident alien." Baumgarten, "Exclusion" 89–93,
attempts to explain how the gentile came to be associated with the *mamzer* in this legislation.
38. See the index of biblical passages in volume 10 of Colson's edition of Philo. Josephus, *AJ* 4.290, may be following the same exegetical path; eunuchs are to be driven out
of the community, a paraphrase of Deut. 23:2.
39. *On Virtues* 108, ed. Colson, 8.228–229.
40. See, for example, Origen, *De Oratione* 20.1 (trans. J. E. L. Oulton and H. Chadwick, in *Alexandrian Christianity* [Philadelphia: Westminster, 1954] 277–278). An Arabic
catena, which may or may not reflect the exegesis of the church father Hippolytus, translates Deut. 23:3 as follows: "And no man who commits fornication [a misunderstand-

Deuteronomy 23:4 in Philonic fashion, because he narrates, without the least sign of disapproval, the circumcision and conversion of Achior, an Ammonite general. In fact, Philo's interpretation cannot be correct. Deuteronomy 23:2–9 cannot prohibit conversion to Judaism since such a concept did not yet exist in preexilic times.[41] The rabbis therefore were correct to accept Ammonite and Moabite converts.[42] But this was not the sort of problem to disturb a philosopher or a church father.

Medieval Jewish exegetes, including Karaites such as Aaron b. Joseph (ca. 1260–1320), accepted the rabbinic interpretation of *to enter the congregation of the Lord:* the verse prohibits marriage. Medieval Christian exegetes, like Nicolas of Lyra (ca. 1270–1340), followed the interpretation that (unknown to them, of course) had been accepted by the Jews of Qumran: the verse prohibits entrance into the temple.[43] Modern students of Deuteronomy are similarly divided.[44]

---

ing of the Septuagint's *ek pornēs*] may enter the house of God, for he is unclean" (H. Achelis, *Hippolyt's kleinere exegetische und homiletische Schriften* [GCS 1,2; 1897], p. 114). This seems to be a continuation of the Qumran understanding of the verse.

41. Milgrom, "Religious Conversion." See chapter 4 above.

42. M. Yadayim 4:4; B. Berakhot 28a; etc. The only rabbinic passage known to me that might follow a Philonic reading of Deut. 23:2–9 is the statement of R. Yosi in Y. Demai 2:1 22c, but the passage is ambiguous. In a note on Jth. 14:10 in the *Oxford Annotated Bible,* the editors write: "The author seems to have forgotten that the conversion of an Ammonite to Judaism is strictly forbidden by the law (Deuteronomy 23:3)"; a similar note appears in *The New Oxford Annotated Bible.* The same mistake appears in Zeitlin cited in M. S. Enslin, *Judith,* Dropsie College Apocrypha Series (Philadelphia, 1972) 24–25; G. W. E. Nickelsburg cited in M. Stone, ed., *Jewish Writings of the Second Temple Period* (Philadelphia: Fortress, 1984) 49; Smith, "Gentiles" 1:307; Feldman, *Jew and Gentile* 288: "the statement (Deut. 23:4) prohibiting Ammonites and Moabites from entering the assembly of the Lord seems to imply that other peoples might be permitted to enter the Jewish fold."

43. See Aaron b. Joseph the Karaite, *Sefer hamivhar* (Eupatoria, 1835) commentary on Lev. 24:10 and Deut. 23:2–3. Nicolas of Lyra, *Biblia Sacra cum Glossis . . . Nicolai Lyrani,* 7 vols. (Lugdunum, 1545), 1:357a–b, discusses three interpretations: that of the Jews (marriage), that of the *doctores Catholici* (entrance into the temple), and that of "others" (the assumption of office within the Jewish polity). See further the detailed discussions of Thomas de Vio Cajetan (or Caietanus; 1469–1534), *Opera Omnia Quotquot in Sacrae Scripturae Expositionem Reperiuntur,* 5 vols. (Lugdunum, 1639), and à Lapide (1567–1637), *Commentaria* ad loc.

44. See, for example, S. R. Driver, *A Critical and Exegetical Commentary on Deuteronomy,* 3d ed. (Edinburgh, 1895; reprint, 1965) 259; Gerhard von Rad, *Deuteronomy: A Commentary* (Philadelphia: Westminster, 1966) 146; Carmichael, *Laws of Deuteronomy* 171–173; Eduard Nielsen, *Deuteronomium,* HAT, vol. 1, no. 6 (Tübingen: Mohr [Siebeck], 1995) 221.

Leviticus 18:21

Do not allow any of your offspring [lit., *your seed*] *to be of-fered up to Molekh, and do not profane the name of your God* (Lev. 18:21). A prohibition of Molekh worship would seem to have its logical place among prohibitions of idolatry and magic;[45] why does it appear in Leviticus 18, a chapter devoted to forbidden sexual relationships? We may assume that the Jews of antiquity, no less than modern commentators, were perplexed by this question. They concluded that the verse must prohibit some sexual offense that could be equated with idolatry (Lev. 20:5 speaks of those who *go whoring after Molekh*), and since the chapter otherwise omits intermarriage, the obvious conclusion was that Leviticus 18:21 prohibits sexual intercourse with idolaters.[46] This, I suggest, was the logic behind the exegesis of Jubilees, Targum Jonathan, and R. Ishmael.[47] First, Jubilees:

And if there is any man in Israel who wishes to give his daughter or his sister to any man who is from the seed of the gentiles, let him surely die, and let him be stoned because he has caused shame in Israel. And also the woman will be burned with fire, because she has defiled the name of her father's house and so she shall be uprooted from Israel. And do not let an adulteress or defilement be found in Israel all of the days of the generations of the earth because Israel is holy to the Lord. And let any man who causes defilement surely die, let him be stoned because thus it is decreed and written in the heavenly tablets concerning all of the seed of Israel, "Let anyone who causes defilement surely die. And let him be stoned."

And there is no limit of days for this law. And there is no remission or forgiveness except that the man who caused defilement of his daughter will be rooted out from the midst of all Israel because he has given some of his seed to Molekh, and sinned so as to defile it. And you, Moses, command

45. Lev. 20:2–5; cf. 2 Kings 23:10 and Jer. 32:35.

46. Philo too (*On the Special Laws* 3.29) inserts into Leviticus 18 his discussion of the Mosaic prohibition of intermarriage. He omits any reference to Molekh because, as Colson notes, the Septuagint version of Lev. 18:21 is incomprehensible (instead of *molekh* the Septuagint read *melekh*). Stephen Bigger, "The Family Laws of Leviticus 18," *JBL* 98 (1979) 187–203, at 202, suggests that the Molekh law has its place in Leviticus 18 by literary association (laws about *zera,* semen, forbidden intercourse, leading to a law about *zera,* offspring, forbidden child sacrifice).

47. Moshe Weinfeld, "The Worship of Molech and of the Queen of Heaven and Its Background," *Ugarit Forschungen* 4 (1972) 133–154, esp. 142–144 (and, in summary form,

the children of Israel and exhort them not to give any of their daughters to the gentiles, and not to take for their sons any of the daughters of the gentiles, for this is contemptible before the Lord.[48]

In connection with the story of Dinah and Shechem (Genesis 34) the author of Jubilees inserts this tirade against intermarriage, and although he prohibits marriage with both the sons and the daughters of the gentiles, he clearly regards the union of an Israelite woman with a gentile man as the more serious offense. If a man defiles his daughter by giving her to a gentile, the father must be stoned because "he has given some of his seed (*zera* = offspring) to Molekh" and the daughter must be burnt "because she has defiled the name of her father's house" (cf. Lev. 21:9). Since the crime was deemed equivalent to idolatry, it was punished capitally.[49]

Rabbinic circles were familiar with this exegesis. Targum Jonathan to Leviticus 18:21 reads: "Do not give your seed (*zera* = semen) in sexual intercourse with a gentile woman so that she becomes pregnant for foreign worship." R. Ishmael comments on this verse: "this is a man who has sexual intercourse with a gentile woman and raises up children (*zera* = offspring) who are the enemies of God." In any case, for an unknown reason the Mishnah strongly disapproves of this exegesis and forbids its recitation in synagogue.[50] Perhaps the disapproval was directed against

Encyclopedia Judaica 12:230–233), argues that this exegesis is correct, at least in part, because the verse prohibits not the burning of infants in an idolatrous cult but the dedication of one's *zera*, either "offspring" or "semen," to a pagan god. This is not the place for a discussion of Weinfeld's interpretation; the matter is far from settled. See Morton Smith, "A Note on Burning Babies," *Journal of the American Oriental Society* 95 (1975) 477–479; Moshe Weinfeld, "Burning Babies in Ancient Israel," *Ugarit Forschungen* 10 (1978) 411–413; George C. Heider, "Molech," *Anchor Bible Dictionary* (1992) 4.895–898.

48. Jubilees 30:7–11, trans. Wintermute, in Charlesworth, *Old Testament Pseudepigrapha* 2:112–113.

49. For intermarriage as a capital crime, see the texts discussed by G. Alon, *Jews, Judaism, and the Classical World* (Jerusalem: Magnes Press, 1977) 114–119; see too Josephus, *AJ* 11:144. I. Ta-Shema, "On the Interpretation of a Section of the Book of Jubilees" (in Hebrew), *Beth Miqra* 11 (1966) 99–102, suggests that the death penalty was deduced from the fact that most of the sexual offenses in Leviticus 18 were capital crimes.

50. Megillah 4:9; Y. Megillah 4:10 75c = Sanhedrin 16:11 27b; B. Megillah 25a. The Peshitta follows Targum Jonathan. See Weinfeld, "Worship of Molech" 142 n. 76, who translates the Targum differently. Instead of "so that she becomes pregnant," Weinfeld offers "to make [the children] pass over to another worship." In any case, a pun on *leha'avir* ("to cause to pass" and "to impregnate") is clearly intended. Sifrei Deuteronomy 171 (218F) attaches R. Ishmael's comment to Deut. 18:10. For a full discussion see G. Vermes, "Leviticus 18:21 in Ancient Jewish Bible Exegesis," in *Studies in Aggadah, Targum, and Jewish Liturgy in Memory of Joseph Heinemann*, ed. J. J. Petuchowski and E. Fleischer

the proponents of the exegesis, who were suspected of "heresy," rather than against the exegesis itself.

Deuteronomy 21:10–14
(and Numbers 31:17–18)

When you take the field against your enemies, and the Lord your God delivers them into your power and you take some of them captive, and you see among the captives a beautiful woman and you desire her and would take her to wife, you shall bring her into your house, and she shall trim her hair, pare her nails, and discard her captive's garb. She shall spend a month's time in your house lamenting her father and mother; after that you may come to her and possess her, and she shall be your wife. Then, should you no longer want her, you must release her outright. You must not sell her for money: since you had your will of her, you must not enslave her. (Deut. 21:10–14)

This law allows the Israelite warrior to bring home and marry a beautiful war captive. Since Deuteronomy elsewhere prohibits marriage with Canaanites and even orders their extermination, we may presume that our text is speaking of non-Canaanites.[51] Nevertheless the law is remarkable, for here Moses permits marriage between an Israelite warrior and a foreign woman. Similarly Deuteronomy 20:14 permits the Israelites, after conquering a town that has refused to surrender, to "take as your booty the women, the children, the livestock, and everything in the town . . . and enjoy the use of the spoil of your enemy which the Lord your God gives you." If the range of activities covered by the word "enjoy the use" (the Hebrew literally means "eat") is not clear here, the implications of Numbers 31:17–18 are unambiguous. Moses enjoins upon the returning warriors to kill their Midianite female captives who have lain with a man, but "spare for yourselves every young woman who has not had carnal relations with a man"; we may be sure that *for your-*

(Jerusalem: Magnes, 1981) 108–124. In the 250 years between Jubilees 30 and R. Ishmael the exegetical link between Molekh and intermarriage underwent a subtle but significant shift. In the rabbinic texts, the primary intent of the verse is to prohibit sexual unions between Israelite men and gentile women, whereas Jubilees understood it to refer to marriages between Israelite women and gentile men. This change probably reflects the growth of the matrilineal principle; see chapter 9 below.

51. The Sifrei (and B. Sotah 35b) says that the law applies also to Canaanites who were in the midst of the conquered people (or perhaps who had been conquered by the people now conquered by the Israelites).

selves means that the warriors may "use" their virgin captives sexually.[52] The law in Numbers differs from the law in Deuteronomy—perhaps the most significant distinction is that the law in Deuteronomy does not care whether the captive is a virgin or not[53]—but it too permits an Israelite warrior to marry (or "marry") a foreign woman.

Neither Philo nor Josephus seems to have been disturbed by these texts,[54] but the author of the Temple Scroll clearly was. After citing Deuteronomy 21:10–13 (with only slight variations from our Hebrew text) the Temple Scroll adds the following:

But she shall not touch your pure stuff for seven years, and she shall not eat a sacrifice of peace offering until seven years pass; only then she may eat.[55]

Moses may have permitted the Israelite warrior to marry his beautiful war captive, but she remains an outsider. Exclusion from the purities of the group is a standard punishment in the Qumran scrolls, and the period of seven years is the maximum duration of punishment within the framework of the sect (even if, as far as I know, this precise penalty— exclusion from purities for seven years—is not attested elsewhere in the Qumran scrolls).[56] The Temple Scroll, of course, is not yet aware of a procedure or ritual for the conversion of women; apparently the Temple Scroll imagines that the captive is naturalized merely through her marriage to an Israelite man, but for seven years she remains an outsider with respect to her husband's—and, we may presume, the community's—pure foods and sacrificial offerings.

With the creation of a procedure for conversion to Judaism by

52. I do not know why the new Jewish version omits *for yourselves;* the Hebrew *lakhem* is unambiguous. That the intent of *for yourselves* is sexual or matrimonial is obvious; the passage is correctly understood by R. Simeon b. Yohai in the Sifrei ad loc. (157 212H), even if the parallel rabbinic passages (B. Qiddushin 78a, Yevamot 60b; Y. Qiddushin 4:6 66a) also present the view that *for yourselves* meant "as servants." Later apologists, both Jewish and Christian, adopted the latter interpretation. Note à Lapide, *Commentaria* 903 on Num. 33:17: *eas [virgines] reservarunt Hebraei, vel ad hoc, ut eas venderent, vel ut eis quasi ancillis uterentur;* for the same apologetic reading, see Hertz, *Pentateuch* ad loc.

53. According to the Sifrei, the law applies even to a married woman.

54. On Num. 31:17–18 see Philo, *On the Virtues* 43 and *Life of Moses* 1.311; Josephus, *AJ* 4.162–163. On Deut. 21:10–14 see Philo *On the Virtues* 110–115; Josephus, *AJ* 4.257– 259 and *CAp* 2.212. In none of these passages do either Philo or Josephus react to the fact that Moses is permitting sexual union with a gentile woman.

55. Temple Scroll 63:14–15, trans. Yadin.

56. See Yadin's discussion in *Temple Scroll* 2:365–367. Manfred R. Lehmann, "The Beautiful War Bride and Other *Halakhoth* in the Temple Scroll," in *Temple Scroll Studies,* ed. George J. Brooke, JSOT Supplement no. 7 (Sheffield, England: JSOT, 1989) 265–271, adds nothing.

women, the difficulties raised by Numbers 31:17–18 and Deuteronomy 21:10–14 disappear easily and automatically. Surely Moses permitted marriage with foreign women only after they had converted to Judaism. The Sifrei on Numbers assumes that the Midianite virgins will have converted before their marriage to their captors. The point is assumed, not argued.[57] Targum Jonathan on Deuteronomy 21:13 reads as follows:

And she shall remove the clothing of her captivity from herself, and you shall immerse her and convert her in your house, and she shall lament the error of the house of her father and mother, and she shall abide for three months so that you should know whether she is pregnant, and after that you shall go to her and give her a marriage settlement and she shall be your wife.

The Targum has reshaped the biblical verse to make it conform to rabbinic halakhic expectations: after the captive converts through immersion and endures the three-month waiting period prescribed for all female converts, she may become a proper Israelite wife.[58]

Targum Jonathan is following the exegesis of R. Akiva as recorded in the Sifrei:

She shall spend a month's time in your house lamenting her father and mother: her actual father and mother—(these are) the words of R. Eliezer. R. Akiva says, her father and mother does not mean anything other than idolatry, as it says, They said to wood [i.e., an image made of wood] "You are my father" (Jer. 2:27).

Thus, according to R. Akiva, she laments her idolatry; that is, she converts to Judaism. Perhaps R. Eliezer would agree that she must convert before marriage and simply disagrees with R. Akiva in the construction of the phrase her father and mother. In the next paragraph the anonymous Sifrei comments on the phrase you must release her outright (lit., to herself) "to herself—and not to the house of her god(s)."[59] That is, even if the warrior decides not to take her to wife, she is not to return

57. Sifrei 157 (212H) on Num. 31:18 and 31:19.

58. On the three-month waiting period see T. Yevamot 6:6 19L and 6:8 21L, and parallels. Targum Jonathan is applying to the captive the halakhic norms that apply to a normal female convert; some circles (Karaite?) in the Middle Ages did the same; that is, the captive became a paradigm for female converts. A document of the Cairo genizah reports the conversion of two sisters; as part of the conversion process they shaved their heads and pared their nails. See Mordecai A. Friedman, Jewish Polygyny in the Middle Ages (in Hebrew) (Jerusalem: Bialik Institute, 1986) 338 n. 11.

59. Sifrei on Deuteronomy 213 (246F) and 214 (247F). Instead of "and not to the house of her god(s)," Nahmanides and one other medieval testimonium read: "and not to the house of her father." See below.

to her god(s), for she has become a convert. R. Eliezer does not demur. Or perhaps R. Eliezer would argue that indeed she remains unconverted, for no matter how it is construed, this scriptural law is problematic and exceptional.

The Bavli assumes that the captive is indeed a convert, but explicitly acknowledges the problematic and exceptional nature of this law. The law is a *hiddush,* an innovation, a departure from expected norms, a concession to men's lust: "The Torah stated (this law) only in response to the evil inclination [i.e., lust]. Better that Israelites should eat meat of dying animals that have been slaughtered and not eat meat of dying animals that have become carrion."[60] In other words, the Torah would have preferred that Israelite warriors not bring home beautiful captives. But as a concession to men's passions, and out of a realization that men will bring home beautiful captives whether permitted to or not, the Torah attempted to regulate that which was inevitable.[61] An animal dying of natural causes will probably be deemed unfit to be eaten (*terefah*) even if slaughtered, but certainly will be deemed unfit (*nevelah*) if allowed to die on its own. The parable assumes that the Israelite is going to eat the meat in any case; the warrior is going to have the captive in any case. Better that the animal be slaughtered first, even if the slaughtering may not in fact succeed in rendering the meat fit to eat; better that the captive be converted first, even if the conversion may not in fact succeed in rendering her fit to be married.

If the captive converts, why is she unfit to be married? Why does she remain the meat of an animal about to die of natural causes? The answer is that she is compelled to convert, and under normal circumstances forced conversions are invalid.[62] That her conversion can be forced

60. B. Qiddushin 21b–22a. *Besar temutot,* which I have translated as "meat of dying animals," is a unique phrase, which, as far as I have been able to determine, occurs nowhere else in ancient rabbinic literature. But its meaning seems clear.

61. Compare Mark 10:5 and Matt. 19:8: Moses gave the Israelites a commandment "in response to their hardness of heart." Although rabbinic exegesis conceded the nonidealistic nature of this law, it did not attempt to uproot it or abrogate it entirely. For contemporary women these passages of Numbers and Deuteronomy, which depict women as war booty, are "texts of terror." See the collection of essays *Women, War, and Metaphor* = *Semeia* 61 (1993). Neither Jews nor Christians of antiquity had this perspective. (Of course, what ancient Jewish and Christian women thought is something that we do not know.)

62. Maimonides, who assumes that the essence of conversion is the philosophical recognition of God (see chapter 7 above, note 35), could not understand how the Torah could validate a forced conversion. Maimonides explicitly says that the captive is not forced to convert (*Hilkhot Melakhim* 8:5–10). (Maimonides, however, also says that if the

upon her, just as it can be forced upon a slave, is stated explicitly in
B. Yevamot 47b–48a. In his commentary on Deuteronomy 21:12 Nahmanides explains:

And the reason for this law [i.e., the requirement that she mourn] is because
she is converting against her will, and we do not ask her whether she wishes
to abandon her religion and to become a Jew, as is the practice with converts, but the husband tells her that she will observe the Torah of Israel
against her will and that she will abandon her superstition. And this is the
reason for *and she shall cry for her father and mother,* because she is abandoning her nation and her gods, and this is the midrash of R. Akiva . . . The
point is that she is lamenting because she is abandoning her religion and is
joining another nation. And it would appear likely that the court immerses
her against her will just as they do with slaves, and, because she is not becoming Jewish properly, Scripture keeps her distant [from her captor] all
this time.[63]

Nahmanides is following the exegetical tradition according to which
the warrior is permitted to have sex with his captive only after she has
observed all the rituals laid out in verses 12–13—that is, only after she
has converted. In recognition of the warrior's overpowering lust the
Torah permits him to have his way with his captive, but only after he
has brought her home, converted her to Judaism (against her will, if
necessary), and left her unmolested for thirty (or ninety! see Targum
Jonathan) days; even overpowering lust must be controlled temporarily![64] Since her conversion is against her will, Nahmanides says, if
she is rejected by her captor, a possibility discussed in verse 14, her
conversion is void and she is deemed to be not Jewish. She may (in

---

captive does not voluntarily accept the seven Noahide laws, she is to be killed; she is pressured to accept the Noahide laws, but she is not pressured to convert to Judaism. This
apparently is a Maimonidean innovation, not a relic of a lost ancient midrash as Finkelstein suggests [see his note on Sifrei 214 p. 247 line 6].) How Maimonides would explain
"Better that Israelites should eat meat of dying animals that have been slaughtered etc."
I do not know.

63. Nahmanides [R. Moshe ben Nahman], *Commentary on the Torah,* ed. H. D.
Chavel (Jerusalem: Rav Kook Institute, 1959; frequently reprinted) 2.441.

64. Rabbenu Tam objects that this interpretation does not have the Torah concede
very much to the evil inclination. He suggests rather that the Torah permits an initial act
of intercourse, when the captive is still a gentile, after which the warrior must leave her
alone and follow the outlined procedures before marrying her and having intercourse
with her again. See Tosafot, B. Qiddushin 22a, s.v. "*shelo yilhatzenah,*" and Sanhedrin 21a,
s.v. "*de'i.*" Maimonides follows the same view; see *Hilkhot Melakhim* 8:2–5. This debate
is anticipated by Y. Makkot 2:7 31d (= Midrash Samuel 25 p. 62a ed. Buber), cited by
Tosafot and Nahmanides.

contradiction with our texts of the Sifrei) return to the house of her god(s).[65]

Ancient and medieval Christian exegetes, no less than their Jewish counterparts, assumed that the beautiful war captive of Deuteronomy 21:10–14 must shed her pagan ways and convert before becoming an Israelite wife. But Christian exegetes, unlike their Jewish counterparts, read the text allegorically. Jerome cites this passage as part of his defense for his use of pagan literature in his writings.

What wonder is it if I too wish to take secular Wisdom, on account of the charm of her speech and the beauty of her limbs, and make her an Israelite woman out of a slave and a captive, if I cut off or shave whatever in her is dead, whether idolatry, pleasure, error, or lust, and, joining with her most pure body, father domestics from her for Lord Sabaoth?[66]

In this conceit, which Jerome seems to have derived from Origen,[67] the "beautiful captive" is pagan wisdom—which, when shorn of its evils, is an appropriate mate for a warrior like Jerome. Other exegetes based other allegories on this passage, but they all understood the passage to be a description of the captive's purification of her foreign and sinful ways.[68] Like the rabbis, these Christian exegetes could not otherwise imagine how Moses could have permitted the union of an Israelite warrior with a foreign woman, even if both the warrior and the woman were to be interpreted allegorically.

Conclusion

A general prohibition of intermarriage between Jews and non-Jews does not appear anywhere in the Tanakh. Leviticus lists nu-

65. See Nahmanides' commentary on verse 14 (2:443–444 ed. Chavel) and see note 59 above for Nahmanides' text of the Sifrei. Even more remarkable than Nahmanides here is the *Moshav Zeqenim* p. 506 ed. Sasoon: if she is rejected by her captor "she is within her rights to be a convert or to return to her gentile state" (*hi bireshut atzmah leheyot giyoret o lahazor legoyutah* [a correction for *legerutah*]).

66. Jerome, Epistle 70.5 (CSEL 54 p. 702): quid ergo mirum, si et ego sapientiam saecularem propter eloquii venustatem et membrorum pulchritudinem de ancilla atque captiva Israhelitin facere cupio, si, quidquid in ea mortuum est idolatriae, voluptatis, erroris, libidinum, vel praecido vel rado et mixtus purissimo corpori vernaculos ex ea genero domino sabaoth?

67. Origen, Homily on Leviticus 7.6, pp. 390–391, ed. Baehrens (GCS 29).

68. Cyril of Alexandria, *Glaphyra* (PG 69:649–657); Ambrose, epistle 31.11–13 (PL 16:1065–1068); Jerome, Cyril, and Ambrose are cited by à Lapide, *Commentaria* 991, in his commentary on Deuteronomy.

merous sexual taboos (chapters 18 and 20) but fails to include intermarriage among them. Exodus 34:15 and Deuteronomy 7:3–4 prohibit intermarriage with the seven Canaanite nations, and Deuteronomy 23:2–9 prohibits four additional nations from *entering the congregation of the Lord*—perhaps (but probably not) a prohibition of marriage. But neither Exodus nor Deuteronomy prohibits intermarriage with all non-Israelites, and both of them prohibit intermarriage with Canaanites only because it might lead to something else that was prohibited (idolatry). Biblical Israel was a nation living on its own land and had no need for a general prohibition of intermarriage with all outsiders. Attitudes changed when conditions changed. In the wake of the destruction of the temple in 587 B.C.E., Judaea lost any semblance of political independence, the tribal structure of society was shattered, and the Israelites were scattered among the nations. In these new circumstances marriage with outsiders came to be seen as a threat to Judaean (Jewish) identity and was widely condemned. The Judaeans sensed that their survival depended upon their ideological (or religious) and social separation from the outside world.

The process that yielded these innovations had already begun by the time of Ezra and Nehemiah, was well under way by the time of the Maccabees, and was substantially complete by the time of the Talmud. Ezra and Nehemiah attempted to expel the "foreign women" from the Judaean community (Ezra 9–10; Nehemiah 13), and justified their action by implicit appeal to Deuteronomy 7:3–4, alleging that all gentiles who were like the Canaanites of old were subsumed under the same prohibition as the Canaanites themselves. Theodotus, an author of the Hasmonean period, paraphrases Genesis 34:14 by having the patriarch Jacob state: "For indeed this very thing is not allowed for Hebrews, to bring home sons-in-law and daughters-in-law from another place, but only one who boasts of being of the same race," a substantial modification of the biblical source.[69] Various works of this period either excuse or extol the massacre of Shechem by Simon and Levi, although in Genesis 34 (and 49:5–7) the patriarch Jacob condemned it.[70] Intermarriage and other violations of fundamental norms were deemed worthy of capital punishment. Jubilees, aware of those who disguised their circumcision and flouted the law, denounces all who would marry a

---

69. Theodotus cited in Eusebius, *Praeparatio Evangelica* 9.22.6 = Holladay, *Fragments* 2.116–117. Scholars have long debated whether Theodotus was a Judaean or a Samaritan; I prefer the former.

70. See chapter 4 above, note 37.

gentile or allow a gentile to marry a daughter of Israel. Unlike Ezra, however, Jubilees attaches its rhetoric not to Deuteronomy 7:3–4 but to Leviticus 18:21. Similarly, of the other works of the Hasmonean period that protest against intermarriage, none bases its argument on Deuteronomy 7:3–4. In contrast, Philo and Josephus also protested against intermarriage but relied on Deuteronomy 7:3–4, extending that prohibition from the seven Canaanite nations to all gentiles.

The rabbis of the Talmud were the first to develop a sustained and detailed exegesis justifying the prohibition of intermarriage, even if some of them also realized that the prohibition, historically considered, was actually a product of the second-temple period. The prohibition was derived from Deuteronomy 7:3–4 and 23:2–9. The Talmud discusses in some detail the applicability of the prohibition and the consequences of its violation—the status of the offspring of intermarriage (see next chapter). The law of the beautiful war captive, in which Moses seems to allow, under specific circumstances, the marriage of Israelite men with non-Israelite women, was rendered unproblematic by rabbinic exegesis: the woman, of course, had to convert to Judaism first. The laws of Scripture were thoroughly rabbinized.

CHAPTER 9

The Matrilineal Principle

According to the Torah and our eternal tradition, he is a Jew who was born [of Jewish parents,] at least of a Jewish mother. No force in the world may or can possibly invalidate this principle which is the very basis of the totality of Judaism.

Rabbi Yehudah Leib Maimon

Why is a child [of a non-Jewish mother] as his mother? The answer is not quite clear.

Rabbi Yechiel Y. Weinberg

According to rabbinic law, from the second century C.E. to the present, the offspring of a gentile mother and a Jewish father is a gentile, while the offspring of a Jewish mother and a gentile father is a Jew. Each of these two rulings has its own history, as I shall discuss below, but it is convenient to group them together under the general heading "the matrilineal principle." Anthropologists and sociologists use the term *matrilineal* to describe societies in which kinship is determined through the females and not the males. Such societies once existed in ancient Egypt and Mesopotamia, and can still be found in parts of Africa, India, and Polynesia.[1] Although rabbinic society and family

The epigraphs are from, respectively, Rabbi Yehudah Leib Maimon, in *Jewish Identity,* ed. Litvin and Hoenig, 20; and Rabbi Yechiel Y. Weinberg, in *Jewish Identity,* ed. Litvin and Hoenig, 92.

1. See, for instance, Koschaker, "Fratriarchat"; David M. Schneider, *Matrilineal Kinship* (Berkeley: University of California Press, 1961; reprint, 1974); *Kinship: Selected Readings,* ed. Jack Goody (Baltimore: Penguin, 1971); idem, *Comparative Studies in Kinship*

law have not yet been studied in the light of modern anthropological and sociological theories, it seems clear that the kinship patterns that characterize matrilineal societies are thoroughly foreign to rabbinic society. With only a few exceptions rabbinic family law is patrilineal. Status, kinship, and succession are determined through the father. As the rabbis say, "The family of the father is considered family, the family of the mother is not considered family.[2] Why, then, did the rabbis adopt a matrilineal principle for the determination of the status of the offspring of mixed marriages?

In the first section of this chapter I examine the Bible and the texts of the second-temple period in order to determine the earliest attestation of the matrilineal principle in Jewish sources. The second section is dedicated to the Mishnah, the Tosefta, and the two Talmudim. In the third section I assess various explanations for the origins of the matrilineal principle, and in the fourth I attempt to reach a conclusion.[3]

The Biblical and Second-Temple Periods

THE BIBLICAL PERIOD

The preexilic portions of the Tanakh are not familiar with the matrilineal principle. Numerous Israelite heroes and kings married foreign women; for example, Judah married a Canaanite, Joseph an Egyptian, Moses a Midianite and an Ethiopian, David a Philistine, and Solomon women of every description.[4] Although Exodus 34:16 and Deuteronomy 7:1–3 prohibit intermarriage only with the Canaanites, a prohibition that was supposed to have originated with the patriarchs

---

(Stanford: Stanford University Press, 1969) chap. 3; and many others. On matriliny in contemporary India, see, for example, *New York Times,* February 15, 1994, p. A21.

2. B. Bava Batra 109b.

3. The most important scholarly contributions to the study of the matrilineal principle are: Aptowitzer, "Spuren des Matriarchats"; Epstein, *Marriage Laws,* esp. 174 and 194–197; B. Cohen, "Law of Persons," esp. 12–24; Schiffman, "Crossroads," esp. 117–122 = *Who Was a Jew?* 9–17; and Gruber, "Matrilineal Determination." The abundant literature spawned by the ongoing debates in the state of Israel on the question "Who is a Jew?" (see, e.g., *Jewish Identity,* ed. Litvin and Hoenig, a book brought to my attention by Rabbi Wolfe Kelman) is important for the student of contemporary Jewry but not for the historian of antiquity. The same judgment applies to the recent pronouncements of the Reform movement justifying a patrilineal (actually, a nonlineal) system (see, e.g., the winter 1983 issue of the *Journal of Reform Judaism*).

4. A convenient collection of the material is Patai, *Sex,* 31–35. It was first collected in modern times by Löw, "Studien" 112–143. On Solomon see my "Solomon."

Abraham and Isaac, some Israelites thought that the prohibition should extend even to others—Philistines, for example.[5] But it never occurred to anyone in preexilic times to argue that such marriages were null and void. Marriage was the nonsacramental, private acquisition of a woman by a man, and the state had little legal standing in the matter.[6] The foreign woman who married an Israelite husband was supposed to leave her gods in her father's house, but even if she did not, it never occurred to anyone to argue that her children were not Israelites. Since the idea of "conversion to Judaism" did not yet exist (see chapter 4 above), it never occurred to anyone to demand that the foreign woman undergo some ritual to indicate her acceptance of the religion of Israel. The woman was joined to the house of Israel by being joined to her Israelite husband; the act of marriage was functionally equivalent to the later idea of "conversion." In some circumstances biblical law and society did pay attention to maternal identity—the children of concubines and female slaves sometimes rank lower than the children of wives[7]—but it never occurred to anyone to impose legal or social disabilities on the children of foreign women.

Although Deuteronomy 7:3 prohibits Israelite men from marrying Canaanite women, and Israelite women from being given in marriage to Canaanite men, the legislator is particularly concerned about the former possibility, because "their daughters will lust after their gods and

5. Abraham: Gen. 24:3. Isaac: Gen. 27:46–28:1. Philistines: Judg. 14:3. See chapter 8 above.

6. Most legal systems of antiquity shared this attitude. See, for example, Elias Bickerman, "La conception du mariage à Athènes," *Bulletino dell' Istituto di Diritto Romano* 78, n.s. 17 (1975) 1–28 = Elias Bickerman, *Religions and Politics in the Hellenistic and Roman Periods,* ed. Emilio Gabba and Morton Smith (Como, Italy: New Press, 1985) 561–588.

7. See, for example, Gen. 21:10, 22:20–24, and 25:5–6; Judg. 9:1–5 and 11:1–2; cf. Exod. 21:4. There are many parallels in other legal systems of antiquity; see G. R. Driver and John Miles, *The Babylonian Laws,* 2 vols. (Oxford: Clarendon, 1952) 1:350–353; Gruber, "Matrilineal Determination." Similarly, in 1662 the Virginia assembly declared that "mulatto children of slave mothers would be slaves. In so deciding, the assembly wrenched itself away from the English rule that the child followed the status of its father." See Joel Willimason, *New People: Miscegenation and Mulattoes in the United States* (New York: Free Press, 1980) 8. A notable exception is Egyptian law, according to which the offspring of a slave mother and a free father is legitimate (Diodorus of Sicily 1.80.3). The text edited by Bezalel Porten and Ada Yardeni in their *Textbook of Aramaic Documents from Ancient Egypt 2: Contracts* (Jerusalem: Hebrew University, 1989) no. B3.6 clearly shows that the offspring of a female slave is a slave "like her," even when the father of the offspring is the owner. The document is quite clear that the father of Yehoishma is Meshullam, the owner of the mother; I do not know why Porten thinks that Ananiah, her adoptive father, is her natural father (Porten, *Archives* 221 and 225).

will cause your sons to lust after their gods."[8] This concern indicates
not a matrilineal principle but a patriarchal society in which the cult, as
well as everything else of importance, was the domain of men. If Israelite men are incited by their foreign wives to abandon the worship of
the true God, the result could be catastrophic; if Israelite women are
turned astray by their foreign husbands, who would notice?[9] Furthermore, when an Israelite woman was married to a foreigner she usually
became part of her husband's family (just like the foreign woman who
was married to an Israelite husband) and was no longer under the jurisdiction or authority of her native people. Hence the legal and narrative texts pay little attention to marriages between Israelite women and
foreign men. Like the women themselves, they were easily overlooked.
A similar phenomenon can be observed not only in the Mishnah (see
below) but also in the literature of other societies that enacted prohibitions of marriage with foreigners.[10]

The meager biblical data about such marriages suggest that the offspring of Israelite women and foreign men were judged matrilineally
only if the marriage was matrilocal—that is, only if the foreign husband joined the wife's domicile or clan.[11] First Chronicles 2:34–35 describes the marriage between an Egyptian slave and the daughter of his
Israelite owner. The marriage was probably a form of adoption.[12] Other
instances of matrilocal marriage involving a foreign male are recorded
by Leviticus 24:10 and 1 Chronicles 2:17.[13] If the marriage was not matrilocal—that is, if the Israelite woman joined the house of her foreign husband—, I assume that the fellow nationals of both the husband
and the wife would have considered the children to be of the same

8. Exod. 34:16, cf. Deut. 7:4 (see below).

9. The Bible seldom notices idolatrous acts by Israelite women: see 2 Kings 23:7; Jeremiah 44 and Jer. 7:18 (the whole family); and Ezek. 8:14.

10. On Periclean Athens see below, notes 15, 19, 32, and 139.

11. On matrilocal marriage in general see Edward Westermarck, *The History of Human
Marriage*, 3 vols. (New York: Allerton, 1922) 1.296–297. On matrilocal marriage in the
ancient near East, see Koschaker, "Fratriarchat" 84–85; G. R. Driver and John C. Miles,
The Assyrian Laws (Oxford: Clarendon, 1935) 134–142; Neufeld, *Marriage Laws* 56–67;
E. Neufeld, *The Hittite Laws* (London: Luzac, 1951) 126, 140–141, and 151–153; Werner
Plautz, "Zur Frage des Mutterrechts im alten Testament," *ZAW* 74 (1962) 9–30, at 18–
26; Patai, *Sex*, 52–53.

12. For the legitimation of the offspring of a slave father and a free mother, cf. Driver
and Miles, *Babylonian Laws*, 1.353–356.

13. Lev. 24:10 carefully contrasts the "son of an Israelite woman" with "the Israelite,"
thereby implying that the former was marked by a social stigma; see further the Sifra on
Lev. 24:10, cited in chapter 10 below, note 17. With 1 Chron. 2:17 contrast 2 Sam. 17:25.

nationality as their father. Unfortunately, little evidence confirms this assumption.[14]

EZRA

The situation becomes less clear in the fifth century B.C.E. At about the time that Pericles was enacting a law restricting Athenian citizenship to those born of an Athenian woman lawfully wedded to an Athenian man (451 B.C.E.), Ezra was promoting a similar reform in Judaea.[15] After exacting a pledge from the notables of Jerusalem to refrain from marriages with foreigners, Ezra attempted to expel from the community approximately 113 foreign wives with their children. Only two aspects of this obscure episode need to be treated here. First, why did Ezra virtually ignore the marriages between Israelite women and foreign men?[16] Second, why did he attempt to expel the children of the foreign wives as well as the wives themselves? The usual answer to these questions is that Ezra introduced the matrilineal principle. He attacked marriages between Israelite (at this period we probably should say "Judaean") men and foreign women because their consequences were serious; like their mothers, the offspring are not Jewish. In contrast, he could ignore (at least temporarily) the marriages between Jewish women and foreign men because their consequences were relatively benign; like their mothers, the offspring are Jewish.[17]

This view *may* be correct, but is not necessarily so; other explanations are possible. Perhaps Ezra ignored the marriages between native women and foreign men because, as I have just mentioned, such mar-

---

14. 1 Kings 7:13–14, cf. 2 Chron. 2:12–13.

15. On the citizenship law of Pericles, see, for example, Lacey, *Family* 100–103; Hannick, "Droit de cité"; John K. Davies, "Athenian Citizenship: The Descent Group and the Alternatives," *Classical Journal* 73 (1977) 105–121; Cynthia Patterson, *Pericles' Citizenship Law of 451–50 B.C.* (New York: Arno, 1981) and "Those Athenian Bastards"; Boegehold, "Perikles' Citizenship Law"; Ogden, *Greek Bastardy* 59–70. The parallel between Pericles and Ezra was observed by G. F. Moore, *Judaism* 1.20, and by Solomon Zeitlin, *The Rise and Fall of the Judean State*, 3 vols. (Philadelphia: Jewish Publication Society, 1968–1978), 1.17.

16. He briefly mentions these marriages in his penitential prayer (Ezra 9:12) but otherwise ignores them. So too his contemporary Malachi (2:11–16).

17. Chaim Tchernowitz, *History of Hebrew Law*, 4 vols. (New York: n.p., 1943–1944), 3.108–111; Belkin, "Paul's Background" 47–48; Zeitlin, *Judean State*, 1.27, referring to his own "Offspring of Intermarriage"; Schiffman, "Crossroads" 121 = *Who Was a Jew?* 16. The amora R. Haggai also deduces the matrilineal principle from the Ezra story (see below).

riages were generally ignored by both biblical and nonbiblical texts. Ezra's jurisdiction extended only to the members of his people,[18] and he could do nothing to a foreign man who had married an Israelite woman. Even the attempted expulsion of the children of the foreign wives does not necessarily presume a matrilineal principle. Perhaps, like Pericles, Ezra introduced a bilateral requirement for citizenship. This innovation affected offspring of foreign mothers more than offspring of foreign fathers in both Athens and Jerusalem, since the former had previously been regarded as citizens while the latter had always been regarded as foreigners.[19] Furthermore, the attempted expulsion of the children was an act of supererogation by one Shekaniah ben Yehiel and was not demanded by Ezra himself.[20] If we insist on seeing the matrilineal principle in this story, we must ascribe its origin not to Ezra but to an unheralded member of the clan of Elam.

THE SECOND-TEMPLE PERIOD

The likelihood that Ezra (or a contemporary) introduced the idea that the offspring of a Jewish father and a gentile mother is a

18. Ezra 9:25, reading *ammak* or *ammeh* instead of *amma*. See See H. L. Ginsberg, *The Israelian Heritage of Judaism* (New York: Jewish Theological Seminary, 1982) 17 n. 18.

19. Christophilopoulos, *Dikaion* 69 (part of his article "Marriage with a Foreign Woman according to Ancient Hellenic and Hellenistic Law"); Vatin, *Recherches* 120–122. On the Periclean citizenship law see the studies listed in note 15 above. Isaeus, *Orations* 8:43 summarizes the Periclean law as follows: "If our mother was not a citizen, we are not citizens" (quoted by Lacey, *Family,* 282 n. 14). Aristophon in 403–402 B.C.E. proposed a law that "whoever is not born of a citizen mother is a *nothos*" (Athenaeus, *Deipnosophists* 14.577b–c; Ogden, *Greek Bastardy* 77–78), but citizenship, of course, required a citizen father. On *mētroxenoi,* "those born of foreign mothers," see Pollux, *Onomasticon* 3.21, vol. 1, p. 161, ed. E. Bethe; the passages listed in Bethe's note, especially the scholium to Euripides, *Alcestis* 989; and the discussion in Ogden, *Greek Bastardy* passim (see 422, index, s.v. "*mētroxenoi*").

20. Contrast Ezra 10:2–3 with Ezra 10:11. This point was sensed by Thomas de Vio Caietan (1469–1534) in his commentary on Ezra 10:5, 11, and 44; see his *Opera Omnia quotquot in Sacrae Scripturae Expositionem Reperiuntur,* 5 vols. (Lugdunum: Jacobus et Petrus Prost, 1639), 2:370–371. Similarly, according to some Karaite exegetes Ezra did not even attempt to expel the children; see below, note 70. Some modern Jewish apologists explain that Ezra did *not* regard the women and their children as gentiles; he was merely purifying the lineage of the aristocracy from admixture with Jews of poor pedigree. See Heinrich Graetz, *Geschichte der Juden,* 2d ed., vol. 2, pt. 2 (Leipzig: O. Leiner, 1902) 130–136, with the critique of Kaufmann, *Religion of Israel* 4.340–342; F. Rosenthal, *Monatschrift für die Geschichte und Wissenschaft des Judentums* 30 (1881) 120–122; and Lewi Freund, "Über Genealogien und Familienreinheit in biblischer und talmudischer Zeit," in *Festschrift Adolf Schwarz,* ed. Victor Aptowitzer and Samuel Krauss (Berlin and Vienna: R. Löwit, 1917) 168–169.

gentile is further diminished by the fact that this half of the matrilineal principle is never attested explicitly, and is frequently contradicted implicitly, by the later literature of the second-temple period.[21] When confronting the biblical narratives about the heroes of Israel who married foreign women, exegetes committed to the matrilineal principle and to the prohibition of intermarriage with all gentiles have only three options: (1) they can assert that the principle and the prohibition were in effect in biblical times, but were occasionally ignored; (2) they can admit that the principle and the prohibition were not in effect in biblical times; or (3) they can argue that the principle and the prohibition were in effect and were observed by all. The first two possibilities were near impossibilities for anyone who believed in the harmony of sacred Scripture and Jewish law. Some rabbis could admit that Jacob and his sons did not observe the legal distinctions between clean and unclean animals because before the revelation at Mount Sinai the Israelites were not bound to observe the laws of the Torah, but the general tendency of rabbinic literature, like that of Jubilees and other pre-rabbinic works, is to claim that the patriarchs observed the law in a manner consonant with later beliefs.[22] And even if an excuse could be found for the marriages of the sons of Jacob, what excuse could be found for Moses himself and for the figures who lived after the revelation of the Torah at Mount Sinai? Rabbinic midrash, therefore, generally chose the third course, and argued that the foreign women were not foreign at all, either because they really were of Israelite origin or because they had converted to Judaism before their marriages.[23] This exegesis does not nec-

---

21. Of course, one could argue that this fact is merely further testimony to Ezra's relative lack of success; see, for example, Morton Smith, *Palestinian Parties and Politics That Shaped the Old Testament* (New York: Columbia University Press, 1971) 121–122. The documents of Elephantine describe several cases of intermarriage, but the matrilineal principle is nowhere in evidence (except in the case of the offspring of slave mothers; see above, note 7). See Porten, *Archives,* 148–149, 203–213, and 252–258.

22. M. Hulin 7:6. See Urbach, *Sages* 1.335–336; Moshe Potolsky, "The Rabbinic Rule: No Laws Are Derived from before Sinai'" (in Hebrew), *Dine Israel* 6 (1985) 195–230. The Sifra frequently distinguishes the law that was normative before the Sinaitic revelation from the law that was normative afterward; see chapter 10 below, note 19. The medieval midrashic collection *Pitron Torah* argues that Moses was permitted to marry Zipporah not only because she converted to Judaism but also because they were married before the revelation of the Torah at Mount Sinai; in contrast, Zimri's liaison with Kozbi (Numbers 25) was sinful because she did not convert and because their liaison occurred after the revelation of the Torah (pp. 206–207, ed. Urbach). See below, note 30.

23. Ginzberg, *Legends,* index, s.v. "converts, conversion, and proselytes"; Victor Aptowitzer, "Asenath, the Wife of Joseph," *Hebrew Union College Annual* 1 (1924): 239–306; and Bamberger, *Proselytism* 174–217.

essarily presume the matrilineal principle—the removal of the blot of intermarriage is sufficient incentive to invent stories about Israelite lineage and conversions to Judaism—but without it the matrilineal principle cannot be maintained in the presence of the biblical data. Therefore, the absence of this exegesis from the vast majority of the midrashic and exegetical works of the second-temple period implies that these works are not familiar with the matrilineal principle.

Some examples follow. The Testament of Joseph mentions without comment Joseph's marriage to the daughter of the priest of Heliopolis; rabbinic midrash (and the book *Joseph and Asenath*) explains away the intermarriage.[24] Egyptian Jews told many wonderful stories about Moses' Ethiopian wife, but one story they did not tell was that of her conversion to Judaism; that motif appears only in the rabbinic version of the tale.[25] The rabbis insist that a female war captive must convert to Judaism before being married by her Israelite captor; Deuteronomy neglects this provision, as does the Temple Scroll, a work closely related to Jubilees.[26] The book of Jubilees has Abraham, Rebecca, and Isaac admonish their sons not to marry Canaanite women, "for the seed of Canaan will be rooted out of the land." Thus Er and Onan, Judah's sons from his Canaanite wife, were killed by God.[27] But the destruction of the matrilineal descendants of Canaan has nothing to do with the rabbinic matrilineal principle. Jubilees is disturbed by marriages of biblical heroes with Canaanites;[28] their marriages with women of other ancestries, however, were acceptable. According to Jubilees, Tamar, the daughter-in-law and paramour of Judah—and, most importantly, the mother of his children "who would not be uprooted"—was an Aramean; in rabbinic lore (and in Philo) she was a convert to Judaism.[29] As

---

24. Testament of Joseph 18:3; see Aptowitzer, "Asenath."

25. Tessa Rajak, "Moses in Ethiopia: Legend and Literature," *JJS* 29 (1978) 111–122, and Avigdor Shinan, "Moses and the Ethiopian Woman," in *Studies in Hebrew Narrative Art*, Scripta Hierosolymitana, vol. 27 (Jerusalem: Magnes, 1978) 66–78.

26. See chapter 8 above.

27. Abraham: Jubilees 20:4, 22:20, and 25:5; Rebecca: 25:1–3; Isaac: 27:10. Er and Onan: 34:20 and 41:2–5. On Jubilees see G. Anderson, "Status of the Torah" 22–29. Anderson is slightly inaccurate on p. 27 when he refers to Shelah (in the eyes of Jubilees) as a Canaanite. Shelah, like Er and Onan, was the offspring of a Canaanite mother, and thus the bearer of Canaanite blood; the Canaanite mother wanted her sons to marry Canaanite wives (41:2 and 7; cf. Hagar and Ishmael); but Jubilees nowhere calls the sons Canaanites.

28. Jubilees 34:20. In contrast, these marriages were sanitized by rabbinic exegesis; see Genesis Rabbah on Gen. 38:2 and 46:10.

29. Tamar an Aramean: Jubilees 41:1 (and Testament of Judah 10:1). Children "who would not be uprooted": 41:27. In some midrashim, notably Targum Jonathan on Gen.

normative Jewish practice Jubilees opposes all intermarriage. In the middle of its paraphrase of Genesis 34, the story of Shechem's rape of Dinah, Jubilees inserts a tirade against intermarriage. It condemns the unions of Israelite men with foreign women and the unions of Israelite women with foreign men, but, influenced by the scriptural text that it is paraphrasing, it directs the brunt of its anger toward the latter, not the former. A man who gives his daughter to a gentile is guilty of handing his seed over to Molekh, and therefore both the man and his daughter deserve death. In rabbinic texts, by contrast, the prohibition of Molekh worship is understood to refer to unions between Israelite men and foreign women: "this is a man who has sexual intercourse with a gentile woman and raises up children who are the enemies of God." Jubilees does not know the matrilineal principle; the rabbis do.[30]

Following the Biblical tradition, few texts of the second-temple period indicate the status of the offspring of unions between Jewish women and gentile men. Some scholars have adduced Acts 16:1–3 to prove that such offspring were considered to be Jewish, but the passage is ambiguous, and may in fact serve as evidence to the contrary. Because of its importance and ambiguity, this passage requires extended discussion.[31]

Philo, Paul, and Josephus, three authors of the first century C.E., are unfamiliar with either half of the matrilineal principle. Philo applies the Greek term *nothos* (often translated as "bastard") to the offspring of

38:6, Tamar is the daughter of Shem. (Her loyalty to God is indicated in Targum Jonathan and Fragment Targum to Gen. 38:25.) See Marshall Johnson, *The Purpose of the Biblical Genealogies* (Cambridge: Cambridge University Press, 1969) 156, 159–162, and 270–272 (who omits pseudo-Philo, *Biblical Antiquities* 9:5). For Philo (*On the Virtues* 40.220–222) Tamar plays the same role as Asenath in *Joseph and Asenath:* she is the perfect archetype of the female proselyte, just as Abraham is of the male. See Marc Philonenko, *Joseph et Aséneth* (Leiden: Brill, 1968) 55.

30. Jubilees 30:7–11, esp. 10. See chapter 8 above, note 50. I freely concede that the argument of the preceding paragraphs is suggestive at best. Ancient and medieval exegetes, for whom the matrilineal principle and the prohibition of intermarriage were fixed and immutable, are still capable of surprising comments that otherwise might be thought to deny the principle and the prohibition. Thus, for example, Rashi on Gen. 50:13 says that Jacob did not want his bier carried by his grandchildren because they were the offspring of Canaanite mothers. This comment seems to be inspired by a passage of Genesis Rabbah, quoted by Rashi on Gen. 37:35, that the sons of Jacob married Canaanite women (at least this is the view of R. Nehemiah). Are we to presume that these Canaanite women converted to Judaism? Neither Genesis Rabbah nor Rashi says so. As G. Anderson, "Status of the Torah" correctly notes, the midrashic strategies concerning the observance of the Torah by the biblical patriarchs need more thorough and nuanced study than they have heretofore received.

31. See appendix D.

both types of mixed marriage: Israelite mothers with gentile fathers, and Israelite fathers with gentile (or slave) mothers. However this usage is explained, it certainly does not presume familiarity with the matrilineal principle.[32] Paul thinks that either a Christian father or a Christian mother could "consecrate" the children to Christ.[33] Josephus knows that priestly lineage can be debased if a priest's wife is raped or is unfaithful,[34] but he does not know that a gentile woman married to a Jewish man produces gentile children. Josephus carefully narrates the conversion (or, in some cases, nonconversion) of the gentile men who married the princesses of the Herodian house, but he never mentions the conversion (or nonconversion) of the gentile women who were married to the princes of the house, and Josephus obviously has no doubt that their children are Jewish. The biblical principle still applies: a gentile woman "converts" by being married to a Jewish husband.[35] Herod the Great is labeled an "Idumaean" and a "half-Jew" because of his paternal ancestry; the fact that his mother was an "unconverted"

---

32. Israelite mother and gentile father: *On the Life of Moses* 2.36.193 (referring to Lev. 24:10). Israelite father and gentile (or slave) mother: *On the Virtues* 40.224 and cf. *Allegorical Interpretation* 2.24.94 (referring to the offspring of Bilhah and Zilpah); *On the Life of Moses* 1.27.147 (referring to the mixed multitude, the offspring of Egyptian women and Hebrew men). Philo is using the term in the sense that it had in classical Greece: the offspring of an unequal union (i.e., a union in which the status of one partner is lower than that of the other). Thus in some Greek cities the offspring of a citizen mother and a noncitizen father was a *nothos* (see Demosthenes, *Against Aristocrates* 23.213, referring to Oreus in Euboea; Ogden, *Greek Bastardy* 282), and Pericles' citizenship law conferred the same status on the offspring of citizen fathers and noncitizen mothers. On this usage see Patterson, "Those Athenian Bastards"; Ogden's criticisms, *Greek Bastardy* 15–17, do not affect my point. *Nothos* also was often used in a nonlegal sense: "of impure lineage" or "a product of improper breeding." Similarly in rabbinic Hebrew *mamzer* sometimes designates the offspring of any forbidden or disapproved union; see below, notes 62 and 69. Samuel Belkin argues that Philo knew the rabbinic matrilineal principle, but the merits of his argument need not be considered (and they are few) because he mistakenly believes that Philo restricts the term *nothos* to the offspring of Israelite fathers and gentile mothers. See his *Philo and the Oral Law* (Cambridge: Harvard University Press, 1940) 233–235. The mistake originates with Isaak Heinemann, *Philons griechische und jüdische Bildung* (Breslau: Marcus, 1932) 313–314, but Heinemann, at least, realized that Philo's usage is not compatible with rabbinic law. See too B. Cohen, "Law of Persons" 24 n. 71.

33. Cor. 7:14.

34. *AJ* 3.276, 13.292, 13.372; cf. 11.71 and *CAp* 1.35.

35. *AJ* 16.225; 18.109; 18.139 and 141; and 20.139–147 (Josephus does not say whether he regards Agrippa, the son of Drusilla and the uncircumcised Felix [20.143], as Jewish). Josephus does not comment on the marriage of (Philippion son of) Ptolemy son of Menneus with a daughter of Aristobulus II, perhaps because he was circumcised (*AJ* 14:126//*BJ* 1.185–186). On all these passages, see Hadas-Lebel, "Mariages mixtes." On the conversion of women, see chapter 5 above, conclusion.

Arab woman is ignored.[36] According to Josephus, free Israelite men ought not to marry slave women or prostitutes because the offspring of these unions will not have "spirits that are liberal and uprightly set toward virtue"; Josephus does not know the matrilineal principle and consequently does not know that the offspring of gentile slave women are supposed to be gentile slaves. Their spirits are illiberal, but their bodies are free, even if socially stigmatized.[37]

CONCLUSION

I conclude that the matrilineal principle was not yet known in second-temple times. This conclusion is supported by an argument from silence and an argument from positive testimony. The argument from silence is that none of the works of "the Apocrypha," "the Pseudepigrapha," or the Qumran scrolls[38] knows, assumes, mentions, or applies the rabbinic matrilineal principle. The argument from positive testimony is that in various scattered passages Philo, Paul, Josephus, and Acts make statements or assumptions that cannot be squared with the rabbinic matrilineal principle. Perhaps the matrilineal principle was already known and regarded as normative in some pre-rabbinic circles of the late second-temple period, but none of those circles has left behind any documentation of this fact. The matrilineal principle is first attested in the Mishnah.

The Mishnah and Talmudim

THE MISHNAH

The central rabbinic text on the matrilineal principle is M. Qiddushin 3:12:

(A) Wherever there is potential for a valid marriage and the sexual union is not sinful, the offspring follows the male. And what [fem.] is this? This is the daughter of a priest, Levite, or Israelite who was married to a priest, Levite, or Israelite.

---

36. Herod: AJ 14.8–10, 14.121, and 14.403; cf. Eusebius, *Ecclesiastical History* 1.7.11–14. See my discussion in chapter 1 above. Joseph Justus Scaliger noticed this problem and solved it by arguing that Herod's mother converted to Judaism; see the *Animadversiones in Chronologica Eusebii* p. 149 in his *Thesaurus Temporum: Eusebii Pamphili . . . Chronicorum Canonum . . . Libri Duo* (Leiden: T. Basson, 1606).

37. *AJ* 4.244–245.

38. Including *Miqtzat Ma'asei HaTorah* (*MMT*).

(B) Wherever there is potential for a valid marriage but the sexual union is sinful, the offspring follows the parent of lower status.[39] And what [fem.] is this? This is a widow with a high priest, a divorcee or a "released woman"[40] with a regular priest, a *mamzeret* or a *netinah* with an Israelite, an Israelite woman with a *mamzer* or a *natin*.[41]

(C) And any woman who does not have the potential for a valid marriage with this man but has the potential for a valid marriage with other men, the offspring is a *mamzer*. And what [masc.] is this? This is he who has intercourse with any of the relations prohibited by the Torah.

(D) And any woman who does not have the potential for a valid marriage either with this man or with other men, the offspring is like her. And what [masc.] is this? This is the offspring of a slave woman or a gentile woman.[42]

This Mishnah is carefully constructed out of four paragraphs that share a common literary structure (each states a general rule followed by one or more examples of the rule) but differ from each other in style. Paragraphs A and B begin with "wherever there is potential for a valid marriage" (*kol maqom sheyesh qiddushin*), ask whether the union is sinful or not, ignore the potential of the woman to contract a legal marriage with other men, and introduce women as their examples. Paragraphs C and D begin with "and any woman who does not have the potential for a valid marriage" (*vekol mi she'ein lah alav qiddushin*), ask whether the woman has the potential to contract a legal marriage with other men, ignore the sinfulness of the union, and introduce men (more precisely, a man in C and a masculine noun in D) as their examples.[43] In their examples A and C use a verb (*sheniset/sheba*); B and D do not. The four

---

39. All the manuscripts listed in note 42 below read: *(ha)pagum shebishneihen.*

40. *Halutzah,* a widow released by her levir (Deut. 25:5–10).

41. A *mamzer* is a male or female Jew (the feminine form of the noun is *mamzeret*) who, because of the circumstances of his or her birth, may not marry a native-born Jew; if he or she does, the children are *mamzerim.* I leave *mamzer* untranslated because the English terms "illegitimate" and "bastard" derive from a completely different legal system and do not accurately reflect the meaning of the Hebrew. A *natin* (feminine form: *netinah*) is a temple slave (Ezra 2:43–58, etc.). Temple slaves (*netinim*) and *mamzerim* formed two of the constitutive lineage groups of Israelite society according to M. Qiddushin 4:1. On *netinim* see chapter 4 above, note 28.

42. I translate Albeck's text. For representative variants I have checked facsimiles of the following codices: Parma De Rossi 138 and 984, Budapest Kaufmann A 50, Paris 328–329, Leiden Scal. 3 (the most important manuscript of the Yerushalmi), and Munich 95 (the most important manuscript of the Bavli).

43. Albeck's edition uses *ve'eizo zo* to introduce the examples of A and B, and *ve'eizeh zeh* to introduce the examples of C and D. Most of the manuscripts are not so exact.

paragraphs of the Mishnah exemplify the four theoretical possibilities in determining status by birth: the offspring follows the father (A), the mother (D), either parent (B), or neither parent (C). These interlocking patterns perhaps imply that the examples are an intrinsic part of each paragraph (i.e., the examples are not later additions to an earlier text), but the point cannot be pressed.[44]

Whether or not it is a literary unit, the Mishnah certainly is a thematic unity. The Mishnah is based on a two-part legal theory unknown to the Bible: first, a marriage may be valid or invalid; second, the status of offspring is determined not by the marriage of the parents but by the potential of the parents to contract a valid marriage with each other (*qiddushin*).[45] Biblical law knows nothing of invalid marriages and of the potential to contract a valid marriage, concepts that are central to this Mishnah. Paragraph A treats unions that are permitted and potentially valid, B unions that are prohibited but potentially valid, and C and D unions that have no potential validity because they are prohibited (although this point is left unstated).

The thematic unity should not mask the fact that the specific rulings of this Mishnah are of disparate origins. Some of the rulings have biblical warrant, others do not. The basic principle enunciated by A is biblical (the offspring of a union between Israelites follows the father). C's assumption that *mamzer* in Deuteronomy 23:3 means the offspring of an incestuous union may be correct, as some scholars have argued.[46]

---

44. There are two indications that the examples may be not intrinsic to the Mishnah but additions to an earlier text. First: paragraph A requires *qiddushin,* the potential for a valid marriage, for an offspring to assume the status of its father, but the example seems to require not potential marriage but actual marriage (note the verb *niset*). Second: two of the four examples in paragraph B are inappropriate. Examples three and four (*mamzer/et* and *netin/ah* with an Israelite) well illustrate the principle that the offspring of certain unions follows the parent with the lower status, but examples one and two (widow with a high priest, divorcee and *halutzah* with a priest) do not. The children of these unions do not follow either parent; they are *hallalim,* a status held by neither the father nor the mother. In his commentary on this Mishnah, Maimonides tries to answer this difficulty. The simplest explanation is that these four examples constituted a fixed list (see M. Yevamot 2:4 and 6:2; Gittin 9:2), and the entire list was transcribed here, even though two of its four items were irrelevant in this context.

45. "Potential to contract a valid marriage" is the only possible meaning of the term in paragraphs C and D, a point not appreciated by many translators of this Mishnah. See B. Cohen, "Law of Persons" 14. The rabbis do not require marriage of the parents for a child to have the status of its father; see below. Sifra p. 92b ed. Weiss (p. 379 in Codex Vaticanus 66) uses *ishut* instead of *qiddushin,* but the meaning is the same: "potential to contract a valid marriage."

46. The meaning of *mamzer* in Deut. 23:3 is obscure; as Zech. 9:6 shows, it seems to mean Ashdodite. See chapter 8 above, note 31. See further Neufeld, *Marriage Laws*

Half of D may be biblical (the offspring of a slave woman follows the mother, at least to some extent and at least in some circumstances).[47] Two important rulings, however, have no biblical basis. The Bible knows nothing of B's ruling that under certain circumstances an offspring follows the parent of lower status. Nor, as I have argued above, does the Bible know that the offspring of a gentile mother (and a Jewish father) follows the mother. This ruling, which appears in paragraph D (and is assumed in M. Yevamot 2:5), constitutes half of the matrilineal principle.

THE OTHER HALF OF
THE MATRILINEAL PRINCIPLE

As noted by the two Talmudim, the Tosefta,[48] and various rabbinic commentators, M. Qiddushin 3:12 does not account for all the anomalies of the rabbinic law of status. Among its many omissions is the union of a Jewish woman with a gentile man. Like the Bible, the Mishnah is interested primarily in those who may or may not be married by Israelite men. As the Yerushalmi says, "Israelite men of good pedigree are prohibited from marriage with women who are unfit, but Israelite women of good pedigree are not prohibited from men who are unfit."[49] Elsewhere, however, the Mishnah does refer to this half of the matrilineal principle. M. Yevamot 7:5 states that the offspring of a Jewish mother and a gentile or slave father is a *mamzer:*

(If) the daughter of an Israelite (was married) to a priest, or (if) the daughter of a priest (was married) to an Israelite, and she bore him a daughter; and (if) that daughter went and was married to a slave or to a gentile and bore him a son[50]—he is a *mamzer.*

Why is this offspring a *mamzer?* M. Yevamot 7:5 does not explain. Perhaps the ruling is a development of the principle stated by paragraph D of M. Qiddushin 3:12, which declares that the offspring of a woman who does not have *qiddushin* follows the status of the mother. The logic of the argument is not spelled out, but most commentators assume, as

---

224–227; *Encyclopaedia Biblica* (in Hebrew) vol. 5 (1968), s.v. *"mamzer"*; Carmichael, *Laws of Deuteronomy* 173–174.

47. See note 7 above.

48. T. Qiddushin 4:16 292L, cited below.

49. Y. Qiddushin 3:14 64c; cf. B. Qiddushin 73a and parallels.

50. Normally I translate *ben* as "child," but here the context requires "son."

I shall discuss below, that the mother's incapacity to enter a valid marriage renders her child fatherless. Since there is no potential for de jure paternity, the child follows the mother.[51] Perhaps, then, this logic was extended also to men who lack *qiddushin*. The offspring of a Jewish woman by a slave or a gentile does not have a legal father and therefore follows the status of the mother. But just as the law penalizes a Jewish man who has fathered a child on a gentile woman (the child is a gentile), the law had to penalize a Jewish woman who conceived a child from a gentile man: the child is a Jew but a *mamzer*. Roman law provides a good analogy to this process (see below). If this exegesis is correct, paragraph D of M. Qiddushin 3:12, as elaborated by M. Yevamot 7:5, testifies explicitly to one half of "the matrilineal principle," and implicitly to the other.

The Talmudim, however, use not paragraph D but paragraph C for determining the consequences of a union between a Jewish woman and a gentile or a slave. The Talmudim cite Tosefta Qiddushin 4:16:

A gentile or a slave who had intercourse with an Israelite woman and she gave birth to a child—the offspring is a *mamzer*.

R. Simeon b. Judah says in the name of R. Simeon,[52]
there is no *mamzer* except (for the offspring) of a woman whose prohibition is among the relations prohibited by scripture[53] and on account of whom (those who have intercourse with her) are liable to extirpation.[54]

The first opinion, which is that of M. Yevamot 7:5, declares that the offspring of a Jewish mother and a gentile father is a *mamzer*. The Talmudim explain that, since the mother does not have the capacity to contract a valid marriage with the father (because he is a gentile) but does have that capacity with other (i.e., Jewish) men, her offspring therefore is a *mamzer*.[55] If this explanation is correct, one half of the matrilineal principle comes from paragraph C, the other from paragraph D.

Another possibility is suggested by the language of R. Simeon in the Tosefta. R. Simeon says that the offspring of a union between a Jewish

---

51. This is not, however, the logic of paragraph C; incestuous and various other prohibited relations produce a *mamzer*, not a fatherless child who follows its mother.

52. Instead of "R. Simeon b. Judah says in the name of R. Simeon," the Erfurt manuscript of the Tosefta reads "R. Simeon b. Eleazar says."

53. *issurah issur ervah*.

54. T. Qiddushin 4:16 292L.

55. See Y. Qiddushin 3:14 64d and B. Yevamot 45b (and parallels). The counterargument in both Talmudim is difficult to understand. That the principle of paragraph C includes male gentiles and slaves seems to be confirmed by M. Gittin 9:2.

woman and a gentile or a slave is not a *mamzer*. R. Simeon's view that a *mamzer* can issue only from a union that entails extirpation (*karet*) echoes that of Simeon the Temanite in M. Yevamot 4:13:

> Who is a *mamzer*?
> (The offspring of a union with) any of one's own flesh who is included in the (scriptural) prohibition of intercourse.
> (These are) the words of R. Aqiva.
> Simeon the Temanite says,
> (The offspring of a union with) any of those on account of whom they are liable to extirpation at the hands of heaven.
> And the law is according to his words.
> R. Joshua says,
> (The offspring of a union with) any of those on account of whom they are liable to death (at the hands of) a court.

Clearly R. Simeon in the Tosefta is paraphrasing, or alluding to, Simeon the Temanite in M. Yevamot 4:13. This fact suggests that the anonymous opening statement of the Tosefta is an expansion not of paragraph C of our Mishnah, as the Talmudim explain, but rather of the view of R. Aqiva in M. Yevamot 4:13. For R. Aqiva a *mamzer* must issue from a prohibited incestuous union, but the anonymous authority in the Tosefta argues that a *mamzer* issues from any prohibited union, even a nonincestuous one. If this is correct, the Mishnah is unfamiliar with a single matrilineal principle. The status of the offspring of a Jewish father and a gentile or slave mother was determined by one legal principle (paragraph D of M. Qiddushin 3:12: the offspring lacks paternity), while the status of the offspring of a Jewish mother and a gentile or slave father was determined by another (M. Yevamot 4:13 as expanded by the Tosefta: a *mamzer* is the offspring of any prohibited union).

DATE

As we have seen, one half of the matrilineal principle (the offspring of a Jewish father and a gentile mother) is attested in M. Qiddushin 3:12 and M. Yevamot 2:5, and one half (the offspring of a Jewish mother and a gentile father) is attested in M. Yevamot 7:5 and T. Qiddushin 4:16. Can these texts be dated?

Jacob Neusner argues that M. Qiddushin 3:12 is Yavnean (end of the first century and beginning of the second century C.E.) because two sages of the Yavnean period, R. Eliezer and R. Tarfon, refer to it in M.

Qiddushin 3:13, but this exegesis is not exact.[56] R. Tarfon suggests that a *mamzer* can produce unimpaired offspring by marrying a slave woman; her child will be a slave who can be manumitted and marry into the community of Israel. Thus R. Tarfon assumes that the offspring of a slave woman is "like her," as our Mishnah says. But R. Eliezer rejects R. Tarfon's argument and advances a view that is hard to square with our Mishnah. Further, perhaps R. Tarfon based his ruling not on the anterior Mishnah but on the Torah—which, as I have already remarked, implies that a slave woman bears a slave (or, at least, a child of impaired status). Thus there is no sign that R. Eliezer knew M. Qiddushin 3:12, and there is no certainty that R. Tarfon knew it. J. N. Epstein argues that M. Qiddushin 3:12 opens a tractate titled "Pedigrees and Prohibited Relations" that extends through 4:14 and that, aside from various interpolations, is an "ancient mishnah" of second-temple times.[57] Unfortunately, this "tractate" is neither a thematic nor a literary unit, and the principles of 3:12 nowhere recur within it. The discussion of the ten "genealogical stocks" in chapter 4 of M. Qiddushin includes many of the anomalous unions omitted by 3:12 (see above). Thus Epstein's literary argument is not entirely convincing. But Neusner and Epstein, taken together, are correct to the extent that M. Qiddushin 3:12–4:14 (or 4:12) is a series of anonymous texts on genealogical matters, into which comments by named authorities, almost all of them Yavnean, have been inserted. This implies that 3:12 is Yavnean (if not earlier).

A Yavnean date is also suggested by the fact that in two separate traditions R. Ishmael attests the matrilineal principle, once explicitly and once implicitly. The explicit attestation is in the Mekhilta, which has R. Ishmael paraphrase paragraph D of our Mishnah, claiming that its ruling can be deduced from Exodus 21:4 (see below); the implicit attestation is in the Talmudim, which attribute to R. Ishmael the statement "He who marries a gentile woman and raises up children from her, raises up enemies against God."[58]

I see no way of dating either M. Yevamot 2:5 (one half of the matri-

---

56. Neusner, *Law of Women* 5:173 and 200–201.

57. J. N. Epstein, *Introduction to Tannaitic Literature* (in Hebrew), ed. E. Z. Melamed (Jerusalem: Magnes, 1957) 54 and 414–415. See Schiffman, "Crossroads" 118 = *Who Was a Jew?* 10.

58. Explicit attestation: Mekhilta Neziqin 2 251H-R on Exod. 21:4. Implicit attestation: Y. Megillah 4:10 75c; B. Megillah 25a; cited above at note 30 and chapter 8 above, note 50.

lineal principle) or 7:5 (the other half).[59] T. Qiddushin 4:16 adduces the view of R. Simeon b. Judah, a *tanna* of the fourth generation (late second century C.E.),[60] in the name of R. Simeon, a *tanna* of the third generation (mid second century C.E.). Thus, if these attributions be reliable, his anonymous disputant would also be a figure of the third (Ushan) generation, if not earlier.

The two halves of the matrilineal principle are combined explicitly for the first time in the Babylonian discussion of M. Qiddushin 3:12. In order to prove the scriptural origin of the ruling that the offspring of a gentile woman follows the status of its mother, the two Talmudim quote (in slightly different forms) a statement of R. Yohanan in the name of R. Simeon b. Yohai. The Babylonian version appends the following comment of Ravina: "Learn from this [the exegesis of R. Simeon] that your daughter's son who is fathered by a gentile is called 'your son.'" The Yerushalmi has nothing comparable to Ravina's comment, perhaps because it thought that R. Simeon's exegesis extends also to the offspring of Israelite mothers and gentile fathers (see below).[61] If the Yerushalmi's assumption is correct, the two halves of the matrilineal principle were first connected by R. Simeon (middle of the second century). According to the Bavli, however, the credit for this connection belongs not to R. Simeon but to Ravina (late fourth century).

DISSENTING OPINIONS

The anonymity of M. Yevamot 2:5, 7:5, and Qiddushin 3:12 implies that the mishnaic editor regarded their rulings as beyond dispute. The consensus was not unanimous, however. Rabbinic literature outside the Mishnah preserves several traces of an anti-mishnaic view (relics of the pre-mishnaic view?). Some rabbis believed that the offspring of a gentile mother and a Jewish father was a *mamzer,* not a gentile. R. Zadoq in Rome excused himself from spending the night with a woman who had been offered to him because, he said, he feared that he might "multiply *mamzerim* in Israel."[62] Even more extreme is

---

59. Neusner, *Law of Women* 5:68, leaves M. Yevamot 7:5 unassigned.

60. Simeon b. Eleazar, the reading of the Erfurt manuscript, is also a *tanna* of the fourth generation.

61. Y. Qiddushin 3:14 64d; B. Qiddushin 68b; and parallels.

62. *AdRN* A 16 p. 32a. Cf. *Darkhe teshuvah* in *Responsa of Maharam Rothenburg,* ed. Moshe Bloch (Budapest, 1895) 160c (= *Hilkhot teshuvah* of R. Eleazar Roqe'ah?): if a man fathers a child on a gentile woman, he requires special penance for bothering God to create a *mamzer.* Aptowitzer's interpretation ("Spuren des Matriarchats" [1926] 266–267) is far-fetched: R. Zadoq feared that he might father a gentile son who might, in turn, marry

the view of Jacob of Kefar Neburya, who argued that such offspring was Jewish: [63]

> Jacob of Kefar Neburya went to Tyre.
>
> They came (and) asked him, what is (the law concerning) circumcising the son of an Aramaean woman (and a Jewish man) on the Sabbath?
>
> He considered permitting them, based on this verse *they were registered by the clans of their fathers' houses* (Num. 1:18). [This verse shows that lineage follows the father. Therefore the son of a Jewish man and a non-Jewish woman should be deemed Jewish by birth, and therefore may be circumcised on the Sabbath.]
>
> R. Haggai heard (this). He said, let him (Jacob) come and be whipped! [64]
>
> (Jacob) said to him, On what basis are you whipping me?
>
> (R. Haggai) said to him, from this (verse), *Now then, let us make a covenant with our God to expel all these foreign women and those who have been born to them* (Ezra 10:3).
>
> (Jacob) said to him, you are whipping me on the basis of a tradition [i.e., a verse not in the Torah]?
>
> (R. Haggai) said to him, *and let it be done according to the Torah* (Ezra 10:3). [The verse states that Ezra and his court established this law to have the force of Torah law, and therefore offenders may be whipped.]
>
> (Jacob) said to him, where is this (in the) Torah?
>
> (R. Haggai) said to him, from this verse, for R. Yohanan said in the name of R. Simeon b. Yohai, *You shall not intermarry with them* (Deut. 7:3) etc.[65]
>
> (Jacob) said to him, strike your blows, for it is good to receive (them).[66]

---

a Jewish woman and father *mamzerim*. See the ingenious suggestion of I. Heinemann, *Zion* 4 (1939) 284 n. 55 (*mamzer* is here used as a translation of the Greek *nothos*) and the discussion of M. Herr, *Scripta Hierosolymitana Volume 22: Studies in Aggadah and Folk Literature* (Jerusalem: Magnes, 1971), 137. Some medieval commentators found the same view in the statement of R. Asi in B. Yevamot 16b: "A gentile who betroths (a Jewish woman) at this time—we suspect that the betrothal might be valid because he might be a descendant of the ten lost tribes." See the Tosafot ad loc. with the comments of Halivni, *Sources and Traditions: Nashim* 703–704, on B. Qiddushin 68a.

63. I translate the version of Qiddushin and indicate the variants from Yevamot; the versions in Genesis Rabbah and the later midrashim contain variants too numerous to be catalogued here.

64. The version in Yevamot reads: "let him come. They brought him so that he would be whipped."

65. Yevamot here repeats in full the statement of R. Yohanan.

66. Y. Qiddushin 3:14 64d; Y. Yevamot 2:6 4a; Genesis Rabbah 7:2 51–52T-A; and parallels. I offer the translation of the final line merely to give the general sense, but the phrase is very difficult, perhaps corrupt; see the discussion in Genesis Rabbah, ed. Theodor and Albeck, ad loc.

I cannot discuss here all the aspects of this fascinating story. Jacob of Kefar Neburya, who seems to have been something of a free thinker, thought that the offspring of a Jewish father and non-Jewish mother was Jewish in all respects—the old patrilineal view of the Bible![67] After a lashing from R. Haggai, both linguistic and literal, he retracted his opinion.[68] R. Haggai proved the error of Jacob's ruling by appeal to Ezra 9 and Deuteronomy 7:3–4 as interpreted by R. Yohanan in the name of R. Simeon b. Yohai. I shall return to this below.

Regarding the offspring of a Jewish mother and a gentile or a slave father, there was vigorous debate among the *amoraim*. Some, following the Mishnah, declared the offspring to be a *mamzer;* others declared the offspring to be legitimate but blemished (*pasul* [unfit], or *mezuham* [tainted], or *mequlqal* [blemished]), and, if female, unfit for marriage to a priest; still others, following R. Simeon, declared the offspring to be *kasher* (fit), legitimate and unblemished. The lenient view came to prevail.[69] A few rabbinic passages suggest that some rabbis regarded the offspring of a Jewish mother and a gentile father as a gentile. I shall return to these problematic passages in chapter 10 below.

All in all, these exceptions do not amount to much. Perhaps outside the rabbinic pale the matrilineal principle was either ignored or rejected, but within rabbinic society it commanded almost universal assent.[70]

67. For a full discussion of Jacob of Kefar Neburya, see Irsai, "Ya'akov." (I am grateful to Dr. Marc Hirshman for this reference.) Irsai 157–163 suggests that Jacob regarded the child as a gentile but merely meant that a child convert could be circumcised on the eighth day even if it was a Sabbath. This suggestion is not likely because the proof texts from Ezra would seem to be irrelevant. Certainly the editor of the Yerushalmi did not understand Jacob in this manner.

68. For another case of one rabbi whipping another see Y. Berakhot 3:1 6a.

69. See B. Yevamot 44b–45b, Y. Yevamot 4:15 6c, and Y. Qiddushin 3:14 64c–d. The Talmudim ignore the evidence of 1 Chron. 2:34–35. On this debate see B. Cohen, "Law of Persons" 15–19; Francus, "Status"; Touati, "Le *mamzer*" 44–45. Maimonides, in his *Epistle to Yemen* (in D. Hartman and A. Halkin, *Crisis and Leadership* [Philadelphia: Jewish Publication Society, 1985] 98), writes that Jesus "was Jewish because his mother was a Jewess although his father was a gentile, and our principle is that a child born of a Jewess and a gentile or a slave is legitimate. Only figuratively do we call him an illegitimate child (*mamzer*)."

70. The evidence for practices of the non-rabbinic Jews of antiquity is meager. If gentiles were allowed to erect epitaphs in the Jewish catacombs for their relatives who had converted to Judaism, the sepulchral inscriptions of Rome provide no instance against the rabbinic matrilineal principle. See Leon, *Jews of Ancient Rome,* appendix, inscriptions nos. 68 and 222. Compare nos. 256 and 462. No. 21 is difficult to understand, matrilineal principle or no; see the full discussion by Kraemer, "The Term 'Jew'" 38–41. A sarcophagus from Termessos in Pisidia bears a dedication from M. Aurelius Hermaeus "to his daughter Aurelia Artemis *Ioudea*." The editor, R. Heberdey, comments that Artemis is Jewish, born of a Jewish mother; the suggestion is approved by L. Robert, *Hellenica* 11–12 (1960)

The Origins of the Matrilineal Principle

The matrilineal principle is not attested in either the Bible or the literature of the second-temple period, including the Qumran scrolls. Even in the first century of our era it is still unknown to Philo, the New Testament, and Josephus. All of these texts seem to be familiar with a patrilineal system. The Mishnah, however, states the matrilineal principle (or, more accurately, the two halves of the matrilineal principle) as if it were agreed upon by all, and provides no reason or justification. It appears in the Mishnah like a bolt out of the blue.

The rabbinic matrilineal principle is surprising within the context of ancient culture, especially ancient Jewish culture. Throughout the ancient world the parent who mattered was, of course, the father. The children born of a marriage are *his* children, not the mother's. In the words of Aeschylus, "The woman you call the mother of the child is not the parent: she is merely the nurse of the seed that was sown inside her. The man who makes her fertile is the parent; she, like a stranger, protects the young shoot."[71] Ancient embryology, both Greek and Jewish, did not always reduce the mother to being a mere vessel for the father's seed, but even systems that allowed a maternal contribution to the formation of the fetus treated that contribution as less significant than that made by the father. Scientific thinking mirrored social and legal reality.[72] The ancients, both Jewish and gentile, recognized the intimate

---

386. But surely *Ioud(a)ea* can indicate a convert to Judaism (see Kraemer, "The Term 'Jew'"). There is no reason to believe either that Artemis had a Jewish mother or that she was called *Ioud(a)ea* because of a Jewish mother. According to the Karaites the child of a gentile mother and a Jewish father is a Jew. Therefore, they argued, Ezra expelled the foreign women (because they had not converted to Judaism) but did *not* expel their children (since they, like their fathers, were Jewish). See Revel, "Karaite Halakah" 375–376. Compare the latter-day apologists for Ezra (n. 20). (The Karaites followed the rabbis in presuming that the Bible knew the institution of conversion for women; see, e.g., Aaron b. Joseph the Karaite, *Sefer hamivhar* [Eupatoria, 1835] 17b, commentary on Deut. 21:10–11 [the law of the female war captive].)

71. *Eumenides* 658–661, as cited by Nicole Loraux, *The Children of Athena*, trans. Caroline Levine (Princeton: Princeton University Press, 1993) 120.

72. Thus, the male contributes the form, the female the material; the male contributes the soul, the female the body; the male contributes the "white" parts, the female the "red" parts. See Lesley A. Dean-Jones, *Women's Bodies in Classical Greek Science* (Oxford: Clarendon, 1994) chap. 3, "The Female's Role in Reproduction." Some rabbis, echoing Aristotle, knew that a fetus was formed from matter contributed by both the mother and the father; see B. Niddah 30b–31a [and parallels] with the comments of J. Needham, *A*

and emotional bond between mother and child, but refrained from
drawing legal inferences from this intimacy.[73] A mother had no rights
to her children; in the sixteenth century the jurist Henry Swinburne
could write "the mother is not of kin to her child." Indeed, it was not
until the nineteenth century that the legal systems of Europe began to
recognize the legal rights of a mother to her children and began in the
case of divorce to assign to the mother the custody of minor children.
For example, in England it was only the Custody of Infants Act of 1839
that allowed courts to give a mother access to her children in case of divorce; previously, only the husband and always the husband received
custody.[74] According to rabbinic law a woman's obligation to care for
her children derives more from her status as a wife than from her status
as a mother. It is the duty of the father to raise the children and it is the
duty of the wife to assist him. The mishnaic list of the responsibilities a
wife must fulfill for her husband includes "giving suck to her child."
Her children are *his*.[75]

History of Embryology, 2d ed. (Cambridge: Cambridge University Press, 1959) 77–79;
David Winston, *The Wisdom of Solomon,* Anchor Bible (Garden City, N.Y.: Doubleday,
1979) 164; and Pieter van der Horst, "Sarah's Seminal Emission," in van der Horst, *Hellenism* 203–223.

73. Intimacy of motherhood: Philo, *On the Virtues* 128; Lacey, *Family* 169 (quoting
Xenophon, *Memorabilia* 2:2:5–10, and Aristotle, *Nicomachean Ethics* 8:12:3 [1161B]);
Suzanne Dixon, *The Roman Mother* (Norman: University of Oklahoma Press, 1988)
chap. 5. The rabbis know that a child often "honors" his mother more than his father (B.
Qiddushin 30b–31a and parallels). Legal rights: Dixon, *Roman Mother* chap. 3.

74. Priscilla Robertson, *An Experience of Women: Pattern and Change in Nineteenth
Century Europe* (Philadelphia: Temple University Press, 1982), p. 648, index, s.v. "child
custody" (I owe this reference to Professor Paula Hyman); Mary Ann Mason, *From Father's Property to Children's Rights* (New York: Columbia University Press, 1994), esp.
chaps. 1 ("Fathers/Masters: Children/Servants") and 2 ("From Fathers' Rights to Mothers' Love"). "The mother is not of kin to her child," writes Henry Swinburne, *A Treatise
of Testaments and Last Wills* (1591), quoted by Laurence Sterne, *The Life and Opinions of
Tristram Shandy,* vol. 4, chap. 29.

75. Obligation of mother: M. Ketuvot 5:5, cf. T. Niddah 2:4–5 642Z. Obligation of
father to raise his children: M. Qiddushin 4:14 and T. Qiddushin 5:15–16 297–298L.
There is little rabbinic discussion of child custody in case of divorce; the rabbis seem to
have recognized that a nursing child, perhaps even any child up to the age of six, belongs
with his or her mother (B. Ketuvot 59b–60b, 65b), and that a girl should be raised by her
mother (B. Ketuvot 102b), but these rulings are justified by a sense of what is best for the
child, not by any notions of maternal rights. The spare talmudic rulings on this subject
were discussed and augmented by the medieval codifiers; see, for example, the responsum
of Ritva (R. Yom-Tov ben Avraham) no. 61 (ed. Kafih, p. 69), and Shulhan Arukh, *Even
HaEzer* 82:5–8. I am puzzled by a will summarized by Goitein in which a pregnant
woman, fearing death in childbirth, entrusts her assets and her newborn to her mother
(the baby's grandmother). Where was the husband and father? Would not the baby be his

What, then, are the reasons for the rabbinic matrilineal principle? Why did the rabbis break with previous practice, which determined the status of offspring patrilineally and which in terms of ancient culture had been quite reasonable and rational? I should state at the outset that neither of these questions is fully answerable. I shall survey a number of proposed explanations, some of them more plausible than others, but I see no way of discovering which—if any—of them are determinative. Nor have I succeeded in discovering what circumstances allowed or compelled the rabbis of the Mishnah to break with previous practice.

What are the reasons for the matrilineal principle?

EXPLANATION NO. I: SCRIPTURE

Both Talmudim usually try to find a basis in Scripture for the rulings of the Mishnah, and both Talmudim adduce the exegesis of R. Yohanan in the name of R. Simeon b. Yohai to prove the scriptural origin of half of the matrilineal principle. Here is the version of the Yerushalmi:

It is written, *You shall not intermarry with them: do not give your daughter to his son* (Deut. 7:3), and it is written, *For he shall turn your son away from me* (Deut. 7:4). Your son from an Israelite (woman) is called *your son,* but your son from a gentile woman is not called *your son* but her son.[76]

This version differs from the Babylonian chiefly by having R. Simeon quote Deuteronomy 7:3 as well as 7:4,[77] but how the verse or verses lead to the requisite conclusion is equally obscure in both sources.

In their commentaries on the Bavli, Rashi (1040–1105) and Rabbenu Tam (ca. 1100–1171) suggest that R. Simeon's deduction is based on the anomalous syntax of Deuteronomy 7:4. Scripture prohibits the marriage of Israelite men with Canaanite women as well as the marriage of Israelite women with Canaanite men. Why, then, does Scripture say, "For *he* shall turn your *son* away from me"? The verse should have read either "For *she* (or: *they*) shall turn your son away from me" or "For he

---

to dispose of as he likes? Perhaps the will required the husband's approval before being put into effect. See S. D. Goitein, *A Mediterranean Society,* vol. 3, *The Family* (Berkeley: University of California Press, 1978) 232 n. 54.

76. Y. Qiddushin 3:14 64d, cf. Y. Yevamot 2:6 4a.

77. B. Qiddushin 68b and parallels. In the Bavli it is the anonymous redactor (the *setam*) who quotes Deut. 7:3, thereby splitting R. Simeon's exegesis in half.

shall turn your *daughter* away from me." It is this anomaly that impelled R. Simeon to deduce that the son of a gentile woman by an Israelite man is "her son" and not "your son." So far Rashi and Rabbenu Tam agree; how the anomaly leads to the requisite conclusion, however, is the subject of debate. Rashi argues that R. Simeon understood Deuteronomy 7:4 to refer to the marriage of an Israelite woman with a gentile man: *for he* (the gentile who married the Israelite woman) *shall turn your son* (the son of his Israelite wife) *away from me.* R. Simeon deduced that the son of an Israelite woman by a gentile man is "your son" but that the son of a gentile woman by an Israelite man is not "your son." Rashi's interpretation is perhaps corroborated by the Yerushalmi's version, which has R. Simeon quote *Do not give your daughter to his son* in addition to the first part of Deuteronomy 7:3. This implies that R. Simeon thought that the anomalous syntax of Deuteronomy 7:4 referred to the marriage of an Israelite woman with a gentile man, just as Rashi says.[78]

According to Rashi's interpretation R. Simeon finds a basis in Scripture for both halves of the matrilineal principle. According to Rabbenu Tam, however, R. Simeon understood Deuteronomy 7:4 to refer to the marriage of an Israelite man with a gentile woman: *for he* (the gentile father-in-law) *shall turn your son* (his Israelite son-in-law) *away from me.* R. Simeon deduced that the Israelite son-in-law is "your son," but that his son (the offspring of the Israelite son-in-law and his gentile wife) is not "your son." Rabbenu Tam's interpretation has two distinct advantages over Rashi's: first, it derives only half of the matrilineal principle from Scripture, and thus is supported by Ravina, who did not think, as Rashi does, that R. Simeon treated marriages between Israelite women and gentile men (see above); second, it is rather close to the simple meaning of Deuteronomy 7:4. For if we exclude the obvious possibilities that the text of sacred Scripture has suffered corruption, or that the singular *he* and *son* should be understood as equivalent to "they" and "sons," the simple meaning of the text is that of R. Simeon as explained by Rabbenu Tam.[79] As Exodus 34:16 demonstrates, Scripture is con-

78. The reading in Y. Qiddushin 3:14 64d is confirmed by Codex Leiden Scal. 3. The parallel in Y. Yevamot 2:6 4a (even in Codex Leiden Scal. 3), however, omits the phrase *Do not give your daughter to his son.* Since scribes often exercised great freedom in copying biblical quotations in the Talmud, my argument is, at best, suggestive.

79. Targum Neofiti, Targum Jonathan, Targum Onqelos, and Saadiah Gaon, followed by the new (1962) Jewish Publication Society version, understand *he shall turn* to mean "they shall turn" (Neofiti even supplies a subject: "their daughters shall turn"). Most of these also take *son* to be the equivalent of "sons" ("children" in the JPS version). Rashi's exegesis is followed by R. Meyuhas b. Eliyahu, *Commentary on the Book of Deuter-*

cerned primarily about the marriage of Canaanite women with Israelite men. But even in Rabbenu Tam's interpretation, R. Simeon's conclusion can be extracted from the scriptural text only with great difficulty.[80] The Yerushalmi admits as much when R. Haggai, in order to silence the obstreperous Jacob of Kefar Neburya, deduces the matrilineal principle chiefly from Ezra 9–10, not Deuteronomy 7:4 (see above).[81]

After adducing R. Yohanan in the name of R. Simeon b. Yohai, the Bavli adduces Ravina, who supplies the other half of the matrilineal principle (see above). Then the Bavli argues as follows: Deuteronomy 7:3–4 speaks of Canaanites, not of all gentiles in general; these laws can be thought to apply to all gentiles only if we are willing to broaden the laws' applicability based on the reasons for the laws stated by Scripture; R. Simeon, indeed, does state that the applicability of laws should be broadened in consonance with their reasoning; therefore R. Simeon would argue that Deuteronomy 7:3–4 would apply to all gentiles, since the reason stated by Scripture *For he shall turn your son away from me* (Deut. 7:4) applies equally to all gentiles.[82] But what of the sages who disagree with R. Simeon? For them Deuteronomy 7:3–4 applies only to Canaanites; whence do they learn the matrilineal principle? The Bavli continues:

Scripture states, *If man has (two wives . . .) and they have borne him sons* (Deut. 21:15). Wherever we can proclaim *if he has,* we proclaim *they have borne him;* and wherever we cannot proclaim *if he has,* we do not proclaim *they have borne him.*[83]

---

onomy (in Hebrew), ed. Yehiel Katz (Jerusalem: Mosad Harav Kook, 1968) 27–28; Rabbenu Tam's exegesis is followed by R. Joseph Bekhor Shor in his Torah commentary (ed. Yoshafat Nebo [Jerusalem: Mosad Harav Kook, 1994]), by Hizquni (ed. Chavel), and by Aaron b. Joseph the Karaite, *Sefer hamivhar,* p. 6b (who discusses two other interpretations as well). Rabbenu Tam's interpretation is also advanced, apparently independently, by R. Eliezer b. Nathan of Mainz (known as the Raavan), *Even ha'ezer, she'elot uteshuvot* 66 (29a ed. Albeck). Tosafot Ri hazaqen on B. Qiddushin 68b proposes yet another explanation, this one derived by implication from Maimonides, *Hilkhot Yibbum* 1:4 and *Hilkhot Issurei Bi'ah* 12:7–8: *for it* (the marriage) *shall turn your son* (the offspring of your son from his gentile wife) *away from me* (so that he will be no longer be deemed "your son").

80. Some modern Jewish apologists imply that the matrilineal principle really is to be found in the sacred text. See S. D. Luzzatto, *Commentary to the Pentateuch* (in Hebrew) (Tel Aviv: Dvir, 1965; first published in 1871) 520; David Z. Hoffmann, *Das Buch Deuteronomium,* 2 vols. (Berlin: Poppelauer, 1913–1922) 1:91; and Hertz, *Pentateuch* 775.

81. In the Genesis Rabbah version R. Haggai does not even quote Deut. 7:4 at all.

82. For this (alleged) view of R. Simeon b. Yohai, see chapter 8 above, note 21.

83. This midrash appears in somewhat different form in Sifrei Deuteronomy 215 (249F).

The basis of this exegesis is the principle, to which I shall return below, that only Jews possess *qiddushin,* the capacity to contract valid marriages. Gentiles lack *qiddushin.* When Deuteronomy 21:15 speaks of a man "having" two wives, it means that both he and they have the capacity to be legally married to each other: he has the capacity to have them, and they have the capacity to be his. Only in this situation does Scripture say *they have borne him;* that is, only in this situation is paternity recognized. If there is no potential for a valid marriage, there is no legal paternity, and the offspring follows the mother.

This scriptural proof is extremely clever and has the advantage of actually following the Mishnah's stated logic, unlike the proof from Deuteronomy 7:3–4, but as a specimen of scriptural exegesis it is very weak. It is most unlikely that Deuteronomy 21:15 really is aware of the rabbinic doctrine of *qiddushin,* or that the phrase *If man has two wives* (lit., *if there be two wives to a man*) is intended to refer only to those cases in which wives have the potential of being had by their husbands, or that the mishnaic ruling really derives from this verse.

The Mekhilta supplies a similar derivation from yet another verse:

> *If his master gave him a wife, and she has borne him children, the wife and her children shall belong to the master* (Exod. 21:4).
> *the wife and her children*—what does Scripture come to teach?
> It teaches that her offspring are like her.
> Thus I know that in the case of a slave woman her offspring are like her—how do I know that the same law applies to a gentile woman?
> R. Ishmael said:[84]
> Just as in the case of a Canaanite slave woman, who does not have the potential for a valid marriage with any man, her offspring are like her;
> so too any woman, who does not have the potential for a valid marriage with any man, her offspring are like her.
> And what [masc.] is this? This is the offspring of a slave woman or a gentile woman.[85]

This scriptural proof, like the one just cited, is extremely clever and has the advantage of actually following the Mishnah's stated logic, unlike

---

84. Some testimonia here add "it is a *qal vahomer* (an argument from the lesser to the greater)." Horovitz and Rabin relegate this reading to the apparatus, whereas Lauterbach places it in the text. The reading is difficult because the argument that follows ("Just as in the case . . .") is not an argument from the lesser to the greater but an argument by analogy. If this reading is correct, we must assume that R. Ishmael's argument has fallen out of the text, and that the argument that appears belongs to the anonymous editor of the Mekhilta, not R. Ishmael (see Lauterbach's note). I suppose that the principle of *lectio difficilior* would militate for this reading, but I am content to follow Horovitz and Rabin.

85. Mekhilta Neziqin 2, 251H-R, 3.11L, on Exod. 21:4.

the proof from Deuteronomy 7:3–4. Exodus states that if a Hebrew slave (whom the rabbis identify as a Jew sold into slavery in order to repay his debts) is given a wife (whom the rabbis identify as a Canaanite or gentile slave) by his master, the wife and children remain behind as slaves when the Hebrew slave goes free. In other words, the offspring of a Jewish man and a slave woman is a slave, following her status ("like her"). R. Ishmael, arguing by analogy and citing Mishnah Qiddushin 3:12, extends this ruling to the offspring of all gentile women. This is not an unreasonable way to read the verse, and one modern scholar even believes that R. Ishmael has correctly explained the origins of the matrilineal principle![86] The problem, of course, is that although the verse *can* be read this way, there is nothing in the verse to suggest that it *should* or *must* be read this way. The verse refers to the offspring of a male Hebrew slave and a female slave. To apply the scriptural law to all male Jews, free as well as slave, is one extension of the verse, and to apply it to all female gentiles, free as well as slave, is another. Nothing in the text demands or warrants either extension. Further, as I remarked in the previous paragraph concerning Deuteronomy 21:15, it is most unlikely that the Torah is aware of the rabbinic notion of *qiddushin,* the potential to contract valid marriages, but it is this notion that is central to R. Ishmael's extension of the law by analogy.

I conclude that Exodus 21:4 and Deuteronomy 21:15 are excellent scriptural hooks upon which to hang the matrilineal principle after it exists, but neither is the source of the idea that the offspring of all gentile women, free as well as slave, follow the status of the mother. Deuteronomy 7:3–4 is an even weaker proof text. In the Middle Ages some scholars continued the quest for a scriptural origin to the matrilineal principle.[87]

EXPLANATION NO. 2: EZRA

In his refutation of Jacob of Kefar Neburya, R. Haggai anticipates the modern scholars who suggest that the matrilineal principle was introduced by Ezra. I argued above that this view is wrong, or

---

86. Gruber, "Matrilineal Determination."

87. See, for example, the *She'iltot de Rab Ahai Gaon,* chap. 25, 1:158–163 ed. Mirsky (a novel arrangement and application of the biblical verses cited on this topic by the Talmud), and B. M. Lewin, *Otzar hage'onim: Qiddushin* 167 par. 376 (a citation from some editions of the *Halakhot Gedolot*). Some medieval rabbis were not convinced by any of these proof texts; see the comment by R. Israel in the Responsa of R. Asher b. Yehiel 55.9 (Vilna, 1881, p. 52c).

at least is not necessarily correct, but perhaps R. Haggai and his modern followers are correct to the extent that the rabbis *deduced* the matrilineal principle from the Ezra episode. Since the rabbis tried to avoid basing law on any part of the Bible other than the Pentateuch, we can understand their hesitation to admit that the matrilineal principle was derived from the book of Ezra (see Jacob's objection to R. Haggai!).

EXPLANATION NO. 3:
THE UNCERTAINTY OF PATERNITY

Many have suggested that the matrilineal principle is based on the uncertainty of paternity. In the *Digest* 2.4.5, the jurist Paulus states: *semper [mater] certa est, etiam si vulgo conceperit, pater vero is est quem nuptiae demonstrant,* "the mother is always known, even if she conceived out of wedlock, whereas the father is he whom the marriage indicates." The identity of a mother is always knowable, but the identity of a father is never knowable; if a woman is married, law and society presume that her husband is the father of her child, but this presumption always lacks certainty. Perhaps the rabbis too believed that paternity was always unknowable and felt that a child's identity should be determined in the first instance by its mother and not by its putative father. Hence the matrilineal principle.[88]

This explanation is unsatisfactory for two reasons. First, as I remarked in the first paragraph of this essay, the rabbis restricted the matrilineal principle to cases of intermarriage, but paternity is no more uncertain in these marriages than it is in unions between Jews. Paulus too adduces the uncertainty of paternity not in connection with the Roman matrilineal principle (which will be discussed below) but in connection with something else entirely (respect for one's parents). Second, unlike the Romans, the rabbis did not require marriage between the father and

88. Paulus' comment is usually summarized by the phrase *mater certa, pater incertus.* This is a widely held explanation of the matrilineal principle. The certainty of maternal identity is still invoked in defense of laws that reflect a matrilineal principle. According to U.S. immigration law, a child born overseas to an unmarried American woman is considered a citizen by birth, but a child born overseas to an unmarried American man has no rights of citizenship unless the father acknowledges paternity and formally agrees to support his child before the age of eighteen. In defense of this law, one Supreme Court judge remarked that the identity of the mother "is established at the moment of birth, no matter where the birth takes place," while there often are "a lot of questions that have to be resolved" about the father's identity. See *New York Times,* November 5, 1997 ("Justices Argue Facet of Immigration Law").

the mother for the offspring to inherit from his father or receive his status. If an unmarried woman is pregnant and declares that the father of her child is a priest, R. Gamaliel and R. Eliezer say that she is to be believed; if a woman becomes pregnant as the result of rape, the offspring is presumed to have the same status as the majority of the people where the rape occurred. In these cases paternity is very uncertain, but the rabbis did not judge the offspring matrilineally.[89]

EXPLANATION NO. 4:
THE INTIMACY OF MOTHERHOOD

Instead of emphasizing the uncertainty of paternity, some have suggested that the matrilineal principle is the result of the natural closeness between mother and child.[90] The offspring of a gentile mother and a Jewish father is a gentile because the intimate connection between a mother and her children makes it certain that she will influence them and instruct them in the ways of the gentiles. This suggestion too is unconvincing. The ancients, both Jewish and gentile, recognized the intimacy of motherhood, but, as I remarked above, drew no legal inferences from this intimacy. The emotional bond between mother and child had no affect on law before modern times and cannot be the basis of the rabbinic matrilineal principle.

EXPLANATION NO. 5:
PRIMITIVE MATRIARCHY

Victor Aptowitzer suggests that the matrilineal principle is a relic of very ancient times when Israelite kinship was matrilineal and Israelite society was matriarchal. Aptowitzer offers a striking parallel to the rabbinic law from Herodotus' description of the Lycians:

Their customs are in part Cretan and in part Carian. But they have one which is their own and shared by no other men; they take their names not

89. Rabbis not require marriage: M. Yevamot 2:5. Unmarried woman: M. Ketuvot 1:9–10. See Zeitlin, "Offspring of Intermarriage" 136. The uncertainty of paternity probably is the explanation for the prominence of matronymy in magic (see the comment of Abbaye in B. Shabbat 66a: all magical spells that are to be repeated several times use the name of the mother). (See the comment of R. Solomon Luria ad loc.) Under the influence of Jewish mysticism, matronymy spread from magic to prayer; see M. Halamish cited in D. Sperber, *Minhage Yisrael*, vol. 3 (Jerusalem: Mosad HaRav Kook, 1994) 195.
90. This is another widely held explanation of the matrilineal principle.

from their fathers but from their mothers; and when one is asked by his neighbor who he is, he will say that he is the son of such a mother, and recount the mother of his mother. Nay, if a woman of full rights marry a slave, her children are deemed pure-born; and if a true-born Lycian man take a foreign wife or concubine, the children are dishonored, though he be the first in the land.[91]

This is the passage that launched J. J. Bachofen on his quest for *das Mutterrecht,* and this is the passage cited by Aptowitzer to prove that the rabbinic law is a relic of primitive times.[92] Aptowitzer supports this thesis by the discovery of numerous other "relics," in both the Bible and the Talmud, none of them more striking than two mishnaic laws that appear on the page following M. Qiddushin 3:12. M. Qiddushin 4:4 ordains: "He who wishes to marry the daughter of a priest must investigate her lineage through four mothers which are eight"—the pedigree of the bride's mother and grandmothers is checked, but not the pedigree of her father and grandfathers. M. Qiddushin 4:7 ordains that a daughter of a convert to Judaism may not be married to a priest unless her father, the convert, has a native-born Jewish mother.

Is the matrilineal principle a relic of prehistoric times? Various scholars have attempted to find traces of matrilineal organization in the legal systems of antiquity, but Aptowitzer does not aid his case when he confuses *matriliny* (determination of kinship through females) with *matriarchy* (rule by females), a social form that never existed.[93] Whether ancient Israelite society was ever matrilineal I leave for others to deter-

---

91. Herodotus 1.173. The translation is that of A. D. Godley in the Loeb Classical Library, slightly modified. For an erudite but disjointed discussion of this passage see Pembroke, "Women in Charge." There is some evidence that the passage is not entirely Greek ethnographic fantasy; see Trevor Bryce, *The Lycians* (Copenhagen: Museum Tusculanum, 1986) 1.143–150.

92. J. J. Bachofen, *Das Mutterrecht: Eine Untersuchung über die Gynaikokratie der alten Welt* (Stuttgart, 1861); *Myth, Religion, and Mother Right: Selected Writings of J. J. Bachofen,* trans. R. Manheim and with an introduction by J. Campbell (Princeton: Princeton University Press, 1967). Aptowitzer, "Spuren des Matriarchats," forgot to cite Bachofen.

93. E. Kornemann, "Mutterrecht," in *Realencyclopädie der klassischen Altertumswissenschaft,* ed. Pauly, Wissowa, and Kroll, Supplementband 6 (1935): 557–558; J. Bamberger, "The Myth of Matriarchy," in *Woman, Culture, and Society,* ed. M. Z. Rosaldo and L. Lamphere (Stanford: Stanford University Press, 1974), pp. 263–280; Eva Cantarella, *Pandora's Daughters: The Role and Status of Women in Greek and Roman Antiquity* (Baltimore: Johns Hopkins University Press, 1987) chaps. 1 and 8; Pembroke, "Women in Charge." I am aware that in recent years some feminist romantics have fantasized about utopian prehistoric worlds ruled by goddesses and women, but I, a phallogocentric male, am unconvinced.

mine, but the alleged relics of that alleged society collected by Aptowitzer are, for the most part, trivial or debatable.[94] Matronymy, a characteristic of the Lycians according to Herodotus, is attested occasionally in the Bible and in Jewish sources, but it too can be explained in various ways and is unlikely to be a relic of ancient matriliny.[95] I am not sure how M. Qiddushin 4:4 should be explained; priestly lineage is traced through the father, and one would therefore expect a priest to check the paternal lineage of a prospective bride as least as carefully as the maternal.[96] I shall return to M. Qiddushin 4:7 in chapter 10 below; it too is not evidence for matriliny. Perhaps a methodologically sophisticated study of rabbinic family law and kinship patterns will reveal traces of a matrilineal society, but in the absence of such a study, Aptowitzer's suggestion is unconvincing.

EXPLANATION NO. 6: ROMAN LAW

Perhaps the matrilineal principle entered rabbinic Judaism under the influence of Roman law. The parallel between the Roman and the rabbinic law of persons was observed by various eighteenth- and nineteenth-century scholars, but it was Louis M. Epstein in 1942 who first suggested that the Roman law influenced the rabbinic.[97]

---

94. For a critique of Aptowitzer, see Walter Koshland, *Mother-Right and Biblical Judaism* (Jerusalem: P. Freund, 1943) 87–91. Aptowitzer argues that the rabbinic predilection for uncle-niece marriages is a relic of matrilineal society; see "Spuren des Matriarchats" (1925) 232–237, citing Samuel Krauss, "Die Ehe zwischen Onkel und Nichte," in *Studies in Jewish Literature in Honor of Kaufmann Kohler* (Berlin: G. Reimer, 1913) 165–175. This is very unlikely, however. See Ginzberg, *Jewish Sect* 23–24; Baron, *Social and Religious History* 1.310 n. 20 and 2.230 with 411 n. 14; and Adiel Schremer, "'Son of the Sister': Kinship Expressions and Endogamy at the Time of the Mishnah and Talmud" (in Hebrew), *Zion* 60 (1995) 5–31. Some modern scholars still hunt the scriptures in search of relics of matriliny; see, for example, Nancy Jay, *Throughout Your Generations Forever* (Chicago: University of Chicago Press, 1992) 99.

95. On matronymy in Jewish sources see Ilan, "'Man Born of Woman . . .'" Add to her references: Lieberman, *Tosefet Rishonim* 3.160; Lewin, *Otzar hage'onim: Berakhot* 43; Bamberger, *Proselytism* 230–231. For a parallel problem see Christophilopoulos, *Dikaion* 60–67 ("Matronymy among the Ancient Greeks").

96. In his discussion of priestly marriages, Josephus states explicitly that the paternal lineage (*patrothen*) of the bride is checked (CAp 1.33).

97. Wetstenius, *Novum Testamentum Graecum* 2:552 (commentary on Acts 16:3); Isaac Weil, *Prosélytisme chez les Juifs selon la Bible et la Talmud* (Strassburg, 1880) 79 ff., a work that I know only through the citation by Bamberger, *Proselytism* 89–90; M. Mielziner, *The Jewish Law of Marriage and Divorce* (New York: Bloch, 1884; reprint, 1901) 95–97; Epstein, *Marriage Laws* 194–197. In his "Law of Persons" 12–15, B. Cohen follows

The suggestion, therefore, is not new, but it has not received sufficient attention.

According to Roman law, a child is the legal heir of his father and is in his father's custody (*potestas*) only if his father and mother were joined in a legal marriage (*justum matrimonium*). The capacity to contract a legal marriage was called *conubium* (or *ius conubii*), and was possessed almost exclusively by Roman citizens. Marriage between a person with *conubium* and a person without *conubium* was valid, but it was not a *justum matrimonium;* and without *justum matrimonium,* the status of the child follows that of its mother. Consequently, if a Roman citizen marries a noncitizen woman, the offspring are noncitizens. If a Roman citizen has intercourse with a slave woman, the offspring are slaves. According to the legal theory, if a Roman matron marries a noncitizen, the offspring are citizens, except that the *Lex Minicia,* a law probably enacted during the first century B.C.E., declared that the children of such unions follow the parent with the lower status; that is, the children follow the father. Similarly, the children of a Roman matron by a slave ought to be, according to the theory, free citizens like their mother, except that a law, enacted under Claudius, declared them to be slaves.[98]

The differences between the Roman and the rabbinic systems are numerous and important. For a son to follow his father the Romans demand not only *conubium,* the potential for a legal marriage, but also *justum matrimonium,* the legal marriage itself.[99] A child born of a *matrimonium injustum* was considered *spurius* or *vulgo quaesitus.* In M. Qiddushin 3:12, however, the rabbis use *qiddushin* to mean not "legal marriage" (*justum matrimonium*) but the capacity to contract a legal

---

Epstein (without acknowledgement) in noting the striking parallels between the Roman law and and the rabbinic, but leaves open the question of influence (see 34–36).

98. M. Kaser, *Privatrecht,* par. 66 I 2, par. 68 I, par. 73 II, and par. 84 II; P. R. C. Weaver, "The Status of Children in Mixed Marriages," in *The Family in Ancient Rome,* ed. Beryl Rawson (Ithaca: Cornell University Press, 1986) 145–169; Treggiari, *Roman Marriage* 43–51. The major primary texts are: *Digesta* 1:5; Ulpian, *Tituli* 5; Gaius, *Institutiones* 1:48–96. For the law of Claudius see Tacitus, *Annals* 12:53. *Conubium* is sometimes spelled *connubium.* For various aspects of the Roman law in practice, see Youtie, "*Apatores,*" and Roger S. Bagnall, "Freedmen and Freedwomen with Fathers?" *Journal of Juristic Papyrology* 21 (1991) 7–8. On the *Lex Minicia,* see Roger S. Bagnall, "Egypt and the *Lex Minicia,*" *Journal of Juristic Papyrology* 23 (1993) 25–28, a response to David Cherry, *Phoenix* 44 (1990) 244–266.

99. Of course, the Roman means of effecting a state of marriage were far less formal than the Jewish or Christian (Treggiari, *Roman Marriage* 161–170; Cantarella, *Pandora's Daughters* 136–137 with bibliography), but this point does not affect our discussion.

marriage (*conubium*). Marriage between the father and the mother is not essential, according to rabbinic law, for the offspring to follow or inherit the father. The rabbis do not have a category corresponding to the *spurius,* and the Romans do not have a category corresponding to the *mamzer.*[100] In Roman law, even the offspring of an incestuous relationship is nothing more than a *spurius.*[101] A final distinction: the Romans allow their rules to be affected by the intention of the actors. If a Roman citizen, either male or female, marries a noncitizen in the erroneous belief that the noncitizen is a citizen, and can demonstrate that the mistake was an honest one, the noncitizen spouse and the children automatically become citizens.[102] The rabbis have no parallel to this remarkable law, although they often accord intention an important place in their rulings. In the law of status they make no such allowances.[103]

These differences, however, cannot mask the conceptual similarity between the Roman and the rabbinic systems. Only Roman citizens possess *conubium;* only Jews possess *qiddushin.*[104] Marriages between those who possess *conubium/qiddushin* produce offspring whose status is determined patrilineally. Even though noncitizens do not possess *conubium,* and even though gentiles do not possess *qiddushin,* both legal systems recognized the paternal filiation of the offspring produced by sexual unions of two outsiders; the child of two *peregrini* (noncitizens), like the child of two gentiles, has the status of his father.[105] Mixed

---

100. The closest rabbinic approximations to the *spurius* are the *shetuqi* and *asufi* (M. Qiddushin 4:1–2). Marriage not essential for inheritance: M. Yevamot 2:5.

101. Gaius, *Institutes* 1:64, and Ulpian, *Tituli* 5:7.

102. Gaius, *Institutes* 1:67–68; see too *Gnomon of the Idios Logos* pars. 39, 46, and 47.

103. The importance of intention in the Mishnah is analyzed and exaggerated by Neusner, *Evidence of the Mishnah* 270–281.

104. The gentiles' lack of *qiddushin* is mentioned frequently in rabbinic texts. See, for example, B. Sanhedrin 57b and Y. Yevamot 2:6 4a, and Z. W. Falk, "On the Historical Background of the Talmudic Laws regarding Gentiles" (in Hebrew) *Zion* 44 (1979) 57–65 = "On the Historical Background of the Talmudic Laws Regarding Gentiles," *Immanuel* 14 (1982) 102–113.

105. The offspring of gentiles follows the father: see R. Yohanan in B. Yevamot 78b and B. Qiddushin 67a; cf. R. Hanina in B. Sanhedrin 57b. Rabbinic opinion was divided on this matter: according to Resh Laqish gentiles have no filiation (Y. Yevamot 2:6 4a). On the paternity of gentiles in rabbinic law, see S. Stern, *Jewish Identity* 37 n. 267. The offspring of *peregrini* follow the father: see the Roman sources analyzed by Kaser, *Privatrecht* par. 73 II; Treggiari, *Roman Marriage* 49–51; and P. E. Corbett, *The Roman Law of Marriage* (Oxford: Clarendon, 1930) 96–106. Slaves, of course, did not have legal fathers in Roman law; see Bagnall, "Freedmen" 7–8. The offspring of a marriage between *peregrini* might follow the status of the mother if her nationality received a *privilegium* from the Romans to this effect; see *Digesta* 50.1.1.2.

marriages between citizens and noncitizens produce offspring whose status, in theory at least, is determined matrilineally; if there is no *conubium/qiddushin,* there is no legal paternity, and without legal paternity the offspring follows the status of the mother. Both legal systems tried to equalize the consequences for male and female citizens who strayed from the fold. A Roman matron impregnated by a noncitizen or a slave bears a noncitizen or slave, not a citizen; a Jewish woman impregnated by a gentile or a slave bears (at least according to the Mishnah) a *mamzer,* a citizen of impaired status.[106]

Even the language of M. Qiddushin 3:12 echoes Roman legal terminology. Ulpian, in *Tituli* 5:8, provides a brief summary of the Roman law of status, and its phraseology is closely paralleled by M. Qiddushin 3:12. "When *conubium* intervenes [between the father and the mother] the children always follow the father[107] (compare the Mishnah's "Wherever there is potential for a valid marriage . . . the offspring follows the male"); when *conubium* does not intervene, they accrue to the status of the mother[108] (compare the Mishnah's "And any woman who does not have the potential for a valid marriage either with this man or with other men, the offspring is like her"), except that he who has a noncitizen father and a citizen mother is born a noncitizen, because the Minician law ordains that one born of a noncitizen mother or father follows the status of the lower parent[109] (compare the Mishnah's "The offspring follows the parent of lower status")." M. Qiddushin 3:12 is one of the few sections of the Mishnah that can be translated easily into classical Latin.[110]

Although it is generally very difficult to prove the influence of one le-

---

106. I note also that the rabbinic idea (presumed by paragraph B of the Mishnah) that a marriage can be sinful and yet valid is strikingly similar to the Roman idea of a *lex minus quam perfecta,* a legal prohibition that does not rescind the validity of an act that violates the prohibition.

107. *Conubio interveniente liberi semper patrem sequuntur.* Compare *cum legitimae nuptiae factae sint, patrem liberi sequuntur,* Celsus in *Digesta* 1.5.19.

108. *Non interveniente conubio matris condicioni accedunt.* Compare *ex eis inter quos non est conubium, qui nascitur . . . matris condicioni accedit,* Gaius, *Institutes* 1:78.

109. *Excepto eo qui ex peregrino et cive Romana peregrinus nascitur, quoniam lex Minicia ex alterutro peregrino natum deterioris parentis condicionem sequi iubet.* Compare *Gnomon of the Idios Logos* par. 39, *ta tekna hettoni genei akolouthei.*

110. A point unappreciated by Guilielmus Surenhusius, *Seder Naschim sive Legum Mischnicarum Liber qui Inscribitur De Re Uxoria* (Amsterdam: Borstius, 1700), p. 377, who translates the Mishnah literally (*quocunque in loco obtinent desponsationes et non obtinet transgressio infans sequitur virum* etc.). On this translator of the Mishnah, Willem Surenhuis, see Frank E. Manuel, *The Broken Staff: Judaism through Christian Eyes* (Cambridge: Harvard University Press, 1992) 95–97.

gal system upon another, here the evidence is rather strong.[111] The Roman law, whose principles are clearly attested in republican times,[112] antedates the earliest attestation of the rabbinic law. As far as I have been able to determine, if the rabbinic law had an external source, Roman law is the only real possibility. The Greek law of the classical and Hellenistic periods is not comparable, nor is the law of Egypt or the other kingdoms of the ancient Orient.[113] This suggestion accounts for the phraseology of the Mishnah as well as its dominant ideas. It also takes seriously the Mishnah's explanation of itself, since the Mishnah ignores Scripture and emphasizes the notion of *qiddushin* (a translation of *conubium*). It also is economical, since it accounts at once for both halves of the matrilineal principle.

A full assessment of this suggestion must await a detailed study of other possible influences of Roman ideas and institutions upon ancient Judaism. If the matrilineal principle can be shown to be but one of the many legacies of Rome to Jerusalem, the suggestion will gain force. This study will also have to address several difficult questions. How did the rabbis learn the principles of the Roman law of status? Surely not from the study of Roman law books. How, then? Why did they allow themselves to draw on Roman wisdom when hatred of Rome must have been widespread in Judaean society, even among those opposed to war

111. For the methodological difficulties see, for example, Reuven Yaron, "Jewish Law and Other Legal Systems of Antiquity," *JSS* 4 (1959) 308–331; Zeev Falk, "Zum fremden Einfluss auf das jüdische Recht," *Revue internationale des droits de l'antiquité*, 3d ser. 18 (1971) 11–23; Bernard Jackson, "On the Problem of the Roman Influence on the Halakah," in *Jewish and Christian Self-Definition*, vol. 2, *Aspects of Judaism in the Greco-Roman Period*, ed. E. P. Sanders et al. (Philadelphia: Fortress, 1981) 157–203 (with extensive bibliography).

112. Cicero, *De Natura Deorum* 3:18 45 and *Topica* 20. Livy 43.3.1–4 (a reference I owe to David Cherry) seems to imply that the principle was already in force in 171 B.C.E.

113. The status of the offspring of mixed marriages varied from one Greek state to another; see Vatin, *Recherches* 123–128; Hannick, "Droit de cité"; Ogden, *Greek Bastardy* 277–317. On the law of Hellenistic Egypt, see Ogden, *Greek Bastardy* 328–361, and the various studies of Joseph (Mélèze) Modrzejewski, especially "Un aspect du 'couple interdit' dans l'antiquité: Les mariages mixtes dans l'Egypte hellénistique," in *Le couple interdit: Entretiens sur le racisme*, ed. Léon Poliakov (Paris: Mouton, 1980) 53–73, and "Dryton le cretois et sa famille: Les marriages mixtes dans l'Egypte hellénistique," in *Aux origines de l'hellénisme: La Crète et la Grèce: Hommages à Henri van Effenterre* (Paris: Université de Paris, 1984) 353–377. On the novelty of the Roman law in Egypt, see Youtie, "*Apatores.*" In Roman Athens the offspring of an Athenian mother and a slave or noncitizen father was a noncitizen; see Dio Chrysostom, *Orations* 15:3. Some Greek cities bestowed citizenship *even* on the offspring of a citizen mother and a noncitizen father (Aristotle, *Politics* 3.1278a26); this too is not the rabbinic system. For the law of the ancient Orient see notes 7 and 11 above.

with Rome? These questions are analogous to those that must be asked in any study of rabbinic "Hellenism," and the answers remain elusive.[114]

EXPLANATION NO. 7:
FORBIDDEN MIXTURES

My next suggestion sees the matrilineal principle not as the product of external influence but as an organic development of rabbinic thought. Before turning to Deuteronomy 7:3–4 and R. Yohanan in the name of R. Simeon b. Yohai (see above), the Bavli asks whether there is scriptural support for the notion that slaves lack the capacity to contract a valid marriage (*qiddushin*). In response the Bavli adduces Genesis 22:5, Abraham's statement to his servants, *You stay here with the ass*. This is interpreted, in a very unecumenical pun, as "You stay here, you who are a race similar to an ass" (*im hahamor / am hadomeh lahamor*). And since asses are unable to contract valid marriages, so too gentile slaves are unable to contract valid marriages.[115] I am not about to suggest that this oft-repeated exegesis accurately portrays the ideological origins of our Mishnah—I am not even sure of its real intent[116]—

---

114. Gustav Hölscher once suggested that the Sadducees were influenced by Roman law; see his *Der Sadduzäismus* (Leipzig: Hinrichs, 1906) 30–32. David Daube, *The Duty of Procreation* (Edinburgh, 1977), argues that rabbinic legislation regarding procreation may have been influenced by Roman legislation on the same subject (Ilan, *Jewish Women* 106 n 23). Many other such suggestions can be cited, but all are hard to prove—or disprove.

115. B. Qiddushin 68a and parallels.

116. Joseph Heinemann, "'A Race Similar to an Ass': The Transformations of a Midrash" (in Hebrew), *Molad* 22, nos. 193–194 (October 1964) 456–462, observes that the application of this exegesis to halakhic matters characterizes the Bavli, not the Yerushalmi. Heinemann argues that the original purpose of the exegesis was anti-Christian polemic. More convincing is his argument that the exegesis should not be taken as rabbinic "philosophy." Many rabbinic passages compare gentiles in general, or gentile slaves in particular, with animals (S. Stern, *Jewish Identity* 35–39, 59, 165), but Jews too can be so compared (M. Bekhorot 7:7, the prohibition of presenting the altar with an animal and its offspring on the same day might be thought to apply to priests too; B. Baba Qamma 34b–35a, comparison of human to ox with respect to the laws of damages; B. Baba Metzia 88b, the prohibition of muzzling an ox while it is threshing also applies to human farm laborers; B. Hulin 5a, the sinners of Israel resemble animals); cf. S. Stern, *Jewish Identity* 82, and Morton Smith, "On the Shape of God and the Humanity of Gentiles," in M. Smith, *Studies* 1.150–160. Cf. Eusebius, *Preparation for the Gospel* 7.8.6 (307a–b), p. 371 ed. Mras: Enosh is the first true man, because he attains knowledge of God and piety; but those who differ [from him] differ not from irrational animals; the Hebrew scripture teaches us to call them beasts rather than men. Peter the Venerable, in his *Adversus Judaeos,* likens Jews to animals because they refuse to accept a Christological reading of the Old Testament no matter how many times it is explained to them; see Anna Sapir Abulafia, *Christians and Jews in the Twelfth Century Renaissance* (London and New York: Routledge 1995) 116.

but I am suggesting that the Mishnah's treatment of the consequences of intermarriage should be juxtaposed to its discussion of the results of mixed breeding in the animal kingdom.

Scripture prohibits the breeding of animals of different species (Lev. 19:19), but if the prohibition is violated, what is the status of the resulting offspring? Does it belong to the species of the father or the species of the mother? Or is it a new species altogether? In other words, what is a mule? The rabbis know that the mule is sterile,[117] but this fact did not free them from the necessity of determining its status. The Torah, as understood by the rabbis, prohibits not only the mating of animals of diverse species but also the yoking together of animals of diverse species. Hence the question: what is a mule? In the Tosefta the sages argue that a mule is neither a horse nor a donkey, but a new and distinct species. It makes no difference whether the mule's mother is a horse or a donkey; a mule is a mule.[118] The Mishnah, however, seems to ignore this opinion in favor of that of R. Judah:[119]

R. Judah says: All those born from a (female) horse, although their father is a donkey, are permitted one with another. Thus too, those born from a (female) donkey, although their father is a horse, are permitted one with another. But those born from a (female) horse with those born from a (female) donkey, they are prohibited one with the other.[120]

R. Judah seems to mean that a mule whose mother is a horse and whose father is a donkey is permitted to mate (or be yoked) not only with other such mules but even with purebred horses, since a mule follows the status of its mother. This interpretation is supported by another Mishnah that declares that an animal is pure (may be eaten) if its mother is pure, and that an animal is impure (may not be eaten) if its mother is impure.[121] If this interpretation is correct, the Mishnah rules that the results of mixed breeding in both the animal kingdom and the human kingdom are to be judged matrilineally. The offspring of a gentile mother and a Jewish father belongs to the species of its mother, just as a mule belongs to the species of its mother. The view of the sages (a mule is a separate species, and thus may not mate or be yoked with the

117. Sifrei Deuteronomy 119 178F.

118. T. Kilayim 5:5 222L.

119. "Seems to ignore" because there is room for doubt; see M. Kilayim 1:6 with T. Kilayim 1:8 204L.

120. M. Kilayim 8:4.

121. M. Bekhorot 1:2. In their commentaries on M. Kilayim 8:4, R. Samson of Sens and R. Yom Tob Lipman Heller recognize that this is the simple meaning of R. Judah's statement. See too H. Albeck ad loc.

kind of either its father or its mother) has its analogue in M. Yevamot 7:5, according to which the offspring of a Jewish mother and a gentile father is a *mamzer* (and thus unable to marry either a gentile or a Jew of good standing).[122]

It is most regrettable, therefore, that the Talmudim reject this interpretation and suggest that R. Judah posits two types of mules, those whose mothers are horses and those whose mothers are donkeys. Mules may mate (or be yoked) only with their own kind.[123] According to this interpretation, the parallel between the human and the animal kingdoms is not exact. In the mixed breeding of humans, the result is either Jew or gentile, and the matrilineal principle serves to determine whether the offspring is the former or the latter; in the mixed breeding of animals, the result is a hybrid, a mulatto, and the matrilineal principle serves to distinguish one sort of hybrid from another.

In any case, the important point is that the laws of *kilayim*, prohibited mixtures, provide an ideological context for the matrilineal principle. Jacob Neusner has well demonstrated the Mishnah's deep and abiding fascination with mixtures and with creatures that, like hermaphrodites, Samaritans, and the land of Syria, straddle the boundaries between defined entities.[124] Perhaps the Mishnah's rulings about gentiles who have become Jews (converts) and about Jews who mate with gentiles should be understood in the light of its larger interests. The off-

122. This is just an analogy: a *mamzer* is a member of the community of Israel, whereas a mule is neither a horse nor a donkey.

123. B. Hulin 78b–79a; Y. Berakhot 8:5 11b; see too T. Kilayim 5:5 p. 222L. The discussion of Irving Mandelbaum, *A History of the Mishnaic Law of Agriculture: Kilayim* (Chico, Calif.: Scholars Press, 1982), is not entirely helpful. In his commentary on T. Kilayim 1:8, Mandelbaum writes (p. 47 n. 156, referring to p. 324), "Cf. M[ishnah] 8:4, where Judah distinguishes between the mule (the dam of which is a mare) and a hinny (the dam of which is a she-ass) and does not allow one to be mated with the other. T[osefta] (which makes no such distinction) and M[ishnah] thus represent two different traditions of Judah concerning the same issue." On p. 270, however, Mandelbaum explains R. Judah's opinion of T. Kilayim 5:5 in the light of M. Kilayim 8:4, so the Tosefta is aware of the Mishnah's view. On p. 267, commenting on M. Kilayim 8:4, Mandelbaum writes: "According to Judah two mules which were born of dams of a single kind (and, of course, of sires of a single kind as well) may be paired with one another, for these animals themselves form a single 'kind.'" His parenthetic remark is far from obvious and needs greater support than an introductory "of course." B. Hulin 78b adduces another instance of the matrilineal principle in the animal kingdom: the prohibition of slaughtering an animal with its young on the same day applies only to a mother and her young. See further Sifra on Lev. 22:28 (99bW) and B. Bekhorot 45b.

124. *Evidence of the Mishnah* 256–270. Neusner is applying to the Mishnah the interpretation of Leviticus by Mary Douglas, *Purity and Danger* (London and Boston: Routledge & Kegan Paul, 1966; reprint, 1979) 52–53.

spring of mixed marriage is a form of *kilayim,* mixed breeding. R. Yosef Bekhor Shor, a French Talmudist of the twelfth century, observes in his commentary on Deuteronomy 7:4 that the offspring of a gentile or a slave follows the mother "just like an animal."

This suggestion is supported by the fact that many texts—the Bible, Ben Sira, Qumran, Philo, Paul, the Talmud, and medieval rabbinic literature—explicitly or implicitly liken prohibited sexual relationships, especially sexual unions between Jews and gentiles, to violations of the laws of mixed breeding. Some texts explicitly liken the forbidden sexual partner to an animal. Here are the examples I have found; I have no doubt that there are many others. *Bible:* Calum Carmichael has suggested that the Deuteronomic prohibition of plowing with an ox and an ass together (Deut. 22:10) is a veiled allusion to the prohibition of mixed marriage, especially to the story of the violation of the prohibition (and the violation of Dinah) in Genesis 34. Moshe Weinfeld has suggested that the prohibition of adultery in the Ten Commandments is the basis for Leviticus 19's prohibitions of mixed seeds, of having intercourse with a slave girl, and of eating premature fruit. Weinfeld further observes that the Deuteronomic prohibition of mixing diverse kinds (Deut. 22:9–11) immediately precedes a section on adultery (Deut. 22:13 ff). These suggestions are strengthened by Howard Eilberg-Schwartz's insight that in several biblical laws animals metaphorically represent Israel and Israelites.[125] *Ben Sira:* Ben Sira 25:8, at least in the Syriac version, thinks that a happy domestic life is connected with observing the prohibition of Deuteronomy 22:10 ("Happy is the one who dwells with a sensible wife, and who does not plow with an ox and a donkey combined"). *Qumran:* The document known as *Miqtzat Ma'asei HaTorah* implicitly likens prohibited marriages to *kilayim:*

And concerning the illicit sexual relations that are practiced among the people: (these are wrong, because the people) are sons of holy seed, as it is written, *Israel is holy* (Jer. 2:3). And concerning his (Israel's) pure animal, it is written that one must not let it mate with another species; and concerning his clothes it is written that they should not be of mixed stuff; and he

---

125. Carmichael, *Laws of Deuteronomy* 159–163. He expands upon this thesis in his "Forbidden Mixtures," *Vetus Testamentum* 32 (1982) 394–415, and *Women, Law, and the Genesis Traditions* (Edinburgh: University of Edingurgh Press, 1979) 33–48 and 57–73. Moshe Weinfeld, *Deuteronomy 1–11,* Anchor Bible (New York: Doubleday, 1991) 252. Howard Eilberg-Schwartz, *The Savage in Judaism* (Bloomington: Indiana University Press, 1990) chap. 5.

must not sow his field and vineyard with mixed kinds (Lev. 19:19). Because they (Israel) are holy, and the sons of Aaron are most holy.[126]

The holy seed of Israel must protect its holiness by abstaining from prohibited marriages and all sorts of prohibited mixtures. *Philo:* Philo explicitly interprets the prohibitions of Leviticus 19:19 and Deuteronomy 22:9–11 as including adultery and all other prohibited sexual relationships.[127] *Paul:* In 2 Corinthians 6:14, Paul (or someone else) says, "Do not be mismated with unbelievers." The word translated as "mismated" (or "mismatched") is *heterozugountes,* a word derived from the Septuagint rendering of Leviticus 19:19. According to the writer of this piece in 2 Corinthians, any intimate association with unbelievers is a violation of the law of mixed seeds. *Talmud:* In one passage the Bavli explicitly compares the *mamzer* (the offspring of incest) to the mule: Ana, the *mamzer* son of Esau, was the first man to mate a horse with a donkey.[128] Another passage declares that a sage who has sexual intercourse with the daughter of a boor (an *am ha-aretz*) has violated the prohibition of copulating with a beast.[129] *Medieval rabbinic literature:* Maimonides rules that a gentile woman who has had sex with a Jewish man should be stoned "like an animal"—that is, just as we stone an animal with which a person has had sex.[130] One medieval rabbinic text says explicitly, "He who has intercourse with a gentile woman is guilty of (violating) fourteen negative precepts: *You shall not sow your vineyard with a second kind of seed* (Deut. 22:9), *You shall not plow with an ox and an ass together* (Deut. 22:10), *You shall not wear cloth combining wool and linen* (Deut. 22:11)."[131]

126. *Miqtzat Ma'asei HaTorah* B 75–79, as edited by Elisha Qimron and John Strugnell, in *Discoveries in the Judaean Desert X: Qumran Cave 4 V* (Oxford: Clarendon, 1994) 54–57. (I have modified Qimron's translation somewhat.) On this text see the note of Y. Zussman, *Tarbiz* 59 (1990) 26 n. 67. Perhaps relevant too is 4Q418 fr. 103 ii (translated in Geza Vermes, *The Complete Dead Sea Scrolls in English* [New York: Penguin, 1997] 411).

127. *On the Special Laws* 3.46–47; 4.203.

128. B. Pesahim 54a, based on Gen. 36:24. A slightly different version appears in Y. Berakhot 8:5 60a; see Theodor and Albeck's discussion in their edition of Genesis Rabbah 82:14 993–994T-A. (I am grateful to Dr. David Lieber for bringing this passage to my attention.) On the common association of donkeys or mules with gentiles, see S. Stern, *Jewish Identity* 37–39.

129. B. Pesahim 49a–b.

130. Lev. 20:16; *Laws of Forbidden Intercourse* (Issurei Biah) 12:10, apparently an innovation of Maimonides.

131. This text is known as *Masekhet Arayot.* See chapter 8 above, note 26. I translate the text in Ms. Kaufmann A 50, p. 254 in the facsimile ed. G. Beer; it is cited by the Yalqut Shimoni on Deut. 22:10. For parallels and variants see M. Higger, ed., *The Treatises Derek*

Nor is this way of thinking peculiar to the Israelites or the Jews. Cyrus the Great was a "mule" because he was the son of a Persian father and a Median mother.[132] In medieval Christian law sexual intercourse of a Christian with a Jew was regarded as sex with an animal.[133] In the first century of Islam, the non-Arab converts to the new religion were looked down upon by their Arab conquerors. According to one poem of the period, miscegenation of Arab with non-Arab resembles intercourse with donkeys and mules.[134] The Spanish word *mulatto*, which originally was the designation for the offspring of a Negro (slave) father and a Spanish (free) mother and later in popular usage came to refer to the offspring of any interracial union, of course derives from Latin *mulus*, mule. In the American South the products of miscegenation were routinely called mules.[135]

In sum, in the rabbinic mind the sexual union of a Jew with a gentile was akin to the sexual union of a human with an animal, or of animals of diverse species. It was a union that violated the natural order established by God and the scriptural prohibition of mixing seed. Rabbinic law and lore, or at least some strands of rabbinic law and lore, regarded the offspring of such forbidden unions, paradigmatically represented by the mule, as belonging to the class of its mother.

Why Did the Rabbis Break with Previous Practice?

I have surveyed seven explanations for the origins of the matrilineal principle. Of these, the last two are far more compelling than the first five. The major difficulty with all of them, however, is that they explain *how* the rabbis might have come to the matrilineal principle but not *why* they would have wanted to come to it. What, if anything, compelled them to depart from the biblical tradition and from the prac-

Erez 273 (where the text reads "He who has intercourse with a slave woman"; the same reading is in Taubes, *Otzar heGeonim: Sanhedrin* 445 no. 1028).

132. Herodotus 1.55.2.

133. Joshua Trachtenberg, *The Devil and the Jews* (New Haven: Yale University Press, 1944; frequently reprinted) 187.

134. Bulliet, *Conversion* 146 n. 19.

135. Davis, *Who Is Black?* 89 (the original use of *mulatto*) and 55 (the American South).

tice of the second-temple period?[136] Did some societal need dictate the new law? It has been suggested that many Jewish women were raped by Roman soldiers during the wars of 66–70 and 132–135, and that the rabbis, out of pity for their plight, declared the resulting offspring to be Jewish, not gentile.[137] This suggestion draws an implausible inference from a plausible hypothesis. It is safe to assume that many Jewish women were, in fact, raped by Roman soldiers during the two wars. Rape of women by victorious soldiers is a normal part of ancient (and, alas, modern) warfare.[138] Some scholars have suggested that their plight prompted a reform to the *ketuvah,* the rabbinic marriage contract; henceforth the rabbis demanded that every marriage contract contain the clause "and if you are captured, I shall redeem you and return you to me to be my wife."[139] Might the same setting explain a change in the law of status?

Probably not. Telling an unfortunate woman who has been raped that she is about to bear a *mamzer* is only slightly more consolatory than telling her that she is about to bear a gentile. In some respects it is less consolatory: a gentile, at least, can convert to Judaism, but a *mamzer* can never be legitimated. And yet, as we have already seen, the Mishnah, the earliest stratum of rabbinic law, assumes that the offspring of a Jewish mother and a gentile father is a *mamzer.* Further, if the rape

136. It is not impossible that the matrilineal principle entered rabbinic Judaism from the marriage regulations of pre–70 C.E. sectarianism (cf. Neusner, *Law of Women* 5.179–192), but I see no evidence to support this conjecture. Levinskaya, *Book of Acts* 15–17, argues that Luke and the Jews of Asia Minor thought of Timothy as a Jew, and that the matrilineal principle may have come to the rabbis from the Jews of Asia Minor, who in turn instituted it under Roman influence; this argument is based on an implausible reading of Acts 16:1–3 (see appendix D below), and still does not explain why either the Jews of Asia Minor or the rabbis would have wanted to institute the matrilineal principle.

137. This suggestion is widely accepted, especially in contemporary rabbinic circles, but I have not found its original author; it is repeated by Daube, *Ancient Jewish Law* 27–30, but he too does not indicate his source (or is Daube the author?).

138. On the rape of women in ancient warfare, see Isa. 13:16 and Zech. 14:2; S. G. Cole, "Greek Sanctions against Sexual Assault," *Classical Philology* 79 (1984) 97–113, at 111–113, who refers to David Schaps, "Women of Greece in Wartime," *Classical Philology* 77 (1982) 203–204. I have not yet seen S. Deacy and K. F. Pierce, *Rape in Antiquity: Sexual Violence in the Greek and Roman Worlds* (London: Duckworth, 1997). It is likely therefore that many women were raped during the wars of 66–70 and 132–135, an assumption that is confirmed by M. Ketuvot 2:9 with the Talmudim ad loc., and by Song of Songs Zuta, end, as presented by Lieberman, *Greek in Jewish Palestine* 179–184.

139. Ranon Katzoff, "Philo and Hillel on Violation of Betrothal in Alexandria," in *The Jews in the Hellenistic-Roman World: Studies in Memory of Menahem Stern* (Jerusalem: Shazar Center, 1996) 39*–57*, at 55*–56* (discussing the views of M. A. Friedman and Y. Gilat).

of Jewish women prompted the emergence of the matrilineal principle, why declare the offspring of a Jewish father and a gentile mother to be a gentile?

Perhaps the half of the matrilineal principle governing the offspring of a Jewish father and a gentile mother had a specific social setting and purpose. Perhaps, like the Athenian citizenship law, its purpose was to discourage intermarriage by Jewish men and thus to improve the marriageability of Jewish women.[140] Perhaps in the wake of the war of 66–70 C.E. there was a shortage of unmarried Jewish men and a surfeit of unmarried Jewish women. Perhaps. There simply is no evidence to substantiate this suggestion. In general, the incidence of intermarriage by Jews in antiquity, especially in Judaea and especially within the rabbinic orbit, seems to have been relatively low, so that the restraint of intermarriage will probably not have been the main motive.[141] And, if the primary motivation was to restrain intermarriage, the rabbis should have introduced a bilateral requirement for citizenship, just as Pericles did in Athens and Ezra did (perhaps) in Jerusalem (see above).

Why, then, did the rabbis break with previous practice? I do not know.

Summary and Conclusions

In the Bible a mixed marriage between an Israelite and a non-Israelite produced offspring whose status was determined patrilineally. Many Israelite men married foreign women, and there was never any doubt that their offspring were Israelite. The offspring of a slave mother and an Israelite father did, apparently, suffer from some social disabilities, but no one questioned their Israelite status. Various works of the late second-temple period still presume the biblical system. The Mishnah, however, explicitly states that the offspring of an Israelite father and a gentile mother (either slave or free) are gentile, following the status of their mother. This ruling is not modified or disputed in the Talmudim. As far as I have been able to determine, the transition from biblical patriliny to mishnaic matriliny cannot be dated before the pe-

140. According to some scholars the purpose of the Periclean citizenship law (see note 15 above) was to improve the marriageability of noble Athenian women; see Boegehold, "Pericles' Citizenship Law" 59.

141. On the low rate of intermarriage, see chapter 8 above, note 14.

riod of the Mishnah itself. There is no evidence that Ezra attempted to introduce the matrilineal principle, and even if he did, there is abundant evidence that it was still unknown in the first century of our era. Why did the rabbis of the early second century C.E. depart from previous practice? [142]

Of the seven explanations I surveyed, two are the most attractive. The matrilineal principle accords nicely with the mishnaic laws regarding the mixture of diverse kinds (*kilayim*). The union of a Jew with a gentile is akin to the forbidden union of a horse with a donkey. In both cases the Mishnah judges the resulting offspring matrilineally. Even more striking is the parallel afforded by the Roman law of status. The terminology, ideas, and conclusions of M. Qiddushin 3:12 are thoroughly Roman: if one parent does not possess the capacity to contract a legal marriage (*conubium* in Latin, *qiddushin* in Hebrew), the offspring follows the mother. The rabbis, like the Romans, departed from this principle in order to penalize a citizen woman who married a noncitizen or a slave: the Romans declared that the offspring follows the parent of lower status (in this case, the father); the rabbis (at least in the Mishnah) declared that the offspring is a *mamzer*. I am unable to decide between these two explanations; indeed we probably should not decide between them. On an issue as complex and diffuse as the rabbinic matrilineal principle, we must allow for a multiplicity of motives. Perhaps even the "wrong" explanations, notably the derivation from Ezra (explanation no. 2), contributed.

Another factor is relevant too. As I discussed in chapter 4 above, the idea of conversion to Judaism and enfranchisement within the Judaean community is a creation of the Hasmonean period. At first it was an option only for men; its ritual was circumcision. A gentile woman "converted" to Judaism through marriage with a Jewish husband, a procedure presumed by the Bible and still presumed by Josephus. [143] Gradually, however, conversion for women was introduced; its ritual was immersion (a practice that also became part of the conversion ritual for men). This facilitated the rise of the matrilineal principle, since the gentile woman was now a person whose Jewishness could be determined without reference to her Jewish husband. If she converts to Judaism, the children she bears to her husband are Jewish; if she does not, they are

---

142. In this short summary I omit the more complicated case of the offspring of Israelite mothers and gentile fathers.

143. See the conclusion to chapter 5 above.

gentiles, in spite of the Jewishness of her husband. This new ideology mandated the reinterpretation of the biblical narratives that glibly admitted that the heroes of ancient Israel married foreign women. These developments form part of the ideological background to the emergence of the matrilineal principle.

All of these suggestions are exercises in intellectual history. Did social history too play a role in the creation of the matrilineal principle? Numerous Jewish scholars have argued that rabbinic law was determined, at least in part, by the social and economic needs of contemporary Jewry. The matrilineal principle has had enormous social consequences for modern Jews, and it is easy to believe that the rabbis in antiquity must have been compelled by some societal need to institute it. But there is little evidence to support this belief. Intermarriage was not a severe problem in rabbinic society, and even if it was, the logical response would have been the institution of a bilateral system, requiring both a Jewish father and a Jewish mother for an offspring to be reckoned Jewish by birth. Perhaps elsewhere the rabbis were legislators listening attentively to the demands of their constituency. In their statement of the matrilineal principle, however, the rabbis were philosophers, and, like most philosophers, they did not always live in the real world.

CHAPTER 10

Israelite Mothers, Israelite Fathers
Matrilineal Descent and the Inequality of the Convert

Only a community based on common blood feels the warrant of eternity warm in its veins . . . The peoples of the world are not content with the bonds of blood. They sink their roots into the night of the earth . . . We were the only ones who trusted in blood and abandoned the land.

Franz Rosenzweig, *The Star of Redemption*

This chapter focuses on a single extraordinary Mishnah, which stands at the intersection of several of our central concerns. Here is M. Bikkurim 1:4–5.

A. The following people (are obligated to) bring (first fruits to the temple) but do not recite (the declaration prescribed by Deuteronomy 26:3–11):

B. The convert brings but does not recite,

C. because he cannot say *(the land) which God has sworn to our fathers to give us* (Deut. 26:3).

D. But if his mother was of Israel, he brings and recites.

E. And when he prays by himself, he says, "God of the fathers of Israel."

F. And when he is in synagogue (with the community), he says, "God of your fathers."

The epigraph is from Franz Rosenzweig, *The Star of Redemption*, trans. William Hallo (New York: Holt, Rinehart and Winston, 1970) 299.

G. But if his mother was of Israel, he says, "God of our fathers."

H. R. Eliezer b. Jacob says,

J. A woman who is the daughter of converts may not marry into the priesthood,

K. unless her mother is of Israel.

L. (This rule applies equally to) converts and emancipated slaves;

M. even until ten generations, (the daughters of converts or emancipated slaves may not marry into the priesthood) unless their mother is of Israel.[1]

This Mishnah treats three areas in which converts suffer legal disability because of their non-Jewish lineage: when bringing their first fruits to the temple, converts may not recite the declaration prescribed by Deuteronomy (A–D); converts may not say "God of our fathers"[2] in their prayers (E–G); and the daughter of converts may not be married to a priest (H–M). In all three areas the legal disability disappears if the convert has a mother who is "of Israel" (or Jewish, as we would say).

This Mishnah raises two important questions. First, as I discussed in chapter 9 above, according to rabbinic law, from the second century C.E. to the present, the status of the offspring of intermarriage (a sexual union between a Jew and a non-Jew) is determined by the status of the mother: a Jewish mother bears a Jewish child, even if the father is a non-Jew, and a non-Jewish mother bears a non-Jewish child, even if the father is a Jew. Thus a gentile cannot have a Jewish mother, and, it would seem, a convert to Judaism (i.e., a gentile who has become a Jew) also cannot have a Jewish mother. M. Bikkurim 1:4–5, however, seems to speak of a convert who has a Jewish mother. How is this Mishnah to be explained? Second, as I discussed in chapter 5 above, the boundary separating Jews and Judaism from gentiles and the ways of gentiles was permeable to a degree: gentiles could cross the boundary and become Jews even if they would always retain something of their gentility and never attain full equality with the native born. This principle is illustrated by our Mishnah, which lists three areas in which the convert is legally inferior to the native. But, our Mishnah continues, the inequality disappears if the convert has a Jewish mother. To what extent,

1. For the manuscript evidence, see *Seder Zera'im,* ed. Nissan Sacks (Jerusalem: Institute of the Complete Israeli Talmud, 1975) 404–406. This edition also provides a rich collection of medieval testimonia, which I exploit in the second part of this chapter.

2. In our egalitarian and gender-conscious age we would prefer to translate *avot* as "ancestors" rather than "fathers," and *avotenu* as "our ancestors" rather than "our fathers," but the writers of the Mishnah and their successors meant "fathers."

then, is the convert really "just like" the native? The disparate parts of this chapter are held together by their common focus on M. Bikkurim and on the place of birth (pedigree) within the rabbinic definition of Jewishness.

Israelite Mothers and Matrilineal Descent

Three times M. Bikkurim says of a convert "but if his mother is of Israel . . ." According to the rabbinic matrilineal principle, however, a gentile (and therefore a convert) cannot have a Jewish mother. How can this Mishnah be explained? In order to answer this question, I shall first propose my own answer (i.e., the "correct" answer), and then consider three different ways of construing the Yerushalmi's explanation of the Mishnah. In the course of the discussion, I shall also treat two other ancient rabbinic texts (both from the Sifra) that seem to contradict the rabbinic matrilineal principle.

FIRST EXPLANATION

The simplest and best way to construe the Mishnah is to assume that clauses D, G, and K are speaking of the offspring of a native mother and a convert father.[3] According to our Mishnah, a convert is obligated to bring first fruits but may not recite the declaration, while the offspring of a Jewish mother and a convert father is obligated both to bring and to recite.

The offspring of a Jewish mother and a convert father, although a Jew by birth, nevertheless has, or might be thought to have, the status of a convert. According to R. Judah the status of convert (*gēr*) is inherited in precisely the same way as the status of priest (*kohen*), Levite, and Israelite: just as the status of priest, Levite, and Israelite is inherited from the father,[4] so too the status of convert is inherited from the father. The legal and social disabilities that apply to the convert father also apply to the offspring, even though the offspring was conceived and born as a Jew. According to R. Eliezer b. Jacob (H–K), however, the

3. This is the explanation of R. Solomon Sirilio (d. ca. 1558) ad loc. For the text of R. Sirilio's commentary, see Kalman Kahana, ed., *Masekhet Bikkurim: Heqer ve'iyun* (Jerusalem, 1989) 36.

4. M. Qiddushin 3:12, par. A; see chapter 9 above.

status of convert is not inherited in precisely the same way as the status of priest, Levite, and Israelite. The offspring of two convert parents has the status of a convert, but the offspring of a native parent and a convert parent, no matter which parent is the native and which is the convert, does not. A native parent, either father or mother, prevents his or her offspring from acquiring the status of convert from the convert parent.[5] Against both R. Judah and R. Eliezer b. Jacob, R. Yosi argues that there is no parallel at all between the status of convert and the three hierarchical categories of Israel. Even the offspring of two convert parents does not inherit the status of convert from his or her parents. This debate appears in M. Qiddushin 4:6–7, with amplifications in the Tosefta.

Thus, at least according to R. Judah and R. Eliezer b. Jacob, the mishnaic term "convert" (*gēr*) has two different senses: a *gēr* is either a first-generation convert—that is, a gentile who has converted to Judaism—or a second-generation convert—that is, the offspring of a convert.[6] Mishnah Bikkurim 1:4–5 ignores the view of R. Yosi, implicitly rejects the view of R. Judah, and explicitly cites the view of R. Eliezer b. Jacob. Three disabilities affect the *gēr* according to the Mishnah. They affect not only first-generation converts but also second-generation converts who are the offspring of two convert parents (J). They do not, however, affect a second-generation convert who is the offspring of a convert father and a native mother. And if the disabilities do not apply to the offspring of a convert father and a native mother, *a fortiori* they do not apply to the offspring of a convert mother and a native father. Even R. Judah would admit that such offspring is not deemed a convert.[7]

---

5. This is how the editor of M. Bikkurim understands and summarizes the view of R. Eliezer b. Jacob. The original setting of the statement of R. Eliezer b. Jacob is M. Qiddushin 4:7, as is correctly noted here by the *Melekhet Shelomo* of R. Solomon Adni (1567–ca.1624), and there the Mishnah seems to imply that a daughter of a male convert to Judaism may not be married to a priest unless her father, the convert, has a native-born Jewish mother. There are variant readings, however, in M. Qiddushin, and various possible interpretations. Translators have had trouble with M. Qiddushin 4:7; see Porton, *Stranger* 229 n. 19.

6. That is, the offspring born after the conversion of the parent. Offspring born before the conversion of the parent is the offspring of a gentile, and the subsequent conversion of the parent does not bestow Jewishness retroactively on the offspring.

7. R. Judah argues that the offspring of a convert father and a native mother has the status of a convert; at least this is R. Judah's position in M. Qiddushin. According to the Tosefta (T. Bikkurim 1:2 286L) R. Judah maintains this position here as well: "R. Judah says, all converts, all of them, bring (first fruits to the temple) but do not recite (the declaration)." The tautology of "all converts, all of them" would seem intended to include even the offspring of a convert father and a native mother. But the Yerushalmi ascribes a

In sum: in clauses B, E, and F the Mishnah is speaking of first-generation converts, whereas in clauses D, G, and J–M it is speaking of second-generation converts. Hence the Mishnah speaks of a convert (i.e., someone with the legal status of a convert or who might be thought to have the legal status of a convert) who has a Jewish mother.[8]

THE YERUSHALMI

This explanation of the Mishnah is assumed and then rejected by the Yerushalmi:

(In clauses A–J, the Yerushalmi discusses two versions of a statement of R. Samuel b. R. Isaac concerning converts who are descendants of the Kenite, the father-in-law of Moses.)

K. R. Yosi says:

L. Benjamin b. Ashtor, in the presence of R. Hiyyah b. (Ab)ba, construed the Mishnah as referring to a gentile who had sinful intercourse with an Israelite woman (and the offspring of that union is the one of whom the Mishnah says *if his mother was of Israel he brings and recites*).

M. R. Jonah did not say (the interpretation of Benjamin b. Ashtor) in this manner, but (rather applied it to a different clause in the Mishnah):

N. Rabbi X^9 heard those of the house of b. Ashtor, who are converts

---

very different view to R. Judah: "R. Judah says, a first-generation convert brings and recites." How to reconcile the positions attributed to R. Judah by the Tosefta and the Yerushalmi (if indeed they can be reconciled), and how the ruling(s) of R. Judah relate to the ruling of the Mishnah, are questions that have been much discussed; see Lieberman, *Tosefta K'Fshutah* ad loc.

8. This explanation also applies to B. Yevamot 102a and Qiddushin 76b, two passages that refer to a convert with a Jewish mother. See the commentaries of R. Menahem Me'iri (pp. 369–370 ed. Dyckman) and R. Solomon b. Avraham ibn Adret (known as the Rashba, cols. 523–526 ed. Dyckman) on Yevamot 102a, and R. Isaac Alfasi (known as the Rif) on Sanhedrin 36b. In Yevamot 45b (the story about R. Mari b. Rachel), the context suggests that R. Mari is the offspring of a Jewish mother and a non-Jewish father, but the story by itself is better understood if R. Mari's father was a convert; see Rashi, Tosafot, and the Me'iri ad loc. These passages are misconstrued by Daube, *Ancient Jewish Law* 24–25. Porton, *Stranger* 231 n. 32, is unable to distinguish between implausible and plausible interpretations of the Mishnah.

9. The Leiden manuscript and the vulgate editions of the Yerushalmi read: "Rabbi heard those of the house of b. Ashtor," but this reading is difficult because Rabbi (Judah the Patriarch) lived several generations before Benjamin b. Ashtor. R. Sirilio reads: "R. Ze'ira heard those of the house of b. Ashtor." R. Eleazar of Worms, *Sefer Roqe'ah* sec. 331 reads: "R. Simeon the Righteous instructed those of the house of b. Ashtor." The name "Simeon" (*shimon*) is clearly a corruption of the verb "heard" (*shama*), and the epithet "the Righteous" (*hasida*) may be a corruption of the name "Ze'ira." The Vilna Gaon emended the text to "R. Hiyya b. (Ab)ba heard those of the house of b. Ashtor."

the sons of converts, saying (in their prayers) "God of our fathers." But did we not learn (in the Mishnah) *But if his mother was of Israel, he says, "God of our fathers"?* (Does this not imply) that converts who are the sons of converts do not (say "God of our fathers")?

P. (It was in response to this objection, R. Jonah says, that) R. Yosi says[10] that Benjamin b. Ashtor, in the presence of R. Hiyyah b. (Ab)ba, construed the Mishnah—

Q. (or, according to another tradition) R. Hezekiah (says) in the name of R. Hiyyah b. (Ab)ba: b. Ashtor, in our presence, construed the Mishnah—

R. as referring to a gentile who had sinful intercourse with an Israelite woman (and the offspring of that union is the one of whom the Mishnah says *if his mother was of Israel he says "God of our fathers,"* thus implying that second generation converts like those of the house of b. Ashtor, who are the sons of converts, may say "God of our fathers" even if they do not have Israelite mothers.[11]

Benjamin b. Ashtor, a student of the third-generation *amora* R. Hiyyah b. Abba,[12] explains that the Mishnah's statement *if his mother was of Israel* refers to the offspring of a gentile father and a Jewish mother. R. Yosi (Yosa), R. Jonah, and R. Hezekiah, three fourth-generation *amoraim,* debate the formulation of this exegesis. According to R. Yosi (K–L), Benjamin's exegesis centered on clause D, which deals with the first-fruits declaration. What prompted the exegesis R. Yosi does not explain.[13] According to R. Jonah and R. Hezekiah in the name of R.

10. I know of no textual variants, but "R. Jonah says" would be much smoother: "(It was in response to this objection,) R. Jonah says, that Benjamin b. Ashtor, in the presence etc." R. Meir Marim in the *Sefer Nir* 75c is disturbed by this problem too.

11. Y. Bikkurim 1:4 64a. See vol. 1, p. 300, of the facsimile of the Leiden manuscript of the Yerushalmi (Jerusalem: Makor, n.d.). Porton, *Stranger* 273–274 n. 56, paraphrases this text but does not explain it. As a result, the paraphrase is incomprehensible.

12. Benjamin spoke "in the presence of" or "in front of" R. Hiyya; this expression implies that Benjamin was the student of R. Hiyya. Benjamin bar Ashtor is not mentioned anywhere else in the Yerushalmi, but the family of b. Ashtor (or b. Ashtin) is mentioned in two other passages, both of which place the family in the city of Emesa (*Hamatz*). In one passage the family of b. Ashtor asks R. Haggai a question about the tithing of produce (Y. Demai 6:1 25b, parallel in Y. Avodah Zarah 1:9 40b); in the other passage the family of b. Ashtor asks R. Yosa whether converts are permitted (or obligated) to perform levirate marriage (Y. Yevamot 11:2 11d). The first passage gives no information on the family's ethnic origins; the second might suggest that the family was a family of converts and therefore interested in laws regarding converts, but this conclusion is tentative at best. R. Jonah, who says explicitly (N) that the house of b. Ashtor was a family of converts, does not reveal the source of his information.

13. Here is one possibility: as I discussed above, the simplest way to interpret the Mishnah is to posit that the Mishnah is speaking of two generations of converts. Benjamin apparently was unhappy that the Mishnah would change subjects; if a first-generation

Hiyya, however, Benjamin's exegesis centered on clause G of the Mishnah, which deals with prayer. The bar Ashtor family was a family of converts. A rabbi (whose name has been lost or corrupted) overheard the members of the family saying "God of our fathers" in their prayers and objected to this practice, because the Mishnah allows a convert to say "God of our fathers" only if he has a native Jewish parent. The Yerushalmi's initial assumption is that clause G applies to a second-generation convert, the offspring of a convert father and a native mother. If so, clause G would imply that second-generation converts (like those of the house of bar Ashtor) who are not the offspring of a native parent would not be allowed to say "God of our fathers." Benjamin b. Ashtor came to the rescue of his family by reinterpreting the Mishnah. Second-generation converts may say "God of our fathers" even if, like the house of Ashtor, they have no native Jewish ancestry at all; when the Mishnah says "but if his mother is of Israel," the Mishnah is referring not to the offspring of a native Jewish mother and a convert father, but to the offspring of a native mother and a *gentile* father. Perhaps influenced by R. Yosi of M. Qiddushin 4:6–7 (see above), Benjamin believed that the offspring of two converts ought not to be affected by the legal disabilities that affect the parents.

Until Benjamin b. Ashtor reinterpreted the Mishnah, the Yerushalmi assumed that clause G (and, presumably, clause D) of the Mishnah was speaking of the offspring of a native mother and a convert father (what I have presented above as "the first explanation"). The Yerushalmi explains why Benjamin rejected this interpretation, but Benjamin's own interpretation is not clear. I shall here consider three ways in which to interpret Benjamin's interpretation of the Mishnah. (Since I have already proposed one explanation of the Mishnah, these three ways are my second, third, and fourth proposed explanations of the Mishnah.) All three of these ways fit Benjamin's words in the Yerushalmi, but none of the resulting explanations of the Mishnah fits the Mishnah as well as my first explanation. The advantage of my first explanation is that it explains all three of the mishnaic references to a native Jewish mother: clauses D (first fruits), G (prayer), and K–M (R. Eliezer b. Jacob on marriage). In contrast, Benjamin's explanation, no matter how it is construed, does not fit the statement of R. Eliezer b. Jacob. The editor of

---

convert was the subject of B–C, a first-generation convert ought to be the subject of D as well. If this explanation is correct, Benjamin clearly envisions a first-generation convert with a Jewish mother. In his notes on the Yerushalmi, R. Elijah Gaon of Vilna proposes a different explanation of Benjamin's reasoning; see below.

the Mishnah, who imported R. Eliezer's statement from M. Qiddushin, must have believed that it formed a piece with the two clauses native to M. Bikkurim. All three discuss the status of second-generation converts, the offspring of convert fathers and native mothers. But Benjamin b. Ashtor clearly says that clauses D and G do not refer to second-generation converts. In other words, no matter which of the following is a correct explanation of Benjamin's exegesis, it is an incorrect explanation of the Mishnah.

SECOND EXPLANATION

Benjamin b. Ashtor means that the Mishnah speaks alternately of converts and Jews by birth. Benjamin construes the Mishnah in the following manner: clauses B and C refer to converts, D refers to the offspring of a Jewish mother; E and F refer to converts, G refers to the offspring of a Jewish mother. Clauses D and G refer to all those who are the offspring of a Jewish mother and thus, according to the matrilineal principle, are Jews by birth no matter who their father is, whether native Jew, convert, or even a gentile. First-generation converts may not recite the declaration or say "God of our fathers," but the offspring of a native Jewish mother may do so. Benjamin argues that the Mishnah implies that all second-generation converts, no matter what their parentage, may recite the declaration and say "God of our fathers." [14]

This is probably the simplest and best way to explain Benjamin's exegesis of the Mishnah. The result seems awkward, especially in translation, but in its defense Benjamin could point to the fact that in clauses J–K too the Mishnah abruptly changes subject. Clause J speaks of the offspring of two converts, but clause K does not:

H. R. Eliezer b. Jacob says,

J. A woman who is the daughter of converts may not marry into the priesthood,

K. unless her mother is of Israel.

If a woman's mother is of Israel (K), she cannot be the daughter of two converts (J)! The explanation is that clause K simply presents a new

14. With some variations this way of construing Benjamin's statement is endorsed by the following commentators: R. Shelomo Sirilio; R. Elijah Gaon of Vilna (Kahana, *Masekhet Bikkurim*, 94–95); R. Jacob David Wil(l)owsky (known as the Ridvaz, 1845–1913); and Lieberman, *Tosefta Ki-Fshutah* 2.824 n. 6. In conversation with me Israel Francus argued that this was the correct interpretation not only of Benjamin b. Ashtor but also of the Mishnah itself.

condition that changes the case under discussion, from the offspring of two converts (J) to the offspring of one convert and one native (K). Similarly, Benjamin could argue, clauses B–C speak of converts but D does not, clauses E–F speak of converts but G does not. This is good mishnaic style, to be sure,[15] but the problem with this reading, as I have already remarked, is that it cannot apply to the statement of R. Eliezer b. Jacob.

THIRD EXPLANATION: DISSENTS
FROM THE MATRILINEAL PRINCIPLE

Benjamin b. Ashtor assumes that the clauses D and G of the Mishnah refer to a first-generation convert, just as clauses B–C and E–F do. Clauses D and G address the case of the offspring of a native Jewish mother and a gentile father. The offspring is a gentile by birth (following its father) and after converting attains the status of a convert with a Jewish mother. Because of his or her Jewish parentage, this convert, unlike converts who are the offspring of two gentile parents, is not hampered by the legal disabilities that otherwise affect converts. Benjamin b. Ashtor either rejects or does not know the rabbinic matrilineal principle.[16]

As I discussed in chapter 9 above, the status of the offspring of a Jewish mother and a gentile father was much debated in rabbinic antiquity. The opinions ranged from *mamzer* to *kasher* (fit), with several interme-

---

15. Cf. M. Yevamot 11:2:

A. A female convert whose sons converted with her—

B. (the sons) perform neither *halitzah* (the ceremony described in Deut. 25:7–10) nor levirate marriage (Deuter. 25:5–6),

C. even if the conception of the first (brother) was not in holiness and his birth was in holiness, and the conception and birth of the second were in holiness.

Clause A refers to a female convert and her convert sons, but clause C refers to a female convert and her nonconvert sons who were born in holiness—that is, after her conversion. Thus according to clause C the verb *converted* in clause A is entirely inappropriate. Cf. too M. Ketuvot 4:3.

16. This explanation is advanced by R. Moshe Margaliot in the *Penei Moshe*. Several modern scholars, without knowing the Yerushalmi, have explained the Mishnah as an exception to the dominant matrilineal view. See, for example, F. F. Bruce, *The Acts of the Apostles* (London: Tyndale, 1951) 86 n. [the note is deleted from the third edition of 1990, p. 118], and Daube, *Ancient Jewish Law* 24. The connection between converts and their natural mothers was not completely broken by conversion; cf. Sifra on Lev. 20:9, *Qedoshim* pereq 9.9 (92aW); B. Yevamot 97b–98b; Y. Yevamot 11:2 11d–12a. Hence it is not impossible to imagine a gentile convert with ties to his Jewish mother.

diary positions. None of the participants in this debate suggests that the offspring is a gentile. Benjamin b. Ashtor's position, however, is not unparalleled. The same position is presumed by the Sifra on Leviticus 24:10:[17]

An Israelite woman's son, who was also the son of an Egyptian man, went out among the people of Israel. And they fought in the camp, that son of an Israelite woman, and an Israelite man.

A. *An Israelite woman's son went out*—whence did he go out?

B. (He went out) from the court house of Moses.

C. He had gone to pitch his tent in the camp of Dan, (but) they said to him, "Who are you to pitch your tent in the camp of Dan?" He said to them, "I am (the son of one) of the daughters of Dan." They said to him, "Scripture says (Num. 2:2), *The Israelites shall camp each with his standard, under the banners of their fathers' house.* (Since your father is Egyptian, you may not join the tribe of Dan although your mother is a Danite.)" (As a result of this rebuke) he entered the courthouse of Moses (to plead his case); he went out, having been condemned, and he stood up and blasphemed.

D. *Who was also the son of an Egyptian man*—Even though at that moment there were no *mamzerim*, he was like a *mamzer*.

E. *Among the people of Israel*—this demonstrates that he converted.

The language of Leviticus 24:10 clearly implies a difference in status between the two participants in the fight. One participant was an *Israelite man;* the other, the blasphemer, was the *son of an Israelite woman.* The blasphemer clearly was not a full Israelite. What was he? The Sifra says that he was like his father—that is, an Egyptian (C); that he was just like (or, in an alternative reading, was)[18] a *mamzer* (D); and that he was a convert (E). How these three suggestions cohere is not clear. Many medieval exegetes explain that "at that moment" (D) means before the revelation at Mount Sinai, and this explanation is the simplest way to understand the passage.[19] The Sifra, like the Mishnah, presumes that the

17. Emor parashah 14.1 104c.

18. "He was like a *mamzer*" (*hu hayah kemamzer*) is the reading of most printed editions and Codex Vatican Assemani 66 p. 465, ed. Finkelstein. However, Midrash HaGadol on Leviticus p. 673, ed. Steinsaltz, R. Abraham ben David and R. Samson of Sens in their commentaries on the Sifra, and some other testimonia read: "he was a *mamzer*" (*hu hayah mamzer*).

19. The Sifra frequently distinguishes between the periods before and after the revelation at Mount Sinai. See, for example, Sifra on Lev. 13:2 (Nega'im pereq 1.1 59d–60a),

offspring of a Jewish mother and a gentile father is a *mamzer,* but "at that moment"—that is, before the revelation at Mount Sinai—this law was not yet in effect so that he was not a *mamzer* although he was "just like" a *mamzer* (D). Before the revelation at Mount Sinai, he was an Egyptian like his father (C) and had to convert in order to remain in the community (E). Had the blasphemer been born after the revelation at Mount Sinai instead of before it, he would have had the status of a *mamzer,* and conversion would have been completely irrelevant to his situation. (And he still would not have been able to pitch his tent with the tribe of Dan!) Here, then, is the same ruling as that of Benjamin b. Ashtor: the son of a native Jewish mother and a gentile father is a gentile like his father and requires conversion in order to be admitted into the community. For the Sifra, however, this ruling was applicable only in the period before the Sinaitic revelation.[20]

Another passage in the Sifra may reflect the same ruling. Leviticus 17:10 reads: *And if any man of the house of Israel or of the strangers who reside among them partakes of any blood, I will set my face against that person* . . . The Sifra comments as follows:

A. *Israel*—these are (male) Israel(ites).

B. *strangers*—these are (male) converts.

C. *who reside*—to include the wives of converts.

D. *among them*—to include women and slaves.

E. If so (i.e., if the scriptural law applies only to Israelites, converts, and slaves), why does it say *if any man* (which would seem to include even non-Israelites)?

Lev. 13:18 (Nega'im pereq 6.6 64c), and Lev. 13:24 (Nega'im pereq 7.4 65a). See chapter 9 above, note 20.

20. For a different explanation of the Sifra (the passage is a conflation of two contradictory statements) see Francus, "Status" 100–101. My explanation is based on the commentary of Rabbenu Hezqiya b. Manoah (known as Hizquni) on Lev. 24:10; see p. 410 in Chavel's edition. In his commentary on Leviticus, Nahmanides (vol. 2, pp. 162–163 ed. Chavel) cites and rejects this explanation, but his own is more difficult ("he converted" means "he stood at the foot of Mount Sinai with the Israelites"—an implausible extension of the word *converted*). The same explanation is advanced by the Tosafist commentary *Hadar Zeqenim;* see too *Moshav Zeqenim* (ed. S. Sasoon, p. 396), and R. Hayyim Paltiel. In their commentaries on the Sifra, R. Abraham b. David and R. Samson of Sens argue that the subject of "he converted" is not the blasphemer but his Egyptian father; this too is difficult. Weiss, the editor of the Sifra, argues that "even though at that moment there were no *mamzerim*" means that the Israelites were chaste and that this blasphemer was the only *mamzer* in their midst, but this explanation stumbles on the preposition in the phrase "he was like a *mamzer*" (which I think is the correct reading). Rabbenu Hillel wisely comments on D, "the meaning of this is not clear to me." The end of T. Eduyyot refers to Lev. 24:10, but the text is corrupt.

F. R. Eleazar said in the name of R. Simeon,

G. to include the offspring of a daughter of Israel by a gentile or a slave.[21]

This passage well illustrates a common exegetical strategy in the Sifra. A verse specifies that its law is to apply to "Israel," and yet also specifies that its law is to apply to "any man" (or "any person"), which would seem to include even non-Israelites. How is this tension in the verse to be resolved? The standard answer in the Sifra is that the phrase "any man" broadens the scope of the law to include some category of persons who otherwise would not have been included. Exegesis of this sort (with numerous variations) occurs dozens of times in the Sifra. The specific formulation represented here in A–E recurs verbatim in four other Sifra passages. In all five passages the Sifra understands the biblical phrase *the house of Israel or the strangers who reside among them* to refer to male Israelites, male converts and their wives, female Israelites, and (male and female) slaves.[22] Of the other four passages, the inclusive phrase "any man" (*ish ish*) in two cases is said to include certain actions that might have been thought to have been excluded by the scriptural laws (both concerning the slaughter of animals outside the sanctuary), and in two cases is said to include gentiles (to render gentiles liable for punishment if they engage in illicit sexual acts, and to allow gentiles to bring voluntary offerings to the central sanctuary).[23] In the fifth passage, R. Eleazar said in the name of R. Simeon that the phrase "any man" comes to teach us that the prohibition of eating blood is binding even on the offspring of an Israelite woman ("a daughter of Israel") by a gentile or a slave.

The commentators on the Sifra explain R. Eleazar's comment as follows: gentiles may eat blood, because the scriptural prohibition does not apply to them, but the offspring of an Israelite woman may not eat blood, because the prohibition does apply to them. In consonance with the rabbinic matrilineal principle, the offspring of an Israelite mother

---

21. Sifra, *aharei*, parasha 8.1–2 84c (Codex Assemani 66, p. 363). The correct reading in the final clause is *lehavi velad bat yisrael min hagoy umin ha'eved;* this is the reading of Codex Assemani, R. Hillel, and Weiss in his note on the text.

22. The absence of female converts is striking, as if the Sifra knows nothing of non-marital conversion for women. The phrase *neshei hagērim* must be translated as "wives of converts," not "female converts"; see Sifra on Lev. 18:26, *aharei*, pereq 13:18, 86c (Codex Assemani 390).

23. Slaughter: Sifra, *aharei*, pereq 10, 84a (Codex Assemani 361), and pereq 11, 84c (Codex Assemani 364). Gentiles: *qedoshim*, parashah 10, 91b (Codex Assemani 409); *emor*, parashah 7, 98a (Codex Assemani 434).

and a gentile or slave father is Israelite, and the phrase "any man" comes to extend the scriptural prohibition to such offspring. This explanation is possible but difficult, for if R. Eleazar accepts the rabbinic matrilineal principle, why is a special phrase needed to include the offspring of an Israelite mother? We already know that the offspring of an Israelite mother is Israelite! And if special inclusion is needed because such offspring has the status of *mamzer* (see above), R. Eleazar should have said simply that the phrase comes to include even *mamzerim*. Perhaps, then, R. Eleazar in the name of R. Simeon does not accept the matrilineal principle; perhaps he believes that the offspring of an Israelite mother and a gentile father is a *gentile*. The force of his remark is that although most gentiles are not bound by the prohibition of eating blood, a gentile who has a Jewish mother, is.[24] Slight support for this suggestion comes from the fact that in the four parallel passages in the Sifra, when the phrase "any man" is said to include a category of persons, those persons are gentiles; when the phrase is said to include a category of actions, those actions are performed by Israelites. The offspring of an Israelite mother and a gentile father is a category of persons, and perhaps the Sifra intends us to see those persons as gentiles.

As far as I have been able to determine, the Mishnah exegesis of Benjamin b. Ashtor, the Sifra on Leviticus 24:10, and the Sifra on Leviticus 17:10 are the only rabbinic passages of antiquity that can be construed as ruling that the offspring of a Jewish mother and a gentile father is a gentile. However, some medieval and early modern rabbinic authorities revived (or independently arrived at) this ruling, at least for the purposes of talmudic exegesis if not for the purposes of legal practice. According to one of the opinions advanced in the Talmud, as I just mentioned, the offspring of a Jewish mother and a gentile father is *kasher* or "fit"—that is, a Jew of unimpaired status. An anonymous Tosafist (one of the commentators on the Talmud who lived in northern France in the twelfth and thirteenth centuries) suggests that *kasher* simply means "not a *mamzer*." According to this interpretation the Talmud means that the offspring of a Jewish mother and a gentile father is a *gentile* who, after conversion, will be a *kasher* Jew (i.e., a Jew able to marry other Jews) and not a *mamzer* (i.e., a Jew unable to marry other Jews). In his gloss on this Tosafot, R. Samuel Eliezer Edels of Poland (known as the Maharsha; 1555–1631) is troubled by this interpretation and re-

---

24. I refrain from speculating on the connection between Israelite motherhood and the prohibition of eating blood.

writes the Tosafot in such a way that the interpretation disappears.[25] But the Maharsha's troubles are not over, because he also claims to find this unsettling interpretation in a comment of Rashi (R. Solomon b. Isaac of Troyes; 1040–1105) on another talmudic passage.[26]

Numerous jurists and talmudic exegetes of the subsequent generations grappled with the problematic Tosafot, the ambiguous Rashi, and indeed with the larger question of whether the offspring of a Jewish mother and a non-Jewish father was a Jew by birth. Most jurists decided the legal question affirmatively (the offspring is a Jew by birth), but some remained ambivalent or undecided.[27] A novel thesis was advanced by R. Yom-Tov Algaze of Jerusalem (1727–1802), following a suggestion of R. Solomon Luria of Poland (known as the Maharshal; 1510–1573). When the Talmud says that the offspring of a gentile father and a Jewish mother is *kasher*, the Talmud means that the offspring is a Jew, but this ruling obtains only if the child was raised by his/her mother and

25. Tosafot Qiddushin 75b s.v. *"verabbi yishmael"* with the Maharsha ad loc. See too the *Pisqei Tosafot* (quoted by the Maharsha). This interpretation also seems to appear in Tosafot Yevamot 16b s.v. *"amora'ei"*; see the Maharsha ad loc. Elsewhere the Tosafot explain that *kasher* means "not a *mamzer*," and that the gentile status of the father prevents the offspring from becoming a *mamzer*; see Tosafot Yevamot 23a s.v. *"qasavar"* and Bekhorot 47a s.v. *"velo teima."* But these Tosafot do not take the next logical step; that is, they do not state that the gentile status of the father determines that the offspring too is a gentile.

26. Rashi Qiddushin 68b s.v. *"leima qasavar."* The Maharsha's reading of Rashi is not convincing. Rashi is echoing a geonic discussion like that of the *Sheiltot* 25 (vol. 1, p. 161 ed. Mirsky): the offspring of a gentile father and a Jewish mother follows either the father or the mother. If the former, the offspring is a gentile; if the latter, the offspring is a Jew but because the union between the mother and the father was sinful, the question arises whether the offspring is *kasher* or a *mamzer*. The Maharsha takes Rashi to imply that the offspring is *kasher* in that it is a gentile like its father and can convert, but while this reading is possible it is certainly unnecessary and probably wrong. Similarly R. Isaac Nuñez (Belmonte; eighteenth century), *Sha'ar hamelekh* (Jerusalem, 1911; reprint, 1962) 59a–b (on Maimonides, *Hilkhot Issurei Biah* 15:3), rejects the Maharsha's reading of Rashi. See too the discussion of R. Noah Hayyim Berlin (1737–1802), *Atzei Arazim* (1789; reprint, Jerusalem, 1974) 14b–15a (on *Shulhan Arukh, Even HaEzer* 4:19). Rashi clearly and explicitly explains *kasher* correctly in Bekhorot 47a. Regarding the Rashi on Yevamot 23a, see below. Aptowitzer, "Spuren des Matriarchats" 268, follows the Maharsha.

27. See R. Solomon Kluger (1783–1869), *Hokhmat Shelomo* on *Shulhan Arukh, Even HaEzer* 4:19 (R. Kluger suggests that if the mother was a married woman, the offspring requires conversion, but if the mother was unmarried, the offspring does not); R. Akiva Eger (1761–1837) on *Shulhan Arukh, Yoreh De'ah* 266:12; R. Joshua Volk, *Derishah* and *Perishah* on *Tur, Yoreh De'ah* 266 end; and others. For discussions of the Rashi and Tosafot, see the *Sha'ar Hamelekh* and *Atzei Arazim* cited in the previous note; see too R. Meir Simhah Kahan (1845–1926), *Or Same'ah* on Maimonides, *Issurei Biah* 15:3, and R. Ovadia Yosef, *Yabia Omer*, vol. 2, Even HaEzer 4, p. 218.

given a Jewish identity. If, however, the offspring was raised by the gentile father and not given a Jewish identity, the offspring is reckoned a gentile who requires conversion before being able to become a Jew.[28] This position, which found support among some exegetes and jurists of the eighteenth, nineteenth and twentieth centuries, adumbrates that of contemporary Reform, which assigns upbringing and identity an equal place with lineage in the determination of the status of the offspring of intermarriage.[29]

In sum: within rabbinic tradition the matrilineal principle was occasionally susceptible to contradiction or modification. According to some authorities the offspring of a Jewish mother and a gentile father is a gentile. It is striking that none of these authorities cited Benjamin b. Ashtor for support. Whatever it was that Benjamin meant in his Mishnah exegesis, later rabbinic tradition did not see him as an advocate of the gentile status of the offspring of a Jewish mother and a non-Jewish father.[30] This argument is no proof, of course, that Benjamin was not such an advocate.

FOURTH EXPLANATION

Benjamin b. Ashtor argues that clauses D and G of the Mishnah refer to the offspring of a native Jewish mother and a gentile

---

28. R. Yom-Tov Algaze, sec. 65 of the commentary on Nahmanides, *Laws of the First Born* (in the Vilna edition of the Talmud, p. 56a of Nahmanides, *Hilkhot Bekhorot,* an appendix to tractate Bekhorot). R. Algaze cites for support the novellas of R. Solomon Luria on Yevamot 16b. R. Algaze seems not to know the Maharsha from Qiddushin cited above, although he cites—and rebuts—the Maharsha in Yevamot where the Maharsha rebuts the Maharshal.

29. For contemporary rabbinic discussions of R. Algaze's position, see Shelomo Yaluz, "In the Matter of Conversion" (in Hebrew), *Noam: A Forum for the Clarification of Contemporary Halakhic Problems* 14 (1971) 282–295 (a request to the chief rabbinate of Israel to consider R. Algaze's position as normative law); J. David Bleich, "Survey of Recent Halakhic Periodical Literature," *Tradition,* fall 1977, 79–91, at 85–88; idem, "The Patrilineal Principle: The Crucial Concern," *Tradition* 34, no.1 (winter 1985) 14–19, at 16.

30. The *Sha'ar Hamelekh* cites for support the Sifra on Lev. 24:10 but not our Yerushalmi. None of the medieval or modern authorities cited in the preceding notes adduces Benjamin for support. It is difficult to argue that the medievals did not know this Yerushalmi; the Roqeah knew it (see below) and numerous authorities (including the Tosafists) cite and discuss the concluding sections of this Yerushalmi (see the second part of this chapter). Thus medieval Talmudists knew this Yerushalmi but did not cite it in this connection.

father. This offspring, in accordance with the matrilineal principle, is a Jew by birth, but is deemed to possess the legal status of a convert. This Jew has a non-Jewish father and thus is more like a convert than a native Jew. Native Jews inherit their status (priest, Levite, Israelite) from their fathers, but this Jew, like a convert, does not. Native Jewish women (whether the daughters of priests, Levites, or Israelites) are permitted to be married to priests, but this Jew, like a female convert, may not be married to a priest.[31] Thus when Benjamin says that the mishnaic phrase *but if his mother was of Israel* refers to the offspring of a native mother and a gentile father, he does not mean that the offspring really is a convert. Rather, he means that the term *gēr* can be applied to this offspring, because the offspring suffers from the same legal and social disabilities that affect the convert.

This explanation of Benjamin's exegesis seems to be followed by R. Eleazar of Worms (1160–1237), who, in his paraphrase of the Yerushalmi, remarks that the offspring of a Jewish mother and a gentile father "is itself a first-generation convert."[32] Independently of the Yerushalmi and Benjamin b. Ashtor, some medieval exegetes of the Talmud commented on the similarity of the convert to the offspring of a Jewish mother and gentile father. The *Halakhot Gedolot*, a Babylonian work of the ninth or tenth century, explains the conclusion of the discussion in B. Yevamot 45b as follows:

(If) a gentile or slave had intercourse with an Israelite woman, the offspring is *kasher* (i.e., fit to marry other Jews), whether the woman is unmarried or married. However, if the offspring is a male, he is an Israelite of good standing and is fit (to marry) the daughter of a priest; for even if he is reckoned only a convert, the law is established that a convert is fit (to marry the daughter of a priest); if the offspring is female, she is permitted (to be married) to a Levite or an Israelite, but is prohibited to a priest.[33]

---

31. That the (female) offspring of an Israelite mother and a gentile father may not be married to a priest is one of the positions advanced in Y. Qiddushin 3:14 64c–d and B. Yevamot 45a. See the analysis of Francus, "Status" 102–103 and 105–107. A female convert may not be married to a priest: see M. Yevamot 6:5 and M. Qiddushin 4:1.

32. *havelad atzmo gēr rishon.* See *Sefer Roqeah* sec. 331. The text is substantively the same in the first edition (Fano, 1505) as in the vulgate editions (Jerusalem, 1967, p. 229). It is possible that the Roqeah means that the offspring is a gentile who requires conversion (see my third explanation), but this is not what he says.

33. See *Halakhot Gedolot*: ed. Warsaw 64b; ed. Hildesheimer (1888) 308; ed. Hildesheimer (1980) 2.130. For parallels see *Otzar HaGeonim: Yevamot,* ed. B. M. Lewin 106, secs. 238 and 240. "For even if he is reckoned only a convert" translates *velo yehei ela gēr.*

Similarly, Rashi on B. Yevamot 23a explains that *kasher* means that the offspring is just like a convert[34]—precisely the view of Benjamin b. Ashtor.

Israelite Fathers and the Inequality of the Convert

Let us turn now from mothers to fathers and return to the Mishnah. M. Bikkurim 1:4–5 clearly assumes that converts are Jews. Like other Jews they are obligated to bring first fruits to the temple (B) and to pray, whether by themselves (E) or in synagogue with the community (F). They are members of the matrimonial congregation of Israel (J); that is, they may marry and be married to other Jews. But the Mishnah's validation of conversion is offset by its assertion of the legal inferiority of the convert. Other Jews recite the Deuteronomic declaration upon presenting their first fruits, but converts may not. Other Jews say "God of our fathers" in their prayers, but converts may not. Other Jews may give their daughters in marriage to priests, but converts may not. According to the Mishnah only native Jews have Abraham, Isaac, Jacob, and Jacob's twelve sons as their "fathers." The fact that a gentile has changed religious allegiance and now observes the commandments of the Torah does not change the fact that a convert does not have Jewish ancestry. Converts are members of the Jewish community, but their unconverted ancestors are not. A convert's past cannot be rewritten or wished away. Therefore, the Mishnah concludes, converts may not recite liturgical references to "our fathers" and are excluded by marriage laws that require native extraction. Converts constitute a separate lineage or "caste" within Jewish society because they lack Jewish "fathers."

As we have seen in chapter 7 above, at the conclusion of the rabbinic conversion ceremony, converts to Judaism are declared to be Jews "in all respects."[35] Like native Jews they are obligated to observe all the

---

34. Rashi on Yevamot 23a, s.v. *"veli nireh."* The Tosafot s.v. *"qasavar"* apparently did not have this comment in their texts of Rashi, and as a result this comment is deleted by R. Joel Sirkes and R. Solomon Luria in their marginal notes ad loc. However, all manuscripts and printed editions of Rashi on Yevamot include this comment, and it is cited in Rashi's name by R. Isaac b. Moses of Vienna, *Or Zarua* pt. 1, sec. 607. See *The Babylonian Talmud with Variant Readings: Yevamot,* ed. Abraham Liss, 3 vols. (Jerusalem: Institute for the Complete Israeli Talmud, 1983), 1.261 n. 56. This Rashi is misinterpreted by Aptowitzer, "Spuren des Matriarchats" 268 n. 19.

35. B. Yevamot 47b.

commandments of the Torah.[36] In spite of this ringing declaration, rabbinic law—and not just M. Bikkurim—ascribes legal inferiority to the convert on the basis of his failure to have Israelite "fathers." The Mishnah has many passages that demonstrate that, in a legal system that puts much value on pedigree and the purity of genealogical descent, converts, the descendants of gentiles, rank below natives. As a result of their base descent, converts are distinctly inferior to the mass of Israelites in matrimonial law: they may not contract certain marriages permitted to lay Israelites and they may contract certain marriages prohibited to lay Israelites. Because converts do not have Israelite fathers, they also do not have a share in the land, and as a result may not recite the standard liturgical formula that all Israelites recite in years three and six of the tithing cycle. They may not serve as judges in capital cases, and are "preceded" by native Jews, even those of low standing. Converts are not only the descendants of gentiles, they were once gentiles themselves, and this fact too had legal implications. Female converts are presumed not to be virgins at conversion, and therefore their marriage contracts are worth less than those of native women.[37]

The ambiguous status of the convert is not an innovation of rabbinic law. Second-temple texts show that even in pre-rabbinic times, especially in circles infused with priestly conceptions of the peoplehood of Israel, converts were sometimes deemed inferior to the native born. To the extent that Jewish identity is based on belief and practice, a convert can become fully equal with the native, because a convert can affirm Jewish beliefs and observe Jewish practices. To the extent that Jewish identity is based on birth and lineage, however, a convert is not, and can never be, fully equal with the native, because a convert was born a non-Jew and has non-Jewish lineage. Unlike native Jews, converts have non-Jewish fathers and mothers, and this fact cannot be effaced by conversion. Religion (or "culture") can be changed, but birth cannot. Thus gentiles can change their religion, convert to Judaism, and join the community of Israel, but within that community they remain legally and socially distinct, because they are not absolutely equal with natives under the law and because their foreign extraction prevents them from becoming true "insiders." They become "insiders" only when they have

36. Mekhilta on Exod. 12:49, Pisha 15 (1.128L; 57H–R).
37. Converts rank below natives: M. Qiddushin 4:1 and M. Horayot 3:8. Marriages: M. Yevamot 8:2 and M. Qiddushin 4:1–7. Tithing formula: M. Ma'aser Sheni 5:14. Judges: M. Horayot 1:4. "Preceded" by natives: M. Horayot 3:8. Virgins: M. Yevamot 6:5, Ketuvot 1:2–4, 3:1–2. See my "On Murdering or Injuring a Proselyte" (forthcoming).

Israelite (Jewish) blood—either an Israelite mother, an Israelite father, or "our fathers." [38]

An excellent parallel to these rabbinic ideas is provided by classical Athens. In the classical Greek *polis* all citizens were linked by kinship; in the *polis*

> . . . citizenship goes by descent. Membership of a society based on the principle of blood can be acquired only by birth in that society, though the society may resolve, by general consent expressed in its assembly, to "adopt" new members . . . When citizenship was thus regarded as membership of a society, based on blood and united by a common cult, it was a natural corollary that it could not easily, if at all, be extended . . . the State . . . is essentially a living group of kinsmen. The State is a family circle; and it is divided into smaller family circles, arranging itself by the principle of blood in brotherhoods and clans . . . [39]

When Athens did resolve to adopt new members, they were not always immediately equal to the native born. After the citizenship law of Pericles, Athenian archons had to present proof that they were descended on both the father's and the mother's side from three generations of citizens. This requirement effectively excluded newly enfranchised citizens from archonships.[40] An exceptional incident brought forth an exception to this rule. During the Peloponnesian war, in 427 B.C.E., 212 men escaped Plataea, a city allied with Athens and under siege by Sparta, and arrived at Athens. There, as reward for their loyalty to Athens and as recompense for the sufferings that they had endured, they were awarded Athenian citizenship by a grateful public. The Athenian assembly passed a law that stated:

> that the Plataeans be Athenians from this day forward; that they have full citizenship rights, like other Athenians; and that they have a share in all things, both sacred and profane, in which the Athenians have a share; except for any hereditary priesthood or ceremony, nor of the nine archonships. But the descendants of these (Plataeans) may have a share (in these things).

38. See chapter 5 above, text at notes 70–75. On the tension between "ethnicity" and "religion" in rabbinic Judaism, see Porton, *Stranger* 1–8 and 211–215.

39. Ernest Barker, *Greek Political Theory: Plato and His Predecessors* (London: Methuen, 1961; originally published in 1918) 29.

40. Aristotle, *Constitution of the Athenians* 55.3. On the citizenship law of Pericles, see chapter 9 above, notes 15 and 19. By the time of Marcus Aurelius the three-generation rule no longer meant three generations of citizens on both sides but three generations of non-servile birth on the paternal side; see Oliver, *Marcus Aurelius* 45–57.

The Plataeans are to be Athenians and to have the same rights as all other Athenians, except that their foreign birth disqualifies them from all functions that are hereditary (i.e., based on birth) and from the most prominent posts of government. The descendants of these Plataeans, however, do not share the legal disabilities of their parents. Our source for this decree, a fourth-century Athenian orator, explains this last clause as follows: descendants of these Plataeans may attain priesthoods and archonships provided that *they have been born of a native Athenian woman married according to the law.*[41] Here, then, is a remarkable parallel to M. Bikkurim 1:4–5. First-generation Athenian "converts" are Athenian citizens in all respects except that they are barred from rituals that require Athenian birth ("fathers" in rabbinic terminology); however, second-generation Athenian citizens, the offspring of Plataean fathers and Athenian mothers, do have Athenian birth ("fathers") and therefore may participate fully in Athenian civic and religious life. I am not suggesting, of course, that the rabbis knew Athenian history or somehow were influenced by the work of an Athenian orator; the Athenian example simply helps to illuminate the logic that is at work in M. Bikkurim 1:4–5.[42]

THE YERUSHALMI

According to our Mishnah, if a convert has an Israelite mother (or, *a fortiori*, an Israelite father) he may recite prayers containing the phrase "God of our fathers." The Yerushalmi comments (this follows immediately upon the passage cited above):

S. R. Zeriqan said: R. Ze'ira posed a question:

T. Does he (the convert when reciting the verse *the land which God has sworn to our fathers to give us*) not refer to Abraham, Isaac, and Jacob?

41. Apollodorus [Demosthenes], *Against Neaera* 59.104 (decree), 92 and 106 (explanation). For text and discussion see Osborne, *Naturalization* 1.28 and 2.11–16; Christopher Carey, *Apollodorus: Against Neaira [Demosthenes] 59* (Westminster: Aris and Phillips, 1992). I am grateful to my colleague Alan Boegehold for discussing this text with me and assisting me in translating it.

42. For another illuminating parallel, cf. Bulliet, *Conversion* 41: ". . . non-Arabs who converted to Islam were obliged [in the first century of Islam's growth] to become *mawali*, that is, fictive members of Arab tribes. Only thus could they obtain social identity as Muslims. Yet being a *mawla* of an Arab tribe was fraught with disadvantages. *Mawali* were regarded as racially inferior by many Arabs because they did not truly share the pure blood lineage that was the focus of tribal honor and loyalty. They were discriminated against in marriage, denied inclusion on the military payroll, and made to suffer revilement and social slights."

And were Abraham, Isaac, and Jacob their fathers? Did not God swear (only) to the males? Or (did God swear) to the females? (Of course not. How then does having an Israelite mother allow a convert to say recite the declaration? The question remains unanswered.)

U. It was taught in the name of R. Judah:

V. A first-generation convert brings and recites.

W. What is the reason? (Because God said to Abraham) *for I have made you the father of a multitude of nations* (Gen. 17:5). In the past you were a father to Aram, but now, henceforth, you are a father to all the nations.

X. R. Joshua b. Levi says:

Y. The law follows R. Judah.

Z. A case came before R. Abbahu and he rendered a decision according to R. Judah.

R. Zeriqan in the name of R. Ze'ira, each of them a Palestinian *amora* of the third generation, asks a string of questions directed against the Mishnah. How does having an Israelite mother allow a convert to recite the Deuteronomic declaration *the land which God has sworn to our fathers to give us?* The fathers to whom Scripture refers are Abraham, Isaac, and Jacob, and God swore to give the land to their male descendants. Thus converts are excluded because they are not descendants of the three patriarchs, and the offspring of Israelite mothers ought to be excluded because the land was promised only to men. How then does having an Israelite mother help the convert? This question is left unanswered, perhaps because it so weak: anyone who has an Israelite mother also has, by definition, Israelite fathers, male ancestors who are heirs to the promised land.[43] R. Zeriqan in the name of R. Ze'ira has confused the absence of an Israelite father (in the singular) with the absence of Israelite fathers (in the plural).

The Yerushalmi concludes with a citation of R. Judah: "A first-generation convert brings and recites." W explains that all converts, even first-generation converts, have an Israelite father in Abraham. (R. Ze'ira would probably object that both the scriptural and the liturgical phrases mention *fathers* in the plural, but W is content with one father alone.) R. Judah accepts the Mishnah's logic that all those who recite the Deuteronomic declaration must have "our fathers," but denies the Mishnah's assumption that converts fail to meet this criterion. According to R. Judah converts do, in fact, have "our fathers"—their Jewish

---

43. See the commentary of R. Samson of Sens on the Mishnah.

father is Abraham. And how is Abraham a father to all converts? Because he is a father to all gentiles. When God changed Abram's name to Abraham, he said to the patriarch *for I have made you the father of a multitude of nations* (Gen. 17:5). The sentence is expounded midrashically: "In the past you were a father to Aram (Abram = *av aram*), but now, henceforth, you are a father to all the nations (Abraham = *av hamon*)." The original setting of this exegesis is a long passage in the Tosefta whose goal is to show how the name changes of the patriarchs exemplify the principle that the new obliterates the old. Abraham replaces Abram, Sarah replaces Sarai, and so forth. Someone, probably an anonymous editor, extracted clause W from that discussion, where it recurs almost verbatim, and transferred it here. Thus a piece of fanciful exegesis with homiletical intent—what of the gentiles who descend not from Abraham but from Noah?—has become an important proof in a legal discussion. Converts may say "our fathers" because Abraham is a (the?) father to all gentiles—or, in the language of the Tosefta, "father to the whole entire world." [44]

R. Judah's statement, a direct and unambiguous rejection of the Mishnah's ruling, is endorsed by R. Joshua b. Levi, a Palestinian *amora* of the first generation, and by R. Abbahu, a Palestinian amora of the third generation. R. Joshua b. Levi declared that the law ought to follow R. Judah (X–Y), and R. Abbahu decided an actual case in accord with the view of R. Judah (Z). In the mid third century C.E., when R. Abbahu lived, there was no temple in Jerusalem and no one brought first fruits and recited the declaration. If R. Abbahu decided a case in accordance with the statement of R. Judah, it must have been a case involving the right of a convert to say "God of our fathers" while praying. [45] R. Abbahu ruled that the convert may indeed say "God of our fathers," and adduced R. Judah for support. Thus R. Abbahu extended R. Judah's ruling from first fruits to prayer.

Whereas the Yerushalmi rejects the Mishnah, the Bavli accepts it. There is no Bavli tractate on Bikkurim, but in another context in an-

---

44. T. Berakhot 1:12 5L (and parallels). The idea that the fatherhood of Abraham establishes kinship between the Jews and the other peoples of the world is attested already in the second century B.C.E.; see 1 Macc. 12:21 and Josephus, *AJ* 12.226 (kinship of Spartans and Jews through common descent from Abraham).

45. Perhaps a convert asked R. Abbahu whether he could recite "God of our fathers" in his prayers, and R. Abbahu replied in the affirmative. Alternatively, a native Israelite complained to R. Abbahu that he overheard some converts saying "God of our fathers" (cf. the family of b. Ashtor, cited above), and R. Abbahu upheld them.

other tractate the Bavli cites our Mishnah as authoritative and offers no reason or source to reverse it.[46] Thus the debate between the Mishnah and the Yerushalmi is also a debate between the Bavli and the Yerushalmi. There were a fair number of converts in rabbinic circles in antiquity in both the land of Israel and Babylonia,[47] so this debate may have had practical consequences. This plausible assumption cannot be confirmed, however. The case cited by the Yerushalmi in Z is the only extant rabbinic evidence showing how converts were instructed to behave when praying, and the case cited in N (the house of bar Ashtor) is the only extant rabbinic evidence showing how converts actually behaved when praying.

THE DEBATE BETWEEN THE MISHNAH AND THE YERUSHALMI IN MEDIEVAL JUDAISM

The *Halakhot Gedolot,* a compendium of rabbinic law written in Babylonia in the ninth century, is the first post-talmudic work to cite the Mishnah under discussion here. It is striking, however, that this citation does not occur in the section of the work dealing with converts and the laws of conversion, but in a chapter containing miscellaneous rules about the temple and temple rituals.[48] This author, then, under the influence of the Bavli, accepts the Mishnah and ignores the Yerushalmi, but apparently does not realize that the ruling concerning

46. B. Makkot 19a (citing the paragraph on the Deuteronomic declaration concerning first fruits). Sifrei 299 p. 318F on Deut. 26:3 also supports the Mishnah.

47. Bamberger, *Proselytism* 221–266; Isaiah M. Gafni, *The Jews of Babylonia in the Talmudic Era* (in Hebrew) (Jerusalem: Shazar Center, 1990) 137–148.

48. *Halakhot Gedolot, Hilkhot Menahot,* ed. Hildesheimer (1988), 3.330. A more logical home for the citation would have been in *Hilkhot Milat Gērim,* vol. 1, pp. 216–223. Some Ashkenazic sources of the twelfth and thirteenth centuries claim that the authorities of the previous generations (seventh to eleventh centuries) followed the position of the Yerushalmi. R. Asher in his commentary on Mishnah Bikkurim, the anonymous author of the *Responsa and Decisions of the Sages of Germany and France,* ed. Kupfer (see note 54 below), and R. Hezekiah b. Jacob of Magdeburg (see note 61 below) claim that the *Sefer Vehizhir* endorses the Yerushalmi; the Roqeah, also cited below in note 61, says that "all the geonim" decided in accordance with R. Judah in the Yerushalmi. I do not know how to evaluate these claims. The extant portion of *Sefer Vehizhir* nowhere mentions the view of either the Yerushalmi or the Mishnah (see Freimann's edition, 1873, p. vi). The Roqeah does not name any of the geonim who allegedly followed the Yerushalmi, and if the word *geonim* has its usual meaning of "masters of the talmudic academies in Babylonia," the claim seems inherently implausible (why would Babylonian geonim follow the Yerushalmi rather than the Bavli?). If the word means simply "rabbis of olden times," the claim is too vague to be helpful.

"our fathers" affects converts even in the absence of the temple. How converts behaved in ninth-century Babylonia—and they probably were very few[49]—we do not know.

The debate between the Yerushalmi and the Mishnah was revived in the latter part of the twelfth century. Here are excerpts from three reports of actual cases in which a convert's right to say "our fathers" was challenged. The reports derive from three of the major Jewish communities of the time: Egypt, Germany, and northern France.

The fullest and most detailed report is a letter of Maimonides (1135–1204) to Obadiah the Convert. Maimonides wrote the letter from Cairo, but Obadiah's origins and location are unknown.[50]

You ask me if you too are allowed to say in the blessings and prayers you offer alone or in the congregation: "Our God and God of our fathers,"[51] "Who has sanctified us through his commandments and commanded us," "Who has separated us," "Who has chosen us," "You who have given to our fathers to inherit (a pleasant, good, and spacious land),"[52] "You who have brought us out of the land of Egypt," "You who have worked miracles to our fathers," and more of this kind.

Yes, you may say all this in the prescribed order and not change it in the least. In the same way as every Jew by birth says his blessing and prayer, you too, shall bless and pray alike, whether you are alone or pray in the congregation. The reason for this is that Abraham our Father taught the people,

---

49. In ninth-century Babylonia virtually all converts will have been emancipated slaves to whom special rules apply; see Ben Zion Wacholder, "The Halakah and the Proselyting of Slaves during the Geonic Era," *Historia Judaica* 18 (1956) 89–106.

50. In the extract that follows, I have somewhat modified the translation of Isadore Twersky, *A Maimonides Reader* (New York: Behrman House, 1972) 475–476, who in turn has somewhat modified the translation of Franz Kobler, *Letters of Jews through the Ages,* 2 vols. (reprint, Philadelphia: Jewish Publication Society, 1978) I.194–196. For the original text see *R. Moses b. Maimon: Responsa,* ed. Jehoshua Blau, 2d ed., vol. 2 (Jerusalem: R. Mass, 1986) 548–550 no. 293. See too Maimonides, *Hilkhot Bikkurim* 4:3.

51. Here and below Twersky (following Kobler) translates "'Our God' and 'God of our fathers.'" In this translation the convert's right to say "Our God" is as much an issue as his right to say "God of our fathers." I think this translation is wrong, because I see no evidence that converts were ever prohibited from saying "our God." The words "our God" are simply the first part of the phrase "our God and God of our fathers." The only text I know that might suggest that converts should not say "our God" is Mekhilta on Exod. 23:19, Kaspa 20 (3.187 L; 335 HR), which states that the phrase *the Lord your God* excludes converts and slaves, but surely this text is irrelevant to Maimonides.

52. Here and below this phrase is mistranslated by Twersky (following Kobler). It is a quote from the second paragraph of the Grace after Meals. The Maimonidean version differs slightly from the one in use today; see "The Oxford Manuscript of Maimonides' Book of Prayer," in Daniel Goldschmidt, *On Jewish Liturgy: Essays on Prayer and Religious Poetry* (Jerusalem: Magnes, 1978) 215–216.

opened their minds, and revealed to them the true faith and the unity of God . . . Ever since then whoever converts and confesses the unity of the Divine Name, as it is prescribed in the Torah, is counted among the disciples of Abraham our Father . . .

In the same way as he converted his contemporaries through his words and teaching, he converts future generations through the testament he left to his children and household after him. Thus Abraham our Father, peace be with him, is the father of his pious posterity who keeps his ways, and the father of his disciples and of all converts who adopt Judaism.

Therefore you shall pray "Our God and God of our fathers," because Abraham, peace be with him, is your father. And you shall say "You who have given to our fathers to inherit (a pleasant, good, and spacious land)," for the land has been given to Abraham . . . As to the words "You who have brought us out of the land of Egypt" or "You have done miracles to our fathers"—these you may change, if you will, and say, "You who have brought Israel out of the land of Egypt" and "You who have done miracles to Israel." If, however, you do not change them, it is no transgression, because since you have come under the wings of the divine presence and confessed the Lord, no difference exists between you and us, and all miracles done to us have been done as it were to us and to you . . . There is no difference whatever between you and us. You shall certainly say the blessing, "Who has chosen us," "Who has given us (his Torah)," "Who has taken us for his own" and "Who has separated us": for the Creator, may He be extolled, has indeed chosen you and separated you from the nations and given you the Torah . . .

The letter concludes with a citation of the Yerushalmi to prove that a convert may say "God of our fathers."

The second report is transmitted by R. Eliezer b. Joel Halevi (known as the Ravyah; ca. 1140–ca. 1225) in the name of his father. The incident that concerns us took place in Würzburg.

A spirit came forth from God and rested on the heart of this man, R. Abraham b. Abraham our Father. And when the spirit rested on him he drew near to the work of God to seek out the Lord and to study scripture and the holy language. He dwelt with us for a long time and was meek and upright, "a dweller of tents." One day I, who am signed below, found him sitting and copying a Pentateuch from a book belonging to (Christian) priests and unfit for use. I said to him, "What is this that you have?" He replied and said to me, "I know the language of (Christian) priests but I do not know the holy language. It (the book of the Christian priests) is like a commentary (on scripture) for me. Furthermore, the sages of Speyer lent me books belonging to (Christian) priests in order to copy them and have not interfered with me. If this is wrong in your eyes, I shall cease and desist." I replied to him, "Know that this action in my opinion is wrong." . . . (R. Joel discusses his decision and concludes that it was wrong, because in reality the convert's action was not prohibited.) . . .

Furthermore, he told me that in Würzburg he was prevented from praying as a cantor. It seems to me that they (who prevented him) went diving in mighty waters and brought up clay in their hands, for even though we learn in the Mishnah (here R. Joel quotes the Mishnah cited above) . . . nevertheless in the Yerushalmi it states (here R. Joel quotes the Yerushalmi cited above) . . . and the law follows the Yerushalmi. And he (the convert R. Abraham) prevailed upon me to make my opinion public, and this I did . . .[53]

The third report comes from the school of the Tosafists, glossators on the Talmud who lived in northern France (and Germany) in the twelfth and thirteenth centuries. The authorities mentioned here are R. Jacob of Ramerupt (known as Rabbenu Tam; ca. 1100–1171) and his nephew R. Isaac of Dampierre.

It once happened that a convert was leading the assembled diners in the grace after meals, and they began to complain against him: how could he say "You who have given to our fathers to inherit a pleasant, good, and spacious land"? [The case came before Rabbenu Tam.] Rabbenu Tam responded (that the convert may not lead the grace after meals): we learn in tractate Bikkurim (here R. Tam quotes the Mishnah cited above) . . . But R. Isaac disagrees with this, and adduces proof from the Yerushalmi (here R. Isaac quotes the Yerushalmi cited above) . . . Converts at this time are accustomed to say "God of our fathers" in accordance with R. Judah (in the Yerushalmi) . . . (R. Tam and R. Isaac proceed to debate the correct interpretation of the Yerushalmi.)[54]

These reports show that, in certain circles throughout the medieval Jewish world, the liturgical disabilities imposed on the convert by the Mishnah not only remained in force but had been extended and strengthened. In Egypt advocates of the Mishnah sought to prohibit a convert from saying the phrase "our fathers" wherever it appears in the liturgy. In Germany and France advocates of the Mishnah prohibited a convert from leading the daily prayer (Germany) and the Grace after Meals (France), because converts and native Jews cannot use the same

53. *Sefer Ravyah,* ed. V. Aptowitzer, vol. 2, pp. 253–256, no. 549.

54. *Responsa and Decisions of the Sages of Germany and France,* ed. Efraim Kupfer (Jerusalem: Mekize Nirdamim, 1973) 101–105 no. 60. This is the fullest version of the debate between R. Tam and R. Isaac; for other versions see Tosafot Bava Batra 81a s.v. *"limutei"* and the commentary of R. Asher on M. Bikkurim 1:4.

wording when reciting these texts.[55] In Egypt, advocates of the Mishnah went even further: since converts cannot say "our fathers," they should also abstain from all liturgical first-person-plural references to the sacred history and divine election of Israel.

In response to these developments, Maimonides, R. Joel Halevi, and R. Isaac rejected not only the expansions of the mishnaic ruling but also the mishnaic ruling itself. All three appealed for support to the Yerushalmi cited above, even though in normal cases a Mishnah endorsed by the Bavli would clearly outweigh a counterposition taken by the Yerushalmi. Maimonides' statement, the fullest of the three, reveals that the debate does not turn on the technical question of whether a passage of the Yerushalmi can overturn a Mishnah. The heart of the matter is the status of the convert. The mishnaic position, especially as extended by its medieval advocates, does not allow a convert to attain a position of normalcy within the Jewish community. Every time the congregation turns to prayer, every time Jews eat together and prepare to recite the Grace after Meals, the convert is reminded of his foreign extraction and anomalous status. For Maimonides this was intolerable:[56] "Since you have come under the wings of the divine presence and confessed the Lord, no difference exists between you and us." We may presume that R. Joel Halevi and R. Isaac were motivated by similar sentiments.

The fatherhood of Abraham undergoes a subtle but significant shift between the Yerushalmi and Maimonides. According to the Yerushalmi a convert may say "God of our fathers" because Abraham is the father of all nations; all gentiles share kinship with Israel through Abraham. Thus for the Yerushalmi, no less than for the Mishnah, the claim to possess Israelite "fathers" is historical and real. The Yerushalmi argues that converts in fact have an Israelite father, just as native Jews do. According to Maimonides, however, the claim to possess Jewish "fathers" is metaphorical and mythic. Converts do not really have Jewish ancestry, but they have a Jewish father in Abraham, the archetype or "father" for all converts. As the first convert and the first Jew, Abraham shows

55. Or, as some jurists explained in the case of the Grace after Meals, because their obligation is of a lower degree than that of native Jews. The convert encountered by R. Joel Halevi clearly had some difficulty with Hebrew, and perhaps this fact, which simply highlighted his foreignness, contributed to the decision of the community of Würzburg not to allow him to officiate as a cantor.

56. It is striking, however, that even Maimonides recommended that converts not say "our fathers" when the phrase referred to the sacred history of Israel. In spite of his protestations even Maimonides cannot quite convince himself that converts really are like natives.

the way to all who would abandon false gods and recognize the true God. Since the acceptance of converts means the triumph of religion over pedigree, Maimonides wanted to interpret the fatherhood of Abraham accordingly: it is a spiritual fatherhood, not a genealogical one.[57]

These reports also show clearly that in the latter part of the twelfth century the debate between the Mishnah and the Yerushalmi had practical consequences. The eleventh and twelfth centuries witnessed a perceptible rise in the number of converts, perhaps rivaling or surpassing the number in the talmudic period. Statistics and percentages obviously are unattainable, but the extant evidence leaves the impression that the number of converts was not small and that encounters between native Jews and converts would not have been unusual either in western Europe or in Egypt.[58] As a result the status of converts became a live issue for many communities of the period. Some communal authorities appealed to the Mishnah to justify their sense that converts, whose education and background were so different from those of native Jews, were not readily assimilable into the community. In contrast, others appealed to the Yerushalmi to justify their sense that converts, who had endured hardship and danger to join the Jewish community, should be treated like natives from the moment of their conversion.[59]

Maimonides' immense authority and prestige guaranteed the victory of his position among Sefardim (the Jews of Spain and their descendants).[60] Among Ashkenazim (the Jews of central and eastern Europe),

57. That Abraham, as the first "convert" to Judaism, serves as the archetype for (or "father" to) all subsequent converts is an idea that appears implicitly in Mekhilta on Exod. 22:20, Neziqin 18 (3.140 L; 312 HR).

58. Ben Zion Wacholder, "Cases of Proselytizing in the Tosafist Responsa," *Jewish Quarterly Review* 51 (1961) 288–315 (who discusses the question of "our fathers" on p. 302), and Norman Golb, *Jewish Proselytism—A Phenomenon in the Religious History of Early Medieval Europe,* University of Cincinnati Judaic Studies Program, Rabbi Louis Feinberg Memorial Lecture(1987).

59. Ben Zion Wacholder argues that Sefardic authorities were more rigorous than Ashkenazim in testing the sincerity of potential converts but that in return they treated converts more as equals than the Ashkenazim did. See his "Proselyting in the Classical Halakah," *Historia Judaica* 20 (1958) 77–96, esp. 90–91, where he discusses our debate. This distinction does not hold up, however, as there are too many exceptions to the proposed pattern. R. Isaac is no less Ashkenazic than Rabbenu Tam; R. Judah HaLevi, who in his *Kuzari* treats converts as lower-level Jews, is no less Sefardic than Maimonides. Those authorities who (like Judah HaLevi) have an ethnic conception of Judaism will inevitably assign converts a lower place than those authorities who (like Maimonides) have a philosophical conception. (See the useful discussion by Lippman Bodoff, "Was Yehudah Halevi Racist?" *Judaism* 38, no. 2 [spring 1989] 174–184.) I do not know the ideological underpinnings of the debate between Rabbenu Tam and R. Isaac.

60. Maimonides is cited, or followed rather closely, by these Spanish scholars: Nahmanides (known as the Ramban; 1194–ca. 1270) in his novellas on Bava Batra 81a; R. Solo-

however, the question was debated for some time: the authority and prestige of R. Joel Halevi and R. Isaac were more than balanced by the authority and prestige of Rabbenu Tam.[61] By the sixteenth century, however, the position of Maimonides, R. Joel Halevi, and R. Isaac had triumphed. In the *Shulhan Arukh*, the code of Jewish law that would become canonical for virtually all Jews, Ashkenazim and Sefardim alike, the Sefardic R. Joseph Karo (1488–1575) follows Maimonides, and his Ashkenazic glossator R. Moses Isserles (ca. 1525–1572) does not demur. Converts may say "God of our fathers," and may lead the congregation in prayer and Grace after Meals.[62]

Conclusion: Israelite Mothers and Israelite Fathers

Mishnah Bikkurim 1:4–5 wonderfully illustrates some of the tensions that beset the rabbinic construction of Jewishness. The

---

mon b. Adret (known as the Rashba; 1235–1310), a disciple of Nahmanides, in his novellas on Bava Batra 81a (whose endorsement of Maimonides is much more muted than that of his teacher); R. Yom Tov b. Abraham of Seville (known as the Ritba; first half of the fourteenth century; a disciple of the Rashba), in his novellas on Makkot 19a; R. Eshtori Ha-Parhi (born c. 1280), *Kaftor vaFerah* chap. 42, pp. 566–567 ed. Luncz; R. Nissim b. Reuben of Gerona (known as the Ran; d. 1380), in his novellae on Bava Batra 81a; R. Joseph Haviva (first half of the fifteenth century), *Nimuqei Yosef* on Bava Batra 81a (in the *Nimuqei Yosef* on Nedarim 31a R. Joseph explains that converts are "children of Abraham," *benei Avraham,* but are not "the seed of Abraham," *zera Avraham*). In addition two Provençal scholars follow a Maimonidean position: R. Abraham b. Nathan of Lunel (fl. ca. 1200), *Sefer HaManhig, Hilkhot Se'udah* 17, and R. Aaron HaKohen of Lunel (fl. ca. 1300), *Orhot Hayyim,* pt. 1, *Hilkhot Tefilah* 18. The Ritba and R. Abraham of Lunel confirm R. Isaac's statement that converts are accustomed to recite "God of our fathers."

61. R. Joel Halevi is followed by R. Mordekhai b. Hillel (ca. 1240–1298), Megillah chap. 1, sec. 786. Rabbenu Tam's view is endorsed by R. Isaac b. Moses of Vienna (ca. 1190–ca. 1260), *Or Zaru'a,* pt. 1, sec. 107, p. 20a, and by R. Meir b. Barukh of Rothenburg (known as the Maharam; d. 1293) in his responsa, ed. Moses Bloch (Berlin, 1901), p. 66 no. 511; cf. too *Moshav Zeqenim* on Deut. 26:5 (ed. Sassoon, p. 512). Rabbenu Tam may have been following the view of his grandfather R. Solomon b. Isaac (known as Rashi; 1040–1105); see Rashi's commentary on Deut. 26:11. R. Isaac's view is endorsed by his disciple R. Samson b. Abraham of Sens (ca. 1150–ca. 1215) in his commentary on M. Bikkurim, and by R. Eleazar of Worms (1160–1237), *Sefer Roqeah* sec. 331. The following authorities summarize the views of Rabbenu Tam and R. Isaac but do not decide between them: R. Jacob b. Asher (ca. 1270–ca. 1343), in *Tur, Orah Hayyim* 199; R. Hezekiah b. Jacob of Magdeburg (second half of the thirteenth century) as cited by R. Israel of Krems (middle of the fourteenth century), *Hagahot Oshri* on the Rosh, Bava Batra 81a; and *Hagahot Maimoniot* on Maimonides, *Laws of Prayer* 8:11.

62. *Shulhan Arukh, Orah Hayyim* 53:19 and 199:4.

people "Israel" are linked to each other by common descent from a single set of "fathers." The category "Israel," as a concrete social reality, is first and foremost a function of pedigree, genealogy, and birth.[63] A good part of the Mishnah and of subsequent rabbinic texts concerns itself with marriage, divorce, remarriage, inheritance, and related matters. In the rabbinic communities of both the land of Israel and Babylonia, birth mattered. And yet, although the system laid great store on birth and pedigree, the rabbis did permit gentiles to enter: converts could take their place within the community of Israel, become Jews, and marry Israelites of good standing. As the rabbinic conversion ceremony declares, the convert "is like an Israelite in all respects."

Of course, a convert is not like an Israelite in all respects, because a convert is a Jew who once had been a gentile. Hence the convert is anomalous, liminal, ambiguous. Within rabbinic texts and the rabbinic community, the free adult Israelite male is the paragon of normality. Those who are not free, not adult, not Israelite, and not male constitute the Other against whom free adult Israelite males are defined and define themselves. In this binary universe, divided between slave and free, child and adult, gentile and Israelite, female and male, there are anomalous creatures who straddle or cross the boundary. Some persons once had been slaves but were emancipated; others were half-slave and half-free. Some young persons, at crucial moments in their lives, precisely straddled the border between childhood and adulthood. Hermaphrodites were both male and female, and those without sexual characteristics were neither male nor female. Converts are Jews who once had been gentiles. The Mishnah and subsequent rabbinic texts devote attention to these anomalies, who are both Us and Them, Normal and Other, at the same time.

The anomalousness of the convert is clearly illuminated not only by law but also by scriptural exegesis. Many passages in the tannaitic midrashim ask whether the scriptural term "Israel" (in such locutions as "a person of Israel," "anyone of Israel," etc.) includes converts. The standard rhetorical pattern is: "I might have thought that 'Israel' excludes converts, but Scripture adds some other phrase to imply their inclusion." In other words, the exegete imagines that it would have been a perfectly reasonable inference to conclude that verses directed to "Is-

---

63. The ethnic reality of Israel in rabbinic law is creatively suppressed by Jacob Neusner, "Was Rabbinic Judaism Really 'Ethnic'?" *Catholic Biblical Quarterly* 57 (1995) 281–305, reprinted in *Approaches to Ancient Judaism,* n.s., vol. 7, ed. Jacob Neusner, South Florida Studies in the History of Judaism, no. 110, (Atlanta: Scholars Press, 1995).

rael" exclude converts because they are not "Israel." Converts are not Israel because they lack Israelite birth; their fathers are not our fathers, their history is not our history. But, in the end, the exegete almost always concludes that the scriptural verse actually does include converts within its purview. Whether or not converts are "Israel," the scriptural laws apply to them. In only three passages in the tannaitic midrashim does the exegete conclude that the scriptural references to "Israel" definitively exclude converts from the law. The Mekhilta declares that converts are exempt from the obligation to participate in the pilgrimage festivals because converts do not belong to "all Israel." In two passages the Sifrei on Deuteronomy excludes converts from the laws of levirate marriage on the grounds that they are not "Israel."[64] Converts, then, are Israel and are not Israel.

These are the issues addressed by M. Bikkurim 1:4–5. Like all other Jews ("Israel"), converts are obligated to observe the commandments. They are obligated to bring first fruits to the temple and to pray; as Jews of good standing they may marry other members of the community. But converts are not the same as natives. Because they do not have Israelite fathers, in some contexts they suffer legal impairment and rank below natives. They are obligated to bring first fruits, but they may not recite the declaration prescribed by Deuteronomy, because they cannot truthfully declare that the fruits come from the land *which God has sworn to our fathers to give us:* God swore nothing to their fathers! Similarly, they are obligated to pray but they may not use the common phrase "God of our Fathers," because our God was not the god of their fathers. Converts may marry into the native Israelite community, but because of their blemished pedigree, the daughter of converts may not be married to a priest. The Mishnah further assumes that the status of "convert" can, in theory at least, be inherited; converts constitute a "caste" or genealogical status within the community of Israel, so that these legal impairments might affect even people who were born as Jews but who inherited their status as "converts" from their parents.

A puzzling aspect of the Mishnah is the Mishnah's thrice-repeated statement that these legal impairments disappear "if his mother was of Israel," which seems to mean "if the convert has a native Jewish

---

64. On this tendency in the tannaitic midrashim, see Bamberger, *Proselytism* 60–63. The three exceptions are Mekhilta on Exod. 23:14, Kaspa 20 (3.182–183 L; 333 HR); Sifrei 289 on Deut. 25:7 (308F); Sifrei 291 on Deut. 25:10 (310F). In his discussion of the tannaitic midrashim, Porton completely misses this important motif and these three important exceptions; see Porton, *Stranger* 51–70 (the motif is briefly noticed on p. 61).

mother." The requirement of "fathers" can be met if the convert has an Israelite mother; motherhood is sufficiently powerful to remove the blot of convert and to bestow "fathers." This is puzzling, for how can a convert to Judaism have an Israelite mother? In the patriarchal world of the Mishnah, status and pedigree are inherited from the father. The father's status is determinative. Only in the case of mixed unions between Jews and gentiles does the Mishnah determine status of offspring matrilineally. How then can a convert to Judaism, a Jew who was born a gentile, have a Jewish mother, if a Jewish mother always bears a Jewish child?

I have reviewed four possible explanations. The simplest and best explanation is that the Mishnah is speaking of second-generation converts, the offspring of native Jewish mothers and *convert* fathers. The native mother prevents her offspring from inheriting the status of convert from the father. The second, third, and fourth explanations, each one an attempt to explain a comment of Benjamin b. Ashtor in the Yerushalmi as much as an attempt to explain the Mishnah, agree that the Mishnah is speaking of the offspring of native Jewish mothers and *gentile* fathers, but disagree how to construe the Mishnah. In the second explanation the Mishnah is speaking not of converts but of native Jews; this explanation assumes that, in accordance with the rabbinic matrilineal principle, the offspring of a Jewish mother and a gentile father is Jewish by birth, and that the Mishnah alternates between converts and natives. In the third explanation, the Mishnah is speaking of first-generation converts; this explanation assumes that, in opposition to the rabbinic matrilineal principle, the offspring of a Jewish mother and a gentile father is gentile by birth. This view is clearly attested not only in pre-rabbinic antiquity (as I discussed in chapter 9) but also in the Sifra and a series of medieval and early modern authorities. In the fourth explanation, the Mishnah is speaking of people who possess the status of converts; this explanation assumes that the offspring of a Jewish mother and a gentile father is Jewish by birth (following the matrilineal principle) but is deemed to be of the same status as a convert.

According to Rabbi Judah in the Yerushalmi, the identification of the mother and the father in the Mishnah is unimportant because even first-generation converts are deemed to be descendants of Abraham and thus to possess Israelite "fathers." And if first-generation converts do not suffer any liturgical impairment as a consequence of their lowly (non-Israelite) birth, surely second-generation converts suffer no such impairment. Perhaps R. Judah would concede that in other areas converts suffer legal disabilities as a result of their foreign extraction, but at least in the liturgical recitation of the phrase "God of our fathers" they are equal to the native born. The debate between the Yerushalmi and the Mishnah was revived in the high Middle Ages, with a string of important rabbinic authorities endorsing the Mishnah, and another string endorsing the Yerushalmi. In the end, the Yerushalmi triumphed; insofar as Judaism is a religion or way of life, the foreign born can indeed cross the boundary and become Jews. Religion overcame ethnicity.

Jews, Judaism, and Jewishness

Us and Them

Jewishness, the conscious affirmation of the qualities that make Jews Jews, presumes a contrast between Us and Them. The Jews constitute an Us; all the rest of humanity, or, in Jewish language, the nations of the world, the gentiles, constitute a Them. Between Us and Them is a line, a boundary, drawn not in sand or stone but in the mind. The line is no less real for being imaginary, since both Us and Them agree that it exists. Although there is a boundary that separates the two, it is crossable and not always distinct.

This book is a study of the creation of this boundary during the formative period of Judaism, the second century B.C.E. to the fifth century C.E. The theme of part I is that the boundary between Jews and gentiles in antiquity was not always clearly marked; the degree of social interaction between Jews and non-Jews was sufficiently great that it was not always easy to tell who was a Jew and who was not. In the diaspora, especially, it was relatively easy for a Jew to "pass" as, or to be mistaken for, a gentile. Associating with Jews and observing Jewish rituals and practices would establish a presumption of Jewishness but not certainty, since gentiles too associated with Jews and even observed some Jewish rituals. In the land of Israel matters were sometimes just as complicated. Was Herod the Great Jewish? The range of answers given to this question by our ancient sources is quite astonishing, from blue-blooded Judaean to Idumaean to "half-Jew" (or "half-Judaean") to gentile slave. These responses reflect Herod's posthumous reputation at least as much as they reflect lingering doubts about his Jewishness during his lifetime,

341

but they clearly show nonetheless that Jewishness was not a function of objective or empirical criteria. Complicating the issue further is the inherent ambiguity of the Greek word *Ioudaios,* which originally designated a member of the ethnic polity of Judaea (in English, a Judaean), but which subsequently also came to designate anyone who venerates the God whose temple is in Jerusalem (in English, a Jew).

The theme of part I is that the boundary between Jew and gentile is not well marked; the theme of part II is that the boundary is crossable. The development of *Ioudaios* from "Judaean" to "Jew" testifies to a momentous development in the history of Judaism, the growth of a nonethnic conception of Jewishness. Such a conception is not securely attested until the second century B.C.E., when the Hasmoneans, under the influence of Greek political ideas, extended citizenship in the Judaean state to the Idumaeans and Ituraeans. The new citizens remained Idumaeans and Ituraeans even as they became Judaeans. With the opening of the boundary in the second century B.C.E., gentiles crossed it and became Jews in a variety of ways, whether by political enfranchisement, religious conversion, veneration of the Jewish God, observance of Jewish rituals, association with Jews, or other means. The same period also provides the first secure attestation of the notion of conversion to Judaism, the idea that a gentile can deny his (there is no need to say "her" at this period, because conversion to Judaism was first conceived as a prerogative of males) polytheism and accept the one true God. The rabbis in the second century C.E. standardized the conversion process by demanding that all converts accept the commandments of the Torah, that men be circumcised, that all converts immerse properly, and that these steps be taken publicly and thus be verifiable. When a gentile has complied with all the rabbinic requirements and performed the prescribed ceremony, the rabbis declare him (or her) to be "like an Israelite in all respects." The gentile has become a Jew.

Even as they permitted gentiles to convert to Judaism, the rabbis proscribed all sexual contact, whether marital or nonmarital, between Jews and gentiles. This is the subject of part III. In stating and justifying the prohibition, the rabbis were following a tradition that reached back—again—to the Hasmoneans in the second century B.C.E. However, when dealing with the consequences of intermarriage, the rabbis of the second century C.E. seem to have been entirely innovative. They established the matrilineal principle, which decreed that the status of the offspring of intermarriage follows that of the mother. Thus a non-Jewish woman bears non-Jewish children even if they are fathered by a

Jewish man, and a Jewish woman bears Jewish children even if they are fathered by a non-Jewish man. This principle appears for the first time in the Mishnah but without explanation or justification. It seems likely that this principle entered rabbinic law either under the influence of the Roman law of persons, or as the result of rabbinic reflection on the nature of mixtures, the crossbreeding of diverse kinds. The matrilineal principle and the prohibition of intermarriage are expressions of the rabbinic concern for proper pedigree and genealogical purity. The offspring of improper marriages rank lower than the offspring of proper marriages, and even the offspring of proper marriages can be ranked in accordance with a genealogical hierarchy. In this system converts, because of their foreign birth, rank lower than native Israelites. A gentile can become a Jew but can never efface his gentile birth and consequently can never attain full equality with the native.

The boundary between Us and Them is a combination of religion or "culture" (part II) and ethnicity or birth (part III). In a number of passages Philo, Josephus, and the rabbis explicitly acknowledge the duality of the boundary, but do not seem to realize that its two aspects are fundamentally irreconcilable. The identity system that would attain canonical form in rabbinic Judaism was a union of disparate elements, Jewishness as a function of religion and Jewishness as a function of descent.

• • •

Rabbinic hegemony and the political setting of Jewish communities from late antiquity to early modern times jointly ensured that Jewishness would be neither elusive nor problematic. As we have seen in chapter 2, many rabbinic texts imagine that Jews are distinctive, identifiable, unassimilable; indeed, rabbinic texts are the only texts of antiquity to make such statements. Rabbinic law strengthened the boundary between Jews and gentiles, and defined the process of conversion, the place of the convert within Jewish society, the status of the offspring of intermarriage, and the marriageability of all those within the community of Israel. The rabbis of antiquity did not—could not—resolve every ambiguity and doubt about Jewishness, conversion, and intermarriage; rabbis of later times devoted (and are still devoting!) much energy to the fine tuning of the rabbinic system and to the elucidation of questions that the rabbis of antiquity had never considered. In particular, the rabbis of the Middle Ages devoted a great deal of attention to the status of the apostate, the Jew who crossed the boundary and became a gentile, one of Us who became one of Them. Ancient rabbinic law paid little attention to apostates, but in the Middle Ages, in both the Christian and Islamic spheres, apostasy was a serious and real problem that demanded attention. Was the apostate a Jew? This was the only major question for which the ancient legacy was entirely inadequate.[1] Otherwise, the rabbis of antiquity bequeathed to posterity a system that defined membership within the community of Israel and that clearly established the meaning and limits of Jewishness.

The political setting of the Jewish communities of Europe, the Mediterranean, and the Near East also contributed to the naturalness and inevitability of Jewishness. The Christian states of Europe and the Islamic states of Africa and the Near East recognized the rabbis as the religious leaders of their Jewish communities and, what is just as significant, supported the maintenance of the boundary between the Jews and their Christian or Muslim neighbors. In their formative periods both Christianity and Islam defined themselves against Judaism, and that legacy carried forward into the Middle Ages. Just as the Jews were interested in defining themselves as an Us against the Christian and Muslim Them, the Christians and Muslims were interested in defining themselves as an Us against the Jewish Them. Christian and Muslim states encouraged Jews to defect, and one of the ways they accomplished that goal was to ensure that everyone knew who was a Jew and who was not. For centuries, then, living in Christian and Muslim states under rabbinic hegemony, Jews knew who they were. Jewishness was not an issue.

Jewishness became an issue when these internal and external factors disappeared. In the nineteenth century the Emancipation of the Jews and the general restructuring of European society meant the collapse of the intellectual, political, and social boundaries that traditionally had kept Jews "in" and gentiles "out." Jews emerged from their ghettos and entered western society. Fueled by a great desire to belong, many Jews shed their ethnic and religious distinctiveness in order to become "good" Germans, good Frenchmen, and so forth. Even in Eastern Europe, where the Emancipation came later and with much less effect than in Western Europe, traditional Jewish life in the villages and small towns was in great distress by the last decades of the nineteenth century due to the corrosive forces of antisemitism, impoverishment,

---

1. Edward Fram, "Perception and Reception of Repentant Apostates in Medieval Ashkenaz and Premodern Poland," *Association for Jewish Studies Review* 21 (1996) 299–339 (with bibliog.).

emigration, and revolution. In the United States the separation of church and state meant that rabbis never had any legal power in the eyes of the government, and that the Jewish community had no greater legal standing than that of a voluntary association. Everywhere, it seemed, rabbinic hegemony had disappeared, or was much reduced, and the state no longer enforced Jewish identity. This is the context in which the modern "Who is a Jew?" question was born.

The nineteenth century was the age of the great modern Jewish ideologies. Reform, Orthodox, and (to use a term that was coined later) Conservative thinkers defined Judaism in terms of religion, akin to, and in contrast with, Christianity. Reform thinkers were the most outspoken and the most logically consistent in their assertion that Judaism was *just* a religion, not a people and not a nation. German Jews, they said, had no more in common with French Jews than German Catholics had with French Catholics. The end of the century saw the emergence of two ideologies that defined Judaism in nonreligious terms. Zionists defined Judaism as a nationality: Jews needed a state of their own so that they could attain the normalcy that eluded them as a diaspora people. For most of the Zionists, Judaism as a religion was dead; the new Judaism was Jewish nationalism. Among the early Zionists were some who would have welcomed as members even Jews who had converted to Christianity; if Germans can be either Catholic or Protestant, why cannot Israelis (to use a term that was coined much later) be either Jewish or Christian? In contrast, the Bundists argued that Judaism was peoplehood, and that the solution to the Jewish problem in Europe was not nationalism but socialism. Through socialism the masses of the Jewish working poor would be liberated from their poverty and ennobled. In Western Europe there were fierce struggles between the forces of Reform and the forces of Orthodoxy, in Eastern Europe between the Zionists and the Bundists, and between both of them and the religious traditionalists. Religion, nationality, ethnicity—what the rabbis, following the Hasmoneans, had joined, now came asunder.[2]

The forces of chaos and confusion have not diminished in the twentieth century. True, Bundists have disappeared. Reform and virtually all organized expressions of Judaism as a religion support the state of Israel and recognize that nationality is a component of Jewish identity. But

2. There is, of course, abundant bibliography on these topics; perhaps the best place to begin is Michael A. Meyer, *Jewish Identity in the Modern World* (Seattle: University of Washington Press, 1990).

the creation of the state of Israel has led to new challenges: there is a growing sense that Jewish identity in the Jewish state is different from Jewish identity in the diaspora, and that this difference is growing. In the United States the growth of intermarriage and the attenuation of a religious identity among broad reaches of the Jewish population have caused a great deal of concern among rabbis, sociologists, demographers, and communal leaders: what sort of Jewish identity do these Jews have? How strong is it? Can it be transmitted to the next generation? In the 1990s there is scarcely an issue of a Jewish periodical in this country that does not have at least one article on this constellation of topics.

The uncertainty of Jewishness in antiquity curiously prefigures the uncertainty of Jewishness in modern times. Then as now, individual Jews are not easily recognizable; they simply are part of the general population. Then as now, the word *Jew* or *Ioudaios* has come to have a wide range of meanings. Before the rabbis came and standardized the rules of conversion, there were numerous ways by which gentiles crossed the boundary and became Jews. Before the rabbis came and invented the matrilineal principle, the offspring of Jewish fathers were deemed Jews, and the offspring of gentile fathers were deemed gentiles. In our age outside the small but influential communities that still adhere to traditional rabbinic law, the rabbinic standards for conversion and the rabbinic matrilineal principle no longer obtain. In some communities, males do not even need to be circumcised in order to be accepted as converts (a degree of openness that, as I have argued several times in this book, is unparalleled in antiquity). Now, as in the non-rabbinic communities of antiquity, gentiles affiliate with the Jewish community in numerous ways and for numerous reasons. Now, as in the non-rabbinic communities of antiquity, the offspring of Jewish fathers and non-Jewish mothers are deemed Jews (at least in some circles). According to rabbinic law there is no such thing as a "half-Jew," but in American society there is a growing category of people who regard themselves as "half-Jews." There is even a small but growing group of "God-fearers," gentiles who see themselves no longer as Christians but as gentiles on the periphery of Judaism.[3] Our post-rabbinic world mirrors the pre-rabbinic world of antiquity.[4]

3. On "half-Jews," see my reflections "Bring Back the 'God-Fearers'?" *Sh'ma* 27, no. 534 (May 16, 1997) 3–5. On modern "God-fearers," see J. David Davis, *Finding the God of Noah: The Spiritual Journey of a Baptist Minister from Christianity to the Laws of Noah* (Hoboken, N.J.: Ktav, 1996).

4. For a similar series of observations, see Martin Goodman, "Identity and Authority in Ancient Judaism," *Judaism* 39 (1990) 192–201.

The major difference between our world and theirs is that the existential contrast between Us and Them was a reality for the Jews of antiquity, even for the pre-rabbinic Jews and the non-rabbinic Jews, whereas it is not a reality for many contemporary Jews of the diaspora. The majority of the Jews of the United States, perhaps the vast majority, do not feel alienated from gentile society. Certainly our neutral society does nothing to reinforce Jewish identity or to compel Jews to remain Jews. Antisemitism is negligible. The dramatic rise of the rate of intermarriage shows not only that large numbers of American Jews do not see gentiles as a Them, but also that large numbers of American gentiles do not see American Jews as a Them. The development of a Holocaust religion among American Jews, which attempts to invest Jewishness with meaning on the basis of the destruction of European Jewry, is an attempt to give American Jews some sense of alienation or Otherness from American society. Whether it has succeeded or can continue to succeed is not clear. American Jews have simply become white, middle-class, Americans. There is no sign that any group of Jews in antiquity attained this level of integration in their society, this level of acceptance and ethnic self-abnegation.

Jewish communal leaders wonder and worry: does the disappearance of the Other portend the disappearance of the Self? Without a Them can there be an Us?

• • •

Throughout this book I have spoken in the first-person singular. I am white, middle-class, middle-aged, heterosexual, right-handed, American, Jewish, male, married, and father of four. I would be happy to share with the reader my entire personal and academic biography except that I imagine that the publisher would object. I offer this personal information because I, like most of my peers in academe, realize that all scholarship is conditioned by the setting and identity of its authors. Hence you, the reader, should know something about me, the author. At the Jewish Theological Seminary in New York, where I was ordained as rabbi and taught for many years, I was educated in the "historical-positive" school of Judaism. Even if I learned the hermeneutics of suspicion from Morton Smith, my doctoral mentor at Columbia University, I remain a positivist: I study the past in order to make positive statements about what I believe happened or did not happen. I study not only the historical traditions about an event but also the event itself. Like most historians I find discontinuity and change more interesting than continuity and tradition. Hence in this book I have emphasized the crucial turning points at which a given law or idea receives its earliest attestation. I have sketched a history of Jewishness, from membership in a people to citizenship in a state to adherence to a religion, and finally, as evidenced in rabbinic texts, to membership in an ethnoreligion. If my reconstruction is correct, this is a remarkably interesting history. Perhaps historians who know the ancient world better than I will find more Greco-Roman parallels than I did to elucidate it; perhaps historians of other regions of the world will find parallels to these developments in the history of other groups;[5] perhaps historians of the Jewish experience will show how any number of these ideas survive and develop in later centuries; perhaps historians who are more conversant with the social sciences than I will be able to illuminate these developments through the application of social theory and models. I have done my best as a historian.

I am a rabbi, but I am not writing as a rabbi. That is, in this book I am not consciously advocating the retention, reform, or removal of any rabbinic law. If my historical approach is correct, conversion to Judaism, the matrilineal principle, the general prohibition of intermarriage, and the nexus of religion, ethnicity, and nationality were not revealed to the people of Israel by Moses at Mount Sinai but were created by historical Jews living in historical time. Does this fact imply that these ideas and laws consequently have no authority over contemporary Jews, that they can be amended or discarded at will? The answer depends entirely on one's theory of revelation, authority, tradition, and law in Judaism. Traditionalist Jews will either dispute the very principles on which my historical scholarship is predicated, or will accept my arguments but contend that my historical theories have no consequences for those who wish to be faithful to tradition and to observe normative rabbinic law. History is history, they will say, and *halakhah* (normative rabbinic law) is *halakhah*. Reform Jews may seize my historical argumentation as justification for the reform of traditional practices, but they argue in this manner only because they have already decided for other reasons that these laws need reforming. In other words, historical scholarship has no necessary consequences for Jewish observance. Those who wish to maintain tradition can do so, those who wish to reform tradition can do so; the former will deny the relevance of historical scholarship to ac-

5. The Armenians are often cited alongside the Jews as a paradigm of a diaspora people; do the Armenians too develop from *ethnos* to ethnoreligion?

tual practice, the latter will affirm it. The crucial issue is not history but hermeneutics.[6]

6. This point is unappreciated by Alan Segal, *Paul the Convert* (New Haven: Yale University Press, 1990) 343–344 n. 34. In one area of law—the treatment of converts to Judaism—I hope that my work will have an effect on the mores of the contemporary Jewish community. I hope that contemporary rabbinic authorities will welcome potential converts with the same moderate stance that forms the basis of the rabbinic conversion ceremony (see chapter 7 above), and that contemporary Jewish society will learn from the Yerushalmi and its medieval continuators to regard converts as equal to the native born (see chapter 10 above). But these hopes have not directed my scholarship and its conclusions—at least not consciously.

Was Martial's Slave Jewish?

Martial has one explicit reference to Jewish circumcision and one implicit reference. The explicit reference is 7.30.5 (= M. Stern, *Authors* no. 240): *nec recutitorum fugis inguina Iudaeorum* (see chapter 2 above, note 56); the implicit reference is 11.94 (= M. Stern, *Authors* no. 245), the fourfold repetition of *verpe poeta* in reference to someone born in Jerusalem (see chapter 2 above, notes 57 and 58). Stern sees two other references to circumcision in the epigrams of Martial, but in one case (7.35, treated here) his interpretation is almost certainly wrong, and in the other (7.82, treated below, in appendix B) the text is ambiguous.

Here is Martial 7.35:

> Inguina succinctus nigra tibi servos aluta
> stat, quotiens calidis tota foveris aquis.
> Sed meus, ut de me taceam, Laecania, servos
> Iudaeum nuda sub cute pondus habet.
> Sed nudi tecum iuvenesque senesque lavantur.
> An sola est servi mentula vera tui?
> Ecquid femineos sequeris, matrona, recessus,
> secretusque tua, cunne, lavaris aqua?

Line 4: *nuda sub cute:* some testimonia have *nulla sub cute.*

This text appears as no. 241 in Menahem Stern's *Greek and Latin Authors on Jews and Judaism*, but, unlike his usual practice, Stern does not give an English translation. Instead he reprints an Italian translation drawn from the old (1925) Loeb edition of Martial, whose editor,

Walter C. A. Ker, apparently believed that Italian was a more appropriate language than English for the translation of "obscenity."[1] Less inhibited, the 1968 and 1993 Loeb editions of Martial contain rather literal English translations,[2] which form the basis of my own. My goal is to be as literal as possible.

A slave, girt under his groin with a black leather strap,
waits on you, whenever you are being soothed all over with warm
     water.
But my slave, Laecania—to say nothing of myself—
has a Jewish load under his bare skin.
But bare are the youths and old men who wash themselves with you.
Is the cock of your slave the only true one?
Why don't you, O matron, go to the women's rooms,
and why don't you, O cunt, wash yourself in secret with your own
     water?

Line 4: *under his bare skin:* a different reading yields *under no skin* or *under his lack of skin.*

Many commentators have observed that the theme of lines 1–2 and 5–6 recurs in epigram 11.75. There Martial mocks Caelia, who makes sure that her slave covers himself with a brass sheath when he goes with her to the bath, although there is a crowd of naked men all about her.[3] Here Martial mocks the pretended modesty of Laecania. Her slave wears a black leather thong when he waits upon his mistress in the bath (lines 1–2).[4] But this show of modesty is a sham, for Laecania has no hesitation to bathe with naked men, young and old (line 5). Does Laecania mean to imply that only her slave, and no other man, has a real *mentula*[5] that must be covered up in the presence of a woman (line 6)? She should go bathe in the company of other women (lines 7–8).[6]

1. Ker writes, xvi n. 3: "All epigrams possible of translation by the use of dashes or paraphrases have been rendered in English, the wholly impossible ones only in Italian."

2. I am not sure who is to get the credit for the 1968 translation. E. H. Warmington, the editor of the series? The 1993 Loeb edition of Martial is by D. R. Shackleton Bailey.

3. There are many references to mixed bathing in the Roman empire. See, for example, Fikret Yegül, *Baths and Bathing in the Roman Empire* (New York: Architectural History Foundation; Cambridge: MIT Press, 1992) index, s.v. "Sexes, separation of."

4. The "black leather strap" is a thong that covers the penis; Hall, "Epispasm" 73, erroneously thinks it a reference to infibulation.

5. *Mentula* was an "obscene" word, avoided in polite company and respectable discourse (Adams, *Sexual Vocabulary* 9–12). Hence it should be translated not as "penis" but as "cock."

6. The nuance and meaning of lines 7–8 are not clear. Do *femineos recessus* and *tua aqua* have sexual meaning? Does line 7 imply female homoeroticism, and does line 8 imply masturbation?

In the middle of the epigram Martial contrasts Laecania's supposed modesty with his own supposed immodesty: your slave wears a thong, but "my slave—to say nothing of myself—has a Jewish load (*Iudaeum pondus*) under his bare skin" (*nuda sub cute*) or "under no skin" (*nulla sub cute*). Many scholars see in *Iudaeum pondus* or in *nulla sub cute* a reference to circumcision, and take *Iudaeum* as explicit evidence that Martial's slave was Jewish. Stern's comment is typical: "Martial alludes to his Jewish slave as being circumcised."[7] Although Martial regularly talks about slaves in his epigrams, this would be the only passage in which he refers to one of his own slaves as a circumcised Jew—indeed the only passage in which he refers to a Jewish slave, either his or anyone else's.[8] In spite of Martial's silence on the subject, there is nothing inherently implausible in the suggestion that there were Jewish slaves in Rome, and that one of them was owned by our poet.[9] The issue here simply is the correct interpretation of lines 3–4 of our epigram. Do the phrases *Iudaeum pondus* and *nuda/nulla sub cute* necessarily imply that Martial's slave was a circumcised Jew?

Iudaeum pondus has often been understood to refer to circumcision, called a "load" or burden because of the Jewish tax (the *fiscus Judaicus*) imposed on the Jews after the destruction of the temple in 70 C.E.[10] This interpretation is supported by two facts: first, book 7 of the epigrams was published in 92 C.E., precisely when the emperor Domitian was collecting the tax vigorously, and any circumcised man

---

7. J. A. Hild, "Les juifs à Rome devant l'opinion et dans la littérature," *Revue des études juives* 11 (1885) 171: "le poète lui-même est servi par un esclave juif, vigoureux gaillard"; T. Reinach, *Textes d'auteurs grecs et romains relatifs au judaïsme* (Paris, 1895; reprint, Hildesheim: Olms, 1963) 288 n. 1: "Martial, grand railleur des juifs, avait donc un esclave juif à son service"; Leon, *Jews of Ancient Rome* 39: "Martial has, or pretends to have, a circumcised Jewish slave"; Solin, "Juden und Syrer" 659: "Martial besass wahrscheinlich einen jüdischen Sklaven"; Martial mentions that "his own slave was circumcised" according to John Gager, *The Origins of Anti-Semitism* (New York: Oxford University Press, 1983) 56; etc.

8. On slaves and slavery in Martial see Marguerite Garrido-Hory, *Martial et l'esclavage* (Paris: Les Belles Lettres, 1981).

9. On Jewish slaves in Rome see G. Fuks, "Where Have All the Freedmen Gone?" *JJS* 36 (1985) 25–32, and Dale B. Martin, "Slavery and the Ancient Jewish Family," in *The Jewish Family in Antiquity*, ed. Shaye J. D. Cohen, Brown Judaic Studies, no. 289 (Atlanta: Scholars Press, 1993). Barrett, "Martial" 44, writes: "one would hardly expect Martial to own a Jewish slave"; why not?

10. Barrett, "Martial," remarks: "*Iudaeum pondus* is commonly translated 'the Jewish burden,' that is, the mark of circumcision, a burden because it leads to discrimination and, in particular, to the *fiscus Iudaicus* (cf. 7.55.8)." On *Iudaeum pondus* see now the excellent discussion in Allen Kerkeslager, "Maintaining Jewish Identity in the Greek Gymnasium," *Journal for the Study of Judaism* 28 (1997) 12–33.

was assumed to be a Jew and liable to the tax;[11] second, another epigram from book 7 explicitly refers to the *fiscus Iudaicus* (7.55 = M. Stern, *Authors* no. 242). Since I will need to refer to that epigram again I present it here in full:

Nulli munera, Chreste, si remittis,
nec nobis dederis remiserisque:
credam te satis esse liberalem.
Sed si reddis Apicio Lupoque
et Gallo Titioque Caesioque,
linges non mihi—nam proba et pusilla est—
sed quae de Solymis venit perustis
damnatam modo mentulam tributis.

My translation is inspired by the versions of the 1968 and 1993 Loeb editions:[12]

If you return services to no one, Chrestus,
give and return none to me either.
I will believe you to be generous enough.
But if you give them to Apicius and Lupus
and Gallus and Titius and Caesius,
you shall lick a cock—not mine (for it is chaste and puny)
but one that comes from burnt-out Jerusalem,
one recently condemned to pay taxes.

Chrestus is a pathic who specializes in fellatio (see epigram 9.27). The "services" (*munera*) that he renders are sexual.[13] If Chrestus intends to repay some favor by performing fellatio on his benefactors, Martial dares him to use his tongue not on the poet (Martial here pretending that his *mentula* is "chaste and puny") but on the *mentula* of "a man from Jerusalem"—that is, a Jew.[14] The implication of the epigram is that a Jew's *mentula* will be large (unlike Martial's), and thus a chal-

---

11. Smallwood, *Jews under Roman Rule* 377; on Domitian and the Jewish tax, see chapter 2 above, note 62.

12. Stern reprints the old translation of Ker, which is filled with paraphrases.

13. For this meaning of *munus/munera*, see Adams, *Sexual Vocabulary* 164 (although he does not list our passage among his examples).

14. Similarly epigram 11.94 = M. Stern, *Authors* no. 245, refers to a poet "born in the very midst of Jerusalem" (*Solymis . . . natus in ipsis*)—that is, a Jew. Sara Mandell, "Martial 7.55 and the *Didrachmon*," *Classical Bulletin* 62 (1986) 26–27, sees antisemitism and political propaganda in this epigram; I see neither. Mandell thinks Martial is calling a Jew a *mentula*. Not so; since the subject is fellatio, the Jew's *mentula* is the part that matters. *Quae de Solymis venit perustis* must mean "which comes from burnt-out [or: scorched] Jerusalem," not, as Mandell translates, "which leaps up from fiery Jews."

lenge to the linguistic skills of Chrestus.[15] I shall return to this point below. Martial adds that the Jew's *mentula* has recently been condemned to tribute: circumcised Jews are subject to the *fiscus Iudaicus*. Hence the suggestion that in our epigram *Iudaeum pondus* too is a reference to a circumcised *mentula* subject to the *fiscus Iudaicus*.

This interpretation of *Iudaeum pondus* was tacitly rejected by the famous poet and Latinist A. E. Housman. In an article written in Latin and published in 1931, Housman argued that *nulla sub cute* was the correct reading and that the variant *nuda* was a corruption of *nulla* inspired by the *nudi* of the next line. He paraphrased the line as follows: "servus meus, qui Iudaeus est, mentulam, et eam quidem grandem, ne cute quidem tectam habet" ("my slave, who is a Jew, has a cock—indeed, a large one—not even covered by a foreskin"). In this interpretation circumcision is alluded to not by *Iudaeum pondus,* which is explained to mean "a Jew with a large *mentula,*" but by *nulla sub cute*. Housman argued that in this passage (and various others) *cutis* must mean not "skin" or "body" but "foreskin." Martial's Jewish slave has a large *mentula* not covered by any foreskin.[16]

Housman correctly felt that the sense of the epigram demands that *Iudaeum pondus* refer not to circumcision and the *fiscus Iudaicus* but to penile magnitude. Laecania thinks that only her slave has a true *mentula,* but, says Martial, my slave has a *Iudaeum pondus!* Housman's paraphrase indicates that he thought that *pondus* alone would mean *mentula grandis,* so that the adjective *Iudaeum* must refer to the Jewishness of the slave. But while *pondus* regularly refers to the testicles, or by extension the male genitals in general, it does not by itself mean a large *mentula*.[17] What makes this *pondus* large is the fact that it is *Iudaeum*. Epigram 7.55, cited above, also implies that Martial thought of

15. Or is Martial implying that the fellator of a circumcised *mentula* is even more despicable than the fellator of one that is uncircumcised? I know of no other text that suggests this.

16. A. E. Housman, "Praefanda," *Hermes* 66 (1931) 409–410 = *The Classical Papers of A. E. Housman,* ed. J. Diggle and F. R. D. Goodyear, 3 vols. (Cambridge: Cambridge University Press, 1972) 3:1181–1182. Housman is followed by Adams, *Sexual Vocabulary* 73, and D. R. Shackleton-Bailey in the 1990 Teubner edition and the 1993 Loeb edition of Martial.

17. On *pondus/pondera* see Adams, *Sexual Vocabulary* 71, and the *Oxford Latin Dictionary* s.v. "*pondus*" 5b: "applied to the testicles or genitals." I have checked all the occurrences of *pondus* listed in Edgar Siedschlag, *Martial-Konkordanz* (Hildesheim: Olms, 1979). Similarly, in Shakespeare's *Merchant of Venice,* "pound of flesh" is probably an allusion to the penis (and perhaps circumcision); see James Shapiro, *Shakespeare and the Jews* (New York: Columbia University Press, 1996) 121–126 (I am grateful to Ivan Marcus for reminding me of this reference).

Jewish men as well endowed. Martial is employing the topos that the "other" or the "barbarian" is characterized by large genitals and/or excessive lust. Following the same typology Tacitus (*Histories* 5.5.2 = M. Stern, *Authors* no. 281) says that the Jews are a nation "most prone to lust" and that "among themselves nothing is unlawful" (*proiectissima ad libidinem gens . . . inter se nihil illicitum*).[18] On classical Greek vases Greeks are depicted with small penises, barbarians with large ones.[19] Martial's slave has a *Iudaeum pondus*—that is, a large *mentula*, a *mentula* worthy of a Jew. The *pondus* is *Iudaeum* but the slave is not necessarily a Jew; to be a Jew and to have a *mentula* large enough to be worthy of a Jew are two different things.

Is this well-endowed slave circumcised? With all due respect for Housman's extraordinary command of Latin, I think that *nuda* is by far a better reading than *nulla,* and *nuda sub cute* does not imply circumcision. Sense requires *nuda*. My slave, Martial is saying, has a *mentula* at least as large as (if not larger than) that of your slave, Laecania, but my slave goes to the bath naked—so why does yours wear a thong? Furthermore, line 3 demonstrates that line 4 cannot refer to circumcision. In 7.55 Martial contrasts his own puny *mentula* with the mighty *mentula* of a man from Jerusalem, but here he explicitly likens his own equipment to that of his slave. "My slave—to say nothing of myself—has a Jewish-sized *mentula* under his bare skin." Martial thus intimates that his own *mentula* rivals that of his slave.[20] Therefore Martial cannot be saying that his slave is circumcised, because this would imply that he too is circumcised![21] The only solution is (following Housman) to deny that *Iudaeum pondus* has anything to do with circumcision and (against Housman) to retain the reading *nuda*.[22]

18. See Stern's commentary ad loc. The text is cited in full in chapter 2 above, at note 65. This typology was correctly adduced here by Barrett, "Martial," and Gilula, "Jewish Slave."

19. K. J. Dover, *Greek Homosexuality* (Cambridge: Harvard University Press, 1978; reprint, 1989) 127–129. See also idem, *Aristophanes Clouds* (Oxford: Clarendon, 1968), commentary on line 1014 (a reference I owe to David Konstan).

20. I leave it for the biographers of Martial to determine whether his *mentula* was large (7:35) or small (7:55).

21. This argument is correctly emphasized by Barrett, "Martial," and Gilula, "Jewish Slave." Schäfer, *Judeophobia* 250 n. 62, is also aware of the problem.

22. The reading *nulla* could be retained if *cutis* were understood not as "foreskin" but as "leather," a synonym with *aluta*. Thus the line would mean "my slave has a large *mentula* not covered by any leather." Gilula, "Jewish Slave" 533 n. 6, calls this rendering "quite preposterous" but does not explain why. *Cutis* in the sense of "flayed hide, leather" is well attested (see the *Oxford Latin Dictionary* s.v. "*cutis*" 2) and appears in Martial 1.103.6. But this reading, although far from preposterous, is inferior to *nuda sub cute*.

The phrase *nuda sub cute* can be construed in two different ways, depending on the meaning of *cutis*. If (against Housman) *cutis* is understood to mean "skin" or "body," Martial is saying that his slave—to say nothing of himself—has a Jewish-sized *mentula* hanging[23] below his naked body. If (following Housman) *cutis* is understood to mean "foreskin," Martial is saying that his slave—to say nothing of himself—has a Jewish-sized *mentula* under his naked foreskin. This rendering is preferable, because it gives the line great irony. Jews do not have foreskins, or at least are not supposed to have foreskins, but this slave combines a naked foreskin with a Jewish-sized *mentula*. Far from saying that his slave is circumcised, Martial says precisely the opposite: his slave has a *cutis*, a foreskin.[24]

In sum: did Martial have a circumcised Jewish slave? Perhaps he did, perhaps he did not. Epigram 7.35 has no bearing on the question.

---

23. The notion of "hanging" is implied, of course, by the word *pondus*.

24. Gilula, "Jewish Slave," argues that the reading *nulla sub cute* arose as a correction of *nuda* in order to do away with the Jewish slave's foreskin. Perhaps.

Was Menophilus Jewish?

The interpretation of Martial 7.82 (= M. Stern, *Authors* no. 243) turns on the ambiguous word *verpus*. In this passage Martial describes a comic actor or singer, one Menophilus, who wore a fibula, ostensibly to protect his voice. While he was exercising in public, however, his fibula fell off, revealing to everyone that he was *verpus*. A fibula is a pin or a ring worn through the foreskin and designed to make erection either painful or impossible. The infibulated man would thus abstain from sex and thereby (it was believed) improve his voice and/or his strength.[1] The epigram can be construed in two ways. "I had thought that Menophilus wore a fibula in order to spare his voice, but now that his fibula fell out in public I realize that he wore it to hide his circumcision." This is how the epigram has usually been understood.[2] However, there is an alternative. "I had thought that Menophilus wore a fibula in order to spare his voice, but now that his fibula fell out in public I realize that he wore it to restrain his aggressive and unseemly homosexual lust" (i.e., his fibula fell out when he had an enormous erection). *Verpa* means "erection" in Martial 11.46. Perhaps both meanings are intended here as in 11.94 (*verpe poeta*). If Menophilus was circumcised and had no foreskin, how did he affix a fibula? If Menophilus was circumcised and

---

1. Kay, *Martial Book XI* 229–231 (commentary on 11.75).

2. See, for example, M. Stern, *Authors,* commentary ad loc.; Smallwood, *Jews under Roman Rule* 377; Kay, *Martial Book XI* 229; Hall, "Epispasm" 73; Williams, "Domitian" 203.

still managed to affix a fibula, it is easy to see how it might have fallen off! It is not clear if this epigram has anything to do with circumcision.

J. P. Sullivan, on page 189 of *Martial: The Unexpected Classic,* writes: "There are a number of sneers (e.g. 7.82) at those *verpi* ('skin-backs') who have been circumcised by their masters in order to gratify their perverse sexual tastes." I have been unable to verify this statement. Neither 7.82 nor 11.94—the only two passages in Martial to use the word *verpus*—refers to slaves who were circumcised in order to gratify their masters' perverse sexual tastes. I know of no references to circumcision in Martial aside from those discussed here and in the text above.

Was Trophimus Jewish?

Acts 21:27–29 reports the following:

When the seven days [of the purification of the Nazirites] were almost completed, the Jews from Asia, who had seen him [Paul] in the temple, stirred up all the crowd, and laid hands on him, crying out, "Men of Israel, help! This is the man who is teaching men everywhere against the people and the law and this place; moreover, he also brought Greeks into the temple, and he has defiled this holy place." For they had previously seen Trophimus the Ephesian with him in the city, and they supposed that Paul had brought him into the temple. Then all the city was aroused, and the people ran together; they seized Paul and dragged him out of the temple, and at once the gates were shut.

Paul is almost beaten to death by the crowd, but is arrested (and thus rescued) by Roman troops, and after a long series of interviews and hearings is sent off to Rome for trial before the emperor.

Paul is the target of two separate accusations: first, of teaching against the people (i.e., against the Jews), against the law (i.e., against the laws of the Torah), and against the place (i.e., against the temple); second, of bringing Greeks—that is, gentiles—into the temple, thereby defiling it. Acts, of course, implies that both accusations are false, but anyone who has read the Pauline epistles, especially Galatians, will have to concede that the first accusation, at least, has merit. Against this accusation the Paul of Acts speaks eloquently of his Jewish upbringing, his loyalty to Jews and Judaism, and his "conversion." But it is the second accusation that concerns us here. Acts explains that the accusation arose because Paul had been seen in the city with Trophimus of Ephesus, a man thought to be a gentile, and the Jews of Asia Minor—themselves, like Paul, pilgrims to the holy city—were convinced that Paul had brought Trophimus into the temple. Trophimus and any other alleged gentiles allegedly introduced into the temple by Paul were certainly liable to be killed if apprehended.[1] Presumably they were nowhere to be found; the mob turned its anger instead against Paul.

How does Paul respond to this accusation? He ignores it. In the subsequent narrative the accusation is mentioned again in 24:6 by one of Paul's prosecutors, but Paul does not deign to reply. "Let my accusers (the Jews of Asia) confront me directly," he says (24:19). The accusation that Paul introduced gentiles into the temple is probably pre-Lucan tradition (i.e., Luke, the author of Acts, did not invent it but learned of it from one of his sources),[2] and it is striking, then, that Luke (or his source) did not see fit to record Paul's response, especially if Paul's response had been "I did not bring Trophimus or any other gentile into the temple." Perhaps Acts suppresses Paul's defense because the defense did not accord well with Acts' picture of a Jewishly pious and non-antinomian Paul. Perhaps Paul said, "I brought Trophimus, a gentile, into the temple, but the distinction between Jew and gentile no longer exists in God's eyes, and gentiles may worship freely in the house of God just as Jews do." If this was Paul's defense one can understand why Luke would have suppressed it, because it would have run counter to his image of a Paul who never speaks the sort of theology that is central to Galatians.[3]

There is yet a third way in which Paul might have responded to the accusation. He might have said, "Yes, I brought Trophimus into the temple, but Trophimus is really a Jew, not a gentile." This response is full of uncertainties, for how would the Jews of Asia Minor have attempted to prove Trophimus to be a gentile, and how would Paul have attempted to prove him to be a Jew? Presumably everyone would have checked Trophimus' genealogy, or would have asked him to verify that he was a convert. Perhaps they would have checked his circumcision.[4] If

---

1. See chapter 2 above, note 166.

2. This seems to be the general consensus; see Gerd Lüdemann, *Das frühe Christentum nach den Traditionen der Apostelgeschichte* (Göttingen: Vandenhoeck & Ruprecht, 1987) 243–244.

3. Morton Smith, "The Reason for the Persecution of Paul and the Obscurity of Acts," in M. Smith, *Studies* 2.87–94.

4. Or perhaps not; see chapter 2 above, note 96.

this was Paul's defense, we may imagine that it was suppressed by Luke because Luke had no doubt that Trophimus was indeed a gentile. In any case, this story, like the story about R. Judah b. Beteira cited above in chapter 2, shows that even in connection with the one Jewish institution that required clear distinction between Jews and gentiles, Jewish identity was not always easy to determine and separation between Jews and gentiles was not always easy to enforce.

Was Timothy Jewish?

And he [Paul] came also to Derbe and to Lystra. A disciple was there, named Timothy, the son of a Jewish woman who was a believer; but his father was a Greek. He was well spoken of by the brethren at Lystra and Iconium. Paul wanted Timothy to accompany him; and he took him and circumcised him because of the Jews that were in those places, for they all knew that his father was a Greek. (Acts 16:1–3)[1]

How could Paul have circumcised Timothy? In Galatians Paul asserts that circumcision has no value. At best, it is worthless; at worst, it might lead to the erroneous belief that salvation is possible through works of the Law. Paul tells the men of (either ethnic or provincial) Galatia that he opposed the circumcision of Titus, his gentile traveling companion (Gal. 2:3–4), but Acts would have us believe that in a village of (provincial) Galatia Paul circumcised Timothy in order to make him his traveling companion. In Acts 15, at the great council, the pillars of the church come to accept Paul's view that gentile converts to Christianity need not be circumcised, but Acts 16 begins with Paul's circumcision of Timothy. How can this incongruity be explained?

Although the Paul of Acts never preaches freedom from the Law and never denigrates circumcision, the author of Acts 16:1–3 seems a little uneasy with the circumcision of Timothy.[2] Timothy was circumcised, he

1. One Greek uncial manuscript and several representatives of the Old Latin and the Vulgate omit *Ioudaias* from 16:1, but this reading appears to be secondary.

2. This was sensed by Ammonios (fifth century), who writes: "By explaining the reason why he circumcised Timothy, Paul escapes the censure of the fault-finders" (*PG* 85.1553).

says, *because of the Jews, all of whom knew that his father was a Greek.* In order to win the Jews, Paul had to behave like a Jew, a motif common in Acts[3] and supported by Paul's famous utterance in 1 Corinthians 9:20: *To the Jews I became as a Jew, in order to win Jews.* This is Luke's explicit apology for Paul's action. He mentions another point too that *may* be an implicit apology: Timothy had a Jewish mother. Thus, in addition to the social setting of the incident ("because of the Jews"), Timothy's "Jewishness" seems to excuse Paul.

Not all scholars have been convinced by Luke's apologetic. Some, led by Ferdinand Christian Baur, argue that the Lukan narrative is fictional. The man who refused to circumcise Titus would not have circumcised Timothy. Luke (or his source) invented the story in order to minimize the contradiction between Paul's radical rejection of the Law (suppressed by Acts) and the continued observance of the Law by the pillars of the church in Jerusalem. Perhaps some of Paul's other acts of simulated Jewish piety are believable, but the circumcision of Timothy is not. It is too inconsistent with the central teaching of Galatians, no matter the social setting of the incident or the "Jewishness" of the circumcised.[4]

Many scholars, however, accept Luke's apologetic. They concede that Paul's circumcision of Timothy seems irreconcilable with his theology, but they accept the Lukan portrait of a flexible apostle ready to compromise in order to make converts for Christ. Since Paul could make himself a Jew to the Jews, why could he not circumcise Timothy

---

3. Morton Smith, "The Reason for the Persecution of Paul and the Obscurity of Acts," in *Studies in Mysticism and Religion Presented to Gershom G. Scholem* (Jerusalem: Magnes, 1967) 261–268 = M. Smith, *Studies* 2.87–94.

4. Ward Gasque, *A History of the Criticism of the Acts of the Apostles,* BGBE 17 (Tübingen: Mohr [Siebeck], 1975; reprint, Peabody, Mass.: Hendrickson, 1989) 66: ". . . of all Paul's Jewish practices mentioned in the Book of Acts, the circumcision of Timothy was considered to be the most flagrant contradiction to Pauline doctrine. The Paul of the epistles could *never* have agreed to such action; of this the Tübingen critics were certain." The most detailed defense of this view remains that of Franz Overbeck in *Kurzgefasstes Exegetisches Handbuch zum Neuen Testament,* vol. 1, pt. 4, by W. M. L. de Wette, 4th ed., ed. F. Overbeck (Leipzig: S. Hirzel, 1870) 248–252. For modern versions see E. Haenchen, *The Acts of the Apostles* (Oxford: Blackwell, 1971) 478–482 (the seventh German edition [1977] does not add anything to the discussion); P. Vielhauer, "On the 'Paulinism' of Acts," in *Essays Presented in Honor of Paul Schubert: Studies in Luke-Acts,* ed. L. E. Keck and J. L. Martyn (Nashville and New York: Abingdon, 1966) 40–41; G. Bornkamm, "The Missionary Stance of Paul in 1 Corinthians 9 and in Acts," in *Studies in Luke-Acts* 203–204; W. O. Walker, "The Timothy-Titus Problem Reconsidered," *Expository Times* 92 (1980–1981) 231–235.

because of the Jews? The circumcision did not render Timothy subject to the Law. In fact, it was theologically meaningless, and was solely for the benefit of the mission. The rumor that Paul denies at Galatians 5:11 (*If I still preach circumcision, why am I still persecuted?*) could well have arisen as a result of the circumcision of Timothy. A circumcision justified by practical reasons was intentionally misinterpreted by Paul's opponents to indicate that even he believed that works of the Law were necessary for salvation. As we shall see, the advocates of this view follow Jerome's interpretation of Acts 16:1–3.[5]

Some scholars defend the historicity of Acts 16:1–3 by a completely different route. Freedom from the Law and rejection of circumcision were preached by Paul to gentiles, not Jews (or Jewish Christians). Paul certainly believed that Christ superseded the Law for both Jew and gentile, but though he found fault with gentile Christians who wished to *begin* observing the Law, he never found fault with Jews (or Jewish Christians) who wished to *continue* observing the Law. He condemned Jews who did not accept Christ and he condemned Jewish Christians who sought to impose the Law on gentile Christians, but he never attacked the observance of the Law per se. Hence, Paul's public displays of loyalty to the Law, including his circumcision of Timothy, are *not* inconsistent with his theology. As we shall see, the advocates of this view follow Augustine's interpretation of Acts 16:1–3.[6]

In this appendix I shall not attempt to treat all the complex problems

5. See, for example, H. H. Wendt, *Die Apostelgeschichte,* 5th ed. (Göttingen: Vandenhoeck & Ruprecht, 1913) 241; E. Meyer, *Ursprung und Anfänge des Christentums,* 3 vols. (Stuttgart and Berlin: Cotta, 1921–1923), 3.201–202; C. S. C. Williams, *A Commentary on The Acts of the Apostles* (London: Black, 1957) 188; G. Schneider, *Die Apostelgeschichte,* HThKNT 5, 2 vols. (Freiburg, Switzerland; Basel; and Vienna: Herder, 1980–1982) 2.200–201.

6. A. von Harnack, *Die Apostelgeschichte: Beiträge zur Einleitung in das Neue Testament 3* (Leipzig: Hinrichs, 1908) 180–181; T. Zahn, *Die Apostelgeschichte des Lucas,* 2 vols. (Leipzig: A. Deichter, 1919–1921) 2.558–9; *The Beginnings of Christianity,* ed. F. J. Foakes-Jackson and K. Lake, 5 vols. (London: Macmillan, 1920–1933) 4.184; Belkin, "Paul's Background" 43–48; J. W. Packer, *Acts of the Apostles* (Cambridge: Cambridge University Press, 1966) 132; R. P. C. Hanson, *The Acts in the Revised Standard Version* (Oxford: Clarendon, 1967) 166; J. C. O'Neill, *The Theology of Acts in Its Historical Setting,* 2d ed. (London: SPCK, 1970) 104–105; G. Stählin, *Die Apostelgeschichte,* NTD 5, 7th ed. (Göttingen: Vandenhoeck & Ruprecht, 1980) 277 (comment on Acts 21:21); S. G. Wilson, *Luke and the Law,* SNTSMS 50 (Cambridge: Cambridge University Press, 1983) 64–65; F. F. Bruce, *The Acts of the Apostles,* 3d ed. (Grand Rapids, Mich.: Eerdmans, 1990) 352. Haenchen, *Acts of the Apostles,* does not discuss this view; if he had, we may be sure that he would have rejected it. Instead he discusses (and rejects) two versions of Jerome's explanation and an incomprehensible interpretation advanced by Bauernfeind.

raised by Acts 16:1–3 and Galatians 2:3–5. Which of the three views sketched above is correct (i.e., those of Baur, Jerome, and Augustine) is not my concern. Instead, I am interested in one specific question: did the narrator of Acts ("Luke") think he was narrating the circumcision of a Jew or the circumcision of a gentile? In other words, is Acts 16:1–3 aware of the rabbinic matrilineal principle?

The plain meaning of Acts 16:3 is fairly clear. *Because of the Jews that were in those places, for they all knew that his father was a Greek* implies that Timothy was a gentile like his father. The advocates of a matrilineal understanding of Timothy's pedigree must interpret the passage as follows: for the Jews all knew [that Timothy's mother was Jewish and therefore that Timothy was Jewish as well; they also knew] that his father was a Greek [and therefore that Timothy was not circumcised]. In this interpretation the crucial part of the argument is missing from the text.[7] Furthermore, if Luke means to imply the falsehood of the rumor spread abroad about Paul's antinomianism (*and they have been told about you that you teach all the Jews who are among the Gentiles to forsake Moses, telling them not to circumcise their children or observe the customs;* Acts 21:21) and if Luke's portrait of Paul is consistent—two debatable assumptions—Acts 16:1–3 cannot refer to the circumcision of a Jew. The phrase *because of the Jews in that vicinity* implies that, were it not for them, Paul would have left Timothy uncircumcised. This implication confirms the charge that the Lukan Paul tries to deny in Acts 21:21. The two passages are consistent only if Timothy is a gentile.[8]

Neither of these arguments "proves" anything, but each implies that the author of Acts 16:1–3 thought that he was narrating the circumcision of a gentile who had a Jewish mother. Patristic exegesis confirms this interpretation. Ancient and medieval scholars seldom doubt the veracity and harmony of Scripture, but they are not prevented by their faith from seeing many of the difficulties that modern scholars see. The fathers of the third, fourth, and fifth centuries, and their medieval continuators, are disturbed by the apparent discrepancy between the Paul of Acts and the Paul of Galatians. Incapable of the skepticism that would later characterize the Tübingen school, these scholars explain Paul's circumcision of Timothy by appealing to the social setting of the

7. Overbeck, *Exegetisches Handbuch* 249; H. Conzelmann, *Acts of the Apostles,* Hermeneia (Philadelphia: Fortress, 1987) 125 (". . . a reference to the mother—instead of the father—would have been better . . . Apparently Luke does not have a precise understanding of Jewish law."); Daube, *Ancient Jewish Law* 25–26.

8. Jerome assumes that the rumor of Acts 21:21 is true, but Augustine and most modern exegetes assume that it is false; see below.

incident (*because of the Jews*). The vast majority of them, however, do not appeal to Timothy's Jewishness, because an exegete who is not pre-conditioned by a knowledge of the rabbinic law of status cannot imagine that Timothy's identity will have been determined by his mother and not his father. These exegetes follow the plain meaning of Acts 16:1–3.[9]

Tertullian, Clement of Alexandria, and Origen deduce from Paul's strange behavior in Derbe[10] that Paul could occasionally act against his own principles if the setting demanded it. To some extent Clement and Origen anticipate Jerome; they also anticipate most of modern scholar-ship by citing 1 Corinthians 9:20 in this connection. There is no sign, however, that any of them regarded Timothy as a Jew.[11] John Chrysos-tom is clearer. He explains that Paul circumcised Timothy "in order to abolish circumcision." Although Timothy "was half-gentile, being the son of a Greek father and a Christian mother" (Chrysostom omits her Jewishness), he consented to the circumcision in order to abolish the Law and propagate the faith in Christ. Timothy was not a Jew.[12]

9. Jewish and, to some extent, Christian scholarship has long recognized the contin-uing value of much of medieval Jewish exegesis for an understanding of the Hebrew Bible, and I do not understand why contemporary scholarship on the New Testament (exclud-ing, of course, textual criticism) ignores practically all works that predate the nineteenth century. For example, the scholars listed in notes 5 and 6 seem not to know that their opin-ions are virtually identical with those of Jerome and Augustine. Haenchen, *Acts of the Apostles,* imagines that the world of scholarship began in Tübingen in 1830 and ignores everything before that date, even J. J. Wetstein.

10. Or was it Lystra?

11. Tertullian, *De Monogamia* 14.1 (*CChr* 2.1249); *Adv. Marc.* 5.3.5 (*CChr* 1.669); *Praescr.* 24.3 (*CChr* 1.206); *De Pudicitia* 17.19 (*CChr* 2.1317). Clement of Alexandria, *Str.* 6.124.1 (*GCS* 52.494) and 7.53.3 (*GCS* 17,2.39). Origen, *Joh. Comm.* 1.42, 10.30, and 13.111 (*GCS* 10.12, 177, and 242); *Mat. Comm.* 11.8 (*GCS* 40.46). I owe these references to F. Overbeck, *Über die Auffassung des Streits des Paulus mit Petrus in Antiochien (Gala-tians. 2,11 ff.) bei den Kirchenvätern* (Basel, 1877; reprint, Darmstadt: Wissenschaftliche Buchgesellschaft, 1968), and to *Biblia Patristica,* ed. J. Allenbach et al., 4 vols. (Paris: Cen-tre National de la Recherche Scientifique, 1975–1987). Jerome claims that he is merely fol-lowing Origen in his interpretation; see M. A. Schatkin, "The Influence of Origen upon St. Jerome's Commentary on Galatians," *Vigiliae Christianae* 24 (1970) 49–58, at 53.

12. *Hom. ad Acta Apost.* 34 (*PG* 60.247–249); *Hom. ad Galatians.* 2 (*PG* 61.636); cf. *Hom. ad II Tim.* 1 (*PG* 62.602). The poor state of the text of these homilies (see F. Bovon, *De Vocatione Gentium: Histoire de l'interprétation d'Act.10,1–11,18 dans les six premiers siè-cles,* BGBE 8 [Tübingen: Mohr [Siebeck], 1967] 6–7) does not affect our discussion. Two works that closely follow Chrysostom say explicitly that Timothy was "from the Greeks"; see the commentary of Theophylactus (PG 125.725) and the note of an anonymous writer in J. A. Cramer, *Catenae Graecorum Patrum in Novum Testamentum,* 8 vols. (Oxford: Oxford University Press, 1838–1844), 3.262. Ephraem (or Ephrem) the Syrian (ed. F. C. Conybeare in Foakes-Jackson and Lake, *Beginnings of Christianity,* 3.428–429), whose commentary is closely related to Chrysostom, also omits the Jewishness of Timothy's mother. Jerome also claims Chrysostom as his forerunner.

The most detailed patristic contribution to our question is the epistolary debate between Jerome and Augustine concerning Paul's rebuke of Peter in Galatians 2:11–14.[13] After the arrival of certain friends of James, men of the circumcision, Peter stopped eating with gentile Christians, and Paul rebuked him for his duplicity. But did not Paul himself often act like a Jew with the Jews? How could he rebuke Peter for conduct of which he himself was guilty? Pagan critics of Christianity attacked Paul's insolence.[14]

Jerome suggests that Paul's rebuke of Peter was as insincere as Peter's observance of the Law in the presence of the men of the circumcision. Both actions were "white lies," Peter simulating Jewish piety in order to keep the Jews loyal to Christ, Paul simulating a rebuke in order to

13. The debate was provoked by Jerome's commentary (written about 387) on these verses of Galatians (*PL* 26.363–367; see also the commentary on Gal. 5:11, *PL* 26.431–432 [these are the column references for the 1884 printing of *PL* 26; in other printings the numeration is different]). Augustine first sketched his position circa 394–395 in his commentary on Gal. 2:11–16, 5:1–3, and 6:15–16 (CSEL 84.69–71, 112–113, and 139–140), and in his *De Mendacio* 8 (CSEL 41.422–424). Between 395 and 405 Augustine and Jerome debated the issue. Augustine opened the debate with two epistles to Jerome, numbers 56 and 67 in the collected letters of Jerome (CSEL 54.496–503 and 666–674), which are identical with numbers 28 and 40 in the collected letters of Augustine (CSEL 34,1.103–113 and 34,2.69–81). Jerome responded with epistle 112 (CSEL 55.367–393) = epistle 75 (CSEL 34,2.280–324) and was answered by Augustine in epistle 116 (CSEL 55.397–422) = epistle 82 (CSEL 34,2.351–387). The other matters discussed in these epistles and the further ramifications of the debate in the other works of Jerome and Augustine do not concern us here. For a detailed analysis see Overbeck, *Über die Auffassung* 49–70. For more recent bibliography see R. Kieffer, *Foi et justification à Antioche* (Paris: du Cerf, 1982) 96 n. 60; R. J. O'Connell, "The Correspondence between Augustine and Jerome," *Thought* 54 (1979) 344–364; Virginia Hellenga, "The Exchange of Letters between St. Augustine and St. Jerome," in *Daidalikon: Studies in Memory of Raymond V. Schoder*, ed. Robert F. Sutton (Wauconda, Ill.: Bolchazy-Carducci Publishers, 1989) (non vidi). I cite the epistles of both fathers from the collection of Jerome (CSEL 54 and 55, ed. I. Hilberg). Some commentators on Galatians refer to this debate (see J. B. Lightfoot, "Patristic Accounts of the Collision at Antioch," in *St Paul's Epistle to the Galatians* [London: Macmillan, 1865] 128–132; T. Zahn, *Der Brief des Paulus an die Galater*, 2d ed. [Leipzig: A. Deichert, 1907] 110–111 n. 39; Franz Mussner, *Der Galaterbrief*, HTKNT 9 (Freiburg, Switzerland: Herder, 1974] 146–167), but, as far as I know, Overbeck is the only modern commentator on Acts to refer to it.

14. Jerome writes that his interpretation refutes the blasphemies of Porphyry, who had accused Paul of *procacitas* (Jerome, *Epist.* 112.6 [CSEL 55.372–373] and commentary on Gal. 2:11–13 [*PL* 26.366]; Augustine, *Epist.* 116.22.3 [CSEL 55.413]). See A. von Harnack, *Porphyrius, "Gegen die Christen,"* Abhandlungen der preussischen Akademie der Wissenschaften Jahrgang 1916, Nr. 1 (Berlin: Reimer, 1916) 53 no. 21, and 56 no. 26; and M. Stern, *Authors* no. 459d (2.450–453). Centuries later Acts 16:1–3 still provided ammunition to anti-Christian writers; see Isaac Troki (1533–1594), *Faith Strengthened*, trans. M. Mocatta (London, 1851; reprint, New York: Ktav, 1970) 88 (pt. 1, chap. 19) and 279 (pt. 2, chap. 74).

keep the gentiles loyal to Christ. Jerome develops this interpretation by demonstrating that both Peter and Paul believed the Law to be totally devoid of sanctity but that both feigned loyalty to it when the occasion demanded. One of his proofs for Paul's ability to simulate is, of course, the circumcision of Timothy. Jerome turns to Paul and asks:

O blessed apostle Paul, you who found fault with the insincerity through which Peter withdrew himself from the gentiles on account of his fear of the Jews who came from James, why were you compelled, against your own belief, to circumcise Timothy, the son of a gentile man and likewise a gentile himself and not a Jew, inasmuch as he had not been circumcised? You will answer me "*Because of the Jews that were in those places.*" Therefore, you who pardon yourself for your circumcision of a disciple coming from the gentiles, pardon Peter too, your predecessor, for doing something through fear of the Jewish Christians.[15]

Jerome deduces that Paul only pretended to rebuke Peter.

Jerome absolves Paul of the charge of insolence. His explanation, however, lays Paul open to the charge of hypocrisy and mendacity.[16] One fourth-century father had to respond to the following question: "Why does Paul say that he makes himself all things for all people, when this appears to be the work of a sycophant and a hypocrite?"[17] This was the point that so deeply disturbed Augustine about Jerome's interpretation. Refusing to believe that the heroes of sacred Scripture could promote any kind of untruth, even "white lies" (*officiosa mendacia*), Augustine argued that in Paul's time it was still theologically permissible for a Jew (and a Jewish Christian) to continue observing the Law. Jerome believed that the arrival of Christ rendered the Law not only *mortua* (dead) but also *mortifera* (lethal). Christianity was *bonum,* Judaism and paganism alike were *mala*.[18] Hence, if Peter and Paul occasionally observed the Law, they must have been acting out a charade. Augustine, however, believed that the observance of the Law, during

---

15. *Epist.* 112.9.3 (CSEL 55.378). That Paul was "compelled" to circumcise Timothy appears also in Ambrosiaster; see below.

16. An objection well made by Augustine, *Epist.* 116.22.3 (CSEL 55.413).

17. Pseudo-Augustine, *Quaestionum Novi Testamenti Appendix* 48 (CSEL 50.443). This text is generally ascribed to "Ambrosiaster"; see below. For a fine critique of Paul's adaptability, see Clarence Glad, *Paul and Philodemus: Adaptability in Epicurean and Early Christian Psychagogy* (Leiden: Brill, 1995).

18. The ceremonies of Judaism are *perniciosae et mortiferae Christianis* (Jerome, *Epist.* 112.14.2 [CSEL 55.382]). See too *Epist.* 112.16.2 (CSEL 55.386): *Observare autem legis caerimonias non potest esse indifferens, sed aut bonum est aut malum est.*

the period when grace through faith was first revealed, was neither *bonum* nor *malum*. It had become (for Jews) indifferent.[19] The ceremonies of the Jews once had been holy, the foreshadowings of what was to come, and although they were now being cast aside, they were not to be treated with the contempt that was appropriate for pagan observances. Jewish Christians could continue to observe these ceremonies as their ancestral custom (*mos patrius* and *consuetudo*). Hence Paul, a Jew by birth, observed the Law when dealing with the Jews, not through simulation and deceit but through compassion and pity (*non fallaciter sed misericorditer*), in order to win them for Christ. And why did he circumcise Timothy?

He circumcised Timothy for the following reason, lest the gentiles who believed in Christ appear to the Jews, and especially to Timothy's maternal relations, to detest circumcision just as idolatry is to be detested, although the former was commanded by God and the latter was induced by Satan. And he did not circumcise Titus for the following reason, lest he give support to those who were saying that believers in Christ could not be saved without such circumcision and who, in order to deceive the gentiles, boasted that Paul himself thought the same way.[20]

Paul circumcised Timothy so that gentile converts to Christianity should not seem to the Jews (including Timothy's Jewish relations) to revile the Jewish ceremonies—which, unlike those of paganism, are of divine origin.

In sum, for both Jerome and Augustine, Timothy is a gentile because he is the son of a gentile father and is uncircumcised; his Jewish mother

---

19. Augustine, *Epist.* 116.13–17 (CSEL 55.405–409). According to Augustine, the history of the Law is tripartite: the period before Christ (in which the Law was still *bonum*), the period of transition (in which observance of the Law was indifferent), and the period after Christ (in which observance of the Law is *malum*). This aspect of the debate is well analyzed by Thomas Aquinas, *Summa Theologiae* prima secundae, q. 103 art. 4 (with a parallel discussion in his commentary on Galatians; see Kieffer, *Foi* 100–101). For a modern discussion see B. Blumenkranz, *Die Judenpredigt Augustins* (Basel, 1946; reprint, Paris: Etudes Augustiniennes, 1973) 135–137. Augustine states that the transition period ended with the promulgation of the gospel, but does not specify a date. Lenain de Tillemont suggests that Augustine means 70 C.E.; see *Memoires pour servir à l'histoire ecclésiastique,* 2d ed. (Paris: C. Robustel, 1701) 1.227–228. The transition period certainly ended sometime in the first century; after that date the ceremonies of Judaism are *perniciosae et mortiferae* for Augustine as well (*Epist.* 116.18.1 [CSEL 55.409]). Augustine is not the originator of the view that in the apostolic period the observance of the Law was indifferent; it is as old as Justin Martyr. See Overbeck, *Über die Auffassung* 9 and 61, and T. Stylianopoulos, *Justin Martyr and the Mosaic Law,* SBLDS 20 (Missoula, Mont.: Scholars Press, 1975) 127–130.

20. *Epist.* 116.12.1 (CSEL 55.404); see also *De Mendacio* 8 (CSEL 41.423).

does not affect his status at all. Jerome had little incentive to emphasize Timothy's Jewishness since he argued that even Jews were no longer to observe the Law after the appearance of Christ. Augustine, however, had great incentive to emphasize Timothy's Jewishness, and his failure to do so is remarkable. Rather than appeal to the insult that would have been felt by Timothy's Jewish relations had Timothy remained uncircumcised, Augustine should have appealed to Timothy's Jewishness, which would have made his circumcision licit. Later commentators on Acts and Galatians, confronted by a debate between two doctors of the church, generally chose to follow Augustine, but they too did not take the step that Augustine refused to take. For them too Timothy was a gentile.[21]

The first scholar to argue that Timothy was a Jew by birth was the older contemporary of Jerome and Augustine known to modern scholarship as "Ambrosiaster." A set of Latin commentaries on the Pauline epistles, ascribed by both the manuscript tradition and medieval scholarship to Ambrose, the fourth-century bishop of Milan, was declared by Erasmus to be the work of someone else whom he named "Ambrosiaster" (or "ps.-Ambrose"). Scholars have not yet succeeded in determining the identity of this author and the number of his works. The commentaries were written in Rome during the second half of the fourth century, but who wrote them remains a mystery. Most scholars ascribe to Ambrosiaster not only the Pauline commentaries but also the *Questions on the Old and New Testament,* which is attributed to Augustine by the manuscripts. Numerous other works too have been be-

---

21. On the triumph of the Augustinian view see Overbeck, *Über die Auffassung* 70–72; Lightfoot, *Galatians* 132; Mussner, *Galaterbrief* 146–167. It is no surprise that all of the modern followers of Jerome listed in note 5 above regard Timothy as a gentile, and that most of the Augustinians listed in note 6 above regard Timothy as a Jew (see below). The followers of Augustine include Bede, *Expositio Actuum Apostolorum et Retractatio,* ed. M. L. W. Laistner (Cambridge, Mass.: Mediaeval Academy of America, 1939) 134–135; John Calvin, *Ioanni Calvini in Novum Testamentum Commentarii,* vol. 4, *In Acta Apostolorum,* ed. A.Tholuck (Berlin: G. Eichler, 1833) 316–317; and Cornelius à Lapide, *Commentaria in Acta Apostolorum* (Antwerp: vidua I. Meursy, 1684) 251. Bede paraphrases Augustine's distinction between the circumcision of Timothy and the noncircumcision of Titus. (He adds an ingenious chronological note: Paul's circumcision of Timothy prompted rumors that he too preached a gospel of circumcision, and in order to refute these rumors Paul refused to circumcise Titus.) Calvin's *sepelienda synagoga cum honore* echoes Augustine *Epist.* 116.20.5 (CSEL 55.412). Cornelius à Lapide adopts Aquinas' summary of Augustine's position: *legalia enim erant mortua, sed necdum mortifera* (on Aquinas see below). Cassiodorus, *Complexiones in Actus Apostolorum* 38 (PL 70.1394), seems to follow Jerome. All of these scholars either say or imply that Timothy was a gentile. For the followers of Chrysostom see note 12 above. Thomas Aquinas and Nicolaus of Lyra follow Augustine but add that Timothy was a Jew; see below.

stowed upon this unknown by enthusiastic source critics. In addition to
these uncertainties, the manuscript tradition of both the Pauline commentaries and the *Questions* is very complex because each work was revised at least once or twice by the author (or by someone else). Here I
assume that "Ambrosiaster" is the author of all the extant versions of the
Questions on the New Testament and the commentaries on the Pauline
epistles.[22]

Ambrosiaster anticipates the major points of Augustine's interpretation:[23] Paul did not "lie" or simulate piety; circumcision and the other
Jewish ceremonies were not *periculosae* (dangerous, harmful) but *superfluae et inanes* (superfluous and empty); Paul rebuked Peter because
Peter sought to impose the Law upon the gentiles.[24] When he explains
the circumcision of Timothy, however, Ambrosiaster makes a significant
addition: Timothy was a Jew because of his Jewish mother. In the following quotation from Ambrosiaster's commentary on Galatians 2:4–
5, square brackets enclose words that are found only in the first edition,
and braces enclose words that are found only in the later edition.[25]

*But because of false brethren secretly brought in, who slipped in to spy out our
freedom which we have in Christ Jesus, that they might subject us to bondage:*
that is, they slipped in with guile and deceit for this purpose, in order to
subject our liberty to bondage by forcing us to be subject to the law of circumcision. *For the moment we yielded to subjection:* that is, for the moment

22. G. Bardy, "Ambrosiaster," *Dictionnaire de la Bible, supplement* 1.225–241; A. Stuiber, "Ambrosiaster," *Theologische Realenzyklopädie* 2.356–362. For a recent study of Ambrosiaster, see David G. Hunter, "*On the Sin of Adam and Eve:* A Little Known Defense
of Marriage and Childbearing by Ambrosiaster," *HTR* 82 (1989) 283–299. I cite the
Quaestiones from CSEL 50 (ed. A. Souter) and the commentaries from CSEL 81 (ed. H. I.
Vogels).

23. In *Epist.* 116.24.1 (CSEL 55.414) Augustine claims that he is following the interpretation of "Ambrose," by which he probably means the author of the commentaries on
the Pauline epistles. See J. H. Baxter, "Ambrosiaster Cited as 'Ambrose' in 405," *JTS* 24
(1922–1923) 187. As far as I have been able to determine, Ambrosiaster deems the observance of the Law in Paul's time *res superflua* (see next note) but does not clearly articu-
late Augustine's theory of a tripartite history of the Law. Ambrosiaster says instead that
Paul was "compelled" by the circumstances to judaize (*Appendix Quaest.* 60.2 [CSEL
50.455] and commentary on Gal. 2:12 [CSEL 81,3.26]), a notion that is not easily reconciled with Augustine (it appears in Jerome; see note 15 above).

24. Paul did not lie or simulate: *Appendix Quaest.* 48 and 60.2 (CSEL 50.443–444
and 455); commentary on 1 Cor. 9:20 (CSEL 81,2.103–104). Jewish ceremonies are not
periculosae but *superfluae: Appendix Quaest.* 48 (CSEL 50.443); commentary on Gal. 2:14
(CSEL 81,3.27). Peter sought to impose the Law upon gentiles: *Appendix Quaest.* 60
(CSEL 50.453–455); commentary on Gal. 2:14 (CSEL 81,3.26–27).

25. CSEL 81,3.20–21; part of this text reappears verbatim in the commentary on Gal.
2:14 (CSEL 81,3.27). I ignore the minor variations between the editions because they do
not affect our discussion.

we subjected ourselves to servitude, humbling ourselves to the Law, so that by the circumcision of Timothy the guile and scandal of the Jews should cease. For they were prepared, as is readily understandable, to rouse a tumult and an uprising against him. Indeed, there was a reason that they had an opportunity for making a slanderous accusation. Timothy was born of a mother who was a Jew but a father who was a Greek [, that is, a proselyte]. Consequently, he was not circumcised as an infant according to the Law [because his mother was already a believer]. The apostle, however, wishing to take him and ordain him bishop, as he in fact did, because, he says, everyone provided good testimony about him, suffered an ambush from the Jews. For they were spying on him, to see whether he would take an uncircumcised son of a Jewish woman, and were preparing an uprising against him, because if he replied that the men of the Greeks were not to be circumcised {as had been decided in an epistle on this subject from the apostles}, he ought not to forbid the circumcision of the sons of Israel {because the apostles indicated nothing about them in that epistle. By its authority the Jews who were believers attacked with even greater ferocity, because that epistle did not prohibit the Jews from circumcising their own sons}. Then, he says, taking him, *he circumcised him on account of the Jews that were in those places.* They did not, however, have a scandal about the gentiles, whence Titus was not compelled to be circumcised.

Following a "Western" reading of Galatians 2:5, which omits the negative particle (texts with the negative particle read *Even for the moment we yielded not to subjection*), Ambrosiaster explains that Paul yielded to the Jews when he circumcised Timothy. As we have seen, most exegetes differentiate between the circumcision of Timothy and the noncircumcision of Titus on the basis of the social setting of each incident. Ambrosiaster, however, regards the settings as identical—in each case Paul is confronted by Jews and Law-observant Christians—and therefore substitutes a different distinction. The council of Acts 15 decreed that gentiles need not be circumcised but made no such declaration concerning the Jews. Titus was a gentile; therefore, in his case, there was no scandal and no compulsion. Timothy, however, was a Jew. In the first edition of his commentary, Ambrosiaster suggested that Timothy's father was a proselyte, a convert to Judaism. The point of this suggestion, I suppose, is to explain how a pious woman like Eunice (2 Tim. 1:5) could have married a "Greek." If his mother was a Jew and his father a proselyte, why was Timothy not circumcised? Because, as a good Christian, Timothy's mother would not permit it! This ingenious but somewhat far-fetched explanation was replaced in the second edition by the simple statement that Timothy was not circumcised because his father was a gentile. What is important for us is that Ambrosiaster, in both the first and the second editions, regards Timothy as a Jew because he was born of a Jewish mother.[26]

Here then is an "Augustinian" interpretation of Acts 16:1–3 (actually written in anticipation of Augustine) that is more elegant than that of Augustine himself. In Timothy's time Jews could still observe the Law licitly. Timothy was a Jew; therefore his circumcision is unobjectionable. Thomas Aquinas (ca. 1225–1274) preferred Augustine's argument to Jerome's, but when he came to explain the circumcision of Timothy he abandoned Augustine's exegesis for Ambrosiaster's.

> Those who converted to Christianity from Judaism were able to observe the works of the law licitly . . . For those, however, who converted to Christianity from paganism, there was no reason that they should observe them. Therefore Paul circumcised Timothy, who was born of a Jewish mother, but refused to circumcise Titus, who was born of pagan parents.[27]

Ambrosiaster's influence is also apparent on Nicolaus (or Nicholas) of Lyra (ca. 1270–1340) in his commentary on Acts 16:1–3:

> This circumcision was not insincere (*ficta*), as Jerome says, but sincere (*vera*), as Augustine says, because at that time those born under Judaism and converted to Christ were able to observe the Law licitly. Indeed, offspring follows the womb. Because there is greater certainty about the mother than about the father, and, by contrast, although his father was a gentile, he was considered then to be a Jew.[28]

Nicolaus prefers Augustine to Jerome and, following Ambrosiaster, says explicitly that Timothy "was considered then to be a Jew." Nicolaus also makes an important original contribution. Why was Timothy considered to be a Jew? Because "offspring follows the womb" and "there is greater certainty about the mother than about the father." These phrases echo the Roman legal texts surveyed above in chapter 9,[29] and

26. Parallel to *explorabant enim (Iudaei) si filium Iudaeae incircumcisum susciperet* on p. 21 is *explorantes si eum qui Iudaeus natus erat incircumcisum adsumeret* on p. 27. Ambrosiaster's commentary on Gal. 2:4–5 is copied verbatim by Rabanus Maurus (*PL* 112.267–268).

27. Thomas Aquinas, *Summa Theologiae* prima secundae, q. 103 art. 4 (Blackfriars edition [1969] 29.248–249).

28. *Biblia Sacra cum Glossis . . . Nicolai Lyrani,* 7 vols. (Lyons, 1545), 6.192b.

29. *Proles enim sequitur ventrem* is a paraphrase of Ulpian 5.5, *partus sequitur matrem. Maior est certitudo de matre quam de patre* echoes the *Digest* 2.4.5, *semper [mater] certa est.*

Nicolaus is implying that the Roman matrilineal principle will explain how Timothy came to be regarded as a Jew.[30] What is implicit in Nicolaus is made explicit by J. J. Wetstein (or Wettstein; 1693–1754), who, in his commentary on Acts 16:1–3, adduces various Roman legal texts to prove that the status of the offspring of intermarriage is determined by the mother, not the father.[31] Wetstein also adduces various rabbinic texts to prove the same point. With Wetstein we have our first explicit linkage between Acts 16:1–3 and the rabbinic matrilineal principle.[32]

Nicolaus implies that a matrilineal understanding of Timothy's Jewishness derives from Roman law; Wetstein states that it derives from either Roman or rabbinic law. It is likely that Ambrosiaster too read Acts 16:1–3 in the light of either the Roman or the rabbinic law. Ambrosiaster knew Roman law well (indeed, some scholars have suggested that he was a jurist) and was familiar with the Jews and Judaism of his day (indeed, some scholars have suggested that he was a born Jew who converted to Christianity).[33] Inspired by his knowledge of either Roman or rabbinic law, Ambrosiaster suggested that Timothy was Jewish. Wet-

30. It is possible that Nicolaus may have been influenced here also by his knowledge of the rabbinic matrilineal principle; he was one of the finest Christian Hebraists of the Middle Ages. On his knowledge of Hebrew see Herman Hailperin, *Rashi and the Christian Scholars* (Pittsburgh: University of Pittsburgh Press, 1963), and Jeremy Cohen, *The Friars and the Jews* (Ithaca: Cornell University Press, 1982) 174–191.

31. It is unclear whether Nicolaus and Wetstein believed that the Roman law applied to the marriage of Timothy's parents, or whether they adduce the Roman law merely to indicate a parallel to their understanding of Acts 16:1–3. If the former, Nicolaus and Wetstein are in error, because there is no sign that either Timothy's mother or father was a Roman citizen. Furthermore, the Roman law of persons determined whether one was citizen or peregrine, free or slave, in the eyes of the state; it did not determine whether one was a Jew or a gentile, and it certainly did not determine whether one was a Jew or a gentile in the eyes of the Jews of Asia Minor, the point at issue here. Therefore I prefer the latter possibility: Nicolaus and Wetstein are adducing the Roman law merely as an analogy.

32. Wetstenius, *Novum Testamentum Graecum* 2.552.

33. On Ambrosiaster's knowledge of Judaism and Roman law see Bardy, "Ambrosiaster"; Stuiber, "Ambrosiaster"; and the chapter on Ambrosiaster in A. Souter, *The Earliest Latin Commentaries on the Epistles of St. Paul* (Oxford: Clarendon, 1927). Many scholars identify Ambrosiaster with a Jew named Isaac who converted to Christianity. Some of the enthusiastic source critics mentioned above ascribe to him the *Mosaicarum et Romanarum Legum Collatio*. Souter (p. 72) notes that a study of Ambrosiaster's knowledge of Judaism is a *desideratum*. In particular, it would be important to determine the sort of Judaism with which he is familiar. On Ambroisiater and Judaism, see now Leonard Rutgers, *The Jews in Late Ancient Rome* (Leiden: Brill, 1995) 229–231, who refers to L. Speller, "Ambrosiaster and the Jews," *Studia Patristica* 17 (1982) 72–77, which I have not been able to locate.

stein's commentary ensured a secure place for this view in modern scholarship.[34]

This lengthy survey of the history of the exegesis of Acts 16:1–3 demonstrates that the vast majority of exegetes, from the second century to the eighteenth, did not explain Paul's conduct by appeal to Timothy's Jewishness. As the son of a gentile father Timothy was a gentile. The reference to the Jewishness of Timothy's mother was considered by these scholars to be inconsequential and virtually irrelevant.[35] This approach is all the more remarkable because Augustine and his followers would have found the circumcision easier to explain had they insisted that Timothy, as the son of a Jewish mother, was a Jew. But this interpretation was advanced only by some proponents of the Augustinian view (Ambrosiaster, Thomas Aquinas, and Nicolaus of Lyra), and they, at least to some extent, read Acts 16:1–3 in the light of data (Roman and rabbinic) not contained in the text itself. When read on its own terms, Acts 16:1–3 clearly implied, and implies, that Timothy was a gentile.

A final note. Although Timothy is mentioned a dozen times in the New Testament (aside from Acts 16:1–3), not a single passage implies that he was a Jew by birth. Even the two passages that speak of his home life (2 Tim. 1:5 and 3:15) do not imply that he was a Jew.[36]

34. Haenchen, *Acts of the Apostles*, says that this view was introduced to modern scholarship in 1852 by H. Thiersch. Among the scholars who regard Timothy as a Jew are Lake and Cadbury, Belkin, Packer, Hanson, O'Neill, Stählin, Wilson, and Bruce listed in note 6 above as followers of Augustine. Other advocates of this view are E. Preuschen, *Die Apostelgeschichte*, HNT, vol. 4, no. 1 (Tübingen: Mohr [Siebeck], 1912) 98–99 (who quotes Wetstein); Strack and Billerbeck, *Kommentar* 2.741; O. Bauernfeind, *Kommentar und Studien zur Apostelgeschichte*, WUNT 22 (Tübingen: Mohr [Siebeck], 1980; the commentary was first printed in 1939) 204; Conzelmann, *Acts* 125; J. Munck, *Acts of the Apostles*, Anchor Bible 31 (New York: Doubleday, 1967) 155; M. Hengel, *Acts and the History of Earliest Christianity* (Philadelphia: Fortress, 1979) 64. Most of these scholars refer to the rabbinic principle; a few quote the Roman principle as well.

35. I would argue that, even if Timothy is to be considered a gentile, the reference to the Jewishness of his mother is not irrelevant. Prof. J. Louis Martyn suggests to me that Luke imagines that the early Christians confront a world consisting of three groups: Jews, gentiles, and those in between—i. e., "sympathizers," "God-fearers," and the like. Timothy, by virtue of his mixed lineage, is a member of this middle group. He is neither wholly a Jew nor wholly a gentile. See Jack T. Sanders, "Who Is a Jew and Who Is a Gentile in the Book of Acts?" *New Testament Studies* 37 (1991) 434–455.

36. They do not even imply that his mother was a Jew, a point unappreciated by Haenchen, *Acts of the Apostles* 478 n. 3. And no text, of course, implies that he was a *mamzer* (according to the Mishnah, as the offspring of a Jewish mother and a gentile father, Timothy will have been a *mamzer*; see M. Yevamot 7:5, cited in chapter 9 above, at note 50).

Was Timothy Jewish? In all likelihood Luke did not think so. The vast majority of ancient and medieval exegetes did not think so. Ambrosiaster and his medieval followers did think so, but in all likelihood this interpretation is wrong because there is no evidence that any Jew in pre-mishnaic times thought that the offspring of an intermarriage follows the status of the mother. Was Timothy Jewish? The answer must be no.[37]

37. Christopher Bryan argues that my interpretation of Acts 16:1–3 may or may not be correct, a sentiment with which I fully concur; see "A Further Look at Acts 16:1–3," *JBL* 107 (1988) 292–294. Levinskaya, *Book of Acts* 15–17, thinks that both Luke and the Jews of Asia Minor thought of Timothy as a Jew, but I am not convinced; see chapter 9 above, note 136.

Glossary of Some Hebrew Terms

Bavli. "Babylonian," convenient designation for the Babylonian Talmud.

Beraita. "An outside teaching," a statement not found in the Mishnah although ostensibly by an authority of the Mishnaic period.

Karet. Usually translated as "extirpation." In the Torah *karet* is one of the punishments inflicted on those who violate God's commands, but the content of the punishment is no clearer to us than it was to the rabbis, who speculated that it meant premature death or the death of one's children.

Mamzer. Usually translated as "bastard," but because *bastard* in English often means "offspring born out of wedlock," this is a poor translation, since the term seems not to have that meaning in Deuteronomy 23:3, and definitely does not have that meaning in rabbinic texts. In rabbinic law a *mamzer* is the offspring of a severely prohibited union; as a result of his/her parentage a *mamzer* is not permitted to marry a Jew of good standing. If a *mamzer* does in fact cohabit with a Jew of good standing, the resulting offspring is a *mamzer*.

Setam. "Plain." The anonymous voice of the Mishnah and the Talmud is the *setam,* as opposed to statements that are attributed to named authorities. Modern scholars also occasionally use the term to refer to the anonymous editors of the Talmud.

Yerushalmi. "Jerusalemite," the standard if incorrect epithet for the Talmud of the land of Israel, sometimes called the Palestinian Talmud.

Tanakh. The Bible; what Christians call the Old Testament, what the politically correct call the Hebrew Bible. Acronym for *Torah, Nevi'im* (Prophets) and *Ketuvim* (Writings).

Bibliography and Abbreviations

Books and articles that are cited only once or twice are not listed here. The works of Josephus and Philo are cited from the editions of the Loeb Classical Library. All of the classical authors cited in this book can readily be found in the Loeb Classical Library; if I have used other editions, I have indicated the editor's name after the citation.

Rabbinic Texts

Note: rabbinic texts are generally cited according to the following paradigm: (abbreviation of) name of work, name of section or tractate, section number (in the case of the tannaitic midrashim), page number in the indicated edition. All of the following editions have been reprinted frequently.

AdRN = *Avoth de Rabbi Nathan* (*Fathers according to Rabbi Nathan*). Edited by Solomon Schechter. Vienna, 1887.

B. = Babylonian Talmud (Bavli). Vilna: Romm, 1880–86.

Genesis Rabbah. Ed. J. Theodor and H. Albeck. Berlin, 1912–1936.

Leviticus Rabbah. Ed. M. Margulies. Jerusalem, 1953–1960.

M. = Mishnah. Ed. H. Albeck. Jerusalem: Bialik Institute, 1952–58.

Mekhilta. HR = ed. H. S. Horovitz and I. A. Rabin (Frankfurt, 1931). L = ed. Jacob Lauterbach (Philadelphia: Jewish Publication Society, 1933–1935).

Sifra on Leviticus. Ed. I. H. Weiss. Vienna, 1862.

Sifrei on Deuteronomy. Ed. L. Finkelstein. Berlin, 1939.

Sifrei on Numbers. Ed. H. S. Horovitz. Leipzig, 1917.

T. = Tosefta. L = ed. Saul Lieberman (New York: Jewish Theological Seminary, 1955–1988: for the orders Zeraim through Nashim and the first three tractates of Neziqin). Z = ed. M. S. Zuckermandel (Passewalk, Germany, 1880).

Y. = Yerushalmi (Talmud of the Land of Israel). Cited according to the pagination of the first edition, Venice, 1523–24.

Other References

AJ = Josephus, *Antiquitates Judaicae* (*Jewish Antiquities*)

Adams, J. N. *The Latin Sexual Vocabulary.* Baltimore: Johns Hopkins University Press, 1982. Reprint, 1991.

à Lapide, Cornelius. *Commentaria in Pentateuchum Mosis.* Antwerp, 1630.

Amir, Yehoshua. "The Term *Ioudaismos,* a Study in Jewish-Hellenistic Self-Identification." *Immanuel* 14 (1982) 34–41.

Anderson, Benedict. *Imagined Communities: Reflections on the Origin and Spread of Nationalism.* Rev. ed. London: Verso, 1991.

Anderson, Gary. "The Status of the Torah before Sinai: The Retelling of the Bible in the Damascus Covenant and the Book of Jubilees." *Dead Sea Discoveries* 1 (1994) 1–29.

ANRW = *Aufstieg und Niedergang der römischen Welt*

Aptowitzer, Victor. "Spuren des Matriarchats im jüdischen Schrifttum." *Hebrew Union College Annual* 4 (1925) 207–240 and 5 (1926) 261–297.

Balsdon, J. P. V. D. *Romans and Aliens.* London: Duckworth, 1979.

Bamberger, Bernard J. *Proselytism in the Talmudic Period.* New York: Hebrew Union College, 1939. Reprint, New York: Ktav, 1968.

Barclay, John M. G. *Jews in the Mediterranean Diaspora: From Alexander to Trajan.* Edinburgh: T. & T. Clark, 1996.

Baron, Salo. *Social and Religious History of the Jews: Ancient Times.* 2d ed. 2 vols. New York: Columbia University Press, 1952.

Barrett, D. S. "Martial, Jews, and Circumcision." *Liverpool Classical Monthly* 9, no. 3 (March 1984) 42–46.

Belkin, Samuel. "The Problem of Paul's Background." *JBL* 54 (1935) 41–60.

Beth She'arim. Vol. 2, *The Greek Inscriptions,* ed. Moshe Schwabe and Baruch Lifshitz. New Brunswick, N.J.: Rutgers University Press, 1974. Vol. 3, *The Excavations, 1953–1958,* by Nahman Avigad. New Brunswick, N.J.: Rutgers University Press, 1976.

Bi(c)kerman(n), Elias (Elie). "Beiträge zur antiken Urkundengeschichte: I. Der Heimatsvermerk." *Archiv für Papyrusforschung* 8 (1927) 216–239.

———. *Institutions des Séleucides.* Paris: Paul Guethner, 1938.

———. *Studies in Jewish and Christian History.* 3 vols. Leiden: Brill, 1976–1986.

———. *The Jews in the Greek Age.* Cambridge: Harvard University Press, 1988.

Bilde, Per, et al., eds. *Ethnicity in Hellenistic Egypt.* Aarhus, Denmark: Aarhus University Press, 1992.

Birnbaum, Ellen. *The Place of Judaism in Philo's Thought: Israel, Jews, and Proselytes.* Brown Judaic Studies, no. 290. Atlanta: Scholars Press, 1996.

BJ = Josephus, *Bellum Judaicum* (*Jewish War*)

Boegehold, Alan. "Perikles' Citizenship Law of 451/0 B.C." In *Athenian Identity and Civic Ideology,* ed. A. Boegehold and A. Scafuro, 57–66. Baltimore: Johns Hopkins University Press, 1994.

Boswinkel, E., and P. W. Pestman. *Les archives privées de Dionysios.* Papyrologica Lugduno-Batava, vol. 22A. Leiden: Brill, 1982.

Bruneau, Philippe. "'Les Israelites de Délos' et la juiverie délienne." *Bulletin de correspondance hellenique* 106 (1982) 465–504.

Bulliet, Richard W. *Conversion to Islam in the Medieval Period.* Cambridge: Harvard University Press, 1979.

CAp = Josephus, *Contra Apionem* (*Against Apion*)

Carmichael, Calum M. *The Laws of Deuteronomy.* Ithaca and London: Cornell University Press, 1974.

CChr = *Corpus Christianorum* (Turnholt: Brepols)

Charlesworth, J. H., ed. *The Old Testament Pseudepigrapha.* 2 vols. Garden City, N.Y.: Doubleday, 1983–1985.

Chesnutt, Randall. *From Death to Life: Conversion in Joseph and Aseneth.* Journal for the Study of the Pseudepigrapha Supplement no. 16. Sheffield, England: Sheffield Academic Press, 1995.

Christophilopoulos, Anastasios. *Dikaion kai Historia.* Athens: n.p., 1973.

CIJ = *Corpus Inscriptionum Judaicarum.* See Frey.

Clarysse, Willy. *The Petrie Papyri.* 2d ed. Vol. 1, *The Wills.* Collectanea Hellenistica, no. 2. Brussels, 1991.

———. "Jews in Trikomia." In *Proceedings of the 20th International Congress of Papyrology, Copenhagen, 1992,* ed. A. Bülow-Jacobsen, 193–203. Copenhagen: Museum Tusculanum Press, 1994.

Cohen, Boaz. "Some Remarks on the Law of Persons in Jewish and Roman Jurisprudence." *Proceedings of the American Academy for Jewish Research* 16 (1946–1947) 1–37. Reprinted in Boaz Cohen, *Jewish and Roman Law* (New York: Jewish Theological Seminary, 1966) 1.122–158.

Cohen, Shaye J. D. "Alexander the Great and Jaddus the High Priest according to Josephus." *Association for Jewish Studies Review* 7–8 (1982–1983) 41–68.

———. "Solomon and the Daughter of Pharaoh: Intermarriage, Conversion, and the Impurity of Women." *Journal of the Ancient Near Eastern Society of Columbia University* 16/17 (1984–1985) 23–37.

———. "Respect for Judaism by Gentiles in the Writings of Josephus." *HTR* 80 (1987) 409–430.

———. "History and Historiography in the *Against Apion* of Josephus." *History and Theory Beiheft 27: Essays in Jewish Historiography* (1988) 1–11.

———. "*Ioudaios to Genos* and Related Expressions in Josephus." In *Josephus and the History of the Greco-Roman Period: Essays in Memory of Morton Smith,* ed. F. Parente and J. Sievers, 23–38. Leiden: Brill, 1994.

———. "Is 'Proselyte Baptism' Mentioned in the Mishnah? The Interpretation of M. Pesahim 8:8 (= M. Eduyot 5:2)." In *Pursuing the Text: Studies in Honor of Ben Zion Wacholder,* ed. John Reeves, 278–292. Sheffield, England: Sheffield Academic Press, 1994.

Collins, John. "The Epic of Theodotus and the Hellenism of the Hasmoneans." *HTR* 73 (1980) 91–104

Cotton, Hannah M., and Joseph Geiger. *Masada: The Yigael Yadin Excavations, 1963–1965: Final Reports.* Vol. 2, *The Latin and Greek Documents.* Jerusalem: Israel Exploration Society, 1989.

CPJ = Corpus Papyrorum Judaicarum. See Tcherikover.

CPR = Corpus Papyrorum Raineri

CPR 13. See Harrauer.

CPR 18. See Kramer.

CSEL = Corpus Scriptorum Ecclesiasticorum Latinorum

Dán, Róbert. "'Judaizare': The Career of a Term." In *Antitrinitarianism in the Second Half of the Sixteenth Century,* ed. R. Dán and A. Pirnát, 25–34. Budapest: Hungarian Academy of Sciences, 1982.

Daube, David. *The New Testament and Rabbinic Judaism.* London: Athlone, 1956.

———. *Ancient Jewish Law: Three Inaugural Lectures.* Leiden: Brill, 1981.

Davies, J. K. "The *Polis* Transformed and Revitalized." In *The Cambridge Ancient History,* 2d ed., vol. 7, pt. 1, ed. F. W. Walbank et al., 304–315. Cambridge: Cambridge University Press, 1984.

Davies, Philip R. "Who Can Join the 'Damascus Covenant'?" *Journal of Jewish Studies* 46 (1995) 134–142.

Davis, F. James. *Who Is Black? One Nation's Definition.* University Park, Pa.: Pennsylvania State University Press, 1991.

Delia, Diana. *The Alexandrian Citizenship.* Atlanta: Scholars Press, 1991.

de Lange, Nicholas. *Origen and the Jews.* Cambridge: Cambridge University Press, 1976.

de Romilly, Jacqueline. *The Rise and Fall of States according to Greek Authors.* Ann Arbor: University of Michigan Press, 1977.

Donaldson, Terence. "Proselytes or 'Righteous Gentiles'? The Status of Gentiles in Eschatological Pilgrimage Patterns of Thought." *Journal for the Study of the Pseudepigrapha* 7 (1990) 3–27.

Dulière, L. "La seconde circoncision pratiquée entre juifs et samaritains." *L'antiquité classique* 36 (1967) 553–565.

Engel, Helmut. *Die Susanna-Erzählung.* Freiburg, Switzerland: Universtitätsverlag; Göttingen: Vandenhoeck & Ruprecht, 1985.

Epstein, Louis M. *Marriage Laws in the Bible and the Talmud.* Cambridge: Harvard University Press, 1942.

Feldman, Louis H. *Jew and Gentile in the Ancient World.* Princeton: Princeton University Press, 1993.

FGrH = Felix Jacoby, *Die Fragmente der Griechischen Historiker.* Berlin: Weidmann, 1923–1954.

Figueras, Pau. "Epigraphic Evidence for Proselytism in Ancient Judaism." *Immanuel 24/25* (1990) 194–206.

Fishbane, Michael. *Biblical Interpretation in Ancient Israel.* Oxford: Clarendon, 1985.

Flesher, Paul V. M. *Oxen, Women, or Citizens? Slaves in the System of the Mishnah.* Brown Judaic Studies, no. 143. Atlanta: Scholars Press, 1988.

Francus, Israel. "The Status of the Offspring of Mixed Marriages in Rabbinic Sources" (in Hebrew). *Sidra* 4 (1988) 89–110.

Fraser, P. M. *Ptolemaic Alexandria.* 3 vols. Oxford: Clarendon, 1972.

Frey, Jean-Baptiste. *Corpus Inscriptionum Judaicarum* (cited as *CIJ*). Vol. 1, *Europe.* Vatican City: Pontificio Istituto di Archeologia Cristiana, 1936. Reprint, New York: Ktav, 1975, with prolegomenon by B. Lifshitz. Vol. 2, *Asie-Afrique.* Vatican City: Pontificio Istituto di Archeologia Cristiana, 1952.

Gager, John. *Moses in Greco-Roman Paganism.* Nashville: Abingdon, 1972.

Gavin, Frank. *The Jewish Antecedents of the Christian Sacraments.* London: SPCK, 1928. Reprint, New York: Ktav, 1969.

GCS = Die griechischen christlichen Schriftsteller

Gilula, Dwora. "Did Martial Have a Jewish Slave?" *Classical Quarterly* 81 (1987) 532–533.

Ginzberg, Louis. *Legends of the Jews.* 7 vols. Reprint, Philadelphia: Jewish Publication Society, 1967–1968.

———. *An Unknown Jewish Sect.* New York: Jewish Theological Seminary, 1976.

Goldstein, Jonathan. *I Maccabees.* Garden City, N.Y.: Doubleday, 1976

———. *II Maccabees.* Garden City, N.Y.: Doubleday, 1983

Goodenough, E. R. *Jewish Symbols in the Greco-Roman Period.* 13 vols. Princeton: Princeton University Press, 1953–1968.

Goodman, Martin. "Nerva, the *Fiscus Judaicus,* and Jewish Identity." *JRS* 79 (1989) 40–44.

———. "Proselytising in Rabbinic Judaism." *JJS* 40 (1989) 175–185.

———. *Who Was a Jew?* Yarnton Manor (Oxford): Oxford Centre for Postgraduate Hebrew Studies, 1989.

———. *Mission and Conversion.* Oxford: Clarendon, 1994.

Goudriaan, Koen. *Ethnicity in Ptolemaic Egypt.* Dutch Monographs on Ancient History, no. 5. Amsterdam: Gieben, 1988.

———. "Ethnical Strategies in Graeco-Roman Egypt." In *Ethnicity in Hellenistic Egypt,* ed. Per Bilde et al., 74–99. Aarhus, Denmark: Aarhus University Press, 1992.

Gruber, Mayer. "Matrilineal Determination of Jewishness: Biblical and Near Eastern Roots." In *Pomegranates and Golden Bells: Studies . . . in Honor of Jacob Milgrom,* ed. David P. Wright et al., 437–443. Winona Lake, Ind.: Eisenbrauns, 1995.

Habicht, Christian. "Royal Documents in Maccabees II." *Harvard Studies in Classical Philology* 80 (1976) 1–18.

———. *2. Makkabäerbuch.* Vol. 1 of *Jüdische Schriften aus hellenistisch-römischer Zeit.* (Gütersloh, Germany: Mohn, 1976)

Hadas-Lebel, Mireille. "Les mariages mixtes dans la famille d'Hérode et la *halakha* prétalmudique sur la patrilinéarité." *REJ* 152 (1993) 397–404.

Halivni, David [Weiss]. *Sources and Traditions: A Source-Critical Commentary on Seder Nashim* (in Hebrew). Tel Aviv: Dvir, 1968.

Hall, Robert G. "Epispasm and the Dating of Ancient Jewish Writings." *Journal for the Study of the Pseudepigrapha* 2 (1988) 71–86.

Hannick, Jean-Marie. "Droit de cité et marriages mixtes dans la Grèce classique." *L'antiquité classique* 45 (1976) 133–148.

Hanson, Ann Ellis. "Egyptians, Greeks, Romans, *Arabes,* and *Ioudaioi* in the First Century A.D. Tax Archive from Philadelphia." In *Life in a Multi-Cultural Society: Egypt from Cambyses to Constantine and Beyond,* ed. J. H. Johnson, Studies in Ancient Oriental Civilization, no. 51, 133–145. Chicago: Oriental Institute, 1992.

Harrauer, Hermann. *Griechische Texte IX: Neue Papyri zum Steuerwesen im 3. Jh. v. Chr.* CPR 13. Vienna: Brüder Hollinek, 1987.

Hengel, Martin. *Die Zeloten.* Leiden: Brill, 1961. 2d ed., 1976.

Hertz, Joseph J. *The Pentateuch and Haftorahs.* 1936. Reprint, London: Soncino, 1961.

Holladay, Carl. *Fragments from Hellenistic Jewish Authors.* Vol. 1, *Historians.* Atlanta: Scholars Press, 1983. Vol. 2, *Poets.* Atlanta: Scholars Press, 1989.

Honigman, Sylvie. "The Birth of a Diaspora: The Emergence of a Jewish Self-Definition in Ptolemaic Egypt in the Light of Onomastics." In *Diasporas in Antiquity,* ed. Shaye J. D. Cohen and Ernest Frerichs, Brown Judaic Studies, no. 288, 93–127. Atlanta: Scholars Press, 1993.

Horbury, William, and Dov Noy. *Jewish Inscriptions of Graeco-Roman Egypt.* Cambridge: Cambridge University Press, 1992.

HTR = Harvard Theological Review

Ilan, Tal. "'Man Born of Woman . . .': The Phenomenon of Men Bearing Metronymes at the Time of Jesus." *Novum Testamentum* 34 (1992) 23–45.

——. *Jewish Women in Greco-Roman Palestine.* Tübingen: Mohr (Siebeck), 1995. Reprint, Peabody, Mass.: Hendrickson, 1996.

Irsai, Oded. "Ya'akov of Kefar Niburaia—A Sage Turned Apostate." *Jerusalem Studies in Jewish Thought* 2, no. 2 (1982–1983) 153–168.

JBL = Journal of Biblical Literature

JIGRE = Jewish Inscriptions of Graeco-Roman Egypt. See Horbury and Noy.

JIWE = Jewish Inscriptions of Western Europe. See Noy.

JJS = Journal of Jewish Studies

Jocelyn, H. D. "A Greek Indecency and Its Students: *Laikazein.*" *Proceedings of the Cambridge Philological Society* 26 (1980) 12–66.

JRS = Journal of Roman Studies

JSJ = Journal for the Study of Judaism

JSNT = Journal for the Study of the New Testament

JSS = Journal of Semitic Studies

JTS = Journal of Theological Studies

Juster, Jean. *Les juifs dans l'empire romain.* 2 vols. Paris: Guethner, 1914.

Kahana, Avraham. *Hasefarim hahitzonim.* 2 vols. Reprint, Jerusalem: Makor, 1978.

Kahana, Kalman. *Masekhet Bikkurim: heker ve'iyun.* Jerusalem: The Institute for the Study of the Commandments that Pertain to the Land of Israel, 1988. Hebrew.

Kajanto, Iiro. *The Latin Cognomina.* Helsinki, 1965. Reprint, Rome: Bretschneider, 1982.

Kaser, Max. *Das römische Privatrecht.* 2d ed. Munich: Beck, 1971.

Kasher, Aryeh. *The Jews in Hellenistic and Roman Egypt.* Tübingen: Mohr (Siebeck), 1985.

——. *Jews, Idumaeans, and Ancient Arabs.* Tübingen: Mohr (Siebeck), 1988.

——. *Jews and Hellenistic Cities in Eretz-Israel.* Tübingen: Mohr (Siebeck), 1990.

——. "The Civic Status of the Jews in Ptolemaic Egypt." In *Ethnicity in Hellenistic Egypt,* ed. Per Bilde et al., 100–121. Aarhus, Denmark: Aarhus University Press, 1992.

Kaufmann, Yehezkel. *History of the Religion of Israel.* Vol. 4, *From the Babylonian Captivity to the End of Prophecy.* Trans. C. W. Efroymson. New York: Ktav, 1977.

Kay, Nigel. *Martial Book XI: A Commentary.* London: Duckworth, 1985.

Koschaker, Paul. "Fratriarchat, Hausgemeinschaft, und Mutterrecht in Keilschriftrechten." *Zeitschrift für Assyrologie* 41 n.F. 7 (1933) 1–89.

Kraabel, A. T. "The Roman Diaspora: Six Questionable Assumptions." *JJS* 33 (1982) [= *Essays in Honour of Yigael Yadin*] 445–464.

Kraemer, Ross. "On the Meaning of the Term 'Jew' in Greco-Roman Inscriptions." *HTR* 82 (1989) 35–53

Kramer, Bärbel. *Griechische Texte XIII: Das Vertragsregister von Theogenis.* CPR 18. Vienna: Brüder Hollinek, 1991.

Lacey, W. K. *The Family in Classical Greece.* Ithaca: Cornell University Press, 1968.

Launey, Marcel. *Recherches sur les armées hellénistiques.* 2 vols. Paris: de Boccard, 1950.

Légasse, S. "Baptême juif des proselytes et baptême chrétien." *Bulletin de littérature ecclésiastique* 77 (1976) 3–40.

Leon, Harry J. *The Jews of Ancient Rome.* Philadelphia: Jewish Publication Society, 1960.

Levinskaya, Irina. *The Book of Acts in Its First Century Setting.* Vol. 5, *Diaspora Setting.* Grand Rapids, Mich.: Eerdmans, 1996.

Lewis, David M. "The First Greek Jew." *JSS* 2 (1957) 264–266.

Lieberman, Saul. *Tosefet Rishonim.* 4 vols. Jerusalem: Bamberger et Wahrmann, 1939.

——. *Greek in Jewish Palestine.* New York: Jewish Theological Seminary, 1942; reprint, Feldheim, 1965.

——. *Hellenism in Jewish Palestine.* New York: Jewish Theological Seminary, 1950.

——. *Tosefta Ki-Fshutah.* 10 vols. New York: Jewish Theological Seminary, 1955–1988.

Lifshitz, B. *Donateurs et fondateurs dans les synagogues juives.* Paris: Gabalda, 1967.

Lifshitz, *CIJ.* See Frey.

Linder, Amnon. *The Jews in Roman Imperial Legislation.* Detroit: Wayne State University Press, 1987.

Litvin, Baruch, and Sidney Hoenig, eds. *Jewish Identity: Modern Responsa and Opinions.* New York: Feldheim, 1965.

Lloyd, Alan B. *Herodotus, Book II: Introduction and Commentary.* 3 vols. Leiden: Brill, 1976–1988.

Löw, Leopold. "Eherechtliche Studien." In *Gesammelte Schriften,* vol. 3, ed. Immanuel Löw, 108–200. Szegedin, 1893. Reprint, Hildesheim: Olms, 1979.

Lowe, Malcolm. "Who Were the *Ioudaioi?*" *Novum Testamentum* 18 (1976) 101–130.

———. "*Ioudaioi* of the Apocrypha." *Novum Testamentum* 23 (1981) 56–90.

LSJ = Liddell, Henry George, Robert Scott, and Henry Stuart Jones. *Greek-English Lexicon.* Oxford: Clarendon, 1940. Frequently reprinted.

Lüderitz, Gerd. *Corpus jüdischer Zeugnisse aus der Cyrenaika.* Wiesbaden: Reichert, 1983.

Mandell, Sara. "Who Paid the Temple Tax When the Jews Were under Roman Rule?" *HTR* 77 (1984) 223–232.

McKnight, Scot. "*De Vita Mosis* 1.147: Lion Proselytes in Philo?" *Studia Philonica Annual* 1 (1989) 58–62.

———. *A Light among the Gentiles.* Minneapolis: Fortress, 1991.

Mélèze-Modrzejewski, Joseph. "Le statut des Hellènes dans l'Egypte Lagide." *Revue des études grecques* 96 (1983) 241–268.

———. *The Jews of Egypt from Rameses II to Emperor Hadrian.* Trans. Robert Cornman. Philadephia: Jewish Publication Society, 1995.

Mendelson, Alan. *Philo's Jewish Identity.* Brown Judaic Studies, no. 161. Atlanta: Scholars Press, 1988.

Milgrom, J. "Religious Conversion and the Revolt Model for the Formation of Israel." *JBL* 101 (1982) 169–176.

Mitchell, Stephen. *Anatolia: Land, Men, and Gods in Asia Minor.* Vol. 2, *The Rise of the Church.* Oxford: Clarendon, 1993.

Moore, Carey A. *Daniel, Esther, and Jeremiah: The Additions.* Garden City, N.Y.: Doubleday, 1977

Moore, George Foot. *Judaism in the First Centuries.* 3 vols. Cambridge: Harvard University Press, 1927.

Neufeld, E. *Ancient Hebrew Marriage Laws.* London and New York: Longmans Green, 1944.

Neusner, Jacob. *A History of the Mishnaic Law of Women.* 5 vols. Leiden: Brill, 1980.

———. *Judaism: The Evidence of the Mishnah.* Chicago: University of Chicago Press, 1981.

NewDocs = *New Documents Illustrating Early Christianity.* Macquarie University: Ancient History Documentary Research Centre.

Newman, L. I. *Jewish Influence on Christian Reform Movements.* New York: Columbia University Press, 1925.

Niebuhr, Karl-Wilhelm. *Gesetz und Paränese.* Tübingen: Mohr (Siebeck), 1987.

Noy, Dov. *Jewish Inscriptions of Western Europe.* Vol. 1, *Italy.* Cambridge: Cambridge University Press, 1993.

Oates, John F. "The Status Designation *Persēs, tēs epigonēs.*" *Yale Classical Studies* 18 (1963) 1–129.

Ogden, Daniel. *Greek Bastardy in the Classical and Hellenistic Periods.* Oxford: Clarendon, 1996.

Oliver, James H. *Marcus Aurelius: Aspects of Civic and Cultural Policy in the East.* Hesperia Supplement no. 13. Princeton: American Schools of Classical Studies at Athens, 1970.

Osborne, M. J. *Naturalization in Athens.* 2 vols. Verhandelingen van de

Koninklijke Academie voor Wetenschappen . . . van België, Klasse der
    Letteren, no. 98 (1981) and no. 101 (1982). Brussels.
Overman, Andrew. "The God-Fearers: Some Neglected Features." *JSNT* 32
    (1988) 17–26.
Patai, Raphael. *Sex and Family in the Bible.* New York: Doubleday, 1959.
Patterson, Cynthia B. "Those Athenian Bastards." *Classical Antiquity* 9
    (1990) 40–73.
Pembroke, Simon. "Women in Charge: The Function of Alternatives in Early
    Greek Tradition and the Ancient Idea of Matriarchy." *Journal of the
    Warburg and Courtauld Institutes* 30 (1967) 1–35.
PG = Patrologia Graeca
PGL = Patristic Greek Lexicon. Ed. G. W. H. Lampe. Oxford: Clarendon,
    1961. Frequently reprinted.
PL = Patrologia Latina
Polster, Gottfried. "Der kleine Talmudtraktat über die Proselyten." *Angelos* 2
    (1926) 2–38.
Porten, Bezalel. *Archives from Elephantine.* Berkeley: University of California
    Press, 1968.
———. "The Jews in Egypt." In *The Cambridge History of Judaism,* vol. 1,
    The Persian Period, ed. W. D. Davies and L. Finkelstein, 372–400.
    Cambridge: Cambridge University Press, 1984.
Porten, Bezalel, and Ada Yardeni. *Textbook of Aramaic Documents from
    Ancient Egypt.* 3 vols. Jerusalem: Hebrew University, 1986–1993.
Porton, Gary G. *The Stranger within Your Gates: Converts and Conversion in
    Rabbinic Literature.* Chicago: University of Chicago Press, 1994.
Pummer, R. "Genesis 34 in Jewish Writings of the Hellenistic and Roman
    Periods." *HTR* 75 (1982) 177–188.
Rajak. Tessa. "Jews and Christians as Groups in a Pagan World." In *"To See
    Ourselves as Others See Us": Christians, Jews, "Others," in Late Antiquity,*
    ed. Jacob Neusner and E. Frerichs, 247–262. Atlanta: Scholars Press, 1985.
———. "The Jewish Community and Its Boundaries." In *The Jews among
    Pagans and Christians,* ed. J. Lieu, J. North, and T. Rajak, 9–28. London:
    Routledge, 1992.
Rap(p)aport, Uriel. "Hellenistic Cities and the Judaization of Palestine in the
    Hasmonean Age" (in Hebrew). In *Doron: Studies . . . Presented to Prof.
    B. Z. Katz,* ed. S. Perlman and B. Shimron, 214–230. Tel Aviv: University
    of Tel-Aviv, 1967.
———. "Les Iduméens en Égypte," *Revue de philologie* 43 (1969) 73–82.
REJ = Revue des études juives
Revel, Bernard. "The Karaite Halakah." *Jewish Quarterly Review* 3 (1912–1913)
    337–396.
Reynolds, Joyce, and Robert Tannenbaum. *Jews and Godfearers at Aphrodisias.*
    Cambridge Philological Society Supplementary Volume 12. 1987.
Richardson, Peter. *Herod: King of the Jews and Friend of the Romans.*
    Columbia: University of South Carolina Press, 1996.
Rubin, Nisan. "The Stretching of the Foreskin and the Enactment of *Periah*"
    (in Hebrew). *Zion* 54 (1989) 105–117.

Runia, David T. "Philonic Nomenclature." *Studia Philonica Annual* 6 (1994) 1–27.

Samet. Moshe. "Conversion in the First Centuries c.e." (in Hebrew). In *Jews and Judaism in the Second Temple, Mishna, and Talmud Period: Studies in Honor of Shmuel Safrai,* ed. I. Gafni et al., 316–343. Jerusalem: Yad Izhak Ben-Zvi, 1993.

Sanders, E. P. *Jewish Law from Jesus to the Mishnah.* London: SCM, 1990.

———. *Judaism: Practice and Belief, 63 b.c.e.–66 c.e.* Philadelphia: Trinity Press, 1992.

Schäfer, Peter. *Judeophobia: Attitudes toward the Jews in the Ancient World.* Cambridge: Harvard University Press, 1997.

Scherer, Jean. *Le commentaire d'Origène sur Rom. III.5–V.7.* Institut Français d'Archéologie Orientale, Bibliothèque d'Étude, no. 27. Cairo, 1957.

Schiffman, Lawrence. "At the Crossroads: Tannaitic Perspectives on the Jewish-Christian Schism." In *Jewish and Christian Self-Definition,* vol. 2, *Aspects of Judaism in the Greco-Roman Period,* ed. E. P. Sanders et al., 115–156. Philadelphia: Fortress, 1981.

———. *Who Was a Jew?* Hoboken, N.J.: Ktav, 1985.

Schneemelcher, Wilhelm, ed. *New Testament Apocrypha.* Trans. R. McL. Wilson. Rev. ed. 2 vols. Louisville: Westminster/John Knox, 1992.

Schürer, Emil. *The History of the Jewish People in the Age of Jesus Christ.* Ed. G. Vermes, F. Millar, M. Goodman, et al. 3 vols. in 4. Edinburgh: T. & T. Clark, 1973–1987.

Schwartz, Daniel R. "Priesthood and Priestly Descent: Josephus, *Jewish Antiquities* 10.80." *JTS* 32 (1981) 129–135.

———. "Wilderness and Temple: On Religion and State in Judaea in the Second Temple Period" (in Hebrew). In *Priesthood and Kingship* 61–78. Jerusalem: Zalman Shazar Center, 1987.

———. *Agrippa I.* Tübingen: Mohr (Siebeck), 1990.

———. "On Two Aspects of a Priestly View of Descent at Qumran." In *Archaeology and History in the Dead Sea Scrolls,* ed. Lawrence H. Schiffman, Journal for the Study of the Pseudepigrapha Supplement no. 8 (Sheffield, England: JSOT, 1990) 157–179.

Schwartz, Seth. "Language, Power, and Identity in Ancient Palestine." *Past and Present* 148 (1995) 3–47.

Schwarz, Eberhard. *Identität durch Abgrenzung: Abgrenzungsprozesse in Israel im 2. vorchristlichen Jahrhundert.* Frankfurt: Peter Lang, 1982.

SEG = Supplementum Epigraphicum Graecum

Segal, Eliezer. *The Babylonian Esther Midrash.* 3 vols. Brown Judaic Studies, nos. 291–293.Atlanta: Scholars Press, 1994.

Select Papyri V. 2. Non-Literary Papyri: Public Documents. Ed. A. S. Hunt and C. C. Edgar. Loeb Classical Library, 1934. Reprint, Cambridge: Harvard University Press, 1970.

Sheppard, A. R. R. "Pagan Cults of Angels in Roman Asia Minor." *Talanta* 12–13 (1980–1981) 77–101.

Siegert, Folker. "Gottesfürchtige und Sympathisanten." *Journal for the Study of Judaism* 4 (1973) 109–164.

Simon, Marcel. *Verus Israel.* Trans. H. McKeating. Oxford: Oxford University Press for the Littman Library, 1986.

Smallwood, E. Mary. *The Jews under Roman Rule.* Leiden: Brill, 1981.

———. *Philonis Alexandri Legatio ad Gaium.* Leiden: Brill, 1970.

Smith, Anthony D. *The Ethnic Origins of Nations.* Oxford: Blackwell, 1986. Reprint, 1995.

Smith, Morton. "Rome and Maccabean Conversions." In *Donum Gentilicium: New Testament Studies in Honour of David Daube,* ed. E. Bammel et al., 1–7. Oxford: Clarendon, 1978.

———. *Studies in the Cult of Yahweh.* Ed. Shaye J. D. Cohen. 2 vols. Leiden: Brill, 1996.

———. "The Gentiles." In *Studies* 1.263–319.

———. "On the Wine God in Palestine." In *Studies* 1.227–237.

Solin, Heikki. *Die griechischen Personennamen in Rom: Ein Namenbuch.* 3 vols. Berlin: W. de Gruyter, 1982.

———."Juden und Syrer im westlichen Teil der römischen Welt." In *ANRW* 2.29.2 (= *Principat: Sprache und Literatur*) 587–789. Berlin and New York: de Gruyter, 1983.

Standhartinger, Angela. "'Um zu sehen die Töchter des Landes': Die Perspektive Dinas in der jüdisch-hellenistischen Diskussion um Gen 34." In *Religious Propaganda and Missionary Competition in the New Testament World: Essays Honoring Dieter Georgi,* ed. Lukas Bormann et al., Supplements to Novum Testamentum, no. 74, pp. 89–116. Leiden: Brill, 1994.

Stern, Menahem. *The Documents on the History of the Hasmonean Revolt* (in Hebrew). Israel: Hakibbutz Hameuchad, 1965.

———. *Greek and Latin Authors on Jews and Judaism.* 3 vols. Jerusalem: Israel Academy of Sciences, 1974–1984.

Stern, Sacha. *Jewish Identity in Early Rabbinic Writings.* Arbeiten zur Geschichte des antiken Judentums und des Urchristentums, no. 23. Leiden: Brill, 1994.

Strack, Hermann, and Paul Billerbeck. *Kommentar zum Neuen Testament aus Talmud und Midrasch.* 4 vols. in 5. Munich: Beck, 1924–1928.

Sullivan, J. P. *Martial: The Unexpected Classic.* Cambridge: Cambridge University Press, 1991.

TAPA = Transactions of the American Philological Association

Tcherikover, Victor, et al., eds. *Corpus Papyrorum Judaicarum.* 3 vols. Cambridge: Harvard University Press, 1957–1964.

Tomson, Peter J. "The Names Israel and Jew in Ancient Judaism." *Bijdragen: Tijdschrift voor filosofie en theologie* 47 (1986) 120–140.

Touati, Charles. "Le *mamzer,* la *zona* et le statut des enfants issus d'un mariage mixte en droit rabbinique." In *Les juifs au regard de l'histoire: Mélanges en l'honneur de Bernhard Blumenkranz,* ed. Gilbert Dahan, 37–47. Paris: Picard, 1985.

Trebilco, Paul. *Jewish Communities in Asia Minor.* Society for New Testament Studies Monograph Series, no. 69. Cambridge: Cambridge University Press, 1991.

Treggiari, Susan. *Roman Marriage: Iusti Coniuges from the Time of Cicero to the Time of Ulpian.* Oxford: Clarendon, 1991.

Urbach, Ephraim Elimelech. *The Sages.* Trans. I. Abrahams. 2 vols. Jerusalem: Magnes, 1979.

van der Horst, Pieter. *Ancient Jewish Epitaphs.* Kampen, Netherlands: Kok Pharos, 1991.

———. *Hellenism—Judaism—Christianity: Essays on Their Interaction.* Kampen, Netherlands: Kok Pharos, 1994.

Vandersleyen, Claude. "Suggestion sur l'origine des *Persai, tēs epigonēs.*" In *Proceedings of the Eighteenth International Congress of Papyrology* 191–201. Athens, 1988.

van Houten, Christiana. *The Alien in Israelite Law.* JSOT Supplement Series, no. 107. Sheffield: Sheffield Academic Press, 1991.

van Unnik, W. C. *Sparsa Collecta . . . Part Three: Patristica, Gnostica, Liturgica.* Novum Testamentum Supplements, no. 31. Leiden: Brill, 1983.

Vatin, C. *Recherches sur le mariage et la condition de la femme mariée à l'époque hellénistique.* Paris: E. de Boccard, 1970.

Vidman, Ladislaus. *Sylloge Inscriptionum Religionis Isiacae et Sarapiacae.* Berlin: de Gruyter, 1969.

Wacholder, B. Z. "The Halakah and the Proselyting of Slaves during the Geonic Era." *Historia Judaica* 18 (1956) 89–106.

Wetstenius (Wetstein or Wettstein), J. J. *Novum Testamentum Graecum.* 2 vols. Amsterdam: Officina Dommeriana, 1752.

Wilken, Robert. *John Chrysostom and the Jews.* Berkeley: University of California Press, 1983.

Will, Edouard, and Claude Orrieux. *Ioudaïsmos-Hellènismos.* Nancy: Presses Universitaires, 1986.

Williams, Margaret H. "Domitian, the Jews, and the 'Judaizers.'" *Historia* 39 (1990) 196–211.

Wolfson, Harry. *Philo.* 2 vols. Cambridge: Harvard University Press, 1968.

Wong, C. K. "Philo's Use of *Chaldaioi.*" *Studia Philonica Annual* 4 (1992) 1–14

Yadin, Yigael. *Bar Kochba.* New York: Random House, 1971.

———. *The Temple Scroll.* English-language ed. Jerusalem: Israel Exploration Society, Institute of Archaeology of the Hebrew University of Jerusalem, Shrine of the Book, 1983.

Youtie, Herbert C. "*Apatores:* Law vs. Custom in Roman Egypt." In *Le monde grec: Hommages à Claire Préaux* 723–740. Brussels, 1975. Reprinted in *Scriptiunculae Posteriores,* 2 vols. (Bonn: Habelt, 1981) 1:17–34.

ZAW = *Zeitschrift für die alttestamentliche Wissenschaft*

Zeitlin, Solomon. "The Offspring of Intermarriage." *Jewish Quarterly Review* 51 (1960) 135–140. Reprinted in *Solomon Zeitlin's Studies in the Early History of Judaism,* 4 vols. (New York: Ktav, 1974) 2:418–423.

General Index

393

Ioudaios and, 71–78, 137; Israelite, 337–40. *See also* children; ethnic group; fathers; genealogies; lineage; mothers
Blacks: American, 8–9; partial, 18
blood: eating, 54, 319–20. *See also* lineage
Bodo-Eleazar, 167
Boeotia, 113n
boundaries, 5–10; crossing, 13–14, 138, 140–74, 218, 309, 342; fluid, 4, 218, 342; Us and Them, 1–2, 5–10, 341–49; violated, 239. *See also* conversion; Jewishness; separatism
Britain: army, 100; Custody of Infants Act (1839), 284
Bundists, 8, 345
Burton, Richard Francis, 66
Byzantine period, 154

Caecilius, 180–81
Caelia, 41, 352
Caesarea, riots, 15–16
Caligula, 32, 179
Canaanites: conquest of, 119; intermarriage/offspring, 241–49n, 255n, 261, 264–66, 270, 285–88
Caracalla, emperor, 35
Carnaim, 118
Carthage, clothing, 31, 32n
catacombs, Jewish, 282n
ceremonies. *See* rituals
Cestius Gallus, 64
Chenephres, Egyptian king, 32
children: circumcision of, 227n, 236n; conversion of, 226; custody in divorce cases, 284; of intermarriage, 4, 19, 23, 263–340, 342–43; sacrificed, 253n. *See also* birth
Chrestus, 354–55
Christians, 99, 145; baptism, 99, 209n, 222, 236; conversion of prostitutes, 164; food laws, 55n, 187; on Genesis 49:10, 19, 22; Greek of, 185–92, 193; growth of early, 154; and intermarriage with beautiful war captive, 260; internecine conflicts of early, 153; as *Ioudaios*, 26–27; *ioudaïzein* in texts of, 180, 185–92, 193–95; Jewish, 154, 345, 365–70; and Judaism terms, 71n; "judaizing," 4, 175n, 182, 185–97; medieval, 37, 167; and mixed breeding, 303; Novatian, 196n; Paul on Law and, 365, 368–70; as political setting, 344; as sinister and secret society, 44

Christology, 191, 193, 298n. *See also* Jesus
circumcision, 138, 346; Antiochus proscription, 91; Arab, 45–46, 115, 227–28; biblical political, 120–21, 123–25; checking, 48–49; conversion ceremony and, 207, 214–15, 218, 219–21, 223, 235; as conversion sign, 137–38, 155–58, 169, 218, 219–20; forced, 115, 116, 136–37; Herod, 22–23, 46n; Idumaean, 48n, 115, 116, 117, 136–37; vs. immersion or both, 219–21, 223, 225; intent, 124, 225, 226–28; involuntary, 226; *ioudaïzein* and, 183, 188–89, 193; Ishmaelite, 124, 165; Ituraean, 48n, 113, 115–17, 136–37; as Jewish distinction, 30, 39–49, 67, 158, 193; and Jews identifying gentiles, 66; by Jews of non-Jews, 213; laws against, 46–47, 91, 155, 212–13, 225; Martial references, 41, 351, 353–57, 359; Menophilus, 358–59; Middle Ages, 39n, 235n, 236n; non-Jew, 42–46, 113, 115–16, 123–24, 213; Paul and, 26, 158, 360–77; pre-rabbinic, 215–16; "proselyte," 150–51; public, 223–24; reason for, 43–44; slave, 115–16, 124, 155, 169, 351–57, 359; Syrian, 44–45, 46, 47, 115; tannaitic period (early), 215–16, 219, 223; technical requirements, 225–26; Timothy, 363–77
citizenship, 81, 126–27; Athenian, 267, 305, 326–27; Judaean, 81–82, 105, 109–29, 136–37, 218, 267–68; and matrilineal descent, 267, 295–96, 305; Periclean law, 267, 268n, 272n, 326; *politeia*, 125–29, 136–39; Roman, 51–52
Claros, oracle at, 143
Claudius, emperor, 52, 74, 76, 294
Clearchus of Soli, 72
Cleitomachus, 77n
Cleopatra, 73–74
clothing, 30–34, 59
Colchians, circumcision, 44–45
colonialism, 138
Columbia University, 347
commandments: conversion ceremony and, 204–7, 212–19, 223, 229–31, 234–35, 324–25; for females, 216; fourteen negative, 248, 302; "light," 205–6; public performance of, 223–24; "severe," 205; Ten, 33, 301. *See also* Jewish laws; observances; prohibitions; Torah
common origins, 6, 131, 337. *See also* lineage

Index of Premodern Sources

411

Index of Modern Scholars

419

Designer:	Ina Clausen
Compositor:	G & S Typesetters
Printer:	Thomson-Shore
Binder:	Thomson-Shore
Text:	10/13 Galliard
Display:	Galliard